Lecture Notes in Computer Science

Lecture Notes in Computer Science

Edited by G. Goos and J. Hartmanis

210

STACS 86

3rd Annual Symposium on Theoretical Aspects of Computer Science
Orsay, France, January 16–18, 1986

Edited by B. Monien and G. Vidal-Naquet

Springer-Verlag
Berlin Heidelberg New York Tokyo

Editors

B. Monien
Universität-Gesamthochschule Paderborn
Fachbereich Mathematik/Informatik
Warburgerstr. 100, 4790 Paderborn, FRG

G. Vidal-Naquet
Laboratoire de Recherche en Informatique
Bâtiment 490, Université de Paris-Sud, 91405 Orsay Cedex, France

Symposium on Theoretical Aspects of Computer Science
Program Committee:

F.J. Brandenburg, Passau
B. Courcelle, Bordeaux
P. Flajolet, Rocquencourt
M. Hennessy, Edinburgh
J. Loeckx, Saarbrücken
G. Longo, Pisa
B. Monien, Paderborn
Th. Ottman, Karlsruhe
E. Ukkonen, Helsinki
J.E. Pin, Paris
J. Savage, Providence
J. van Leeuwen, Utrecht
G. Vidal-Naquet, Orsay

CR Subject Classifications (1985): B.7.2, C.2, C.1, F.1, F.2, F.3, F.4, H.2.1

ISBN 3-540-16078-7 Springer-Verlag Berlin Heidelberg New York Tokyo
ISBN 0-387-16078-7 Springer-Verlag New York Heidelberg Berlin Tokyo

Printed in Germany

Printing and binding: Beltz Offsetdruck, Hemsbach/Bergstr.
2145/3140-543210

FOREWORD

This volume contains the papers presented at the Third Symposium on Theoretical Aspects of Computer Science (STACS 86) held at the University Paris-Sud January 16-18, 1986.

This Symposium is organized jointly by the Special Interest Group for Theoretical Computer Science of the "Gesellschaft für Informatik" (G.I.) and the special interest group for applied mathematic of the "Association Française des Sciences et Techniques de l'Information, de l'Organisation et des Systèmes" (AFCET). It is held alternatively in France and Germany.

In response to the call for papers 122 papers were submitted.

The program committee met on September 27th and selected 29 papers chosen on the basis of their scientific qualities and relevance to the Symposium. Three invited talks were given.

On behalf of the program committee the symposium chairmen would like to thank all those who submitted papers and the referees who helped for the task of selecting papers.

Our thanks also to the sponsoring organizations, the secretariat of AFCET and Sylvie Congnard for the preparation of the symposium.

B. MONIEN - University of Paderborn

G. VIDAL-NAQUET - University of Paris-Sud, Ecole Supérieure d'Electricité

LIST OF REFEREES

E. AESTESIANO
A. ALBANO
J. ALBERT
V. AMBRIOLA
A. ARNOLD
J. AUTEBERT
R. BACK
R. BADE
R. BARBUTI
G. BAUDET
J. BEAUQUIER
M. BELLIA
J. BERMOND
J. BERSTEL
E. BERTINO
A. BERTOSSI
M. BIDOIT
G. BILLAUD
A. BLIKLE
N. BLUM
L. BOASSON
L. BOUGE
A. BRANDSTÄDT
A. BRAUGGEMANN-KLEIN
G. BREBNER
M. BROY
P. CAMION
R. CAPOCELLI
H. CARSTENSEN
I. CASTELLANI
M. CASTERAN
P. CHARPIN
C. CHOPPI
H. COHEN
R. CORI
G. COSTA
P. COUSOT
R. COUSOT
M. CROCHEMORE
P. DEGANO
P. DEMBINSKI
R. DE NICOLAS
W. DIEKERT
T. DOEPPNER
P. DOLLAND
A. DOUCET
J. EBERT
G. EDELSBRUNNER
J. FALLOT
E. FEHR
J. FERBUS
A. FILE
A. FINKEL
A. FISCHER
U. FISSGUS
M. FLE
P. FRAISSE
L. FRIBOURG
C. FROUGNY
M. GAUDEL
E. GHELLI
S. GNESI
D. GOUYOU-BEAUCHAMPS
A. HEINZ
N. HOLSTI
P. INVERARDI
M. JANTZEN
M. JERRUM
M. KANELLAKIS
S. KAPLAN
V. KERÄNEN
R. KLEIN
J. KORTELAINEN
K. KOSKIMIES
T. KRETSCHMER
M. KUDLEK
G. LALLEMENT
J. LAMBERT
K. LANGE
M. LATTEUX
D. LAZARD
C. LERMEN
T. LETTMANN
A. MAGGIOLO
V. MANCA
H. MANNILA
K. MELHORN
R. MIGNOTTE
P. MOLITOR
E. NETT
F. NICKL
M. NIELSON
O. NURMI
E. OLDEROG
P. ORPONEN
R. ORSINI
F. OTTO
J. PANSIOT
E. PENAUD
M. PENTONEN
P. PEPPER
M. PROTASI
L. PUEL
F. RADEMACHER
K. RAIHA
J. RAOULT
W. RULLING
A. SALIBRA
A. SALOMAA
D. SANNELLA
J. SCHMIDT
D. SCHOETT
T. SCHRÖDER
P. SCHUSTET
S. SCHWER
G. SENIZERGUES
K. SIEBERD
M. SIMI
S. SIPPU
E. SOISALON SOININEN
G. SONTACHI
J. STERN
C. STIRLING
H. STORK
A. STOUGHTON
T. STROHOTTE
J. TARHIO
P. TURAKAINEN
F. TURINI
R. VALK
M. VANNESCHI
R. VAUQUELIN
J. VAUTHERIN
R. VERBEEK
K. WAGNER
L. WALLEN
R. WANKMÜLLER
P. WEGNER
P. WIDMAYER

CONTRIBUTED PAPERS

INVITED LECTURES

* Contributions not submitted in time for publication

ABSTRACT INTERPRETATION OF DENOTATIONAL DEFINITIONS

(A survey)

Flemming Nielson
Institute of Electronic Systems
Aalborg University Centre
Strandvejen 19, 4
9000 Aalborg C.
Denmark

ABSTRACT

Abstract interpretation is a framework for describing data flow analyses and for proving their correctness. Traditionally the framework is developed for flow chart languages, but this paper extends the applicability of the idea to a wide class of languages that have a denotational semantics. The main idea is to study a denotational metalanguage with two kinds of types: one kind describes compile-time entities and another describes run-time entities. The run-time entities will be interpreted differently so as to obtain different semantics from the same denotational definition: the standard semantics is the ordinary semantics, an approximating semantics describes a data flow analysis and the collecting semantics is a convenient tool in relating the previous two semantics.

1. INTRODUCTION

Often the acceptability of using some high-level programming languages depends critically on the quality of the code produced by the compiler: sometimes the code must execute fast and sometimes the code must be short. Consider the fragment

<u>if</u> -9 × -3 + 5 > 0 <u>then</u>...<u>else</u>...

and the problem of generating suitable code for it. For this it would help to know at compile-time that -9 × -3 + 5 is positive because then no code needs to be generated for the test and the else branch. To obtain such information a compiler performs some <u>data flow analyses</u> [AhUl 78, Hec 77]. For example the properties

negative, positive, zero, integer, true, false, boolean

may be used in a calculation showing that

negative × negative + positive > zero

yields positive > zero and hence true.

The formulation of data flow analyses depends on the way programs are modelled. When they are modelled as flow charts the monotone framework of [KaUl 77] provides a very general setting for the formulation. The work by Patrick and Radhia Cousot on <u>abstract interpretation</u> [CoCo 77, CoCo 79] extends this by incorporating a correctness relation between properties and values. In this way many data flow analyses can be specified and proved correct. However, it is often more convenient to have a more structural model of programs. In this setting the high-level data flow analyses of [Ros 77] provides a framework for formulating data flow analyses, but no theory of correctness has been developed.

Denotational semantics is a structural method for expressing the meaning of programs. This paper surveys a framework of abstract interpretation that is applicable to all programming languages that have a denotational definition using the metalanguage of section 3. Previously such developments have only been performed for particular languages (e.g. [Don 78, Don 81, Nie 82, MyNi 83, BuHA 85]). The detailed development is given in [Nie 84]. Here no details of particular data flow analyses will be given as such examples can be found elsewhere (e.g. [CoCo 78]). Such examples include constant propagation [AhUl 78], array bound checking, type checking in a typed language and type inference in an untyped language [Ten 74].

2. INTRODUCTORY EXAMPLE

For the benefit of the reader unacquainted with abstract interpretation we shall begin with an example. The framework to be developed should include the flow charts so consider the following program:

```
a: if x<y then goto b
   x:=x-y
   goto a
b: skip
```

For positive integers x and y the program calculates the remainder of dividing x by y. The semantics of the program may be viewed as a partial function

$$f: Z \times Z \hookrightarrow Z \times Z$$

over pairs of integers. In the terminology of [MiSt 76] this function is called the standard semantics of the program. It is formally defined by

$$f = \mathrm{FIX}(\lambda(\phi_a,\phi_b).((\lambda s.f_1(s) \rightarrow \phi_b(s),(\phi_a \cdot f_2)(s)),f_3))\downarrow 1$$

where FIX is the least fixed point operator, $f_1(x,y)=x<y$, $f_2(x,y)=(x-y,y)$, $f_3(x,y)=(x,y)$ and $\ldots\rightarrow\ldots,\ldots$ is conditional.

A data flow analysis amounts to giving the program a non-standard semantics h which will be called an approximating semantics. In a data flow analysis for detecting the signs of integers one may have

$$h: L \times L \rightarrow L \times L$$

where L is a set of properties of the integers. A central notion is that of a property safely approximating another, e.g. "integer" safely approximates "positive". This is modelled by equipping L with a partial order $\sqsubseteq$ such that $l_1 \sqsubseteq l_2$ whenever l_2 safely approximates l_1. In the detection of signs example from section 1 one may use:

L =

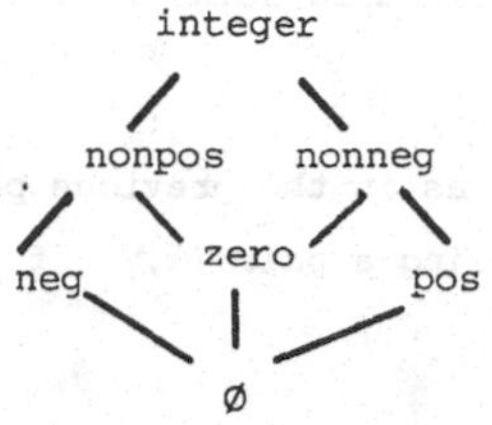

The definition of h is given by

$$h = \mathrm{FIX}(\lambda(\psi_a,\psi_b).((\lambda\sigma.\psi_b(h_{1t}(\sigma)) \sqcup (\psi_a \cdot h_2)(h_{1f}(\sigma))),h_3))\downarrow 1$$

The intention of $h_{1t}(\sigma)$ is that it should be a safe approximation to the part of the argument for which x<y may be true. It is common to use $h_{1t}(\sigma)=\sigma$ but one could be more precise and specify e.g. $h_{1t}(\mathrm{pos},\mathrm{neg})=(\emptyset,\emptyset)$ etc. The definition of h_{1f} is similar and h_2 and h_3 should be straightforward. It is common to require L to be a complete lattice so that the effect of combining the results along the then and else branches is modelled by the binary least upper bound operator $\sqcup$.

When x and y are initially both positive the resulting value of x will be non-negative and y will remain positive. Therefore one might hope that h(pos,pos)=(nonneg,pos) but the definition of h gives the less precise h(pos,pos)=(integer,pos) because $h_2(\mathrm{pos},\mathrm{pos})=(\mathrm{integer},\mathrm{pos})$. The problem is that h_{1f} is unable to record the connection between the values of x and y. This means that the data flow analysis is an <u>independent attribute method</u> [JoMu 81]. It does not suffice to replace L with a more extensive set of properties such as the powerset $\mathcal{P}(Z)$ ordered by subset inclusion $\subseteq$. What is required is to use an adequate description of pairs of integers and $\mathcal{P}(Z\times Z)$ is a good candidate. The <u>collecting semantics</u> (static semantics [CoCo 77])

$$g\colon \mathcal{P}(Z\times Z) \rightarrow \mathcal{P}(Z\times Z)$$

may then be defined by

$$g = \mathrm{FIX}(\lambda(\phi_a,\phi_b).((\lambda\underline{\sigma}.\ \phi_b(g_{1t}(\underline{\sigma}))\cup(\phi_a \cdot g_2)(g_{1f}(\underline{\sigma}))),g_3))\downarrow 1$$

where

$$g_{1t/f}(\underline{\sigma}) = \{(x,y)\in\underline{\sigma} \mid f_1(x,y) = \mathrm{true/false}\}$$

$$g_{2/3}(\underline{\sigma}) = \{(u,v) \mid \exists (x,y)\in\underline{\sigma}\colon f_{2/3}(x,y)=(u,v)\}.$$

It is a relational method [JoMu 81] and gives

$$g(\{x|x \text{ is positive}\}\times\{y|y \text{ is positive}\})$$

$$\subseteq \{x|x \text{ is non-negative}\}\times\{y|y \text{ is positive}\}$$

because g_{1f} does record the connection between the values of x and y.

The collecting semantics is of interest because it intuitively is the most precise data flow analysis consistent with the standard semantics, i.e.

$$g(\underline{\sigma}) = \{(u,v)|\exists(x,y)\in\underline{\sigma}: (u,v)=f(x,y)\}.$$

This is the case whenever g_{1t}, g_{1f}, g_2 and g_3 are as in the previous paragraph. The connection between g and h is established using a pair (α,γ) of adjoined functions [CoCo 79]. The upper adjoint

$$\gamma: L\times L \to P(Z\times Z)$$

gives the meaning of pairs of properties and is defined as $\gamma(l_1,l_2)=\overline{\gamma}(l_1)\times\overline{\gamma}(l_2)$ where $\overline{\gamma}: L\to P(Z)$ sends pos to $\{z|z \text{ is positive}\}$ etc. The lower adjoint

$$\alpha: P(Z\times Z) \to L\times L$$

is uniquely determined by the adjoinedness condition

$$\alpha(\underline{\sigma})\sqsubseteq(l_1,l_2) \Leftrightarrow \underline{\sigma} \subseteq \gamma(l_1,l_2).$$

This implies that α and γ are both monotonic, i.e. that they preserve the relation "safe approximation". Furthermore $\gamma(\alpha(\underline{\sigma}))\supseteq\underline{\sigma}$, which means that $\alpha(\underline{\sigma})$ is a safe representation of $\underline{\sigma}$, and $\alpha(\gamma(l_1,l_2))\sqsubseteq(l_1,l_2)$ which means that $\alpha(\underline{\sigma})$ is as precise a description as possible. The desired relation between g and h then is

$$g(\underline{\sigma})\subseteq\gamma(h(\alpha(\underline{\sigma})))$$

which is abbreviated to $g\sqsubseteq\gamma\cdot h\cdot\alpha$. This relation is equivalent to

$$g\cdot\gamma\sqsubseteq\gamma\cdot h$$

because (α,γ) is a pair of adjoined functions. The relation holds whenever there are similar relations between g_2 and h_2, g_3 and h_3, g_{1t} and h_{1t} as well as g_{1f} and h_{1f}.

3. METALANGUAGE

The denotational semantics of a programming language may be viewed as consisting of:

- a structurally defined mapping from programs to terms in a semantic metalanguage, and
- an interpretation of the primitives of the metalanguage.

Usually only one interpretation is considered and the standard semantics results.

We shall aim at obtaining the approximating and collecting semantics as well by changing the interpretation. This places certain demands upon the metalanguage.

Usually the metalanguage is a typed λ-calculus so let us begin with consideration of the types. As an aid we shall concentrate upon the functionality of the arguments to FIX in the definitions of f, h and g:

$$(Z\times Z\to Z\times Z)\times(Z\times Z\to Z\times Z)\ \to\ (Z\times Z\to Z\times Z)\times(Z\times Z\to Z\times Z)$$

$$(L\times L\to L\times L)\times(L\times L\to L\times L)\ \to\ (L\times L\to L\times L)\times(L\times L\to L\times L)$$

$$(\mathcal{P}(Z\times Z)\to\mathcal{P}(Z\times Z))\times(\mathcal{P}(Z\times Z)\to\mathcal{P}(Z\times Z))\ \to\ (\mathcal{P}(Z\times Z)\to\mathcal{P}(Z\times Z))\times(\mathcal{P}(Z\times Z)\to\mathcal{P}(Z\times Z))$$

To obtain these as different interpretations of a formal type we shall use the type:

$$\underline{Z\times Z\to Z\times Z}\times\underline{Z\times Z\to Z\times Z}\to\underline{Z\times Z\to Z\times Z}\times\underline{Z\times Z\to Z\times Z}.$$

It should be clear that the first two functionalities can be obtained by suitably interpreting the underlined symbols, e.g. $\underline{Z}$ as Z and L respectively. The same holds for the third functionality if $\underline{\times}$ is interpreted as the operator ⊗ temporarily defined by $\mathcal{P}(A)\otimes\mathcal{P}(B)=\mathcal{P}(A\times B)$. It should also be clear from this example that it is <u>necessary</u> to distinguish between $\underline{\times}$ and × etc.

Based on this experience one may consider the system TMLs of types [+]:

$$ct::=A_i\,|\,ct_1+\ldots+ct_k\,|\,ct_1\times\ldots\times ct_k\,|\,ct_1\to ct_2\,|\,\mathrm{rec}X.ct\,|\,X\,|\,ft$$

$$ft::=rt_1\underline{\to}rt_2$$

$$rt::=\underline{A}_i\,|\,rt_1\underline{+}\ldots\underline{+}rt_k\,|\,rt_1\underline{\times}\ldots\underline{\times}rt_k\,|\,\underline{\mathrm{rec}}\ \underline{X}.rt\,|\,\underline{X}.$$

Imagine for a moment that ct::=ft is omitted. The types ct then are those usually found in a semantic metalanguage: A_i are the base types, + gives disjoint sum, × gives cartesian product, → gives function space and rec X.ct stands for the type of the solution to the equation X=ct. The types rt resemble ct except that rt::=ft has been omitted for simplicity. The best way to view the types ct is as being the type of <u>compile-time</u> (or static) entities. Similarly the types rt correspond to <u>runtime</u> (or dynamic) entities. The functions of type ft then are the <u>state transformations</u> which are of prime interest in abstract interpretation. It therefore makes sense to connect the two systems with ct::=ft. Also it becomes clear that the absense or rt::=ft means that "storable procedures" cannot be accomodated.

\+ With respect to [Nie 84] it appears that * and $\underline{*}$ have been omitted. However, from section 4 it will emerge that $\underline{\times}$ here corresponds to $\underline{*}$ in [Nie 84] so that it is really * and $\underline{\times}$ of [Nie 84] that have been omitted. The use of $\underline{X}$ rather than X is a notational improvement.

Remark The development of the present paper constitutes one example of a non-standard semantics (in the sense of [MiSt 76]) where the distinction between compile-time and run-time types is indispensable. Another example where this is the case is when specifying code generation [NiNi 85a], where $rt\underline{\rightarrow}rt$ essentially is a domain of code for state transformations over the state rt. Perhaps it is more interesting that the distinction may also prove useful when defining the standard semantics (in the sense of [MiSt 76]) for actual programming languages. One example is the distinction in [Ten 81] between expression procedures and static expression procedures. Ignoring side effects and free variables some typical types would be $\underline{Z\rightarrow Z}$ and $Z\rightarrow Z$ respectively, so that the metalanguage does allow to distinguish between the two concepts. Another example is the programming language type array [...] of integer where ... denotes a static expression determining the size. Here one might allow a run-time type construction $\underline{\Pi}(e)rt$ to denote the product of e copies of rt assuming that e denotes a compile-time integer. In general one would expect one notion of type for each binding time [JoMu 78]. □

Turning to the expressions of the metalanguage the goal is to obtain the definitions of f, h and g by suitably interpreting a formal expression. For this we shall use the expression

$$FIX(\lambda(\delta_a,\delta_b).(cond(lt,\delta_b,\delta_a \,\square\, [\![x\leftarrow x-y]\!], id))\downarrow 1.$$

It is straightforward to verify that the definitions of f, h and g can be achieved by suitably interpreting lt, id, □, cond and $[\![x\leftarrow x-y]\!]$. As an example $cond(\delta_1,\delta_2,\delta_3)$ will be $\lambda s.\delta_1(s)\rightarrow\delta_2(s),\delta_3(s)$ in the standard semantics. In the remainder of this section some of the expressions will be surveyed but it is impractical to cover all aspects.

All expressions have a formal type ct. It makes sense to require such types to be closed, i.e. not to contain any free domain variables. Since ct includes $rt\underline{\rightarrow}rt'$ it is possible to have expressions that denote state transformations. The constants lt (for less than) and id (for identity) are two such examples. The only restriction imposed upon constants is that their type must be contravariantly pure [Nie 84]: essentially this means that each $ct'\rightarrow ct''$ occurring in the type must satisfy that ct' does not contain a type ft. The need for this restriction will become clear in section 4 in the context of transforming constants from the standard semantics and to the collecting semantics.

The constructs whose types are not contravariantly pure are FIX and a few functionals: these are functions whose type is of the form $ft^n\rightarrow ft$. One functional is composition

$$\square\colon\ (rt'\underline{\rightarrow}rt'')\times(rt\underline{\rightarrow}rt')\rightarrow(rt\underline{\rightarrow}rt'').$$

Another is conditional

$$\text{cond}: (rt \underline{\rightarrow} \underline{T}) \times (rt \underline{\rightarrow} rt') \times (rt \underline{\rightarrow} rt') \rightarrow (rt \underline{\rightarrow} rt')$$

where $\underline{T}$ is the type of the run-time truth values. This differs from the conditional $\ldots\rightarrow\ldots,\ldots$ of type $T\times ct\times ct\rightarrow ct$ that was used in section 2. However, both conditionals will be used in the metalanguage: the former conditional expresses a run-time test whereas the latter will be used to express a compile-time test.

The distinction between syntax for compile-time operations and run-time operations permeate all of the metalanguage. Related to the compile-time cartesian product we have notation $(e_1,\ldots,e_k)$ and $e{\downarrow}i$ for forming tuples and selecting components. Related to the run-time product $\underline{\times}$ the analogous notations are

$$\text{tuple}: (rt \underline{\rightarrow} rt_1)\times\ldots\times(rt \underline{\rightarrow} rt_k)\rightarrow(rt \underline{\rightarrow} rt_1 \underline{\times}\ldots\underline{\times} rt_k)$$

$$\text{take}_i: rt_1 \underline{\times}\ldots\underline{\times} rt_k \underline{\rightarrow} rt_i.$$

In the standard semantics one has $\text{tuple}(f_1,\ldots,f_k)(v)=(f_1(v),\ldots,f_k(v))$ and $\text{take}_i(v)=v{\downarrow}i$. The use of the functional tuple and constant take_i is illustrated by the definition

$$[\![x\leftarrow x\text{-}y]\!] = \text{tuple}(\text{sub},\text{take}_2)$$

where sub: $\underline{Z\times Z\rightarrow Z}$ is a constant subtraction function. Turning to compile-time sum + we have injection in_i, projection out_i and test is_i. For run-time sum $\underline{+}$ we have

$$\text{case}: (rt_1 \underline{\rightarrow} rt)\times\ldots\times(rt_k \underline{\rightarrow} rt)\rightarrow(rt_1 \underline{+}\ldots\underline{+} rt_k \underline{\rightarrow} rt)$$

$$\text{in}_i: rt_i \underline{\rightarrow} rt_1 \underline{+}\ldots\underline{+} rt_k.$$

In the standard semantics we will have $\text{case}(f_1,\ldots,f_k)(\text{in}_i(v))=f_i(v)$. We refer to [NiNi 85b] for a discussion of the pragmatic aspects of the notation.

4. STANDARD AND COLLECTING SEMANTICS

An interpretation of the primitives of the metalanguage amounts to defining the meaning of types and expressions. We begin with defining the standard semantics $\underline{S}$ upon the run-time types rt. The programme is to follow the categorical approach of [SmPl 82] rather than the universal domain approach. The presentation needs to be rather terse so consult [ArMa 75] for general categorical concepts and [SmPl 82] for special notions. (A detailed development is given in [Nie 84].) The main idea is to define the semantics as a locally continuous covariant functor

$$\underline{S}[\![rt]\!] : \underline{\underline{ACCs}}^N \rightarrow \underline{\underline{ACCs}}$$

where N is the number of free domain variables in rt. The category $\underline{\underline{ACCs}}$ has as objects the (ω-) algebraic consistently complete (ω-) cpo's and as morphisms the strict (ω-) continuous functions.

The definition of $\underline{S}[\![rt]\!]$ is by induction on the structure of rt. So $\underline{S}[\![\underline{A}_i]\!]$ is defined to be a constant functor and $\underline{S}[\![\underline{X}_i]\!]$ is a projection functor. If $rt_1,\ldots,rt_k$ all have the same free domain variables we get

$$\underline{S}[\![rt_1 \underline{+} \ldots \underline{+} rt_k]\!] = + \cdot (\underline{S}[\![rt_1]\!], \ldots, \underline{S}[\![rt_k]\!])$$

where + is the coalesced sum functor, $\cdot$ is composition of functors and (...,...,...) denotes tupling of functors. We shall write $\underline{S}(\underline{+})=+$ as a record of this. The use of coalesced sum is motivated by the isomorphism $S_\perp + S_\perp \cong (S \uplus S)_\perp$ where $\uplus$ is disjoint union and $(\ )_\perp$ constructs a flat cpo. Similarly $rt_1 \underline{\times} \ldots \underline{\times} rt_k$ is handled by using $\underline{S}(\underline{\times})=*$ which is the smash product functor. If differs from cartesian product in that all tuples with a $\perp$ component are identified and is motivated by $S_\perp * S_\perp \cong (S \times S)_\perp$. When interpreting $\underline{S}(\underline{\rightarrow})$ as the strict continuous function space constructor $\rightarrow_s$ one then obtains e.g.

$$S_\perp + S_\perp \rightarrow_s S_\perp * S_\perp \cong S \uplus S \rightarrow S \times S$$

so that the formal definition of the standard semantics $\underline{S}$ is close to the "naive" definition in section 2.

Finally we consider the recursive domain $\underline{rec}\ \underline{X}_1.rt$ and suppose that $\underline{X}_1$ and $\underline{X}_2$ are the only free domain variables or rt. Let $\underline{S}[\![rt]\!]^0$ be $\underline{S}[\![\underline{X}_1]\!]$ and let $\underline{S}[\![rt]\!]^{n+1}$ be $\underline{S}[\![rt]\!] \cdot (\underline{S}[\![rt]\!]^n, \underline{S}[\![\underline{X}_2]\!])$. We shall feel free to write $\underline{S}[\![rt^n(\underline{X}_1)]\!]$ for $\underline{S}[\![rt]\!]^n$ where $rt^0(\underline{X}_1)=\underline{X}_1$ and $rt^{n+1}(\underline{X}_1)=rt[rt^n(\underline{X}_1)/\underline{X}_1]$. To define $\underline{S}[\![\underline{rec}\ \underline{X}_1.rt]\!]$ we must define its effect upon an object D and a morphism f: D→D'. Let (r_n,E) be the limiting cone for the chain $(\underline{S}[\![rt]\!]^n(U,D), \underline{S}[\![rt]\!]^n(\perp,id))$ and similarly (r'_n,E'). As usual the r_n and r_n' are embeddings with upper adjoints r_n^u and $r_n'^u$, i.e. they are morphisms of the subcategory $\underline{\underline{ACCe}}$. Then

$$\underline{S}[\![\underline{rec}\ \underline{X}_1.rt]\!](D)=E$$

$$\underline{S}[\![\underline{rec}\ \underline{X}_1.rt]\!](f)=\bigsqcup_n r_n' \cdot \underline{S}[\![rt]\!]^n(\perp,f) \cdot r_n^u$$

completes the definition.

Before proceeding with the definition of $\underline{S}$ let us consider the definition of the collecting semantics $\underline{C}$ upon the run-time types rt. The example in section 2 used powersets and the corresponding analogue within domain theory is the so-called relational powerdomain $\mathcal{P}_R$. This is a locally continuous and covariant functor from $\underline{\underline{ACCs}}$ to the category $\underline{\underline{ACLs}}$ of algebraic complete lattices and strict continuous functions. It is defined by

$$\mathcal{P}_R(D)=(\{Y \subseteq B_D \mid Y \neq \emptyset \wedge Y=LC(Y)\}, \subseteq)$$

$$\mathcal{P}_R(f)=\lambda Y.\{e \mid \exists d \in Y: e \sqsubseteq f(d)\}$$

where B_D is the set of finite elements of D and

$$LC(Y) = \{d' \in B_D \mid \exists d \in Y: d' \sqsubseteq d\}.$$

The motivation for using P_R rather than e.g. the Smyth or Plotkin powerdomains is that $P_R(S_\perp)\cong P(S)$ so that the development is still close to section 2. It is then natural to define $\underline{C}[\![\underline{A}_i]\!]$ as $P_R\cdot\underline{S}[\![\underline{A}_i]\!]$ and to let $\underline{C}[\![\underline{X}]\!]$ be a projection functor. For $\underline{C}(\underline{+})$ we shall use cartesian product $\times$ because $P_R(D_1)\times\ldots\times P_R(D_k)\cong P_R(D_1+\ldots+D_k)$. For $\underline{C}(\times)$ we shall use the tensor product $\circledast$. For k=2 it is defined by

$$L\circledast M = (L\to_{as} M^{op})^{op}$$

$$f\circledast g = \lambda h.\lambda l'.\bigsqcup\{g(h(l))\,|\,l'\sqsubseteq f(l)\}$$

where "as" means strict, additive and continuous and $(L\sqsubseteq)^{op}=(L\sqsupseteq)$. The motivation for this choice is that $P_R(D)\circledast P_R(E)\cong P_R(D^*E)$. Unfortunately $\circledast_k$ is not a functor from $\underline{\underline{ACLs}}$ to $\underline{\underline{ACLs}}$ because the composition law

$$\circledast(f\cdot f',g\cdot g')=\circledast(f,g)\cdot\circledast(f',g')$$

may fail. In general we have only

$$\circledast(f\cdot f',g\cdot g')\sqsubseteq\circledast(f,g)\cdot\circledast(f',g').$$

However, equality holds whenever f and g are additionally additive and then $\circledast(f,g)$ is also additive. We shall use the term $\underline{\underline{\text{semifunctor}}}$ for such a mapping. A semi-functor specializes to a covariant functor over the category $\underline{\underline{ACLe}}$. This means that $\underline{C}[\![\underline{rec}\ \underline{X}.rt]\!]$ can be defined analogously to $\underline{S}[\![\underline{rec}\ \underline{X}.rt]\!]$. In summary we obtain a locally continuous semi-functor $\underline{C}[\![rt]\!]:\underline{\underline{ACLs}}^N\to\underline{\underline{ACLs}}$.

The motivational remarks in the definition of $\underline{C}[\![rt]\!]$ have already hinted at the following connection between the functionalities in the standard and collecting semantics.

Lemma 1. For a closed type rt the object $P_R(\underline{S}[\![rt]\!])$ is isomorphic to the object $\underline{C}[\![rt]\!]$. □

Proof. The proof proceeds by structural induction and this means that it will be necessary to consider types that are not closed. The inductive hypothesis therefore considers a type rt with free domain variables $\underline{X}_1,\ldots,\underline{X}_n$ and asserts that:

> there is a natural equivalence nat_{rt}
>
> from $P_R\cdot\underline{S}[\![rt]\!]$
>
> to $\underline{C}[\![rt]\!]\cdot(P_R\cdot\underline{S}[\![\underline{X}_1]\!],\ldots,P_R\cdot\underline{S}[\![\underline{X}_N]\!])$.

The proof also gives a structural definition of nat_{rt}. The details may be found in [Nie 84, Theorem 3.3:4]. □

When rt is closed we shall write nat_{rt} for the isomorphism from the object $P_R(\underline{S}[\![rt]\!])$ to the object $\underline{C}[\![rt]\!]$.

We now continue the definition of the standard semantics $\underline{S}$ upon types. It would be natural to define $\underline{S}[\![ct]\!]$ as a locally continuous and covariant functor over the category $\underline{\underline{CPOs}}$ of cpo's and strict continuous functions. However, the contravariance of the function space construction motivates considering so-called symmetric functors over another category $\underline{\underline{CPO2s}}$. In this category an object is a cpo, a morphism $f{:}A\to B$ is a pair $(f'{:}A\to B, f''{:}B\to A)$ of strict continuous functions and composition is given by $(f',f'')\cdot(g',g'') = (f'\cdot g', g''\cdot f'')$. A symmetric functor (domain functor [Rey 74]) $F{:}\underline{\underline{CPO2s}}^N\to\underline{\underline{CPO2s}}$ is a covariant functor that satisfies

$$F(f_1,\ldots,f_N)^R = F(f_1^{\,R},\ldots,f_N^{\,R})$$

where $(f',f'')^R = (f'',f')$.

The definition of $\underline{S}[\![ct]\!] : \underline{\underline{CPO2s}}^N\to\underline{\underline{CPO2s}}$ as a locally continuous symmetric functor (abbreviated l.c.s. functor) then has $\underline{S}[\![A_i]\!]$ to be the constant functor over the appropriate cpo and $\underline{S}[\![X]\!]$ to be a projection functor. All $rt\underline{\to}rt'$ considered will be closed so $\underline{S}[\![rt\underline{\to}rt']\!]$ may be defined to be the constant functor over the cpo of strict continuous functions from $\underline{S}[\![rt]\!]$ to $\underline{S}[\![rt']\!]$. For $\underline{S}(+)$ we use the symmetric variant of coalesced sum +. It is defined as + upon objects but as

$$\underline{S}(+)((f_1',f_1''),\ldots,(f_N',f_N'')) = (f_1'+\ldots+f_N', f_1''+\ldots+f_N'')$$

upon morphisms. Similarly $\underline{S}(\times)$ is the symmetric variant of cartesian product $\times$. The symmetric functor $\underline{S}(\to)$ is defined as $\to$ upon objects but as

$$S(\to)((f_1',f_1''),(f_2',f_2'')) = (f_1''\to f_2', f_1'\to f_2'')$$

upon morphisms. (In a sense the contravariance has been hidden in the composition of $\underline{\underline{CPO2s}}$.) Since embeddings have unique upper adjoints it is still possible to specialize a l.c.s. functor to a suitable functor over $\underline{\underline{CPOe}}$. This means that recursive domains may be solved much as before and furthermore the solution may be turned into a l.c.s. functor.

The l.c.s. functor $\underline{C}[\![ct]\!]$ is defined analogously to $\underline{S}[\![ct]\!]$. The difference between $\underline{S}[\![rt]\!]$ and $\underline{C}[\![rt]\!]$ was motivated by the different perceptions of run-time entities in the standard and collecting semantics. There seems to be no reason for why compile-time entities should be perceived as differently and therefore the only difference in the definition is that $\underline{C}[\![rt\underline{\to}rt']\!]$ corresponds to the cpo of strict continuous functions from $\underline{C}[\![rt]\!]$ to $\underline{C}[\![rt']\!]$.

To relate $\underline{S}[\![ct]\!]$ and $\underline{C}[\![ct]\!]$ we define a "relation" sim_{ct}. It has the form

$$sim_{ct}(Q_1,\ldots,Q_N){:}\ \underline{S}[\![ct]\!](D_1,\ldots,D_N)\times\underline{C}[\![ct]\!](L_1,\ldots,L_N)\to\{true,false\}$$

where $Q_i{:}\ D_i\times L_i\to\{true,false\}$ is a relation corresponding to the free domain variable X_i of ct. When ct is $rt\underline{\to}rt'$ the relation is true upon (d,l) iff

$$l = nat_{rt'}\cdot\mathcal{P}_R(d)\cdot nat_{rt}^{-1}$$

as should be expected given Lemma 1 and the development in section 2. When $ct=A_i$ we require that $l=d$ and when $ct=X_i$ we require that $Q_i(l,d)$. In the remaining cases the definition is "componentwise". So when $ct=ct_1\times\ldots\times ct_k$ it is

$$\forall i:\ sim_{ct_i}(Q_1,\ldots,Q_N)(d\downarrow i, l\downarrow i)$$

and when ct=ct'→ct" it is the so-called logical relation

$$\forall(u,v):\ sim_{ct'}(Q_1,\ldots,Q_N)(u,v) \Rightarrow sim_{ct''}(Q_1,\ldots,Q_N)(d(u),l(v)).$$

When $ct = rec\ X_{N+1}.ct'$ the definition roughly is

$$\forall n:\ sim_{ct'^n(X_{N+1})}(Q_1,\ldots,Q_N,\lambda(d',l').true)(r_n^u(d),s_n^u(l))$$

for appropriate embeddings r_n and s_n.

The definition of sim_{ct} fits well with the definition of the functors $\underline{S}[\![ct]\!]$ and $\underline{C}[\![ct]\!]$. To make this precise define a category SIM as follows. An object is a triple (D,Q,L) where D and L are cpo's and Q: $D\times L\rightarrow\{true,false\}$ is an admissible relation (i.e. is true of $(\bot,\bot)$ and truth is preserved when taking least upper bounds of chains). A morphism from (D,Q,L) to (D',Q',L') is a pair of CPO2s morphisms

$$((f',f''):D\rightarrow D',(g',g''):L\rightarrow L')$$

fulfilling that

$$Q(d,l) \Rightarrow Q'(f'(d),g'(l))$$
$$Q(f''(d'),g''(l')) \Leftarrow Q'(d',l').$$

Composition is defined componentwise. Next define a functor-like mapping

$\underline{SC}[\![ct]\!] : SIM^N \rightarrow SIM$ by

$$\underline{SC}[\![ct]\!]((D_1,Q_1,L_1),\ldots) = (\underline{S}[\![ct]\!](D_1,\ldots),sim_{ct}(Q_1,\ldots),\underline{C}[\![ct]\!](L_1,\ldots))$$
$$\underline{SC}[\![ct]\!]((f_1,g_1),\ldots) = (\underline{S}[\![ct]\!](f_1,\ldots),\underline{C}[\![ct]\!](g_1,\ldots)).$$

We then have (in analogy with the relational functors of [Rey 74]).

Lemma 2. $\underline{SC}[\![ct]\!]$ is a locally continuous covariant functor over SIM. □

Proof. The proof is by structural induction on ct. Full details are given in [Nie 84, Theorem 3.3:13] and the discussion after that theorem. □

We are now ready to consider the semantics of expressions. The definition of $\underline{S}[\![e]\!]$ is by structural induction on e. The notation pertaining to compile-time types ct is rather standard and is interpreted as usual, so for example FIX gives the least fixed point. For the notation pertaining to run-time types rt the explanatory remarks in section 3 indicate what their standard semantics is.

The definition of $\underline{C}[\![e]\!]$ corresponds to that of $\underline{S}[\![e]\!]$ as long as no run-time types are involved. Furthermore, FIX is interpreted so as to give the least fixed point. For a constant f of contravariantly pure type ct define the type ct' to be ct with all $rt_i \underline{\rightarrow} rt_i'$ replaced by X_i. The contravariantly purity of ct enforces that $\underline{S}[\![ct']\!]$ $(=\underline{C}[\![ct']\!])$ is the symmetric variant of a covariant functor $F_{ct}: \underline{\underline{CPOs}}^N \rightarrow \underline{\underline{CPOs}}$. It is then natural to define

$$\underline{C}[\![f]\!] = F_{ct}(\lambda d_i.nat_{rt'_i} \cdot P_R(d_i) \cdot nat_{rt_i}^{-1})(\underline{S}[\![f]\!]).$$

When $ct=rt\underline{\rightarrow}rt'$ this gives the expected $\underline{C}[\![f]\!] = nat_{rt'} \cdot P_R(\underline{S}[\![f]\!]) \cdot nat_{rt}^{-1}$. This method is not applicable to functionals.

When considering the functionals it is instructive to assume that the isomorphisms in Lemma 1 are the identities (but see [Nie 84] for the general case). Composition is straightforward

$$\underline{C}[\![e\square e']\!] = \underline{C}[\![e]\!] \cdot \underline{C}[\![e']\!].$$

Building on the development of section 2 it is natural to put +

$$\underline{C}[\![cond(e_1,e_2,e_3)]\!] = \underline{C}[\![e_2]\!] \cdot true(\underline{C}[\![e_1]\!]) \mathbf{U} \underline{C}[\![e_3]\!] \cdot false(\underline{C}[\![e_1]\!]).$$

Here $\mathbf{U}$ means "set-union pointwise",

$$true(g) = \lambda Y.LC(\{d \in Y | g(LC(\{d\})) \ni true\})$$

and false(g) similarly. Recalling that $\underline{C}(\underline{+})=\times$ we shall use

$$\underline{C}[\![case\ e_1,\ldots,e_k]\!] = \lambda(Y_1,\ldots,Y_k).\underline{C}[\![e_1]\!](Y_1) \cup \ldots \cup \underline{C}[\![e_k]\!](Y_k).$$

Finally,

$$\underline{C}[\![tuple\ e_1,\ldots,e_k]\!] = \lambda Y.\cup\{\underline{C}[\![e_1]\!](LC(\{y\})) * \ldots * \underline{C}[\![e_k]\!](LC(\{y\})) | y \in Y\}.$$

We cannot just use $\lambda Y.\underline{C}[\![e_1]\!](Y) * \ldots * \underline{C}[\![e_k]\!](Y)$ because then $\underline{C}[\![tuple\ id,id]\!]$ $(LC(\{2,3\}))$ gives $LC(\{(2,2),(2,3),(3,2),(3,3)\})$ rather than the desired $LC(\{(2,2),(3,3)\})$.

The correctness of these definitions is guaranteed by

Theorem 1. For all expressions e of type ct we have $sim_{ct}(\underline{S}[\![e]\!], \underline{C}[\![e]\!])$. □

We shall omit the proof (but see [Nie 84, Theorem 3.3:14]) which is by structural induction on e using Lemma 2. When $ct=rt\underline{\rightarrow}rt'$ and nat... are the identities the Theorem asserts that

$$\underline{C}[\![e]\!](Y) = LC(\{\underline{S}[\![e]\!](d) | d \in Y\}).$$

This is the analogue within domain theory of the connection expressed in section 2.

+ This agrees with [Nie 84] because here $\underline{C}[\![e_2]\!]$ and $\underline{C}[\![e_3]\!]$ are strict.

5. ABSTRACT INTERPRETATION

The main design principle underlying the metalanguage is that data flow analyses should be obtainable by interpreting the primitives adequately. However, not all interpretations may meaningfully be viewed as specifications of data flow analyses. We shall therefore define an approximating interpretation I to be a specification of:

- constant functors $I(A_1)$,... over ACLs; these correspond to the approximations desired in the particular data flow analysis,
- locally continuous semifunctors I(+) and I(×) over ACLs; these correspond to the data flow analysis methods used (e.g. relational method),
- constant functions $I(f_1)$,... of contravariantly pure type,
- functionals I(cond), I(tuple),...

The collecting interpretation C is an approximating interpretation but the standard interpretation S is not (e.g. S(+) does not map into ACLs). The use of ACLs means that the sets of data flow values (like L in section 2) must be complete lattices and this is a common assumption. The additional assumptions of algebraicity of objects and strictness and continuity of morphisms is a technical convenience that hardly limits the applicability of the framework.

Consider now how to relate two data flow analyses described by approximating interpretations I and J. (A natural choice for I might be C.) The first task is to relate the complete lattices I[[rt]] and J[[rt]] for closed types rt. Motivated by section 2 we use a morphism

$$\gamma rt: J[\![rt]\!] \rightarrow I[\![rt]\!]$$

of ACLs to describe the meaning of elements of J[[rt]] in terms of those of I[[rt]]. In keeping with section 2 we shall require that γ_{rt} is an upper adjoint (relative to ACLs). This means that there must be a (necessarily unique) morphism (of ACLs)

$$\alpha_{rt}: I[\![rt]\!] \rightarrow J[\![rt]\!]$$

called a lower adjoint such that $\alpha_{rt}(l) \sqsubseteq m$ iff $l \sqsubseteq \gamma_{rt}(m)$. It now remains to give a structural definition of $(\alpha_{rt}, \gamma_{rt})$.

We shall use section 2 as a guide in this. So let rt=A×A with $I(A)=P(Z)$, $J(A)=L$ and $\gamma_A=\bar{\gamma}$. Suppose first that $I(\times)=J(\times)=\times$. It is then natural to define γ_{rt} as the componentwise application of $\bar{\gamma}$ so that e.g. γ_{rt}(pos,neg) is $(\{z|z\geq 0\},\{z|z<0\})$. This suggests the general definition

$$\gamma_{rt} = J(\times)(\bar{\gamma},\bar{\gamma}).$$

Suppose next that $I(\times)=\otimes$ (as defined in section 2) whereas $J(\times)=\times$.

The definition of γ_{rt} used in section 2 may be written

$$\gamma_{rt} = \Gamma_{\underline{\times}} \cdot \underline{J}(\underline{\times})(\overline{\gamma},\overline{\gamma})$$

where $\Gamma_{\underline{\times}}(X,Y)=X\times Y$ so that $\gamma_{rt}(\text{pos},\text{neg})$ is $\{(z,z')|z>0\wedge z'<0\}$. This amounts to applying $\overline{\gamma}$ componentwise and then passing from $\underline{J}(\underline{\times})$ to $\underline{I}(\underline{\times})$. There is no reason for this particular order so

$$\gamma_{rt} = \underline{I}(\underline{\times})(\overline{\gamma},\overline{\gamma}) \cdot \Gamma_{\underline{\times}}$$

would be just as natural and it is desirable that the two definitions agree. This suggests that $\Gamma_{\underline{\times}}$ should be a natural transformation.

The formal definition of γ_{rt} is complicated by two issues. One is that $\underline{I}(\underline{\times})$ etc. are not necessarily functors. However, they are semifunctors and therefore specialize to functors over the categories ACLsu and ACLsl of upper and lower adjoints respectively. Another problem is that the structural definition necessitates consideration of types that are not closed. So if rt has its free domain variables in the list $\underline{X}_1,\ldots\underline{X}_N$ we define

$$\Gamma_{rt}(\gamma_1,\ldots,\gamma_N):\underline{J}[\![rt]\!](M_1,\ldots,M_N)\rightarrow\underline{I}[\![rt]\!](L_1,\ldots,L_N)$$

assuming that $\gamma_i:M_i\rightarrow L_i$. For a closed type rt we then use $\gamma_{rt}=\Gamma_{rt}(\ )$. The definition proceeds as follows:

$$\Gamma_{\underline{A}}(\gamma_1,\ldots,\gamma_N) = \text{some previously specified } \gamma_{\underline{A}}.$$

When $rt=rt_1\underline{\times}\ldots\underline{\times}rt_k$ we put

$$\Gamma_{rt}(\gamma_1,\ldots,\gamma_N) = \Gamma_{\underline{\times}}(\underline{I}[\![rt_1]\!](L_1,\ldots,L_N),\ldots)\cdot\underline{J}(\times)(\Gamma_{rt_i}(\gamma_1,\ldots,\gamma_N),\ldots)$$

where $\Gamma_{\underline{\times}}(\ldots)$ is the instantiation of a natural transformation $\Gamma_{\underline{\times}}$ from $\underline{J}(\underline{\times})$ (specialized to ACLsu) to $\underline{I}(\underline{\times})$ (specialized to ACLsu). The case $rt=rt_1\underline{+}\ldots\underline{+}rt_k$ is similar and

$$\Gamma_{\underline{X}_i}(\gamma_1,\ldots,\gamma_N) = \gamma_i.$$

Finally, the definition for rt = $\underline{\text{rec}}\ \underline{X}_{N+1}.rt'$ roughly is

$$\Gamma_{rt}(\gamma_1,\ldots,\gamma_N) = \bigsqcup_n r_n\cdot\Gamma_{rt'}{}^n{}_{(\underline{X}_{N+1})}(\gamma_1,\ldots,\gamma_N,\perp)\cdot s_n^u$$

for appropriate embeddings r_n and s_n.

The actual choices of $\underline{I}(\underline{A}),\gamma_{\underline{A}}$ and $\underline{J}(\underline{A})$ depend on the particular data flow analyses and will not be considered here. A special case in the choice of $\underline{I}(\underline{\times}),\underline{J}(\underline{\times})$ etc. is when $I(\underline{\times})=\underline{J}(\underline{\times})$ and $\underline{I}(\underline{+})=\underline{J}(\underline{+})$. Then it is natural to define $\Gamma_{\underline{\times}}(\ldots)$ and $\Gamma_{\underline{+}}(\ldots)$ as the identity functions. For a closed type rt one then gets

$$\Gamma_{rt}(\ ) = \underline{I}[\![rt']\!](\gamma_{\underline{A}_1},\ldots) = \underline{J}[\![rt']\!](\gamma_{\underline{A}_1},\ldots)$$

where rt' is rt with each $\underline{A}_i$ replaced by $\underline{X}_i$. When $\underline{I}(\underline{\times})\neq\underline{J}(\underline{\times})$ or $\underline{I}(\underline{+})\neq\underline{J}(\underline{+})$ a shift in data flow analysis method occurs and the definition of $\Gamma_{\underline{\times}}$ and $\Gamma_{\underline{+}}$ are not so straightforward. We refer to [Nie 84, Nie 85a, Nie 85b] for particular examples.

The definition of α_{rt} is similar. Here it is assumed that all $\alpha_{\underline{A}}$ are given and that (relative to ACLs1) there are natural transformations $\underline{A}_{\underline{\times}}$ from $\underline{I}(\underline{\times})$ to $\underline{J}(\underline{\times})$ and $\underline{A}_{\underline{+}}$ from $\underline{I}(\underline{+})$ to $\underline{J}(\underline{+})$. When all of

$$(\alpha_{\underline{A}},\gamma_{\underline{A}})$$
$$(\underline{A}_{\underline{\times}}(L_1,\ldots,L_k),\Gamma_{\underline{\times}}(L_1,\ldots L_k))$$
$$(\underline{A}_{\underline{+}}(L_1,\ldots,L_k),\Gamma_{\underline{+}}(L_1,\ldots,L_k))$$

are pairs of adjoined functions then also all

$$(\alpha_{rt},\gamma_{rt})$$

will be. This completes the first task of relating the complete lattices

$\underline{I}[\![rt]\!]$ and $\underline{J}[\![rt]\!]$.

The next task is to relate the compile-time entities in $\underline{I}$ and $\underline{J}$. So consider a closed type ct and the definition of the relation

$$\underline{<}_{ct,(\gamma,\Gamma)}:\underline{I}[\![ct]\!]\times\underline{J}[\![ct]\!]\rightarrow\{true,false\}.$$

Here γ abbreviates the list of $\gamma_{\underline{A}}$'s and Γ abbreviates $\Gamma_{\underline{\times}}$ and $\Gamma_{\underline{+}}$. The interesting case is when ct=rt$\underline{\rightarrow}$rt'. Then elements $u \in \underline{I}[\![ct]\!]$ and $v \in \underline{J}[\![ct]\!]$ will be functions from rt to rt'. Building on section 2 we define

$$u\underline{<}_{rt\underline{\rightarrow}rt',(\gamma,\Gamma)}v \text{ iff } u\cdot\gamma_{rt}\sqsubseteq\gamma_{rt'}\cdot v$$

so that the results produced by v are safe approximations to those produced by u. The remaining cases are analogous to the definition of sim_{ct} because it is only run-time state transformations that are perceived differently in $\underline{I}$ and $\underline{J}$. (So to cater for non-closed types ct we should index $\underline{<}_{ct,(\gamma,\Gamma)}$ with predicates for the free domain variables of ct.)

The relation $\underline{<}_{ct,(\gamma,\Gamma)}$ can be extended componentwise so as to relate the approximating interpretations $\underline{I}$ and $\underline{J}$. We shall write $\underline{I}\underline{<}_{(\gamma,\Gamma)}\underline{J}$ whenever γ and Γ are as assumed above and

- $\underline{I}(cond)\underline{<}_{ft^3\rightarrow ft,(\gamma,\Gamma)}\underline{J}(cond)$ etc. hold for all functionals
- $\underline{I}(f)\underline{<}_{ct,(\gamma,\Gamma)}\underline{J}(f)$ for all constant functions f.

This relation means that the data flow analysis $\underline{J}$ is a safe approximation to $\underline{I}$:

Theorem 2. $\underline{I}\underline{<}_{(\gamma,\Gamma)}\underline{J}$ iff for all expressions e of type ct that $\underline{I}[\![e]\!]\ \underline{<}_{ct,(\gamma,\Gamma)}\underline{J}[\![e]\!]$. □

The proof is analogous to that to Theorem 1 and is therefore omitted.

The relation $\underline{<}_{(\gamma,\Gamma)}$ satisfies a transitive property, namely that

$$\underline{I}\underline{<}_{(\gamma,\Gamma)}\underline{J}\wedge\underline{J}\underline{<}_{(\gamma',\Gamma')}\underline{K} \Rightarrow \underline{I}\underline{<}_{(\gamma\cdot\gamma',\Gamma\cdot\Gamma')}\underline{K}$$

where $(\gamma \cdot \gamma')_{\underline{A}} = \gamma_{\underline{A}} \cdot \gamma_{\underline{A}}'$ etc. In practice this means that the task of proving one data flow analysis ($\underline{K}$) correct (with respect to $\underline{I}$) may be broken down into smaller and more amenable parts. Furthermore the reflexive law

$$\underline{I} \underset{(\text{id},\text{ID})}{<} \underline{I}$$

holds where $\underline{\text{ID}}_{\underline{x}}(\ldots) = \text{id} \ldots$ etc. Similar remarks apply to $\underset{\text{ct}, (\gamma, \Gamma)}{<}$.

6. INDUCING A DATA FLOW ANALYSIS

To describe a data flow analysis by means of an approximating interpretation $\underline{J}$ involves the specification of many components. In this section we consider how to ease this by using an already specified data flow analysis $\underline{I}$ (which may well be $\underline{C}$). It is to be expected that each $\underline{J}(\underline{A})$ is to be specified because it is usually the choices made here that determine the data flow analysis. Similar remarks apply to $\underline{J}(\underline{x})$ and $\underline{J}(+)$ although previous treatments have regarded these as fixed (e.g. $\underline{J}(\underline{x}) = \times$). It is when specifying the functionals and constants that there is room for ingenuity.

We shall write (α, γ) for the pairs $(\alpha_{\underline{A}}, \gamma_{\underline{A}})$ of adjoined functions. Similarly we shall write (A, Γ) for the pairs $(\underline{A}_{\underline{x}}, \overline{\Gamma_{\underline{x}}})$ and (A_+, Γ_+) of natural transformations and assume that all $(A \ldots (\ldots), \overline{\Gamma \ldots} (\ldots))$ are pairs of adjoined functions. Consider now a constant f of type $\text{rt} \rightarrow \text{rt}'$. The diagram

$$
\begin{array}{ccc}
\underline{I}[\![\,\text{rt}\,]\!] & \xrightarrow{\;\;\underline{I}(f)\;\;} & \underline{I}[\![\,\text{rt}'\,]\!] \\[2mm]
\Big\uparrow{\scriptstyle \gamma_{\text{rt}}} & & \Big\downarrow{\scriptstyle \alpha_{\text{rt}'}} \\[2mm]
\underline{J}[\![\,\text{rt}\,]\!] & & \underline{J}[\![\,\text{rt}'\,]\!]
\end{array}
$$

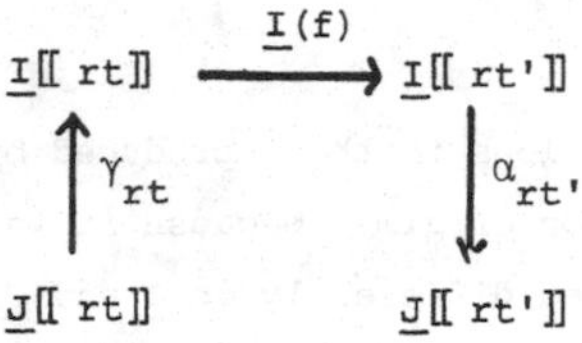

suggests using $\underline{J}(f) = \alpha_{\text{rt}'} \cdot \underline{I}(f) \cdot \gamma_{\text{rt}}$. The function $\underline{J}(f)$ is said to be __induced__ from $\underline{I}(f)$ [CoCo 79] and is intuitively the best version of $\underline{I}(f)$ that is possible using the approximative spaces $\underline{J}[\![\,\text{rt}\,]\!]$ and $\underline{J}[\![\,\text{rt}'\,]\!]$. Formally we have

$$\underline{I}(f) \cdot \gamma_{\text{rt}} \sqsubseteq \gamma_{\text{rt}'} \cdot \underline{J}(f)$$

showing that $\underline{J}(f)$ is a correct approximation to $\underline{I}(f)$, and

$$\underline{I}(f) \cdot \gamma_{\text{rt}} \sqsubseteq \gamma_{\text{rt}'} \cdot h \Leftrightarrow \underline{J}(f) \sqsubseteq h$$

showing that $\underline{J}(f)$ is as precise as possible.

The first task is to extend the concept of inducing to all types ct. Inducing $\underline{J}(f)$ from $\underline{I}(f)$ is analogous to transforming $\underline{S}(f)$ in the standard semantics into $\underline{C}(f)$ in the collecting semantics. However, here the situation is more "symmetric" so that types need not be contravariantly pure. So for a function or functional ϕ of closed type ct we shall use

$$\underline{J}(\phi) = \underline{I}[\![ct']\!] (f_1,\ldots,f_N)\downarrow 1 \ (\underline{I}(\phi))$$

$$= \underline{J}[\![ct']\!] (f_1,\ldots,f_N)\downarrow 1 \ (\underline{I}(\phi)).$$

Here ct' is ct with all $rt_i \underline{\to} rt_i'$ replaced by X_i and

$$f_i = (f_i', f_i'') = (\lambda f.\alpha_{rt'_i} \cdot f \cdot \gamma_{rt_i}, \lambda g.\gamma_{rt'_i} \cdot g \cdot \alpha_{rt_i}).$$

For a constant f of type $rt \underline{\to} rt'$ this gives the same result as above. For the functional □ we get

$$\underline{J}(\square)(g_1,g_2) = \alpha \cdot \underline{I}(\square)(\gamma \cdot g_1 \cdot \alpha, \gamma \cdot g_2 \cdot \alpha) \cdot \gamma$$

(omitting the indexes to α and γ). Intuitively $\gamma \cdot g \cdot \alpha$ is the effect of g when operating on the complete lattices $\underline{I}[\![\ldots]\!]$.

The transformations $\underline{I}[\![ct']\!] (\ldots)\downarrow 1$ and $\underline{I}[\![ct']\!] (\ldots)\downarrow 2$ preserve safe approximation. This means that they are monotonic in the following sense (as may be proved by structural induction on ct)

$$u \le_{ct,(id,ID)} v \Rightarrow \underline{I}[\![ct']\!] (\ldots)\downarrow 1(u) \le_{ct,(id,ID)} \underline{I}[\![ct']\!] (\ldots)\downarrow 1(v)$$

$$u \le_{ct,(id,ID)} v \Rightarrow \underline{I}[\![ct']\!] (\ldots)\downarrow 2(u) \le_{ct,(id,ID)} \underline{I}[\![ct']\!] (\ldots)\downarrow 2(v).$$

Furthermore they satisfy

$$u \le_{ct,(\gamma,\Gamma)} v \Leftrightarrow I[\![ct']\!] (f_1,\ldots,f_N)\downarrow 1(u) \le_{ct,(id,ID)} v$$

$$\Leftrightarrow u \le_{ct,(id,ID)} \underline{I}[\![ct']\!] (f_1,\ldots,f_N)\downarrow 2(v).$$

Since $\le_{ct,(id,ID)}$ is reflexive this means that

$$\underline{I}(\phi) \le_{ct,(\gamma,\Gamma)} \underline{J}(\phi)$$

so that $\underline{J}(\phi)$ is a safe approximation to $\underline{I}(\phi)$. Furthermore

$$\underline{I}(\phi) \le_{ct,(\gamma,\Gamma)} h \Leftrightarrow \underline{J}(\phi) \le_{ct,(id,ID)} h$$

so that $\underline{J}(\phi)$ is as precise as possible.

The next task is to define $\underline{J}$. We write

$$\underline{J} = \text{induce } (\underline{I},(\alpha,\gamma),(A,\Gamma),(J(\underline{A}))_{\underline{A}},\underline{J}(\underline{\times}),\underline{J}(\underline{+}))$$

and define

$$\underline{J}(\phi) = \underline{I}[\![ct']\!] (f_1,\ldots,f_N)\downarrow 1(\underline{I}(\phi))$$

for every constant or functional ϕ. The correctness and preciseness of $\underline{J}$ follows from

<u>Theorem 3</u>

- $\underline{I} \le_{(\gamma,\Gamma)}$ induce $(\underline{I},\ldots)$
- $\underline{I} \le_{(\gamma,\Gamma)} \underline{J}' \Leftrightarrow$ induce$(\underline{I},\ldots) \le_{(id,ID)} \underline{J}'$ □

Proof This is a consequence of the results above. □

Just as $\leq_{(\gamma,\Gamma)}$ satisfied reflexive and transitive laws one can show that induced(...) has "functor-like" properties. This means that it is unimportant whether a data flow analysis is induced in one big step or as a sequence of smaller steps.

For implementation purposes the induced data flow analysis may be too precise. For example a constant $\underline{J}(f)$ may be computationally too costly to use. Little can be said in general about such constants except that it is always safe to replace $\underline{J}(f)$ by a more approximative $\underline{J}'(f)$, i.e.

$$\underline{J}(f) \leq_{ct,(id,ID)} \underline{J}'(f) \Rightarrow I \leq_{(\gamma,\Gamma)} \underline{J}'.$$

For a functional there is the additional phenomenon that one might expect its definition to be of a certain form and that inducing does not preserve this. A simple example is □ which might be expected to be functional composition. Even if this is so for $\underline{I}(\square)$ it needs not be the case for $J(\square)$ since then

$$\underline{J}(\square)(g_1,g_2) = (\alpha\cdot\gamma)\cdot g_1\cdot(\alpha\cdot\gamma)\cdot g_2\cdot(\alpha\cdot\gamma).$$

In this case it is clear that it is safe to replace $\underline{J}(\square)$ by $\underline{J}'(\square)=\lambda(g_1,g_2).g_1\cdot g_2$. Similar considerations apply to the remaining functionals [Nie 85b].

7. CONCLUSION

The main achievement of the work reported here is that it develops a rather general setting in which abstract interpretation can be performed. The distinction between run-time types and compile-time types is the fundament that makes this possible. A major limitation in the syntax of the metalanguage is the absence of rt::=ft so that storable procedures cannot be handled.
None the less a variant of M. Gordon's language SMALL [Gor 79] can be handled [Nie 84], and it is conjectured that also PASCAL can be handled. The present treatment generalizes previous approaches in allowing the interpretation of functionals and domain constructors to vary. However, it is too restrictive always to treat FIX as the least fixed point and rec X.rt as the limit of $rt^n(U)$. Another natural extension is to include backward data flow analyses (e.g. for type inference).

8. REFERENCES

[AhUl 78] A.V. Aho, J.D. Ullman: Principles of Compiler Design, Addison-Wesley, 1978.

[ArMa 75] M.A. Arbib, E.G. Manes: Arrows, Structures and Functors: The Categorical Imperative, Academic Press, 1975.

[BuHA 85] G.L. Burn, C.L. Hankin, S. Abramsky: The Theory and Practice of Strictness Analysis for Higher Order Functions, Research Report DoC 85/6, Imperial College of Science and Technology, London.

[CoCo 77] P. Cousot, R. Cousot: Abstract Interpretation: A Unified lattice model for static analysis of programs by construction or approximation of fixpoints, in: Conf. Record of the 4th ACM Symposium on Principles of Programming Languages, 1977.

[CoCo 78] P. Cousot, R. Cousot: Static determination of dynamic properties of recursive procedures, in: Formal Descriptions of Programming Concepts, E.J. Neuhold (ed.), North-Holland Publishing Company, 1978.

[CoCo 79] P. Cousot, R. Cousot: Systematic design of program analysis frameworks, in: Conf. Record of the 6th ACM Symposium on Principles of Programming Languages, 1979.

[Don 78] V. Donzeau-Gouge: Utilisation de la sémantique dénotationelle pour l'étude d'interprétations non-standard, IRIA report No. 273, France, 1978.

[Don 81] V. Donzeau-Gouge: Denotational definition of properties of program computations, in: Program Flow Analysis: Theory and Applications, S.S. Muchnick, N.D. Jones (eds.), Prentice-Hall, 1981.

[Gor 79] M. Gordon: The Denotational Description of Programming Languages - An Introduction, Springer-Verlag, 1979.

[Hec 77] M.S. Hecht: Flow Analysis of Computer Programs, North-Holland, 1977.

[JoMu 78] N.D. Jones, S.S. Muchnick: TEMPO: A Unified Treatment of Binding Time and Parameter Passing Concepts in Programming Languages, Lecture Notes in Computer Science No. 66, Springer Verlag, 1978.

[JoMu 81] N.D. Jones, S.S. Muchnick: Complexity of flow analysis, inductive assertion synthesis and a language due to Dijkstra, in: Program Flow Analysis: Theory and Applications, S.S. Muchnick, N.D. Jones (eds.), Prentice-Hall, 1981.

[KaUl 77] J.B. Kam, J.D. Ullman: Monotone data flow analysis frameworks, Acta Informatica, vol. 7 (1977), pp. 305-317.

[MiSt 76] R. Milne, C. Strachey: A Theory of Programming Language Semantics, Chapman and Hall, London, 1976.

[MyNi 83] A. Mycroft, F. Nielson: Strong abstract interpretation using power domains, in: Proceedings ICALP 1983, Springer LNCS no. 154, pp. 536-547.

[Nie 82] F. Nielson: A denotational framework for data flow analysis, Acta Informatica, vol. 18 (1982), pp. 265-287.

[Nie 84] F. Nielson: Abstract Interpretation Using Domain Theory, Ph.D. thesis, University of Edinburgh, Scotland, 1984.

[Nie 85a] F. Nielson: Tensor Products Generalize the Relational Data Flow Analysis Method, 4'th HCSC, 1985.

[Nie 85b] F. Nielson: Expected Forms of Data Flow Analysis, to appear in: Proceedings of "Programs as Data Objects", Springer LNCS, 1986.

[NiNi 85a] F. Nielson, H.R. Nielson: Code Generation from Two-Level Denotational Meta-Languages, to appear in: Proceedings of "Programs as Data Objects", Springer LNCS, 1986.

[NiNi 85b] H.R. Nielson, F. Nielson: Pragmatic Aspects of Two-Level Denotational Meta-Languages, report R-85-13, Aalborg University Centre, Denmark.

[Rey 74] J.C. Reynolds: On the Relation between Direct and Continuation Semantics, in: Proceedings 2nd ICALP 1974, Lecture Notes in Computer Science 14, pp. 141-156.

[Ros 77] B.K. Rosen: High-level data flow analysis, CACM vol. 20 No. 10 (1977), pp. 712-724.

[SmPl 82] M.B. Smyth, G.D. Plotkin: The category-theoretic solution of recursive domain equations, SIAM J. Comput., vol. 11 No. 4 (1982), pp. 761-783.

[Ten 74] A. Tenenbaum: Automatic Type Analysis in a Very High Level Language, Ph.D. thesis, New York University, 1974.

[Ten 81] R.D. Tennent: Principles of Programming Languages, Prentice-Hall, 1981.

TEMPORAL REASONING UNDER GENERALIZED FAIRNESS CONSTRAINTS[1]
(Extended Abstract)

E. Allen EMERSON and Chin-Laung LEI

Department of Computer Sciences
University of Texas at Austin
Austin, Texas 78712
U.S.A.

1. Introduction

A variety of systems of temporal logic have been proposed for use in the design of correct concurrent programs (cf. [PN77], [PA78], [PR79], [EC80], [BMP81], [EC82], [OL82]). These systems offer differing modalities and notation. However, we can usually classify them into two groups: linear time logics (LTLs) and branching time logics (BTLs) (cf. [LA80], [EH83]). In an LTL, the temporal modalities are defined with respect to a single path which intuitively represents the future that the program will actually follow. Typical linear time operators include G ("always"), F ("sometime"), X ("nexttime"), and U ("until"). When LTLs are used to specify correctness properties of a concurrent program, there is an implicit universal quantification over all possible futures that could turn out to be the actual future. In contrast, branching time modalities are true or false of a state and are usually of the general form A ("for all futures") or E ("for some future") followed by some combination of linear time operators thus allowing explicit quantification over possible futures starting in the state. Some basic branching time operators are AFp ("for all futures, sometime p"), EFp ("for some future, sometime p"), and AGp ("for all futures, always p "). The first two properties (often called *inevitability* and *potentiality*, resp.) are *eventuality* properties which assert that something will eventually happen while the last property is an *invariance* property.

Two important characteristics of a temporal logic are (1) its expressive power (what correctness properties are (and are not) expressible in the logic), and (2) the complexity of the decision procedure for testing satisfiability (or equivalently, testing validity) in the logic. A great deal of attention has been devoted to classifying and comparing various logics in terms of these two characteristics. These matters are not only of theoretical interest, but are also of great practical significance as well. A logic that is very expressive is desirable since it may provide great generality and ease of use for specification in applications. At the same time, the

[1]Work supported in part by NSF Grant MCS8302878

complexity of the decision procedure is of concern in mechanical verification efforts. It is also of crucial importance in applications such as program synthesis from temporal logic specifications (cf. [EC82], [MW84]) where the decision procedure is used to construct a model of the specification formula from which a concurrent program is extracted. Since, as a general rule, the more expressive a logic the greater the complexity of its decision procedure, it is a challenge to get a logic with a satisfactory tradeoff between expressive power and cost of testing satisfiability.

As discussed in [EH83], there are certain advantages to doing temporal reasoning in a BTL. For example, in concurrent program synthesis applications the ability to assert the existence of alternative computation paths as allowed in a BTL (but not in an LTL) can be used to enforce lower bounds on nondeterminism so that the synthesized concurrent program exhibits an adequate degree of parallelism. On the other hand, a criticism often levelled at branching time logic is the inability to express correctness under fair scheduling assumptions (cf. [LA80], [LP84]). Indeed, the temporal logic (CTL) used in the branching time approach of [EC82] cannot express inevitability under fair scheduling assumptions. While another BTL, CTL*, does have a sufficiently rich syntax to allow expression of most any correctness property including fair inevitability, the best known deterministic time decision procedure is of triple exponential complexity (cf. [ES84]), and almost certainly unsuitable for use in applications. To have any hope of practical utility, we need a logic of exponential time complexity.

An inspection of the literature does not reveal any BTL sufficiently expressive to allow specification of correctness properties under fair scheduling constraints which also has an exponential time decision procedure We are thus left with the question: does there exist such a logic? We are now able to answer in the affirmative. We describe a BTL which we call *Fair Computation Tree Logic* (FCTL). FCTL generalizes the (ordinary) CTL as used in [EC82] and [CES83] by having all path quantifiers relativized to a fairness assumption Φ_0 specified by a boolean combination of the infinitary linear time temporal operators $\overset{\infty}{F}p$ (which abbreviates GFp and means "infinitely often p") and $\overset{\infty}{G}p$ (which abbreviates FGp and means "almost everywhere p"). Its basic modalities are thus of the form A_Φ ("for all fair paths") or E_Φ ("for some fair path") followed by a single linear time operator: F, G, X, or U. The infinitary operators of Φ_0 make it possible to express and reason under a wide variety of "practical" fairness assumptions from the literature including impartiality [LPS81], weak fairness ([LA80]), strong fairness ([LA80]), fair reachability of predicates ([QS83]), state fairness ([PN83]), generalized fairness ([FK84]), as well as the technical notion of "limited looping" fairness ([AB80]). We show that when Φ_0 is in a restricted canonical form $\bigwedge_{i=1}^{n}(\overset{\infty}{F}a_i \vee \overset{\infty}{G}b_i)$, FCTL has the *Small Model Property*: any satisfiable FCTL specification has a small (exponential size) finite model. Since most all "practical" types of fairness considered in the literature (including all those listed above) can be directly specified using a Φ_0 in restricted canonical form, we immediately get a nondeterministic exponential time, and, hence, deterministic double exponential time decision procedure for a BTL which allows reasoning about many useful types of fairness. This is an exponential time improvement over the decision procedure for CTL*. We go on to show that when Φ_0 is further restricted to be of the form $\bigwedge_{i=1}^{n} \overset{\infty}{F} a_i$, we can give a decision procedure for FCTL of *deterministic, single exponential time* complexity. Such a Φ_0 still suffices for expressing important types of fairness including impartiality, weak fairness, and unconditional fairness ([FK84]).

In broad outline, our decision procedure follows that for CTL (cf. [EC82], [EH82]). Given an FCTL specification, we show that we can collapse any (possibly infinite) model by identifying states which agree on the Fischer-Ladner ([FL79]) closure of the specification. The resulting quotient structure can be viewed as a small, "pseudo-model" which can be unwound into a small, genuine model of p. The unwinding is accomplished by detecting small subgraphs of the quotient structure which certify fulfillment of the eventualities and then splicing the fragments together appropriately. The decision procedure can be implemented by building a *tableau* which essentially contains the quotient structure as a subgraph. This method has been generalized in automata-theoretic terms in [VW84] and is somewhat similar to that used in [KO83] to decide a fragment of the propositional Mu-Calculus.

However, there are significant technical differences between our approach here and that described above. We believe that these differences may account for our being able to handle branching time modalities in exponential time that no previous approach could. A crucial limitation of the previous approaches seems to be that the subgraphs they used to certify fulfillment of eventualities could not contain cycles. For example, for ordinary CTL the subtree certifying fulfillment in the original (say, without loss of generality, tree-like) model of the eventuality AFp collapses to a directed acyclic subgraph embedded (in a special way) in the quotient structure. Similarly, in [VW84] finite subtrees certify fulfillment of eventualities. In our approach however, the subgraphs do contain (disciplined) cycles: For example, the subgraph certifying fulfillment of A_ΦFp will in general contain unfair cycles (corresponding to paths which violate the fairness specification Φ_0.) while the subgraph for E_ΦFp will contain a fair cycle. Some additional, somewhat subtle, technical constraints are also placed on the subgraphs certifying fulfillment of eventualities. A further complicating factor is that E_ΦGp and E_ΦXp are essentially eventuality properties since we must check that there really exist fair paths.

We can gain some insight into the possible significance of our techniques by expressing correctness properties in the propositional Mu-Calculus (cf. [EC80], [DB80]). The propositional Mu-calculus provides a *least fixpoint* operator (μ) and a *greatest fixpoint* operator (ν) which make it possible to give *fixpoint characterizations* of the branching time modalities. Intuitively, the Mu-Calculus makes it possible to characterize the modalities in terms of recursively defined tree-like patterns (and, thus, may itself be viewed as a BTL). For example, the ordinary CTL modality for potentiality $EFP = \mu Z.[P \vee EXZ]$, the least fixpoint of the functional $P \vee EXZ$ where Z is an atomic proposition variable (intuitively ranging over sets of states).[2] Similarly, ordinary inevitability $AFP = \mu Y.[P \vee AXY]$. The fixpoint characterizations for correctness properties under fair scheduling can be significantly more complicated however. For even a simple type of fairness, specified by, say, $\Phi_0 = \overset{\infty}{F}\neg P$, fair inevitability $A_\Phi FQ \equiv A[\overset{\infty}{F}\neg P \Rightarrow FQ] \equiv A[\overset{\infty}{G}P \vee FQ] = \mu Y.\nu Z.[AX((P \vee Y) \wedge Z) \vee Q]$. Hence while fair inevitability is expressible in the Mu-Calculus, it is not expressible in the *aconjunctive* μ-calculus shown to be decidable in deterministic exponential time in [KO83] (because Y is active in both conjuncts $AX(P \vee Y)$ and Z). We also note that alternating nestings of μ's and ν's in the above fixpoint characterization of fair inevitability lead to discontinuities so that transfinite ordinals are needed in well-foundedness arguments to prove fair inevitability (cf. [AO83], [LPS81], [GFMD81]). Moreover, all the eventuality properties that are handled in deterministic exponential time in the automata-theoretic approach of [VW84] are definable by Buchi automata on infinite trees (cf. [RA68]) whereas properties such as fair inevitability are not.

The limitation of both the [KO83] and [VW84] approaches can be viewed as an inability to cope with certain well-foundedness conditions corresponding to transfinite ordinals and for fulfillment of eventualities, a limitation reflected in the absence of cycles in the certifying subgraphs for eventualities. We thus believe that generalizations of our approach here might lead to deterministic exponential time decision procedures more expressive logics suitable for applications, and, in particular (i) for a larger fragment of the propositional Mu-Calculus than that of [KO83] and (ii) in a broader automata-theoretic framework than [VW84].

Finally, by way of comparison with [QS83], we remark that the main result of [QS83] is that (in effect) their "temporal logic for reasoning about fairness (FCL)" is translatable into (ordinary) CTL. (They are using a rather restricted form of fairness.) Since our FCTL subsumes CTL, it also subsumes their FCL.

The remainder of the paper is organized as follows: Section 2 presents important preliminary definitions including the characterization of the subgraphs certifying fulfillment of eventualities. Section 3 proves the small model theorem for FCTL while the decision procedure is given in section 4.

---

[2]PDL enthusiasts should think of EXZ as <R>Z and AXZ as [R]Z where R is the program letter corresponding to the underlying transition relation of the (Kripke) structure.

2. The Specification Language

A Fair Computation Tree Logic (FCTL) specification (p_0,Φ_0) consists of a functional assertion p_0 and an underlying fairness assumption Φ_0. The functional assertion p_0 is expressed in essentially CTL syntax with basic modalities of the form either A_Φ ("for all fair paths"), or E_Φ ("for some fair path") followed by one of the linear time operators Fp ("sometimes p"), Gp ("always p"), Xp ("nexttime p"), or [p U q] ("p holds until q becomes *true*"). We subscript the path quantifiers with the symbol Φ to emphasize that they range over paths meeting the fairness constraint Φ_0, and to syntactically distinguish FCTL from CTL. A fairness constraint Φ_0 is build up from atomic propositions, the infinitary linear time operators $\overset{\infty}{F}$p ("infinitely often p") and $\overset{\infty}{G}$p ("almost always p"), and boolean connectives. Note that p_0 is a state formula (*true* or *false* of states) whereas Φ_0 is a path formula (*true* or *false* of paths).

2.1. Syntax. Formally, the class of functional assertions in FCTL specifications is defined inductively as follows:

1. Any atomic proposition P is a functional assertion.
2. If p, q are functional assertions then so are $\neg$p, and (p $\wedge$ q).
3. If p, q are functional assertions then so are A_ΦXp, E_ΦXp, A_Φ(pUq), and E_Φ(pUq).

A propositional formula is one formed by rules 1, 2 above. A fairness constraint is then formed by the following rules:

4. If p, q are propositional formulae then $\overset{\infty}{F}$p, $\overset{\infty}{G}$p are fairness constraints.
5. If p, q are fairness constraints then so are $\neg$p, and (p $\wedge$ q).

The other connectives can then be defined as abbreviations in the usual way: p $\vee$ q abbreviates $\neg(\neg p \wedge \neg q)$, p $\Rightarrow$ q abbreviates $\neg p \vee q$, A_ΦFq abbreviates A_Φ[*true* U q], E_ΦFq abbreviates E_Φ[*true* U q], A_ΦGq abbreviates $\neg E_\Phi F \neg q$, E_ΦGq abbreviates $\neg A_\Phi F \neg q$, ΦA_Φ[p W q] abbreviates $\neg E_\Phi$[p U q], E_Φ[p W q] abbreviates $\neg A_\Phi$[p U q] etc.

Remark: Recall that CTL* is the full branching time logic in which the basic modalities have the form: A or E followed by an arbitrary combination (involving boolean connectives and nesting) of linear time operators F, G, X, and U. We could thus view the assertions of FCTL as a sublanguage of CTL* where, eg., the A_ΦFp is an abbreviation for the CTL* formula A[$\Phi_0 \Rightarrow$ Fp]. However, the corresponding CTL* formula might be rather unwieldy due to the need to repeatedly write down multiple copies of the actual fairness formula Φ_0.

2.2. Semantics. Let AP be the underlying set of atomic propositions. A *prestructure* M=(S, R, L) is a labelled transition graph, where

- S is a nonempty set of states.
- R is a binary relation on S which gives the possible transitions between states.
- L is a labeling which assigns to each state a set of formulae .

We say that prestructure M = (S,R,L) is a *subprestructure* of prestructure M' = (S',R',L') provided that S ⊆ S', R ⊆ R', and L = L'|S. We also say that M is *contained in* M'. The size of a prestructure M=(S, R, L), written |M|, is defined to be the number of states in S. A *structure* is a prestructure with R total. A *fullpath* x is an infinite sequence of states $(s_0, s_1, s_2, \ldots)$ such that $\forall i \geq 0[(s_i, s_{i+1})] \in R]$. We use x^i to denote the suffix of x beginning at state x_i, i.e. $x^i=(x_i, x_{i+1}, \ldots)$. We write $M, x \models \Phi_0$ to mean that fullpath x in prestructure M meets fairness constraint Φ_0. We define the $\models$ relation inductively in the usual way:

1. $M, x \models P$ iff $P \in L(s_0)$, for any atomic proposition P.
2. $M, x \models \neg p$ iff not$(M, x \models p)$
3. $M, x \models p \wedge q$ iff $M, x \models p$ and $M, x \models q$
4. $M, x \models \overset{\infty}{F}p$ iff there exists infinitely many $i \geq 0$ such that $M, x^i \models p$
5. $M, x \models \overset{\infty}{G}p$ iff $\exists i \geq 0[\forall j \geq i(M, x^j \models p)]$

We write $M, s \models E\Phi_0$ if there is a fullpath x starting at s such that $M, x \models \Phi_0$. We say that fullpath x is a fair path in prestructure M under fairness assumption Φ_0 if $M, x \models \Phi_0$ holds. A state is fair iff it lies on some fair path.

An FCTL specification (p_0, Φ_0) is interpreted with respect to a prestructure M. We write $M, s \models_{\Phi_0} p_0$ to mean that functional assertion p_0 is *true* at state s of prestructure M under fairness assumption Φ_0. We define $\models_{\Phi_0}$ inductively on the prestructure of the functional assertion p_0:

1. $M, s \models_{\Phi_0} P$ iff $P \in L(s)$, for any atomic proposition P.
2. $M, s \models_{\Phi_0} \neg p$ iff not$(M, s \models_{\Phi_0} p)$
3. $M, s \models_{\Phi_0} p \wedge q$ iff $M, s \models_{\Phi_0} p$ and $M, s \models_{\Phi_0} q$
4. $M, s_0 \models_{\Phi_0} E_\Phi Xp$ iff there exists a path $x=(s_0, s_1, s_2, \ldots)$ such that $M, x \models \Phi_0$, and $M, s_1 \models_{\Phi_0} p$
5. $M, s_0 \models_{\Phi_0} A_\Phi Xp$ iff for all paths $x=(s_0, s_1, s_2, \ldots)$ $[M, x \models \Phi_0 \Rightarrow M, s_1 \models_{\Phi_0} p]$
6. $M, s_0 \models_{\Phi_0} E_\Phi(p\ U\ q)$ iff there exists a path $x=(s_0, s_1, s_2, \ldots)$ such that $M, x \models \Phi_0$ and $\exists j \geq 0[M, s_j \models_{\Phi_0} q \wedge \forall i<j(M, s_i \models_{\Phi_0} p)]$
7. $M, s_0 \models_{\Phi_0} A_\Phi(p\ U\ q)$ iff for all paths $x=(s_0, s_1, s_2, \ldots)$, $M, x \models \Phi_0$ implies $\exists j \geq 0[M, s_j \models_{\Phi_0} q \wedge \forall i<j(M, s_i \models_{\Phi_0} p)]$

A model w.r.t. fairness assumption Φ_0 is a structure M=(S,R,L) such that for all s ∈ S, and for every functional assertion p, $M,s \models_{\Phi_0}$ p iff $p \in L(s)$.

In the sequel we will assume that a functional assertional has been written in positive normal form where all negations have been pushed as deep as possible using duality and DeMorgan's laws. We use *not(p)* to indicate the formula, also in positive normal form, obtained from $\neg p$ by driving the $\neg$ in as far as possible and eliminating double negations.

Remarks: (1) The restricted form of $\Phi_0 = \wedge_{i=1}^{n} \overset{\infty}{F} a_i$ suffices to handle unconditional fairness of [FK84], impartiality of [LPS81] as $\bigwedge_{i=1}^{n} (\overset{\infty}{F} executed_i)$, where $executed_i$ is a proposition which asserts that process i is being executed, and weak fairness of [LA80] (also known as justice in [LPS81]) as $\bigwedge_{i=1}^{n}$ $(\overset{\infty}{G} enabled_i \Rightarrow \overset{\infty}{F} executed_i) \equiv \bigwedge_{i=1}^{n}$ $(\overset{\infty}{F}(\neg enabled_i) \vee \overset{\infty}{F} executed_i) \equiv \bigwedge_{i=1}^{n}$ $(\overset{\infty}{F}(\neg enabled_i \vee executed_i))$.

(2) It is routine to extend the semantics of FCTL to be interpreted over PDL-like (cf. [FL79]) structures $M = (S, A_1, ... A_k, L)$ in order to formalize the distinction between a process being enabled and being executed. Alternatively, we can encode the extended semantics into the present semantics as is done in [PN77], [QS83], or [CES83].

(3) The reader wishing additional information on FCTL, its generalizations and range of applicability, is referred to the companion papers [EL85a] and [EL85b] which consider the - technically much simpler - problem of model checking.

3. Preliminaries.

Remark: To simplify the exposition, we will just deal with $A_\Phi Fq$ and $E_\Phi Fq$; the generalization to $A_\Phi[p \ U \ q]$ and $E_\Phi[p \ U \ q]$ is routine and left to the full paper.

In the next section, we will prove the Small Model Theorem for FCTL as follows: Suppose M is a model of (p_0, Φ_0). Identify those states which agree on the *closure* of (p_0, Φ_0). The resulting *quotient structure* M' is a *Pseudo-Hintikka Structure* which can be unwound into a small model of (p_0, Φ_0). More precisely, for each state s of M' and for each eventuality p in the label of s, we show that there is a "fragment" contained in M' which certifies that p is fulfilled at s. These fulfilling fragments can then be spliced together in such a way as to get a small model of (p_0, Φ_0). We now give some terminology to the make the above precise. (We suggest that the reader go over this section quickly on first reading and then refer to it in detail as needed while reading the subsequent sections.)

3.1. Quotient Construction. We define the *Extended Fischer-Ladner Closure* (cf. [FL79]} of an FCTL specification (p_0,Φ_0), written $EFL(p_0,\Phi_0)$ to be the least set such that,

EFL1. $p_0 \in EFL(p_0,\Phi_0)$
EFL2. $p \in EFL(p_0,\Phi_0) \Rightarrow not(p) \in EFL(p_0,\Phi_0)$
EFL3. $p \wedge q \in EFL(p_0,\Phi_0) \Rightarrow p, q \in EFL(p_0,\Phi_0)$
EFL4. $p \vee q \in EFL(p_0,\Phi_0) \Rightarrow p, q \in EFL(p_0,\Phi_0)$
EFL5. $E_\Phi Xp \in EFL(p_0,\Phi_0) \Rightarrow p \in EFL(p_0,\Phi_0)$
EFL6. $A_\Phi Xp \in EFL(p_0,\Phi_0) \Rightarrow p \in EFL(p_0,\Phi_0)$
EFL7. $E_\Phi Fp \in EFL(p_0,\Phi_0) \Rightarrow p, E_\Phi XE_\Phi Fp \in EFL(p_0,\Phi_0)$
EFL8. $A_\Phi Fp \in EFL(p_0,\Phi_0) \Rightarrow p, A_\Phi XA_\Phi Fp \in EFL(p_0,\Phi_0)$
EFL9. $E_\Phi Gq \in EFL(p_0,\Phi_0) \Rightarrow q, E_\Phi XE_\Phi Gq \in EFL(p_0,\Phi_0)$
EFL10. $A_\Phi Gq \in EFL(p_0,\Phi_0) \Rightarrow q, A_\Phi XA_\Phi Gq \in EFL(p_0,\Phi_0)$
EFL11. All (atomic) propositional subformulae of Φ_0 are in $EFL(p_0,\Phi_0)$.
EFL12. $E_\Phi X\mathit{true} \in EFL(p_0,\Phi_0)$

Note that $|EFL(p_0,\Phi_0)| = O(|p_0| + |\Phi_0|)$.

A subset s of $EFL(p_0,\Phi_0)$ is said to be *maximal* if for every formula $q \in EFL(p_0,\Phi_0)$, either $q \in s$ or $not(q) \in s$. The *quotient structure* of a prestructure M=(S, R, L) w.r.t. (Φ_0,p_0), written $M/EFL(p_0,\Phi_0)$, is defined as the structure M'=(S', R', L') such that $S'=\{[s]: [s] = \{t\in S: L(t) \cap EFL(p_0,\Phi_0) = L(s) \cap EFL(p_0,\Phi_0)\}\}$, $R'=\{([s],[t]): (s,t)\in R\}$, and $L'([s]) = L(s)\cap EFL(p_0,\Phi_0)$. Intuitively, it is the structure obtained from M by identifying and collapsing together all states that have the same closure. [s] is the equivalence class of states t in M satisfying the same formulae in the closure as s.

3.2. Hintikka Structure. A Hintikka structure for an FCTL specification (p_0,Φ_0) is a structure M=(S,R,L) such that $p_o \in L(s)$ for some $s \in S$ which satisfies the following constraints:

H1. $E_\Phi X\mathit{true} \in L(s)$ iff $\exists$fullpath $x[M,x \models \Phi_0]$
H2. $E_\Phi X\mathit{true} \in L(s)$ or $A_\Phi X\mathit{false} \in L(s)$
H3. $not(p) \in L(s) \Rightarrow p \notin L(s)$
H4. $p \wedge q \in L(s) \Rightarrow p,q \in L(s)$
H5. $p \vee q \in L(s) \Rightarrow p \in L(s)$ or $q \in L(s)$
H6. $E_\Phi Fq \in L(s) \Rightarrow E_\Phi X\mathit{true} \in L(s)$ and $[q \in L(s)$ or $E_\Phi XE_\Phi Fq \in L(s)]$
H7. $A_\Phi Fq \in L(s) \Rightarrow A_\Phi X\mathit{false} \in L(s)$ or $q \in L(s)$ or $A_\Phi XA_\Phi Fq \in L(s)$
H8. $E_\Phi Gq \in L(s) \Rightarrow q, E_\Phi X\mathit{true}, E_\Phi XE_\Phi Gq \in L(s)$
H9. $A_\Phi Gq \in L(s) \Rightarrow A_\Phi X\mathit{false} \in L(s)$ or $q, A_\Phi XA_\Phi Gq \in L(s)$
H10. $E_\Phi Xp \in L(s) \Rightarrow E_\Phi X\mathit{true} \in L(s) \wedge \exists(s,t) \in R[p, E_\Phi X\mathit{true} \in L(t)]$
H11. $A_\Phi Xp \in L(s) \Rightarrow \forall(s,t) \in R[p \in L(t) \vee A_\Phi X\mathit{false} \in L(t)]$
H12. $E_\Phi Fq \in L(s) \Rightarrow$ for some fair path x starting at s and some state t on x, $q \in L(t)$.
H13. $A_\Phi Fq \in L(s) \Rightarrow$ for all fair paths x starting at s and some state t on x, $q \in L(t)$
H14. $E_\Phi Gq \in L(s) \Rightarrow$ there is a fair path x starting at s such that for all t on x, $q \in L(t)$.

Remarks: A Hintikka structure M is a structure with certain syntactic constraints on its labelling which guarantee that if formula p appears in L(s) for state s, then p is actually true at s in M. (Hence, if M is a Hintikka structure for (p_0,Φ_0) it defines a model of (p_0,Φ_0); the converse is also true.) Rules H1-H2 guarantee that fair paths are handled correctly, rules H4-10 guarantee propositional consistency, rules H10-11 guarantee local consistency, while rules H1,12-14 guarantee that eventualities are fulfilled. Note that $A_\Phi Gq$ is automatically handled by the local consistency rule H9.

Proposition 3.2.1: An FCTL specification (p_0, Φ_0) is satisfiable iff there exists a structure $M'=(S',R',L')$, a state $s' \in S'$, such that $M', s' \models_{\Phi_0} p_0$, and either (1) $\forall t \in S'[M', t \models_{\Phi_0} E_\Phi X\mathit{true}]$ or (2) $\forall t \in S'[M', t \models_{\Phi_0} A_\Phi X\mathit{false}]$.

proof: It suffices to show the only-if part since the if-part is trivial. Assume that (p_0, Φ_0) is satisfiable. Then there exists a structure $M=(S,R,L)$ and a state $s \in S$ such that $M, s \models_{\Phi_0} p_0$.

Case 1: $M, s \models_{\Phi_0} E_\Phi X\mathit{true}$. Let $S'=\{t \in S\colon M, t \models_{\Phi_0} E_\Phi X\mathit{true}\}$, $R' = R|S'\times S'$, and $L' = L|S'$. It is easily argued by induction on formula length that $\forall$ subformula p' of p_0 $\forall t \in S'[M, t \models_{\Phi_0} p'$ iff $M', t \models_{\Phi_0} p']$. In particular, $M, s \models_{\Phi_0} p_0$ iff $M' s \models_{\Phi_0} p_0$. Moreover, condition (1) holds on structure M'.

Case 2: $M, s \models_{\Phi_0} A_\Phi X\mathit{false}$. Since $A_\Phi X\mathit{false} \equiv A[\Phi_0 \Rightarrow X\mathit{false} \equiv A[\neg\Phi_0]$, it is clear that $\Phi_0 \not\equiv \mathit{true}$ (otherwise, $M, s \models_{\Phi_0} \mathit{false}$ -- which is impossible). Hence we can find in M an unfair path starting at s. More precisely, take $S' = \{t \in S\colon M, t \models_{\Phi_0} A_\Phi X\mathit{false}$ and t is reachable from s$\}$, $R' = R|S'\times S'$, and $L' = L|S'$. It is quite obvious that R' is total and every path in M' is unfair. . Again, it can be proved easily by induction on formula length that $\forall$ subformula p' of p_0 $[M, s \models_{\Phi_0} p'$ iff $M', s \models_{\Phi_0} p']$.

Note that for any state s in a structure, if $A_\Phi \mathit{false}$ holds at s then every formula of the form $E_\Phi p$ is false at s and every formula of the form $A_\Phi p$ is true at s. Let prop(p) denote the formula obtained from p by substituting *true* (*false*) for each subformula $A_\Phi p'$ ($E_\Phi p'$) of p.

Corollary 3.2.2: Let (p_0, Φ_0) be an FCTL specification, $M = (S,R,L)$ be a structure and s be a state in S. If $M, s \models_{\Phi_0} A_\Phi X\mathit{false}$ then $M, s \models_{\Phi_0} p_0$ iff $M, s \models_{\Phi_0} \mathrm{prop}(p_0)$.

Note that $\mathrm{prop}(p_0)$ is a pure propositional formula whose truth value at a state s in a structure $M = (S,R,L)$ depends on the labelling function L only and has nothing to do with the fairness assumption Φ_0.

Thus, to test satisfiability of (p_0,Φ_0), it suffices to check whether (1) (p_0,Φ_0) is satisfiable in a structure all of whose states satisfy $E_\Phi X\mathit{true}$ or (2) the propositional formula $\mathrm{prop}(p_0)$ is satisfiable. In what follows, we will concentrate on how to check condition (1). We therefore assume that every state in a structure satisfies $E_\Phi X\mathit{true}$.

3.3. Fragments. We say that the A-formula $A_\Phi Fq$ is *not violated* in M provided that $\forall s \in S[E_\Phi X$*true*$, A_\Phi Fq \in L(s) \Rightarrow$ for all fair fullpaths x starting at s, q appears (in the label of some node) on x]. An A-formula $A_\Phi Fq$ is *fulfilled* in M provided that $\forall s \in S[E_\Phi X$*true*$, A_\Phi Fq \in L(s) \Rightarrow$ q appears in the label of some node along every path starting at s which is infinite and fair or finite and has $E_\Phi X$*true* at the last node]

An E-formula $E_\Phi Fq$ appearing in the label of a node s of M is said to be *fulfilled* at s if there exists a fair fullpath x in M starting at s such that q appears in the label of some node on x; we say that $E_\Phi Fq$ is *pending* at s if it is not fulfilled at s but there is a finite maximal path y in M starting at s, such that either $E_\Phi Fq$ appears everywhere on the path, or q appears on y and $E_\Phi X$*true* appears at the last node of y.

An E-formula $E_\Phi Gq$ appearing in the label of an node s of M is said to be *fulfilled* at s if there exists a fair fullpath x in M starting at s such that q appears in the label of every node on x; we say that $E_\Phi Gq$ is *pending* at s if it is not fulfilled at s but there is a finite maximal path y in M starting at s, such that $E_\Phi Gq$ and $E_\Phi X$*true* appear everywhere on y.

If $E_\Phi g$ (g is either Fq or Gq) is either fulfilled or pending at a state s, we say that $E_\Phi g$ is *not violated* at s. We say that $E_\Phi g$ is *not violated in a prestructure* M=(S,R,L) provided that $E_\Phi g$ is not violated at any state of S.

We define *fulfillment* and *violation* for an E-formula $E_\Phi Xp$ similarly.

A node in a prestructure M is said to be a *frontier* node provided it does not have any successor in M. On the contrary, nodes with successor(s) are *interior* nodes.

A *fragment* (rooted) at state s is a prestructure which satisfies the following 5 conditions:

1. All nodes are reachable from s.
2. No A-formulae are violated.
3. No E-formulae are violated.
4. All the interior nodes of the prestructure satisfy H2-H11.
5. All the frontier nodes of the prestructure satisfies H2-H9.

Note that all eventualities appearing in the root of a fragment are either fulfilled in the fragment or propagated to the frontier nodes in order to be fulfilled later.

In the following definitions for A/E/full-fragments, we only consider nodes including in their label $E_\Phi X$*true* because the A/E/full-fragment for node s containing $A_\Phi X$*false* can be defined to be to be an unfair path starting at s with $A_\Phi X$*false* in all its nodes.

An *E-fragment at a state s for an E-formula* $E_\Phi g$ (g = Fq, Gq, or Xq) is a fragment such that $E_\Phi g$ is fulfilled at s.

An *A-fragment at a state s for an A-formula* $A_\Phi Fq$, is a fragment M=(S,R,L) which satisfies the following conditions:

1. There is no fair path in M.
2. For all exterior nodes u of M, q L(u).

3. Each interior node containing $E_\Phi X\mathit{true}$ can reach some frontier node.

Note that in such a fragment $A_\Phi Fq$ is fulfilled.

A *full fragment* for a state s is a prestructure M such that every eventuality $A_\Phi Fq$, $E_\Phi Fq$, $E_\Phi Gq$, $E_\Phi Xq$ in s is fulfilled in M. Note that every formula that appears in the label of some node of a full fragment will not be violated.

A *pseudo-fair component (PFC)* C of structure M is a strongly connected subprestructure of M such that

1. C contains a fair fullpath.
2. Every fullpath in C which goes through each node of C infinitely often is fair.
3. If any $A_\Phi Fq$ appears in (the label of some node in) C then q also appears in (the label of some, in general, different node in) C.
4. $E_\Phi X\mathit{true}$

3.4. Pseudo Hintikka Structure. A Pseudo Hintikka Structure (PHS) for an FCTL specification (p_0,Φ_0) is a structure M=(S,R,L) with $p_0 \in L(s)$ for some $s \in S$ which satisfies the consistency requirements H2-H12 of Hintikka Structure and the following conditions (which certify "pseudo-fulfillment of the eventualities"):

H1'. $E_\Phi X\mathit{true} \in L(s) \Rightarrow \exists$ a path starting at s leading to a PFC in M.
H12'. $E_\Phi Fq \in L(s) \Rightarrow \exists$ in M a path starting at s leading to a state t such that $p \in L(t)$ and a PFC is reachable from t.
H13'. $A_\Phi Fq \in L(s) \Rightarrow \exists$ an A-fragment for s w.r.t. $A_\Phi Fq$ that is contained in M.
H14'. $E_\Phi Gq \in L(s) \Rightarrow \exists$ in M a finite path from s leading to a PFC such that all nodes on the finite path and in the PFC contain p in their label.

4. Small Model Theorem for FCTL

4.1. Theorem. Suppose (p_0,Φ_0) is an FCTL specification with Φ_0 of the form $\bigwedge_{i=1}^{k} (\overset{\infty}{F}a_i \vee \overset{\infty}{G}b_i)$, and $|EFL(p_0,\Phi_0)|=n$. Then the following are equivalent:

(1) (p_0,Φ_0) is satisfiable.
(2) There is a PHS for (p_0,Φ_0) of size $\leq O(2^n)$.
(3) There is a Hintikka structure for (p_0,Φ_0) of size $\leq O(n\cdot 2^{4n})$.
(4) (p_0,Φ_0) has a model of size $\leq O(n\cdot 2^{4n})$.

proof. (1) $\Rightarrow$ (2): In the sequel, let M=(S,R,L) be a model for (p_0,Φ_0), where $\Phi_0=\wedge_{i=1}^{n}(\overset{\infty}{F}a_i \vee \overset{\infty}{G}b_i)$, and $|EFL(p_0,\Phi_0)|=n$. We can assume w.l.o.g. M is a model such that, for each s, L(s) is exactly all the formula in $EFL(p_0,\Phi_0)$ that are true at s in M Let M'=(S',R',L') be the quotient structure of M w.r.t. $EFL(p_0,\Phi_0)$. In order to establish that M' is a PHS for

(p_0,Φ_0) we will prove a series of lemmas asserting that each eventuality is "pseudo-fulfilled" in M'.

4.1.1. Lemma. If $A_\Phi Fq \in L'([s])$ then there is an A-fragment N at [s] for AFq contained in M' (such that all frontier nodes of N contain q in their label).

proof sketch. Since $A_\Phi Fq \in L'([s]) = L(s)$ it follows that there is a fragment N_1 in M rooted at s which certifies fulfillment of $A_\Phi Fq$ at s (just follow every path out from s as long as q has not occurred.) Since some nodes may have (infinitely) many successors, for each node t in N_1 and each formula $E_\Phi Xp$ in t choose a successor u of t such that $p \in L(t)$. Delete all successor nodes that are not so chosen. Each node of the resulting structure, $N_2=(S_2,R_2,L')$, has at most n successors. Moreover, N_2 is still a fragment for AFq. If N_2 is finite then we are done; otherwise, we can now give a Ramsey-type argument collapsing N_2 into a finite fragment N_3. We can then eliminate nodes with duplicate labels to get a fragment N_4 contained in M'. Details are given in the full paper. □

4.1.2. Lemma. If $E_\Phi Gp \in L'([s])$ then there exists in M' a finite path from [s] leading to a PFC such that all nodes on the finite path and in the PFC contain p in their label.

proof sketch. Since $E_\Phi Gp \in L'([s]) = L(s)$ and M is an actual model of (p_0,Φ_0), $E_\Phi Gp$ is true at s in M. Thus, there is a fair fullpath $x = (s{=}s_0,s_1,s_2,...)$ starting at s in M each of whose states contains $E_\Phi Gp$ and p in its label. Consider the "image" of x in M': $([s_0],[s_1],[s_2],...)$. It consists of a finite prefix (those $[s_i]$ which appear only finitely often) followed by an infinite suffix (those $[s_i]$ which appear infinitely often). The nodes of M' appearing in the infinite suffix define a strongly connected subprestructure of M' which is a PFC and the finite prefix defines a finite path leading to it. Since $p \in L(s_i) = L([s_i])$ for each s_i on x, we thus have the desired finite path leading to a PFC. □

Arguments similar to that for Lemma 4.1.2 can be used to prove the following two lemmas:

4.1.3. Lemma. If $E_\Phi X\mathit{true} \in L'([s])$ then there is a path from [s] leading to a PFC contained in M'. □

4.1.4. Lemma. If $E_\Phi Fp \in L'([s])$ then there exists in M' a path starting at [s] leading to a state [t] such that $p \in L'([t])$ and a PFC contained in M' is reachable from [t]. □

Thus M' is the desired PHS for (p_0,Φ_0) of size $\leq O(2^n)$, and we have established that (1) ⇒ (2).

(2) ⇒ (3): We must show how to unwind a PHS M = (S,R,L) for (p_0,Φ_0) of size $O(2^n)$ into an HS for (p_0,Φ_0) of size $O(n\cdot 2^{4n})$.

4.1.5. Lemma. If $E_\Phi Gp \in L(s)$, then we can construct an E-fragment for $E_\Phi Gp$ at s of size $O(2^{2n})$.

proof sketch. Since M is a PHS, there exists in M a (shortest) finite path from s leading to a PFC; all of the nodes appearing therein have p in their label. Unwind the finite path into a finite simple path and the PFC into a finite simple cycle duplicating nodes as needed. (This can cause a quadratic blowup.) Each node u' in the resulting graph is a copy of some node u in M. For each such u' and for each $E_\Phi Xq \in L(u)$, add as a successor to u' a copy v' of some successor in M of u such that $q \in L(v)$. This final graph is the desired E-fragment for $E_\Phi Gp$ at (a copy of) s. □

We can similarly establish the following two lemmas:

4.1.6. Lemma. If $E_\Phi Fp \in L(s)$, then we can construct an E-fragment for $E_\Phi Fp$ at s of size $O(2^{2n})$. □

4.1.7. Lemma. If $E_\Phi Xp \in L(s)$, then we can construct an E-fragment for $E_\Phi Xp$ at s of size $O(2^{2n})$. □

We then splice together the E-fragments and A-fragments to get a full fragment at each state s of size $O(n \cdot 2^{3n})$. These full fragments are then spliced together to get a Hintikka Structure for (p_0,Φ_0) of size $O(n \cdot 2^{4n})$. The details are similar to those in [EC82] and [EH82].

The proofs that (3) ⇒ (4) and (4) ⇒ (1) are immediate. □

5. Decision Procedure

It follows from the Small Model Theorem that satisfiability for FCTL specifications (p_0,Φ_0) with Φ_0 in canonical form is decidable in nondeterministic exponential time: just guess a small structure M and check that it is a model. This model checking can be done in time polynomial in the size of M and (p_0,Φ_0). (Actually, the model checking can be done in linear time; see [EL84a], [EL84b] for details.) However, when Φ_0 is further restricted we can do much better:

5.1. Theorem. There is an algorithm for deciding whether a given FCTL specification (p_0,Φ_0) with $\Phi_0 = \wedge_{i=1}^{k} \overset{\infty}{F} a_i$ is satisfiable which runs in deterministic time 2^{cn} for some constant $c>0$, where $n=|EFL(p_0,\Phi_0)|$.

Proof sketch. We define a "tableau" M=(S,R,L) where S={s: s ∈ $EFL(p_0,\Phi_0)$ and s is maximal}, L(s)=s, and R is a binary relation on S consisting of all pairs (s,t)∈S×S *except* those for which $A_\Phi Xp \in s$, $E_\Phi X$*true* ∈ t, and p ∉ t or (ii) $E_\Phi X$*true* ∉ s and $E_\Phi X$*true* ∈ t.

We then repeatedly scan through the tableau checking for states that have no R-successor or violate one of the PHS rules H1', H2-H11, H12', H13', H14'. Any such state detected is deleted along with all incident arcs. This continues until no more nodes can be deleted.

Let M'=(S',R',L') be the (stablized) tableau upon termination. If S' is nonempty then M' is a PHS. So if $p_0 \in s$ for some $s \in S'$, (p_0, Φ_0) is satisfiable by the small model theorem of FCTL. Conversely, if (p_0, Φ_0) is satisfiable by a model N, then the nodes in the quotient structure of N (which trivially are a subset of S) will not be eliminated. Hence, for some node $s \in S'$, we have $p_0 \in s$.

Checking that rules H2-H11 are not violated is routine. But, it remains to show how to check H1', H12'-H14'. To handle rules H1', H12' and H14' we must be able to compute PFCs. To compute PFCs, we first compute strongly connected components (SCCs) of the tableau. An SCC will be a PFC iff each a_i appears in some node of the SCC, $E_\Phi X$*true* appears in every node of the SCC, and for every $A_\Phi Fg \in EFL(p_0, \Phi_0)$, if $A_\Phi Fg$ appears somewhere in the SCC then so does g. This method allows us to detect the nodes which can reach a PFC making it routine to check H1', H12'. To check H14', for $E_\Phi Gq$, delete all nodes not containing q in the label. Then compute PFCs in the resulting subprestructure and check that there is a path from s to a PFC in the subprestructure.

To check the fulfillment for an A-formulae $A_\Phi Fq$, we only have to consider nodes with $E_\Phi X$*true* appearing on their labels because nodes with $A_\Phi X$*false* satisfy all A-formulae. To check H13' (for $A_\Phi Fq$), we proceed as follows:

A. for all $t \in S$ do if $q \in L(t)$ then mark t GREEN;

B. for each conjunct $\overset{\infty}{F} a_i$ do the following:

B.1. for each $t \in S$ do if t has enough GREEN successors then mark t GREEN;
B.2. repeat

```
        for all unmarked nodes t ∈ S such that ¬a_i ∈ L(t) do
            if t has enough successors u such that
                either ¬a_i ∈ L(u) or u is marked (GREEN or BLUE)
            then mark t BLUE
    until no more node can be marked;
```

B.3. repeat

```
        for all BLUE nodes t ∈ S do
            if t does not has enough marked successors
                or t cannot reach a GREEN node via a BLUE path
            then erase the marker of t
    until no more makers can be erased;
```

B.4. Change BLUE markers to GREEN.

C. Repeat step B until no more changes can be made.

Claim: A state s ∈ S is marked GREEN by the above algorithm iff s satisfies H13'.

The proof of the claim is given in the full paper.

Since all the above processing can be implemented in time polynomial in the size of the tableau, the algorithm has the desired 2^{cn} complexity. □

6. References

[AB80] Abrahamson, K., *Decidability and Expressiveness of Logics of Processes*, PhD Thesis, University of Washington, 1980.

[AO83] Apt, K. R., Olderog, E. R. *Proof Rules and Translations Dealing with Fairness*, Science of Computer Programming 3 (1983), pp. 65-100.

[BMP81] Ben-Ari, M., Manna, Z., and Pnueli, A., *The Temporal Logic of Branching Time*, 8th Annual ACM Symp. on Principles of Programming Languages, 1981.

[CES83] Clarke, E. M., Emerson, E. A., and Sistla, A. P., *Automatic Verification of Finite State Concurrent System Using Temporal Logic*, 10th Annual ACM 10th Annual ACM Symp. on Principles of Programming Languages, 1983.

[DB80] DeBakker, J. W., *Mathematical Theory of Program Correctness* (Prentice-Hall, Englewood Cliffs, NJ, 1980).

[EC80] Emerson, E. A., and Clarke, E. M., *Characterizing Correctness Properties of Parallel Programs Using Fixpoints*, Proc. ICALP 80, LNCS Vol. 85, Springer Verlag, 1980, pp. 169-181.

[EC82] Emerson, E. A., and Clarke, E. M., *Using Branching Time Temporal Logic to Synthesize Synchronization Skeletons*, Tech. Report TR-208, Univ. of Texas, 1982.

[EH82] Emerson, E. A., and Halpern, J. Y., *Decision Procedures and Expressiveness in the Temporal Logic of Branching Time*, 14th Annual ACM Symp. on Theory of Computing, 1982.

[EH83] Emerson, E. A., and Halpern, J. Y., *"Sometimes" and "Not Never" Revisited: On Branching Versus Linear Time*, 14th Annual ACM Symp. on Theory of Computing, 1982.

[EL85a] Emerson, E. A., and Lei, C. L., *Temporal Model Checking Under Generalized Fairness Constraints*, to be presented at the 18th Annual Hawaii International Conference on System Sciences.

[EL85b] Emerson, E. A., and Lei, C. L., *Modalities for Model Checking: Branching Time Strikes Back*, to be presented at the 12th Annual ACM Symposium on Principles of Programming Languages.

[ES84] Emerson, E. A., and Sistla, A. P., *Deciding Branching Time Logic*, 16 Annual ACM Symp. on Theory of Computing, 1984.

[FK84] Francez, N., and Kozen, D., *Generalized Fair Termination*, 11th Annual ACM Symp. on Principles of Programming Languages, 1984, pp. 46-53.

[FL79] Fischer, M. J., and Ladner, R. E, *Propositional Dynamic Logic of Regular Programs*, JCSS vol. 18, pp194-211, 1979.}

[GFMD81] Grimberg, O., Francez, N., Makowsky, J. A., and deRoever, W. P., *A proof rule for fair termination of guarded commands*, Proc. International Symp. on Algorithmic Languages (North-Holland, Amsterdam, 1981).

[KO83] Kozen, D., *Results on the Propositional Mu-calculus*, Theoretical Computer Science, pp. 333-354, December 83.

[LA80] Lamport, L., *Sometimes is Sometimes "Not Never" - on the temporal logic of programs*, 7th Annual ACM Symp. on Principles of Programming Languages, 1980, pp. 174-185.

[LPS81] Lehmann. D., Pnueli, A., and Stavi, J., *Impartiality, Justice and Fairness: The Ethics of Concurrent Termination*, ICALP 1981, LNCS Vol. 115, pp 264-277.

[LP84] Lichtenstein, O. and Pnueli, A., *Checking that Finite State Concurrent Programs Satisfy their Linear Specification*, unpublished manuscript, July 84, (to appear in POPL85.)

[MP79] Manna, Z., and Pnueli, A., *The modal logic of programs*, Proc. 6th Int. Colloquium on Automata, Languages, and Programming, Springer-Verlag Lecture Notes in Computer Science #71, pp. 385-410, 1979.

[MW84] Manna, Z., and Wolper, P., *Synthesis of Communicating Processes from Temporal Logic Specifications*, TOPLAS, Vol. 6, #1, pp. 68-93.

[OL82] Owicki, S. S., and Lamport, L., *Proving Liveness Properties of Concurrent Programs*, ACM Trans. on Programming Languages and Syst., Vol. 4, No. 3, July 1982, pp. 455-495.

[PA78] Parikh, R., *A Decidability Result for a Second Order Process Logic*, 17th Annual Symp. on Foundations of Computer Science, 1978.

[PN77] Pnueli, A., *The Temporal Logic of Programs*, 19th annual Symp. on Foundations of Computer Science, 1977.

[PN83] Pnueli, A., *On The Extremely Fair Termination of Probabilistic Algorithms*, 15 Annual ACM Symp. on Theory of Computing, 1983, 278-290.

[PR79] Pratt, V., *Process Logic*, 6th Annual ACM Symposium on Programming Languages, 1979.

[QS83] Queille, J. P., and Sifaki, J., *Fairness and Related Properties in Transition Systems*, Research Report #292, IMAG, Grenoble, 1982.

[RA68] Rabin, M. O., *Weakly Definable Relations and Special Automata*, in Mathematical Logic and Foundations of Set Theory, Y. Bar-Hillel, editor, North-Holland, Amsterdam, 1968, pp. 1-23.

[VW84] Vardi, M. and Wolper, P., *Automata Theoretic Techniques for Modal Logics of Programs*, pp. 446-455, STOC84.

DECIDABILITE DE L'EGALITE DES LANGAGES ALGEBRIQUES INFINITAIRES SIMPLES

D. Caucal

IRISA . Campus de Beaulieu . 35042 Rennes . France

1. Introduction

Un schéma récursif de programmes [Ni 72], [Ni 75], noté R. P. S., est un système d'équations algébriques où chaque équation est une définition récursive d'une fonction. Plus précisémment, un R. P. S. est un schéma récursif [Ga-Lu73] où aucune fonction de base n'est interprétée.

Les problèmes de l'équivalence des R. P. S. sans fonction d'arité nulle [Co 78] et de l'équivalence des schémas récursifs monadiques [Fr 77] sont inter-réductibles à celui des D. P. D. A. (automate à pile déterministe). Ce dernier problème est ouvert depuis une vingtaine d'années [Gi-Gr66]. Par contre, l'équivalence (syntaxique) des R. P. S. monadiques réduits et sans fonction d'arité nulle, se ramenant à celle des grammaires algébriques simples [Ko-Ho 66], est décidable. Le problème de l'équivalence pour tous les R. P. S. monadiques a été posé par [Co-Vu 76].

Il est aisé de s'apercevoir que le problème de l'équivalence des R. P. S. monadiques est inter-réductible [Ca 85] à celui de l'égalité des langages algébriques infinitaires simples [Ni77], [Ni78]. On établit, et c'est là où réside toute la difficulté, que l'équivalence infinitaire, notée $\equiv_G$, sur l'ensemble des non-terminaux (mots de lettres non-terminales) d'une grammaire algébrique simple G est finiment engendrée, c'est à dire qu'il existe un ensemble fini R_G de paires équivalentes telle que la plus petite congruence sur les non-terminaux contenant R_G soit égale à $\equiv_G$. La relation R_G, dite système générateur de $\equiv_G$, est construite de telle façon qu'elle soit un système de réécriture [Hu80] noethérien. Ceci permet de minimiser le nombre de paires de R_G et d'éviter de compléter la grammaire avec de nouvelles production [Co84]. Enfin, en reprenant les travaux de [Co83b] montrant que l'équivalence des R. P. S. est décidable si elle est finiment engendrée, on en déduit que l'égalité des langages algébriques infinitaires simples est décidable et qu'il en est donc de même de l'équivalence des R. P. S. monadiques.

2. Langage infinitaire; Congruence de Thue; Grammaire algébrique

On note Σ^* (respectivement Σ^ω) l'ensemble des ***mots*** de longueur finie (resp. infinie) que l'on peut constituer par ***concaténation*** à partir de l'ensemble de symboles (***lettres***) Σ. Le symbole du mot vide est ε et celui de la concaténation est le point (pouvant être omis). Soient Σ^∞ la réunion de Σ^* et Σ^ω, $\mathbb{N}$ (resp. $\mathbb{N}_+$) l'ensemble des entiers positifs (resp. strictement positifs). On pose pour $i \in \mathbb{N}_+$, $[i] = \{1, \ldots, i\}$ avec $[0] = \emptyset$. On représente, pour $i \in \mathbb{N}_+$ et $u \in \Sigma^\infty$, la longueur (nombre de lettres) de u par $|u|$, la i^{eme} (en commençant par la gauche) lettre de u par $u(i)$, le préfixe (ou ***facteur gauche***) de longueur $\min(|u|, i)$ par $u|i$ et le suffixe de u à partir de sa i^{eme} lettre par $u\backslash i$, avec $u(i)$ et $u\backslash i$ réduits au mot vide si $i \notin [|u|]$. On munit Σ^∞ d'un ordre partiel, dit facteur gauche strict et noté $<_{FG}$, défini par : pour $u, v \in \Sigma^\infty$, $u <_{FG} v$ si $u \neq v$ et pour tout $i \in [|u|]$, $u(i) = v(i)$. Un ***langage*** sur Σ est une partie de Σ^∞; il est dit ***finitaire*** s'il est inclus dans Σ^* et ***infinitaire*** sinon. Un langage L est un ***langage préfixe*** si la relation $<_{FG}$ restreinte sur L est vide. Pour E ensemble quelconque, on désigne par Card(E) la cardinalité de E et par $P(E)$ (resp. $P_0(E)$) l'ensemble des parties (resp. parties finies) de E. La ***clôture*** d'un langage L est l'ensemble des mots infinis ayant une infinité de facteurs gauches dans L. L'***adhérence*** d'un langage L est l'ensemble des mots infinis dont tout facteur gauche est facteur gauche de L.

Pour R relation binaire quelconque, on définit $Dom(R) = \{x / (x, y) \in R\}$ le ***domaine*** de R; $Im(R) = R(Dom(R))$ avec $R(A) = \{y / (x, y) \in R \text{ et } x \in A\}$ l'***image*** de l'ensemble A par R; $R^{-1} = \{(y, x) / (x, y) \in R\}$ la relation ***inverse*** de R. Pour R relation binaire <u>sur</u> un ensemble E, on note R^0 la relation identité sur E; pour i entier, $R^i = \{(x, y) / (x, z) \in R \text{ et } (z, y) \in R^{i-1}\}$ la relation ***composée*** i fois de R; R^*, la réunion des R^i pour i entier, la ***fermeture réflexive et transitive*** de R. Un ***système semi-Thue*** sur Σ est une relation sur Σ^*. Soit R un système semi-Thue quelconque sur Σ. R est dite ***stable par concaténation*** si pour tout $(u, v), (u', v') \in R$, $(u.u', v.v') \in R$. R est une ***congruence*** *si* R est une équivalence stable par concaténation. On note $\underset{R}{\rightarrow}$ le plus petit système de Thue contenant R et stable par concaténation. On pose $\underset{R}{\leftrightarrow} = \underset{R}{\rightarrow} \cup (\underset{R}{\rightarrow})^{-1}$; $\underset{R}{\overset{*}{\rightarrow}} = (\underset{R}{\rightarrow})^*$ l'opération de ***dérivation*** selon R; la plus petite congruence contenant R $\underset{R}{\overset{*}{\leftrightarrow}} = (\underset{R}{\leftrightarrow})^*$ appelée ***la congruence de Thue*** engendrée par R. On note pour n entier $\underset{R}{\overset{n}{\rightarrow}} = (\underset{R}{\rightarrow})^n$ et $\underset{R}{\overset{n}{\leftrightarrow}} = (\underset{R}{\leftrightarrow})^n$. Un mot u de Σ^* est ***irréductible*** selon R si $\underset{R}{\rightarrow}(\{u\})$ est vide. R est ***noethérien*** si aucun mot de Σ^* n'admet de dérivation infinie ce qui implique que tout mot dérive en un mot irréductible. R est ***confluent*** si R satisfait la propriété : pour tout u, v, $w \in \Sigma^*$ tels que w dérive en u et v, il existe un $w' \in \Sigma^*$ tels que u et v dérivent en w'. R est ***canonique*** si R est noethérien et confluent c'est à dire que tout mot de Σ^* dérive en un unique mot irréductible.

Une ***grammaire algébrique*** G sur Σ d'axiome S est une relation finie dans $N \times (\Sigma \cup N)^*$ avec S élément de N=Dom(G) ensemble de symboles disjoint de Σ. Toute lettre de N (resp. Σ) est appelée ***non-terminale*** (resp. ***terminale***) de G. Tout mot de N^* (resp. Σ^∞) est appelé ***non-terminaux*** (resp. ***terminaux***) de G. G étant un système semi-Thue sur $(\Sigma \cup N)^*$, on définit pour tout $U \in (\Sigma \cup N)^*$, L(G, U) le langage finitaire des terminaux qui dérivent de U selon G et, $L^\infty(G, U) = L(G, U) \cup L^\omega(G, U)$ où $L^\omega(G, U)$ est l'ensemble des mots u de Σ^ω tel que pour tout entier i, U dérive en $(u|i).V_i$ avec $V_i \in (\Sigma \cup N)^*$. $L^\omega(G, U)$ est alors la fermeture par clôture ou par adhérence de l'ensemble des terminaux qui sont facteurs gauches d'une dérivation de U selon G. Un langage L sur Σ est dit ***algébrique*** (resp. ***algébrique infinitaire***) s'il existe une grammaire algébrique G sur Σ d'axiome S tel que L=L(G, S) (resp. $L=L^\infty(G, S)$). Soit G une grammaire algébrique sur Σ. G est dite ***en forme normale de Greibach***, noté F.N.G., si $Im(G) \subset \Sigma.N^*$, est dite ***réduite*** (resp. ***ε-libre***; ***préfixe***) si pour tout non-terminale A, L(G, A) est non vide (resp. ε n'est pas élément de L(G, A) ; L(G, A) est préfixe). Si G est en F.N.G., $L^\infty(G, U)$ est le langage algébrique infinitaire, au sens de [Ni 77] [Ni 78], engendré par G à partir de U. G est une ***grammaire simple*** si G est en F.N.G. et pour tout $A \in N$ et $a \in \Sigma$, si $(A, a\alpha)$, $(A, a\beta) \in G$ alors $\alpha = \beta$. Tout langage finitaire (resp. infinitaire) sur Σ engendré par une grammaire algébrique simple à partir de son axiome est appelé ***langage algébrique simple*** (resp. ***langage algébrique infinitaire simple***).

3. Le problème de l'équivalence infinitaire des grammaires simples

Pour C une classe de grammaires sur Σ, on note $L(C) = \{L(G,S) / G \in C$ d'axiome $S\}$ (resp. $L^\infty(C) = \{L^\infty(G,S) / G \in C$ d'axiome $S\}$) la famille des langages algébriques finitaires (resp. infinitaires) sur Σ engendrés par une grammaire de C à partir de son axiome. Le ***problème de l'équivalence*** (resp. équivalence infinitaire), noté P.E., pour deux classes C, C' (ou une classe si C = C') de grammaires est celui de la décidabilité de l'égalité dans $L(C) \times L(C')$ (resp. dans $L^\infty(C) \times L^\infty(C')$). On sait [Ca 85] que résoudre le P.E. des R.P.S. monadiques est identique à résoudre le P.E. infinitaire des grammaires simples. Remarquons que le P.E. finitaire (resp. infinitaire) des grammaires simples est identique à : peut-on décider, pour n'importe quelle grammaire simple G et A, B $\in$ Dom(G), si $L(G,A) = L(G,B)$ (resp. $L^\infty(G,A) = L^\infty(G,B)$). Indiquons que le P.E. finitaire et infinitaire sont identiques pour des classes de grammaires quelconques réduites.

Proposition 1 Soit G une grammaire sur Σ réduite

$$\forall\ U,V \in (\Sigma \cup \mathrm{Dom}(G))^*,\quad L^\infty(G,U) = L^\infty(G,V) \iff L(G,U) = L(G,V)$$

On appelle ***équivalence infinitaire*** d'une grammaire simple G, la relation sur $\mathrm{Dom}(G)^*$, notée $\equiv_G$, et définie pour tout $\alpha, \beta \in (\mathrm{Dom}(G))^*$ par $\alpha \equiv_G \beta$ si et seulement si $L^\infty(G,\alpha) = L^\infty(G,\beta)$. On montre dans ce chapitre que, pour toute grammaire simple G, $\equiv_G$ est la congruence de Thue sur Dom(G) engendrée par un système <u>fini</u> : $\equiv_G$ est alors dite ***finiment engendrée***. Autrement dit, l'étude de $\equiv_G$ se ramène à celle d'un ensemble fini de paires qui l'engendre. On en déduit au chapitre suivant que l'équivalence infinitaire de toute grammaire simple est décidable et qu'il en est de même du P.E. infinitaire des grammaires simples.

La ***valuation*** d'une grammaire algébrique G, notée τ_G, est l'application qui à tout $U \in (\Sigma \cup \mathrm{Dom}(G))^*$ associe $\tau_G(U)$, la plus petite longueur des mots de $L(G,U)$ si ce dernier est non vide sinon ∞. On note pour G grammaire en F.N.G. sur Σ, $u \in \Sigma^*$ et $\alpha \in (\mathrm{Dom}(G))^*$, $R_G(\alpha,u) = \{\beta \in (\mathrm{Dom}(G))^* / \alpha$ dérive selon G en $u.\beta\}$ qui possède au plus un élément si G est simple. Dorénavant G est une grammaire simple quelconque sur Σ. On note $N = \mathrm{Dom}(G)$, N_0 (resp. N_1) l'ensemble des éléments de N de valuation infinie (resp. finie). Par la suite, on ne considère des éléments de N^* que ceux de $N^*_1.(N_0 \cup \{\varepsilon\})$. On dit que deux non-terminales A, B sont ***unifiables*** s'il existe α, β non-terminaux tel que $A\alpha \equiv_G B\beta$. On munit N d'un ordre total $<_N$

croissant avec τ_G et on se donne une application Val de N_1 dans Σ^* qui à tout $A \in N_1$ associe Val(A) un mot de L(G, A) de longueur minimale ($|Val(A)| = \tau_G(A)$). On définit la valuation finie τ_f comme étant l'homomorphisme de $(N^*, .)$ dans $(\mathbb{N}, +)$ identique à τ_G sur N_1 et nulle sur N_0, c'est à dire pour tout α de N^*, $\tau_f(\alpha)$ vaut $\tau(\alpha)$ si $\alpha \in N^*_1$ et sinon $\tau(\alpha(\ |\alpha|-1))$. On étend τ_f sur $N^* \times N^*$ en posant pour tout $\alpha, \beta \in N^*$, $\tau_f(\alpha, \beta) = \max(\tau_f(\alpha), \tau_f(\beta))$.

On reprend [Ha 78] la ***transformation parallèle extèrieure***, notée T_A, application de $N^* \times N^*$ dans $P_0(N^* \times N^*)$, définie par :

$$\forall\, \alpha,\beta \in N^*,\ T_A(\alpha,\beta) = \begin{cases} \{(\xi,\xi)\} & \text{si } \alpha = \beta = \xi \\ \emptyset & \text{si pour } \{\alpha',\beta'\} = \{\alpha,\beta\},\ \exists\, a \in \Sigma \ /\ R_G(\alpha',a) = \emptyset \neq R_G(\beta',a) \\ \{(\alpha',\beta') \in N^* \times N^* \ /\ \{\alpha'\} = R_G(\alpha,a)\ ,\ \{\beta'\} = R_G(\beta,a)\ ,\ a \in \Sigma\} & \text{sinon} \end{cases}$$

On étend T_A sur $P_0(N^* \times N^*)$ par

$$\forall\, E \subset N^* \times N^*,\ T_A(E) = \begin{cases} \emptyset & \text{si } \exists\, (\alpha,\beta) \in E \ /\ T_A(\alpha,\beta) = \emptyset \\ \bigcup_{(\alpha,\beta) \in E} T_A(\alpha,\beta) & \text{sinon} \end{cases}$$

T_A (ou plus exactement son graphe) étant une relation binaire sur $P_0(N^* \times N^*)$, on note pour n entier, T^n_A l'application composant T_A n fois. On notera $T^n_A(\alpha,\beta)$ à la place de $T^n_A(\{(\alpha,\beta)\})$. L'application T_A satisfait la propriété suivante :

Lemme 1 Soient $\alpha,\ \beta \in N^*$ et $n \in \mathbb{N}_+$

$$T^n_A(\alpha,\beta) \neq \emptyset \iff (\forall\, u \in \Sigma^*,\ |u| \leq n\ ,\ R_G(\alpha,u) \neq \emptyset \iff R_G(\beta,u) \neq \emptyset)$$

et dans ce cas, $T^n_A(\alpha,\beta) = \{(\alpha',\beta') /\ \{\alpha'\} = R(\alpha,u),\ \{\beta'\} = R(\beta,u),\ u \in \Sigma^n\}$

L' égalité des langages algébriques infinitaires simples est alors caractérisée par :

Proposition 2 Soient G une grammaire simple sur Σ et $\alpha,\ \beta \in (Dom(G))^*$

Les propiétés suivantes sont équivalentes

a) $\alpha \equiv_G \beta$ i.e. $L^\infty(G,\alpha) = L^\infty(G,\beta)$

b) $\forall\, n \geq 0$, $T^n_A(\alpha,\beta) \neq \emptyset$

c) $\forall\, u \in \Sigma^*$, $R_G(\alpha,u) \neq \emptyset \iff R_G(\beta,u) \neq \emptyset$

d) $L(G,\alpha) = L(G,\beta)$ si G est réduite

On définit l'application de ***divergence gauche***, notée Divg, de $N^* \times N^*$ dans $\mathbb{N}_+ \cup \{\infty\}$ par :

$$\forall\ \alpha,\ \beta \in N^*,\ \mathrm{Divg}(\alpha,\beta) = \begin{cases} \infty \text{ si } \alpha \equiv_G \beta \\ \inf\ \{n \in \mathbb{N}\ /\ T_A^n(\alpha,\beta) \neq \emptyset\} \text{ sinon} \end{cases}$$

Exemple : Soit $G = \{(S,a)\ ,\ (S,bSTS)\ ,\ (T,aS)\ ,\ (T,bTST)\}$ la grammaire simple réduite sur $\{a,b\}$

on a $\forall\ n \in \mathbb{N}\ ,\ R_G(TS,b^n) = (TS)^n\ ;\ \tau_G(A) = 1\ ,\ \tau_G(B) = 2\ ;\ \mathrm{Divg}(S,T) = 2\ ;\ ST \equiv_G TS$

$\equiv_G$ est la congruence de Thue engendrée par l'unique paire (T,SS)

D'après la proposition 2, l'opérateur Divg est bien défini et de plus satisfait

Lemme 2 $\forall\ \alpha,\ \beta,\ \gamma,\ \delta \in N^*\ /\ \gamma \equiv_G \delta$

$$1 \leqslant \mathrm{Divg}(\alpha,\beta) \leqslant \mathrm{Divg}(\alpha.\gamma,\beta.\delta) \leqslant \mathrm{Divg}(\alpha,\beta) + \tau_G(\gamma) = \mathrm{Divg}(\gamma.\alpha,\delta.\beta)$$

On utilisera le lemme 1 et le fait que G est préfixe pour prouver le lemme 2.

Avant d'établir que $\equiv_G$ est finiment engendrée, on doit montrer la

Proposition 3 Soient $A,\ B \in N\ /\ B <_N A\ ,\ B \in N_1$ et $\exists\ \alpha,\ \beta \in N^*$ tel que $A.\alpha \equiv_G B.\beta$

Alors $\{\gamma\} = R_G(A,\mathrm{Val}(B))$ existe et de plus

a) $\gamma.\alpha \equiv_G \beta$ et si $\tau_G(\alpha) < \infty$ alors $A \equiv_G B.\gamma$

b) si $A \not\equiv_G B.\gamma$ alors $\forall\ \lambda,\ \mu \in N^*\ /\ A.\lambda \equiv_G B.\mu$

on a $\alpha \equiv_G \lambda$ et $\beta \equiv_G \mu$

Cette proposition signifie que toute paire équivalente $(A\alpha, B\beta)$ peut être "découpée" en deux autres paires équivalentes :

soit en $(A,B\gamma)$, $(\gamma\alpha,\beta)$. Notons R l'ensemble de ces deux paires

soit en (α,λ), (β,μ) avec A, B non unifiables et $(A\lambda,B\mu)$ une paire équivalente. Notons R l'ensemble de ces trois paires.

et on remarquera alors que $(A\alpha,B\beta) \in \overset{*}{\underset{R}{\longleftrightarrow}}$

On peut maintenant montrer que $\equiv_G$ est finiment engendrée :

Théorème 1 Soit G une grammaire simple quelconque

$\exists$ R relation binaire <u>finie</u> sur $(\mathrm{Dom}(G))^*$ tel que $\equiv_G = \overset{*}{\underset{R}{\longleftrightarrow}}$

Preuve :

i) Construction d'un système fini R de $\equiv_G$.

Soit R_1 <u>un</u> plus grand (au sens de l'inclusion) ensemble de $(Nx(N-\mathrm{Dom}(R_1))^+) \cap \equiv_G$ et qui soit fonctionnel : $\forall\ (A,\alpha),\ (A,\beta) \in R_1\ ,\ \alpha = \beta$

Notons $N' = N-\mathrm{Dom}(R_1)\ ;\ N'_0 = N' \cap N_0\ ;\ N'_1 = N' \cap N_1$

On définit un ordre partiel $\ll$ sur $(N')^*.N'_0$, pour $\alpha,\ \beta \in (N')^*.N'_0$ et $\alpha(1) \neq \beta(1)$, par

$$\alpha \ll \beta \iff (\tau_f(\alpha) < \tau_f(\beta))\ \text{ou}\ (\tau_f(\alpha) = \tau_f(\beta))\ \text{et}\ \beta(1) <_N \alpha(1))$$

Soit R_2 un plus grand (au sens de l'inclusion) ensemble de

$$\{(A\alpha, B\beta) \in \equiv_G \,/\, A,\ B \in N';\ A\alpha \ll B\beta \text{ et } \tau_f(\alpha,\beta) \leqslant \tau_f(\lambda,\mu) \text{ si } A\lambda \equiv_G B\mu \text{ et } \lambda,\ \mu \in (N')^*\}$$

et tel que $\forall\ (\alpha,\beta),\ (\lambda,\mu) \in R_2\ ,\ \{\alpha(1),\beta(1)\} \neq \{\lambda(1),\mu(1)\}$ si $(\alpha,\beta) \neq (\lambda,\mu)$

On pose alors $R = R_1 \cup R_2$ qui est donc fini et inclus dans $\equiv_G$

ii) R_1 est canonique, R_2 et R sont noethériens.

$\forall\ \alpha \in \mathrm{Im}(R_1)\ ,\ \forall\ i \in [\,|\alpha|\,]\ ,\ \alpha(i) \notin \mathrm{Dom}(R_1)$

donc α est irréductible selon R_1 d'où R_1 est noethérien

de plus, R_1, n'admettant pas de paire critique, est confluent (théorème de Knuth-Bendix)

enfin, la noethériennité de R_2 et R proviennent de celle de $\ll$

iii) $\equiv_G = \overset{*}{\underset{R}{\longleftrightarrow}}$?

$R \subset \equiv_G \Rightarrow \overset{*}{\underset{R}{\longleftrightarrow}} \subset \equiv_G$

Montrons l'inclusion inverse : soit $(\alpha,\beta) \in \equiv_G$.

prenons $\bar\alpha$ (resp. $\bar\beta$) un mot irréductible de α (resp. β) selon R alors $(\bar\alpha,\bar\beta) \in \equiv_G$

Montrons par induction sur $\tau_f(\bar\alpha,\bar\beta) \geqslant 0$ pour $\alpha \equiv_G \beta$ que $\bar\alpha \overset{*}{\underset{R}{\longleftrightarrow}} \bar\beta$

Si $\tau_f(\bar\alpha,\bar\beta) = 0$ alors comme $\bar\alpha \equiv_G \bar\beta$

soit $\bar\alpha = \bar\beta = \varepsilon$

soit $\bar\alpha,\ \bar\beta \in N_0$ donc par maximalité de R_1 , $\bar\alpha = \bar\beta$

Si $\bar\alpha \overset{*}{\underset{R}{\longleftrightarrow}} \bar\beta$ pour $\tau_f(\bar\alpha,\bar\beta) \leqslant n \in \mathbb{N}_+$ et $\alpha \equiv_G \beta$

alors montrons le pour $\alpha \equiv_G \beta$ et $\tau_f(\bar\alpha,\bar\beta) = n+1$

soit $\bar\alpha = \bar\beta$ alors $\bar\alpha \overset{0}{\underset{R}{\longleftrightarrow}} \bar\beta$

soit $\bar\alpha \neq \bar\beta$. Or $\bar\alpha \equiv_G \bar\beta$ donc $\tau(\bar\alpha) = \tau(\bar\beta)$

par conséquent $(\bar\alpha,\bar\beta)$ est une paire distinguable, c'est à dire

$\exists\ i \in [\min(\,|\bar\alpha|,\ |\bar\beta|\,)]$ tel que

$\bar\alpha(i) \neq \bar\beta(i)$ et $\forall\ j \in [i-1]\ ,\ \bar\alpha(j) = \bar\beta(j)$

d'après le lemme 2 ou bien la prop. 3, on a $\bar\alpha\backslash i \equiv_G \bar\beta\backslash i$

si $i>1$ alors par hypothèse d'induction $\bar\alpha = (\bar\alpha|i)\bar\alpha\backslash i \overset{*}{\underset{R}{\longleftrightarrow}} (\bar\alpha|i)\bar\beta\backslash i = \bar\beta$

si $i=1$: notons $(A,B) = (\bar\alpha(1),\bar\beta(1))$

Par symétrie, on peut supposer que $B <_N A$.

Alors $B \in N'_1$ car $\tau_f(\alpha,\beta) = n+1 \geqslant 1$

Il nous reste à considérer les 2 cas suivants :

soit $A \in N'_0$ alors par maximalité de R_1, $(\bar\alpha,\bar\beta)$ est de la forme

$(A, B.\gamma.A)$ avec $\gamma \in (N'_1)^*$ et par maximalité de R_2

$\exists\ \alpha_0 \in (N'_1)^* \,/\, (B.\alpha_0.A, A) \in R$ et $\tau(\alpha_0) \leqslant \tau(\gamma)$

d'où $\alpha_0.A \equiv_G \gamma.A$ et

$$\tau_f(\overline{\alpha_0.A}, \overline{\gamma.A}) \leq \tau_f(\alpha_0.A, \gamma.A) = \tau(\gamma) < \tau_f(\bar{\alpha}, \beta)$$

donc par hyp. d'induction $\alpha_0.A \overset{*}{\underset{R}{\longleftrightarrow}} \gamma.A$

ainsi $\bar{\alpha} = A\ R^{-1}\ B.\alpha_0.A \overset{*}{\underset{R}{\longleftrightarrow}} B.\gamma.A = \beta$

<u>soit</u> $A \in N'_1$ alors $(\bar{\alpha}, \beta)$ est de la forme $(A.\lambda, B.\mu)$ avec

$\lambda,\ \mu \in (N'_1)^*.N'_0$ d'après a) de la prop. 3 et par maximalité de R_1

donc par maximalité de R_2, $\exists\ \lambda_0,\ \mu_0 \in (N'_1)^*.N'_0$ /

$(A.\lambda_0, B.\mu_0) \in R \cup R^{-1}$ et $\tau_f(\lambda_0, \mu_0) \leq \tau_f(\lambda, \mu)$

d'après la prop. 3 et par maximalité de R_1,

on en déduit que $\lambda \equiv_G \lambda_0$ et $\mu \equiv_G \mu_0$

donc par hypothèse d'induction, on obtient

$\bar{\alpha} = A.\lambda \overset{*}{\underset{R}{\longleftrightarrow}} A.\lambda_0\ R \cup R^{-1}\ B.\mu_0 \overset{*}{\underset{R}{\longleftrightarrow}} B.\mu = \beta$

en définitive, dans tous les cas $\bar{\alpha} \overset{*}{\underset{R}{\longleftrightarrow}} \beta$

la preuve par induction est terminée et donc $\equiv_G \subset \overset{*}{\underset{R}{\longleftrightarrow}}$

iii) est démontré et le théorème 1 par la même occasion □

On remarquera que

pour G réduite, N_0 et R_2 sont vides et donc que les systèmes R fonctionnels et maximaux pour l'inclusion dans $N\times(N-Dom(R))^+ \cap \equiv_G$, de cardinalité au plus taille de la grammaire moins un, sont systèmes générateurs de l'équivalence (finitaire) des grammaires simples.

On peut aussi définir les systèmes R_1 de la façon suivante :

soit R'_1 un ensemble fonctionnel et maximal pour l'inclusion de $\equiv_G \cap N\times N^+$ tel que

$\forall\ (A, \alpha) \in (R'_1)^+,\ \ \alpha(|\alpha|) \neq A$

R'_1 est un système canonique et R_1 est le système canonique réduit associé, c'est à dire

$R_1 = \{(A, \bar{\alpha})\ /\ (A, \alpha) \in R'_1$ et $\bar{\alpha}$ le mot irréductible de α selon $R'_1\}$

4. Décidabilité de l'équivalence infinitaire d'une grammaire simple

Ce chapitre n'est que l'application aux grammaires simples des travaux de [Co 83b] sur les R.P.S. . A partir de la notion de relation auto-prouvable, on montre, pour G grammaire simple, que $\equiv_G$ est décidable si elle est finiment engendrée. Ainsi, l'équivalence infinitaire des grammaires simples et celle des R.P.S. monadiques sont décidables.

On conserve les notations du chapitre précédent. On dit que R, relation binaire sur N^*, est ***auto-prouvable*** si $\emptyset \neq T_A(R) \subset \xrightarrow[R]{*}$.

Comme $\xrightarrow[R]{*}$ est semi-décidable pour R fini, il est semi-décidable qu'une relation finie soit auto-prouvable. Remarquons que

Lemme 3 Soit R une relation binaire sur N^*
alors $T_A(R) \subset \xrightarrow[S]{*}$ avec $S = R \cup T_A(R)$

et comme $\equiv_G$ est finiment engendrée, on a

Proposition 4 $\forall\, \alpha, \beta \in N^*$, $\alpha \equiv_G \beta \Leftrightarrow \exists$ R relation finie et auto-prouvable / $(\alpha,\beta) \in R$

Il nous reste à établir

Théorème 2 Soit G une grammaire simple quelconque
L'équivalence infinitaire $\equiv_G$ est décidable

Preuve :

Soit Range une procédure qui à A alphabet fini et i entier associe

Range(A, i) une partie finie de A^*xA^* tel que $\cup$ {Range(A, i) / i $\in \mathbb{N}$} = $P_0(A^*xA^*)$

Soit g la bijection de $\mathbb{N}^2$ sur $\mathbb{N}$ qui à (i, j) associe ((i+j)(i+j+1)/2) + j

Comme pour une relation finie, la propriété d'être auto-prouvable est semi-décidable, on peut définir une procédure, appelée Autoprouve, de paramètres une grammaire simple G et une relation finie sur (Dom(G))*, qui s'arrête si et seulement si la relation est auto-prouvable.

Soit la procédure Decide qui à G grammaire simple et α, $\beta \in$ Dom(G)* associe

Decide(G, (α, β)) = Dec(G, (α, β), { (α, β) }, 0)

Avec, pour G grammaire simple, α, $\beta \in$ (Dom(G))*, E $\in P_0$((Dom(G)*)^2) et n $\in \mathbb{N}$,

Dec(G, (α, β), E, n) définie récursivement par

DEBUT

<u>Si</u> $E = \emptyset$ <u>Alors</u> Stop("Faux") <u>fs</u>

$(i,j) \leftarrow g^{-1}(n)$

<u>Si</u> $(\alpha, \beta) \in$ Range(Dom(G), i) <u>Alors</u>

<u>*Si*</u> Autoprouve(G, Range(Dom(G), i)) s'arrête au bout de

j "étapes élémentaires de calcul" <u>*Alors*</u> Stop("Vrai") <u>*fs*</u>

<u>fs</u>

Dec(G, (α, β), $T_A(E)$, n+1)

FIN

On montre alors, pour n'importe quelle grammaire simple G et α, $\beta \in (\mathrm{Dom}(G))^*$, que

$\alpha \equiv_G \beta \iff$ Decide(G, (α, β)) = "Vrai"

et comme la procédure Decide s'arrête toujours, le théorème 2 est alors établi □

4. Conclusion

L'algorithme de Korenjak-Hopcroft [Ko-Ho 66], dit de K-H, décide de l'équivalence infinitaire des grammaires simples réduites. Il décide directement de l'équivalence de deux grammaires en construisant un arbre fini de racine la paire d'axiomes à comparer et dont chaque label est une paire de non-terminaux. Les algorithmes qui reprennent la méthode de K-H pour décider de l'équivalence pour deux classes de grammaires (ou d'automates, de schémas, ...) sont appelés des algorithmes de branchement ou de K-H [Ol-Pn77], [Ha-Ha-Ye 79], [Co 83a], [To 84].

On a montré que l'équivalence infinitaire des grammaires simples est décidable parce que l'équivalence infinitaire associée sur les non-terminaux de toute grammaire simple est finiment engendrée. La connaissance de systèmes générateurs finis de cette équivalence nous a permis de définir un algorithme de branchement pour décider de l'équivalence infinitaire des grammaires simples (et donc de l'équivalence syntaxique des R.P.S. monadiques). Cet algorithme de branchement généralise celui de K-H mais de plus réduit la complexité exponentielle de ce dernier en une complexité polynomiale [Ca 85].

Remerciements

Mes remerciements vont à Laurent KOTT sans lequel ce travail n'aurait été possible.

Références

Bo-Ni 80 L. Boasson , M. Nivat "Adherences of languages " *Journal of computer and System Science 20* . pp 285-309

Ca 85 D. Caucal "Décidabilité de l'équivalence forte des R.P.S. monadiques" *Rapport LITP* . Thèse 3eme cycle Paris 7 .

Co 78 B. Courcelle "A representation of trees by languages" *Theoret. Comput. Scie. 6 & 7*. pp 255-279 & pp 25-55

Co 83a B. Courcelle "An axiomatic approach to the KH algorithms" *Math. Systems Theory 16*. pp 191-231

Co 83b B. Courcelle "Fundamental properties of infinite trees" *Theoret. Comput. Sci. 25* . pp 95-169

Co 84 B. Courcelle . Communication personnelle .

Co-Vu 76 B. Courcelle , J. Vuillemin "Completeness results for the equivalence of recursive schemes " *Journal of computer and System Science 12* . pp 179-197

Fr 77 E.P. Friedman "Equivalence problems for deterministic context-free languages and monadic recursion schemes" *Journal of Computer and System Sciences 14*. pp 344-359

Ga-Lu 73 S. Garland , D. Luckam "Program Schemes, recursion schemes, and formal languages" *Journal of Computer and System Sciences* . pp 119-160

Gi-Gr 66 S. Ginsburg , S.A. Greibach "Deterministic context-free languages" *Information and Control 9* . pp 602-648

Gu 81 I. Guessarian "Algebraic semantics" *Lecture Note of Computer Science 99* .

Ha 78 M.A. Harrisson "Introduction to formal language theory" *Addison-Wesley*

Ha-Ha Ye 79 M.A. Harrison , I.M. Havel , A. Yeduhaï "On equivalence of grammars through transformation trees" *Theoret. Comput. Sci. 9*. pp 191-231

Hu 80 G. Huet "Confluent reductions : abstract properties and applications to term rewriting systems" *Journal of the Assoc. for Comput. Mach. 17*. pp 797-821

Ko-Ho 66 A.J. Korenjak , J.E. Hopcroft "Simple deterministic languages" *Seventh Annual IEEE Switching and Automata Theory Conference* . pp 36-46

Ni 72 M. Nivat "Langages algébriques sur le magma libre et sémantique des schémas de programmes" *Proc. I.C.A.L.P. 1*, North-Holland. Amsterdam.

Ni 75 M. Nivat "On the interpretation of polyadic recursive schemes" *Symposia Mathematica 15* . Academic Press

Ni 77 M. Nivat "Mots infinis engendrés par une grammaire algébrique" *Rairo 11* . pp 311-327

Ni 78 M. Nivat "Sur les ensembles de mots infinis engendrés par une grammaire algébrique" *Rairo 12* . pp 259-278

Ol-Pn 77 T. Olshansky , A. Pnueli "A direct algorithm for checking equivalence of LL(k) grammars" *Theoret. Comput. Sci. 4* . pp 321-349

To 84 E. Tomita "An extended direct branching algorithm for checking equivalence of deterministic pushdown automata" *Theoret. Comput. Sci. 32* . pp 87-120

SOME PROBABILISTIC POWERDOMAINS IN THE CATEGORY SFP

D. Frutos Escrig
Dpto. Ecuaciones Funcionales Fac. C. Matemáticas
Universidad Complutense 28040 MADRID (SPAIN)

ABSTRACT

We define and study some definitions of probabilistic powerdomains over domains in SFP. We give three definitions: the first one is based in the notion of probability distribution over a domain; the second in probabilistic generating trees, that generalize the notion of generating tree, introduced by Smyth; and the last in "informations about probability distributions", that we introduce, getting an information system, as defined by Scott.

INTRODUCTION

Many times, in studying a concrete process we are interested in "ensuring" some property of its final result. The problem roots in expressing such a "security" in a reasonable way.

In practice it seems more reasonable to require that the result has the property with probability 1, than to require that every "possible" result has it.

Consider for instance the program below. We can "ensure" that it stops after some finite time, because the unique infinite computation has probability zero to get executed.

```
Begin
        x := 0;
        While x = 0  do
            (1/2 : x:=1 ; 1/2 : x:=0)
End.
```

As a possible formalization of these ideas we have tried to define powerdomains whose elements have some probabilistic sense. For, we shall work in the category SFP, already shown to have a nice behaviour, by Plotkin |4|.

We define and study some definitions of probabilistic powerdomains over domains in SFP. We begin defining probabilistic distributions over and SFP-object D, introducing an order between them, whose completeness we prove. But the resulting domain, $\mathcal{D}(D)$, can be non algebraic because its order is too close to the usual one over $\mathbb{R}$. In order to get an algebraic powerdomain we consider probabilistic generating trees, gene_ ralizing Smyth's generating trees |7|; we call Sd(D) to the domain obtained in this way. We can embed $\mathcal{D}(D)$ into Sd(D), but we can not project this into the first one. That is because generating trees not only defines a distribution, but also a way to approximate it.

Nevertheless Sd(D) is not, in general, an SFP-object, and if we want to define a semantics of a probabilistic version, SPL, of Plotkin's simple language (that we will call SL), see |4|, we need an admissible functor which constructs probabilistic powerdomains. To get it we have defined an information system |6| about probabilistic distributions, $S_P(D)$, that leads us to a third domain Inf(D). Again we are able to embed Sd(D) into Inf(D), but not to project it into the first, since some informations describe a set of distributions without a least element.

We can extend the functions $f : D_1 \rightarrow D_2$ between two SFP-objects, to the three probabilistic powerdomains, obtaining three functors. In particular the third one is admissible, so that we can solve recursive equations between domains making use of the functor Inf; this allows us to define a semantics, M_p, of SPL. On the other side we can not define, at least in a classical way, such a semantics using the functor Sd instead of Inf; nevertheless we can prove that M_p takes as values only elements that are images of the semantical domain that we can construct, using Sd instead of Inf, via a generalization of the aforementioned embedding. This result allows us to relate M_p and Plotkin's semantics, M, of his language: as we can consider programs in SPL as probabilistic refinements of the ones in SL, we also have that M_p refines M. That is to say: we can forget the probabilities either sintactically or semantically.

1. Definitions

Def. 1.1: a) Let D and E be two domains (ω-algebraic cpo's), we say that $\phi = \langle i,j \rangle$ is a projective pair between them when $i : D \rightarrow E$, $j : E \rightarrow D$ where $j \circ i = Id_D$, $i \circ j \sqsubseteq Id_E$; b) A chain of domains is a sequence $(D_n, \phi_n)_{n \in N}$ where D_n's are domains and ϕ_n's are projective pairs between D_n and D_{n+1}. c) A cone between a chain (D_n, ϕ_n) and domain D is a sequence $(\phi^n)_{n \in N}$ of projective pairs between D_n and D such that $\phi^n = \phi^{n+1} \circ \phi_n$, for all $n \in \mathbb{N}$; d) We say that a cone $(D, (\phi^n))$ is universal when for each other one $(D', (\phi'^n))$ there is a (and unique) projective pair ϕ between D and D' such that $\phi^n = \phi'^n \circ \phi$ for each $n \in N$.

Prop. 1.1: If (D_n, ϕ_n) is a chain of domains, $D = \{(x_n)_{n \in N} \,/\, x_n \in D_n$

$x_n = j_n(x_{n+1})\}$ ordered by the product ordering, is a cpo; and $(D,(\phi^n))$ where $j^n((x_m)_{m\in N}) = x_n$, $i_n(x) = (x_m)_{m\in N}$ with $x_m = i_{m-1} \bullet \dots \bullet i_n(x)$ for $m \geq n$, and $x_m = j_m \bullet \dots \bullet j_{n-1}(x)$ for $m < n$, is an universal cone for (D_n,ϕ_n). We will call D, the limit of the chain.

Def. 1.2: SFP-objects are the limits of the chains constructed by finite domains.

You can find more details about SFP in |4|.

Def. 1.3: Let D be a domain, then a) We call Scott's topology over D, to the one that has as a basis the family $\{U_f \,/\, f \in F\}$ where $U_f = \{x \in D \,/\, f \sqsubseteq x\}$ and F is the set of finite elements from D; b) We call Cantor's topology over D, to the one that has a subbasis the family $\{U_f \,/\, f \in F\} \cup \{N_f \,/\, f \in F\}$ where $N_f = D - U_f$; c) We will call Borel's σ-algebra over D, $\mathcal{B}(D)$, to the one generated by Scott's (eq. Cantor's) topology; d) We will call probability distributions over D to the probability measures over $\mathcal{B}(D)$.

Prop. 1.2: Let D be an SFP-object, then we have a) $B = \{X_{M,N} \,/\, M,N \subseteq F_D$ $|M|, |N| < \infty\}$ where $X_{M,N} = \left[\bigcup_{f\in M} U_f\right] \cap \bigcap_{f\in N} N_f$, is a basis of Cantor's topology; b) B is a semi-ring; c) Cantor's topology over D is compact; d) B has not infinite disjoint unions of nonempty sets from it.

Corollary 1.1: a) If m is a finitely additive function over B, then it is a measure over it; b) If m is a finitely additive function over B, then there is one, and only one, measure over $\mathcal{B}(D)$ that extends m.

Proof: See |1| and |3|.

This result gives us an easy way to define and study probability distributions over an SFP-object.

2. The cpo of probabilistic distributions

Def. 2.1: Given and SFP-object D, the cpo $\mathcal{D}(D)$ of probability distributions over D has them as elements, and is ordered by

$$p \sqsubseteq p' \text{ iff } \forall M \subseteq F_D,\ |M| < \infty \quad p(\bigcup_{f\in M} U_f) \leq p'(\bigcup_{f\in M} U_f).$$

Theorem 2.1: a) $\sqsubseteq$ as defined in def. 2.1 is a partial order; b) $\mathcal{D}(D)$ is a cpo.

Proof (hint): We take $T = \{X_M \,/\, M \subseteq F_D,\ |M| < \infty\}$ where

$X_M = \bigcup_{f \in M} U_f$, and we prove that for each $X_{M,N} \in B$, and $p \in \mathcal{D}(D)$, $p(X_{M,N})$ can be expressed as a linear combination, that does not depend of p, of the values of p over some sets from T.

Remark: You can find more details about this, and the rest of proofs in this paper, in |3|.

3. Probabilistic generating trees

Def. 3.1. Let D be a domain, we call probabilistic generating trees (p.g.t.) over D, to the infinite finitary trees, labelled in their nodes by finite elements from D, so that if t' is a descendant of t, then it is labelled by a label greater or equal than that over t; and in their arcs by probabilities (rational and positive numbers), such that the sum of them below any node is 1.

Def. 3.2: We say that $p \in \mathcal{D}(D)$ is finite ($p \in \mathcal{D}_f(D)$) if p is a discrete distribution concentrated over a finite subset of F_D, and taking rational values.

Def. 3.3: We can associate to any level, k, of a p.g.t. g, a finite distribution p_k^g whose support is the set L_k^g of labels over the nodes of g in that level, assigning to each $x \in L_k^g$ the sum of the products of the probabilities that label the arcs of the paths from the root of g, to nodes of the level k labelled by x.

Prop. 3.1: For each $k \in N$ we have $p_k^g \sqsubseteq p_{k+1}^g$.

Corollary 3.1: We can associate to each p.g.t. g, a probability distribution p^g given by $p^g = \bigsqcup_{n \in N} p_n^g$.

The converse of this result is also true:

Theorem 3.1: For each $p \in \mathcal{D}(D)$ there is some p.g.t. g, such that $p = p^g$.

Proof (hint): As D is an SFP-object, we have $D = \mathrm{Lim}\,(D_n, \varphi_n)$ for some chain whose elements D_n are finite. Then we can define $p_n \in \mathcal{D}(D_n)$ by $p_n(x) = p(\{y \in D \,/\, x = j^n(y)\})$. Via the natural identification of F_D and $\bigcup_{n \in N} D_n$, we can consider p_n as an element in $\mathcal{D}(D)$, and $p = \bigsqcup_{n \in N} p_n$.

This result says us that any distribution over D is finitely generable, what is a bit surpresive (but pleasant) as some subsets of D are not finitely generable.

Definition 2.1 is justified by the following theorem:

Theorem 3.2: Let $p, p' \in \mathcal{D}_f(D)$ and $p \sqsubseteq p'$, then there is some p.g.t. g such that $p = p_1^g$ and $p' = p_2^g$.

Proof (hint): As p and p' take rational values, we can find a common denominator of all of them, so that our problem consists of assigning some weights over the elements of the support of p' among the ones of the support of p, so that if we assign one unity of x to y, then $y \sqsubseteq x$; and the weight assigned to each y agrees with the assigned by p. And we can prove that such a distribution is possible, by induction over the number of unities to distribute.

Now we define our second probabilistic powerdomain.

Def. 3.4: Given a domain D, we have a) If Psd(D) is the set of sequences $(d_n)_{n \in N}$ such that $d_n \in \mathcal{D}(D)$ and $d_n \sqsubseteq d_{n+1}$, we can (pre-) order it by means of $(d_n)_{n \in N} \sqsubseteq (d'_n)_{n \in N}$ iff $\forall n \exists m \; d_n \sqsubseteq d'_m$; b) Sd(D) is the cocient ordered set Psd(D)/$\simeq$, where $\simeq$ is the equivalence relation induced by $\sqsubseteq$.

Prop. 3.2: Sd(D) is a domain, whose finite elements are the classes of the sequences $(d_n)_{n \in N}$, such that there is some $p \in \mathcal{D}_f(D)$, $p = d_n$ for each $n \in N$.

Corollary 3.2: $\mathcal{D}(D)$ is an ω-continuous cpo.

We can embed, as shows th.3.1, $\mathcal{D}(D)$ into Sd(D) via some aplication s. But in general we can not project Sd(D) over $\mathcal{D}(D)$, as we have:

Prop. 3.3: In general the set $\{d \in \mathcal{D}_f(D) \,/\, d \sqsubseteq p\}$, where $p \in \mathcal{D}(D)$ is not directed.

4. Information systems about probability distributions

We will consider basic informations, bi $\in$ BI(D), that are pairs (q:A) such that $q \in [0,1] \cap Q$, $A \subseteq F_D$, $|A| < \infty$; finite informations, fi $\in$ FI(D), that are finite subsets of BI(D); and informations, i $\in$ I(D), that are arbitrary subsets of BI(D).

We say that $p \in \mathcal{D}(D)$ satisfies bi=(q:A), (p $\models$ bi) when $p(\bigcup_{f \in A} U_f) \geq q$; we say that p satisfies i $\in$ I(D), (p $\models$ i) when it satisfies each one of the elements in i. P(bi) (resp. P(fi)) denotes the set $\{p \in \mathcal{D}(D) \,/\, p \models \text{bi}\}$ (resp. $\{p \in \mathcal{D}(D) \,/\, p \models \text{fi}\}$).

We will say that bi (resp. fi) is consistent when P(bi) $\neq \emptyset$ (resp. P(fi) $\neq \emptyset$). And i $\in$ I(D) is consistent when each one of its finite subsets is. CBI(D), CFI(D) and CI(D) will denote the subsets of consistent elements from BI(D), FI(D) and I(D), respectively.

Def. 4.1: a) We will call information system about probability distributions over D, to the system $S_p(D) = (CBI(D), \Delta(D), Con, \vdash)$, where $\Delta(D) = (1:\{\perp\})$, Con is the consistency predicate, and $\vdash$ is given by $fi \vdash bi$ iff $P(fi) \subseteq P(bi)$; b) Following Scott's |6|, $S_p(D)$ induces a domain Inf(D), that is consistently complete, whose elements are the consistent informations that are deductively closed: that is to say $fi \subseteq i \wedge fi \vdash bi \Longrightarrow bi \in i$. Inf(D) is ordered by set inclusion.

Intuitively $i \in Inf(D)$ defines the set of distributions that verify each one of its elements; fortunately it is always a nonempty set, as shown by:

Theorem 4.1: For each $i \in Inf(D)$ the set $P(i) = \{p \in \mathcal{D}(D) \,/\, p \models i\}$ is nonempty.

Proof (hint): First at all we prove it when D is finite, using the fact that $[0,1]^n$ is compact with its usual topology. Then we take $D = Lim\,(D_n)$, where D_n's are finite, and we project i over each D_n, obtaining $i_n \in Inf(D_n)$. $P(i_n)$ is nonempty, and we see that we can take $p_n \in P(i_n)$ each one refining the previous one, so that they define some $p \in \mathcal{D}(D)$ that verifies i. The keys of the proof are compactness and the result in corollary 1.1.

We can embed Sd(D) into Inf(D) in the following way:

Def. 4.2: a) We define $fi : \mathcal{D}_f(D) \to CFI(D)$ by

$fi(p_1:f_1,\ldots,p_k:f_k) = \{(\sum_{i\in J} p_i : \{f_i \,/\, i \in J\}) \,/\, J \subseteq \{1,\ldots,k\}\}$;

b) We define $i : Sd(D) \to Inf(D)$ by $i((d_n)_{n\in N}) = \overline{\bigcup_{n\in N} fi(d_n)}$, where $\overline{}$ denotes the clausure with respect to derivability.

Remark: We have denoted by $(p_1:f_1,\ldots,p_k:f_k)$ the finite distribution that assigns probability p_i to each one of the f_i.

Prop. 4.1: a) i is an embedding of Sd(D) into Inf(D); b) Nevertheless it is in general impossible to complete it to a projective pair, as sometimes $P(fi) \cap \mathcal{D}_f(D)$ is not directed.

5. Extending functions to the probabilistic powerdomains

Def. 5.1: Given $f : D \to E$, we define $f^{\mathcal{D}} : \mathcal{D}(D) \to \mathcal{D}(E)$ by $f^{\mathcal{D}}(p)(X) = p(f^{-1}(X))$ for each $X \in \mathcal{B}(E)$.

Def. 5.2: Given $f : D \to E$, we define $f^{Sd} : Sd(D) \to Sd(E)$ observing that as D and E are SFP-objects, $D \to E$ is too, so that there is a seouence $(f_n)_{n \in N}$ such that $f_n \in F_{D \to E}$, $f = \bigsqcup_{n \in N} f_n$; then we take $f^{Sd}(|(d_n)|) = |(f_n^{\mathcal{D}}(d_n))|$.

Def. 5.3: Given $f : D \to E$, we define an approximable mapping R_f^I between $S_p(D)$ and $S_p(E)$, by $X \, R_f^I \, Y$ iff $X \in CFI(D)$, $Y \in CFI(E)$ and $p \models X \Longrightarrow f^{\mathcal{D}}(p) \models Y$. We will denote by f^{Inf} the induced function $f^{Inf} : Inf(D) \to Inf(E)$ (see |6|).

Prop. 5.1: a) f^{Sd} extends $f^{\mathcal{D}}$, that is to say $s_E.f^{\mathcal{D}} = f^{Sd}.s_D$; b) f^{Inf} extends f^{Sd}, that is to say $i_E.f^{Sd} = f^{Inf}.i_D$; c) $f^{\mathcal{D}}$, f^{Sd} and f^{Inf} are continuous.

Prop. 5.2: If we consider the category SFP-P (whose morphisms are the pairs of functions $<p_1,p_2>$, where $p_1 : D \to E$, $p_2 : E \to D$), and we define $Inf(<p_1,p_2>) = <p_1^{Inf},p_2^{Inf}>$, we have a functor into SFP-P, that is simetric and locally continuous. (See |4|).

Corollary 5.1: We can solve, in SFP, every recursive eouation between domains, whose right side is constructed by applying the functors sum, product, function's space, powerdomain, and our probabilistic powerdomain Inf.

Then we can use Inf to define a semantics of a simple probabilistic language.

6. A semantics of a simple probabilistic language (SPL)

The sintax of SPL is given gy

$v \in Var ::= x_1 \mid \ldots \mid x_n$; $\quad t \in Ter ::= v \mid 0 \mid 1 \mid t_1+t_2 \mid t_1-t_2$;
$s \in Stat ::= v:=t \mid (s_1;s_2) \mid (q_1:s_1,q_2:s_2) \mid (\text{if } v \text{ then } s_1 \text{ else } s_2)$
$\mid (\text{while } v \text{ do } s) \mid (s_1 \| s_2)$. Where $q_1,q_2 \in (0,1) \cap Q$, $q_1+q_2 = 1$.

Note that SPL is exactly as Plotkin's language SL, excepting that his choice construction $(s_1 \text{ OR } s_2)$ is substituted by $(q_1:s_1,q_2:s_2)$. Semantically the only nontrivial difference is that parallelism is implemented in a probabilistic way: we choose between s_1 and s_2 in an uniform way, executing the first atomic action of the chosen statement, and then the rest of it and the other one again in parallel.

We need a domain of probabilistic resumptions to model the semantics of SPL. We will call it PR, and it is the initial solution of the equation $PR \simeq S_\perp \to Inf(S_\perp + (S_\perp \times PR))$, where $S_\perp$ stands for $N_\perp^n$, giving us the values of the variables. Applying corollary 5.1, the existence of such a domain is ensured. Indeed we know (see |8|) that PR is, up to isomorphism, the limit of the chain $(T^{Inf\ n}(\perp\!\!\perp), T^{Inf\ n}(\psi_{Inf}))$ where $\perp\!\!\perp$ is the trivial cpo $\{\perp\}$, T^{Inf} is the functor such that $T(D) = Inf(S_\perp + (S_\perp \times D))$ and ψ_{Inf} is the unique projective pair between $\perp\!\!\perp$ and $T(\perp\!\!\perp)$.

As usual denotational semantics is defined in an structured way; we need three combinators to model sequential, probabilistic and parallel constructions.

Def. 6.1: Let $p_1, p_2 \in (0,1) \cap Q$, $p_1 + p_2 = 1$, then a) If $X, X' \in CFI(D)$, we can find $X'' \in CFI(D)$ such that $p_1.P(X) + p_2.P(X') \subseteq P(X'')$, and if $X''' \in CFI(D)$ verifies $p_1.P(X) + p_2.P(X') \subseteq P(X''')$ then $P(X'') \subseteq P(X''')$. We will denote such an X'' by $(p_1{:}X, p_2{:}X')$; b) If $i_1, i_2 \in Inf(D)$, we define $(p_1{:}i_1, p_2{:}i_2) \in Inf(D)$ by $\overline{\bigcup_{\substack{X \in i_1 \\ X' \in i_2}} (p_1{:}X, p_2{:}X')}$; c) If $r_1, r_2 \in PR$ we define $(p_1{:}r_1, p_2{:}r_2)$ by $(p_1{:}r_1, p_2{:}r_2)(s) = (p_1{:}r_1(s), p_2{:}r_2(s))$.

On the other side, the sequential ($\circledast$) and parallel ($||$) combinators can be defined in a recurrent way, as Plotkin defines his corresponding combinators $*$ and $||$. For instance we have

Def. 6.2: a) We define $r^{\|} : S_\perp + (S_\perp \times PR) \to S_\perp + (S_\perp \times PR)$ by $r^{\|}(s) = \langle s, r\rangle$, $r^{\|}(\langle s, r'\rangle) = \langle s, r' \| r\rangle$; b) Then we take $r_1 \blacksquare r_2 = Inf(r_2^{\|}).r_1$, and finally $r_1 || r_2 = (1/2{:}r_1 \blacksquare r_2, 1/2{:}r_2 \blacksquare r_1)$.

Then our semantics, M_p, of SPL is given by

Def. 6.3: M_p : Stat $\to$ PR is defined by $-M_p[\![x_i := e]\!](\alpha) = Rep(\alpha')$, with $\alpha'_i = E[\![e]\!](\alpha)$, $j \neq i \Longrightarrow \alpha'_j = \alpha_j$, where E is the natural function of evaluation of expressions, and $Rep : D \to Inf(D)$ is the natural embedding $Rep(x) = \overline{\{(1{:}\{f\}) \mid f \in F_D \wedge f \subseteq x}$. $(M[\![x_i := e]\!](\alpha) = [\![\alpha']\!])$

$-M_p[\![(s_1;s_2)]\!] = M_p[\![s_1]\!] \circledast M_p[\![s_2]\!]$ $(M[\![(s_1;s_2)]\!] = M[\![s_1]\!] * M[\![s_2]\!])$

$-M_p[\![(q_1{:}s_1, q_2{:}s_2)]\!] = (q_1{:}M_p[\![s_1]\!], q_2{:}M_p[\![s_2]\!])$

$(M[\![(s_1 \text{ OR } s_2)]\!] = M[\![s_1]\!] ? M[\![s_2]\!])$

$-M_p[\![(s_1 || s_2)]\!] = M_p[\![s_1]\!] || M_p[\![s_2]\!]$

$-M_p[\![(\text{if } x_i \text{ then } s_1 \text{ else } s_2)]\!](\alpha) = COND(EQ(\alpha_i, 0), M_p[\![s_1]\!](\alpha), M_p[\![s_2]\!](\alpha))$

$-M_p[\![(\text{while } x_i \text{ do } s)]\!] = Y(\lambda r \in PR\ \lambda\alpha \in S.COND(EQ(\alpha_i, 0), M_p[\![s]\!] \circledast r(\alpha), Rep(\alpha)))$ $(M[\![(\text{while } x_i \text{ do } s)]\!] = Y(\lambda r \in R\ \lambda\alpha \in S.COND(EQ(\alpha_i, 0), M[\![s]\!] * r(\alpha), [\![\alpha]\!])))$ where Y is the minimal fixed point operator.

Remark: In brackets you can see the more illustrative clauses of the definition of M. Remind that R is given by $R \simeq S_\perp \to P(S_\perp + (S_\perp x R))$, that is to say $R \equiv \mathrm{Lim}(T^n(\perp\!\!\!\perp), T^n(\psi))$ where $T(D) = S_\perp \to P(S_\perp + (S_\perp x D))$ and ψ is the unique projective pair between $\perp\!\!\!\perp$ and $T(\perp\!\!\!\perp)$.

To relate M and M_p, we have first to relate P and Inf. To do it we consider $P(D)^\emptyset = P(D) \cup \{\emptyset\}$, and define

Def. 6.4: $\phi : \mathrm{Inf}(D) \to P(D)^\emptyset$ associates to each $i \in \mathrm{Inf}(D)$ the set of $d \in D$ that verifies i) $\neg \exists (q:A) \in i \;/\; q=1 \wedge d \notin \bigcup_{f \in A} U_f$; ii) $\forall e \in F_D$ $e \sqsubseteq d \Longrightarrow \exists q > 0 \quad (q:\{e\}) \in i$.

Unfortunately $\phi(i)$ can be empty; nevertheless, if $i = i(s)$ for some $s \in Sd(D)$, then $\phi(i) \in P(D)$, and it is given by the generating tree that defines s, once we forget about the probabilities that label the arcs of such a tree.

So things go well if we restrict ourselves to $i(Sd(D))$ instead of working with $\mathrm{Inf}(D)$ as a whole. And we can prove that we can do it.

Def. 6.5: Over the category of domains, we define the functor T^{Sd} given by $T^{Sd}(D) = S_\perp \to Sd(S_\perp + S_\perp x D))$, and we take $PR^{Sd} = \mathrm{Lim}(T^{Sd\ n}(\perp\!\!\!\perp), T^{Sd\ n}(\psi_{Sd}))$, where ψ_{Sd} is the unique projective pair between $\perp\!\!\!\perp$ and $T^{Sd}(\perp\!\!\!\perp)$.

We have an obvious embedding $i_\infty : PR^{Sd} \to PR$, whose image will be denoted by PR^{Sdc}.

Def. 6.6: For each $n \in N$ we define $\phi_n : T^{Sd\ n}(\perp\!\!\!\perp) \to T^n(\perp\!\!\!\perp)$ by $\phi_0 = \mathrm{Id}_{\perp\!\!\!\perp}$; and when ϕ_n is defined we take

$$\psi_n : S_\perp + (S_\perp x T^{Sd\ n}(\perp\!\!\!\perp)) \to S_\perp + (S_\perp x T^x(\perp\!\!\!\perp)) \begin{cases} \psi_n(s) = s \\ \psi_n(<s,x>) = <s, \phi_n(s)> \end{cases}$$

$\gamma_n : Sd(S_\perp + (S_\perp x T^{Sd\ n}(\perp\!\!\!\perp))) \to P(S_\perp + (S_\perp x T^n(\perp\!\!\!\perp)))$ $\quad \gamma_n = \phi \bullet i \bullet \psi_n^{Sd}$, to get ϕ_{n+1} given by $\phi_{n+1}(f) = \gamma_n \circ f$.

Prop. 6.1: The diagrams in the figure below are conmutative.

$$\begin{array}{ccc}
T^{Sd\ n}(\perp\!\!\!\perp) & \xleftarrow{T^{Sd\ n}(\psi^2_{Sd})} & T^{Sd\ n+1}(\perp\!\!\!\perp) \\
\downarrow \phi_n & & \downarrow \phi_{n+1} \\
T^n(\perp\!\!\!\perp) & \xleftarrow[T^n(\psi^2)]{} & T^{n+1}(\perp\!\!\!\perp)
\end{array}$$

$$\begin{array}{ccc} T^{Sd\ n}(\perp\!\!\perp) & \xrightarrow{T^{Sd\ n}(\psi^1_{Sd})} & T^{Sd\ n+1}(\perp\!\!\perp) \\ \downarrow \phi_n & & \downarrow \phi_{n+1} \\ T^n(\perp\!\!\perp) & \xrightarrow[T^n(\psi^1)]{} & T^{n+1}(\perp\!\!\perp) \end{array}$$

<u>Corollary 6.1</u>: a) We can define $\phi_\infty : PR^{Sd} \to R$ by $\phi_\infty((x_n)_{n\in N}) = (\phi_n(x_n))_{n\in N}$; also we will denote by ϕ_∞ the function $\phi_\infty \bullet i_\infty^{-1} : PR^{Sdc} \to R$. b) For each $r \in F_{PR^{Sd}}$, that is identificable with some $r' \in T^{Sd\ n}(\perp\!\!\perp)$ for some $n \in N$, we can also identify $\phi_\infty(r)$ and $\phi_n(r')$.

Finally some lemmata will allow us to relate M and M_p.

<u>Lemma 6.1</u>: For all $r_1, r_2 \in PR^{Sdc}$ we have a) $r_1 \circledast r_2 \in PR^{Sdc}$, and $\phi_\infty(r_1 \circledast r_2) = \phi_\infty(r_1) * \phi_\infty(r_2)$; b) $r_1 || r_2 \in PR^{Sdc}$, and $\phi_\infty(r_1||r_2) = \phi_\infty(r_1)||\phi_\infty(r_2)$; c) $(q_1:r_1, q_2:r_2) \in PR^{Sdc}$, and $\phi_\infty(q_1:r_1, q_2:r_2) = \phi_\infty(r_1) ? \phi_\infty(r_2)$.

<u>Lemma 6.2</u>: Given $r' \in PR^{Sdc}$, $f : PR \to PR$ $f \equiv \lambda r \in PR\ \lambda s \in S.$ $COND(EQ(s_i,0),\ r' \circledast r(s),\ Rep(s))$ and $g : R \to R$ $g \equiv \lambda r \in R\ \lambda s \in S.$ $.COND(EQ(s_i,0),\ \phi_\infty(r') * r(s), [\![s]\!])$, we have $Y(f) \in PR^{Sdc}$, and $\phi_\infty(Y(f)) = Y(g)$.

<u>Theorem 6.1</u>: Let s be an SPL program, if we call s_{nd} its nondeterministic version, which is obtained replacing each statement $(q_1:s_1, q_2:s_2)$ in s, by $(s_1 \text{ OR } s_2)$, we have i) $M_p[\![s]\!] \in PR^{Sdc}$; ii) $\phi_\infty(M_p[\![s]\!]) = M[\![s_{nd}]\!]$.

<u>Acknowledgements</u>

I want to thank M.B. Smyth, who suggested to me the matter of the paper, and to M. Rodríguez Artalejo who listened to me, and gave me new ideas about the matter.

<u>References</u>

|1| C.V. BURRILL, "Measure, integration and probability". Mc.Graw Hill (1970).

|2| D. FRUTOS ESCRIG, "A characterization of Plotkin's order in powerdomains and some of its properties" TCS 31 (1984).

|3| D. FRUTOS ESCRIG, "Algunas cuestiones relacionadas con la semántica de construcciones probabilísticas" Tesis doctoral. Madrid, july 1985.

|4| G. PLOTKIN, "A powerdomain construction" SIAM J. Comput. 5 (1976).

|5| N. SAHEB-DJAHROMI, "CPO's of measures for nondeterminism" TCS 12 (1980).

|6| D. SCOTT, "Domains for denotational semantics", ICALP-82 LNCS 140 Springer-Verlag, (1982).

|7| M. SMYTH, "Powerdomains", J.C.S.S. 16 (1978).

|8| M. SMYTH & G. PLOTKIN, "Category theoretic solution of recursive domain equations" SIAM J. Comput. 11,4 (1982).

IONS AND LOCAL DEFINITIONS IN LOGIC PROGRAMMING

M.A. Nait Abdallah
Department of Computer Science
University of Western Ontario
London, Ontario, Canada

Abstract

In [1] Bowen and Kowalski suggest amalgamating language and metalanguage in logic programming in order to be able to explicitly refer to theories (i.e. collections of clauses), and discuss derivability from these theories. In particular, they use amalgamation in order to give a solution to the locality of definition problem. *In this paper we reconsider this locality of definition problem, and present a new approach for solving it, whithout calling upon language and metalanguage amalgamation. To this end we introduce the notion of an* ion, *and extend to logic programming with ions various results from "classical" logic programming. We give a least fixpoint semantics, a set-theoretic characterization of successful derivations, and a skylight theorem characterizing approximations to the result computed by a given derivation.*

I. Introduction

To place the contribution of this paper, we first recall a few basic definitions of logic programming [2, 5]. These definitions are then generalized by introducing the notion of an ion and the properties of ions are examined.

The basic definitions we are referring to are the following.

A *logic program* is a finite set of definite clauses and procedure calls. A *definite clause* is an expression of the form:

$$A \leftarrow B_1 \ \& \ \dots \ \& \ B_m \qquad m \geq 0$$

where $A, B_1, \dots, B_m$ are atoms. An *atom* is an expression of the form $p(t_1,\dots,t_k)$, where p is a k-ary relation symbol, and $t_1,\dots,t_k$ are terms. A *term* is a variable, a constant, or has the form $f(t_1,\dots,t_n)$, where f is a n-ary function symbol and $t_1,\dots,t_n$ are terms.

A *goal clause* is a formula of the form

$$\leftarrow B_1 \ \& \ \dots \ \& \ B_m \qquad m \geq 0$$

where $B_1, \dots, B_m$ are atoms.

A goal clause may be seen as a database query, or as a recursive function call.

A goal clause where m = 0 is called an *empty clause*, and denoted by the symbol □ .

A *Horn clause* is either a definite clause or a goal clause.

The problem we address is the *locality of definition* problem as presented by Bowen and Kowalski [1]; a feature similar to the locality of definition device is present in QLISP [8], and goes under the name of *APPLY team*. The problem as described in [1] is to construct definitions of predicates which are purely local to a given clause. The following example is given by Bowen and Kowalski:

$$p(x) \leftarrow \text{Local}(aux,\ q(x,\ y,\ z))\ \&\ r(x,\ y,\ z)$$

where *aux* is the *name* of a set of clauses defining q. "The intent of the first condition of the clause is that q(x, y, z) should be demonstrated in that extension of the present theory in which q is defined by the clauses named by *aux*. The expression Local(*aux*,q(x, y, z)) is regarded as a single unitary goal." [1]. The solution presented by the authors uses "language and metalanguage amalgamation" through a special modification of their *Demo* predicate. We argue that, from a theoretical point of view, the meaning of this amalgamation concept bears much fuller investigation, and its *necessity* for the purpose of expressing the above device is not clear.

We now present our solution to the locality of definition problem, which does not call upon language and metalanguage amalgamation. We also believe that our solution is simpler. The solution is obtained by using *generalized atoms* which we call *ions*. The notion of an ion is simply obtained by making the object "Local(*aux*, q(x, y, z))" into an element of the domain containing all the objects of computation. This technique is very much the same as the one used by Dana Scott when he made the object "non termination of a computation" (or undefinedness of the result for some value of the argument) into a value (called bottom) of the domain of computation; thus denotational semantics could talk about non–terminating computations without going into the "language/metalanguage" dichotomy. Also, Bowen and Kowalski's *linking rules* can be avoided by the introduction of this new syntactic item. Another advantage of ions is that they can easily be nested. Finally in the approach given in [1], a *specific* modification of the definition of the predicate *Demo* is required for *each* local definition introduced. This is not so with ions. Intuitively speaking, if we use Ferguson's dominoe description of logic programming, the formalism we are about to define is a game of nested dominoes with nested sets of rules.

II. Logic program schemes

We now give our definitions. Many of the new concepts we introduce are generalized from those defined above, but for the sake of keeping a simple terminology, the prefix *generalized* will be omitted. The definitions we now give will hold throughout the paper.

II.1. The sets Π(Ξ, R, F ∪ V) and Π(∅, R, F ∪ V) of logic programs

Let V be an infinite set of variables. Let F be a set of function symbols. Let R be a set of relation symbols. Let Ξ be a set of procedure names.

A *logic program* is a finite set of definite clauses and procedure calls. A *definite clause* is an expression of the form:

$$A \leftarrow B_1 \ \& \ \ldots \ \& \ B_m \qquad m \geq 0$$

where A ,is an atom and B_1 , ... , B_m are ions. An *ion* is either an atom or an expression of the form :

$$(B_1 \ \& \ \ldots \ \& \ B_m, \ P) \qquad m \geq 0$$

where B_1 , ... , B_m are ions, $m \geq 0$, and P is a logic program. In the ion (B_1 & ... & B_m, P), we say that the set of ions {B_1 , ... , B_m} is the *ionic component* of the ion, and the logic program P is its *program component*.

An *atom* is an expression of the form $p(t_1,...,t_k)$, where p is a k–ary relation symbol, and $t_1,...,t_k$ are terms. A *term* is a variable, a constant, or has the form $f(t_1,...,t_n)$, where f is a n–ary function symbol and $t_1,...,t_n$ are terms.

A *procedure call* is an expression of the form

$$\xi \leftarrow$$

where $\xi \in \Xi$ is a *procedure name*. As a *notational convention* we will abbreviate by ξ the logic program $\{\xi \leftarrow \}$. The purpose of this convention is to try to keep our notation as simple as possible, and it will be used only when no ambiguity is possible.

We designate by $\Pi(\Xi, R, F \cup V)$ the set of all logic programs that can be constructed from symbols of Ξ, R, F and V. Similarly, $\Pi(\emptyset, R, F \cup V)$ designates all logic programs that can be constructed from symbols of R, F and V, and which contain no procedure calls.

Examples of ions are: a, a & b, (a, Q_1), (((, Q_1) & (, Q_2), Q_3), Q_4), (((a, Q_1) & (b, Q_2), Q_3) & c, Q_4), where a, b, c are atoms and the the Q_i's are programs. Notice that the ion before last contains no atom. Such an ion is called an *empty ion*. Note that there are infinitely many empty ions.

We now define contexts. Intuitively, a context is an ion with a hole in it. The formal definition of *contexts* is as follows.

(i) [ ] is a context.

(ii) If C[ ] is a context, and a_1, ... , a_{i-1}, a_{i+1}, ... , a_m are ions, where $0 \leq i \leq n$, and if P is a logic program, then (a_1 & ... & a_{i-1} & C[ ] & a_{i+1} & ... a_n, P) is a context.

If C[ ] is a context, and a is an ion, we define the ion C[a] as being the context C[ ] in which the hole [ ] has been filled by ion a. Let now a and b be ions, and C[ ] be a context ; then we say that C[ ] is the *context of a in* b if and only if C[a] = b, i.e. C[a] and b are the same ion.

If a is an ion, then we define occurrences in ion a as follows. An *occurrence* is any finite string of strictly positive integers. Intuitively, the occurrence provides a path from the "outside shell" of the ion through the nesting of its *ionic* subcomponents. More precisely, let $\lambda \in N^*$ be an occurrence, and a be an ion. Then we define the *ion* $(a{\downarrow}\lambda)$ *of occurrence* λ *in* a as being the ion defined as follows:

(i) If $\lambda = \varepsilon$ is the empty string, then $(a{\downarrow}\lambda) = a$

(ii) If $\lambda = k\lambda'$ and if $a = (a_1 \& \ldots \& a_k \& \ldots \& a_n, P)$, with $k \leq n$, then $(a{\downarrow}\lambda) = (a_k{\downarrow}\lambda')$; otherwise $(a{\downarrow}\lambda)$ is undefined.

We say that an atom u *occurs* in some ion a if and only if $u = (a{\downarrow}\lambda)$ for some occurrence λ. An ion is said to be *variable–free* if and only if each atom *occurring* in that ion is variable–free. In particular, every empty ion is variable–free.

An ion a is *elementary* if and only if every occurrence λ of a is a string containing only 1's, i.e. $\lambda \in \{1\}^*$. Alternatively we may say that a is elementary iff no ion occurring in a has a ionic component which is a conjunction of more than one ion. Thus empty ions are *minimal* elementary ions.

Occurrences in *contexts* are defined in a similar way. All we have to do is to consider the hole [ ] as being a special kind of atom. Similarly a context C[ ] is *elementary* if and only if every occurrence λ of C[ ] contains only 1's.

Let λ be an occurrence in a, where a may be either an atom or a context. Then we define the *clausal scope* (or simply *scope*) scope(λ, a) of occurrence λ in .on a as follows:

(i) if $\lambda = \varepsilon$ then scope$(\lambda,a) = \emptyset$.

(ii) if a is ($a_1 \& \ldots \& a_m$, Q) and if $\lambda = k\lambda'$, with $1 \leq k \leq m$, then scope(λ,a) = scope$(\lambda',a_k) \cup Q$

We define the *scope of an atom* (resp. *hole*) occurring in an ion (resp. context) as being the scope of the occurrence of that atom (resp. hole). (Notice that there may be more than one occurrence of a given atom, in which case we must specify the occurrence which is considered.) Intuitively the scope of an atom u in an ion is the set of rules from that ion which can be used in order to solve atom u.

II.2. Rewriting systems and logic program schemes

A *(parameterless) rewriting system* over $\Pi(\Xi, R, F \cup V)$ is a system Σ of n equations

$$\Sigma : \xi_i = T_i$$

where for $1 = 1, \ldots , n$, $\xi_i \in \Xi$ are procedure names and $T_i \subseteq \Pi(\Xi, R, F \cup V)$ are subsets whose elements are logic programs. We denote by $\vec{t}$ the vector of subsets $(T_1,\ldots,T_n)$.

Let P, P' be logic programs in $\Pi(\Xi, R, F \cup V)$ and Σ be a rewriting system. We say that P is *immediately rewritten* in P', and we write $P \rightarrow^{\Sigma} P'$, if and only if there exists a procedure call $\xi_i \leftarrow$ belonging to P, an equation $\xi_i = T_i$ of Σ and some $Q_i \in T_i$, such that P' is obtained from P by taking $P' = (P_i - \{\xi \leftarrow\}) \cup Q_i$. Thus, intuitively, P' is deduced from P by substituting the body of ξ_i to some call $\xi_i \leftarrow$ to ξ_i in P.

The transitive and reflexive closure of $\rightarrow^{\Sigma}$ is denoted by $\rightarrow^{\Sigma *}$, and its transitive closure is denoted by $\rightarrow^{\Sigma +}$. We define the two sets:

$$L'(\Sigma,P) = \{ P' \in \Pi(\Xi, R, F \cup V) : P \rightarrow^{\Sigma *} P'\}$$

$L(\Sigma,P) = \{ P' \in \Pi(\emptyset, R, F \cup V) : P \rightarrow^{\Sigma*} P' \}$

Let $C = \{<Q_1, \dots, Q_n> : Q_i \subseteq \Pi(\Xi, R, F \cup V) \}$. C is ordered componentwise, by inclusion, and forms a complete lattice.

Definition :

Let $\hat{\Sigma}$ be the mapping from C to C defined by : $\hat{\Sigma}(\vec{q}) = [\vec{q}/\vec{\xi}]\vec{t}$ where $\vec{t} = (T_1, \dots, T_n)$ and $\vec{\xi} = (\xi_1, \dots, \xi_n)$.

Lemma 2.1 :

$\hat{\Sigma}$ is monotone increasing and preserves least upper bounds of increasing sequences.

Lemma 2.2 :

Let $\hat{\Sigma}_1(\vec{q}) = \hat{\Sigma}(\vec{q}) \cup \vec{q}$, and let $\hat{\Sigma}_1^*(\vec{q}) = \cup\{ \hat{\Sigma}_1^n(\vec{q}) : n \in N \}$. Then for any P, P' in $\Pi(\Xi, R, F \cup V)$, $P \rightarrow^{\Sigma*} P'$ implies $[\vec{q}/\vec{\xi}]P' \subseteq [\hat{\Sigma}_1^*(\vec{q})/\vec{\xi}]P$.

Lemma 2.3 :

For any t in $\Pi(\Xi, R, F \cup V)$, $t' \in [\vec{L}/\vec{\xi}]t$ implies $t \rightarrow^{\Sigma*} t'$, where $\vec{L}$ denotes $L(\Sigma,\vec{\xi}) = <L(\Sigma,\xi_1), \dots, L(\Sigma,\xi_n)>$, and $L(\Sigma,\xi_i)$ is the set (language) of all logic programs belonging to $\Pi(\emptyset, R, F \cup V)$ that can be generated from ξ_i by using Σ.

Theorem 2.4 :

$L(\Sigma, \vec{\xi}) = <L(\Sigma,\xi_1), \dots, L(\Sigma,\xi_n)>$ is the least fixpoint of $\hat{\Sigma}$.

A *(parameterless) scheme* on Ξ, R, F ∪ V is a system of n equations :

$\Sigma : \xi_i = Q_i$

where for 1 = 1, ... , n, $\xi_i \in \Xi$ are procedure names and $Q_i \in \Pi(\Xi, R, F \cup V)$ are logic programs. Each such scheme canonically defines a *rewriting system* :

$\xi_i = \{ Q_i, \emptyset \}$

for 1 = 1, ... , n, which, for the sake of keeping a simple notation, will also be called Σ.

A *(parameterless) logic program scheme* (or LPS) is a pair (Σ,P), where Σ is a scheme and P is a logic program in $\Pi(\Xi, R, F \cup V)$.

A *goal clause for LPS* (Σ,P) is an expression of the form

$$\leftarrow (B_1 \,\&\, \ldots \,\&\, B_m,\ P) \quad m \geq 0$$

where B_1 , ... , B_m are ions. The intuitive meaning of a goal clause in the ionic case is the same as in the usual case, namely that of a negation of the (conjunction of) ion(s) it displays.

Example 1:

In this example, the tools defined above are used in order to express the intersection of two algebraic languages defined by their context–free grammars. We consider the following two grammars over the terminal alphabet {a, b, c} :

G_1: $S \rightarrow aSb + \varepsilon$
G_2: $S \rightarrow ASbX + \varepsilon$; $X \rightarrow cX + \varepsilon$

These grammars can be coded into the following scheme Σ over $\Pi(\Xi, R, F \cup V)$:

ξ_1 = { S(a.x.b) ← S(x) ; S(ε) ← }
ξ_2 = { S(a.x.b.y) ← S(x) & X(y)
S(ε) ←
X(ε) ←
X(c.y) ← X(y)
}

The intesection of the two algebraic languages $L(G_1)$, $L(G_2)$ is given by the logic program scheme (Σ,P), where P is the logic program:

$$P = \{\ I(x) \leftarrow (S(x),\xi_1) \,\&\, (S(x),\xi_2)\ \}$$

The goal clause ← (I(x),P) will generate all strings belonging to both languages $L(G_1)$ and $L(G_2)$.

III. Ionic interpretations and models of logic program schemes

In this section we generalize Herbrand interpretations to ionic interpretations. We show a least fixpoint theorem for the ionic case, and give a proof–theoretic characterization of this least fixpoint.

Let (Σ,P) be a logic program scheme. If S is some generating set, let $H_u(\Sigma,P)(S)$ be the free F–algebra on generating set S, i.e. the set of all terms constructed from F and S, the elements of S being taken as 0–ary.

By definition the ***ground Herbrand universe*** (resp. ***Herbrand universe***) of LPS (Σ,P) is the F–algebra $H_u(\Sigma,P)(\emptyset)$ (resp. $H_u(\Sigma,P)(V)$). The ***ionic base*** $I_b(\Sigma,P)$ ***of LPS*** (Σ,P) is the set of all variable–free ***elementary ions*** that can be constructed from programs of $\Pi(\emptyset, R, F \cup V)$ and from atoms with relations symbols from R and entries from $H_u(\Sigma,P)(\emptyset)$.

A ***substitution*** ϑ is a function ϑ: $V \rightarrow H_u(\Sigma,P)(V)$ whose support

$$D(\vartheta) = \{x \in V : \vartheta(x) \neq x\}$$

is finite.

Given a tree $t \in H_n(\Sigma,P)(V)$ and an arbitrary substitution ϑ, we define the ***result*** ***$t\vartheta$ of applying substitution ϑ to t*** as follows:

(i) if $t = x \in V$, then $t\vartheta = \vartheta(x)$

(ii) if $t = c \in F_0$, then $t\vartheta = c$

(iii) if $t = f(t_1, \ldots, t_n)$, where $n \neq 0$ and $f \in F_n$, then $t\vartheta = f(t_1\vartheta, \ldots, t_n\vartheta)$

The above definition is extended to ions t by letting:

(iv) if $t = r(t_1, \ldots, t_n)$, where $n \neq 0$ and $r \in R_n$, then $t\vartheta = r(t_1\vartheta, \ldots, t_n\vartheta)$

(v) if $t = (B_1 \& \ldots \& B_m, Q)$ where the B_i's are ions and P is a logic program, then $t\vartheta = (B_1\vartheta \& \ldots \& B_m\vartheta, Q)$.

In each one of these cases, we will say that $t\vartheta$ is an ***instance*** of t.

A ***ionic interpretation*** I for logic program scheme (Σ,P) is defined as a subset of $I_b(\Sigma,P$.

A ***ionic model*** of LPS (Σ,P) is a ionic interpretation I of (Σ,P) such that the following condition holds : for any clause $A \leftarrow B_1 \& \ldots \& B_n$ of program P, for any variable–free instance $A\vartheta \leftarrow B_1\vartheta \& \ldots \& B_n\vartheta$ of that clause, where ϑ is some substitution, for any elementary context C[ ] whenever $C[B_1\vartheta], \ldots, C[B_n\vartheta]$ are all true under interpretation I, then $C[A\vartheta]$ is also true under interpretation I.

If (Σ,P) is a logic program scheme, then we associate to (Σ,P) a ***subset transformation*** which is generalized from the definition given in [3]. We recall the definition of [3] which is as follows. Let P be a (classical) logic program; to program P we associate ***subset transformation*** T(P) defined on the ***powerset*** $\mathcal{P}(H_b)$ of its Herbrand base (i.e. set of all variable–free atoms constructed from symbols from P) by:

$$T(P) : \mathcal{P}(H_b) \rightarrow \mathcal{P}(H_b)$$

$$S \rightarrow \{ A\vartheta : A\vartheta \leftarrow B_1\vartheta \& \ldots \& B_m\vartheta \text{ is a variable–free instance of a clause of P, and } B_1\vartheta, \ldots, B_m\vartheta \in S \}$$

The generalization of T(P) we now need is two–fold. First we have to manipulate definite clauses whose right–hand side may contain ***ions*** i.e. local definitions. Secondly, we must handle the fact that we are dealing with ***logic program schemes***, and not only with programs. The ionic aspect is taken care of by a simple definition, which we first give. The LPS aspect uses the results obtained in the previous section concerning the existence of a least solution to the system of equations Σ of the scheme. We examine now successively each step.

Let P be a call–free program $P \in \Pi(\emptyset, R, F \cup V)$. Let $I_b(P)$ be the ionic base of P, i.e. the set of all variable–free ions that can be constructed from symbols of P. To program P we associate a subset transformation which is also denoted by T(P). ***Subset transformation*** T(P) is defined on the powerset $\mathcal{P}(I_b(P))$ of the ionic base by:

$$T(P) : \mathcal{P}(I_b(P)) \rightarrow \mathcal{P}(I_b(P))$$
$$T(P) : S \rightarrow T(P)(S) = T_1(S) \cup T_2(S) \cup \mathit{Elem}$$

where

T(P) : S → { C[Aϑ] variable–free ion : (Aϑ ← $B_1\vartheta$ & ... & $B_m\vartheta$) is a variable–free instance of some rule A ← B_1 & ... & B_m belonging to the scope scope([ ],C[ ]), C[ ] is a context, C[$B_1\vartheta$],... , C[$B_m\vartheta$] ∈ S } ∪ *Elem*

where *Elem* is the set of all empty elementary ions.

Definition :

If (T_n) is an increasing chain of self–maps defined on the powerset of the ionic base $I_b(P)$, then its least upper bound is given by the self–map defined by $\cup_n T_n = \lambda S \subseteq I_b(P).\ \cup_n T_n(S)$.

Theorem 3.1 : (continuity of the T operator):

Let {P_n: n ∈ N} be an increasing sequence of programs in Π(∅, R, F ∪ V), all having the same ionic base. Then

(i) $T(\cup_n P_n) = \cup_n T(P_n)$ (i.e. T is continuous on the powerset of Π(∅, R, F ∪ V)).

(ii) lfp(T(∪{P_n : n ∈ N}) = ∪{lfp(T(P_n)) : n ∈ N}.

Theorem 3.2:

Transformation T(P) is Scott–continuous.

We remark that S is a ionic model of program P containing all empty elementary ions if and only if T(P)(S) ⊆ S. The above theorem implies that the least fixpoint of T(P) is given by:

$$\text{lfp}(T(P)) = \cup \{ T(P)^n(\emptyset) : n \in N \}$$

This least fixpoint contains all empty elementary ions, and we now show that it is also the least ionic model of LPS (Σ,P) containing all empty elementary ions.

Lemma 3.3:

The least fixpoint of transformation T(P) is the least ionic model of P containing all empty elementary ions.

Let now (Σ,P) be a logic program scheme. To this LPS we associate a ***subset transformation*** T(Σ,P) defined on the powerset $P(I_b(\Sigma,P))$ of the ionic base as follows:

$$T(\Sigma,P) = T([L(\Sigma,\vec{\xi})/\vec{\xi}]P)$$

where $L(\Sigma,\vec{\xi})$ is the solution to rewriting system Σ given by Theorem 2.4. Then from the continuity of operator T and the definition of T(Σ,P) we deduce the following Mezei–Wright–like theorem:

Lemma 3.4 : (equivalence between the algebraic and "denotational" semantics of LPS (Σ,P)):

$$T(\Sigma,P) = \cup\{ T([\widehat{\Sigma}^{\,n}(\vec{\emptyset})/\vec{\xi}\,]P : n \in N\}.$$

By theorem 3.1 this lemma implies $\mathrm{lfp}(T(\Sigma,P)) = \cup_n \mathrm{lfp}(T([\widehat{\Sigma}^n(\vec{\emptyset})/\vec{\xi}\,]P))$.

IV. Derivations and direct approximations

In this section, we first define derivations on ions, and link results of successful derivations to the least fixpoint of the subset transformation $T(\Sigma,P)$. We then generalize *computed subsets* to *direct approximation* of ions, and use this notion for giving a version of the "skylight theorem" for the ionic case.

We now define derivation steps on ions. Each *derivation step* will be of one of the two kinds: either a simplification step or a rewriting step, depending on whether it acts on an atom or logic program component.

A *simplification step* (or *resolution step*) is defined by: $g \rightarrow g'$ if and only if there exists a triple $<\lambda, r, \vartheta>$ where λ is an occurrence of an atom in g, r is a rule variant $A \leftarrow B_1$ & ... & B_m from the *scope* scope(λ,g) with no variable in common with g, and ϑ is a most general unifier for A and the atom of occurrence λ in g. Goal g' is then obtained from goal g by simply replacing the atom of occurrence λ in g by $B_1\vartheta$ & ... & $B_m\vartheta$, and applying substitution ϑ to the rest of ion g. The result of applying a substitution so an ion has been defined earlier in the paper. This definition corresponds to clause (D2) of Bowen and Kowalski's representation of provability ([1], pp 156).

A *rewriting step* is defined by : $g \rightarrow g'$ if and only if $P \rightarrow^{\Sigma} P'$ is a derivation step in grammar Σ, for some program P occurring in g, and g' is obtained from g by replacing P by P'. In other words there exists some procedure call $\xi_i \leftarrow$ occurring in P, there exists some equation $\xi_i = Q_i$ occurring in scheme Σ such that P' is obtained from P as follows: the call ξ_i is erased from P, and P' is the union of the remaining program and Q_i: $P' = (P - \{\xi_i \leftarrow\}) \cup Q_i$. This is a much more general form of Bowen and Kowalski's "additional clause" (D1.1) ([1], pp 166).

A *finite derivation from g* is defined as a finite sequence

$$\Delta = g_0,\delta_1,g_1, \dots ,\delta_n,g_n$$

such that:

$g_0 = g$

δ_i is either a resolution step $<\lambda_i, r_i, \vartheta_i>$ or a rewriting step from t_{i-1} for every $i = 1, \dots , n$

$t_i = \delta_i(t_{i-1})$ for every $i = 1, \dots ,n$.

A finite derivation is *successful* iff it reaches an empty ion. This definition corresponds to clause (D1) of Bowen and Kowalski's representation of provability:

(D1) Demo(prog,goals) $\leftarrow$ Empty(goals).

Example 2:

(1) Let (Σ,P) be the following logic program scheme:

(a) the logic program P is the empty program $P = \emptyset$.
(b) the equations of the scheme are as follows:

ξ_1 = { smarter(Jimmy, Leonid) ← }
ξ_2 = { smarter(Leonid, Jimmy) ← }
ξ_3 = { happy(x) ← smarter(x, y) ;
happy(Joshua) ← happy(Jimmy) & happy(Leonid) }

In the sequel we designate by Q_i the body of equation ξ_i. We now consider the following goal:

1. ← (happy(Joshua) & ((happy(Jimmy), ξ_1) & (happy(Leonid), ξ_2)), ξ_3)

we then obtain the following computation:

2. ← (happy(Joshua) & ((happy(Jimmy), Q_1) & (happy(Leonid), ξ_2)), ξ_3) 1,Σ(1) call rule

3. ← (happy(Joshua) & ((happy(Jimmy), Q_1) & (happy(Leonid), ξ_2)), Q_3) 2,Σ(3) call rule

4. ← (happy(Joshua) & ((smarter(Jimmy,y), Q_1) & (happy(Leonid), ξ_2)) , Q_3) 3,Q_3(1) MT

5. ← (happy(Joshua) & ((, Q_1) & (happy(Leonid), ξ_2)), Q_3) y = Leonid 4,Q_1(1) MT

6. ← (happy(Joshua) & ((, Q_1) & (smarter(Leonid,z), ξ_2)), Q_3) 5,Q_3(1)

7. ← (happy(Joshua) & ((, Q_1) & (smarter(Leonid,z), Q_2)), Q_3) 6,Σ(2) call rule

8. ← (happy(Joshua) & ((, Q_1) & (, Q_2)), Q_3) z = Jimmy 7,Q_2(1)

The computation is finitely failed as we reach no empty ion. If the atom *happy(Joshua)* were deleted from the original query, we would reach the empty ion

(((, Q_1) & (, Q_2)), Q_3)

i.e. the derivation would be successful.

Example 3:

In the discussion in [1], the following sentence is considered : "*A person is innocent if she cannot be proved guilty.*". This example may be formalized by using ions as follows:

Let (Σ,P) be the following logic program scheme:

(a) the logic program P is the program P = { $\xi_1 \leftarrow$ }.

(b) there is one single equation in the scheme which is as follows:

ξ_1 = { female(Pandora) ← ;
person(x) ← female(x) ;
innocent(x) ← person(x) & ~(guilty(x), ξ_1) }

In the sequel we designate by Q the body of equation ξ_1. We then have the following derivation:

1. ← (innocent(Pandora) , P)

2. ← (innocent(Pandora) , Q) 1,Σ(1) call rule

3. ← (person(Pandora) & ~(guilty(Pandora), ξ_1), Q) 2,Q(3) MT

4. ← (female(Pandora) & ~(guilty(Pandora), ξ_1), Q) 3,Q(2) MT

5. ← (~(guilty(Pandora), ξ_1), Q) 4,Q(1) MT

5.1 ← (guilty(Pandora), ξ_1) 5,beginning of the application of the negation as finite failure rule

5.2 ← (guilty(Pandora), Q) 5.1, Σ(1) call rule

5.1 ← (guilty(Pandora), Q) *finitely fails.*

6. ← (, Q) 5, ~(guilty(Pandora)) finitely fails in {ξ_1 ← }

Thus Pandora, not being provably guilty, is innocent.

Example 4:

The mathematical induction principle cannot be formalized very well in the present framework. Indeed the definite clause:

$$p(x) \leftarrow p(0)\ \&\ (\ p(n+1),\ \xi \cup \{p(n) \leftarrow\ \}\ )$$

(where ξ is the name of the "theory" (i.e. the logic program) in the context of which we are working), amounts to the mathematical induction principle applied to p *only if* we allow ourselves to use n with the following *restriction*: whenever the above clause is used, n is a constant symbol which occurs nowhere else in the current logic program or the segment of derivation constructed so far.

Remark :

Notice that by using ions and the following computation rule: "in a resolution step, always choose the *smallest* scope containing a rule variant whose left-hand side unifies with the atom to be solved, and whenever such a scope has been found, ignore all the super-scopes", we can formalize a form of default reasoning. Consider the following example:

ξ_1 = {color(x, gray) ← elephant(x)}

ξ_2 = {elephant(Clyde) ← ; color(Clyde, pink) ← }

The ionic goal:

$$\leftarrow ((\mathrm{color(Clyde,\ z)},\ \xi_2),\ \xi_1)$$

together with the above computation rule yields the unique answer substitution <z, pink>, whereas without that computation rule we also obtain a second answer substitution <z, gray>. Thus we have the same advantage here as in [1], namely that ions make the underlying data base explicit.

Theorem 4.1 :

Let g be a variable-free elementary ion. Then the following are equivalent:

(i) g is the root of a successful derivation

(ii) $g \in \mathrm{lfp}(T(\Sigma,P)) = \mathrm{lfp}(T([\mathrm{lfp}(\hat{\Sigma})/\vec{\xi}\,]P))$

(iii) $\exists\, n \in N \quad g \in \mathrm{lfp}(T([\hat{\Sigma}^n(\emptyset)/\vec{\xi}\,]P))$

(iv) $\exists\, n \in N\ \forall$ atom u occurring in g, $u \in \mathrm{lfp}(T([\hat{\Sigma}^n(\emptyset)/\vec{\xi}\,]\mathrm{scope}(u,g)))$

(v) $\forall$ atom u occurring in g, $u \in \mathrm{lfp}(T([\mathrm{lfp}(\hat{\Sigma})/\vec{\xi}\,]\mathrm{scope}(u,g)))$.

Definition :

Let (Σ,P) be a logic program scheme. For any *elementary* ion g, we define the *direct approximation* ω(g) of g as follows:

(i) If g is an empty ion, then ω(g) = ∅.

(ii) If g is an atom, then ω(g) is simply the *ground-set*

$$[g] = \{g\vartheta \text{ variable-free: } \vartheta \text{ substitution}\}.$$

(iii) If g is not an atom, and g = (g', P) for some elementary ion g' which is non-empty, then $\omega(g) = (\omega(g'), [\vec{L}/\vec{\xi}\,]P)$ where $\vec{L}$ is the vector of languages which is the least fixpoint of $\hat{\Sigma}$.

Thus for any elementary non-empty ion g, ω(g) has the form $(\ldots(([t],P_1),P_2)\ldots,P_n)$ for some atom t, and logic programs $P_1, \ldots, P_n$. We shall identify $\omega(g) = (\ldots(([t],P_1),P_2)\ldots,P_n)$ with the subset of $I_b(\Sigma,P)$ given by $\{(\ldots((u,P_1),P_2)\ldots,P_n) : u \in [t]\}$. In this way the set of all direct approximants is identified with the powerset of the set of all variable-free elementary ions belonging to $I_b(\Sigma,P)$. The inclusion relation on that powerset canonically induces a partial odering on direct approximants: if x and y are direct approximants, then $x \leq y$ iff, seen as subsets of $I_b(\Sigma,P)$, y contains x. We denote by ∩ (resp. ∪) the greatest lower bound (resp. least upper bound) operation on direct approximants.

If $\Delta = t_0,\delta_1,t_1, \ldots ,\delta_n,t_n$ is a finite derivation starting from an elementary ion t_0, and if for every $i \in [1,n]$, ϑ_i is the most general unifier associated with step δ_i of Δ, then we define the *direct approximant* (or *subset of the ionic base*) *computed by* Δ, [[Δ]] as being given by:

$$[[\Delta]] = [\Delta(t_0)] = \omega(t_0\vartheta_1\vartheta_2\ldots\vartheta_n)$$

We then obtain the following "skylight theorem".(We call a "skylight theorem" any statement relating the amount of information initially contained in a goal, the results of certain computations starting from that goal, and (an approximation of) a fixpoint of transformation T.) The notion of fairness which is used here is, mutatis mutandis, the one given in [4,6].

Theorem 4.2 :

For any elementary ion g we have:

(i) $\omega(g) \cap \mathrm{lfp}(T(\Sigma,P)) = \cup \{ [\Delta(g)] : \Delta$ successful derivation from g $\}$.

(ii) $\omega(g) \cap T(\Sigma,P)^q(I_b(\Sigma,P)) = \cup \{ [\Delta(g)] : \Delta$ derivation from g fair up to q$\}$.

Bibliography

[1]. Bowen K.A. and Kowalski R.A. : Amalgamating language and metalanguage, in Logic Programming, K.L. Clark and T.-S. Taernlund ed, Academic Press (1982), pp 153-172

[2]. Clark K.L. : Logic as a computational formalism, Research monograph 79/59 DOC, Imperial College (1979).

[3]. van Emden M.H. and Kowalski R. : The semantics of predicate logic as a programming language, JACM 23, 4 (1976), pp. 733-742

[4]. van Emden M.H. and Nait Abdallah M.-A. : Top-down semantics of fair derivations in logic programs, Journal of Logic Programming (1985), 1 pp 67-75

[5]. Kowalski R. : Logic for problem solving, Elsevier North Holland, New York (1979).

[6] Nait Abdallah M.-A. : On the interpretation of infinite computations in logic programming, Springer LNCS # 172, pp 358-370 (1984)

[7]. Robinson J.A. : A machine-oriented logic based on the resolution principle, JACM 12, 1 (1965), pp 23-41

[8] Sacerdoti et al. : QLISP, a language for the interactive development of complex systems, SRI AI Center, Technical Note 120 (1976)

Input sensitive, optimal parallel randomized algorithms for addition and identification.

by

Paul G. Spirakis[1]

Courant Institute of Mathematical Sciences
251 Mercer St
NY NY 10012
USA
and
Computer Technology Institute
P.O. Box 1122
26110 Patras
GREECE

Abstract

Although many sophisticated parallel algorithms now exist, it is not at all clear if any of them is sensitive to properties of the input which can be determined only at run-time. For example, in the case of parallel addition in shared memory models, we intuitively understand that we should not add those inputs whose value is zero. A technique which exploits this idea, may beat the general lower bound for addition if the count of nonzero operants is much smaller than the numbers to be added. In this paper, we device such algorithms for two fundamental problems of parallel computation. Our model of computation is the CRCW PRAM. We first provide a randomized algorithm for parallel addition which never errs and computes the result in O (logm) expected parallel time, where m is the count of nonzero entries among the n numbersto be added. This algorithm uses O (m) shared space. We then use this result to solve the following problem of processor identification : n processors are given, each keeping either a 0 or an 1. We want each processor at the end, to know which are the processors with the 1's. Our solution is randomized and sensitive to the number [illegible] of the 1's. It takes

1 This work was supported in part by the NSF grants MCS 8300630 and DCR 8503497 and by the Greek Ministry of Energy , Industry and Technology.

O (min $\{$ m, n logm/logn$\}$) expected parallel time and only O (m) shared memory, capable of holding only O(n) size numbers. Combinatorial techniques of Erdos and Renyi were helpful to a part of this second result.

All our techniques enjoy the following properties : (1) They never produce an erroneous answer (2) if T is the actual parallel time and E (T) its expected value, then Prob $\{T > k.E(T)\} \leq n^{-c}$ where k is arbitrary and $c > 1$ is linear on k and can be specified by the algorithm implementer.

(3) m is initially unknown to our algorithms. They produce an accurate estimate of it.

1. Introduction

Recently there has been much interest in fast parallel algorithms that employ randomization. Although many sophisticated such algorithms now exist (see e.g. the proceedings the 16th STOC Conference), it is not at all clear if any of them are sensitive to properties of the input which can be determined only at runtime. For example, in the case of parallel addition (or multiplication) in shared memory models, we understand intuitively that we should not add(multiply)those inputs whose value is zero (one). Even if we manage to quickly estimate the number of nonzero inputs, we still have to organize them in an appropriate manner (e.g. pack them in shared memory), in order to perform the addition. Our goal here is to device such algorithms (by use of randomization) which are sensitive to such dynamic properties of the input and hence <u>beat the known lower bounds</u> (which hold for the general case).

We use the synchronous Concurrent Read - Concurrent Write (CRCW) model of parallel computation (called WRAM) (see e.g. [SV, 80], [G, 68]). This model assumes the presence of a (potentially) unlimited number of processors with (potentially) unlimited local memory in each processor. We assume our processors capable of doing independent probabilistic choices on a fixed input (This was first used by [R, 82 a,b] and [V, 83]). WRAM is like the PRAM of [W, 79] and [FW, 78] in the sence that different processors can read the same memory location at the same time. However, in the case of a simultaneous write attempt, exactly one processor succeeds in the WRAM model.We make no assumption of which one succeeds but we assume that the failed ones are notified. This can be easily implemented by having processors read the result of the "write".

We first consider the fundamental problem of parallel addition of n numbers. Our technique first provides a probabilistic estimate of the count (m) of the non-zero inputs, and then uses a probabilistic method to lay them out in shared memory and add them. The whole algorithm takes O (logm) expected parallel time, uses O (m) shared space and involves only m processors. To our knowledge, deterministic WRAM algorithms for addition have to take O (logn) parallel time when at most n processors are used and n numbers are to be added.

We then examine the related problem of processor identification : n processors of a WRAM are given, each processor must find out which are the processors with the 1's. We assume that each shared memory location can fit a number of at most O (n) size. We first use a nice technique of Erdos and Renyi (ER, 63), to provide an O (n /logn) parallel time solution to the problem, if counting of O (n) units had unit cost. We then use our first result (about addition) to provide an O (min {m, n logm/logn}) expected parallel time algorithm for the WRAM which uses only O (m) shared space. We also give a matching lower bound for the parallel time.

All our results satisfy the following : If T is the actual parallel time of our algorithm and E(T) is its expected value, then Prob $\{T > k.\ E(T)\} \leq n^{-c}$ where $k > 1$ is any constant and $c > 1$ grows linearly with k and can be controlled by the algorithm designer.

2. The case of parallel addition

2.1. The Algorithm

Let the array M represent the shared memory. Let $\partial \geq$ be a positive integer constant. Let each processor Pi be equipped with a local variable, $TIME_i$, intended to keep the current parallel step. Initially, each processor P_i $(1 \leq i \leq n)$ holds locally a number x_i. The goal is to compute the sum of the x_i's. Let m be the number of the nonzero x_i's. We give the algorithm in two parts : Procedure ADDITION (m') actually performs the addition, assuming an estimate $m' = cm + d$, ($c, d > 1$ constants) known. Function ESTIMATION produces such an estimate. So, the whole algorithm has the following high level description :

<u>begin</u>

  m' ← ESTIMATION

  ADDITION (m')

<u>end</u>

We provide the description of ESTIMATION first. In ESTIMATION, each Pi with $x_i \neq o$ produces k estimates of m (k is a constant) through a probabilistic technique, and then does a variance-reduction process to get the final estimate. The actual value of k is determined in the analysis.

Function ESTIMATION

procedure PRODUCE-AN-ESTIMATE

<u>begin</u>

<u>stage 1</u> (Initialization)

Processor P_1 initializes a special shared memory location (CLOCK) to zero. Them, each P_i executes $TIME_i \leftarrow o$.

<u>stage 2</u> (Estimate)

Processor P_i

if $x_i \neq o$ <u>then</u>

<u>begin</u>

(1) Flip a fair coin (two-sided)
(2) If the autcome is 'tail'then

<u>begin</u>

(2a) $TIME_i : \leftarrow TIME_i + 1$

(2b) CLOCK $\leftarrow TIME_i$

(2c) go to (1)

<u>end</u>

<u>end</u>

comment :This is done by processors which flipped a 'head'

(3) If $x_i \neq o$ then

<u>begin</u>

(4) read CLOCK into a local variable R1

(5) wait for 5 steps

(6) read CLOCK into a local variable R_2

(7) If R1 $\neq$ R2 then go to (4)

<u>end</u>

<u>comment</u> At this point, every Pi with xi $\neq$ o has flipped a 'head'

(8) Each Pi with $x_i \neq o$ reads CLOCK and makes its value to be the current estimate.

<u>end</u> (of procedure PRODUCE-AN-ESTIMATE)

<u>begin</u> (main part of ESTIMATION)

Each Pi with $x_i \neq o$ runs procedure PRODUCE-AN-ESTIMATE k times and produces estimates $E_1, E_2, \ldots, E_k$. Then all compute

$$(1) \quad E \leftarrow (\log 2) \frac{E_1 + \ldots + E_k}{k}$$

$$(2) \quad m' \leftarrow \exp(2) . \exp(E) + d$$

where $d \geqslant 1$ is a constant.

m' is the value returned by ESTIMATION.
We assume that it is written to a special shared memory location, so that it is available to all processors.

<u>end</u>

We now provide a description of procedure ADDITION (m'). It has 3 stages :

PROCEDURE ADDITION (m')

Stage 1 (Initialization)

In one parallel step, processors initialize a.m'+2 shared memory locations to zero, by executing :"Processor P_j writes a zero to M (j), if $j \leqslant am'+2$. "Then, they all execute $TIME_j \leftarrow 0$

Stage 2 (Memory Marking)

Processor P_j

IF $x_j \neq 0$ then

BEGIN

(1) Select y equiprobably at random from $\{1,2,\ldots,am'\}$

(2) $TIME_j \leftarrow TIME_j + 1$

(3) Read M (y); $TIME_j \leftarrow TIME_j + 1$

(4) If M(y) = 0 then write x_j into M (y).
Also, $TIME_j \leftarrow TIME_j + 1$

(5) If the "write" failed then

BEGIN

(5a) write $TIME_j$ into M (am'+1)

(5b) go to (1)

END

END

Comment : This part is executes by P_j with x_j =0 and by "successful"P_j with $x_j \neq 0$.

(6) Read M (am'+1) into a local variable R1

(7) Wait for 8 steps

(8) Read M (am'+1) into a local variable R2.

(9) If R1 ≠ R2 then go to (6)

Comment: R1 = R2 means all processors with $x_i \neq 0$ succeeded into writing x_i in a shared memory location, different for each processor, among M (1),..., M (am'). (If a processor was failing, the value of M(am'+1) would change).

Stage 3 (Addition)

(Processor P_j is assigned to location M(j), $1 \leq j \leq am'$)

From this point on, processors P_j (where $1 \leq j \leq am'$) perform a standard parallel addition of the numbers M(1),..., M(am'). In the ith parallel step of the addition, processor P_j adds M (j) and $M(j+2^i)$ into M(j), for $j=k.2^i+1$, k =0,1,2,... $am'/2^i$. (See e.g. (K, 82) or (FW, 78) on how to do the parallel addition of am' numbers by am' processors in O (m') space and O (log m') parallel time).

2.2. Analysis of the Algorithm

Lemma 1 At the end of each execution of procedure PRODUCE-AN-ESTIMATE, the variable CLOCK is a random variable, whose mean and variance satisfy :

(1) $E\ (CLOCK)\ .\ \log 2 \geq \log m + 0.5$

(2) $(E\ (CLOCK)\ -1).\log 2 \leq \log m + 0.5$

(3) $var\ (CLOCK) \leq 4$

Sketch of Proof (Details in full paper)

CLOCK is the maximum of m independent geometric random variables $X_1, \ldots, X_m$ (the number of coin flips until a head' of the Pi's with $x_i \neq 0$) with density Prob $\{ Xi = j \}$ = $(1/2)^j$ $j \geq 1$. The rest is a relatively easy calculation, since Prob $\{ CLOCK \leq j \} = (Prob\ \{ X_1 \leq j \}\ )^m$

□

<u>Lemma 2</u> Given any $\delta > o$, if we choose $k \geqslant 4/\delta$ then, with probability at least $1-\delta$, we have

(1) $|E - \log m| \leqslant 2$

and (2) The total running time of ESTIMATION is

$$0 \left(\frac{4}{\delta} . \log m \right).$$

<u>Proof sletch</u> (Complete Proof in full paper)

From Chebyshev inequality and Lemma1

we get Prob $\{ |E - \log m| \leqslant 1.2 \} \geqslant 1 - 4/\delta$

Also note that the running time of ESTIMATION is $0 (k.E) = 0 (E_1 + \ldots + E_k)$

□

<u>Corollary 1</u> Given any $\delta > 0$, if we choose $k \geqslant 4/\delta$ then, with probability at least $1-\delta$ we have

$$m \leqslant m' \leqslant m. \exp(4)$$

<u>Proof</u> It follows immediately, by Lemma 2.

□

In the following we assume $k \geqslant {}^4/\delta$ for a fixed small δ.

<u>Lemma 3</u> Conditioned on the event

$\mathcal{E} = \{m \leqslant m' \leqslant m. \exp (4)\}$, the time of stage 2 of procedure ADDITION (m') has an expected value of O(logm). Furthermore, the (conditional on $\mathcal{E}$) probability that the time of stage 2 exceeds $\beta.\log m$ is $\leqslant m^{-\beta \log a+1}$ (and can be made arbitrarily small)

<u>Proof sketch</u> (See full paper for details)

It is easy to see that every time a processor P_j attempts to write its x_j, and if $g \leqslant m$ shared memory locations are already "occupied", the competitors of P_j are $m-g-1$. Even if all of them manage to select different memory locations which were not occupied previously, the maximum number of locations that P_j must "avoid" is $g + m-g-1 = m-1$.
So, P_j will succeed with probability

$$\text{at least } \frac{am' - (m-1)}{am'} \geqslant \frac{am'-(m'-1)}{am'} \geqslant \frac{a-1}{a}$$

in each trial (and this holds for every P_j).

A generalization of Lemma 1 about the maximum of m geometrics with success probability $\geqslant 1 - 1/a$ implies that the average number of parallel steps required for all m processors to succeed is O(logm') =O (logm).

The probability that there exists a processor which continues failing for at least logm rounds is

$$\leqslant m.\ (\frac{1}{a})^{\beta \log m} \leqslant m^{-\beta \log a+1}$$

□

It is easy to see that the algorithm uses O(m') shared memory, O(m') processors, and performs the addition correctly, because, at the end of stage 2 of ADDITION(m') the m nonzero x_i's are placed one in each of m shared memory locations, and these locations are among M (1),..., M (am'). The rest of these locations contain zeros. So, we have :

Lemma 4 Given any $\delta \in (0,1)$, we can choose β 0 such that with probability at least

$1-\max(\delta, m^{-\beta \log a+1})$, our algorithm performs the parallel addition in O (logm) time, uses O(m) shared space and O(m) processors. Our algorithm never errs. With diminishingly small probability, it may choose a bad estimate m' of m and hence it may never exit the loop (6)-(9) of stage 2 of ADDITION(m').

3. The processor identification problem.

3.1. An $O(\frac{n}{\log n})$ parallel time algorithm which assumes unit-cost addition

The processor identification problem assumes that n processors are given, each keeping either a 0 or an 1. The problem is for each processor to find out which are the processors with the 1's. We first solve this problem for the so-called strong W-RAM (SW-RAM) model. This model has the property that simultaneous writes on the same memory location succeed only if they write the same value, and, if that is the case, their sum is recorded. We also assume that each shared memory location can hold only up to O(n) size-numbers. Let us imagine that all the processors are equipped with the same list $L = l_1, l_2, \ldots l_s$ of "testing" sequences, where each l_i is an n-bit sequence of 0's and 1's. Let us also assume that L is independent of the particular assignment of 0's and 1's to processors. In the following, let v be a fixed memory location and let e_i be the value of processor P_i. Processors execute the following sequence of steps, s^1 times :

Round i $(1 \leq i \leq s)$

(1) P_1 erases v's contents by writing a 0

(2) Each P_j $(1 \leq j \leq n)$ looks at the jth position of l_i, If $[l_i](j) = 1$ and $e_j = 1$ then P_j writes e_j to location v.

(3) Each P_j reads v's contents.

At the end of the s rounds, each processor has, for each testing seqeunce, the number of places in which an 1 stands both in the testing seqeunce and in the sequence $e_1 e_2 ... e_n$ to be guessed. If L allows each processor to find $e_1 ... e_n$ after the s rounds, we call L an s-algorithm for the processor identification problem (We allow unrestricted local memory per processor).

An obvious L (which would take O(n) parallel time) is that consisting of n li's with l_i (j) = 0 for $i \neq j$ and $l_i(i) = 1$ for all i.

Erdos and Renyi (ER, 63) considered a very closely related problem, the "coin-weight" problem. Using their techniques, we show that the s needed is Θ (n/logn) and that L can be easily constructed.

Let us view L as an sxn matrix of 0's and 1's.

Lemma 5 (see also (ER, 63)). A matrix L, sxn of 0's and 1's is an s-algorithm for the processor identification problem iff :For each pair c, c' of subsets of the set C of columns of L, such that $c \neq c'$, if we form the row-sums of the submatrices L (c) and L (c') (consisting of the selected columns) and denote by $\vec{V}_c$ and $\vec{V}_{c'}$, the column-vectors consisting of these row-sums, then $\vec{V}_c \neq \vec{V}_{c'}$

Proof sketch After m rounds, each processor has a row-sum vector, v , of L. This corresponds to just one subset c of the set of columns of L. This subset determines the processors with the 1's, because c is exactly the subset of processors with a value equal to 1.

□

Here, the techniques of (ER, 63) can be used to prove :

Lemma 6 A matrix L , sxn, with s= an/(logn), a $\geq$ 6, chosen so that the sn entries are independent random variables each taking on the values 0, 1 with probability 1/2 , is an s-algorithm, with probability tending to 1 as $n \rightarrow +\infty$.

<u>Proof sketch</u> Let p = prob $\{L$ is an s-algorithm$\}$

Let q = 1-p

Let $E(c_1, c_2)$, where c_1, c_2 are subsets of the set of columns C of L, denote the event that $\vec{v}_{c_1} = \vec{v}_{c_2}$ (where $\vec{v}_{c_i}$ is the row-sum vector of L (c_i) If c_1, c_2 are not disjoint, then if $d_1 = c_1 - c_1 \cap c_2$ and $d_2 = c_2 - c_1 \cap c_2$, we have $\vec{v}_{d_1} = \vec{v}_{d_2}$. Hence, if L is not an s-algorithm, there exist <u>disjoint</u> subsets of the set of columns, such that $v_{d_1} = v_{d_2}$. So

$$q \leq \Sigma \quad \text{prob}\{E(d_1, d_2)\}$$

where d_1, d_2 disjoint subsets of C.

One can then get, by some combinatorics, that

$$q \leq 2^{n(\log 3 - a/2) + o(n)}, \text{ for } s = \frac{an}{\log n}$$

So, if we choose $a > \log_2 9 + 2$ then

we get $q \leq 2^{-n}$ and $\lim_{n\to\infty} q = 0$

□

<u>Corollary</u> There exists an s-algorithm, for

$$s = \frac{an}{\log n}, \quad a \geq 6.$$

<u>Proof</u>

Since, from Lemma 6, $q < 2^{-n}$, we get $p > 1-2^{-n} > 0$. (In fact the vast majority of random o-1 sxn matrices are s-algorithms).

□

3.2. An $O(\min\{m, n \frac{\log m}{\log n}\})$ algorithm for the WRAM.

In the following, let m be the number of ones among the $e_1, e_2, \ldots, e_n$.

(a) An 0 (m) parallel-time algorithm for identification.

THE MARKING ALGORITHM

(Stage 1) The WRAM runs the algorithm for parallel addition once (as explained in Section 2) for the values e_j of the processors. At the end of this process (which takes 0 (logm) time with high probability), each processor knows the number of ones among $e_1, e_2, \ldots, e_n$.

(Stage 2)

The WRAM runs the stages 1 (Initialization) and 2 (memory marking) of the procedure ADDITION (m), with the following modification: Each time a processor marks a memory location, it writes its id instead of its value. At the end of this stage, the m id's of the processor with nonzero values have been placed "contiguously" in M(1), M(2),..., M(am).

(Stage 3) Each processor reads the memory locations M(1),..., M(am) in sequence.

Lemma 7 The marking algorithm solves the identification problem in the WRAM, in 0(m), parallel time, with arbitrarily high probability.

Proof sketch

By Lemma 4 of Section 2, the first stage of the algorithm takes 0(logm) time with probability at least 1-max (δ , $m^{-\beta \log a+1}$) where δ and β can be selected by the implementer. The second stage of the algorithm takes 0 (logm) time with probability at least $1-m^{-\beta \log a+1}$, by Lemma 3 of Section 2. The last stage of our algorithm takes am time. Our algorithm never reports an erroneous answer. Hovever, with diminishingly small probability, it may never terminate.

□

(β) An 0 (n $\frac{\log m}{\log n}$) expected parallel time algorithm for the WRAM.'

The WRAM here will simulate the SW-RAM of Section 3.1., as follows :

(stage 1) The WRAM runs the algorithm for parallel addition once, for the values e_j of the processors. At the end of this process, each processor knows the number of ones (m) among the e_i's.

(Stage 2) The WRAM runs the s-algorithm, by simulating step 2 of each round, with the procedure ADDITION (m) (described in Section 2).

Lemma 8 The simulation algorithm described above, runs in $O(n \frac{\log m}{\log n})$ expected parallel time.

Proof sketch Stage 1 runs in $O(\log m)$ expected time, by Lemma 4 of Section 2. Each round of the s- algorithm runs also in $O(\log m)$ expected time, by Lemma 3 of Section 2. □

In the full paper, we also prove that

Lemma 9 If $m = o(n)$, then our simulation algorithm runs in $O(\log m)$ parallel time, with probability at least $1-m^{\frac{-\log n}{\log m}}$

(c) The conbination of the two techniques. We can have the WRAM running both algorithms (a) and (b) interleaved (one parallel step of (a), and then one parallel step of (b). When one of the two techniques terminates, the processors will stop.

4. Remarks and Lower bounds

Lemma 10 No s-algorithm can have $s < \frac{n}{\log(n+1)}$

Proof sketch Each processor needs at least $\log(2^n) = n$ "pieces of information" to distinguish between the 2^n possible assignments of 0's and 1's to processors. On the other hand, if k processors attempt an addition (in step 2 of each round), the amount of information obtained cannot exceed $\log(k+1) \leq \log(n+1)$ because the number of 1's among them are 0,1 or,..., or k. So, s rounds can give at most $s \cdot \log(n+1)$ pieces of information to each processor.

□

Remark

Once the processors have an s-algorithm L, then can construct a table of the possible row-sum vectors $\vec{V}_c$ and their corresponding subset c of L. Then, given any instance of the identification problem, then need O(s) rounds to find $\vec{V}_c$ and one (indexed) table access to find c and solve the problem. Another piece of the preprocessing work is the construction of L itself. It seems to us that the n processors of the WRAM will need $\Theta(n^2/\log n)$ time to agree to a common random L. Clearly, our algorithm of Section 3.1 and of Section 3.2 -(b), becomes practical in dynamic environments, where the values of the n processors change. We pose as a general open problem the construction of input-sensitive parallel algorithms for other problems (so that the "general" lower bounds are beaten). A possible candidate is graph connectivity for special types of graphs.

Acknowledgments

The author wishes to thank C.H. Papadimitriou, D. Shasha and Z. Kedem for helpful comments in previous versions of this work.

REFERENCES

(CLC, 83)
Chin, F., J. Lam and I. Chen, "Oprtimal Parallel Algorithms for the Connected Components Problem,"CACM83.

(C, 80)
Cook, S., "Towards a Complexity Theory of Synchronous Parallel Computations", Specker Symp. on Logic and Algorithms, Zurich, Feb.5-11, 1980.

(DNS, 81)
Dekel, E., D. Nassimi and S. Sahni, "Parallel Matrix and Graph Algorithms, "SIAM J. Comp. 10 (4) 1981.

(ER, 60)
Erdos, P. and A. Renyi, "On the Evolution of Random Graphs," The Art of Counting, J. Spencer Editor, MIT Press, 1973.

(ER, 63)
Erdos, P. and A. Renyi, "On two problems of information theory"Mayar Tud. Akad. Mat. Kut. Int. Kozl. 8 (1963); also in The Art of Counting, J. Spencer, Editor, MIT Press, 1973.

(G, 78)
Goldschlager, L., "A Unified Approach to Models of Synchronous Parallel Machines", Proc. 11 th sub STOC, May 1978

(G, 77)
Goldshlager, L., "Synchronous Parallel Computation", Ph. D. thesis, Univ. of Toronto, C.S Dept., 1977.

(GLR, 80)
Gottlieb, A., B Lubachevsky and L. Rudolph, "Basic Techniques for the efficient coordination of very large numbers of cooperating sequential processors, "Courant Inst. TR No. 028, Dec. 1980.

(HCS, 79)
Hirschberg, D., A. Chandra, D. Sarwate, "Computing Connected Components on Parallel Computers, "CACM 22(8) Aug.1979.

(K, 82)
Kucera L., "Parallel Computation and Conflicts in Memory Access", Info. Processing Letters Vol. 14, April 1982.

(MV, 83)
Melhorn, K., and U. Vishkin, "Randomized and deterministic simulation of PRAMs by parallel machines with restricted

granularity of parallel memories," 9th Workshop on Graph Theoretic Concepts in Computer Science, Univ. Usnabruck, June 1983.

(R, 82)
Reif, J., "Symmetric Complementation," 14th STOC, San Francisco, CA, May 1982.

(R, 82b)
Reif, J., "On the Power of Probabilistic Choice in synchronous Parallel Computations", 9th ICALP, Aarchus, Denmark, July 1982.

(Ru, 79)
Ruzzo, W., "On Uniform Circuit Complexity", Proc. 20th FOCS, Oct. 1979.

(SJ, 81)
Savage, C. and J. Ja'ja', "Fast, Efficient Parallel Algorithms for Some Graph Problems", SIAM J. Comp. 10 (4), Nov. 1981.

(SV, 80)
Shiloach, Y. and U. Vishkin, "Finding the Maximum Merging and Sorting in a Parallel Computation Model", Tech. Rep. Technion Israel, Comp. Sci., March 1980.

(SV, 82)
Shiloah, Y. and U. Vishkin. "An 0 (logn) Parallel Connectivity Algorithm", J. of Algorithms, 1982.

(S, 80)
Schwartz, J.T., "Ultracomputers", ACM TOPLAS 1980, pp. 484-521.

(UW, 84)
Upfal, E. and A. Wigderson, "How to share memory in a distributed system", 25th FOCS, Proceedings, October 1984.

(V. 83a)
Vishkin, U., "A parallel-design, distributed-implementation general purpose parallel computer", to appear, J. TCS.

(V, 83b)
Vishkin, U., "Randomized speeds-ups in parallel computation", 16th STOC, April 1984, Proceedings.

(U. 84)
Upfal, E., "A probabilistic relation between desirable and feasible models of parallel computation", 16th ACM STOC 1984, Proceedings.

(W, 79)
Wyllie, J., "The Complexity of Parallel Computation", Ph. D. Thesis, Cornell University, 1979.

A PARALLEL STATISTICAL COOLING ALGORITHM

E.H.L. Aarts, F.M.J. de Bont,
J.H.A. Habers and P.J.M. van Laarhoven
Philips Research Laboratories,
P.O. Box 80000, 5600 JA Eindhoven, the Netherlands.

Abstract

Statistical Cooling is a new optimization technique based on Monte-Carlo iterative improvement. Here we propose a parallel formulation of the statistical cooling algorithm based on the requirement that quasi-equilibrium is preserved throughout the optimization process. It is shown that the parallel algorithm can be executed in polynomial time. Performance of the algorithm is discussed by means of an implementation on an experimental multi-processor architecture. It is concluded that substantial reductions of computation time can be achieved by the parallel algorithm in comparison with the sequential algorithm.

INTRODUCTION

Most combinatorial optimization problems belong to the class of NP-hard problems [5]. Consequently, exact solutions require prohibitive computational efforts for larger problems. Less time consuming optimization algorithms can be constructed applying heuristic techniques striving for near-optimal solutions. Statistical Cooling (SC)* is a powerful heuristic optimization technique for solving combinatorial problems. Ever since Kirkpatrick et al. [7] introduced the concepts of annealing [9] into the field of combinatorial optimization, much attention has been paid to research on the theory and applications of SC [1]. Important fields of interest include VLSI-design [1] and artificial intelligence [4,6]. The SC-algorithm is based on Monte-Carlo techniques. Salient features of the algorithm are its general applicability and its ability to obtain solutions arbitrarily close to an optimum. The quality of the final solution is determined by the convergence behaviour of the algorithm which is governed by a set of parameters. Due to the fact that SC is based on Monte-Carlo methods the algorithm intrinsically requires large amounts of CPU time. A major problem in the study of SC is to provide

---

(*) Originally, the algorithm drew heavily upon the analogy between combinatorial optimization and the annealing of solids. Therefore, it is commonly denoted as "simulated annealing" [7]. Similar to others [6,10] our formulation of the algorithm is based on the theory of Markov chains and it is this mathematical approach that leads us to prefer the notion "statistical cooling".

appropriate cooling schedules that ensure fast convergence to near-optimal solutions. Besides proper tuning of the parameters of the schedule, a substantial gain in computational effort may be obtained by a parallel SC-algorithm running on a multi-processor architecture. Here we propose such a parallel SC-algorithm.

The present paper first summarizes the most important features of the theoretical framework of the SC-algorithm based on the theory of Markov chains. After discussing the (sequential) cooling schedule we introduce a parallel SC-algorithm. The performance of the algorithm is briefly discussed by means of an implementation for a special class of Traveling Salesman Problems on a multi-processor architecture. The paper concludes with some inferences and remarks.

STATISTICAL COOLING: EQUILIBRIUM THEORY

A combinatorial optimization problem is characterized by a configuration space and a cost function [2]. The configuration space $\mathcal{R}$ is given by the finite set of system configurations (states), each represented by a state vector $\vec{r}_i$, whose components uniquely determine the given configuration. The set $I_{\mathcal{R}} = \{1,2,\ldots,|\mathcal{R}|\}$ denotes the set of state labels of the states contained in $\mathcal{R}$ ($|\mathcal{R}|$ denotes the total number of states). The cost function $C: \mathcal{R} \to \mathbb{R}$ assigns a real number, $C(\vec{r}_i)$, to each state $i \in I_{\mathcal{R}}$. The cost function is defined such that the lower the value of $C(\vec{r}_i)$ the better the corresponding configuration.

The SC-algorithm starts off with a given initial configuration and generates randomly a sequence of new configurations by perturbing the system. New configurations are accepted according to an acceptation criterion which allows of deteriorations of the system in a limited way. Thus the optimization process may be prevented from getting stuck at local optima. The algorithm can be formulated as a sequence of Markov chains, each chain consisting of a sequence of states for which the transition probability from state i to state j is defined as [2,10]

$$\begin{aligned} T_{ij}(\beta) &= B_{ij}(\beta)P_{ij} && \text{if } i \neq j \\ T_{ij}(\beta) &= 1 - \sum_{\substack{k=1\\k\neq i}}^{|\mathcal{R}|} B_{ik}(\beta)P_{ik} && \text{if } i = j, \end{aligned} \qquad (1)$$

where $T_{ij}(\beta)$ denotes the transition probability, P_{ij} the perturbation probability to generate state j from state i, $B_{ij}(\beta)$ the acceptation probability to accept state j if the system is in state i and $\beta \in \mathbb{R}^+$ the cooling control parameter. Note that the probabilities $T_{ij}(\beta)$, P_{ij} and $B_{ij}(\beta)$ are conditional probabilities.
For each state i, $\mathcal{R}_i$ is defined as the set of states that can be reached from i in a single perturbation. The perturbation probability P_{ij} then may be chosen as

$$P_{ij} = \begin{cases} |\mathcal{R}_i|^{-1} & \text{if } j \in I_{\mathcal{R}_i} \\ 0 & \text{if } j \notin I_{\mathcal{R}_i}. \end{cases} \qquad (2)$$

According to [2] a good choice for the $B_{ij}(\beta)$ is given by

$$B_{ij}(\beta) = \begin{cases} \exp(-\Delta C_{ij}/\beta) & \text{if } \Delta C_{ij} > 0 \\ 1 & \text{if } \Delta C_{ij} \leqslant 0, \end{cases} \qquad (3)$$

where $\Delta C_{ij} = C(\vec{r}_j) - C(\vec{r}_i)$. By assuming that the perturbation probabilities are symmetric and that, given a state i, any other state j can be reached by means of a finite number of perturbations, it can be proven that the size of a configuration sub-space $\mathcal{R}_i$ is independent of i. Hence, R can be defined as the size of the configuration sub-spaces.

From the theory of Markov chains it follows [2] that there exists a unique equilibrium vector $\vec{q}(\beta) \in [0,1]^{|\mathcal{R}|}$ satisfying

$$\forall i \in I_{\mathcal{R}} : \quad \lim_{L\to\infty} \vec{e}_i^{\,T} T^L(\beta) = \vec{q}^{\,T}(\beta), \tag{4}$$

where $T(\beta)$ is the transition matrix whose components $T_{ij}(\beta)$ are given by eq. (1), and $\hat{e}_i$ is the i-th unit vector in $\{0,1\}^{|\mathcal{R}|}$. Thus the probability to meet the system after an infinite number of transitions in state j is determined by the component $q_j(\beta)$ and it can be shown that [2]

$$q_j(\beta) = \frac{\exp(-\Delta C_{i_0 j}/\beta)}{\sum_{k=1}^{|\mathcal{R}|} \exp(-\Delta C_{i_0 k}/\beta)}, \tag{5}$$

where i_0 denotes the state label of an optimal configuration. Furthermore, it can be shown that

$$\lim_{\beta\downarrow 0}\left(\lim_{L\to\infty}(\vec{e}_i\, T^L(\beta))_j\right) = \lim_{\beta\downarrow 0} q_j(\beta) = \begin{cases} |\mathcal{R}_0|^{-1} & \text{if } i \in I_{\mathcal{R}_0} \\ 0 & \text{if } i \notin I_{\mathcal{R}_0} \end{cases} \tag{6}$$

where $\mathcal{R}_0$ is the set of optimal states. Thus, for Markov chains of infinite length, eventually (i.e. for $\beta\downarrow 0$) an optimal state will occur with probability equal to 1.

THE (SEQUENTIAL) COOLING SCHEDULE

In practice one obtains Markov chains by repeatedly generating a new configuration from an old one and applying the acceptation criterion of eq. (3) for a fixed value of β. Optimization is performed by starting the chain generation process for a given value of β, say β_0, and repeating it for decreasing values of β approaching 0. This procedure is imposed by approximating the limits of eq. (6) and is governed by the cooling schedule. The parameters determining the cooling schedule are

i) the start value β_0 of the cooling control parameter,
ii) the decrease of the cooling control parameter,
iii) the length of the Markov chains L (clearly the Markov chains cannot be of infinite length) and
iv) a stop criterion Z to terminate the algorithm.

As we shall show, near-optimal results may be obtained by the statistical cooling algorithm in polynomial time by making adequate heuristic choices for these parameters. Determination of adequate, time-efficient cooling schedules has evolved into an important research topic. The literature provides a number of (ad hoc) approaches, most of them based on a decrement in β, given by a fixed multiplication factor smaller than but close to 1, and a variable Markov-chain length [2,7,10]. Hereinafter, we summarize the main features of a cooling schedule that is based on a fixed chain length and a variable decrement of β (for an extensive discussion we refer to [2]).

Initial value of the cooling control parameter

For $\beta \to \infty$, the stationary distribution is the one in which all states have equal probability. Thus, the value of β_0 should be high enough to have a sufficiently large probability for all possible system configurations to be reached initially. This corresponds with an acceptation ratio χ, say χ_0, close to 1 (χ is the ratio between the number of accepted perturbations and the total number of perturbations generated for a given value of β). The value of β_0 can be obtained by monitoring the evolution of the system during a number of perturbations, say m_0, before the actual optimization process starts. Initially β_0 is chosen zero. After each perturbation a new value of β_0 is calculated according to the expression

$$\beta_0 = \overline{\Delta C}^{(+)} \{\ln(m_2/(m_2\chi_0 - (1-\chi_0)m_1))\}^{-1}, \qquad (7)$$

where m_1 and m_2 are the numbers of perturbations obtained so far with $\Delta C_{ij} < 0$ and $\Delta C_{ij} > 0$, resp. (at the end $m_1 + m_2 = m_0$), and $\overline{\Delta C}^{(+)}$ the average value of those ΔC_{ij} values for which $\Delta C_{ij} > 0$. During these m_0 perturbations the acceptation criterion of eq. (3) is applied. The expression of eq. (7) is chosen such that the corresponding acceptation ratio (which clearly depends on β) equals χ_0.

Markov-chain length and cooling control decrease

We require that for each Markov chain generated during the optimization process the distribution of the relative frequencies of the states should be close to the equilibrium vector $\vec{q}(\beta)$. We then say that the process remains in quasi-equilibrium. If the equilibrium vectors for two succeeding values of β (β and β', resp.) are kept close to each other, a short chain length suffices to fulfil the aforementioned requirement. That is, we impose

$$\|\vec{q}(\beta) - \vec{q}(\beta')\| < \varepsilon, \qquad (8)$$

which is equivalent to imposing

$$\forall i \in I_{\mathcal{R}} : \frac{1}{1+\delta} < \frac{q_i(\beta)}{q_i(\beta')} < 1 + \delta \qquad (9)$$

where $\varepsilon, \delta \in \mathbb{R}^+$ are small positive numbers. This condition is satisfied (for $\beta' < \beta$) if [2]

$$\forall i \in I_{\mathcal{R}} : \frac{\exp(-\Delta C_{i_0 i}/\beta)}{\exp(-\Delta C_{i_0 i}/\beta')} < 1 + \delta . \qquad (10)$$

Hereinafter, δ is called the distance parameter. It then can be shown that eq. (10) leads to the following decrement rule

$$\beta' = \beta\{1 + \ln(1+\delta)\beta/3\sigma(\beta)\}^{-1}, \qquad (11)$$

where $\sigma(\beta)$ is the standard deviation of the values of the cost function of the states of the Markov chain at β.
If quasi-equilibrium is maintained throughout the optimization process the chain length can be kept small. However, it is apparent that for larger problems re-establishment of equilibrium will take longer than for smaller problems. The system, furthermore, should have the possibility to investigate at least all configurations belonging to the configuration sub-space of a given configuration. A reasonable value for the chain length L, therefore, may be given by the size of the configuration sub-spaces $\mathcal{R}_i$, i.e.

$$L = R. \qquad (12)$$

Termination of the algorithm

Termination of the algorithm is done by evaluating a stop criterion Z that is based on an extrapolation (towards 0) of the smoothed average $\bar{C}_s(\beta)$ of the values of the cost function obtained during the optimization process, i.e.

$$Z : \left| \frac{d\bar{C}_s(\beta)}{d\beta} \frac{\beta}{\bar{C}(\beta_0)} \right| < \varepsilon_s, \qquad (13)$$

where ε_s is a small positive real number called the stop parameter and $\bar{C}(\beta_0)$ the average value of the cost function at β_0. The smoothed average is calculated over a number of chains in order to reduce the fluctuations of $\bar{C}(\beta)$.

With the cooling schedule presented above the execution time of the statistical cooling algorithm is

$$O(R \ln|\mathcal{R}|), \qquad (14)$$

where the term R originates from the length of the Markov chains (eq. (12)) and the term $\ln|\mathcal{R}|$ is an upper bound for the number of steps in the cooling control parameter [2]. The perturbation mechanism can always be chosen such that the size of the configuration sub-spaces is polynomial in the number of variables of the problem. Consequently, our statistical cooling algorithm is of polynomial time complexity in the number of variables. The cooling schedule presented above is controlled by only three problem-independent parameters, i.e. the initial acceptation ratio χ_0, the distance parameter δ and the stop parameter ε_s.

A PARALLEL STATISTICAL COOLING SCHEDULE

The basic idea underlying the parallel algorithm is to assign a Markov chain to each available processor and thus to let processors generate Markov chains simultaneously. However, the formulation of the SC-algorithm presented in the previous section is based on the sequential nature of the process, i.e. for two subsequent Markov chains M-1 and M, initialization of chain M is given by

$$(\beta_M; \vec{r}_{M,1}) = (\beta'_{M-1}; \vec{r}_{M-1,L}), \qquad (15)$$

where β_M and β'_{M-1} are the corresponding values of the cooling control parameter (β'_{M-1} is given by eq. (11)), $\vec{r}_{M-1,L}$ the last state of chain M-1 and $\vec{r}_{M,1}$ the first state of chain M. This inherent sequentiality is imposed by the strict sequence in which the two limits of eq. (6) are to be evaluated. Reversing the evaluation of the two limits results in stationary frequency distributions that depend on the initial configuration; in fact the optimization process is reduced to a simple iterative improvement algorithm.

The starting point for the parallel algorithm is again given by the requirement that quasi-equilibrium should be preserved. This, however, is achieved in a slightly different way as was done in the sequential algorithm. To overcome the inherent sequentiality imposed by the sequential nature of the process each Markov chain is divided into a number of sub-chains. Generation of a subsequent Markov chain is started after generation of the first sub-chain of the previous Markov chain (before equilibration). Quasi-equilibrium is preserved by adjusting the intermediate results obtained for the subsequent Markov chain after each of its sub-chains. In this way Markov chains can be generated in parallel while the length of each Markov chain can be limited to the minimum value given by eq. (12).

Let K be the number of processors, L the length of the Markov chains, $\ell = \lfloor L/K \rfloor$ the length of the sub-chains, $\beta_{M,m}$ the cooling control parameter for the m-th sub-chain of Markov chain M and $\vec{r}_{M,m,i}$ the i-th state of sub-chain m of Markov chain M, then the initialization of the sub-chains in the parallel algorithm may be formulated as (see also fig. 1)

i) $(\beta_{1,1}; \vec{r}_{1,1,1}) = (\beta_0; \vec{r}_0)$ (16)

ii) $\forall m \in \{2,3,..,K\} : (\beta_{1,m}; \vec{r}_{1,m,1}) = (\beta_0; \vec{r}_{1,m-1,\ell})$ (17)

iii) $\forall M > 1 : (\beta_{M,1}; \vec{r}_{M,1,1}) = (\beta'_{M-1,1}; \vec{r}_{M-1,1,\ell})$ (18)

iv) $\forall M,m>1 : \begin{cases} \Pr\{(\beta_{M,m}; \vec{r}_{M,m,1}) = (\beta'_{M-1,m}; \vec{r}_{M-1,m,\ell})\} = Q_1 \\ \Pr\{(\beta_{M,m}; \vec{r}_{M,m,1}) = (\beta_{M,m-1}; \vec{r}_{M,m-1,\ell})\} = Q_2 \end{cases}$ (19)

where $\beta'_{M,m}$ is defined as

$$\beta'_{M,m} = \beta_{M,m}\{1 + \ln(1+\delta)\beta_{M,m}/3\sigma(\beta_{M,m})\}^{-1}, \tag{20}$$

where $\sigma(\beta_{M,m})$ is the standard deviation of the values of the cost function of the states of the sub-chain at $\beta_{M,m}$. The probabilities Q_1 and Q_2 are defined as

$$Q_1 = p_1/(p_1 + p_2); \qquad Q_2 = p_2/(p_1 + p_2), \tag{21}$$

with

$$p_1 = p_0^{-1}(\beta'_{M-1,m})\exp((C(\vec{r}_{i_0}) - C(\vec{r}_{M-1,m,\ell}))/\beta'_{M-1,m}); \tag{22}$$

$$p_2 = p_0^{-1}(\beta_{M,m-1})\exp((C(\vec{r}_{i_0}) - C(\vec{r}_{M,m-1,\ell}))/\beta_{M,m-1}) \tag{23}$$

and

$$p_0(\beta) = \tfrac{1}{2}\exp((\beta\Delta C_0 + \tfrac{1}{2}\sigma^2(\beta_0))/\beta^2) \\ (1 - \mathrm{erf}(\Delta C_0/\sqrt{2}\sigma(\beta_0) + \sigma(\beta_0)/\sqrt{2}\beta)) \tag{24}$$

where $\Delta C_0 = C(\vec{r}_{i_0}) - \bar{C}(\beta_0)$, and where $\bar{C}(\beta_0)$ and $\sigma(\beta_0)$ are the average and the standard deviation, respectively, of the values of the cost

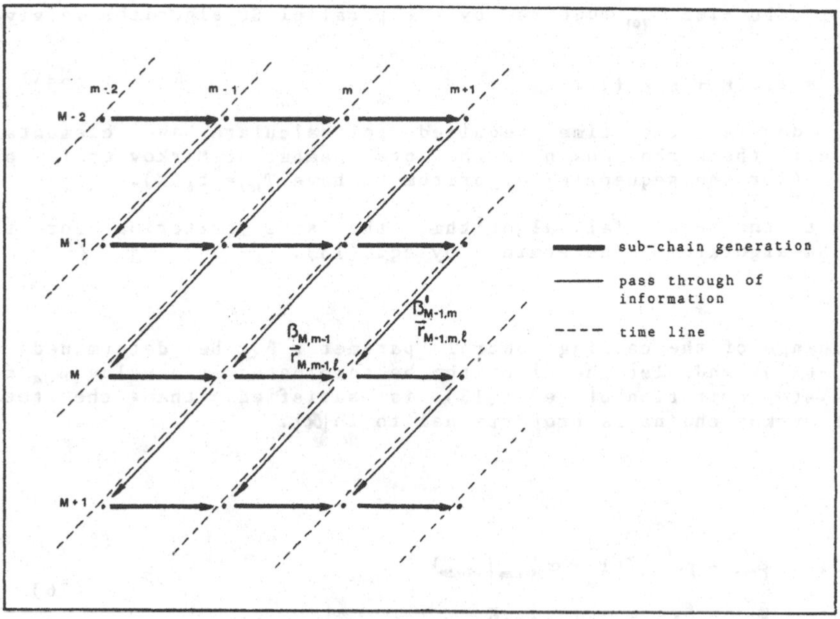

Figure 1. Schematic representation of the parallel SC-algorithm.

function at β_0.

ad i) Initialization of the first Markov chain. Here β_0 is given by eq. (7) and $\vec{r}_0$ denotes the (randomly chosen) initial state.

ad ii) Initialization of the subsequent sub-chains of the first Markov chain.

ad iii) Initialization of the first sub-chain of each subsequent Markov chain.

ad iv) Initialization of the subsequent sub-chains for each subsequent Markov chain. The state $\vec{r}_{M,m,1}$ is chosen probabilistically from the two states $\vec{r}_{M-1,m,\ell}$ and $\vec{r}_{M,m-1,\ell}$ such that the process continues with either one of the two states with a probability that is given by the normalized probability of occurrence of the states in the equilibrium distributions of eq. (5). As to arrive at the expression for the normalization constant $p_0(\beta)$ of eq. (24), the summation of eq. (5) over the configuration space is replaced by an integration over the configuration density function. The latter is approximated by a normal distribution $\mathcal{N}(\mu,\sigma)$ with mean $\mu = \bar{C}(\beta_0)$ and variance $\sigma^2 = \sigma^2(\beta_0)$ [3].

Through the manipulations of initialization (iv), quasi-equilibrium may be preserved during the course of the chain generation process, despite the fact that generation of subsequent Markov chains is started before equilibrium in the previous chain is re-established.

The timing of the parallel SC-algorithm is determined by: i) the length of the time intervals Δt_g required to generate the sub-chains and ii) the length of the synchronization-time intervals Δt_s between two subsequent sub-chains. Here we assume that Δt_g is equally long for all sub-chains and that the synchronization-time intervals may be neglected, i.e. $\Delta t_s \ll \Delta t_g$. Consequently the process is assumed to proceed in a number of equidistant time steps (dashed lines in fig. 1).

The total CPU time T_{TOT} required by the parallel SC-algorithm is given by

$$T_{TOT} = t_0 L(N + K - 1)/K \tag{25}$$

where t_0 denotes the time required to calculate an elementary transition in the Markov chain, N the total number of Markov chains and $\Delta t_s = Lt_0/K$ (for the sequential algorithm we have $T_{TOT} = t_0 LN$).

Similarly to the sequential algorithm, the stop criterion for the parallel SC-algorithm is determined by eq. (13).

Theorem

Let the change of the cooling control parameter $\beta_{M,m}$ be determined by eqs. (16)-(24) and let the algorithm be terminated at a value $\beta_{N,m}$ for which the stop criterion of eq. (13) is satisfied, then the total number of Markov chains is proportional to $\ln|\mathcal{R}|$.

Proof

Define

$$\begin{aligned} &\forall M>1 \ : \ \beta''_{M,m} = \beta''_{M-1,m}/(1 + \alpha_{M-1,m}\beta''_{M-1,m}) \\ &\text{and} \quad \beta''_{1,m} = \beta_0 \ , \ m = 1,\ldots,K, \end{aligned} \tag{26}$$

where

$$\alpha_{M,m} = \min_{i\in\{1,\ldots,m\}} \ln(1 + \delta)/3\sigma(\beta_{M,i}), \tag{27}$$

then it can be shown by induction that for M>0

$$\beta_{M,m} \leqslant \beta''_{M,m}, \ m = 1,2,\ldots,K. \tag{28}$$

For the proof of eq. (28) the reader is referred to the appendix.

For the $\beta''_{N,m}$ generated by the recursive formula of eq. (26) it has been proven that [2]

$$N < (\alpha\beta''_{N,m})^{-1} \tag{29}$$

where $\alpha = \min_M(\min_m \alpha_{M,m})$. Hence

$$N < (\alpha\beta_{N,m})^{-1}. \tag{30}$$

For the final value of the cooling control parameter $\beta_{N,m}$ satisfying the stop criterion of eq. (13) it has been proven that [2]

$$\beta_{N,m} > \bar{C}(\beta_0)\varepsilon_s/\ln|\mathcal{R}|. \tag{31}$$

Consequently the total number of steps is bounded by

$$N < \frac{1}{\alpha\,\varepsilon_s\bar{C}(\beta_0)} \ln|\mathcal{R}|. \tag{32}$$

Combining eqs. (12), (25) and (32) yields a time-complexity for the parallel SC-algorithm that is given by (N+K>>1)

$$\mathcal{O}(R \ln|\mathcal{R}|/K) + \mathcal{O}(R), \qquad (33)$$

which is polynomial in the system complexity for most combinatorial optimization problems.

IMPLEMENTATION AND EXPERIMENTAL RESULTS

The performance of the parallel SC-algorithm is studied by means of an implementation on an experimental multi-processor system. As a test case we used a special class of Traveling Salesman Problems (TSP) in which the cities are positioned on the vertices of a square grid such that all vertices are occupied. Furthermore, it is required that the tour is closed and that it calls at each city exactly once. For this type of TSP the value of the cost function for an optimum is given by simple relations [2]. The fact that the value of the cost function for an optimal configuration is known beforehand is a powerful aid in the analysis of the performance of the algorithm.

The multi-processor system is a general purpose parallel machine consisting of a number of processing units (P.U.'s), presently limited to fifteen, a data bus and a common memory. The P.U.'s have a Motorola 68000 micro-processor as CPU (8Mhz) and a 512 kbyte DRAM local memory. The local memory is dual-ported, i.e. it is possible to perform read and write operations on other P.U.'s. The P.U.'s do not have a floating point co-processor. Consequently, all floating point operations are performed by CPU-expensive software (400 μsec vs 10 μsec for an elementary operation). The data bus is 32 bits wide (integers and reals in one transfer) and runs on 12 Mhz. The common memory consists of 8 Mbyte DRAM. The parallel system is operated through a host computer (VAX-11/780).

Preliminary results obtained with a 8-P.U. parallel system for a 100-city TSP show that a good performance may be obtained for the parallel SC-algorithm. Near-optimal results deviating less than 2% from an optimum are obtained within computation times that are six times smaller than for the sequential algorithm. The sequential algorithm is run on a 1-P.U. machine and is about 5 times slower than on a VAX-11/780 computer. The parameter setting both for the parallel and the sequential algorithm are $\chi_0 = 0.95$, $\delta = 0.1$ and $\varepsilon_s = 0.001$. Results obtained with a 15-P.U. machine reveal that the distance parameter has to be decreased ($\delta = 0.05$) to obtain solutions with the same quality as obtained with the 8-P.U. machine (2% deviation from an optimum). Consequently there is a relative increase in the computational effort; here the parallel algorithm is about nine times faster than the sequential algorithm. As the number of processors is increased the length of the sub-chains becomes smaller. Consequently, for a fixed value of δ, the system is less equilibrated when the generation of the subsequent Markov chain is started and quasi-equilibrium has to be preserved by the manipulations of eqs. (16)-(24). Evidently, as the number of processors becomes larger, these manipulations are not powerful enough to preserve quasi-equilibrium and, therefore, a decrease in δ is required to maintain the same quality of the final solution. As the number of processors is further increased this effect becomes more pronounced and for a given critical number of processors N_c no further gain in computational effort is achieved by increasing the number of processors (extrapolations yield $N_c \sim 30$).

The aforementioned results are confirmed by experiments in which problems from literature, with known optimal solutions, are solved by the parallel SC-algorithm. Kernighan and Lin's well-known 318-city problem ([8]) is solved to 1.5% from optimality with the same parameter setting as above. On an 8-P.U. machine, the CPU time is again six times faster compared to the sequential algorithm.

CONCLUSIONS

Good near-optimal solutions can be obtained by the parallel SC-algorithm with a substantial reduction of the computational effort compared to the sequential algorithm. The parallel SC-algorithm has a polynomial-time complexity. It is argued that the advantage of the parallel algorithm (reduction of the computation time) is restricted to implementations on parallel machines with a limited number of processors (~30). By the time more powerful processor units become available (e.g. Motorola 68020) the parallel SC-algorithm can be executed at least one order of magnitude faster on a 30-P.U. parallel machine than on a conventional computer (VAX-11/780) (this factor even might be increased by equipping the individual processors with dedicated hardware).

APPENDIX

We proof by induction that for $M > 0$

$$\beta_{M,m} \leq \beta''_{M,m}, \quad m = 1,2,\ldots,K, \tag{A1}$$

where $\beta_{M,m}$ and $\beta''_{M,m}$ are given by eqs. (16)-(20) and (26), respectively.

First, we show by induction that for $M>0$

$$\beta''_{M,i} \leq \beta''_{M,m}, \quad i = 1,2,\ldots,m; \; m = 1,2,\ldots,K. \tag{A2}$$

This assertion is true for $M=1$. Assume that

$$\beta''_{M-1,i} \leq \beta''_{M-1,m}, \quad i = 1,2,\ldots,m; \; m = 1,2,\ldots,K, \tag{A3}$$

where $M>1$. By definition, $\alpha_{M-1,i} \geq \alpha_{M-1,m}$, $i=1,\ldots,m$; $m=1,\ldots,K$. Therefore:

$$\begin{aligned} \beta''_{M,i} &= \beta''_{M-1,i}\,(1+\alpha_{M-1,i}\beta''_{M-1,i})^{-1} \leq \beta''_{M-1,i}\,(1+\alpha_{M-1,m}\beta''_{M-1,i})^{-1} \leq \\ &\beta''_{M-1,m}\,(1+\alpha_{M-1,m}\beta''_{M-1,m})^{-1} = \beta''_{M,m}. \end{aligned} \tag{A4}$$

Here, we have used the induction hypothesis (A3) and the strict monotony of the function $f(x) = x(1+\alpha_{M-1,m}x)^{-1}$, for $x>0$.

Using eq. (A2), we now prove eq. (A1) by induction. Again, the assertion is true for $M=1$. Assume that for $M>1$

$$\beta_{M-1,m} \leq \beta''_{M-1,m}, \quad m = 1,2,\ldots,K. \tag{A5}$$

Using the definition of the $\beta_{M,m}$'s, it can be shown that there is an $i\in\{1,\ldots,m\}$, such that $\beta_{M,m} = \beta'_{M-1,i}$. It is, therefore, sufficient to show that

$$\beta'_{M-1,i} \leqslant \beta''_{M,m}\ ,\quad i = 1,2,\ldots,m. \tag{A6}$$

For i = 1,2,...,m, we have:

$$\beta'_{M-1,i} = \beta_{M-1,i}\left(1 + \frac{\ln(1+\delta)}{3\sigma(\beta_{M-1,i})}\beta_{M-1,i}\right)^{-1} \leqslant$$

$$\beta_{M-1,i}(1+\alpha_{M-1,m}\,\beta_{M-1,i})^{-1} \leqslant \beta''_{M-1,i}(1+\alpha_{M-1,m}\,\beta''_{M-1,i})^{-1} = \beta''_{M,i} \tag{A7}$$

Here, we have again used the monotony of the function $f(x) = x(1+\alpha_{M-1,m}x)^{-1}$ as well as the induction hypothesis (A5).
Using eq. (A2), we find, for i = 1,2,...,m,

$$\beta'_{M-1,i} \leqslant \beta''_{M,i} \leqslant \beta''_{M,m} \tag{A8}$$

which completes the proof of eq. (A1).

REFERENCES

[1] Aarts, E.H.L. and P.J.M. van Laarhoven, "Simulated Annealing: State of the Art and Current Trends", to be published.
[2] Aarts, E.H.L. and P.J.M. van Laarhoven, "Statistical Cooling: A General Approach to Combinatorial Optimization Problems", Philips Journ. Res. 40(1985)193.
[3] Aarts, E.H.L. and P.J.M. van Laarhoven, "Quantitative Analysis of the Statistical Cooling Algorithm", Philips Journ. Res., to be published.
[4] Ackley, D.H., G.E. Hinton and T.J. Sejnowski, "A Learning Algorithm for Boltzmann Machines", Cognitive Science 9(1985)147.
[5] R.M. Garey and J.D. Johnson, "Computers and Intractability: A Guide to the Theory of NP-Completeness", W.H. Freeman and Co., San Francisco, 1979.
[6] Geman S. and D. Geman, "Stochastic Relaxation, Gibbs Distributions, and the Bayesian Restoration of Images", IEEE Trans. Pattern Anal. Mach. Intel. 6(1984)721.
[7] Kirkpatrick, S., C.D. Gelatt Jr. and M.P. Vecchi, "Optimization by Simulated Annealing", Science 220(1983)671.
[8] Lin, S. and B.W. Kernighan, "An Effective Heuristic Algorithm for the Traveling Salesman Problem", Operations Res. 21(1973)498.
[9] Metropolis, M. et al. "Equation of State Calculations by Fast Computing Machines", J. Chem. Phys. 21(1953)1087.
[10] Romeo, F. and A.L. Sangiovanni-Vincentelli, "Probabilistic Hill Climbing Algorithms: Properties and Applications", University of Berkeley, Mem. No. UCB/ERL M 84/34, 1984.

SUBGRAPH ISOMORPHISM FOR BICONNECTED OUTERPLANAR GRAPHS IN CUBIC TIME

Andrzej Lingas, Linköping University

1. *Introduction*

The *subgraph isomorphism* problem is to determine whether a graph can be *imbedded* in another graph, i.e. whether the former is isomorphic to a subgraph of the latter. For instance, if H is an n-vertex circuit and G is an n-vertex planar graph of valence 3, $n \in N$, then determining whether H can be imbedded in G is equivalent to the NP-complete problem of determining whether a planar graph of valence 3 has a Hamiltonian circuit [GJ79]. Thus, the subgraph isomorphism problem is NP-complete even if G and H range only over connected planar graphs of valence ≤ 3. Subgraph isomorphism also remains NP-complete when the first input graph is a forest and the other input graph is a tree (see pp. 105 in [GJ79]).

In contrast, the related graph isomorphism problem constrained to planar graphs on n vertices is solvable in time $O(n)$ [HT80]. Also, polynomial time algorithms for graph isomorphism respectively constrained to graphs of bounded genus, bounded valence, bounded eigenvalue multiplicity of adjacency matrix are known [Mit80,Lu80,Mo81].

In [Li85], Lingas shows that subgraph isomorphism for connected graphs with $\leq n$ vertices, $s(n)$-separator [LT80], and valence $\leq d(n)$, can be solved in time $2^{O((d(n)+logn)\Gamma_s(n))}$, where $\Gamma_s(n) = \sum_{i=0}^{\lceil log_{3/2}n \rceil} s((2/3)^i)$. By the planar graph separator theorem [LT80], Lingas' result yields a $2^{O(\sqrt{n}log^2n)}$ time-bound for subgraph isomorphism for connected planar graphs of valence $O(logn)$. The only known polynomial-time algorithms for subgraph isomorphism are those for trees [Ma78,Re77]. Are there other non-trivial classes of graphs for which subgraph isomorphism can be solved in polynomial time?

Trees can be seen as a special case of so called *outerplanar graphs*, i.e. graphs that can be embedded in the plane in such a way that all vertices lie on the exterior face. Since any outerplanar graph has a 2-separator, the mentioned result of Lingas [Li85] implies a quasi polynomial-time bound $n^{O(logn)}$ for subgraph isomorphism constrained to connected outerplanar graphs of bounded valence. In [S82], Sysło proves that if H, G are outerplanar graphs, and H is disconnected or it is connected but not biconnected, and G is biconnected, then the problem of determining whether H is isomorphic to a subgraph of G is NP-complete. Interestingly, the *induced subgraph isomorphism* problem, which is to decide whether a graph is isomorphic to a subgraph of another graph induced by a set of vertices of the other graph, remains NP-complete in the above cases [S82], however, it can be solved for biconnected outerplanar graphs in time $O(n^2)$ [S82]. In [S82], it was also claimed that subgraph isomorphism for biconnected outerplanar graphs remained NP-complete, however the proof, using only graphs of valence ≤ 4, turned out to be not correct [S85]. In this paper, we show that subgraph isomorphism constrained to biconnected outerplanar graphs H, G, with m and n vertices respectively, is solvable in time $O(mn^2)$. The mentioned NP-completeness results of Sysło witness that the simultaneous assumption of outerplanarity and biconnectivity is necessary to obtain the polynomial-time upper bound. To derive the upper bound, we use a dynamic programming algorithm. The recursive reduction of an imbedding problem to smaller ones is solved not by matching technique, as it is in the case of algorithms for subtree isomorphism [Re77,Ma78] , but by finding a simple path in a corresponding graph.

The structure of the paper is as follows: In Section 2, we introduce basic notions, definitions, facts and lemmas necessary to design the algorithm for subgraph isomorphism for biconnected outerplanar graphs. In Section 3, we present the algorithm, prove its correctness and analyse its time complexity.

2. Preliminaries

We shall use standard set and graph theoretic notation and definitions (for instance, see [H69,AHU74]). Specifically, we assume the following set and graph conventions:

1) For a graph G, $V(G)$ denotes the set of vertices of G.
2) A *path* in a graph G is a sequence v_0, v_1, ..., v_k of its vertices such that for $i = 0, ..., k-1$, v_i is adjacent to v_{i+1}. If v_k is also adjacent to v_0 then the sequence can be also called a *cycle*. A path or a cycle is *simple* if all vertices that occur in it are distinct. G is *connected* (*biconnected*, respectively) if for any two vertices v, w in G there is a simple path (simple cycle, respectively) including v and w.
3) A *directed path* in a directed graph D is a sequence v_0, v_1, ..., v_k of its vertices such that for $i = 0, ..., k-1$, there is an edge of D leaving v_i and entering v_{i+1}. As in the undirected case, a directed path is simple if all vertices that occur in it are distinct.
4) Given two vertices v, w in a graph G, v is in the *distance* $\leq k$ from w if there is a simple path in G of length $\leq k$ including both vertices.

An alternative way of defining the concept of subgraph isomorphism discussed in Introduction is as follows.

Let H, G be two graphs. A one-to-one mapping ϕ of $V(H)$ to $V(G)$ is called an *imbedding* of H in G if for any adjacent vertices v, $w \in V(H)$, $\phi(v)$ is adjacent to $\phi(w)$. H can be *imbedded* in G if there exists an imbedding of H in G.

We shall consider the graph imbedding problem (i.e. the subgraph isomorphism problem) for so called outerplanar graphs. An *outerplanar* graph is a graph which can be embedded in the plane in such a way that all vertices lie on the exterior face [Mit79]. We shall call such an embedding of a graph in the plane, an *outerplanar embedding*. By adapting the algorithm of Mitchell for recognition of outerplanar graphs in linear time [Mit79], we can easily deduce the following fact:

Fact 1: Given a biconnected outerplanar graph, we can find the cycle bounding the exterior face of its outerplanar embedding in linear time.

Sketch: At the beginning of our procedure, the current graph C equals G and has all edges uncolored. The procedure is as follows.
Pick a vertex v of C of degree not greater than two in C. Let w, u be the vertices of C adjacent to v (if there is only one vertex adjacent to v, we assume $w = u$). Remove the edges (v, w), (v, u) from C and account each of them to the sought cycle provided it is not green. If $u = w$ then halt. If (u, w) is the only remaining edge of C and (u, w) is not green then add (u, w) to the sought cycle and halt. If (u, w) is not in G, add it to C. Color (u, w) with green, and go to the beginning.
For how to implement the procedure in linear time, see the third section in [M79]. ∎

Using the following definitions of planar figures, we will be able to specify outerplanar embeddings of biconnected outerplanar graphs more precisely.

a) A *polygon* P is a sequence v_0, v_1, ..., v_m of points and the closed straight-line segments

$[v_i, v_{i+1 \ mod \ m+1}]$, $i = 0, 1, ..., m$, in the plane. The points and segments are called *vertices* and *edges of P*, respectively. P is a *simple polygon* if all its vertices are distinct and its edges $[v_i, v_{i+1 \ mod \ n+1}]$ touch only the adjacent edges $[v_{i-1 \ mod \ n+1}, v_i]$, $[v_{i+1 \ mod \ n+1}, v_{i+2 \ mod \ n+1}]$ at their endpoints. P is a *convex polygon* if it is a simple polygon such that for $i = 0, 1, ..., m$, the angle $(v_i, v_{i+1 \ mod \ m+1}, v_{i+2 \ mod \ m+1})$ in the inside of P is of less than 180 degrees. A *diagonal* of P is a segment $[v_i, v_j]$, where $0 \le i, j \le m$ and $j \notin \{i - 1 \ mod \ m + 1, \ i, \ i + 1 \ mod \ m + 1\}$, which touches only the edges of P adjacent to its endpoints.
b) A *partial triangulation* of a simple polygon is a set of non-intersecting diagonals of the polygon. A *partially triangulated* polygon Q is a union of a simple polygon and a partial triangulation of the simple polygon. The vertices of the simple polygon are vertices of Q, whereas the edges of the simple polygon and the diagonals from the partial triangulation of the simple polygon are edges of Q. The former edges of Q are called *boundary edges* of Q, the latter edges of Q are called *diagonal edges* of Q.
By Fact 1, we have:

Fact 2: Given a biconnected outerplanar graph, we can find its outerplanar embedding in the form of a partially triangulated (convex) polygon in linear time.

It follows that a biconnected outerplanar graph has a unique outerplanar embedding (in the topological sense) up to the mirror image (see also [S82]).
In the next section, to design our algorithm, we shall use Fact 2 and two following, technical lemmas. The first lemma easily follows from Fact 2.

Lemma 1: Let F be an outerplanar graph with vertices identified with numbers 0 through n. If the vertex sequence 0, 1, ..., n forms the cycle bounding the exterior face of an outerplanar embedding of F, then any simple path in F that begins with 0 and ends with n is an increasing number sequence.

3. *The Algorithm for Subgraph Isomorphism for Biconnected Outerplanar Graphs*

Let H, G be biconnected outerplanar graphs on m and n vertices, respectively. To determine whether H is isomorphic to a subgraph of G, we proceed as follows.
First, we construct outerplanar embeddings H', G' of H and G respectively, in the form of partially triangulated convex polygons. Such embeddings can be produced in time $O(m + n)$ by Fact 2. We shall identify the vertices on the boundary of G' with numbers 0, 1 ... $n - 1$, in counterclockwise order.
Then, for $F \in \{H, \ G\}$, we consider the class $PE(F')$ of pairs composed of parts of F' and edges of F', defined as follows. (I, e) is in $PE(F')$ if and only if I equals F' and e is a boundary edge of F' or e is a diagonal edge of F' splitting F' into two partially triangulated polygons such that, one of them, including the splitting edge, equals I. Given $M = (I, e)$ in $PE(F')$, we denote by $S(I)$ the subgraph of F represented by I and call e the *root* edge of M. Next, given an edge e of F' and a diagonal edge d of F' different from e, $p(e, d)$ is the unique member (K, d) in $PE(F')$ where e is not an edge of K, see Fig 1. Let b be an arbitrary given boundary edge of H'. We distinguish a subclass $B(H')$ of $PE(H')$ such that (K, d) is in $B(H')$ if and only if $(K, d) = (H', b)$ or $b \ne d$ and $(K, d) = p(b, d)$.

Let us consider *root-imbedding* subproblems of the following form:

Given $M = (I, (v_0, v_1))$ in $B(H')$ and $N = (J, (w_0, w_1))$ in $PE(G')$, can $S(I)$ be imbedded in $S(J)$ such that v_0, v_1 are respectively mapped on w_0, w_1.

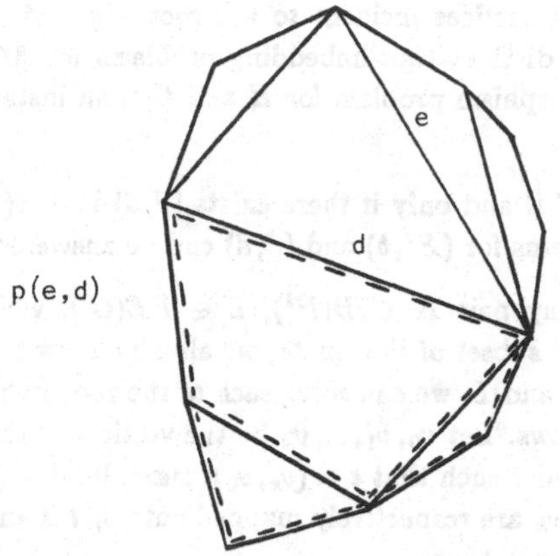

Fig. 1. **The embedding F', edges e, d, and the figure from $p(e, d)$ additionally marked with dashed lines.**

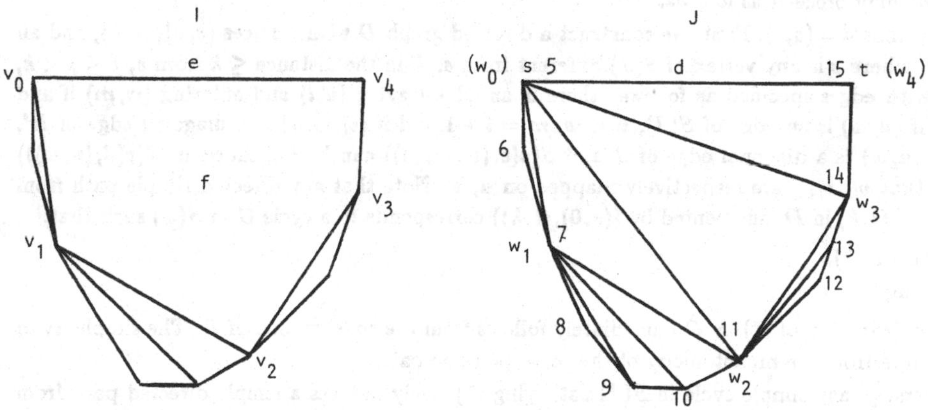

Fig. 2. **An example of the partially triangulated polygons I and J. Note that w_0, w_1, w_2, w_3, w_4 satisfies (*) here.**

Note that depending on the order of vertices incident to the root edges of $M \in B(H')$ and $N \in PE(G')$ one may consider two distinct root-imbedding problems for M and N. By the following remark, the subgraph isomorphism problem for H and G is an instance of the above root-imbedding problems.

Remark 1: H can be imbedded in G if and only if there exists (J,d) in $PE(G')$ such that at least one of the two imbedding problems for (H',b) and (J,d) can be answered positively.

If we inductively assume that for any pair $K \in B(H')$, $L \in PE(G')$, where the partially triangulated polygon in K is a proper subset of that in M, we already know the answers to the two root-imbeddings problems for K and L, we can solve each of the root-imbedding problems for $M = (I,e)$ and $N = (J,d)$ as follows. Let $v_0, v_1, ..., v_k$ be the vertices of the inner face f of I adjacent to e in counterclockwise order such that $e = (v_k, v_0)$. Next, let $d = (s,t)$. Then, $S(I)$ can imbedded in $S(J)$ such that v_0, v_k are respectively mapped onto s, t if and only if there is a *simple cycle* $w_0, w_1, ..., w_k$ in $S(J)$ such that

(*) $w_0 = s$, $w_k = t$, and for $i = 0,1,...,k-1$, if (v_i, v_{i+1}) is a diagonal edge of I then (w_i, w_{i+1}) is a diagonal edge of J and $S(p(e,(v_i,v_{i+1})))$ can be imbedded in $S(p(d,(w_i,w_{i+1})))$ such that v_i, v_{i+1} are respectively mapped onto w_i, w_{i+1} (see Fig. 2).

Note that the vertices of J occur on the outer boundary of J as the sequence s, $s+1$ *mod* $n,...,t$, or as the sequence s, $s-1$ *mod* $n,...,t$, in counterclockwise order. Further, we may assume without loss of generality the former numbering and $s < t$ (see Fig. 2). It follows from Lemma 1 that $w_0, w_1, ..., w_k$, where $w_0 = s$, $w_k = t$, is a simple cycle in $S(J)$ if and only if $w_0 - s$, $w_1 - s, ..., w_k - s$ is an increasing sequence.
By the above observation, to determine whether there exists a simple cycle in $S(J)$ satisfying (*), we may proceed as follows.
Recall that $d = (s,t)$. First, we construct a directed graph D with vertices $(s,0)$, (t,k), and all (z,j), where z is any vertex of $S(J)$ different from s, t, in the distance $\leq k$ from s, $1 \leq j < k$, and with edges specified as follows: there is an edge leaving (u,l) and entering (w,m) if and only if (u,w) is an edge of $S(J)$, $u < w$, $m = l+1$ and if (v_l, v_{l+1}) is a diagonal edge of H', then (u,w) is a diagonal edge of J and $S(p(e,(v_l,v_{l+1})))$ can be imbedded in $S(p(d,(u,w)))$ such that v_l, v_{l+1} are respectively mapped on u, w. Note that any directed simple path from $(s,0)$ to (t,k) in D, augmented by $((s,0),(t,k))$ corresponds to a cycle C in $S(J)$ such that:

C satisfies (*),

C is simple.

The satisfiability of (*) by C immediately follows from the construction of D. The simplicity of C follows from the monotonicity of the corresponding path.
Conversely, any simple cycle in $S(J)$ satisfying (*) easily induces a simple directed path from $(s,0)$ to (t,k) in D, by the construction of D.
By the shown equivalence of the above cycle in $S(J)$ and path in D existence problems, it is sufficient to determine whether there exists a simple directed path in D from $(s,0)$ to $(t,0)$. By breadth-first search we can determine it in time proportional to the size of D. The construction of D also can be done by k-phase breadth-first search in G, in time proportional to the size of D.
The subgraph of $S(J)$ that consists of vertices in $S(J)$ in the distance $\leq k$ from s has $O(n)$ vertices and edges. It follows immediately from the definition of D that D has only $O(kn)$ vertices. Since each edge in the subgraph of $S(J)$ corresponds to at most k edges in D, D has also only $O(kn)$ edges.

Thus, we can determine the root-imbedding problems for $M = (I, e)$ and $N = (J, d)$ in time $O(kn)$. Note that for the face f, $M = (I, e)$ is the only member of $B(H')$ where I includes f and the root edge e of M is adjacent to f. Let $size(f)$ mean the number of vertices adjacent to f. It follows that for all $K \in B(H')$ and given $N \in PE(G')$, all the root-imbedding problems for K and N, can be solved in total time $O(n \cdot \sum_{f \text{ is an inner face of } H'} size(f))$, what is $O(mn)$. By Euler's formula for planar graphs [H69], G' has $O(n)$ edges. Thus, there are $O(n)$ figures in $PE(G')$ and all possible root-imbedding problems for K and L, where $L \in B(H')$, $K \in PE(G')$ can be solved in total time $O(mn^2)$. Hence, by Remark 1, we obtain our main result:

Theorem 1: We can determine whether a biconnected outerplanar graph H on m vertices is isomorphic to a subgraph of another biconnected outerplanar graph G on n vertices in time $O(mn^2)$.

Final Remark: It would be interesting to know whether one could essentially improve the $O(mn^2)$-time bound for subgraph isomorphism constrained to biconnected outerplanar graphs. If we compare biconnected outer planar graphs with trees, for which subgraph isomorphism is solvable in time $O(mn^{1.5})$ [Ma78], the former are more complicated because contain cycles, however, on the other hand, they are simpler because have unique outerplanar embeddings in the plane.

Acknowledgements: I would like to express my appreciation to to Maciej Sysło for posing the problem of the status of subgraph isomorphism constrained to biconnected outerplanar graphs.

References

[AHU74] A.V. Aho, J.E. Hopcroft and J.D. Ullman, *The Design and Analysis of Computer Algorithms*, Addison-Wesley, Reading, Massachusetts.

[GJ79] M.R. Garey, D.S. Johnson, *Computers and Intractability. A Guide to the Theory of NP-completeness*, Freeman, San Francisco.

[H69] F. Harary, *Graph Theory*, Addison-Wesley, Reading, Massachusetts.

[HT80] J. Hopcroft, R.E. Tarjan, *Isomorphism of planar graphs*, Proc. 4th Ann. Symposium on Theory of Computing.

[Li85] A. Lingas, *Subgraph Isomorphism for Easily Separable Graphs of Bounded Valence*, 11th Workshop on Graph-theoretic Concepts in Computer Science, Castle Schwanberg.

[Lu80] E.M. Luks, *Isomorphism of bounded valence can be tested in polynomial time*, in Proc. 21st Ann. Symposium of Foundations of Computer Science, IEEE.

[Ma78] D. W. Matula, *Subtree isomorphism in* $O(n^{5/2})$, Annals of Discrete Mathematics 2, 91-106.

[Mil80] G. Miller, *Isomorphism testing for graphs of bounded genus*, Proc. Ann. 12th ACM symposium on Theory of Computing.

[Mit79] S.L. Mitchell, *Linear algorithms to recognize outerplanar and maximal outerplanar graphs*, Inf. Proces. Let., vol. 9, no. 5.

[Mo81] D.M. Mount, *Isomorphism of graphs with bounded eigenvalue multiplicity*, manuscript, Purdue University.

[Re77] S. W. Reyner, *An analysis of a good algorithm for the subtree problem* , SIAM J. Comput. 6, 730-732.

[S82] M.M. Sysło, *The subgraph isomorphism problem for outerplanar graphs* , Theoretical Computer Science 17, 91-97.

[S85] M.M. Sysło, *Personal Communication*, 1985.

Polynomial Time Algorithms for Finding Integer Relations Among Real Numbers

J. Hastad[1], B. Helfrich[2], J. Lagarias[3] and C. P. Schnorr[2]

[1]MIT, Department of Computer Science, Cambridge, Massachusetts

[2]Universität Frankfurt, Fachbereich Mathematik/Informatik, Germany

[3]AT&T, Bell Laboratories, Murray Hill, New Jersey

Abstract

We present algorithms, which when given a real vector $x \in \mathbb{R}^n$ and a parameter $k \in \mathbb{N}$ as input either find an integer relation $m \in \mathbb{Z}^n$, $m \neq 0$ with $x^T m = 0$ or prove there is no such integer relation with $\|m\| \leq 2^k$. One such algorithm halts after at most $O(n^3(k+n))$ arithmetic operations using real numbers. It finds an integer relation that is no more than $2^{\frac{n-2}{2}}$ times longer than the length of the shortest relation for x. Given a rational input $x \in \mathbb{Q}^n$ this algorithm halts in polynomially many bit operations. The basic algorithm of this kind is due to Ferguson and Forcade (1979) and is closely related to the Lovász (1982) lattice basis reduction algorithm.

1. Introduction

We study the important computational problem of either finding short integer relations m for a given real vector $x \in \mathbb{R}^n$, i.e. $m \in \mathbb{Z}^n$, $m \neq 0$, $x^T m = 0$, or of proving no small integer relation exists. Finding integer relations in the case of two numbers $x = (x_1, x_2)$ can be solved essentially by applying the Euclidean algorithm to x_1, x_2, or equivalently by computing the ordinary continued fraction expansion of x_1/x_2. The problem of finding good algorithms for the case $n \geqq 3$ has been studied under the names of generalizing the Euclidean algorithm ("vector Euclidean algorithm") and of multidimensional continued fraction. Jacobi (1968) already proposed the problem for n=3 and many different multi-dimensional algorithms have been proposed, see Brentjes

(1981) for a more detailed history. The first such algorithm proved to find integer relations in all dimensions, if they exist, is due to Ferguson and Forcade (1979). No time bound is given in their paper. More recently Kannan, Lenstra and Lovász (1984) used a modification of the Lovász lattice basis reduction algorithm to find integer relations for the case that $x = (1,\alpha,...,\alpha^n)$ and α is an algebraic number of degree $\leq n$.

The main algorithm analysed in this paper is a variant of the Forcade, Ferguson (1979) algorithm and has been developped subsequently by Bergman (1980) and Ferguson (1984). In section 2 we present this algorithm, Algorithm A, in a form that is strikingly similar to the Lovász lattice basis reduction algorithm, see A.K.Lenstra, H.W.Lenstra, Jr. and L.Lovász (1982). This close relationship between the Forcade, Ferguson and the Lovász algorithm was not transparent from the original papers. Let $\lambda(x)$ be the minimal length of a non-zero integer relation for x, if such a relation exists, and $\lambda(x) = \infty$ otherwise. Algorithm A gets as input a real vector $x = (x_1,...,x_n) \neq 0$ and an integer parameter k. We prove the following performance bounds.

(1) algorithm A halts after at most $O(n^3(k+n))$ arithmetic operations on real numbers;

(2) it either finds an integer relation m for x with $\|m\|^2 \leq 2^{n-2}\lambda(x)^2$ or proves $\lambda(x) \geq 2^k$;

(3) for an integer input vector x the algorithm can be operated so that it uses at most $O(n^4(k+n))$ arithmetic operations on $O(n+\log\|x\|)$-bit integers.

In section 3 we extend algorithm A to find for a given vector $x\in\mathbb{R}^n$ a basis of the lattice $L_x := \{m\in\mathbb{Z}^n : x^Tm=0\}$ of all integer relations for x. Given a basis of lattice L_x then any lattice basis reduction algorithm can be used to find short integer relations for x.

In section 4 we present an algorithm that finds simultaneous integer relations for linearly independent vectors $x_1,...,x_s\in\mathbb{R}^n$. When given as input $x_1,...,x_s\in\mathbb{R}^n$ and $k\in\mathbb{N}$ this algorithm halts after at most $O(n^3(k+n))$ arithmetic operations with real numbers and either finds a simultaneous integer relation m for $x_1,...,x_s$ or proves no simultaneous integer relation m exists with $\|m\| \leq 2^k$.

2. An algorithm for finding integer relations

Throughout the paper let $x \in \mathbb{R}^n$ be a fixed non-zero vector. We let an n-tuple $b \in \mathbb{R}^n$ be a column vector with corresponding row vector b^T. We denote by $\pi(b) = \pi_x(b)$ the component of $b \in \mathbb{R}^n$ which is orthogonal to x, i.e. $x^T\pi(b) = 0$, $b - \pi(b) \in x\mathbb{R}$ A non-zero vector $m \in \mathbb{Z}^n$ with $x^T m=0$ will be called an integer relation for x. Let $\lambda(x)$ be the euclidean length of the shortest integer relation for x if an integer relation exists, and $\lambda(x) = \infty$ otherwise. The euclidean length of a vector $b \in \mathbb{R}^n$ is $\|b\| = |b^T b|^{\frac{1}{2}}$.

With an ordered basis $b_1,\dots,b_n \in \mathbb{R}^n$ and the fixed vector $x \in \mathbb{R}^n$ we associate the orthogonal system $b_1^*,\dots,b_n^*$ where b_i^* is the component of b_i that is orthogonal to $b_1,\dots,b_{i-1}$ and x. Note that $b_i^* = 0$ for exactly one i which makes a difference to the Lovász algorithm. We can easily compute $b_1^*,\dots,b_n^*$ by the process of Gram- Schmidt orthogonalization using $O(n^3)$ arithmetic operations:

$$b_1^* = \pi(b_1) = b_1 - (b_1^T x \,/\, \|x\|^2) \cdot x$$

$$b_i^* = \pi(b_i) - \sum_{j=1}^{i-1} \mu_{i,j}\, b_j^* \qquad i=1,\dots,n\ ,$$

$$\mu_{i,j} = \pi(b_i)^T \,/\, \|b_j^*\|^2 \qquad \text{for } 1 \leq j < i < n\ .$$

For completeness let $\mu_{i,i}=1$, $\mu_{i,j}=0$ for $i > j$. We denote by $\lceil r \rfloor$ the nearest integer to $r \in \mathbb{R}$.

Algorithm A

(Given as input x and $k \in \mathbb{N}$ it either finds an integer relation m for x or proves $\lambda(x) \geq 2^k$).

1. (initiation) $b_i := [0,\dots,1,0,\dots,0]^T$ for $i=1,\dots,n$.
   compute $\mu_{i,j}$, $\|b_i^*\|$ for $1 \leq j < i \leq n$.
2. (test on termination)

   if $b_n^* \neq 0$ then ($\begin{bmatrix} c_1^T \\ \vdots \\ c_n^T \end{bmatrix} := [b_1,\dots,b_n]^{-1}$, $m := c_n$, output (m), stop)

   if $\|b_i^*\| \leq 2^{-k}$ for $i=1,\dots,n$ then (output "$\lambda(x) \geq 2^k$" , stop)
3. (exchange step)
   choose $i<n$ that maximizes $\|b_i^*\|^2\, 2^i$,
   $b_{i+1} := b_{i+1} - \lceil \mu_{i+1,i} \rfloor\, b_i$, exchange b_i and b_{i+1} ,
   update $\|b_i^*\|$, $\|b_{i+1}^*\|$, $\mu_{i,j}$, $\mu_{i+1,j}$ for $j=1,\dots,n$; go to 2.

We have not included the details on how to compute and how to update the numbers

$\mu_{i,j}$, $\|b_i^*\|$. Algorithm A is essentially identical to the algorithms in Bergman (1980), Ferguson (1984) and is very similar to the Lovász algorithm for lattice basis reduction, see A.K.Lenstra et alii (1982). Unlike the Lovász algorithm the exchange $b_i \Leftrightarrow b_{i+1}$ is chosen as to maximize the progress of convergence whereas the Lovász algorithm exchanges b_i, b_{i+1} for the smallest reasonable i. All arithmetic operations are on real numbers. We did not include reduction steps that achieve $|\mu_{i,j}| \leq 1/2$ for all $i>j$. However these steps will be necessary to keep all integers small when for integer input $x \in \mathbf{Z}^n$ all arithmetic steps are done on integers.

Proposition 1 (Correctness of the algorithm)

(1) The output $m=c_n$ in step 2 is an integer relation for x.

(2) $\lambda(x) \geq 1/\max_i \|b_i^*\|$ holds for every basis $b_1,\dots,b_n$ of $\mathbf{Z}^n$.

Proof (1) Let $b_n^* \neq 0$, then $b_i^*=0$ for some $i<n$. The vectors $b_1,\dots,b_i$ are linearly independent but linearly dependent mod$(x\mathbb{R})$, thus $x \in \Sigma_{j\leq i}\, b_j\mathbb{R}$. Therefore $b_j^T c_k=0$ for $k>i\geq j$ implies $x^T c_k=0$ for $k=i+1,\dots,n$. In particular $x^T m=x^T c_n=0$. The vector m is integer since $[b_1,\dots,b_n]$ is an unimodular matrix.

(2) Let m be an integer relation for x. Since $(x\mathbb{R})^{\perp} = \Sigma_{i=1}^n\, \pi(b_i)\mathbb{R}$ we have $m \in \Sigma_{i=1}^n\, \pi(b_i)\mathbb{R}$. Therefore there exists i with $m^T\pi(b_i) \neq 0$. For the smallest such i we have $m^T b_i^* = m^T\pi(b_i) = m^T b_i \in \mathbf{Z}$, hence $|m^T b_i^*| \geq 1$, and thus $\|m\| \geq \|b_i^*\|^{-1}$. Q.E.D.

By proposition 1(2) the algorithm correctly outputs "$\lambda(x) \geq 2^k$".

Time analysis

The progress of the reduction process is related to the quantity

$$D := \prod_{\substack{j=1 \\ b_j^* \neq 0}}^{n} \|b_j^*\|^{2(n-\tau_j)}, \quad \text{where } \tau_j = \#\{i<j \mid b_i^* \neq 0\}.$$

For each exchange $b_i \Leftrightarrow b_{i+1}$ in step 3 we have $\|b_i^*\|^2 2^i \geq \|b_{i+1}^*\|^2 2^{i+1}$, hence $\|b_{i+1}^*\|^2 \leq \frac{1}{2}\|b_i^*\|^2$. Also step 3 achieves $|\mu_{i+1,i}| \leq 1/2$. Therefore each exchange step $b_i \Leftrightarrow b_{i+1}$ satisfies

$$\begin{aligned} \|b_i^{new*}\|^2 &= \|b_{i+1}^{old*}\|^2 + \mu_{i+1,i}^2 \cdot \|b_i^{old*}\|^2 \\ &\leq \frac{1}{2}\|b_i^{old*}\|^2 + \frac{1}{4}\|b_i^{old*}\|^2 = \frac{3}{4}\|b_i^{old*}\|^2. \end{aligned}$$

From this and $\|b_i^{new*}\|\,\|b_{i+1}^{new*}\| = \|b_i^{old*}\|\,\|b_{i+1}^{old*}\|$ we have

(2.1) $D_{new} \leq \frac{3}{4} D_{old}$ if $b_i^{new*} \neq 0$.

If $b_i^{new*}=0$ then algorithm A terminates directly in step 2 and outputs m; in this case

$D_{new}=D_{old}$.
Unlike the situation of the Lovász algorithm no lower bound is known for the value of D on termination. We overcome this difficulty by writing D as a product

$$D = D_1 \cdot D_2$$

so that initially $D_1 \leqq 1$, on termination $D_1 \geqq 2^{-(2k+n)n^2}$, and for every exchange step $D_1^{new} \leqq \frac{3}{4} D_1^{old}$. We associate with $b_i^* \neq 0$ the real number

$$\alpha(b_i^*) = \max \{\|b_i^*\|^2, 2^{-2k-n}\}.$$

Let $D_1 := \Pi_i \; \alpha(b_i^*)^{n-\tau_i}$, $D_2 := \Pi_i \; (\|b_i^*\|^2/\alpha(b_i^*))^{n-\tau_i}$, where i ranges over the integers i=1,...,n with $b_i^* \neq 0$. Obviously $D=D_1 \cdot D_2$, initially $D_1 \leqq 1$ and on termination of algorithm A $D_1 \geqq 2^{-(2k+n)n^2}$.

<u>Lemma 2</u> Every exchange step that decreases D_2 yields $D_1^{new} \leqq \frac{1}{2} D_1^{old}$.

<u>Proof</u> Every exchange step $b_i \Leftrightarrow b_{i+1}$ satisfies

(2.2) $\|b_{i+1}^{old*}\| \leqq \|b_i^{new*}\|, \quad \|b_{i+1}^{new*}\| \leqq \|b_i^{old*}\|,$

and since i is chosen to maximize $\|b_i^*\| 2^i$ and the algorithm did not previously stop in step 2 we have

(2.3) $\|b_i^{old*}\|^2 > 2^{-2k-i+1} \geqq 2^{-2k-n+1}$.

The exchange step decreases D_2 only if

(2.4) $\|b_i^{new*}\|^2 < 2^{-2k-n}$.

If $b_{i+1}^{old*}=0$ then $b_{i+1}^{new*}=0$ since D_2 decreases, and $D_1^{new} \leqq \frac{1}{2} D_1^{old}$ follows from (2.3), (2.4).
So let $b_{i+1}^{old*}, b_{i+1}^{new*} \neq 0$.
We distinguish two cases.

<u>Case</u> $\|b_{i+1}^{new*}\|^2 \geqq 2^{-2k-n}$.

$$\frac{D_1^{new}}{D_1^{old}} = \frac{\alpha(b_i^{new*})^{n-\tau_i} \, \alpha(b_{i+1}^{new*})^{n-\tau_i-1}}{\alpha(b_i^{old*})^{n-\tau_i} \, \alpha(b_{i+1}^{old*})^{n-\tau_i-1}} \overset{(2.2),(2.3),(2.4)}{=} \frac{(2^{-2k-n})^{n-\tau_i} \, \|b_{i+1}^{new*}\|^{2(n-\tau_i-1)}}{\|b_i^{old*}\|^{2(n-\tau_i)} \, (2^{-2k-n})^{n-\tau_i-1}} \overset{(2.2)}{\leqq} \|b_i^{old*}\|^{-2} \, 2^{-2k-n} \overset{(2.3)}{\leqq} \frac{1}{2}.$$

<u>Case</u> $\|b_{i+1}^{new*}\|^2 < 2^{-2k-n}$.

$$\frac{D_1^{new}}{D_1^{old}} \overset{(2.2),(2.3),(2.4)}{=} \frac{(2^{-2k-n})^{n-\tau_i} \cdot (2^{-2k-n})^{n-\tau_i-1}}{\|b_i^{old*}\|^{2(n-\tau_i)} \, (2^{-2k-n})^{n-\tau_i-1}} \overset{(2.3)}{\leqq} \frac{1}{2} \quad \text{since } n-\tau_i \geqq 1.$$

Q.E.D.

As a consequence of (2.1) and of lemma 2 we have $D_i^{new} \leq \frac{3}{4} D_i^{old}$ for every exchange step except the last one that achieves $b_{n-1}^* = 0$. Since initially $D_i \leq 1$ and on termination $D_i \geq 2^{-(2k+n)n^2}$ there are at most $O(n^2(k+n))$ exchange steps. Each exchange step uses at most $O(n)$ arithmetic steps; this includes the steps to update $\mu_{i,j}$, $\mu_{i+1,j}$ for $j=1,\dots,n$ and $\|b_i^*\|$, $\|b_{i+1}^*\|$. The initial computation of the numbers $\mu_{i,j}$, $\|b_i^*\|$ for $1 \leq j < i \leq n$ can be done using $O(n^3)$ arithmetic operations. Alltogether this shows that the algorithm halts after at most $O(n^3(k+n))$ arithmetic operations on real numbers.

Performance analysis

We show that $\|m\|^2 \leq 2^{n-2} \lambda(x)^2$ holds for the integer relation m found by algorithm A. The number 2^{n-2} arises in the same way as the Lovász algorithm finds a lattice vector that is at most 2^{n-1} times longer than the shortest lattice vector.

When algorithm A finds an integer relation m then $m = c_n$ with $\begin{bmatrix} c_1^T \\ \vdots \\ c_n^T \end{bmatrix} = [b_1,\dots,b_n]^{-1}$ for the terminal basis $b_1,\dots,b_n$ of lattice $\mathbf{Z}^n$. We have $b_i^T c_n = b_i^T b_n^* = 0$ for $i=1,\dots,n-1$, hence

(2.5) $\|c_n\| \, \|b_n^*\| = c_n^T b_n^* = c_n^T \pi(b_n) = c_n^T b_n = 1$.

Before the last exchange $b_n \Leftrightarrow b_{n-1}$ the sequence $\|b_i^*\|^2 \, 2^i$ has its maximum at $i=n-1$, therefore

$$\|m\|^2 \overset{(2.5)}{=} \|b_n^*\|^{-2} = \|b_{n-1}^{old*}\|^{-2} \leq 2^{n-i-1} \|b_i^*\|^{-2} \quad \text{for } i=1,\dots,n-1 .$$

(If there is no exchange step then $\|m\| = 1$ and the claim holds). Thus the terminal basis $b_1,\dots,b_n$ proves the claim:

$\lambda(x)^2 \overset{\text{Prop.1(2)}}{\geq} 1/\max_i \|b_i^*\|^2 \geq 2^{-n+2} \|b_n^*\|^{-2} \overset{(2.5)}{=} 2^{-n+2} \|m\|^2$. So far we have proved the following theorem.

Theorem 3 Algorithm A holds after at most $O(n^3(k+n))$ arithmetical steps on real numbers. It either finds an integer relation m for x with $\|m\|^2 \leq 2^{n-2} \lambda(x)^2$ or proves $\lambda(x) \geq 2^k$.

It is interesting to bound the number of bit operations of algorithm A for the case of an integer input $x \in \mathbf{Z}^n$. Then all arithmetic steps are on rationals and thus can be done on integers. The size of these integers can be kept small by inserting in algorithm A additional reduction steps 'that achieve $|\mu_{i,j}| \leq 1/2$ after the exchange $b_i \Leftrightarrow b_{i+1}$.

(2.6) insertion for algorithm A, step 3

for $j=i-1,\dots,1$ do $b_i := b_i - \lceil \mu_{i,j} \rfloor b_j$.

With these additional reduction steps an exchange step uses at most $O(n^2)$ arithmetic operations. Throughout the computation on input $x \in \mathbb{Z}^n$ the Gramian determinants $\det[(b_i,b_j)]_{0 \le i,j \le k}$ – here let $b_0=x$ – are bounded by $\|x\|^2$. A detailed analysis shows that the nominators and denominators of the rational numbers $\|b_i^*\|^2$ and $\mu_{i,j}$ are bounded by $\|x\|\ 2^n$ throughout the computation. Therefore all arithmetic steps can be done on integers with $O(n + \log\|x\|)$ bits. This proves the following theorem.

Theorem 4 Given an integer input $x \in \mathbb{Z}^n$ and $k \in \mathbb{N}$, algorithm A when supplemented by the reduction steps (2.6) uses at most $O(n^4(k+n))$ arithmetic operations on $O(n+\log\|x\|)$-bit integers.

The next theorem shows that an output "$\lambda(x) \ge 2^k$" of algorithm A implies that no short integer relation exists for any vector $\bar{x}$ that is sufficiently near to x.

Theorem 5 Suppose algorithm A outputs "$\lambda(x) \ge 2^k$" and the final lattice basis of $\mathbb{Z}^n$ satisfies $\|b_1\|,\dots,\|b_n\| \le B$. Then $\lambda(\bar{x}) \ge 2^{k-1}$ holds for every vector $\bar{x} \in \mathbb{R}^n$ such that $\|x-\bar{x}\| \le 2^{-k}\ B^{-1} \min\{\|x\|,\|\bar{x}\|\}$.

Proof Suppose the current basis of lattice $\mathbb{Z}^n$ on termination of algorithm A is $b_1,\dots,b_n$. Let $b_{i,x}^*$ ($b_{i,\bar{x}}^*$, resp.) be the component of b_i that is orthogonal to $b_1,\dots,b_{i-1},x$ (to $b_1,\dots,b_{i-1},\bar{x}$, resp.). It is sufficient to prove $\|b_{i,\bar{x}}^*\| \le 2^{-k+1}$ for $i=1,\dots,n$, which implies $\lambda(\bar{x}) \ge 2^{k-1}$ by Prop. 1 (2).

A detailed calculation shows

$$\|\pi_x(b) - \pi_{\bar{x}}(b)\| \le \|b\|\ \|x-\bar{x}\| \quad \text{for all } b,x,\bar{x} \text{ with } \|x\|,\|\bar{x}\| \ge 1 .$$

This implies for all vectors $x,\bar{x}$

$$\|b_{i,x}^* - b_{i,\bar{x}}^*\| \le \|b_i\|\ \|x-\bar{x}\| \ /\ \min\{\|x\|,\|\bar{x}\|\}$$
$$\le 2^{-k} \text{ by the assumptions on } x,\bar{x} \text{ and } b_i .$$

From this and since on termination of algorithm A we have $\|b_{i,x}^*\| \le 2^{-k}$ for $i=1,\dots,n$ we conclude $\|b_{i,\bar{x}}^*\| \le 2^{-k+1}$ for $i=1,\dots,n$ which proves the claim. Q.E.D.

Remark It makes sense to run algorithm A without the input parameter k and to eliminate the second termination rule from step 2. This variant of algorithm A halts after at most $O(n^3(\lambda(x)+n))$ arithmetical steps and finds an integer relation m for x such that $\|m\| \le \lambda(x)2^{(n-2)/2}$.

3. On finding linearly independent integer relations

We study the lattice L_x of all integer relations for x,

$$L_x = \{m \in \mathbf{Z}^n : x^T m = 0\} .$$

The dimension of L_x is the maximal number of linearly independent integer relations for x. Let $\lambda_1(x) \leqq \lambda_2(x) \leqq \ldots \leqq \lambda_r(x)$ be the successive minima of lattice L_x,

$$\lambda_r(x) = \min_{\substack{m_1,\ldots,m_r \in L_x \\ \text{linearly independent}}} \max_{j \le r} \|m_j\| .$$

For $r > \dim(L_x)$ we define $\lambda_r(x) = \infty$.

Proposition 6 Let $b_1,\ldots,b_n$ be any basis of lattice $\mathbf{Z}^n$. Then $\lambda_r(x) \geqq 1 / \|\pi(b_i)\|$ holds for r distinct vectors b_i.

Proof Let $m_1,\ldots,m_r \in L_x$ be linearly independent vectors so that $\|m_i\| = \lambda_i(x)$ for $i=1,\ldots,r$. Every basis $b_1,\ldots,b_n$ of $\mathbf{Z}^n$ contains at least r distinct vectors b_i such that $\max_{j\le r}|b_i^T m_j| \neq 0$. Hence $\max_{j\le r}|\pi(b_i)^T m_j| = \max_{j\le r}|b_i^T m_j| \geqq 1$. This implies $\lambda_r(x) = \|m_r\| \geqq 1/\|\pi(b_i)\|$ for r distinct basis vectors b_i . Q.E.D.

When given as input $x \in \mathbb{R}^n$ and $r,k \in \mathbb{N}$ the following algorithm B either finds r linearly independent integer relations for x or proves $\lambda_r(x) \geqq 2^k$.

Outline of Algorithm B

1. Let $b_1,\ldots,b_n$ be the standard basis of $\mathbf{Z}^n$, $s := n$.
2. If $s = n-r$ then ($\begin{bmatrix} c_1^T \\ \vdots \\ c_n^T \end{bmatrix} := [b_1,\ldots,b_n]^{-1}$, output $(c_{n-r+1},\ldots,c_n)$, stop)

   If $\|b_i^*\| \leqq 2^{-k-i}$ for $i=1,\ldots,n-r$ then (output "$\lambda_r(x) \geqq 2^k$ stop)
3. Choose i<s that maximizes $\|b_i^*\|^2\, 2^i$.

   $b_{i+1} := b_{i+1} - \lceil \mu_{i+1,i} \rfloor\, b_i$, exchange b_i, b_{i+1}

   If $b_i^*=0$ then $s := i$, go to 2 .

Theorem 7 When given as input $x \in \mathbb{R}^n$, $k \in \mathbb{N}$ then algorithm B either finds r linearly independent integer relations $c_{n-r+1},\ldots,c_n$ for x or proves $\lambda_r(x) \geqq 2^k$. The algorithm halts after at most $O(n^3(k+n))$ arithmetical steps on real numbers.

Proof We consider the situation on termination of algorithm B. If $s = n-r$ then $b_s^* = 0$ implies $x \in \Sigma_{j \le n-r} b_j \mathbf{R}$. In this case $c_{n-r+1},\dots,c_n$ are linearly independent integer relations for x.

If $\|b_i^*\| \le 2^{-k-i}$ for $i=1,\dots,n-r$ holds for the terminal basis $b_1,\dots,b_n$ of $\mathbf{Z}^n$ we can conclude $\lambda_r(x) \ge 2^k$. W.l.o.g. we can assume that $|\mu_{i,j}| \le 1/2$ for $1 \le j < i \le n$ since these inequalities can be achieved without changing $\|b_i^*\|$ for $i=1,\dots,n$. It follows for $i=1,\dots,n-r$

$$\|\pi(b_i)\|^2 \le \|b_i^*\|^2 + \Sigma_{j<i}\, \mu_{i,j}^2\, \|b_j^*\|^2 \le 2^{-2k} .$$

Therefore Proposition 6 implies $\lambda_r(x) \ge 2^k$.

It can easily be seen that the time analysis of algorithm A carries over to algorithm B. Q.E.D.

If algorithm B finds integer relations $c_{n-r+1},\dots,c_n$ for x then $\|c_n\|^2 \le 2^{n-2}\, \lambda_1(x)^2$ holds by theorem 3. The following theorem extends this bound to $c_{n-r+1},\dots,c_{n-1}$ provided that $|\mu_{i,j}| \le 1/2$ for $1 \le j < i \le n$ holds on termination of algorithm B. The inequalities $|\mu_{i,j}| \le 1/2$ can be achieved by $O(n^3)$ arithmetical steps before inverting the matrix $[b_1,\dots,b_n]$ and this does not change the numbers $\|b_1^*\|,\dots,\|b_n^*\|$.

Theorem 8 Suppose algorithm B finds integer relations $c_{n-r+1},\dots,c_n$ for x and $|\mu_{i,j}| \le 1/2$ for $1 \le j < i \le n$ holds on termination. Then $\|c_{n-i+1}\|^2 \le 1.5^{2i}\, 2^n\, \lambda_i(x)^2$ holds for $i=1,\dots,r$.

Proof On termination of algorithm B we have $b_s^* = 0$ for $s := n-r$, and for some matrix W we have

$$[b_1,\dots,b_n] = [x, b_1^*,\dots,b_{s-1}^*, b_{s+1}^*,\dots,b_n^*]\, W^T .$$

The matrix $W = [w_{i,j}]_{1 \le i,j \le n}$ has entries

$$w_{i,j} = \begin{cases} (b_i,x)\, \|x\|^{-2} & j = 1 \\ \mu_{i,j-1} & 1 < j \le s \\ \mu_{i,j} & j > s \end{cases}$$

with $w_{i,i} = 1$ for $i = s+1,\dots,n$ and $|w_{i,j}| \le 1/2$ for $1 < j < i \le n$. The matrix W is lower triangular for the last r columns, i.e. $w_{i,j}=0$ for $j>n-r$ and $i<j$. From the definition of $c_1,\dots,c_n$ and since the vectors x, $b_1^*,\dots,b_n^*$ are pairwise orthogonal we conclude

$$[c_1,\dots,c_n] = [b_1,\dots,b_n]^{-1\,T} = [x,b_1^*,\dots,b_{s-1}^*,b_{s+1}^*,\dots,b_n^*] \begin{bmatrix} \|x\|^{-2} & & & 0 \\ & \|b_1^*\|^{-2} & & \\ & & \ddots & \\ 0 & & & \|b_n^*\|^{-2} \end{bmatrix} W^{-1}.$$

Let the matrix $V := W^{-1}$ have entries $v_{i,j}$ then

$$\|c_{n-i+1}\|^2 = \sum_{j \geq n-i+1} v_{n-i+1,j}^2 \|b_j^*\|^{-2} \quad \text{for } i=1,\dots,r.$$

From this the asserted upper bound on $\|c_{n-i+1}\|^2$ easily follows from the inequalities (3.1), (3.2).

(3.1) $|v_{i,j}| \leq 1.5^{i-j}$ for $n-r < j \leq i \leq n$;

(3.2) $\|b_{n-i+1}^*\|^{-2} \leq \lambda_i(x)^2\, 2^{n-i}$ for $i=1,\dots,r$.

The inequality (3.1) follows from $|w_{i,j}| \leq 1/2$ for $n-r < j < i \leq n$, $w_{i,i}=1$ for $i>n-r$, and since the matrix W is lower triangular for the last r columns.

To prove (3.2) consider the last exchange $b_{n-r} \Leftrightarrow b_{n-r+1}$. Before this exchange the maximum $\|b_j^*\|^2\, 2^j$ for $j \leq n-r$ is at $j=n-r$. Thus we have for $j \leq n-r+1$:

$$\|\pi(b_j)\|^2 = \sum_{\nu \leq j} \mu_{j,\nu}^2 \|b_\nu^*\|^2 \leq \sum_{\nu \leq j} \mu_{j,\nu}^2 \|b_{n-r}^{\mathrm{old}*}\|^2\, 2^{n-r-\nu} \leq \|b_{n-r+1}^*\|^2\, 2^{n-r}.$$

We know from proposition 6 that $\lambda_r(x) \geq \|\pi(b_\nu)\|^{-1}$ for r distinct basis vectors b_ν. By the previous inequalities this yields

$$\lambda_r(x) \geq 1 \Big/ \max_{\nu \leq n-r+1} \|\pi(b_\nu)\| \geq \|b_{n-r+1}^*\|^{-1}\, 2^{(-n+r)/2}.$$

This proves (3.2) for $i=r$. The inequality (3.2) for $i<r$ follows in the same way from the situation of the last exchange $b_{n-i} \Leftrightarrow b_{n-i+1}$. Q.E.D.

The following algorithm C reduces the problem of finding a short integer relation for x to the problem of finding a short vector in a lattice L' contained in L_x.

Outline of algorithm C

1. Given x find $m' \in L_x \backslash 0$ via algorithm A such that $\|m'\|^2 \leq 2^{n-2}\, \lambda(x)^2$.
2. Repeat the exchange steps $b_i \Leftrightarrow b_{i+1}$ as in algorithm B until for some $r \geq 1$ $b_{n-r}^* = 0$ and $\|b_i^*\| \leq \|m'\|$ for $i=1,\dots,n-r-1$.

3. Make sure that $|\mu_{i,j}| \leq 1/2$ for $1 \leq j < i \leq n$. $\begin{bmatrix} c_1^T \\ \vdots \\ c_n^T \end{bmatrix} := [b_1,\dots,b_n]^{-1}$.
4. Apply the Lovász lattice basis reduction algorithm to the basis $c_{n-r+1},\dots,c_n$. This yields an LLL-reduced basis $a_1,\dots,a_r$ of the lattice $L' := \sum_{i=0}^{r-1} c_{n-i}\,\mathbb{Z}$,
5. output $(m := a_1)$.

<u>**Theorem 9**</u> When given as input $x \in \mathbb{R}^n$ with $L_x \neq 0$ algorithm C finds some integer $r \leq \dim L_x$ and some integer relation $m \in L_x \backslash 0$ such that $\|m\|^2 \leq 2^{r-1}\,\lambda(x)^2$. It halts after at most $O(n^3(n + \log \lambda_r(x)))$ arithmetic steps with real numbers.

<u>**Proof**</u>

<u>**Correctness of algorithm C :**</u> We first prove (3.3) and (3.4).

(3.3) $L' \subset L_x$;

(3.4) $\forall\, m \in L_x : \|m\| \leq \|m'\| \Rightarrow m \in L'$.

<u>Proof of (3.3) :</u> On termination of algorithm C we have $b^*_{n-r} = 0$ and thus $x \in \sum_{i=1}^{n-r} b_i\,\mathbb{R}$ and $c_{n-r+1},\dots,c_n \in L_x$.

<u>Proof of (3.4) :</u> If m is linearly independent of $c_{n-r+1},\dots,c_n$ then there exists an integer $i \leq n-r$ such that $m^T b_i \neq 0$. For the smallest such integer i we have $i \leq n-r-1$ and

$$|m^T b_i^*| = |m^T \pi(b_i)| = |m^T b_i| \geq 1 .$$

Hence $\|m\|^2 \geq \|b_i^*\|^{-2} \geq \|m'\|^2$.

If m is linearly dependent on $c_{n-r+1},\dots,c_n$ then $m \in L'$ since $c_1,\dots,c_n$ is basis of the lattice $\mathbb{Z}^n$.

From (3.3), (3.4) we conclude $\|a_1\|^2 \leq 2^{r-1}\,\lambda(x)^2$ since the Lovász lattice basis reduction algorithm finds a lattice vector $a_1 \in L' \setminus 0$ such that $\|a_1\|^2 \leq 2^{r-1}\,\lambda(L')^2$. Here $\lambda(L')$ is the length of a shortest non-zero vector in L'. For the Lovász algorithm see Lenstra at alii (1982).

<u>**Time analysis**</u> Application of algorithm A in step 1 costs $O(n^3(n + \log \lambda(x)))$ arithmetic operations and this bound also covers the cost of steps 2, 3. Since $|\mu_{i,j}| \leq 1/2$ for $1 \leq j < i \leq n$ the proof of theorem 8 shows $\|c_{n-i+1}\|^2 \leq 1.5^{2i}\, 2^n\, \lambda_i(x)^2 \leq 1.5^{2i}\, 2^n\, \lambda_r(x)^2$.

Therefore the Lovász algorithm in step 4 halts after at most $O(r^2(n + \log \lambda_r(x))$ iterations. We apply the Lovász algorithm without performing the reduction steps that are used to keep integers small. Then each iteration only costs $O(r)$ arithmetic steps. This shows that algorithm C halts after at most $O(n^3(n + \log \lambda_r(x)))$ arithmetical steps. Q.e.d.

Remarks (i) If $\dim(L_x) = 1$ then algorithm A finds a shortest integer relation m but it does not prove $\|m\| = \lambda(x)$. Algorithm C in the case $\dim(L_x) = 1$ proves $\|m\| = \lambda(x)$.

(ii) The Lovász algorithm in step 4 of algorithm C can be replaced by any lattice basis reduction algorithm. The time bound of algorithm C and the performance $\|m\| / \lambda(x)$ of the found integer relation m are determined by the lattice basis reduction algorithm that is used in step 4. In particular this reduces the problem of finding a shortest integer relation for x to the problem of finding a shortest non-zero vector in the lattice $L' \subseteq L_x$.

4. Simultaneous Integer Relations

We consider the problem of finding a simultaneous integer relation for linearly independent $x_1,...,x_s \in \mathbb{R}^n$, i.e. we search for a non- zero vector $m \in \mathbb{Z}^n$ such that $x_i^T m = 0$ for $i=1,...,s$. Let the vectors $x_1,...,x_s$ be fixed, and for a basis $b_1,...,b_n$ of lattice $\mathbb{Z}^n$ let b_j^* be the component of b_j which is orthogonal to $x_1,...,x_s$, $b_1,...,b_{j-1}$.

Proposition 1 and theorem 2 can easily be extended to, the case of simultaneous relations. Let $\lambda(x_1,...,x_s)$ be the length of a shortest simultaneous integer relation for $x_1,...,x_s$ and $\lambda(x_1,...,x_s) = \infty$ if no such relation exists.

Proposition 10 Every basis $b_1,...,b_n$ of lattice $\mathbb{Z}^n$ satisfies $\lambda(x_1,...,x_s) \geq 1/\max_i\|b_i^*\|$.

Theorem 11 There is an algorithm which given $x_1,...,x_s$ and k either finds a simultaneous relation m for $x_1,...,x_s$ or proves $\lambda(x_1,...,x_s) \geq 2^k$. The algorithms halts after at most $O(n^3(k+n))$ arithmetic operations with real numbers.

Outline of the algorithm:

Using the vectors b_i^* defined above, repeat the exchange step of algorithm A until either (i) or (ii) holds,

(i) $b_n^* \neq 0$,

(ii) $\|b_i^*\| \leq 2^{-k}$ for $i = 1,...,n$.

Correctness of the algorithm

In case (i) we have dim $(\mathrm{span}(b_1^*,...,b_{n-1}^*)) = n-s-1$, and this implies $x_1,...,x_s \in$ span $(b_1,...,b_{n-1})$. Thus a simultaneous relation c_n for $x_1,...,x_s$ is found in $\mathbb{Z}^n \cap \mathrm{span}(b_1,...,b_{n-1})^{\perp}$ by one matrix inversion

$$\begin{bmatrix} c_1^T \\ \vdots \\ c_n^T \end{bmatrix} = [b_1,...,b_n]^{-1}.$$

In case (ii) proposition 10 implies $\lambda(x_1,...,x_s) \geq 2^k$. The time analysis of algorithm A carries over to the new algorithm . **Q.E.D.**

Remark A particular case of the simultaneous relation problem is the problem of finding the minimal polynomial of an algebraic number. Let $\alpha = (\mathrm{Re}(\alpha)\ ,\ \mathrm{Im}(\alpha)) \in \mathbb{C}$ be an algebraic number with degree at most n. Then every simultaneous relation $m = (m_0,...,m_n)$ for $x_1 = (\mathrm{Re}(\alpha^0,...,\mathrm{Re}(\alpha^n))$, $x_2 = (\mathrm{Im}(\alpha^0),...,\mathrm{Im}(\alpha^n))$ yields a multiple $p(x) = \sum_{i=0}^{n} m_i \cdot x^i$ of the minimal polynomial for α. Hence the minimal polynomial can be found by factoring p(x) over $\mathbb{Z}$.

References

G. Bergman (1980)
Notes on Ferguson and Forcade's Generalized Euclidean Algorithm.
Unpublished paper. University of California at Berkeley.

A. Brentjes (1981)
Multi-dimensional Continued Fraction Algorithms.
Math. Centre Tracts No. 145.
Universiteit Amsterdam.

H.R.P. Ferguson and R.W. Forcade (1979)
Generalization of the euclidean algorithm for real numbers to all dimensions higher than two.

Bulletin of the AMS 1,6 pp. 912–914.

H.R.P. Ferguson (1984)
A non-inductive GL(n,$\mathbb{Z}$) algorithm that constructs integral linear relations. Preprint. Brigham Young University

H.R.P. Ferguson (1985)
A short proof of the existence of vector Euclidean algorithms to appear in Proceedings of the AMS.

C.G.J. Jacobi (1868)
Allgemeine Theorie der Kettenbruchähnlichen Algorithmen.
J. reine Angew. Math. 69 (1969), 29–64.

A.K. Lenstra, H.W. Lenstra Jr., and L. Lovász (1982)
Factoring polynomials with rational coefficients.
Math. Ann. 21, 515–534.

R. Kannan, A.K. Lenstra, and L. Lovász (1984)
Polynomial factorization and nonrandomness of bits of algebraic and some transcendental numbers.
Proc. 16th Ann. ACM Symp. on Theory of Computing, pp. 191–200.

NEW UPPERBOUNDS FOR DECENTRALIZED EXTREMA-FINDING IN A RING OF PROCESSORS

H.L. Bodlaender* and J. van Leeuwen

Department of Computer Science, University of Utrecht
P.O.Box 80.012, 3508 TA Utrecht, the Netherlands

Abstract. We show that decentralized extrema-finding ("election") is more efficient in bidirectional rings than in unidirectional rings of processors, by exhibiting a (non-probabilistic) algorithm for distributed extrema-finding in bidirectional rings that requires fewer messages on the average than any such algorithm for unidirectional rings.

1. Introduction. Consider n processors connected in a network, and distinguished by unique identification numbers. Every processor only has local information about the network topology, viz. it only knows the processors to which it is connected through a direct link. In a number of distributed algorithms it is required that the active processors elect a central coordinator (a "leader"), e.g. as part of an initialisation or restart procedure. The problem arises to design a protocol by means of which any active processor can incite the election and every processor will learn the identification number of the leader in as small a number of message-exchanges as possible. Because the active processor with the largest identification number is normally designated as the leader, the election problem is also known as the "decentralized extrema-finding" problem.

The decentralized extrema-finding problem for rings of n processors was proposed by LeLann [13] in 1977. The problem has been studied for unidirectional rings as well as for general, bidirectional rings. Figures 1 and 2 summarize the solutions presently known for both cases. In 1981 Korach, Rotem, and Santoro [12] gave a probabilistic algorithm for decentralized extrema-finding in bidirectional rings that uses a smaller (expected) average number of messages than any deterministic algorithm for the problem in unidirectional rings requires. In this paper we consider the key question of whether decentralized extrema-finding can be solved more efficiently in bidirectional rings than in unidirectional rings by a deterministic algorithm. (The question was first posed by Pachl, Korach, and Rotem [14].)

---

* The work of this author was supported by the Foundation for Computer Science (SION) of the Netherlands Organisation for the Advancement of Pure Research (ZWO).

Algorithm	Lowerbound	Average	Worst Case
LeLann (1977)		n^2	n^2
Chang & Roberts (1979)		nH_n	$0.5n^2$
Peterson (1982)			1.44..nlogn
Dolev, Klawe, & Rodeh (1982)			1.356 nlogn
Pachl, Korach, & Rotem (1982)	(aver.) nH_n		

Fig. 1 Election Algorithms for Unidirectional Rings

Algorithm	Lowerbound	Average	Worst Case
Gallager et.al. (1979)			5nlogn
Hirschberg & Sinclair (1980)			8nlogn
Burns (1980)	$\frac{1}{4}$nlogn		3nlogn
Franklin (1982)			2nlogn
Korach, Rotem, & Santoro (1981)		(prob.)$\frac{3}{4}nH_n$	(prob.) $\frac{1}{2}n^2$
Pachl, Korach, & Rotem (1982)	(aver.) $\frac{1}{8}$nlogn		
Santoro, Korach, & Rotem (1982)			1.89nlogn
van Leeuwen & Tan (1985)			1.44nlogn
this paper (1985)		(det.)$<\frac{3}{4}nH_n$	(det.)$\frac{1}{4}n^2$

Fig. 2 Election Algorithms for Bidirectional Rings

Consider a ring of n processors with identification numbers X_1 through X_n. Without loss of generality assume that $X \equiv X_1X_2...X_n$ is a random permutation of the numbers 1 to n. In a typical election algorithm due to Chang and Roberts [4] identification numbers are send in the same direction and are annihilated by the first larger processor that is encountered. Thus all identification numbers except the largest are annihilated on their way around the ring, and the "leader" is identified as the only processor that eventually receives its own identification number as a message again.

Given a random sequence (e.g. a time-series), an "upper record" is any element that is larger that all the preceeding ones. Let X be a random sequence. Let $v_o=1$, and let v_i be the index of the first upper record with index larger than v_{i-1} $(i \geq 1)$. Thus v_i is a random variable for the position of the ith upper record in the sequence. Observe that v_1 is the distance to the 'first' upper record of the sequence. The following result repeatedly occurs in the theory (see e.g. [3], [7],

[10]).

Theorem A. The average distance to the first upper record in a random sequence of length n is $H_n - 1 \approx 0.69 \log n$.

The theory of record distributions in random sequences was considerably advanced by Renyi [16] in 1962. He also derived the following useful fact, see also David and Barton [5].

Theorem B. For every $k \geq 1$ and $1 < j_1 < \ldots < j_k$ one has that $P(v_1 = j_1; \ldots; v_k = j_k) = \frac{1}{j_k \prod_{i=1}^{k} (j_i - 1)}$.

The results from the theory of order statistics apply to decentralized extrema-finding by observing that e.g. in the algorithm of Chang and Roberts the message generated by an X_i is propagated to the first upper record in the random sequence $X_i X_{i+1} \ldots$. By theorem A a message will travel over H_n links "on the average", before it is annihilated. It follows that the algorithm of Chang and Roberts uses $nH_n \approx 0.69\, n \log n$ messages on the average. By a result of Pachl, Korach, and Rotem [14] the algorithm is optimal for unidirectional rings. In this paper we show that the algorithm is not optimal for bidirectional rings, i.e., bidirectional rings are "faster".

2. Decentralized extrema-finding in a bidirectional ring using a small number of messages on the average.

We begin by describing a probabilistic algorithm due to Korach, Rotem, and Santoro [12]. We subsequently derive a deterministic algorithm for the problem that uses the same number of messages on the average (over all rings of n processors). In the probabilistic algorithm the processors randomly decide to send their identification number to the left or to the right. With messages going clockwise and counterclockwise on the ring, it is expected that many messages run into "larger" messages and (hence) are annihilated sooner. The algorithm consists of three successive stages, as described below.

Algorithm-P

Each processor X_i keeps the largest identification number it has seen in a local variable MAX_i $(1 \leq i \leq n)$. Each processor X_i goes through the following stages.

Stage 1 (initialisation)

$MAX_i := X_i$;

choose a direction $d \in \{left, right\}$ with probability $\frac{1}{2}$;

send message $\langle X_i \rangle$ in direction d on the ring;

Stage 2 (election)

repeat the following steps, until the end of the election is signalled by receipt of a <!> message:

if two messages are received from the left and the right simultaneously, then ignore the smaller message and proceed as if only the larger message is received;

if message $\langle X_j \rangle$ is received from a neighbour, then

```
    if X_j>MAX_i then MAX_i := X_j;
                      pass messages <X_j> on
    elif X_j = MAX_i then {X_i has won the election}
                      send message <!> on the ring
    fi;
```

Stage 3 (inauguration)

if a message <!> is received, the election is over and MAX_i holds the identification number of the leader;

if this processor was elected in stage 2 then the inauguration is over, otherwise pass message <!> on and stop.

One easily verifies that a processor X_i wins the election if and only if its identification number succeeds in making a full round along the ring in a direction chosen in stage 1. Thus, at the moment that a unique processor X_i finds out that it is the leader, all processors must have set their local MAX-variable to X_i. It follows that it is sufficient to send a simple <!> message around the ring for an inauguration and as a signal that the election is over.

Theorem 2.1 (Korach, Rotem, and Santoro [12]).

(i) Algorithm-P uses $\approx \frac{1}{2}n^2$ messages in the worst case,

(ii) Algorithm-P uses (at most) $\approx \frac{3}{4}nH_n \approx 0.52$ nlogn messages in the expected case.

Proof.

(i) The worst case occurs in a ring $X \equiv n\ n-1 \ldots 2\ 1$, when all processors decide to send their identification numbers to the right. The number of messages adds up to $\frac{1}{2}n(n-1)+n \approx \frac{1}{2}n^2$.

(ii) Observe that the message generated by X_i (in stage 1) will be annihilated by the first upper record in the chosen direction on the ring. If the first upper record had decided to send its identification number in the opposite direction, i.e., towards X_i, then the messages meet "half way" and the $\langle X_i \rangle$-message is killed right there. There is probability $\frac{1}{2}$ that the $\langle X_i \rangle$-message needs to travel only half the distance to the first upper record in either direction on the ring. Using theorem A, the expected number of $\langle X_i \rangle$-messages will be $\frac{1}{2}H_n + \frac{1}{2} \cdot \frac{1}{2}H_n = \frac{3}{4}H_n$. It follows that the total number of messages exchanged is less than $\frac{3}{4}nH_n + n \approx \frac{3}{4}nH_n \approx 0.52$ nlogn in the expected case. □

Observe that Algorithm-P is probabilistic and, hence, no proof in itself that decentralized extrema-finding is more efficient for bidirectional rings than for unidirectional rings. To resolve the problem we devise a version of Algorithm-P in which stage 1 is replaced by a purely deterministic step.

Algorithm-D

Similar to Algorithm-P, except that for each processor X_i stage 1 is replaced by the following stage.

Stage 1*

send message $\langle *X_i \rangle$ to both neighbours on the ring;

wait for the messages $\langle *X_{i-1} \rangle$ and $\langle *X_{i+1} \rangle$ of both neighbours (with the indices "i-1" and "i+1" interpreted in the usual circular sense as indices of the left and right neighbour, resp.);

```
MAX_i := max(X_{i-1}, X_i, X_{i+1});
if MAX_i = X_i then
        if X_{i-1} < X_{i+1} then send messages <X_i> to the left
                             else send message <X_i> to the right
        fi
fi;
```

(Stages 2 and 3 are unchanged.)

Theorem 2.2.

(i) Algorithm-D uses $\approx \frac{1}{4}n^2$ messages in the worst case,

(ii) Algorithm-D uses (at most) $\approx \frac{3}{4}nH_n \approx 0.52$ nlogn messages in the average case.

Proof.

(i) At most $\frac{1}{2}n$ processors are still active after stage 1*, and the active processor are separated by at least one inactive processor. Suppose the largest processor sends its identification number to the right. The worst case occurs if every second processor sends its identification number in the same direction and is not annihilated before it reaches the largest. This generates at most $n + \sum_{i=1}^{n/2} (n-2i) \approx \frac{1}{4}n^2$ messages. The worst case occurs in a ring of the form $X \equiv n\ 1\ n-1\ \lceil \frac{1}{2}n \rceil\ n-2\ \lceil \frac{1}{2}n \rceil -1 \ldots$ (the shuffle of $n\ n-1 \ldots \lceil \frac{1}{2}n \rceil +1$ and $1\ \lceil \frac{1}{2}n \rceil\ \lceil \frac{1}{2}n \rceil -1 \ldots 2$).

(ii) Note that stage 1* only requires 2n messages and leaves at most $\frac{1}{2}n$ processors (peaks) that will send a message on the ring at the end of the stage. By pairing every permutation with one in which the neighbours of X_i are interchanged, one sees that X_i sends its messages to the left or to the right with probability $\frac{1}{2}$ (averaged over all permutations). The message sent by X_i will be annihilated by the first upper record X_j in the direction determined in stage 1*, or by the message of the first upper record that is a peak in the same direction (in case this message was sent towards X_i and collided with the $\langle X_i\rangle$-message between X_i and X_j). We ignore the case that X_i does not have an upper record. Without loss of generality we may in fact assume that X_i and X_j are more than two steps apart, otherwise the $\langle X_i\rangle$-message certainly travels only O(1) steps. As a result we may assume that X_j sends a message towards X_i with probability $\frac{1}{2}$, where we note that the complementary case with probability $\frac{1}{2}$ consists of X_j sending its message away from X_i or not sending a message at all. (This is seen by the following argument, where we use X_j^l and X_j^r to denote the left and right neighbours of X_j as seen from X_i in the direction of X_j. Note that $X_j^l < X_i$, by the assumption that X_j is the first upper record. If $X_j^r < X_i$ then pair the current permutation with the one in which X_j^l and X_j^r are switched. If $X_j^r > X_i$ then pair the current permutation with the one in which X_j and X_j^r are switched. Of every pair precisely one permutation will give a case in which the first upper record of X_i sends a message towards X_i. Note that the pairing of permutations is independent of the choice of a direction by X_i.) By theorem A we know that the average distance of a random processor to its first upper record is H_n. It follows that Algorithm-D uses (at most) $\frac{3}{4}nH_n+O(n)$ messages on the average. □

Corollary 2.3. Decentralized extrema-finding can be achieved strictly more efficiently (i.e., with fewer messages on the average) for bidirectional rings than for unidirectional rings.

3. An improved analysis of Algorithm-P and Algorithm-D. In the proofs of theorem 2.1 and 2.2 the bound of $\frac{3}{4}H_n$ on the average (c.q. expected) number of propagations of an $\langle X_i\rangle$-message is only an upperbound, because the possible effect of higher order upper records was ignored. For a more precise analysis of Algorithm-P, we assume without loss of generality that i=1 and that the $\langle X_1\rangle$-message is sent to the right. Let v_1, v_2, ... be random variables denoting the position of the first and higher order upper records (cf. Section 1). If X_{v_1} to $X_{v_{j-1}}$ randomly choose to send their $\langle X\rangle$-message to the right as well but X_{v_j} sends its message to the left, then the $\langle X_1\rangle$-message is annihilated by the $\langle X_{v_j}\rangle$-message if the messages meet before X_{v_1} is reached, i.e., at processor $X_{1+\frac{\lceil v_j-1\rceil}{2}}$ provided $v_j<2v_1$. (For v_j-1 odd, the messages will not meet but pass over the same link before $\langle X_1\rangle$ is annihilated at the next processor.) Otherwise the $\langle X_1\rangle$-message is simply killed at X_{v_1}.

<u>Definition</u>. $K_n(j)= \sum\limits_{\substack{1<t_1<..<t_j\le n\\ t_j<2t_1}} \frac{t_1-1/2t_j}{(t_1-1)\dots(t_j-1)t_j}$.

Suppose that we take the effect of up to l upper records into account.

<u>Theorem</u> 3.1 The expected number of messages used by Algorithm-P is bounded by
$n(H_n - \sum\limits_{j=1}^{l} (\frac{1}{2})^j K_n(j)) + O(n)$.

<u>Proof</u>.

The expected number of $\langle X_1\rangle$-messages propagated by Algorithm-P is bounded by the expected value of

$$\sum_{j=1}^{l} (1/2)^j\frac{\lceil v_j-1\rceil}{2} + (1/2)^l(v_1-1) =$$

$$= (v_1-1)-\{ \sum_{j=1}^{l} (1/2)^j(v_1-1)- \sum_{j=1}^{l} (1/2)^j\frac{\lceil v_j-1\rceil}{2}\}$$

$$= (v_1-1)- \sum_{j=1}^{l} (1/2)^j\left(v_1-\frac{v_j}{2}\right)+O(1)$$

, where each term in the summation arises with the probability of v_j being less than $2v_1$ (and thus of the $\langle X_{v_j}\rangle$-message serving as the annihilator of the $\langle X_1\rangle$-message). We ignore the effect of rings without a first upper record. The expected value is given by

$$\sum_{1<t_1\le n} P(v_1=t_1)(t_1-1)- \sum_{j=1}^{l} (1/2)^j \sum_{\substack{1<t_1<\dots<t_j\le n\\ t_j<2t_1}} P(v_1=t_1;\dots;v_j=t_j)(t_1-1/2t_j)+O(1)=$$

$$= \sum_{1<t_1\le n}\frac{t_1-1}{(t_1-1)t_1}- \sum_{j=1}^{l} (1/2)^jK_n(j)+O(1)=$$

$$= H_n- \sum_{j=1}^{l} (1/2)^jK_n(j)+O(1),$$

using theorem B. Accumulating this bound for all $\langle X_i\rangle$-messages yields the result. □

<u>Lemma</u> 3.2.

(i) $K_n(1) = \frac{1}{2}H_n + O(1)$,

(ii) $K_n(2) = (\frac{1}{2} - \frac{1}{2}\ln 2)\, H_n + O(1)$,

(iii) $K_n(3) = (\frac{1}{2} - \frac{1}{2}\ln 2 - \frac{1}{4}\ln^2 2)\, H_n + O(1)$,

(iv) $K_n(j+1) < K_n(j)$.

Proof.

Omitted (see [1]). □

Theorem 3.3. The expected number of messages used by Algorithm-P is equal to $0.70\ldots nH_n + O(n)$.

Proof.

By theorem 3.1. the expected number of messages used by Algorithm-P is equal to $n(H_n - \sum_{j=1}^{L} (\frac{1}{2})^j K_n(j)) + O(n)$, for the largest L possible. (Note that no ring has a jth upper record with $t_j < 2t_1$ for $j \geq \frac{1}{2}n+1$.) Using lemma 3.2. this number is bounded from above by

$$(1-\tfrac{1}{2}(\tfrac{1}{2})-\tfrac{1}{4}(\tfrac{1}{2}-\tfrac{1}{2}\ln 2)-\tfrac{1}{8}(\tfrac{1}{2}-\tfrac{1}{2}\ln 2-\tfrac{1}{4}\ln^2 2))nH + O(n) =$$
$$= (+\ln 2+\ln^2 2)nH_n + O(n) =$$
$$= 0.7075nH_n + O(n),$$

and from below by

$$(+\ln 2+\ln^2 2)nH_n - (\tfrac{1}{2}-\tfrac{1}{2}\ln 2-\tfrac{1}{4}\ln^2 2) \sum_{j=4}^{\infty} (\tfrac{1}{2})^j .nH_n + O(n)$$
$$= (\tfrac{1}{2}+\tfrac{1}{4}\ln 2+\ln^2 2)nH_n + O(n) =$$
$$= 0.7033\, nH_n + O(n). \quad \square$$

Because of the analogy to Algorithm-P (cf. theorem 2.2), it is intuitive that the improved bound of $0.70..nH_n + O(n)$ messages also holds for the average number of messages used by Algorithm-D. We give a more rigorous proof of this fact. Note that in its first stage, Algorithm-D expends O(n) messages to eliminate every processor that has a larger neighbour. The active processors that remain are at least one position apart, but must be at least two positions apart if we want to claim the independence of their choice of direction at the end of stage 1*. This motivates the definition of a modified record concept.

Definition. Given a random sequence, and "upper *-record" is any element that is larger than all the preceeding ones (thus an upper record in the traditional sense) for which the two immediately preceeding elements are not upper *-records.

We will bound the average number of messages used by Algorithm-D by taking only the effect of upper *-records into account, by an analysis that is very similar to the analysis of Algorithm-P.

Definition. $L_n(j) = \Sigma\, P^*(v_1=t_1;\ldots;v_j=t_j).(t_1-\frac{1}{2}t_j)$, where the summation is taken over all $t_1,\ldots,t_j$ with $1<t_1<\ldots<t_j\le n$ and $2<t_1$, $t_1+2<t_2,\ldots,t_{j-1}+2<t_j$ and $t_j<2t_1$.

In the definition, $P^*(v_1=t_1;\ldots;v_j=t_j)$ denotes the probability that the ith upper *-record occurs at position t_i $(1i\le j)$. Note that for $2<t_1$, $t_1+2<t_2,\ldots,t_{j-1}+2<t_j$ one has $P^*(v_1=t_1;\ldots;v_j=t_j) \ge P(v_1=t_1;\ldots;v_j=t_j) = \frac{1}{(t_1-1)\ldots(t_j-1)t_j}$, because the upper records in positions t_1 through t_j will automatically be upper *-records. Suppose we only take the effect of 1 upper *-records into account.

Theorem 3.4. The average number of messages used by Algorithm-D is bounded by (at most) $n(H_n - \sum_{j=1}^{l} (\frac{1}{2})^j L_n(j)) + O(n)$.

For simplicity define $L_n'(j) = \Sigma \frac{t_1-1/2t_j}{t_1-1)\ldots(t_j-1)t_j}$, where the summation extends over all $t_1,\ldots,t_j$ as in $L_n(j)$.

Lemma 3.5.

(i) $L_n(j) \ge L_n'(j)$,

(ii) $0\le K_n(j) - L_n'(j) = O(j)$.

Proof.

(i) This follows immediately from the definitions.

(ii) Obviously $K_n(j) \ge L_n'(j)$, as L_n' equals the expression for $K_n(j)$ over a more restricted range. To show that $K_n(j)-L_n'(j) = O(j)$ we define the following auxiliary quantity $M_n(j,i)$ for $0\le i\le j$:

$$M_n(j,i) = \Sigma \frac{t_1-1/2t_j}{(t_1-1)\ldots(t_j-1)t_j},$$ where the summation is taken over all $t_1,\ldots,t_j$ with $1<t_1<\ldots<t_j\le n$ and $t_i+2<t_{i+1},\ldots,t_{j-1}+2<t_j$ and $t_j<2t_1$.

Observe that $K_n(j) = M_n(j,j)$ and $L_n'(j)=M_n(j,0)$, and clearly $M_n(j,i+1)\ge M_n(j,i)$. Note that $\frac{t_1-1/2t_j}{t_j} \le 1$, and that for "fixed" t_1 to t_i one has $\Sigma \frac{t_1-1/2t_j}{(t_1-1)\ldots(t_j-1)(t_{i+1}-1)\ldots(t_j-1)t_j} = O\left(\frac{1}{(t_1-1)\ldots(t_i-1)}\right)$, where the summation extends over all $1<t_{i+1}<\ldots<t_j\le n$ with $t_i+2<t_{i+1},\ldots,t_{j-1}+2<t_j$ and $t_j<2t_1$. Next observe that

$$M_n(j,i+1)-M(j,i)=\Sigma\frac{t_1-1/2t_j}{(t_1-1)\ldots(t_j-1)t_j}$$

where the summation is taken over all $t_1,\ldots,t_j$ with $1<t_1<\ldots<t_j\leq n$ and $t_{i+1}+2<t_{i+2},\ldots,t_{j-1}+2<t_j$ and $t_j<2t_1$, and $t_{i+1}=t_i+1$ or $t_{i+1}=t_i+2$. It follows that

$$M_n(j,i+1)-M(j,i)=O\Big(\sum_{\substack{1<t_1<\ldots<t_{i+1}\leq n\\ t_{i+1}<2t_1\\ t_{i+1}=t_i+1 \text{ or } =t_i+2}}\frac{1}{(t_1-1)\ldots(t_i-1)(t_{i+1}-1)}\Big)=$$

$$=O\Big(\sum_{\substack{(1<t_1<\ldots<t_i\leq n)\\ t_i<2t_1}}\frac{1}{(t_1-1)\ldots(t_i-1)t_i}\Big)==O\Big(\sum_{1<t_1\leq n}\frac{1}{t_1^2}\Big)=O(1).$$

Hence $K_n(j)-L_n'(j)=M_n(j,j)-M_n(j,o)=\sum_{i=0}^{j-1}(M(j,i+1)-M(j,i))=O(j)$. □

Theorem 3.6. The average number of messages used by Algorithm-D is bounded by (at most) $0.7075nH_n+O(n)$.

Proof.

By theorem 3.4. and lemma 3.5. the average number of messages used by Algorithm-D can be bounded as follows (for any fixed l):

$$n(H_n-\sum_{j=1}^{l}(1/2)^jL_n(j))+O(n)\leq n(H_n-\sum_{j=1}^{l}(1/2)^jL_n'(j))+O(n)=$$

$$=n(H_n-\sum_{j=1}^{l}(1/2)^jK_n(j))+O(n.\sum_{j=1}^{l}(1/2)^jj)+O(n)=$$

$$=n(H_n-\sum_{j=1}^{l}(1/2)^jK_n(j))+O(n).$$

The result now follows by using the upper bound on the latter expression, derived in the proof of theorem 3.3. □

4. References.

[1] Bodlaender, H.L. and J. van Leeuwen, New upperbounds for decentralized extrema-finding in a ring of processors, Tech. Rep. RUU-CS-85-15, Dept. of Computer Science, University of Utrecht, Utrecht, 1985.

[2] Burns, J.E., A formal model for message passing systems, Techn. Rep. 91, Computer Sci. Dept., Indiana University, Bloomington, IN., 1980.

[3] Chandler, K.N., The distribution and frequency of record values, J. Roy. Stat. Soc., Series B, 14(1952) 220-228.

[4] Chang, E., and R. Roberts, An improved algorithm for decentralized extrema-finding in circular configurations of processes, C. ACM 22 (1979) 281-283.

[5] David, F.N., and D.E. Barton, Combinatorial chance, Charles Griffin & Comp., London, 1962.

[6] Dolev, D., M. Klawe, and M. Rodeh, An O(nlogn) unidirectional distributed algorithm for extrema finding in a circle, J. Algorithm 3 (1982) 245-260.

[7] Foster, F.G., and A. Stuart, Distribution-free tests in time-series based on the breaking of records, J. Roy. Stat. Soc., Series B, 16(1954) 1-13.

[8] Franklin, W.R., On an improved algorithm for decentralized extrema finding in circular configurations of processors, C.ACM 25(1982) 336-337.

[9] Gallager, R.G., P.A. Humblet, and P.M. Spira, A distributed algorithm for minimum-weight spanning trees, ACM Trans. Prog. Lang. and Syst. 5(1983) 66-77.

[10] Haghighi-Talab, D., and C. Wright, On the distribution of records in a finite sequence of observations, with an application to a road traffic problem, J. Appl. Prob. 10(1973) 556-571.

[11] Hirschberg, D.S., and J.B. Sinclair, Decentralized extrema-finding in circular configurations of processors, C.ACM 23(1980) 627-628.

[12] Korach, E., D.Rotem, and N. Santoro, A probabilistic algorithm for decentralized extrema-finding in a circular configuration of processors, Res. Rep. CS-81-19, Dept. of Computer Science, Univ. of Waterloo, Waterloo, 1981.

[13] LeLann, G., Distributed systems-towards a formal approach, in: B. Gilchrist (ed.), Information Processing 77 (IFIP), North- Holland Publ. Comp., Amsterdam, 1977, pp. 155-160.

[14] Pachl, J., E. Korach, and D. Rotem, A technique for proving lower bounds for distributed maximum-finding algorithms, Proc. 14th ACM Symp. Theory of Computing, 1982, pp.378-382.

[15] Peterson, G.L., An O(nlogn) unidirectional algorithm for the circular extrema problem, ACM Trans. Prog. Lang. and Syst. 4(1982) 758-762.

[16] Renyi, A., Egy megfigyeléssorozat kiemelkedő elemeiről (On the extreme elements of observations), MTA III. Oszt. Közl. 12(1962) 105-121.

[17] Santoro, N., E. Korach, and D. Rotem, Decentralized extrema-finding in circular configurations of processors: and improved algorithm, Congr. Numer. 34(1982) 401-412.

[18] van Leeuwen, J., and R.B. Tan, An improved upperbound for distributed election in bidirectional rings of processors, Tech. Rep. RUU-CS-85-23, Dept. of Computer Science, University of Utrecht, Utrecht, 1985.

ALGORITHMS FOR VISIBILITY REPRESENTATIONS OF PLANAR GRAPHS †

Roberto Tamassia ‡

Coordinated Science Laboratory
and
Department of Electrical and Computer Engineering
University of Illinois at Urbana-Champaign
Urbana, Illinois 61801

Ioannis G. Tollis

Coordinated Science Laboratory
and
Department of Computer Science
University of Illinois at Urbana-Champaign
Urbana, Illinois 61801

ABSTRACT

We investigate *visibility representations* of planar graphs, which are constructed by mapping vertices to horizontal segments, and edges to vertical segments that intersect only adjacent vertex-segments. We consider three types of visibility representations, and present linear time algorithms for testing the existence of and constructing visibility representations. Applications of our results can be found in VLSI layout compaction, and in efficient embedding of graphs in the rectilinear grid.

1. INTRODUCTION

Two parallel segments of a given set are said to be *visible* if they can be joined by a segment orthogonal to them, which does not intersect any other segment. In this paper, we investigate *visibility representations* of graphs, which are constructed by mapping vertices to horizontal segments, and edges to vertical segments drawn between visible vertex-segments. It is easy to see that a graph that admits such a representation must be planar. Applications of visibility representations can be found in several areas, including VLSI layout compaction, [9].

Otten and van Wijk, [8], gave a method for constructing a representation of a planar 2-connected graph such that vertices are represented by horizontal segments and edges by vertical segments having only points in common with the pair of horizontal segments corresponding to

† This research was partially supported by the Joint Services Electronics Program under Contract N00014-84-C-0149. Roberto Tamassia was supported in part by a Fulbright grant.

‡ On leave from: Dipartimento di Informatica e Sistemistica - Universita' di Roma, "La Sapienza" - Via Buonarroti 12 - 00185 Roma, Italy.

the vertices they connect, see fig. 1.b. Note that visible horizontal segments do not necessarily correspond to adjacent vertices in the graph. In the following, this representation will be referred to as *weak-visibility representation*. Duchet et al., [1], proved that every planar graph admits such a representation.

Melnikov, [7], suggested the problem of characterizing the graphs whose vertices can be represented by horizontal line intervals (which may or may not contain the endpoints) in the plane, such that two vertices are adjacent if and only if their associated intervals are visible, see fig. 1.c. Thomassen, [13], showed that all 3-connected planar graphs admit this representation, which will be called *ϵ-visibility representation*.

Another problem that naturally arises in this context is the following: Characterize the class of graphs whose vertices can be represented by horizontal segments such that two vertices are adjacent if and only if their corresponding segments are visible, see fig. 1.d. Such a representation will be called *strong-visibility representation* and it differs from the weak-visibility representation because it *requires* that visible vertex-segments correspond to adjacent vertices. Luccio et al., [6], gave a partial solution to the above problem by requiring that the endpoints of all the horizontal segments have distinct x-coordinates. Namely, they defined a new family of graphs, called *ipo-triangular graphs* (graphs that can be transformed into planar multigraphs with all triangular internal faces, by successive duplications of existing edges), and proved that a graph admits a strong-visibility representation with the above restriction on the x-coordinates if and only if it is ipo-triangular.

The main contributions of this paper are:

a) We unify and extend the results of Otten and van Wijk and of Duchet et al. on the weak-visibility representation by giving a linear time algorithm for constructing a weak-visibility representation of any planar graph.

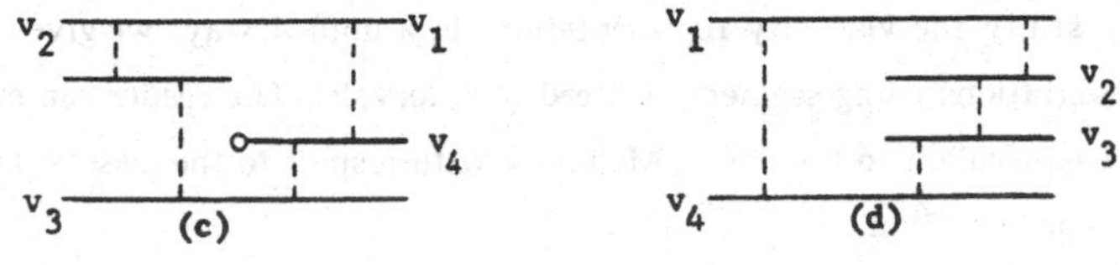

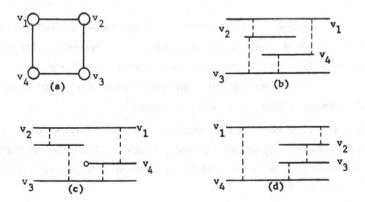

Figure 1 The three visibility representations.

b) We present a complete solution of Melnikov's problem by showing that a graph admits an ϵ-visibility representation if and only if it is is planar and there is a planar embedding for it such that all cutpoints appear on the boundary of the same face.† We also give two linear time algorithms, one for testing the above condition, and the other for constructing an ϵ-visibility representation.

c) Finally, we give a complete characterization of the class of graphs that admit a strong-visibility representation and we show how to efficiently construct one in the case of maximal planar graphs and 4-connected planar graphs.

Another application of our results in the field of VLSI layout is to the problem of *minimal-node-cost* planar embedding. This problem has been considered by Storer, [10], and consists of finding an embedding of a graph in the rectilinear grid where the total number of bends along edges is minimum. The techniques described in this paper can be used as the core of a linear time heuristic algorithm for this problem which yields better performance guarantees than the heuristics given by Storer, [11].

In the next section, we give formal definitions of the three visibility representations. In each of the subsequent sections, we present the results on weak-, ϵ-, and strong-visibility representations, respectively.

2. PRELIMINARIES AND DEFINITIONS

Let S be a set of horizontal nonoverlapping segments in the plane. Two segments s, s' of S are said to be *visible* if they can be joined by a vertical segment not intersecting any other segment of S. Furthermore, s and s' are said to be *ϵ-visible* if they can be joined by a vertical band of nonzero width that does not intersect any other segment of S. This is equivalent to saying that s and s' can be joined by two distinct vertical segments not intersecting any other segment of S.

Definition 1 A *weak-visibility representation* (*w-visibility representation*) for a graph $G=(V,E)$ is a mapping of vertices of G into nonoverlapping horizontal segments (called *vertex-segments*) and of edges of G into vertical segments (called *edge-segments*) such that, for each edge $(u,v) \in E$, the associated edge segment has its endpoints on the vertex-segments corresponding to u and v, and it does not cross any other vertex-segment. □

In order to study the visibility representations in a unified way, we give a definition of ϵ-visibility representations using segments instead of intervals. The reader can easily verify that our definition is equivalent to the one of Melnikov with respect to the class of graphs that admit an ϵ-visibility representation.

† This characterization has been independently discovered by the authors [12] and by Wismath [14].

Definition 2 An *ϵ-visibility representation* for a graph G is a w-visibility representation with the additional property that two vertex-segments are ϵ-visible if and only if the corresponding vertices of G are adjacent. □

Definition 3 A *strong-visibility representation* (*s-visibility representation*) for a graph G is a w-visibility representation with the additional property that two vertex-segments are visible if and only if the corresponding vertices of G are adjacent. □

It is easy to show that if a graph admits any of the three aforementioned visibility representations, then it is planar. In the remaining part of this section, we present some preliminary results that will be used later. A *PERT-digraph* $D=(V,A)$ is an acyclic digraph with exactly one source, s and one sink, t. We usually associate a positive length with each arc of D. A well-known problem on PERT-digraphs is the following: For each vertex v of D, find the length of the longest path from s to v. This quantity will be denoted by $\alpha(v)$. The *critical path method* solves this problem in $O(|A|)$ time, [3].

An *st-numbering* for a graph $G=(V,E)$, where s and t are two distinct vertices of G, is a one-to-one mapping $\xi: V \rightarrow \{1,2,\cdots,|V|\}$, such that: $\xi(s)=1$, $\xi(t)=|V|$, and each vertex $v \neq s,t$ has two adjacent vertices u, w for which $\xi(u) < \xi(v) < \xi(w)$. Given an *st*-numbering ξ for a graph $G=(V,E)$, we construct a digraph $D=(V,A)$ by orienting every edge from the lowest numbered vertex to the highest one. Namely, $[u,v] \in A$ if and only if $(u,v) \in E$ and $\xi(u) < \xi(v)$. The digraph D, which is *induced* by ξ, is clearly acyclic and has exactly one source, s, and one sink, t, i.e. it is a PERT-digraph. Lempel, Even, and Cederbaum [5] showed that, for every 2-connected graph and every edge (s,t), there exists an *st*-numbering. A linear time algorithm for finding it has been presented by Even and Tarjan [2]. Let D be a planar 2-connected digraph, induced by some *st*-numbering, and $\hat{D}$ any planar embedding of D. We denote with $l(f)$ and $h(f)$ the lowest and highest numbered vertices on the boundary of a face f of $\hat{D}$.

Lemma 1 Each face f of $\hat{D}$ consists of two directed paths from $l(f)$ to $h(f)$. □

Lemma 2 All outgoing (ingoing) arcs of any vertex v of $\hat{D}$ appear consecutively around v. □

3. WEAK-VISIBILITY REPRESENTATION

First, we describe a linear time algorithm for constructing a w-visibility representation of a planar 2-connected graph $G=(V,E)$. We use some of the ideas introduced in the construction of Otten and van Wijk, [8]. Next, we extend this algorithm in order to construct a w-visibility representation of any planar graph, thus giving an alternative proof of the result of Duchet et al., [1]. For the sake of simplicity, we will use the same notation for the vertex-segments of the visibility representations and their corresponding vertices in the graph. The same will be done for the edge-segments and their corresponding edges.

Algorithm *W-VISIBILITY*

Input: A planar 2-connected graph $G=(V,E)$.

Output: A w-visibility representation for G such that each vertex- and edge-segment has endpoints with integer coordinates.

1. Select an edge $(s,t)\in E$ and compute an st-numbering for G. Let D be the directed graph induced by the st-numbering.

2. Find a planar representation $\hat{D}$ of D such that the arc $[s,t]$ is on the external face and the rest of D lies on the right side of $[s,t]$, [4]. Use $\hat{D}$ to construct a new digraph D^* as follows: Vertices of D^* are the faces of $\hat{D}$. There is an arc $[f,g]$ in D^* if face f shares an arc $a=[v,w]$, distinct from $[s,t]$, with face g and a is positively oriented with respect to f, i.e., face f is on the left side of a, when a is traversed from the tail to the head. Note that D^* is a 2-connected planar PERT-digraph, with source, s^*, (the internal face containing arc $[s,t]$) and sink, t^*, (the external face).

3. Apply the *critical path method* to D^* with all arc-lengths equal to 2. This gives the function $\alpha(f)$ for each vertex f of D^*.

4. Construct the w-visibility representation as follows:

   4.1 Use the st-numbering computed in step 1 to assign y-coordinates to horizontal vertex-segments.

   4.2 Set the x-coordinate of arc $[s,t]$ equal to -1.

   4.3 For any other arc a of $\hat{D}$, set the x-coordinate of the corresponding vertical edge-segment equal to an integer j, with $\alpha(f)<j<\alpha(g)$, where f and g are the faces of $\hat{D}$ sharing a in their contour.

   4.4 Set the y-coordinates of the endpoints of each edge-segment equal to the ones of the connected vertex-segments.

   4.5 Set the x-coordinates of the left and right endpoint of each vertex-segment equal to the minimum and maximum x-coordinates of their incident arcs, respectively. If a vertex-segment v is incident to exactly two edge-segments with the same x-coordinate, x_v, then set the x-coordinates of the endpoints of v to x_v-1 and x_v, respectively. □

Note A more compact representation can be obtained modifying the algorithm as follows: *(i)* in step 3, set all arc-lengths equal to 1; *(ii)* in step 4.1, assign y-coordinates to horizontal vertex-segments applying the critical path method also to the graph D; *(iii)* in step 4.3, set $j=\min\{\alpha(f),\alpha(g)\}$; *(iv)* do not perform the second part of step 4.5. This last modification causes vertices of degree two, except s and t, to be represented by a single point.

An example of the construction performed by the algorithm *W-VISIBILITY* is given in fig. 2. Figure 2.a shows a planar embedding $\hat{D}$ along with the corresponding D^*. Vertices of $\hat{D}$ and D^* are represented by white and black circles, respectively. The white vertices are numbered

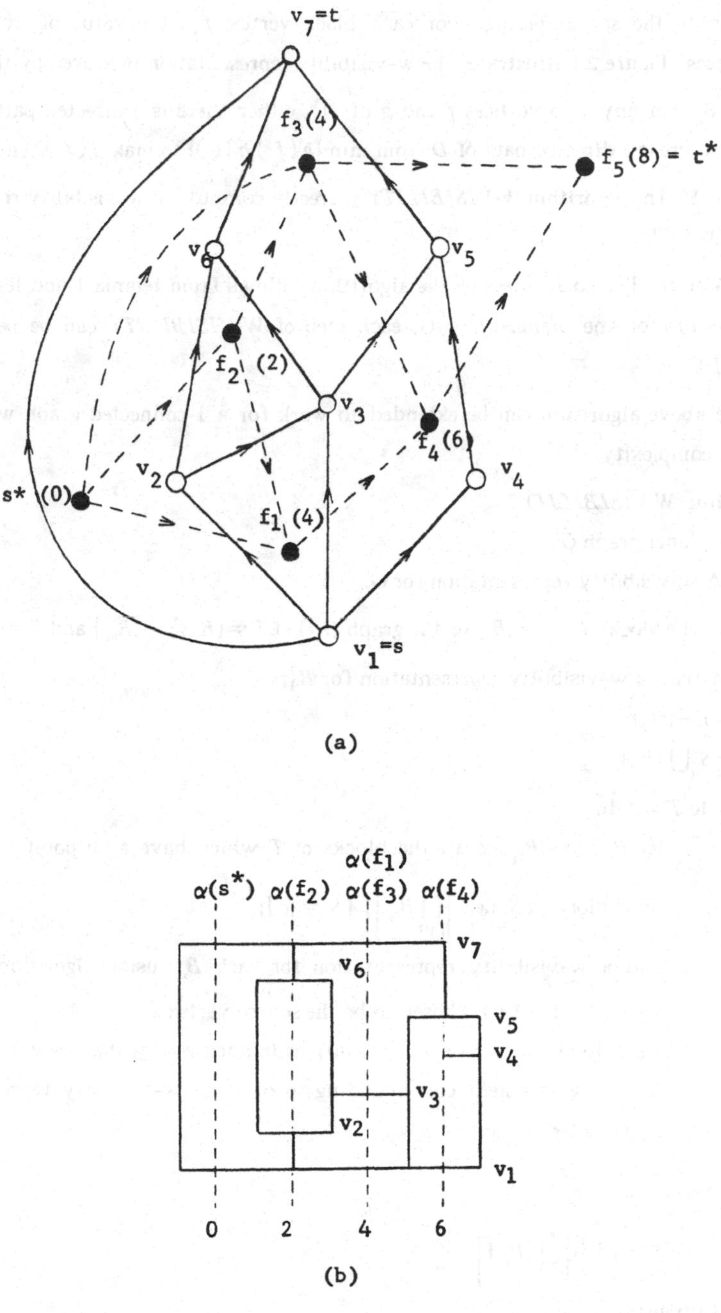

Figure 2 Running example for algorithm *W-VISIBILITY*

according to the st-numbering. For each black vertex f_i, the value of $\alpha(f_i)$ is shown in parentheses. Figure 2.b illustrates the w-visibility representation produced by the algorithm.

Lemma 3 For any two vertices f and g of D^*, either there is a directed path of D^* between them, or there is a directed path of D from $\min\{h(f),h(g)\}$ to $\max\{l(f),l(g)\}$. □

Theorem 1 The algorithm *W-VISIBILITY* correctly computes a w-visibility representation of G in time $O(|V|)$.

Proof Sketch The correctness of the algorithm follows from lemma 1 and lemma 3. Furthermore, because of the planarity of G, each step of *W-VISIBILITY* can be performed in time $O(|V|)$. □

The above algorithm can be extended to work for a 1-connected graph without increasing the time complexity.

Algorithm *W-VISIBILITY2*

Input: A planar graph G.

Output: A w-visibility representation for G.

1. Find the blocks $B_1, \cdots, B_m$ of the graph G. Let $T := \{B_1, \cdots, B_m\}$ and $S := \emptyset$.

2. Construct a w-visibility representation for B_1;

   $T := T - \{B_1\}$;

   $S := S \cup \{B_1\}$;

3. **while** $T \neq \emptyset$ **do**

   let $B_{c_1}, \cdots, B_{c_k}$ be all the blocks of T which have a cutpoint c in common with some block in S, i.e., $\left(\bigcap_{i=1}^{k} B_{c_i}\right) \bigcap S = \{c\}$;

   find a w-visibility representation for each B_{c_i} using algorithm *W-VISIBILITY*, where in step 1 c is chosen to be the source vertex s;

   scale down the above representations in such a way that they all fit on the top of the vertex-segment corresponding to c in the w-visibility representation already constructed for S;

   $T := T - \bigcup_{i=1}^{k} \{B_{c_i}\}$;

   $S := S \cup \left(\bigcup_{i=1}^{k} \{B_{c_i}\}\right)$;

   endwhile □

Theorem 2 A graph admits a w-visibility representation if and only if it is planar. Furthermore, a w-visibility representation for a planar graph can be constructed in linear time. □

4. ϵ-VISIBILITY REPRESENTATION

In this section, we present a complete characterization of the class of graphs that admit an ϵ-visibility representation. Moreover, we give linear time algorithms for testing the existence of and for constructing an ϵ-visibility representation of a planar graph. The following lemma provides a necessary condition for the existence of an ϵ-visibility representation.

Lemma 4 If the graph G admits an ϵ-visibility representation, then there exists a planar embedding $\hat{G}$ of G such that all cutpoints appear on the boundary of the external face. □

The algorithm *W-VISIBILITY* described in the previous section can be extended in order to construct an ϵ-visibility representation for any 2-connected planar graph G, see fig. 3.

Algorithm *ϵ-VISIBILITY*

Input: A 2-connected planar graph G.

Output: An ϵ-visibility representation for G such that each vertex- and edge-segment has endpoints with integer coordinates.

1. Compute a w-visibility representation Γ for G using algorithm *W-VISIBILITY*.
2. **for** each internal face f of Γ **do begin**
   - 2.1 let Λ and Ψ be the sets of vertex segments on the left and right side of f, excluding $l(f)$ and $h(f)$, respectively;
   - 2.2 **for** each $\lambda \in \Lambda$ **do** extend λ moving its right endpoint to the abscissa $\alpha(f)$;
   - 2.3 **for** each $\psi \in \Psi$ **do** extend ψ moving its left endpoint to the abscissa $\alpha(f)$;

   end □

Theorem 3 Algorithm *ϵ-VISIBILITY* correctly computes an ϵ-visibility representation of a planar 2-connected graph $G=(V,E)$ in time $O(|V|)$. □

Lemma 5 Let $\hat{G}$ be a planar embedding of a separable graph $G=(V,E)$ such that every cutpoint of G appears on the external face of $\hat{G}$. Then G admits an ϵ-visibility representation that can be constructed in time $O(|V|)$.

Proof Let B_i, $i=1,\cdots,k$, be the blocks of G that have only one cutpoint c_i, $i=1,\cdots,k$ in common with the rest of G, i.e., the B_i's are the leaves of the block-cutpoint tree of G. Let v_i be a vertex of B_i distinct from c_i, appearing on the external face of $\hat{G}$, $i=1,\cdots,k$. We construct the graph G' from G by adding a new vertex x and connecting it to all the vertices v_i, $i=1,\cdots,k$. G' is 2-connected and planar. Hence, from theorem 3, it admits an ϵ-visibility representation. In particular, consider the one, Γ', produced by algorithm *ϵ-VISIBILITY* when choosing vertex x as the topmost vertex-segment. By removing x from Γ', we obtain an ϵ-visibility representation for G. The above transformation can clearly be performed in linear time. □

Note For every boundary circuit C of $\hat{G}$, there exists another planar embedding $\tilde{G}$, of the same graph G, which has the same boundary circuits, but, in $\tilde{G}$, C is external. Therefore, lemma 5

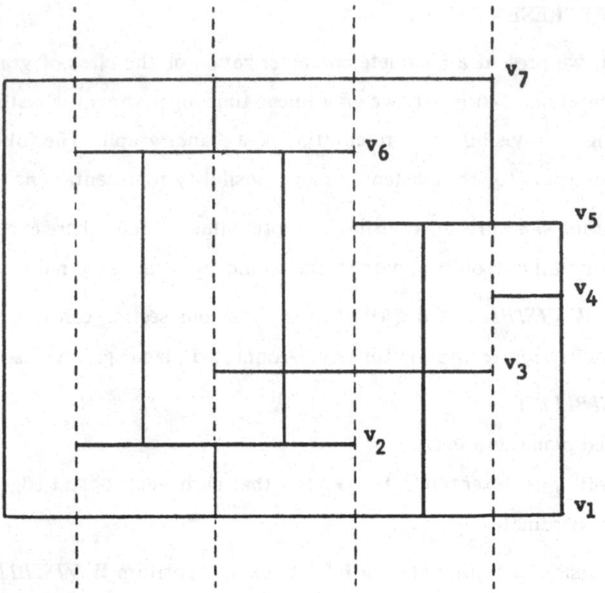

Figure 3 The ϵ-visibility representation for the graph of figure 2.

still holds if the cutpoints of G all lie in some internal face of $\hat{G}$.

An example of a graph that does not admit an ϵ-visibility representation is shown in fig. 4. From lemma 4 and lemma 5, we obtain a complete characterization of the class of graphs that admit an ϵ-visibility representation.

Theorem 4 A graph G admits an ϵ-visibility representation if and only if there is a planar embedding $\hat{G}$ for G such that all cutpoints of G appear on the boundary of the same face. □

The following equivalent characterization may be conveniently used in order to test in linear time whether a graph G admits an ϵ-visibility representation.

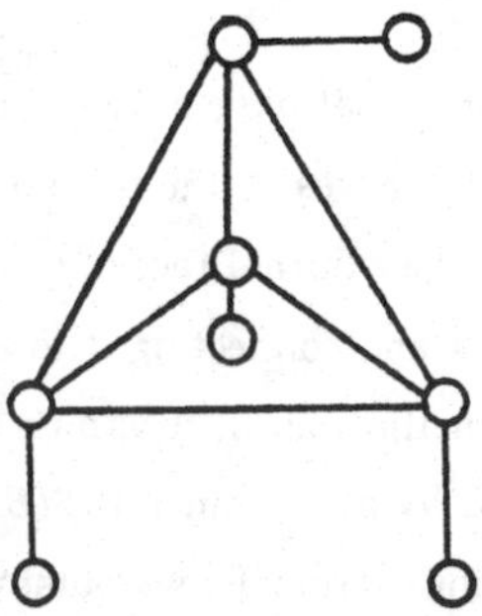

Figure 4 Example of a planar graph that does not admit an ϵ-visibility representation.

Corollary 1 Let G' be the graph obtained from G by adding a new vertex x and connecting it to all cutpoints of G. Then G admits an ϵ-visibility representation if and only if G' is planar. □

5. STRONG-VISIBILITY REPRESENTATION

From the results of section 3, one can immediately derive that:

Theorem 5 Every maximal planar graph $G=(V,E)$ admits an s-visibility representation that can be computed in time $O(|V|)$. □

Furthermore, one could use an argument similar to the proof of lemma 4 to prove the following result:

Lemma 6 If the graph G admits an s-visibility representation, then there exists a planar embedding $\hat{G}$ of G such that all cutpoints appear on the boundary of the external face. □

However, the above necessary condition is not always sufficient to guarantee the existence of an s-visibility representation. In fact, there are 2-connected graphs that do not admit an s-visibility representation. Consider for example the graph $K_{2,4}$. The reason for this is given in the next theorem.

Theorem 6 Let G be a 2-connected planar graph that has a separation pair of non-adjacent vertices v and w. If the removal of v and w separates G into at least four components, then G does not admit an s-visibility representation. □

From the definition of visibility between segments we have that, for each internal face of an s-visibility representation, there is an edge-segment connecting the topmost and bottommost vertex-segments, see fig. 1.d. Let D be the digraph induced by some st-numbering ξ on the planar 2-connected graph G. We say that ξ is a *strong st-numbering* if there is a planar embedding $\hat{D}$ of D such that s and t appear on the boundary of the external face, and for every internal face f of $\hat{D}$, the vertices $l(f)$ and $h(f)$ are joined by the arc $[l(f),h(f)]$.

Theorem 7 A 2-connected graph G admits an s-visibility representation if and only if there is a strong st-numbering for G.

Proof Sketch *Only If:* Let Γ be an s-visibility representation for G. We can assume without loss of generality that each vertex-segment of Γ has a distinct y-coordinate. Then, a strong st-numbering can be obtained by assigning numbers from 1 to $|V|$ to vertices, according to the vertical ordering of the corresponding vertex-segments.

If: Let ξ be a strong st-numbering for G. For simplicity, assume that s and t are adjacent. To construct an s-visibility representation for G, we apply the algorithm *ϵ-VISIBILITY*, where we replace step 2.2 with step 2.2' shown below, using the st-numbering ξ and the associated planar embedding $\hat{D}$.

2.2' **for each** $\lambda \in \Lambda$ **do if** f contains the arc $[l(f),h(f)]$

then extend λ moving its right endpoint to the abscissa $\alpha(f)$

else extend λ moving its right endpoint to the abscissa $\alpha(f)-½$; □

Combining lemma 6, theorem 7, and the construction in the proof of lemma 5, we have a complete characterization of the class of graphs that admit an s-visibility representation.

Corollary 2 A graph G admits an s-visibility representation if and only if it is planar and, for each block B of G, there exists a strong st-numbering such that the associated planar embedding $\hat{B}$ contains all the cutpoints of G in B on the boundary of the external face. □

Now, we give some results that show a connection between hamiltonian paths and s-visibility representations.

Theorem 8 Let G be a planar graph, and Γ a planar embedding of G. If there is a hamiltonian path between two vertices s and t of G that lie on the boundary of the external face of Γ, then G admits an s-visibility representation. □

Corollary 3 Every 4-connected planar graph $G=(V,E)$ admits an s-visibility representation which can be computed in time $O(|V|^2)$. □

ACKNOWLEDGMENTS

We wish to thank Franco Preparata for suggesting the connection between hamiltonian paths and visibility, and Doug West for useful discussion.

REFERENCES

[1] P. Duchet, Y. Hamidoune, M. Las Vergnas, and H. Meyniel, "Representing a Planar Graph by Vertical Lines Joining Different Levels," *Discrete Mathematics*, vol. 46, pp. 319-321, 1983.

[2] S. Even and R.E. Tarjan, "Computing an st-Numbering," *Theoretical Computer Science*, vol. 2, pp. 339-344, 1976.

[3] S. Even, *Graph Algorithms*, Computer Science Press, 1979.

[4] J. Hopcroft and R. Tarjan, "Efficient Planarity Testing," *J. of ACM*, vol. 21, no. 4, pp. 549-568, 1974.

[5] A. Lempel, S. Even, and I. Cederbaum, "An Algorithm for Planarity Testing of Graphs," *Theory of Graphs, International Symposium*, Rome, pp. 215-232, 1966.

[6] F. Luccio, S. Mazzone, and C.K. Wong, "A Note on Visibility Graphs," Manuscript, Pisa, 1983.

[7] L.A. Melnikov, *Problem at the 6th Hungarian Colloquium on Combinatorics*. 1981.

[8] R.H.J.M. Otten and J.G. van Wijk, "Graph Representations in Interactive Layout Design," *Proc. IEEE Int. Symposium on Circuits and Systems*, New York, pp. 914-918, 1978.

[9] M. Schlag, F. Luccio, P. Maestrini, D.T. Lee, and C.K. Wong, "A Visibility Problem in VLSI Layout Compaction," pp. 259-282 in *Advances in Computing Research, vol. 2*, ed. F.P. Preparata, JAI Press Inc., 1985.

[10] J.A. Storer, "On minimal node-cost planar embeddings," *Networks*, vol. 14, pp. 181-212, 1984.

[11] R. Tamassia and I.G. Tollis, "A Provably Good Linear Algorithm for Embedding Graphs in the Rectilinear Grid," Manuscript, Urbana, May 1985.

[12] R. Tamassia and I.G. Tollis, "Plane representations of graphs and visibility betwen parallel segments," Technical Report ACT-57, Coordinated Science Laboratory, University of Illinois at Urbana-Champaign, April 1985.

[13] C. Thomassen, "Plane Representations of Graphs," pp. 43-69 in *Progress in Graph Theory*, ed. J.A. Bondy and U.S.R. Murty, Academic Press, 1984.

[14] S.K. Wismath, "Characterizing bar line-of-sight graphs," *Proc. of ACM Symposium on Computational Geometry*, Baltimore, Maryland, pp. 147-152, June 1985.

SPEEDING UP RANDOM ACCESS MACHINES BY FEW PROCESSORS

(Preliminary Version)

Friedhelm Meyer auf der Heide

FB 20-Informatik, Johann Wolfgang Goethe Universität Frankfurt

6000 Frankfurt a.M.

Fed. Rep. of Germany [1)]

Abstract: Sequential and parallel random access machines (RAMs, PRAMs) with arithmetic operations + and - are considered. PRAMs may also multiply with constants. These machines work on integer inputs. It is shown that, in contrast to bit orientated models as Turing machines or log-cost RAMs, one can in many cases speed up RAMs by PRAMs with few processors. More specifically, a RAM without indirect addressing can be uniformly sped up by a PRAM with q processors by a factor $\frac{(\log\log q)^2}{\log q}$. A similar result holds for nonuniform speed ups of RAMs with indirect addressing. Furthermore, certain networks of RAMs (such as k-dimensional grids) with q processors can be sped up significantly with only $q^{1+\epsilon}$ processors. Nonuniformly, the above speed up can even be achieved for arbitrary bounded degree networks (including powerful networks such as permutation networks or Cube-Connected Cycles), if only few input variables are allowed. It is previously shown by the author, that the speed ups for RAMs are almost best possible.

[1)] This research was done at the IBM Research Laboratory, San Jose, CA, USA.

Introduction

Parallel random access machines (PRAMs) are a widely accepted model of parallel computation. Many algorithms are known in this model which show that sometimes surprisingly strong speed ups of certain sequential algorithms are possible. On the other hand many problems look inherently sequential, i.e. there seems to be no significant speed up possible, at least when only few processors are allowed. It is known [PR] that with many, namely 2^t processors, one can speed up t steps of a Turing machine by a factor $\frac{\log\log\log t}{\log\log t}$, but no speed ups are known with poly(t) processors.

In this paper we show that such speed ups are possible for RAMs with operations + and -, uniform cost measure, and inputs given integer by integer, not bit by bit. We show that such RAMs without indirect addressing (storage addresses are functions in the *number*, but not in the *values* of the inputs) can be sped up by PRAMs with q processors by a factor $\frac{(\log\log q)^2}{\log q}$, if the PRAMs can multiply with constants. Here *uniform* means that , if the RAM computes $f: N^* \to N^*$ in time T(n) (n = #(input variables)), then the PRAM needs time $T(n)\frac{(\log\log q)^2}{\log q}$. We also can speed up RAMs with indirect addressing in a similar way, but only to the expense of nonuniformity, i.e. we need a new PRAM for each new number n of input variables. This is one of the examples where fast algorithms can be designed to the expense of nonuniformity. Other, more surprising examples are the fast nonuniform algorithms for the knapsack or traveling salesman problem [M1], [M2], or the fast nonuniform simulations of probabilistic by deterministic computations [BG], [A], [M3].

We furthermore show that even certain networks of RAMs can be sped up. If q RAMs are for example connected to a k-dimensional grid, a PRAM with $q^{1+\epsilon}$ processors can uniformly speed it up by a factor $\frac{(\log\log q)^2}{(\log q)^\delta}$, where $\delta = \frac{1}{k+1}$. Nonuniformly, we even can speed up arbitrary bounded degree networks, including powerful networks as permutation networks or Cube-Connected Cycles, as long as the number of input variables is very small relative to the number of processors.

The paper is organized as follows. In section I we define our computation models in more detail and state our results. In section II we show how to speed up straight line versions of RAMs. It turns out that, because only operations + and - are allowed, we can achieve dramatic speed ups with few processors. This result is used in the next two sections in order to show the simulations of RAMs and networks.

I. Definitions and Results

A random access machine (RAM) consists of a program and an infinite set of registers labelled by 1,2,..., each able to store one integer. Initially the first n registers contain the input consisting of n integers, finally the first m registers contain the output, m integers. In one step, a RAM1 can execute a direct storage access (i.e. the address of the accessed register only depends on the *number*, but not on the *values* of the input variables, and its computation only uses constant addresses independent on n), write a constant into register 1, add or subtract two contents of registers, or execute an If-question (if (content of register 1) > 0 then ... else...). A RAM2 can, in addition to the above, execute indirect storage accesses, i.e. use any computed value as an address.

A PRAM1 (PRAM2) with q processors P1,...,Pq consists of q RAM1s (RAM2s), the processors, and an infinite shared memory consisting of registers labelled with 1,2,.., each able to store one integer. In addition to its RAM1 (RAM2) capabilities each processor can access directly (and also indirectly) the shared memory. Each processor can also multiply a content of a register with a constant, where a number is constant, if it appears in the program, or, inductively, is the sum or product of two constants. The PRAMs are assumed to be synchronized. We allow to concurrently read in the same register of the the shared memory, but no concurrent write is allowed. (This means that for our simulations we do not need the very strong concurrent write versions of PRAMs, compare [FMRW].)

Straight line RAM1s or RAM2s are those RAM1s or RAM2s which do not use If-questions.

A network M of q RAM1s or RAM2s consists of q processors (RAM1s or RAM2s) which are partially connected according to a (communication) graph. In one step each processor can, in addition to its sequential capabilities, read an information from some register of a neighboring processor. M has no shared memory. If $s:N\to N$ is such that each Pi can reach at most s(t) different processors along paths of length at most t in the communication graph, then s is the ***spreading function*** of M.

A machine as described above is uniform (and T(n) time bounded), if it computes a function $f:N^*\to N^*$ (in time T(n), where n denotes the respective number of input variables). A family of such machines is nonuniform (and T(n) time bounded), if it contains a machine for each n which computes $f|_{N^n}$ (in time T(n)). Well known examples of nonuniform computation models are Boolean and algebraic circuits and all types of computation trees or branching programs.

In this paper we show the following results.

Theorem 1 : A uniform PRAM1 with q processors can simulate a T(n) time bounded RAM1 in time $O(T(n)\frac{(\log\log q)^2}{\log q})$.

Theorem 2 : A family of nonuniform PRAM1s with q processors can simulate a T(n) time bounded RAM2 in time $O((T(n)+n)\frac{(\log\log q)^2}{\log q})$.

Theorem 3 : A uniform PRAM1 with $q^{1+\varepsilon}$ processors can simulate a T(n) time bounded network of q RAM1s with spreading function $O(t^k)$ in time $O(T(n)\frac{(\log\log q)^2}{(\log q)^\delta})$, where $\delta=\frac{1}{k+1}$.

Theorem 4 : Let the number n of input variables the following machines deal with be a constant. A nonuniform PRAM1 with $q^{1+\varepsilon}$ processors can simulate T steps of a bounded degree network of q RAM1s in time $O(T\frac{(\log\log q)^2}{\sqrt{\log q}})$. (n is considered constant in this O-notation.)

Remark 1 : A k-dimensional grid has spreading function $O(t^k)$. Thus theorem 3 applies to it.

Remark 2 : In [M4] the author has shown that the simulations from the theorems 1 and 2 are almost best possible (up to a factor $\log\log q$).

II. Speeding up straight line RAMs

In this section we show that straight line RAM1s can be sped up significantly.

Lemma 1 : A PRAM1 with t^3 processors can simulate t steps of a straight line RAM1 M in $O((\log t)^2)$ steps.

Proof: Assume for a moment that we have computed all at most t addresses used in M. We sort them and compute their ranks, such that equal numbers have the same rank. This can be done in time $O(\log t)$ with t processors [AKS]. For our purpose even the $O((\log t)^2)$ sorting algorithm from [B] is good enough. We now replace each address by its rank. This obviously does not change the computation and has the advantage that we only access the registers 1,...,t.

Let $\bar{c}_i \varepsilon N^{t+1}$ be the vector of the contents of the t registers before step i, $c_{i,0}=1$. Then for each operation of M there is a (t+1)x(t+1) matrix A such that $\bar{c}_{i+1}=A\bar{c}_i$, where i is the time when the operation is executed. For example, if the operation is "store the sum of registers i and j into register i", then $A=E+E_{ij}$, where E is the unity matrix and E_{ij} has a one at position ij and zeros everywhere else. As the first component of $\bar{c}_i$ is 1, we also can create a constant c in register j by the matrix $E+cE_{j0}-E_{jj}$, etc. Thus we can compute in constant time the t matrices $A_1,...,A_t$ (each with the help of t^2 processors) such that $\bar{c}_{t+1}=A_tA_{t-1}\cdots A_1\bar{c}_1$. But in this way we certainly can compute $\bar{c}_{t+1}$, i.e. simulate M with t^3 processors, in time $O((\log t)^2)$, because with t^2 processors we can execute a matrix multiplication in time $O(\log t)$, and because of the associativity of this operation we get the whole product in $\log t$ stages each consisting of at most t parallel matrix multiplications. (Here we need that the processors may multiply with constants.)

It remains to show how to compute the addresses mentioned in the beginning of the proof. This can be done by the same algorithm, if we consider n to be the input variable. For this program the addresses are by the definition of direct addressing only constants which appear explicitly in the program and need not be computed. Thus we get all addresses in time $O((\log t)^2)$, which completes the simulation. q.e.d.

III. Simulating RAMs by PRAMs

We first prove theorem 1.

Let t be chosen such that $2^t t^4 \le q$. Assume we have simulated some number of steps. We now show how to simulate the next t steps. A computation of length t is a sequence of instructions M executes if the results of the If-questions are fixed. There are at most 2^t such computations, $C_1,...,C_{2^t}$. For each of them we reserve t^4 processors. Let $C=C_i$ be fixed. C is a RAM1. For each $t' \le t$ we now use t^3 processors to simulate the prefix of length t' of C. This can be done in time

$O((\log t)^2)$ by lemma 1. Now we check whether C is the computation actually executed by M. This can be done in constant time because we know all prefixes and therefore all values determining the If-questions. The above we do for all C_i in parallel. Now the bunch of processors which has identified the right computation updates the registers maintaining the storage of M. This can be done in constant time because at most t changes are necessary and we have enough processors.

Thereby we have simulated t steps of M in $O((\log t)^2)$ steps. As we may choose $t \sim \log q$ theorem 1 follows. q.e.d.

Now we prove theorem 2.

We unroll the T(n)-time bounded RAM2 for a fixed number n of input variables to a computation tree as described in [M2]. In such a tree, a node representing an arithmetic operation or a direct storage access has one child, a node representing an If-question has two children, one for each possible outcome of the question, a node representing an indirect storage access has s+1 children $v_0, \ldots, v_s$, where s denotes the number of previously accessed registers. The i-th child stands for the case that the i-th of the previously accessed registers is accessed now, i=1,...,s. The 0-th child stands for the case that the register accessed now was never accessed before. (For a detailed description of this computation tree see [M2].)

As shown in [M2] each path of this tree can be looked upon as a straight line RAM1, if we ignore the nodes associated with If-questions.

In order to apply the idea from the last simulation we try to simulate all computations of length t from some time on, for a given parameter t. But as in this case the degree of the tree can be roughly T(n), we would need $T(n)^t t^4$ processors in order to simulate all possible computations of length t as in the previous simulation. Therefore there is no (non-constant) speed up possible, if the number of processors is polynomial in T(n).

Thus we need an additional idea to obtain a speed up as demanded in theorem 2. We first remove all those branches from the computation tree which are not followed by any input. If during this procedure, a node representing an indirect storage access looses all but one of its children, this storage access was ***redundant***, i.e. for all inputs passing through this node the time when the accessed register was previously accessed is the same, or for all these inputs the accessed register was never accessed before. In this case we can clearly replace the indirect by a direct storage access. Note that these modifications can only be done to the expense of nonuniformity!

Now let t be chosen such that $p \leq 2^t t^4$. Suppose we have simulated some number of steps of the RAM2 M. We now want to simulate the next t steps. We have seen above that we do not have enough processors to simulate all computations of length t in parallel. Therefore we only simulate those computations which follow the 0-th branch at each (nonredundant) indirect addressing, i.e. which assume that the accessed register was never accessed before. As there are at most 2^t such computations, we can simulate all of them and all their prefixes in $O((\log t)^2)$ steps, as described in the previous computation.

Now we check whether one of these computations is correct, i.e. whether on one of them all the If questions are answered correctly and whether the choices of the 0-th branches at indirect addressings were correct. If we find such a computation we have simulated t steps in $O((\log t)^2)$ steps and are done.

Otherwise we locate the computation and the time when the first mistake (at an indirect addressing) occured. This can be done in constant time, because we have all the prefixes of the computations and enough processors.

Now we restart the simulation from this time on. First we simulate the indirect addressing correctly (with one processor in constant time). Then we start a new phase of simulating t steps. By this algorithm we clearly simulate M.

Each phase of trying to simulate t steps needs $O(\log(t)^2)$ steps. The number of phases we now have to simulate is not only $\frac{T(n)}{t}$, but $\frac{T(n)}{t}+m$, where m denotes the number of mistakes, i.e. the number of unsuccessful attempts to simulate t steps. The following lemma shows that we do not make too many such mistakes and thereby implies theorem 2 .

Lemma 2 : During the simulation, at most n mistakes occur (n=number of input variables).

Proof : Let B be the set of inputs following the computation of M we consider up to (not including) the indirect read, where we made a mistake. Let L be the affine subspace with smallest dimension containing B. For an input $\bar{x}\varepsilon B$ let $f(\bar{x})$ be the address used in M at this indirect storage access. Suppose that the same cell was previously accessed at time t with address $g(\bar{x})$. Let now A contain all those inputs $\bar{y}$, for which $f(\bar{y})=g(\bar{y})$ holds. One easily checks that f and g are linear functions (see [M4]). As the indirect read is nonredundant we know that $f|_B \neq g|_B$. On the other hand, $f|_A \equiv g|_A$ by construction. Thus $A \subset L' := L \cap \{\bar{y}\varepsilon R^n$, $f(\bar{x})=g(\bar{x})\}$. Thus each mistake reduces the dimension of the set of inputs following the computation we consider. After at most n mistakes this set has dimension 0, i.e. it consists of at most one point. But in this case there are no further nonredundant indirect storage accesses possible. Therefore our simulation makes no further mistakes. q.e.d.

IV. Simulating networks by RAMs

We first prove theorem 3. Let M be a network of RAM1s P1,...,Pq with spreading function s. Let p (>q) be the number of processors of the simulating PRAM1. Choose t such that $(t\, s(t))^4 2^{t\, s(t)} \leq \frac{p}{q}$. We again simulate t steps of M. For each Pi we reserve $(t\,s(t))^4 2^{t\,s(t)}$ processors. We now use an idea from [M5] to simulate t steps of M by only considering relatively small parts of M. Let Mi be the subnetwork of M consisting of all those processors which are connected via a path of length at most t to Pi. Mi has at most s(t) processors. In [M5] it is shown that after t computation steps of M and Mi, the configurations of Pi in M and Mi are the same. Thus it is sufficient to simulate M1,...,Mq for t steps. As each Mi only has s(t) processors, we can simulate it by a RAM1 in $t\,s(t)$ steps. By theorem 1 we can simulate this RAM1 by a PRAM1 with $(t\,s(t))^4 2^{t\,s(t)}$ processors in time $O(\log(t\,s(t))^2)$ steps. Because of our choice of t we have enough processors to execute these simulations for all Mi in parallel. Thus we have simulated t steps of M in $O(\log(t\,s(t))^2)$ steps. If $s(t)=O(t^k)$ for some k, we can choose $t\sim(\varepsilon\log q)^\delta$ with $\delta=\frac{1}{k+1}$ and obtain a PRAM with $q^{1+\varepsilon}$ processors which simulates T(n) steps of M in time $O(T(n)\frac{(\log\log q)^2}{(\log q)^\delta})$. q.e.d.

Now, in order to sketch the proof of theorem 4, we try to apply the same ideas to simulate arbitrary networks of RAM1s with q processors and degree bound c, say. Such a network has spreading function c^t. Let t be fixed. We specify it later. We define the Mi's as in the last proof. But now their number of processors can be exponential in t, namely up to c^t. We now interpret Mi as a PRAM1 with c^t processors which makes t steps. Combining ideas from [DL] and [M4] shows that this PRAM can nonuniformly be simulated in $d=O(2^n t^2)$ steps by a RAM1. Now we apply again theorem 1 to speed up this RAM1. With $d^4 2^d$ processors we can simulate Mi in $O((n+\log t)^2)$ steps. Thus $q d^4 2^d$ processors can simulate t steps of M in $O((n+\log t)^2)$ steps. Now choose $t\sim\sqrt{(\frac{\varepsilon\log q}{2^n})}=\Omega(\sqrt{\log q})$ because n is a constant. Then $d=q^\varepsilon$. Therefore we can simulate $\Omega(\sqrt{\log q})$ steps of M in $O((\log\log q)^2)$ steps using $q^{1+\varepsilon}$ processors. q.e.d.

References

[A] L. Adleman, Two theorems on random polynomial time, 19th IEEE-FOCS, 1978, 75-83.

[AKS] M. Ajtai, J. Komlos, E. Szemeredi, An $O(n\log n)$ sorting network , 15th ACM-STOC, 1983, 1-9.

[B] K. Batcher, Sorting networks and their applications, AFIPS spring joint computing conference 32, 1968, 307-314.

[BG] C. H. Bennett, J. Gill, Relative to a random oracle, $P^A \neq NP^A \neq co-NP^A$ with probability 1, SIAM J. on Comp. 10, 1981, 96-113.

[DL] D. Dobkin, R. Lipton, Multidimensional search problems, SIAM J. on Comp. 5, 1976, 181-186.

[FMRW] F. Fich, F. Meyer auf der Heide, P. Ragde, A. Wigderson, One , two, three ... infinity: lower bounds for parallel computation, 17th ACM-STOC, 1985, 48-58.

[M1] F. Meyer auf der Heide, A polynomial linear search algorithm for the n-dimensional knapsack problem, J. ACM 31(3), 1984, 668-676.

[M2]______,Fast algorithms for n-dimensional restrictions of hard problems, 17th ACM-STOC, 1985, 412-420.

[M3]______, Simulating probabilistic by deterministic algebraic computation trees, to appear in TCS.

[M4]______, Lower bounds for solving linear Diophantine equations on several parallel computational models, to appear in Information and Control.

[M5]______, Efficient simulations among several models of parallel computers, to appear in SIAM J. on Comp.

[PR] W. Paul, R. Reischuk, On alternation II, Acta Informatica 14, 1980, 391-403.

EFFICIENT ALGORITHMS FOR FINDING MINIMUM SPANNING FORESTS OF HIERARCHICALLY DEFINED GRAPHS

Thomas Lengauer
Fachbereich 17
Universität-Gesamthochschule Paderborn

4790 Paderborn
West Germany

Abstract

In [L 85a] a hierarchical graph model is defined that allows the exploitation of the hierarchy for the more efficient solution of graph problems on very large graphs. The model is motivated by applications in the design of VLSI circuits.

We show how to efficiently find minimum spanning forests in this graph model. We solve decision problems pertaining to minimum spanning forests in almost linear time in the length of the hierarchical description, query problems in time linear in the depth of the hierarchy and we construct minimum spanning forests in space linear in the length of the hierarchical description.

1. Introduction

In [L 85a] a hierarchical graph model has been introduced that allows to speed up the solution of graph problems by exploiting the hierarchy. The model is motivated by applications of graph algorithms in the design of hierarchically specified integrated circuits.

The exploitation of the hierarchy is necessary even for simple, e.g., linear time graph problems, because graphs arising from hierarchical descriptions can be too large to fit into the main memory of a computer. Thus running a non-hierarchical graph algorithm on graphs of this size amounts to extraordinary amounts of page swapping. For practical purposes it is important to decrease the space requirement for processing such graphs. This is done by modifying the algorithms such that they exploit the hierarchy of the graph description and need only store the hierarchical description of the graph instead of the fully expanded graph. [L 85a] presents a special method for doing this, the so-called bottom-up method, and applies the method to the solution of connectivity problems on directed and undirected graphs. [L 85b] applies the same method for testing planarity of hierarchically defined graphs.

In this paper, we will apply the bottom-up method to the problem of finding minimum spanning forests of hierarchically defined graphs. Specifically we deal with three problems pertaining to minimum spanning trees, a decision problem, a query problem, and a construction problem that requires the generation of large output.

Thus for the decision and query problem substantial time savings are achieved (over the non-hierarchical solutions up to exponential, depending on the hierarchy). The construction problem can be solved using up to exponentially less space than with a non-hierarchical algorithm.

The paper is organized as follows. Section 2 defines the hierarchical graph model. Section 3 introduces the bottom-up method. Section 4 discusses the decision problem. Section 5 considers the query problem. The construction problem is solved in Section 6. Section 7 gives conclusions.

2. Basic definitions

Definition 1: A hierarchical undirected graph $\Gamma = (G_1, \ldots, G_k)$ is a tuple of undirected graphs G_i called cells. Here the graph G_i has n_i vertices and m_i edges. p_i of the vertices are distinguished and called pins. The other $n_i - p_i$ vertices are called inner vertices. r_i of the inner vertices are distinguished and called nonterminals or hierarchical vertices. The other $n_i - r_i$ vertices are called terminals or proper vertices.

Each pin has a unique label, its name. W.l.o.g. we can assume that the pins are named with numbers between 1 and p_i. Each nonterminal has two labels, a name and a type. The type is a symbol from $\{G_1, \ldots, G_{i-1}\}$. If a nonterminal v has type G_j then v has degree p_j and each proper vertex that is a neighbour of v has a label (v,ℓ) such that $1 \leq \ell \leq p_j$. We say that the neighbour of v labeled (v,ℓ) matches the ℓ-th pin of G_j. (All neighbours of a nonterminal must be terminals.)

We assume that Γ is irredundant in the sense that each G_i is the type of some nonterminal v in some G_j, $j > i$.

The size of Γ is $n := \sum_{1 \leq i \leq k} n_i$, the edge number is $m := \sum_{1 \leq i \leq k} m_i$.

Note that with $\Gamma = (G_1, \ldots, G_k)$ also each prefix $\Gamma_i = (G_1, \ldots, G_i)$, $i < k$ is a hierarchical graph.

A hierarchical edge labelled graph is a graph such that each edge between terminals in a cell is labelled with a positive number, its length.

Definition 1 essentially describes a context-free graph grammar with axiom G_k, where each nonterminal only has one production. Thus the language of the graph grammar has one word. This word is called the expansion of Γ.

Definition 2: The expansion $E(\Gamma)$ of the hierarchical graph Γ is obtained as follows:

$k = 1$: $E(\Gamma) = G_1$. The pins of $E(\Gamma)$ are the pins of G_1.
$k > 1$: Repeat the following step for each nonterminal v of G_k, say, of type G_j:
Delete v and its incident edges. Insert a copy of $E(\Gamma_j)$ by identifying the ℓ-th pin of $E(\Gamma_j)$ with the node in G_k that is labelled (v,ℓ). (In general $E(\Gamma)$ can have multiple edges.)

The size of $E(\Gamma)$, i.e., its number of vertices is denoted by N. The number of edges of $E(\Gamma)$ is denoted by M.

The expansion of Γ naturally has a tree structure, namely the parse tree for the word $E(\Gamma)$ in the graph grammar Γ.

Definition 3: With Γ and $E(\Gamma)$ we associate the so-called hierarchy tree T that is defined as follows. Each node in T has two labels, a name and a type. (The root of T has no name.) A node of type G_i in T has r_i sons. Each son has the name and type of one of the nonterminals in G_i. T is defined inductively:

$k = 1$: T has one node with type G_1.
$k > 1$: T has a root of type G_k. The son of the root that has the name and type of the nonterminal v of type G_j in G_k is the root of the copy of the hierarchy tree for $\Gamma_j = (G_1, \ldots, G_j)$.

Clearly each node of type G_i in the hierarchy tree T corresponds to a copy of G_i in the expansion of Γ. We will sometimes identify the node $x \in T$ with this copy of G_i. (In the context of T we will use exclusively the term node. In the context of Γ we will use exclusively the term vertex.)

The terminology in the above three definitions is taken partly from the area of graph grammars (nonterminals) and partly from the area of CAD for VLSI design (cells, pins). Many subtasks of IC design can be formulated in graph theoretic terms. Examples are functional simulation, circuit extraction and verification, compaction, layout and others. The graph that is the problem instance, can be directly derived from the circuit specification. In this way hierarchical circuit specifications give rise to hierarchical graphs as defined above.

The following example of a hierarchical graph will accompany us throughout the paper.

<u>Example 1:</u> Let $\Gamma = (G_1, G_2, G_3, G_4)$ be the following hierarchical graph:

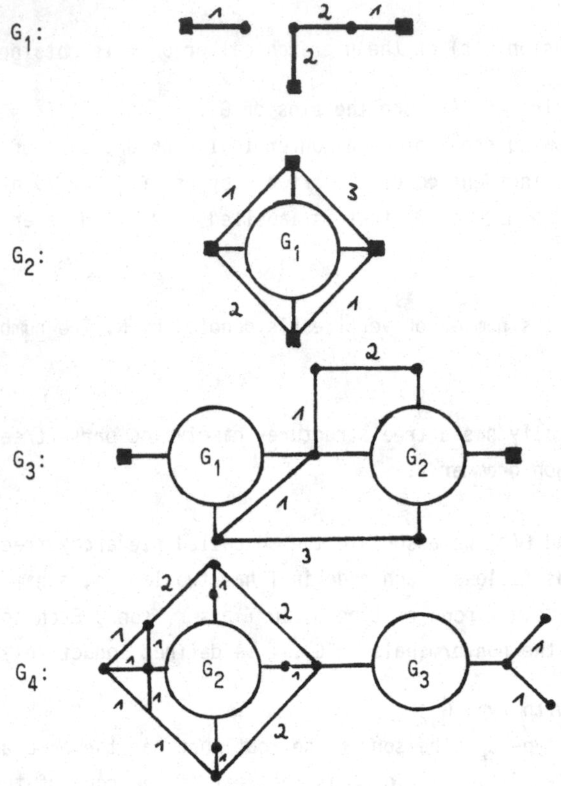

Figure 1

The expansion $E(\Gamma)$ is shown in Figure 2, the hierarchy tree is shown in Figure 3.

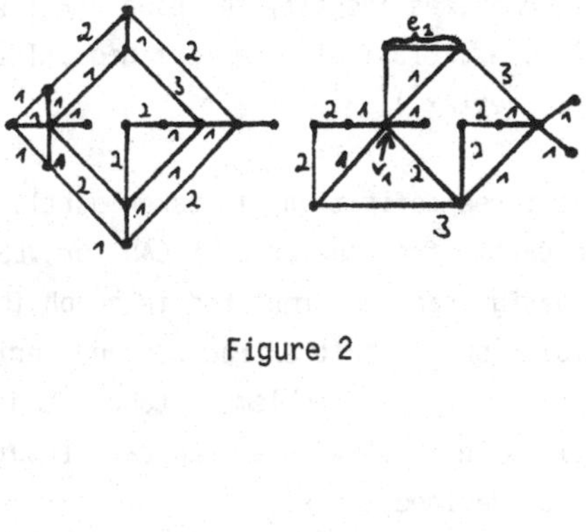

Figure 2

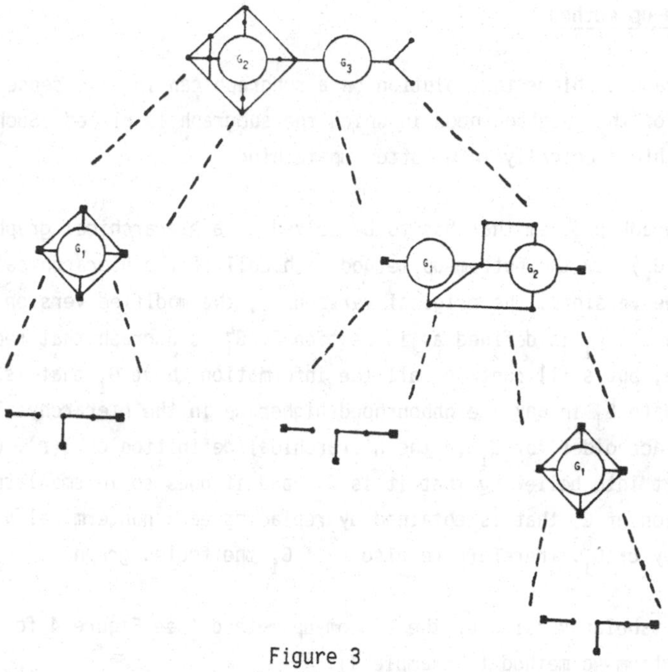

Figure 3

Here again we omitted labels on the vertices. The correspondence between pins of G_j and neighbours of a nonterminal of type G_j in cell G_i is clear by the positions of the vertices in the figure.

Each edge in $E(\Gamma)$ belongs to a unique node $x \in T$. E.g., the edge e_1 in Figure 2 belongs to the unique node in T that is of type G_3. Similarly a vertex in $E(\Gamma)$ belongs to a unique node x in T where that vertex appears as a terminal that is not a pin. E.g., the vertex v_1 belongs to the same node x in T as the edge e_1. (This is even though the vertex v_1 is also represented by pins in two descendants of x in T.) Thus an edge (vertex) in $E(\Gamma)$ can be identified by providing the path from the root of T to the node x in T the edge (vertex) belongs to, and then identifying the edge (vertex) inside x. Thus a path name is a sequence of nonterminals $v_1, \ldots, v_{\ell-1}$ followed by a terminal node v or an edge e. Here, v_1 is a nonterminal in G_k and if v_k is a nonterminal of type G_j, then v_{k+1} is a nonterminal in G_j. For technical reasons we assume path names to start with a dummy nonterminal of type G_k. Note that $E(\Gamma)$ can have multiple edges, in general, even if G_i has no multiple edges, for all i.

3. The bottom-up method

For certain graph problems the solution on a subgraph can in some sense be done independently of the neighbourhood in which the subgraph is placed. Such problems can be solved hierarchically in a bottom-up fashion.

Let P be the graph problem that has to be solved on a hierarchical graph $\Gamma = (G_1, \ldots, G_k)$. In the bottom-up method each cell of the hierarchical graph exists in three versions: the original version G_i, the modified version $\tilde{G}_i$, and the boundary graph G_i^b. G_i is defined as in Section 2. G_i^b is a graph that reduces G_i to a smaller size, but still contains all the information about G_i that is necessary in order to evaluate G_i in any neighbourhood higher up in the hierarchy. The object of G_i^b is to be placeholder for G_i in the hierarchical definition of $E(\Gamma)$. G_i^b "fools" its environment into believing that it is G_i, and it does so in small space. $\tilde{G}_i$ is the modification of G_i that is obtained by replacing each nonterminal v of type G_j in G_i by a copy of G_j^b. Therefore we also call $\tilde{G}_i$ the fooled graph.

We now give a tabular version of the bottom-up method (see Figure 4 for an application of the bottom-up method to Example 1).

	$\tilde{G}_i$	$\tilde{\tilde{G}}_i$	G_i^b	D_i
i = 1				
i = 2				
i = 3				
i = 4				
	column 1	column 2	column 3	column 4

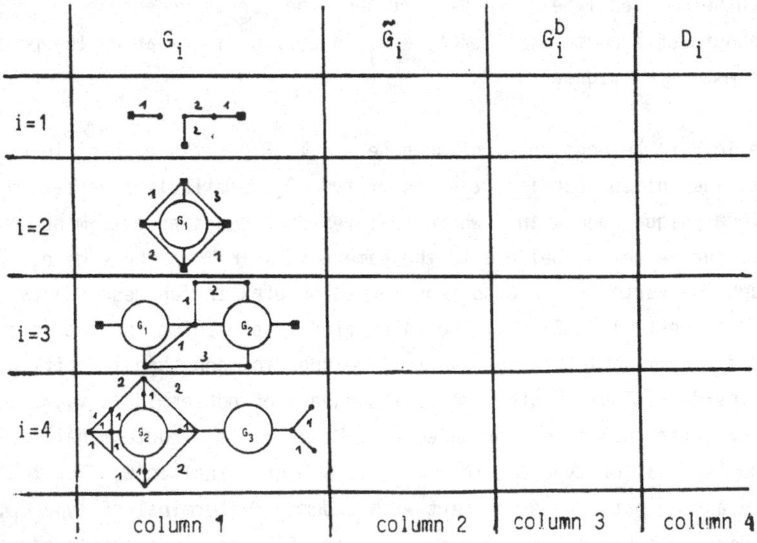

Figure 4

We use a so-called BU-table with one row for each cell in the hierarchical graph. In row i we compute the versions of G_i and the solution D_i pertaining to G_i. Initially only the first column is filled. The bottom-up method fills this table top-down row by row; each row is filled left to right. Let us look at row i. The entry in the second column is computed by simply substituting G_j^b for each nonterminal vertex of type G_j in G_i, i.e., in the graph depicted in the first entry of row i. Since $j < i$, G^b_j can be read out of the third entry of row j at the time row i is computed. The third and forth entry of row i are computed from the second entry by a procedure which is problem-specific, i.e., different for different graph problems. Defining this procedure is called "personalizing" the bottom-up method for a specific graph problem. This procedure also yields additional information stored in the table entry D_i.

The result of the bottom-up method is the filled BU-table of Figure 4. This table contains the solution of the graph problem on $E(\Gamma)$ in some encoded and compressed form. A second pass over this table is necessary to compute the solution of the graph problem. Note that G_i^b does not contain any nonterminals, and therefore $\tilde{G}_i$ does neither. For the bottom-up method to be efficient G_i^b must be small, if possible of size $O(p_i)$ and easy to compute.

In this paper we discuss three problems:

1. The Decision Problem D:

Input: A hierarchical edge-labelled graph $\Gamma = (G_1, \ldots, G_k)$, an integer ℓ.

Question: Does $E(\Gamma)$ have a spanning forest of size $\leq \ell$?

The Decision Problem will be solved in almost linear time in m+n.

2. The Query Problem Q:

Input: A hierarchical edge-labelled graph $\Gamma = (G_1, \ldots, G_k)$. Two vertices v, w of $E(\Gamma)$ given by path names.

Question: What is the cost of the unique path from v to w in a fixed minimum spanning forest of $E(\Gamma)$, if such a path exists? (Otherwise the cost is infinite.)

The Query Problem will be solved using a preprocessing phase in which the BU-table is filled. The complexity of the preprocessing phase is the same as that of solving the decision problem. In this preprocessing phase a minimum spanning forest will be computed that serves as a reference for all queries to follow. Then each query can be answered in time $O(k)$.

3. The Construction Problem C:

Input: A hierarchical edge-labelled graph $\Gamma = (G_1, \ldots, G_k)$

Goal: Generate a minimum spanning forest for $E(\Gamma)$.

The Construction Problem will be solved by starting again with filling up the BU-table in the same time it takes to solve the decision problem. Then a traversal of the hierarchy tree will compute the minimum spanning forest in time $O((M+N)k)$ (in time $O(N)$ on a large subclass of hierarchical graphs) and in space $O(m+n)$.

The following section of the paper describes each problem in turn.

4. The decision problem

We personalize the bottom-up method as follows:

Construction of G_i^b:

Step 1: Use a nonhierarchical minspan algorithm, such as the one described in [GGST 85], to generate a minimum spanning forest T_i for $\tilde{G}_i$. Reduce T_i as follows:

Step 2: Consecutively delete leaves of T_i that are not pins.

Step 3: Collapse paths in T_i as follows: If $p = v_1, \ldots, v_\ell$ is a path such that $v_2, \ldots, v_{\ell-1}$ are degree -2 vertices and v_1, v_ℓ are not, then delete $v_2, \ldots, v_{\ell-1}$ and give the edge between v_1 and v_ℓ the length of the longest edge on p.

The resulting forest is G_i^b.

D_i is a number giving the cost of a minimum spanning forest of $E(\Gamma_i)$. If i = 1 then D_i is the cost of T_i (after Step 1). If i > 1 then D_i is computed as follows: D_i is the sum of the lengths of all edges in G_i that are in T_i (after Step 1), plus the sum of the D_j for each nonterminal v of type G_j minus the length of all edges from a copy of G_j^b that are inside $\tilde{G}_i$ but not inside T_i (after Step 1).

Furthermore we associate the minimum spanning forest T_i of $\tilde{G}_i$ with D_i, i.e., we store T_i along with D_i in the BU-table.

Clearly G_i^b has size $O(p_i)$, since G_i^b is a forest all of whose leaves are pins and whose internal nodes have degree at least 3. Thus G_i has size $O(m_i+n_i)$. Furthermore, constructing G_i^b is no harder than finding a minimum spanning forest of $\tilde{G}_i$. If we use the nonhierarchical minspan algorithm of [GGST 85] this takes time $O(m_i \log\log^* m_i + n_i)$.

Thus filling the BU-table takes time $\sum_{i=1}^{k} O(m_i \log\log^* m_i + n_i) = O(m \log\log^* m + n)$.

Figure 5 gives the BU-table for Example 1.

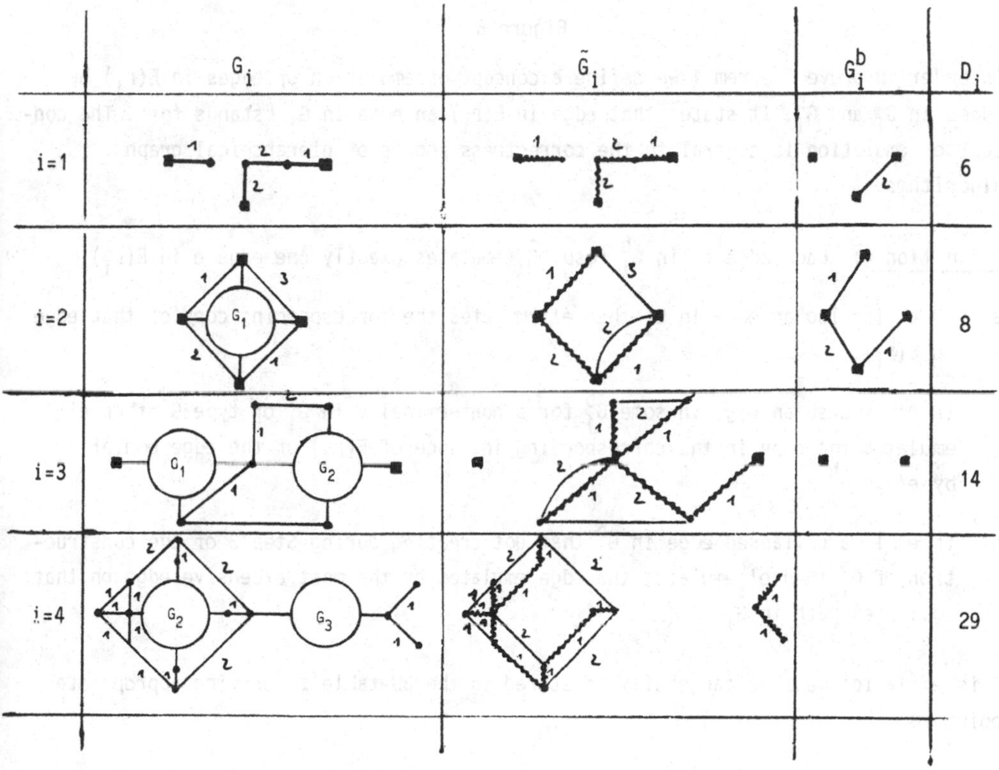
G_i
$\tilde{G}_i$
G_i^b
D_i
i=1
6
i=2
8
i=3
14
i=4
29
G_1
G_2
G_3

Figure 5

The wiggly lines in Figure 5 represent the edges in the minimum spanning forests T_i (after Step 1).

The correctness of the above procedure is given by the following theorem.

<u>Theorem 1:</u> D_k is the cost of a minimum spanning forest of $E(\Gamma)$.

The minimum spanning forest represented by Figure 5 is depicted in Figure 6.

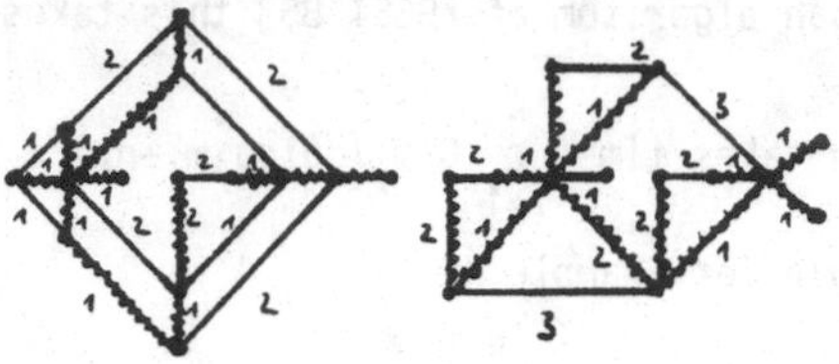

Figure 6

In order to prove Theorem 1 we define a concept of emulation of edges in $E(\Gamma_i)$ by edges in $\tilde{G}_i$ and G_i^b. It states that edge in $E(\Gamma_i)$ an edge in G_i "stands for". The concept of emulation is central to the correctness proofs of hierarchical graph algorithms.

<u>Definition 4:</u> Each edge e' in G_i^b resp. $\tilde{G}_i$ emulates exactly one edge e in $E(\Gamma_i)$:

a) if e' is also an edge in G_i then e' emulates the corresponding copy of that edge in $E(\Gamma_i)$.

b) if e' is also an edge in some G_j^b for a nonterminal v in G_i of type G_j then e' emulates the copy in the corresponding instance of $E(\Gamma_j)$ of the edge emulated by e' in G_j^b.

c) if e' is a collapsed edge in G_i^b that got creating during Step 3 of the construction of G_i^b then e' emulates the edge emulated by the most expensive edge on that collapsed path in $\tilde{G}_i$.

This emulation mapping can easily be stored in the BU-table by proving appropriate pointers.

Theorem 1 is proved using the following fact.

Fact [T 83]: Let G be a graph and T be a spanning forest of G. T is a minimum spanning forest, exactly if for each edge $e = \{v,w\} \notin T$ the path between v and w in T contains no edge e' such that length(e') > length(e).

For the proof of Theorem 1 we describe the minimum spanning forest T of $E(\Gamma)$ that is represented in the BU-table.

<u>Definition 5:</u> For i, $1 \leq i \leq k$ define $T_{min,i}$ inductively to be the following subgraph of $E(\Gamma_i)$:

a) $T_{min,i}$ contains all edges of $E(\Gamma_i)$ emulated by edges of T_i by way of Definition 4a.

b) For each nonterminal v of type G_j ($j < i$) in G_i, $T_{min,i}$ contains all edges of the corresponding copy of $E(\Gamma_j)$ that are also in $T_{min,j}$ except for the edges emulated by edges in the corresponding copy of G_j^b by way of Definition 4b, 4c, that are not in T_i.

By Definition 4 edges in T_i emulate edges in $T_{min,i}$ and edges that are not in T_i emulate edges that are not in $T_{min,i}$. Furthermore, obviously D_i is exactly the cost of $T_{min,i}$.

Thus proving Theorem 1 can be done by showing that $T_{min,i}$ is a minimum spanning forest. The following lemma proves a few simple properties of $T_{min,i}$.

<u>Lemma 1:</u> a) $T_{min,i}$ is a spanning forest.

b) Let p_1, p_2 be two pins of G_i. The length of the longest edge is the same on the path between p_1 and p_2 in G_i^b and in $T_{min,i}$. (Note that by a) if these paths exist they are unique.)

c) Let e' be an edge in $G_i - T_i$. Let e be the edge emulated by e' in $E(\Gamma_i) - T_{min,i}$. Then the length of the longest edge is the same on the path between the two endpoints of e' in T_i and of e in $T_{min,i}$.

We now complete the proof of Theorem 1:

<u>Lemma 2:</u> $T_{min,i}$ is a minimum spanning forest of $E(\Gamma_i)$.

<u>Proof Sketch:</u> We test the property given in the Fact on each edge $e \in E(\Gamma_i) - T_{min,i}$ using induction on i and applying Lemma 1c. □

Note that, for Example 1, $T_{min,k}$ is depicted in Figure 6.

5. The query problem

We want to answer queries of the following type:

Q(v,w): Cost of the unique path from v to w in $T_{min,k}$.

Here v and w are given by path names. If v and w are not connected then $Q(v,w) = \infty$.

In this section we prove the following theorem.

<u>Theorem 2:</u> After filling the BU-table and adding additional information in time $O(m\log\log^* m+n)$ we can answer queries of the type $Q(v,w)$ in time $O(k)$ per query.

<u>Proof:</u> In order to answer such queries efficiently we have to collect more information about paths in $T_{min,k}$ and their cost in the BU-table. To this end we modify the emulation mapping of $E(r)$, such that each edge e in $\tilde{G}_i$ resp. G_i^b emulates all edges in $E(r_i)$ on the path that got collapsed to e. (We omit a formal definition here.)

We now describe the additional information necessary to quickly answer queries, and we sketch, how it is computed. First, with each edge e in $\tilde{G}_i$, G_i^b we associate a value sumlength(e) that is the sum of the lengths of all edges emulated by e. Clearly all sumlength(e) values for edges in $\tilde{G}_i$, G_i^b can be computed in time $O(n_i+m_i)$.

The value sumlength(e) determines the length of the collapsed path in $E(r_i)$ emulated by e in $\tilde{G}_i$ resp. G_i^b. The sumlength values will be used to compute lengths of path segments in $T_{min,k}$. Furthermore, we label vertices in G_i^b with vertices in $\tilde{G}_i$. Intuitively, a vertex w in G_i^b is labelled with a vertex v in $\tilde{G}_i$ if v gets collapsed into w in Step 2 or 3 of the reduction from $\tilde{G}_i$ to G_i^b. There are two ways in which a vertex v can be collapsed into a vertex w.

1. In Step 2 if a subtree of T_i is deleted by cutting it off at vertex w, then all vertices v in the subtree are collapsed into w and thus all of them are labels of w.

2. In Step 3 if a path p is collapsed then the vertices on the path are collapsed into the endpoints of the path. Specifically, let e be the longest edge on p. A vertex v is collapsed into the endpoint of p that is on the same side of e as v.

With each vertex label v of a vertex w we now associate additional information that allows us to compute the cost of the collapsed path from v to w. Specifically, we attach the following values to vertex labels.

1. If v labels a vertex w due to collapsing in Step 2 then in addition to the label v we store

   cc(v) : the cost of the collapsed path from v to w in T_i, i.e., the sum of all sumlength values along the path in T_i from v to w.

2. If v labels a vertex w due to collapsing in Step 3 then in addition to the label v we store

   edge(v) : The edge out of w that represents the collapsed path.

   ccin(v) : The cost (sum of all sumlength values) of the part of the collapsed path p between v and w.

   ccout(v): The cost (sum of all sumlength values) of the collapsed path p between v and the other endpoint of edge(v).

This is ccin is the cost of the portion of the path from v to an endpoint that does not go across the longest edge on p. Analogously, in ccout we store the cost of the portion that goes across the longest edge on p. With an appropriate implementation all of these data can be computed in time $O(n_i)$.

We will now show, how we use this information to answer a query Q(v,w) quickly.

We process the path names of v and w backwards simultaneously. These path names have a left segment that is identical for v and w and right segments for which all prefixes are different in v and w.
In the first phase of the query algorithm we process the right segments (independently) from right to left. In the second phase of the algorithm we process the (identical) left segments of both path names from right to left. We can equivalently think of the algorithm as performing a postorder traversal on the subtree of the hierarchy tree T that is given by the union of the two search paths from the root of T to the nodes in T that v resp. w belong to (see Figure 7).

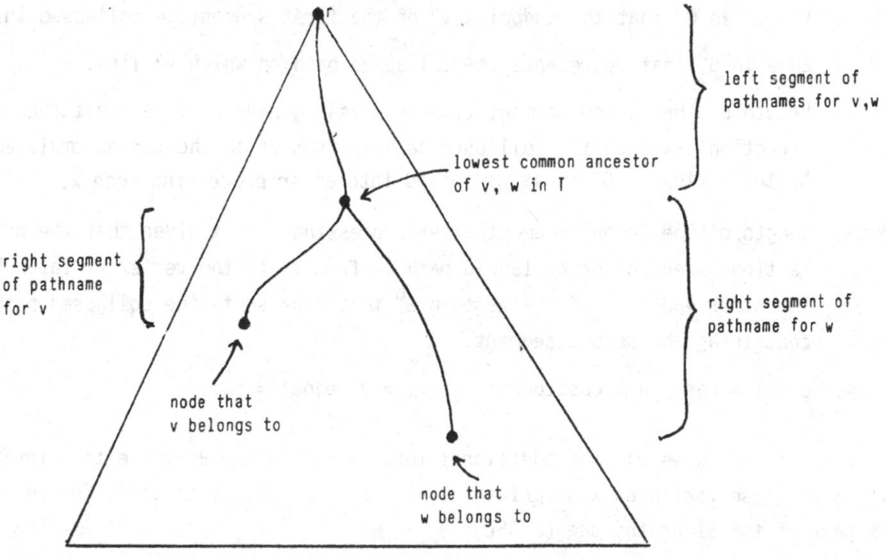

Figure 7

We now describe the first phase of the algorithm.

Let p_{min} be the path from v to w in $T_{min,k}$. In the first phase we successively collapse portions of p_{min} that are adjacent to v resp. w. When working on a node x of type G_j in T, say, on the search path for v, we collapse a portion of p_{min} that runs through the corresponding copy of G_j.

During the bottom-up search of the right segment of the path name for v the path p_{min} will be considered to consist of three segments:

The first segment runs from v through portions of $T_{min,k}$ that have been cut off in Step 2 of the construction of some G_j^b to a vertex v" in $T_{min,k}$ that is located on a collapsed path emulated by an edge e in $\tilde{G}_i$. The second segment runs from v" to the endpoint of the collapsed path. The rest of p_{min} constitutes the third segment.

The first segment of p_{min} we can find while processing node x. The second segment is not completely determined when processing node x. However, there are only two possibilities, namely the portions of the collapsed path emulated by edge e from v" to either endpoint of the path. About the third segment we have no information, whatsoever.

As we move up the search path for v in T we will extend the first segment, move the second segment, and shrink the third segment. In order to do this we keep the following information:

cost1 : Length of the first segment after processing node x.

v' : Vertex in G_i^b that the endpoint v" of the first segment is collapsed into.

edge' : Edge in G_i^b that represents the collapsed path on which v" lies.

cost2in : Length of the second segment after processing node x, given that the direction taken on the collapsed path is from v" to the vertex emulated by the vertex in G_i^b v" is collapsed into after processing node x.

cost2out : Length of the second segment after processing node x given that the direction taken on the collapsed path is from v" to the vertex emulated by the other endpoint of the edge in G_i^b that represents the collapsed path containing the second segment.

Initially: cost1 = cost2in = cost2out = 0, v' = v, edge' = nil.

When processing node x we use the additional information in the BU-table to maintain the values of these variables appropriately. All of this takes time O(1). For details of this part of the algorithm see [L 85c].

This completes the description of the first phase of the query algorithm. The second phase now has to deal with two vertices inside a $\tilde{G}_i$ each representing one of v, w. In the second phase we keep on collapsing these vertices exactly as we did in the first phase, updating the four variables given above for each vertex independently. We do this, until we reach a node y in T of type G_j where after processing y, v and w would get collapsed into the same vertex. At this node in T we do not update the values of the four variables for v, w as in the first phase. Rather, we are now in a position to merge the two ends of p_{min} computed so far, because we know that all of p_{min} has to go through a part of $T_{min,k}$ we already constructed. Merging of the two paths is done as follows. First, if edge' $\neq$ nil for v or w, we add the appropriate cost2in- resp. cost2out-value to cost1. Further collapsing is not done, rather, inside T_j we now ask the following query.

Q'(v',w') = cost of the path between v' and w' in T_j.

Here v', w' are the vertices v and w are collapsed into at this point. Adding this value to the two cost1-values yields the total path cost. Since T_i is not changed between queries an efficient data structure for answering queries of type Q'(v',w') on T_i can be precomputed when filling the BU-table. Using the results of [HT 84] we can prove the following lemma.

<u>Lemma 3:</u> After preprocessing time $O(n_i\alpha(n_i))$ each query Q'(v',w') can be answered in time O(1).

Note that Lemma 3 discusses the nonhierarchical version of the query problem discussed in this section. Since all other steps of the query algorithm process a node in T in time O(1), in the case that a node y as described above exists Theorem 2 is proved.

The case that a node y in T as described above is not found on the way up the hierarchy tree is handled similarly. Merging is done when processing the root of T in this case. This completes the proof of Theorem 2. □

Figure 8 shows an example of the processing of a query. At each relevant node of T the values of the three cost variables used by the query algorithm are given, and the vertex v' is highlighted.

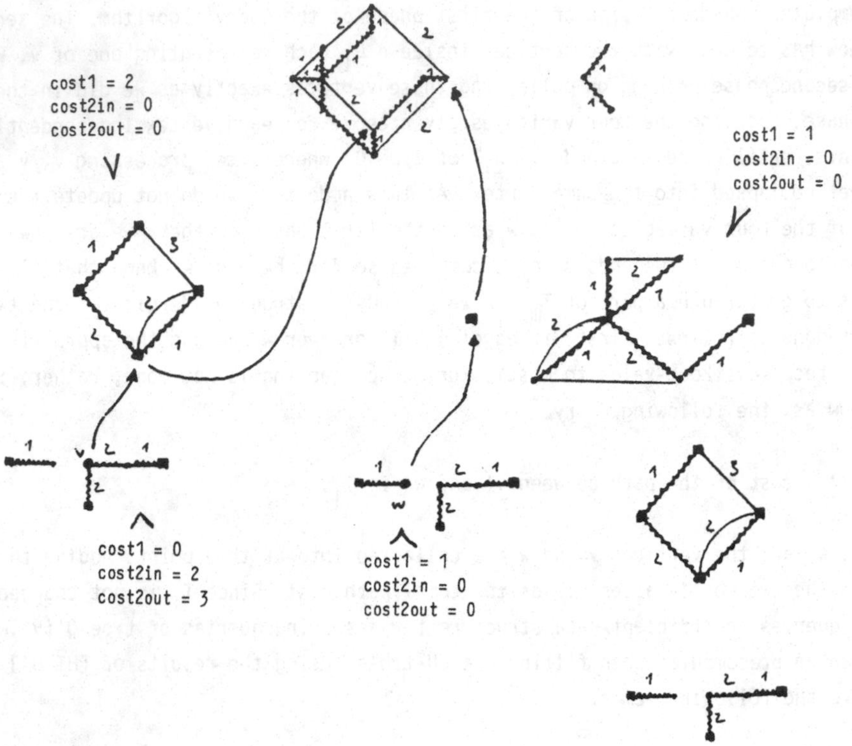

Figure 8: Processing of Q(v,w) = 5

6. The construction problem

If we want to construct the forest $T_{min,k}$ explicitly we cannot hope to spend less than O(N) time. This is, because $T_{min,k}$ does not have to respect the hierarchy of E(Γ). In fact, different instances of a subcell may contribute different parts to $T_{min,k}$. E.g., the two instances of the subcell G_2 in Example 1 contribute different parts to $T_{min,k}$ as shown in Figure 6. (The problem that the solution of a graph problem on a hierarchical graph need not respect the hierarchy has been studied in [L 82] for the shortest path problem.) However, non-hierarchical minimum spanning forest algorithms also need linear space, i.e., a non-hierarchical solution of the construction problem needs space O(N). Using the bottom-up method we can reduce this space requirement to O(n) (except for the output space needed to write the forest $T_{min,k}$). In practice this means that costly paging faults can be avoided. Experience with CAD systems for VLSI design shows that this avoidance of paging often makes the difference between a feasible and an infeasible algorithm.

The hierarchical solution of the construction problem goes as follows:

First we solve the decision problem as in Section 4. In a second pass we use the information stored in the BU-table to generate $T_{min,k}$. We need here also to store the emulation mapping of edges defined in Definition 4. Specifically we assume the existence of pointers between an edge in $\tilde{G}_i$ and its counterpart in G_i^b. These pointers are a hierarchical representation of the emulation mapping of Definition 4. Clearly these pointers can be generated at no extra cost while filling the BU-table.

The second pass performs a preorder traversal of the hierarchy tree. While processing node x of type G_i in T all edges of $T_{min,k}$ that belong to x will be generated and output. We start at the root r by outputting all edges in the copy of T_k that belong to r. At the same time an inspection of $\tilde{G}_k$ tells us which edges of the copy of T_j belonging to a son x of r do not belong to $T_{min,k}$. Those are exactly the edges in the corresponding copy of G_i^b inside $\tilde{G}_k$ that do not belong to T_k. This information we hand down when we continue with processing x. In this fashion we eventually generate a list of all edges in $T_{min,k}$.

The first pass of this procedure takes time $O(m\log\log^* m+n)$ to fill the BU-table. In the second pass the time spent on each node x of type G_i in T is $O(m_i+n_i)$. Thus the second pass runs always in time $O((M+N)k)$. If the same vertex appears only in a bounded number of nodes of T then the second pass runs in time $O(N)$.

7. Conclusions

We introduced a hierarchical graph model and a general procedure, the so-called bottom-up method that allows for the efficient hierarchical solution of graph problems. Then we solved three graph problems pertaining to minimum spanning forests hierarchically using this method. For the decision problem we could achieve great speed-up w.r.t. the non-hierarchical solution. For the query problem the speed-up is modest, since queries can be answered quickly without using hierarchy if enough space is available as we have seen in Section 5. However, hierarchically preprocessing time is cut by a large margin, and we only need space $O(n)$ to answer queries, and this makes the hierarchical query algorithm superior to the non-hierarchical ones. The construction problem cannot be sped up asymptotically, however, space usage can be reduced dramatically here, too. The hierarchical solutions of all three problems eliminate the need for paging on practical problem sizes.

We remark, that the non-hierarchical solution of the graph problems discussed here does not depend on any specific non-hierarchical minimum spanning forest algorithm. Since subcells can be expected to be small, for practical purposes it will often suffice to use a simple non-hierarchical minimum spanning forest algorithm that may not have good asymptotic behavior, but be easy to program and superior to more sophisticated minimum spanning forest algorithms on the problem instances encountered.

Many other graph problems can be solved hierarchically using the bottom-up method. Connectivity problems are discussed in [L 85a] where also the graph model is motivated in more detail. Planarity problems are discussed in [L 85b].

Not all problems can be solved hierarchically using the bottom-up method. [L 85a] gives an example of a problem that becomes P-SPACE complete [GJ 79] when the length of an instance is the length of its hierarchical description. Other hierarchical graph processing methods have to be found that make such graph problems more feasible in practice.

The hierarchical graph model studied here is used as the basis for the hierarchical circuit model of the HILL layout system [HILL].

References

[GGST 85] H.N. Gabow/Z. Galil /T. Spencer/R.E. Tarjan: Efficient Algorithms for Finding Minimum Spanning Trees in Undirected and Directed Graphs. Typescript 1985 , to appear in COMBINATORIKA

[GJ 79] M.R. Garey/D.S. Johnson: Computers and Intractability: A Guide to the Theory of NP-Completeness. Freeman, San Francisco (CA), 1979

[HILL] T. Lengauer/K. Mehlhorn: The HILL-System: A design environment for the hierarchical specification, compaction, and simulation of integrated circuit layouts. Proc. Conference on Advanced Research in VLSI (ed. P. Penfield Jr.) M.I.T. (1984), 139-149

[HT 84] D. Harel/R.E. Tarjan: Fast algorithms for finding nearest common ancestors. In: SICOMP 13.2 (1984), 338-355

[L 82] T. Lengauer: The complexity of compacting hierarchically specified layouts of integrated circuits. 23rd IEEE-FOCS 1982, 358-368

[L 85a] T. Lengauer: Efficient solution of connectivity problems on hierarchically defined graphs. Reihe "Theoretische Informatik" No. 24, FB 17, Universität-Gesamthochschule Paderborn, Paderborn, West-Germany, 1985

[L 85b] T. Lengauer: Hierarchical planarity testing algorithms. Reihe "Theoretische Informatik" No. 25, FB 17, Universität-Gesamthochschule Paderborn, Paderborn, West-Germany, 1985

[L 85c] T. Lengauer: Efficient algorithms for finding minimum spanning forests of hierarchically defined graphs. Reihe "Theoretische Informatik" No. 26, FB 17, Universität-Gesamthochschule Paderborn, Paderborn, West-Germany, 1985

[T 83] R.E. Tarjan: Data structures and network algorithms. SIAM, Philadelphia (PA), 1983

On Sparseness, Ambiguity and other Decision Problems for Acceptors and Transducers

Óscar H.Ibarra and B.Ravikumar
Department of Computer Science
University of Minnesota
Minneapolis,MN-55455.

Abstract. We consider some decision problems on sparseness, degrees of ambiguity and multiple valuedness concerning finite-state and pushdown acceptors and transducers. A language L is sparse if there is a polynomial P such that the number of strings of length n in L is atmost $P(n)$. A recognizer (transducer) is of polynomial ambiguity (valued) if there exists a polynomial P such that the number of derivations (outputs) for any input of length n is at most $P(n)$. We relate these problems and show that they are decidable for finite-state devices. For cfl's, only the sparseness problem is decidable. We also study some properties of structure generating function defined as $f_L(z) = \Sigma a_n z^n$, where a_n is the number of strings of length n in a language L. Our results are useful in proving the non-regularity/ non-context-freeness of some languages.

1.Introduction

The goal of the present study is to consider some decision problems on sparseness, degrees of ambiguity and multiple valuedness of acceptors and transducers recognizing regular and context-free languages(cfl's). For a language $L \subseteq \Sigma^*$, (Σ being a finite alphabet of size at least 2), we define the growth function of L, $g_L: N \rightarrow N$ as follows. $g_L(n)$ (growth function) denotes the number of strings of length n in L, i.e. $g_L(n) = | L \cap \Sigma^n |$, where Σ^n stands for Σ concatenated n times. A language L is said to be *sparse* if there exists a polynomial P such that $g_L(n) \leq P(n)$ for all n. (Otherwise, we call L dense or non-sparse). The notion of sparseness has been considered earlier in the context of NP-complete languages by several researchers(see, e.g.[BERM77].) Let M be a non-deterministic finite automaton (nfa). We define the ambiguity function of $M, a_M: N \rightarrow N$ such that $a_M(n)$ is the maximum number of distinct derivations for any string of length n accepted by M. M is said to be exponentially ambiguous if there is no polynomial P such that $a_M(n) \leq P(n)$ for all n. In a similar way, we define exponential valuedness of a non-deterministic Mealy machine M with accepting states. This device outputs a single symbol of the output alphabet on each transition. These notions can be extended to pushdown automata (pda) in an obvious manner. We consider the decidability of sparseness, exponential ambiguity/valuedness of a given device. We relate all the three problems and show that they are decidable for finite-state devices, but that only the sparseness problem is decidable for pda's.

We consider other problems related to the growth function g_L, such as: 'Is there a regular language L such that $g_L(n) = \Theta(2^{n/logn})$?' We solve these problems by considering the generating function $f_L(z)$ for the sequence $<g_L(0), g_L(1), \cdots >$. Kuich[KUIC70] defined $f_L(z)$ as the structure generating function of a language L. Kuich has shown that, for an unambiguous non-expansive cfg G, $f_{L(G)}(z)$ is a rational function. ($L(G)$ is the language generated by the grammar G). We use this result to show the solvability of a problem on unambiguous, non-expansive cfgs. Some of our results are useful in showing the non-regularity/non-context-freeness of languages. Also, the sparseness problem, whose complexity seems to lie between the infiniteness and the universe problem ('$=\Sigma^*$?') might be useful in sharpening the boundary between decidable and undecidable problems for some families of languages.

Here is the summary of results. Section 2 deals with sparseness problem. We show that, for context-free languages, sparseness is equivalent to boundedness. This implies that sparseness is decidable for cfls. We also show that there are non-cfls (in fact, co-cfls), for which sparseness is not equivalent to boundedness. As an application of the decidability of sparseness of regular languages, we show the decidability of a problem on the growth of a matrix product. In section 3, we study the exponential ambiguity problem and show that it is decidable for regular languages, but not for cfls. As a consequence, we also provide algorithms to test if a given non-deterministic Mealy machine with accepting states is finite valued or exponential valued. In section 4, we use the properties of structure generating function to show the solvability of some problems. For example, we consider a 'birdie' problem due to Ullian[ULLI67]. Suppose G is a cfg such that $L(G)$ is regular. Is it possible to effectively construct a dfa A such that $L(G)=L(A)$? Ullian showed that it is not always possible to do so. We prove that, when G is an unambiguous non-expansive cfg, such a dfa A can be effectively found. We conclude in section 5 with a list of open problems.

In this extended abstract, proofs of the results, except that of the main result of section 3, will be omitted. The complete version with all proofs will be presented in a full paper.

2.The Sparseness Problem

Let $\Sigma = \{a,b\}$. A language $L \subseteq \Sigma^*$ is said to be sparse if there is a polynomial P such that the number of strings of length n in L is atmost $P(n)$ for all n. We use $g_L(n)$ to denote the number of strings of length n in L. The sparseness problem for a family $\mathcal{C}$ of languages is: 'given an arbitrary $L \in \mathcal{C}$, is L sparse'? The main result of this section is that the sparseness problem is decidable for context-free languages (Theorem 2.1). We show this by establishing that, for context-free languages, boundedness is a necessary and sufficient condition for sparseness. (A language L is bounded if there are strings $w_1, w_2, \ldots, w_k$ such that $L \subseteq w_1^* w_2^* \cdots w_k^*$.) This fact does not hold for arbitrary languages. We show this by exhibiting a language L which is sparse and unbounded. Further L is a co-cfl. We also prove some closure properties of sparse cfls. Finally, we use Theorem 2.1. to show the decidability of the sparseness of a 0-1 matrix.

We first establish the equivalence of sparseness and boundedness for cfls. The following condition(*) will be used to prove our result. Before we state this condition, we need a definition.

A language L is said to be commutative if and only if for any $u,v \in L$, $uv = vu$.

Let $G = (V,\Sigma,P,S)$ be a cfg[HOPC79]. We assume that G is reduced,*i.e.*, all the useless variables in G have been removed.

condition(*) A cfg $G = (V,\Sigma,P,S)$ satisfies (*) if and only if, for each non-terminal $A \in V$, the languages

$L_A(G) = \{ u \in \Sigma^* \mid A \overset{*}{\Rightarrow} uAv \text{ for some } v \in \Sigma^* \}$ and

$R_A(G) = \{ v \in \Sigma^* \mid A \overset{*}{\Rightarrow} uAv \text{ for some } v \in \Sigma^* \}$

are commutative.

The following result is known[GINS66].

Lemma 2.1. A context-free language L is bounded if and only if L can be generated by a cfg G which satisfies condition(*), and it is decidable whether an arbitrary cfg G satisfies condition(*).

Lemma 2.2. Let $w_1, w_2, \ldots, w_k \in \Sigma^*$ be arbitrary strings. The language $L = w_1^* w_2^* \cdots w_k^*$ is sparse.

We now present the main result of this section.

Theorem 2.1. Let L be a context-free language. L is bounded if and only if it is sparse. Thus, sparseness is decidable for cfls.

The latter claim in the above theorem follows from the former claim and the decidability of boundedness for cfl's[GINS66]. For regular and linear context-free languages, the boundedness testing algorithm given in[GINS66] runs in time polynomial in the size of the grammar $|G|$, but for general cfl's, a polynomial time algorithm is not known.

In the case of a regular language L, the condition (*) above which we showed to be necessary and sufficient for sparseness means that, if M is a dfa that accepts L, then the graph of M (vertices corresponding to states and the edges corresponding to transitions) has no useful vertex which lies in two loops. (A vertex is useful if there is a path from the starting state to it and from it to a final state.) This fact will be useful in Theorem 2.4.

In the rest of the section, we consider some applications of Theorem 2.1. As an immediate consequence of this result, we have an alternate proof of a result due to Ginsburg[GINS66].

Corollary 2.1. $L = (a+b)^*$ is not bounded.

This follows from the fact that $g_L(n) = 2^n$.

Next we state some closure properties of sparse cfls.

For a language L, define
$PRE(L) = \{w \mid \text{for some } x \in \Sigma^*, wx \in L\}$ and
$SUB(L) = \{w \mid \text{for some } x,y \in \Sigma^*, xwy \in L\}$.

Corollary 2.2. If L is a sparse cfl, then so are $PRE(L)$ and $SUB(L)$.

This result can be shown using the fact that the class of bounded cfl's is closed under *PRE* and *SUB* operations.

For an arbitrary language L, it is obvious that boundedness implies sparseness. Theorem 2.1 shows that the converse also holds in case L is a cfl. A natural question to ask is whether the converse always holds. Our next result shows that this is not the case.

Theorem 2.2. There exists a co-cfl L (*i.e.* $\bar{L}$ is a cfl) which is sparse and unbounded.

One such $L = \{a_1\#a_2\# \cdots \#a_k \mid k \geq 1,\ a_i$ is the binary representation of i with a leading 1 $\}$.

The results above can be used to prove that some languages are not cfls. For example, L defined in Theorem 2.2 is a non-cfl as a consequence of Theorems 2.1 and 2.2.

We conclude this section with an application of Theorem 2.1 to a decision problem on the growth of exponents of a matrix.

Let A be a 0-1 matrix of order $k \times k$. A is said to be *sparse* if there exists a polynomial P such that $[A^n]_{1,k} \leq P(n)$ for all n, where A^n denotes the matrix obtained by multiplying A, n times.

Note that the notion of sparseness used above is different from a conventional use of this term in a qualitative sense. We use this term because of its obvious relation to the sparseness of regular languages.

Theorem 2.3. It is decidable if an arbitrary 0-1 matrix is sparse.

We state below a necessary and sufficient condition for non-sparseness of a matrix.

Theorem 2.4. A matrix A of order $k \times k$ is non-sparse if and only if there exist integers p,d,s and r, $1 \leq p,s,r \leq k$ such that (1) $[A^p]_{1,s} > 0$, (2) $[A^r]_{s,k} > 0$ and (3) $[A^d]_{s,s} \geq 2$.

3. Exponential Ambiguity and Valuedness

In this section, we consider some decision problems that are closely related to the sparseness problem. We define the ambiguity function $a_A : N \rightarrow N$ of a non-deterministic device A such that $a_A(n)$ denotes the number of distinct derivations of any string of length n that is accepted/generated by A. **Note that the ambiguity function is associated with a device, not a language. In the case of cfl's, we** also consider exponential inherent ambiguity. A device A is exponentially ambiguous if a_A is not bounded by P for any polynomial P. The devices we deal with are nfa's, cfg's and non-deterministic Mealy machines. We use the conventional definition for the first two devices, *e.g.* as in [HOPC79]. A non-deterministic Mealy machine is defined as follows. It is a 6-tuple $M = <Q , \Sigma , \Delta , \delta , q_0 , F>$ where Q , Σ , q_0 and F are as in a nfa, Δ is an output alphabet (without loss of generality, we assume that $\Sigma \cap \Delta = \emptyset$) and $\delta : Q \times \Sigma \rightarrow 2^{Q \times \Delta}$. If $\delta(q,a) = \{(q_1,a_1),...,(q_k,a_k)\}$, it means that the machine can non-deterministically select one of the q_i's as the next state and output the corresponding a_i. We can define the language associated with M by ignoring the outputs and considering the remaining nfa. We denote this language by $L(M)$. For any string $s \in L(M)$, we associate $V(s)$, the set of values of s as $V(s) = \{\sigma \mid \sigma$ is a possible output for the input s $\}$. We also define the value function $v_M : N \rightarrow N$ such that $v(n) = \max_{s \in L(M) \cap \Sigma^n} \{|V(s)|\}$. M is exponential valued if v is not bounded by any polynomial. The main result of this section is Theorem 3.1 which shows that it is decidable whether a given nfa is exponentially ambiguous. We use this result to show that the exponential valuedness problem is decidable for non-deterministic Mealy machines. We also show that exponential ambiguity problem is not decidable for linear cfg's.

We first consider the special case of the exponential ambiguity problem for nfas over unary alphabet. This restricted version is shown to be decidable by reducing this problem to the sparseness problem.

Lemma 3.1. Let $M = <Q , \{1\} , \delta , q_0 , F>$ be an nfa over a unary alphabet. We can construct a dfa $M' = <Q , \Sigma' , \delta' , q_0 , F>$ such that $a_M(n) = g_{L(M')}(n)$. Thus M is exponentially ambiguous if and only if $L(M')$ is non-sparse.

The next lemma shows that a reverse transformation is also possible. Thus, there is a one-one correspondence between the instances of the ambiguity problem over unary alphabet and instances of the sparseness problem.

Lemma 3.2. Given a dfa $M_1 = <Q , \Sigma , \delta , q_0 , F>$, we can construct a nfa $M = <Q , \{1\}, \delta' , q_0' , F'>$ such that $g_{L(M_1)}(n) = a_M(n)$.

We now consider the general case when Σ is arbitrary.

Theorem 3.1. Let M be an arbitrary nfa. There is an algorithm to decide if M is exponentially ambiguous.

Proof. Let $M = <Q , \Sigma , \delta , q_1 , F>$ be an arbitrary nfa, where $Q = \{q_1, q_2, \ldots , q_m\}$. Without loss of generality, we may assume that M has only one final state and that M is reduced, *i.e.* all useless states have been removed. (If M has more than one final state, we may define the nfa's $M_1, M_2, \ldots$, considering final states one at a time. It is easy to see that M is exponentially ambiguous if and only if atleast one of the M_i's is.) Let $F = \{q_m\}$.

We associate with M, a digraph G_M with vertex set $V_M = \{1,2,...,m\}$. This graph is a modified form of the conventional transition graph associated with a nfa. The edges of G_M are of two types -call them dotted and straight edges. Let D_M , $S_M \subseteq V_M \times V_M$ be the sets of dotted and straight edges, respectively. To define these sets, we need the following languages. For any pair of vertices i , j, we define the languages
$L_{i,j}^{(s)} = \{w \mid q_j \in \delta(q_i , w)$, there is a unique way in which w can be derived by moving from q_i to $q_j\}$ and
$L_{i,j}^{(a)} = \{w \mid q_j \in \delta(q_i , w)$, there are atleast two distinct ways of deriving w by moving from q_i to $q_j\}$.
Obviously, these two languages are disjoint. For $i,j \in V_M$, $<i , j> \in D_M$ if and only if, $L_{i,j}^{(s)} \neq \emptyset$ and $<i , j> \in S_M$ if and only if $L_{i,j}^{(a)} \neq \emptyset$.

We first show that, given an nfa M, the digraph G_M can be effectively constructed. In fact, we show a stronger result, that the languages $L_{i,j}^{(s)}$ and $L_{i,j}^{(a)}$ are effectively constructible regular languages.

For $i,j \in V_M$, define $M_{i,j} = <Q, \Sigma, \delta, q_i, \{q_j\}>$. Note that $L_{i,j} = L(M_{i,j}) = L^{(d)}_{i,j} \cup L^{(s)}_{i,j}$. Using the subset construction method [HOPC79], we can construct a dfa $M'_{i,j}$ equivalent to $M_{i,j}$. Define an *extended* dfa $M' = <Q, \Sigma, \delta, q_0, F, T>$, where T is an additional component $T \subseteq Q$. Acceptance of a string w by M', an extended dfa, is slightly modified. A string w is accepted by M' if and only if $\delta(q_0, w) \in F$, and the sequence of states visited during the accepatance of w includes a member of T. It is easy to see that the languages accepted by extended dfa's are regular. Now, we augment $M'_{i,j}$ as an extended dfa with $T = \{Q' \mid$ the set $Q' \subseteq Q$ contains atleast two elements$\}$. The language accepted by this extended dfa is $L^{(s)}_{i,j}$ and thus an effectively constructible regular set. Further, we see that $L^{(d)}_{i,j}$ is also regular since it is the difference of two regular sets. This concludes the proof that G_M can be effectively constructed.

We claim that M is exponentially ambiguous if and only if G_M contains a cycle that includes a straight edge (or, equivalently, G_M contains a self-loop through a vertex by a straight edge.) Since it is decidable if G_M contains such a cycle, the result follows once we prove the claim stated above. The rest of the proof is intended to establish the above claim.

(sufficiency) This part is easy. Suppose i is a vertex in G_M containing a loop of straight edge. Let $u \in L_{0,i}, v \in L^{(s)}_{i,i}$ and $w \in L_{i,m}$. The string $uv^t w \in L(M)$ and can be derived in atleast 2^t different ways. This proves that M is exponentially ambiguous.

(necessity) Suppose G_M does not contain any cycle having a straight edge. This means that only cycles in G_M are those all of whose edges are dotted. Figure 3.1. shows two digraphs the former satisfying this condition and the latter not satisfying it. We show that, under the assumption stated above, $a_M(n) \leq n^m$. (Recall that $m = |V_M|$).

Figure 3.1.(a) and (b)

We associate with any string w, a set $S^{i,j}_w$ as follows. $S^{i,j}_w$ will be the set of sequences of states visited for the input w, starting at state q_i and reaching at state q_j. Thus, any string $\sigma \in S^{i,j}_w$ will be a string in $Q^{|w|+1}$ such that its first and the last characters are q_i and q_j respectively. We next define a set of *direct* derivations of w between the states q_i and q_j, $D^{i,j}_w \subseteq S^{i,j}_w$ as follows. Let $\sigma = q_i q_{i_1} \cdots q_{i_r} q_j \in S^{i,j}_w$. σ is in $D^{i,j}_w$ if and only if the following condition holds. For any $\sigma' = q_i q_{j_1} \cdots q_{j_r} q_j \in S^{i,j}_w$, if there exists some s, $1 < s < r$ such that $q_{i_s} = q_{j_s}$ then, $q_{i_1} \cdots q_{i_s} = q_{j_1} \cdots q_{j_s}$ or $q_{i_{s+1}} \cdots q_{i_r} = q_{j_{s+1}} \cdots q_{j_r}$. Intuitively, the concept of direct derivation can be explained as follows. Say that two strings (over the alphabet Q) 'meet' at a vertex i if, the kth letter (from left) in both strings is q_i. A string $\sigma \in S^{i,j}_w$ is a direct derivation if and only if, for any string $\sigma' \in S^{i,j}_w$ that meets σ, either the prefixes (or suffixes) of the two strings upto the common letter ('meeting vertex') are identical, *i.e.*, there exist $\delta_1, \delta_2, \delta_3$ and δ' (possibly empty) such that $\sigma = \delta_1 \delta_2 \delta_3$ and $\sigma' = \delta_1 \delta' \delta_3$. The essential idea behind the direct derivation of a string w between q_i and q_j is that w can not be split into $w = w_1 w_2$ such that $w_1 \in L^{(s)}_{i,k}$ and $w_2 \in L^{(s)}_{k,j}$ for some k. We shall now prove that the number of direct derivations of a string w

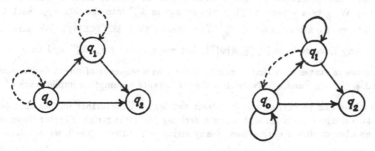

between states q_i and q_j is bounded by $C.|w|$ for some C which depends only on m, the size of M, but not on w.

First, we consider those strings $\sigma \in D_w^{i,j}$ that never meet any string $\sigma' \in S_w^{i,j}$. It is easy to show that the number of such strings is atmost m. Consider the second letter (from left) of such a string. There can be atmost one string σ whose second letter can be q_k for any k, and this shows the desired bound m. Next, we consider the set D of all strings that meet some string $\sigma' \in S_{w'}^{i,j}$. For any $\sigma \in D$, we define $L(\sigma)$ and $R(\sigma)$, where $L,R:Q^* \to Q$ as follows. Let $\sigma' \in S_w^{i,j}$ be such that σ and σ' have the longest common prefix. We define $L(\sigma)$ as the rightmost character of the common prefix of the two strings. In a similar way, $R(\sigma)$ is defined with respect to suffixes. We partition the set D into $D = \cup E_{r,s}$ as follows. A string $\sigma \in D$ belongs to $E_{r,s}$ if and only if $L(\sigma) = q_r$ and $R(\sigma) = q_s$. We shall count the size of $E_{r,s}$ for each pair (r,s) and show that in each case $|E_{r,s}| \leq C_1.|w|$ for some C_1. To do this, we should distinguish two cases. In the first case, for any $\sigma \in E_{r,s}$, q_r occurs in σ only once. It is easy to show, in this case, that $|E_{r,s}| \leq m$. In the other case, there exists a $\sigma \in E_{r,s}$ such that q_r appears atleast twice. Let t be the length of the loop between two successive occurrences of q_i. It is easy to see that, there is atmost one string $\sigma \in E_{r,s}$ that has d occurrences of the above loop for any d. Thus, we can infer that $|E_{r,s}| \leq |w|/t$, thus showing that $|D_w^{i,j}| \leq m + m^2 / t \,.\, |w| \leq C.|w|$ for $C = (1 + m^2/t)$ and for any string w of length atleast m.

The rest of the proof depends on the following intuitive idea. For any $w \in L(M)$ the set of derivations of w can be decomposed into a collection of atmost m direct derivations. This combined with the above bound will yield the desired result. A formal proof is as follows. Let $S_w^{1,m}$ be the set of derivations of the string w. We define a collection of sets $S_{\sigma_1}, \cdots, S_{\sigma_p}$, where p depends on m, but not on w. Infact, the set $I = \{\sigma_1, \cdots\}$ is the set of strings over the alphabet $\{1,2,...,m\}$ such that no string in I has more than one occurrence of any symbol. (Thus, $123 \in I$, but $1412 \notin I$). Clearly, then, $|I|$ is independent of $|w|$. We give a scheme to place the strings in $S_w^{1,m}$ into the sets $S_{\sigma_1}, ...$ such that every string in $S_w^{1,m}$ belongs to atleast one of S_{σ_i}. This means that $|S_w^{1,m}| \leq \sum_i |S_{\sigma_i}|$. We also show that $|S|_{\sigma_i} \leq 0(|w|^m)$ for any i, so we have $|S_w^{1,m}| \leq 0(|w|^m)$. Let $\sigma = q_1 q_{i_1} \cdots q_{i_r} q_m \in S_w^{1,m}$, and let $q_{i_{j_1}} \cdots q_{i_{j_s}}$ be a maximal subsequence of states such that w can be derived as a sequence of direct derivations between q_1 and $q_{i_{j_1}}, q_{i_{j_1}}$ and $q_{i_{j_2}}, \cdots, q_{i_{j_s}}$ and q_m. Note that the maximality assumption implies each of the above mentioned derivations can be carried out in atleast two ways. This further implies that $|s| \leq m$ else, there would be two distinct loops through a state deriving the same string. Further, from our earlier claim that the number of direct derivations of any string w is atmost $0(|w|)$, we conclude the main claim of the result.

The ideas used in the proof of Theorem 3.1 lead to a characterization of finite ambiguity of nfas. Let M be an nfa. M is said to be finitely ambiguous if, for any string $w \in L(M)$, the number of derivations is bounded by some K, which depends only on M, not the length of w. It was shown in [CHAN83] that it is decidable if an arbitrary nfa is finitely ambiguous. The next result can also be used to establish the decidability of finite ambiguity of nfa's.

Corollary 3.1. Let $M = < Q , \Sigma , \delta , q_0 , F >$ be an nfa, and let $Q = \{q_1, ..., q_k\}$. (We assume, with out loss of generality, that useless states in M have been removed). M is not finitely ambiguous if and only if one of the following conditions hold.
(1) There exist $w \in \Sigma^*$, $|w| \leq k^2$ and $1 \leq i , j \leq k$ such that $|S_w^{i,j}| \geq 2$. *i.e.*, there are atleast two derivations of w, beginning with and reaching back q_i.
(2) There exist $w \in \Sigma^*$, $|w| \leq k^{3k}+2$ and integers i,j,r,s and $t, 1 \leq i,j,r,s,t \leq k$ such that $q_i \in \delta(q_i, w^r), q_j \in \delta(q_i, w^s)$ and $q_j \in \delta(q_j, w^t)$.

We present two consequences of the above theorem. First, we show that exponential valuedness of non-deterministic Mealy machines. is decidable.

Theorem 3.2. Let M be an arbitrary non-deterministic Mealy machine. There exists an algorithm to decide if M is exponential valued.

Combining the ideas of Theorem 3.2 and Corollary 3.1, we can obtain an algorithm to test the finite valuedness of nondeterministic Mealy machines.

Next, we persent a generalization of the matrix problem whose decidability was shown in section 2.

Let $\mathcal{A} = \{A_1, A_2, ..., A_r\}$ be a finite collection of $(k \times k)$ 0-1 matrices. $\mathcal{A}$ is said to grow exponentially if max $[A_{i_1} A_{i_2} \cdots A_{i_n}]_{1,k}$ is not bounded by any polynomial, where $A_{i_1} A_{i_2} ... A_{i_n}$ is an arbitrary sequence of n matrices in $\mathcal{A}$.

Theorem 3.3. Given a collection $\mathcal{A}$ of matrices, it is decidable if $\mathcal{A}$ grows exponentially.

Observe that, when $r=1$, the above problem reduces to the matrix problem of section 2. That is the reason for a one-one correspondence between the sparseness problem for regular languages and the exponential valuedness problem for nfas over unary alphabet.

We conclude this section by considering the exponential ambiguity problem for cfg's. For a cfg, the ambiguity is determined by the number of distinct derivation trees.

Theorem 3.4. It is undecidable to determine, given a linear cfg G, whether it is exponentially ambiguous.

4. Structure Generating Function

In this section, we study the generating function $f_L(z)$ for the sequence $<g_L(0), g_L(1), \cdots>$, g_L being the growth function studied in section 2. The function $f_L(z)$ is closely related to a formal power series[CHOM63] and has been studied before [KUIC70]. We use the properties of $f_L(z)$ to prove the decidability of some problems . We first consider the following question : 'When L is regular, what is the asymptotic nature of the function g_L? We characaterize the growth function of regular languages. We illustrate the usefulness of the g function *e.g.* to prove the non-regularity of some languages. Finally, we show a restricted version of Ullian's 'birdie' problem to be effectively solvable.

The following results are well-known.See *e.g.* [STEA81].

Lemma 4.1. Let L be a regular language. Then, $f_L(z)$ is rational, i.e., a ratio of two polynomials $P(z)$ and $Q(z)$. Further, the degree of Q is an upperbound on the number states in an nfa accepting L.

Lemma 4.2. If L is a regular language, $g_L(z)$ satisfies a linear difference equation with constant coefficients,

$g_L(n) = a_1 g_L(n) + \cdots + a_k g_L(n-k)$

with suitable initial conditions, where k is an upperbound on the number of states of an nfa that accepts L.

Our next result characterizes the type of growth function a regular language admits.

An exponential function $E: N \to N$ is a function of the form $E(n) = \sum_{j=0}^{k} r_j^n \cdot P_j(n)$, where P_j's are polynomials and r_j's are algebraic numbers.

Theorem 4.1. If L is regular, there exists an integer $p>0$ such that, for all i, $0 \leq i < p$, and suffiently large n , $g_L(np+i)$ satisfies one of the following:

(1) $E_1(n) \leq g_L(np+i) \leq E_2(n)$, for some exponential functions E_1 and E_2.

(2) $P_1(n) \leq g_L(np+i) \leq P_2(n)$ for some polynomial functions P_1 and P_2.

(3) $C_1 \leq g_L(np+i) \leq C_2$ for some constants C_1 and C_2.

The structure generating function for a cfl appears much harder to characterize. For unambiguous cfl's, [FLAJ85] provides a characterization.

We illustrate how the above result can be used to show the non-regularity of some languages. Let $L = \{a^{2^n} | n \geq 0\}$. Consider the cumulative growth function $c_L(n) = \sum_{i=0}^{n} g_L(i)$. The growth function for the language $L_1 = L_0 1^*$ is c_L. Also, if L_0 is regular, so is L_1. However, $c_{L_0}(n) = \Theta(\log n)$, which shows that L_1 is not regular. As a more non-trivial example, let us consider the language $L \subseteq (0+1)^*$ as follows. L consists of strings that begin with a 1, whose value treated as a binary number is a prime. By prime number theorem, $c_L(n) = \Theta(2^n / n)$. This proves that L is not regular.

Finally, we consider a restricted form of a 'birdie problem' of Ullian [ULLI67]. 'Given a cfg G such that $L(G)$ is regular, is there an effective algorithm to construct an nfa A such that $L(G) = L(A)$?' It was shown that such an algorithm does not exist. But, when G is an unambiguous, non-expansive cfg, we can show that there is an algorithm to solve this problem. (A cfg G is non-expansive if, for no useful variable A, we have A $uAvAw$, for some terminal strings u, v and w.) Kuich [KUIC70] has shown that, if L is generated by an unambiguous non-expansive cfg, then $f_L(z)$ is rational and can be effectively computed from G. Thus, given G, we compute $f_L(z) = P(z) / Q(z)$ where P and Q are polynomials. Now, by Lemma 4.2, s, the degree of Q is an upperbound on the number of states in an nfa A that accepts $L(G)$. Also, the equivalence of a regular language and an unambiguous cfl can be tested [SALO78]. Thus, we generate all the nfa's A with s or fewer states and test for equivalence with $L(G)$. Eventually, we would generate A such that $L(G) = L(A)$.

5.Some Open Problems

We conclude with a list of open problems. We showed in section 2 that sparseness is equivalent to boundedness for cfl's. It is interesting to study other families for which a similar result can be established. Are there families of languages with semilinear Parikh mapping such as presented in [IBAR78] for which equivalence of sparseness and boundedness does not hold? Another problem is to study the complexity of boundedness/sparseness testing for cfl's. This problem was mentioned as an open problem in [HUNT76]. It is possible that Theorem 2.1 (the equivalence of boundedness and sparseness) might throw more light on this problem. In section 3, our study on exponential ambiguity can be extended to more general finite-state devices such as transition systems[HARR78]. The growth function g of cfl's is not well understood. We do not know, *e.g.* how to prove that, for a cfl, the growth can not be of the form $\Theta(2^{\sqrt{n}})$. Also, it would be of interest to apply the structure generating function to solve other problems of formal language theory.

Acknowledgment

This research was supported in part by NSF Grant MCS83-04756.

References

[BERM77] Berman L. and J.Hartmanis, On isomorphism and density of NP and other complete sets, *SIAM Journal of Computing*(1977) 305-322.

[CHAN83] Chan T. and O.H.Ibarra, On the finite-valuedness problem for sequential machines, *Theoretical Computer Science*(1983) 95-101.

[CHOM63] Chomsky N. and M.P.Schutzenberger, The algebraic Theory of Context-free Languages, in *ComputerProgramming* and *Formal Systems* , North-Holland Publishing Company, Amsterdam,1963.

[FLAJ85] Flajolet P., Ambiguity and Transcendence, *Proc .of Inter. Coll. on Automata,Lang. and Programming* (1985)179-188.

[GINS66] Ginsburg S., *Mathematical Theory of Context−free Languages*, McGraw Hill Book Company, (1966).

[HARR78] Harrison M.A., *Introduction to Formal Language Theory*, Addison-Wesley Inc. (1978).

[HOPC79] Hopcroft J. and J.D.Ullman, *Introduction to Automata Theory, Formal languages and Computation*, Addison-Wesley Inc.(1979).

[HOPC69] Hopcroft J., On the equivalence and containment problems for context-free languages, *Mathematical Systems Theory*(1969)119-124.

[HUNT76] Hunt H., D.J.Rosenkrantz and T.Szymanski, On the equivalence, containment and covering problems for the regular and context-free languages, *Journal of Computer* and *System Sciences* (1976) 222-268.

[IBAR78] Ibarra O.H., Reversal bounded multicounter machines and their decision problems, *Journal of Asso. Comp. Mach* 25 (1978) 116-133.

[KUIC70] Kuich W., On the entropy of Context-free languages, *Information and Control*(1970)173-200.

[SALO78] Salomaa A. and M.Soittola, *Automata−theoretic Aspects of Formal Power Series*, Springer-Berlin (1978).

[STEA65] Stearns R. J.Hartmanis and P.M.Lewis, Heirarchies of memory bounded computations, *Conf. Record of Sixth Annual IEEE Symp. on Switching Theory* and *Logical Design* (1965) 179-190.

[STEA81] Stearns R. and H.B.Hunt, On the equivalence and containment problem for unambiguous regular expressions, regular grammars and finite automata, *Proc. 22nd IEEE Annual Symp. on Foundations of Comp. Sci.* (1981) 74-81.

[ULLI67] Ullian J.S., Partial algorithm problems for context-free languages, *Information* and *Control* (1967) 80-101.

VARIETES DE SEMIGROUPES ET MOTS INFINIS *

Jean-Pierre Pécuchet
LITP CNRS
Laboratoire d'Informatique de Rouen
Faculté des Sciences BP 67
76130 Mont-Saint-Aignant

Résumé:

Nous étudions la possibilité d'étendre la théorie des variétés de Eilenberg au cas des mots infinis. La situation est plus complexe et les résultats moins satisfaisants que dans le cas des mots finis. Nous obtenons cependant des descriptions intéressantes des classes associées aux variétés les plus usuelles. Cette étude permet également de mieux saisir la portée du théorème de Mac Naughton.

Abstract:

This paper deals with the possibility of extending Eilenberg's theory of varieties to the case of infinite words. The situation is more complex and the results less satisfactory than in the case of finite words. Nevertheless, we get interesting descriptions of classes associated to the most usual varieties. Furthermore this study brings a better understanding of Mac Naughton's theorem.

0. Introduction

L'étude des ensembles de mots infinis reconnus par des automates finis a été inaugurée par Buchi (1962) sur des préoccupations du domaine de la logique et par Muller (1963) pour l'étude de certains circuits électriques, puis théorisée par Mac Naughton (1966) qui montra que ces ensembles coincident avec les combinaisons booléennes des parties reconnues par les automates finis déterministes.

Enfin plus récemment, l'utilisation des mots infinis par Arnold et Nivat (1982) pour modéliser certains comportements des ordinateurs a suscité de nouveaux travaux, dont ceux de Perrin (1982) tendant à affiner le résultat de Mac Naughton.

* Faute de place, de nombreuses preuves ont du être omises ou écourtées. Une version complète sera disponible en publication interne du LITP.

Landweber (1969) et Wagner (1979) ont procédé à une classification des ensembles reconnaissables de mots infinis basée sur leur position dans la hiérarchie de Borel.

Dans le cas des mots finis une autre classification, basée sur les variétés de semigroupes, fait l'objet de la célèbre théorie des variétés de Eilenberg (1976). Elle associe de façon biunivoque, à chaque variété de semigroupes finis V, la classe V^+ constituée indifféremment des langages reconnus par les V-automates, ou reconnus par les éléments de V, ou dont le semigroupe syntaxique est dans V. De nombreuses classes ont pu être décrites de façon naturelle, dont les plus célèbres sont celles des langages sans étoile ([15]), des langages localement testables ([3], [9], [20]) et des langages testables par morceaux ([16]) associés respectivement aux variétés des semigroupes apériodiques, localement idempotents commutatifs et J-triviaux.

Dans le cas des mots infinis, la situation est beaucoup plus compliquée. La première difficulté provient du fait qu'ici les automates ne peuvent plus être supposés déterministes. On est ainsi amené à distinguer les deux classes V^w des parties reconnues par les V-automates et $\vec{V}$ des combinaisons booléennes des parties reconnues par les V-automates déterministes. La deuxième difficulté est liée au fait que la syntaxe du comportement infini d'un automate ne dépend pas seulement de ses transitions, mais aussi de ses boucles ([1]). On est ainsi amené à distinguer une troisième classe V^s constituée des parties reconnaissables dont le semigroupe syntaxique est dans V. Enfin la troisième difficulté provient du fait que la correspondance entre variétés de semigroupes et classes de parties n'est plus biunivoque.

Nous étudierons ici les classes V^w et $\vec{V}$ dont les relations constituent l'objet même du théorème de Mac Naughton. Nous donnerons des descriptions de ces classes pour les variétés les plus usuelles. L'étude de la classe V^s sera développée dans un prochain article ([11]).

L'article est divisé en quatre parties. La première est consacrée à des définitions et au rappel de quelques résultats. Dans la seconde nous montrons que la classe V^w peut être définie de trois façons distinctes et en déduisons une preuve directe d'un résultat de Thomas (1981). Dans les deux dernières, nous décrivons et comparons les classes V^w et $\vec{V}$ pour les variétés usuelles. La dernière partie est consacrée au cas particulier des parties localement testables et testables par morceaux.

1. Les parties reconnaissables

Dans le cas des mots finis, il y a identité entre les parties rationnelles, les parties reconnues par des automates finis et les parties reconnues par des semigroupes finis. Nous montrons dans ce chapitre qu'il en est de même dans le cas des mots infinis.

Dans ce qui suit, on désigne par A un <u>alphabet</u>, qui sera toujours supposé fini, sauf mention explicite du contraire. On note respectivement A^*, A^+, A^ω, A^∞ l'ensemble des <u>mots</u> respectivement finis, finis non vides, infinis, finis ou infinis, écrits sur l'alphabet A.

Pour $L \subseteq A^+$ on note L^ω l'ensemble des mots infinis de la forme $u=u_1u_2\ldots$ avec $u_i \in L$, et $\vec{L}$ l'ensemble des mots infinis ayant une infinité de facteurs gauches dans L.

$\mathcal{A} = (Q,I,T,F)$ désigne un <u>automate fini</u> sur l'alphabet A dont l'ensemble des états est Q, l'ensemble des états initiaux I, l'ensemble des états finaux T et l'ensemble des flèches $F \subseteq Q \times A \times Q$.

On note $\mathcal{A}^+$ le <u>comportement fini</u> de $\mathcal{A}$, constitué des étiquettes des chemins finis non vides débutant dans I et se terminant dans T, et $\mathcal{A}^\omega$ son <u>comportement infini</u>, constitué des étiquettes des chemins infinis débutant dans I et passant une infinité de fois dans T.

$S(\mathcal{A})$ désigne le <u>semigroupe de transition</u> de $\mathcal{A}$, c'est à dire le semigroupe de relations dans Q image du morphisme $\theta : A^+ \dashrightarrow S(\mathcal{A})$ défini par $\theta(a)=\{(p,q)\in Q^2 / (p,a,q)\in F\}$.

<u>Exemple 1.1</u> L'automate $\mathcal{A}=(\{1,2\}, \{1\}, \{2\}, \{(1,b,1), (1,a,2), (2,b,2), (2,a,1)\})$ sur l'alphabet $A=\{a,b\}$ est représenté de la façon suivante.

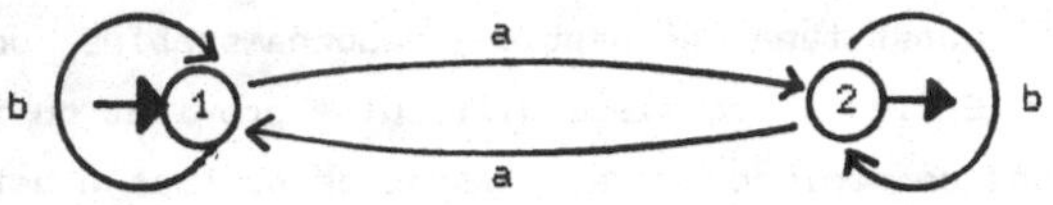

On vérifie que $\mathcal{A}^\omega=b^*a(b+ab^*a)^\omega$ est constitué des mots infinis ayant un nombre impair ou infini d'occurrences de a, et que $S(\mathcal{A})=Z_2$ avec $\theta(a)=1$ et $\theta(b)=0$.

Une partie de A^ω est dite <u>reconnaissable</u> si elle est le comportement infini d'un automate fini. On note $\mathrm{Rec}(A^\omega)$ l'ensemble de ces parties.

Cet ensemble coincide avec celui des parties <u>rationnelles</u> de A^ω, unions finies de parties de la forme XY^ω avec $X,Y\ \mathrm{Rec}(A^+)$. La formule

$$\mathcal{A}^\omega = \bigcup_{(i,t)\in I\times T} (Q,i,t)^+[(Q,t,t)^+]^\omega \qquad (1.1)$$

donne l'inclusion dans le sens direct, l'autre s'obtenant en construisant de façon évidente un automate reconnaissant XY^ω à partir de ceux reconnaissant X et Y.

Etant donné un semigroupe S et un morphisme $f : A^+ \dashrightarrow S$, on appelle <u>partie f-simple</u> (ou plus souvent <u>partie simple</u>) toute partie non vide de A^ω de la forme $f^{-1}(m)f^{-1}(e)^\omega$ pour un idempotent $e \in S$ et un $m \in S$ vérifiant $me=m$. Nous dirons qu'une partie L de A^ω est <u>reconnue</u> par f (ou plus souvent par S) si elle est réunion de parties f-simples.

<u>Remarque 1.1</u> La condition me=m qui n'apparait pas dans [13] se trouvera justifiée dans le chapitre suivant.

Dans ce qui suit, nous poserons $X_s=f^{-1}(s)$ $(s\in S)$ et

$$P_L = \{ (m,e)\in S^2 \ / \ e^2=e,\ me=m,\ \emptyset \neq X_m X_e^w \subseteq L\}.$$

Ainsi L est reconnu par S ssi l'on a l'égalité:

$$L = \bigcup_{(m,e)\in P_L} X_m X_e^w . \qquad (1.2)$$

Notons dès à présent le lemme suivant dont nous ferons un usage constant et qui peut être obtenu comme une conséquence du théorème de Ramsey faible.

Lemme 1.1 Soit A un alphabet quelconque (fini ou infini), S un semigroupe fini et $f:A^+\dashrightarrow S$ un morphisme. Alors tout $\alpha\in A^w$ est contenu dans une partie f-simple.

Autrement dit, A^w est reconnu par tous les semigroupes finis.

Il est clair d'après (1.2) que toute partie de A^w reconnue par un semigroupe fini est rationnelle et donc reconnaissable. La réciproque est assurée par la

---

Proposition 1.2 Le comportement infini d'un automate fini est reconnu par le semigroupe de transition de cet automate.

Preuve: Utiliser la formule (1.1) et le lemme 1.1. ■

Corollaire 1.3 Une partie L de A^w est reconnaissable ssi elle est reconnue par un semigroupe fini.

Nous avons ainsi montré l'identité entre les parties rationnelles de mots infinis, les parties reconnues par les automates finis et les parties reconnues par les semigroupes finis.

2. La classe V^w

Dans ce chapitre nous étendons aux mots infinis l'équivalence, bien connue dans le cas des mots finis, entre être reconnu par un automate dont le semigroupe de transition est dans V et être reconnu par un élément de V.

Rappelons (cf [5],[14]) qu'une variété de semigroupes finis est une classe de semigroupes finis fermée par passage au sous-semigroupe, par image homomorphe (i.e. passage au quotient) et par produit direct fini. Dans la suite, semigroupe sera synonyme de semigroupe fini.

Si V désigne une variété de semigroupes, nous appellerons V-morphisme tout morphisme $f:A^+\dashrightarrow S$ dans un élément $S\in V$, et V-automate tout automate dont le semigroupe de transition est dans V. Nous noterons V^+ la +-variété des langages de A^+ reconnus par les éléments de V.

<u>Théorème 2.1</u> Soit V une variété de semigroupes finis et L une partie de mots infinis. Il y a équivalence entre:

(i) L est reconnu par un V-automate.

(ii) L est reconnu par un V-morphisme.

(iii) L est une union finie de parties de la forme XY^{w} avec XY^{*} et Y^{+} dans V^{+}.

Nous noterons V^{w} la classe des parties de mots finis vérifiant l'une des trois conditions équivalentes ci-dessus. La condition (iii) correspond à celle utilisée dans [12].

<u>Preuve:</u> La partie (i)==>(ii) se déduit de la proposition 1.2, (ii)==>(iii) est immédiat et (iii)==>(ii) s'obtient sans trop de difficulté à l'aide du lemme 1.1.

Enfin pour (iii)==>(i) on construit à partir d'un semigroupe S reconnaissant L, un automate qui reconnait également L et dont le semigroupe de transition est un produit de quotients de S. Le procédé est explicité par le lemme suivant qui fournit une représentation de S par relations dans S^1 et dont la preuve consiste en une simple vérification.

<u>Lemme 2.2</u> Soit S un semigroupe, N un sous-semigroupe de S, S^1 le monoide déduit de S par l'adjonction d'un nouvel élément neutre noté 1, et $\mathcal{B}(S^1)$ le semigroupe des relations binaires sur S^1. Alors l'application $\varphi: S \rightarrow \mathcal{B}(S^1)$ définie par $(r,t) \in \varphi(s)$ ssi $st \in rN^1$ est un morphisme de semigroupes.

Pour tout idempotent e, en posant N={e}, cette représentation vérifie $(1,1) \in \varphi(s)$ ssi s=e, et $(m,1) \in \varphi(s)$ ssi s=m, pour tout m tel que me=m. D'où un V-automate $(S^1, M, \{1\}, \{(r,a,t)/(r,t) \in \varphi(f(a))\})$ reconnaissant $\bigcup_{m \in M} X_m X_e^{w}$, avec $M=\{m/(m,e) \in P_L\}$.

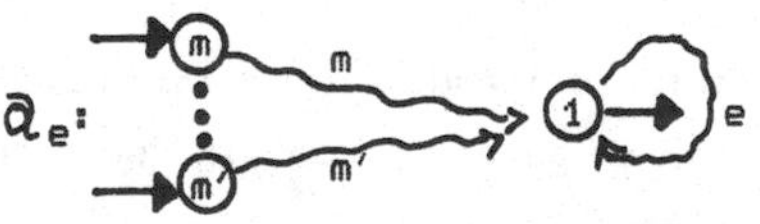

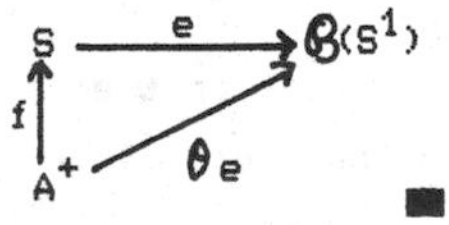

■

Nous terminerons ce chapitre par quelques commentaires.

<u>Remarque 2.1:</u> L'équivalence (i)<==>(iii) a été obtenue dans [18] pour la variété des semigroupes apériodiques à l'aide d'autres méthodes. Le théorème 2.1 en donne une preuve plus directe.

<u>Remarque 2.2:</u> Dans la preuve du théorème 2.1 la condition me=m imposée aux parties simples intervient de façon cruciale. Sans elle on perd les deux implications (ii)==>(i) et (ii)==>(iii). On peut le voir en considérant sur A={a,b} le morphisme

$f:A^+\text{-->}U_1$ défini par $f(a)=0$ et $f(b)=1$, où U_1 désigne le sous-semigroupe $\{1,0\}$ de $(N,.)$. La partie $L=X_1X_0{}^w$, constituée des mots infinis commençant par b et contenant une infinité de a, ne peut pas être reconnue par U_1 ni par aucun autre semigroupe J-trivial (cf théorème 4.3).

<u>Remarque 2.3:</u> Contrairement à ce qui se passe dans le cas des mots finis, il n'y a pas ici de plus petit semigroupe reconnaissant une partie de mots infinis.

Considérons par exemple sur l'alphabet $A=\{a,b\}$ la partie L constituée des mots infinis contenant une infinité de a. Considérons d'autre part les deux semigroupes $B_{1,2}=\{s,s'\}$ et $B_{2,1}=\{t,t'\}$ définis par les multiplications $s=s^2=s's$, $s'=s'^2=ss'$, $t=t^2=tt'$, $t'=t'^2=t't$ et dont les représentations en D-classes sont les suivantes.

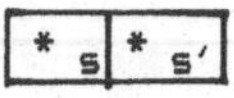

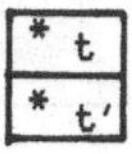

Ces deux morphismes reconnaissent L. Le premier grace à $f:A^+\text{-->}B_{1,2}$ défini par $f(a)=s$ et $f(b)=s'$ qui vérifie $L=f^{-1}(a)^w=(A^*a)^w$. Le deuxième grace à $g:A^+\text{-->}B_{2,1}$ défini par $g(a)=t$ et $g(b)=t'$ qui vérifie $L = g^{-1}(t)^w + g^{-1}(t')g^{-1}(t)^w = (aA^*)^w+bA^*(aA^*)^w$. Ces deux semigroupes ne sont pas isomorphes et les seuls semigroupes à les diviser tous deux sont le semigroupe vide et le semigroupe trivial dont aucun ne reconnait L. A ces deux semigroupes correspondent les deux automates suivants qui peuvent être retrouvés à partir de la construction du lemme 2.2.

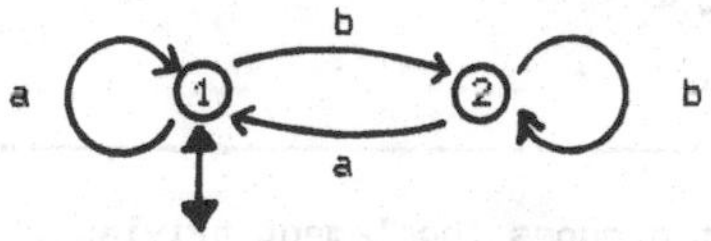

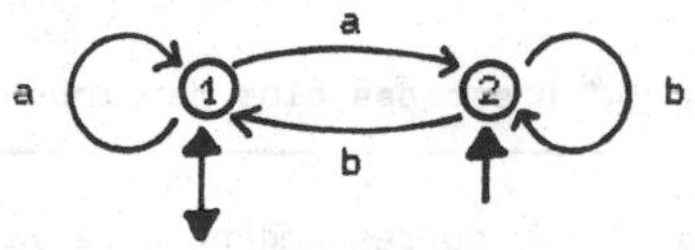

3. Etude de quelques variétés

Les exemples qui suivent montrent que l'on ne peut pas étendre le théorème des variétés aux mots infinis: deux variétés de semigroupes V distinctes peuvent correspondre à des classes V^w identiques. Nous verrons que l'on peut cependant donner des descriptions des classes associées aux variétés les plus usuelles. Une descripton de la classe des parties sans étoile a été obtenue par Thomas (1979). Nous donnerons une description de quelques autres classes, notemment de celles constituées des parties localement testables et des parties testables par morceaux. Nous renvoyons le lecteur à [6] pour ce qui concerne la théorie des semigroupes et à [5] ou [14] pour celle des variétés.

Une partie reconnaissable de A^w est dite <u>déterministe</u> si elle est reconnue par un automate fini déterministe. On note $\vec{V}$ la classe constituée des combinaisons booléennes des parties reconnues par un V-automate déterministe. Ainsi le théorème de Mac Naughton se relativise à la variété V ssi on a l'égalité $V^w=\vec{V}$. Nous verrons qu'en général une seule des deux inclusions est vérifiée.

Nous désignerons par $X^{\mathcal{B}}$ l'algèbre booléenne engendrée par X. La relation $\mathfrak{a}^w = \overrightarrow{\mathfrak{a}^+}$ vérifiée par le comportement infini de tout automate déterministe montre qu'une autre définition de $\overrightarrow{V}$ est donnée par $\overrightarrow{V} = \{\overrightarrow{X} / X \in V^+\}$. Elle montre également les deux faits suivants:

Si $V^w \subseteq \overrightarrow{V}$ on a l'égalité $\overrightarrow{V} = (V^w)^{\mathcal{B}}$. (3.1)

Si V^w est une algèbre booléenne on a l'inclusion $\overrightarrow{V} \subseteq V^w$. (3.2)

Le cas de la variété des semigroupes nilpotents montre que la relation $V \dashrightarrow V^w$ n'est pas injective.

<u>Proposition 3.1</u> Soit $\underline{I} = \{\emptyset, 1\}$ la variété triviale et <u>Nil</u> la variété des semigroupes nilpotents. On a les égalités

$$\underline{I}^w = \overrightarrow{\underline{I}} = \{\emptyset, A^w\} = \underline{Nil}^w = \overrightarrow{\underline{Nil}}.$$

Comme dans le cas des mots finis, on ne dispose pas de description de la classe $\underline{G}_S{}^w$ associée à la variété de semigroupes constituée de tous les groupes finis. On peut cependant remarquer qu'une seule partie du théorème de Mac Naughton se relativise à cette variété.

<u>Proposition 3.2</u> Soit $\underline{G}_S$ la variété de semigroupes constituée de tous les groupes finis. On a l'inclusion stricte

$$\underline{G}_S{}^w \subsetneq \overrightarrow{\underline{G}_S} = (\underline{G}_S{}^w)^{\mathcal{B}} .$$

De plus $\underline{G}_S{}^w$ n'est pas clos par intersection.

La classe correspondant à la variété des semigroupes localement triviaux, et à la variété des semigroupes localement triviaux et R-triviaux, est la première à admettre une description non triviale. Dans cet enoncé comme dans les suivants, les unions portent sur des ensembles finis.

<u>Proposition 3.3</u> Soient $\underline{LI} = \{S / eSe = e$ pour tout idempotent $e\}$ la variété des semigroupes localement triviaux et $\underline{K} = \{S / eS = e$ pour tout idempotent $e\}$ celle des semigroupes localement triviaux et R-triviaux. On a :

$$\overrightarrow{\underline{K}} = \{XA^w / X \text{ fini}\} \subsetneq \underline{K}^w = \{\bigcup XA^*(YA^*)^w / X,Y \text{ finis}\} = \underline{LI}^w \subsetneq \overrightarrow{\underline{LI}} = \{XA^*(YA^*)^w / X,Y \text{ finis}\}^{\mathcal{B}} .$$

De plus $\underline{K}^w$ n'est pas clos par intersection.

Voici un autre exemple intéressant.

<u>Proposition 3.4</u> Soit $\underline{K}^r = \{S / Se = e$ pour tout idempotent $e\}$ la variété des semigroupes L-triviaux et localement triviaux. On a :

$$(\underline{K}^r)^w = \{\bigcup (A^*X)^w / X \text{ fini}\} \subsetneq \overrightarrow{(\underline{K}^r)} = \{(A^*X)^w / X \text{ fini}\}^{\mathcal{B}} .$$

De plus $(\underline{K}^r)^w$ n'est pas clos par intersection.

Vu leur importance, nous réserverons un chapitre à l'étude des deux derniers exemples.

4 Parties testables par morceaux et localement testables

Nous étudierons dans ce chapitre les classes $\underline{J}^{\omega}$ des parties testables par morceaux et $\underline{LJ_1}^{\omega}$ des parties localement testables. Nous aurons besoin du

---

Lemme 4.1 Soit

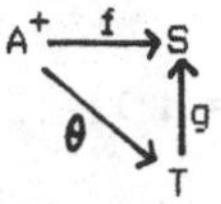

un diagramme commutatif où S et T sont deux semigroupes finis et f, g, θ des morphismes. Alors si f reconnait $L \subseteq A^{\omega}$, il en est de même de θ.

Preuve: On pose $Q=\{(t,h)\in T^2/h^2=h, th=t, (g(t),g(h))\in P_L\}$ et on montre que $L=\bigcup_{(t,h)\in Q} \theta^{-1}(t)\theta^{-1}(h)^{\omega}$ à l'aide du lemme 1.1. ■

Soit $\underline{J}$ la variété des semigroupes J-triviaux. Simon (1975) a montré que $\underline{J}^{+}=\{A^*a_1\ldots A^*a_nA^*/n>=1, a_i \in A\}^{\mathcal{B}}$. Les langages obtenus, appelés testables par morceaux, sont aussi les langages saturés par la congrence σ_k (pour un k>=1) définie par $\sigma_k(u)=\sigma_k(v)$ ssi u et v ont les mêmes sous-mots de longueur inférieure ou égale à k. On peut encore exprimer ces résultats de la façon suivante.

Nous dirons qu'un semigroupe S est k-testable par morceaux si la surjection canonique du semigroupe libre S^+ sur S factorise à travers S^+/σ_k, autrement dit si deux produits $s_1\ldots s_m$ et $t_1\ldots t_n$ sont égaux dans S dès que $\sigma_k(s_1\ldots s_m)=\sigma_k(t_1\ldots t_n)$ dans S^+. On peut alors reformuler le théorème de Simon de la façon suivante.

Théorème 4.2 $\underline{J}$ = { S / S k-testable par morceaux pour un k >= 1}.

En appliquant ce résultat aux mots infinis on obtient le

Théorème 4.3 Soit $\underline{J}$ la variété des semigroupes J-triviaux. On a l'inclusion stricte $\vec{\underline{J}}=\{A^*a_1\ldots A^*a_nA^{\omega}/n>=1, a_i \in A\}^{\mathcal{B}} \subsetneq \underline{J}^{\omega}=\{A^*a_1\ldots A^*a_nA^{\omega}, (A^*b_1\ldots A^*b_m)^{\omega}/n,m>=1\ a_i, b_j \in A\}^{\mathcal{B}}$.

Preuve: La première égalité se déduit immédiatement des formules $\overrightarrow{A^*a_1..A^*a_nA^*}=A^*a_1..A^*a_nA^{\omega}$ et $\overrightarrow{A^*/A^*a_1..A^*a_nA^*}=A^{\omega}/A^*a_1..A^*a_nA^{\omega}$.

Pour la deuxième posons $\mathcal{C}=\{A^*a_1..A^*a_nA^{\omega}, (A^*b_1..A^*b_m)^{\omega}\}^{\mathcal{B}}$ et $L(k,X,Y)=\{\alpha \in A^{\omega}$/l'ensemble des sous-mots de longueur <= k de α coincide avec X et l'ensemble des sous-mots de longueur <= k apparaissant infiniment souvent dans α coincide avec Y}.

Pour k fixé, les L(k,X,Y) constituent une partition de A^{ω} et l'on a pour tout k

$L(k,X,Y)=L(k+1,X+XA,Y,Y+YA)$. D'autre part on vérifie facilement que $A^*a_1...A^*a_nA^w$ est une réunion de $L(n,X,Y)$ et $(A^*b_1..A^*b_m)^w$ une réunion de $L(m,X,Y)$. On en déduit donc que tout élément de $\mathcal{C}$ est une réunion de $L(k,X,Y)$ pour un $k>=1$. La réciproque étant évidente, on obtient:

$$\mathcal{C} = \{ \bigcup L(k,X,Y) \ / \ k >= 1 \ , \ X,Y \text{ fini} \} . \qquad (4.1)$$

D'autre part on vérifie facilement que toute partie simple associée à $\sigma_k(u)= \sigma_k(uv)$ et $\sigma_k(v)= \sigma_k(v^2)$ est définie par

$\sigma_k(u)\sigma_k(v)^w=\{ \alpha$ /les sous-mots de longueur $<=k$ de α sont ceux de u,les sous-mots de longueur $<=k$ apparaissant infiniment souvent dans α sont ceux de v}. (4.2)

De (4.1) et (4.2) on déduit immédiatement l'égalité

$$\mathcal{C} = \{ L \ / \ L \text{ reconnu par } A^+/\sigma_k \text{ pour un } k >= 1 \} . \qquad (4.3)$$

Puisque $A^+/\sigma_k \in \underline{J}$ on en déduit l'inclusion $\mathcal{C} \subseteq \underline{J}^w$.

Réciproquement, si $L \in \underline{J}^w$ est reconnu par $f:A^+\text{-->}S$, on dispose d'après le théorème 4.2 du diagramme commutatif suivant.

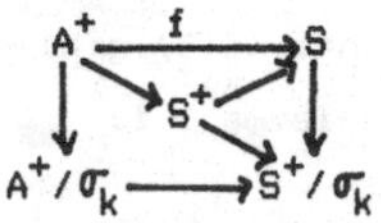

On en déduit d'après le lemme 4.1 que L est reconnu par A^+/σ_k et est donc dans $\mathcal{C}$ d'après (4.3).

On obtient donc $\underline{J}^w \subseteq \mathcal{C}$, d'où l'égalité $\mathcal{C} = \underline{J}^w$ recherchée. ■

Soit $\underline{LJ}_1$={S/eSe est un treillis pour tout idempotent e} la variété des semigroupes localement idempotents commutatifs. Brzozowski-Simon (1973) et Mac Naughton (1974) ont montré que $\underline{LJ}_1{}^+ = \{uA^*,A^*uA^*,A^*u/u\ A^+\}^{\mathcal{B}}$. Les langages obtenus, appelés <u>localement testables</u>, sont aussi les langages saturés par la congruence $\sim_k$ (pour un $k>=1$) définie sur A^+ de la façon suivante.

Pour tout mot $u \in A^+$ de longueur $|u| >= k$ nous noterons $G_k(u)$ le facteur gauche de u de longueur k, $D_k(u)$ le facteur droit de u de longueur k et $I_k(u)$ l'ensemble des facteurs internes de u de longueur k. On définit alors la congruence $\sim_k$ par $u \sim_k v$ ssi

* ou bien $|u| >= k$, $|v| >= k$ et $G_k(u) = G_k(v)$, $D_k(u) = D_k(v)$, $I_k(u) = I_k(v)$.
* ou bien $u = v$.

Nous dirons qu'un semigroupe S est <u>k-testable</u> si la surjection canonique du semigroupe libre S^+ sur S factorise à travers $S^+/\sim_k$, autrement dit si deux produits $s_1...s_m$ et $t_1...t_n$ sont égaux dans S dès que $s_1...s_m \sim_k t_1...t_n$ dans S^+.

Le théorème de Brzozowski-Simon peut alors être formulé de la façon suivante.

<u>Théorème 4.4</u> $\underline{LJ}_1 = \{ S \ / \ S$ localement k-testable pour un $k >= 1 \}$.

Revenons maintenant aux mots infinis.

Nous dirons qu'une partie L de A^w est <u>k-testable</u> si elle est combinaison booléenne de parties de la forme $XA^w/A^+YA^w/A^+(ZA^*)^w$ pour des $X,Y,Z \subseteq A^k$. L sera dite <u>localement testable</u> si elle est k-testable pour un $k >= 1$. Les classes de parties correspondantes seront notées respectivement $\mathcal{C}_k$ et $\mathcal{C} = \bigcup_{k>=1} \mathcal{C}_k$.

On vérifie facilement que $\mathcal{C}_k$ est l'algèbre de Boole engendrée par les parties de la forme $uA^w, A^+uA^w, A^+(uA^*)^w$ lorsque u décrit A^k, et que $\mathcal{C}$ est celle engendrée par les parties de la forme $uA^w, A^+uA^w, A^+(uA^*)^w$ lorsque u décrit A^+.

On obtient alors le

<u>Théorème 4.5</u> Soit $\underline{LJ}_1$ la variété des semigroupes localement idempotents commutatifs. On a les égalités

$$\underline{LJ}_1{}^w = \overrightarrow{\underline{LJ}_1} = \{ uA^w , A^+uA^w, A^+(uA^*)^w / u \in A^+ \}^{\mathcal{B}} .$$

<u>Preuve:</u> Nous noterons $[u]_k$ la classe du mot $u \in A^+$ modulo $\sim_k$. Pour tout mot infini $\alpha \in A^w$ nous noterons $\alpha[k]$ le facteur gauche de longueur k de α et $I_k(\alpha)$ [respectivement $I_k^\infty(\alpha)$] l'ensemble des facteurs internes [infiniment répétés] de longueur k de α.

On constate alors que toute partie simple associée à $[x]_k=[xy]_k$ et $[y]_k=[y^2]_k$ est définie par

$[x]_k[y]_k{}^w = \{ \alpha / \alpha[k]=G_k(x), I_k(\alpha)=I_k(x), I_k^\infty(\alpha)=I_k(y), D_k(y)G_k(y) \in I_{2k}^\infty(\alpha)\}$. (4.4)

L'inclusion dans le sens direct est évidente(les hypothèses impliquent $|x|>=k$ et $|y|>=k$).On obtient la réciproque en choisissant,pour chaque élément α du membre droit, un mot u et une suite $(u_n)_{n>=1}$ vérifiant

$\alpha = G_k(x)uD_k(y)G_k(y)u_1D_k(y)G_k(y)u_2D_k(y)G_k(y)\ldots$ avec $G_k(y)u_nD_k(y) \in [y]_k$ pour tout $n>=1$.

L'égalité (4.4) et l'inclusion $\mathcal{C}_k \subseteq \mathcal{C}_{k'}$ pour $k'>=k$ montrent que l'on a

$\{ L / L$ reconnu par $A^+/\sim_k \} \subseteq \mathcal{C}_{2k}$. (4.5)

Pour tout $k>=1$, posons maintenant $L(k,x,Y,Z) = \{\alpha / \alpha[k]=x, I_k(\alpha)=Y, I_k^\infty(\alpha)=Z\}$. Il est clair que tout élément de $\mathcal{C}_k$ est une union de $L(k,x,Y,Z)$. Or chacune de ces parties est reconnue par $A^+/\sim_k$. En effet si $\alpha \in L(k,x,Y,Z)$ est contenu dans la partie simple $[u]_k[v]_k{}^w$, on a d'après (4.4) $G_k(u)=x$, $I_k(u)=Y$ et $I_k(v)=Z$, d'où $[u]_k[v]_k{}^w \subseteq L(k,x,Y,Z)$. On a donc $\mathcal{C}_k \subseteq \{L/L$ reconnu par $A^+/\sim_k\}$, ce qui associé à (4.5) nous fournit:

$\mathcal{C} = \{ L / L$ reconnu par $A^+/\sim_k$ pour un $k >= 1 \}$. (4.6)

Puisque $A^+/\sim_k \in \underline{LJ}_1$ on en déduit l'inclusion $\mathcal{C} \subseteq \underline{LJ}_1{}^w$.

Réciproquement si $L \in \underline{LJ}_1{}^w$ est reconnu par $f:A^+ \rightarrow S$, on dispose d'après le théorème 4.4 du diagramme commutatif suivant:

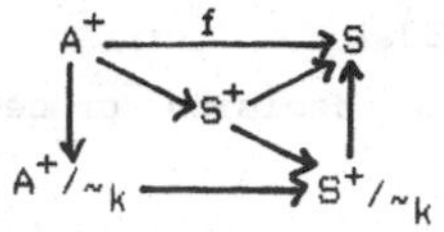

On en déduit d'après le lemme 4.1 que L est reconnu par $A^+/\sim_k$ et est donc dans d'après (4.6). On obtient ainsi $\underline{LJ}_1{}^w \subseteq \mathcal{C}$ d'où finalement l'égalité $\underline{LJ}_1{}^w = \mathcal{C}$.

$\underline{LJ}_1{}^w$ est donc une algèbre booléenne d'où $\overrightarrow{\underline{LJ}_1} \subseteq \underline{LJ}_1{}^w$ d'après (3.2).

Enfin l'inclusion réciproque $\mathcal{C} \subseteq \overrightarrow{\underline{LJ}_1}$ se déduit immédiatement des formules $uA^w=\overrightarrow{uA^*}$, $A^+uA^w=\overrightarrow{A^+uA^*}$ et $A^+(uA^*)^w=\overrightarrow{A^+u}$. ∎

5 Conclusion

Nous avons montré que, pour les variétés les plus usuelles , la classe V^w des parties de mots infinis reconnues par les V-automates pouvait être décrite de façon agréable. D'autres variétés devraient également se prêter à de telles descriptions.

D'autre part nous avons montré la nécessité de distinguer cette classe de la classe $\overrightarrow{V}$ des parties de mots infinis reconnues par les V-automates déterministes. Le théorème de Mac Naughton stipule l'égalité $\overrightarrow{V} = V^w$ dans le cas où V est la variété de tous les semigroupes et Perrin (1982) a donné une condition suffisante pour que cette égalité ait lieu, à savoir que V soit fermée par produit de Schutzenberger. L'exemple de la variété $\underline{LJ}_1$ montre que cette condition n'est pas nécessaire et aucune condition nécessaire et suffisante n'est connue à ce jour.

Enfin un problème reste ouvert qui est de caractériser, par des opérations sur les parties, les classes pouvant être des V^w. La situation est ici plus compliquée que dans le cas des mots finis, puisque les classes V^w ne sont pas des algèbres booléennes et que les relations ne sont pas syntaxiques.

Références

[1] A. Arnold (a paraitre): A syntactic congruence for rational w-languages.

[2] A. Arnold, M. Nivat (1982): Comportement de processus; Colloque des Mathématiques de l'Informatique, Paris, 35-68.

[3] J.A. Brzozowski, I. Simon (1973): Characterizations of locally testable events ; Discrete Math., 4, 243-271.

[4] J.R. Buchi (1962): On a decision method in restricted second order arithmetic; Logic, Methodology and Philosophy of Science, (Proc. 1960 Int. Congr.), Stanford Univ. Press, 1-11.

[5] S. Eilenberg (1976): Automata, Languages and Machines, Vol. B, Academic Press.

[6] G. Lallement (1979): Semigroups and Combinatorial Applications, Whiley, New-York.

[7] L.H. Landweber (1969): Decision Problems for w-automata; Math. Syst. Th., 3, 376-384.

[8] R. Mac Naughton (1966): Testing and generating infinite sequences by a finite automaton; Inf. and Control, 9, 521-530.

[9] R. Mac Naughton (1974): Algebraic decision procedures for local testability; Math. Syst. Th., 8, 60-76.

[10] D. Muller (1963): Infinite sequences and finite machines; Switching Theory and Logical Design, (proc. 4th IEEE Symp.), 3-16.

[11] J.P. Péouchet (en préparation): Etude syntaxique des parties reconnaissables de mots infinis.

[12] D. Perrin (1982): Variétés de semigroupes et mots infinis;C. R. Acad. Sci. Paris,295,595-598.

[13] D. Perrin (1984): Recent Results on Automata and Infinite Words;Math. Found. Comp. Sci.,(Proc. 11th symp. Praha),Goos and Hartmanis ed.,Springer.

[14] J.E. Pin (1984): Variétés de langages et de monoides,Masson,Paris.

[15] M.P. Schutzenberger (1965): On finite monoids having only trivial subgroups;Inf. and Control,8,190-194.

[16] I. Simon (1975): Piecewise testable events;Automata Theory and Formal Languages,(2nd G.I. Conf.),Lect. Notes in Comp. Sci.,33,Springer-Verlag,214-322.

[17] W. Thomas (1979): Star-free regular sets of w-sequences;Inf. and Control, 42,148-156.

[18] W. Thomas (1981): A combinatorial approach to the theory of w-automata;Inf. and Control,48,261-283.

[19] K. Wagner (1979): On w-Regular Sets;Inf. and Control,43,123-177.

[20] Y. Zalcstein (1972): Locally testable langages;J. Comp. Syst. Sci.,6,151-167.

EQUATIONS IN FREE PARTIALLY COMMUTATIVE MONOIDS

Christine DUBOC
Laboratoire d'informatique
Université de Rouen B.P 67
76130 Mont Saint Aignan FRANCE

RESUME: On caractérise les solutions de toutes les équations à deux inconnues dans les monoïdes partiellement commutatifs libres. On montre que les solutions génériques sont cycliques. On définit ensuite les relations de transposition (t et t' sont transposés ssi t=xy et t'=yx) et de conjugaison (t et t' sont conjugués ssi tλ=λt'). On montre que la conjugaison est la fermeture transitive de la transposition et que l'ensemble des facteurs de conjugaison λ est un ensemble reconnaissable du monoïde partiellement commutatif.

ABSTRACT: We characterize the solutions of all the equations in two unknowns in the free partially commutative monoids. We show that the solutions are basically cyclic. Afterwards, we define the transposition (t and t' are transposed iff t=xy and t'=yx) and the conjugacy relations (t and t' are conjugate iff tλ=λt'). We show that the conjugacy is the transitive closure of the transposition and that the set of conjugacy factors λ is a recognizable subset of the partially commutative monoid.

INTRODUCTION:

The free partially commutative monoids (or f.p.c.m.) have been used as a tool in two different areas. Indeed, they were introduced by Cartier and Foata (2) to study rearrangements of words and to give a combinatorial proof of Mac-Mahon's Master Theorem. In purely computer science, they have been proposed by Mazurkiewicz (8) as a model for parallel computation. More precisely, it consists in associating a symbol (a name) with every atomic action (event) in the system and then describing the fact that two actions may be concurrently performed by means of a suitable concurrency relation on the set of actions names.

As an example (cf (6)), let us consider two processes P_1 and P_2 which repetitively compute a given sequence of two actions respectively labelled by a_1, b_1 and a_2, b_2:

P_1	P_2
a_1 : x:=2*x	a_2 : x:=x+1
b1 : y:=2*y	b2 : y:=y+1

The actions a_1 and b_2 may commute, as well as the actions b_1 and a_2 because they do not share the same variable. The set of all valid concurrent behaviours is the set of all the behaviours which are equivalent to some sequential composition of P_1 and P_2.

The free partially commutative monoids have been widely studied for themselves and in particular characterizations of their recognizable and rational subsets have been proposed ((1),(3),(4),(9),(12)).

In this paper, we are interested in solving equations in fpcm.

After having stated some general properties over the free partially commutative monoids, we show that equations in two unknowns which are unbalanced (i.e., at least one unknown has more occurrences on one side of the equation), admit only cyclic solutions. In the case of balanced equations we prove that the solutions whose alphabets are connected (with respect to the concurrency relation) are also cyclic. As consequences, we state two results already obtained in (5) concerning the equations $t^n = t'^m$ and $t\ t' = t't$.

In the last section, we are concerned with the study of conjugacy in fpcm. We recall that two words t and t' of a free monoid A^* are conjugate if and only if they satisfy one of the two following equivalent conditions:

(i) words x and y exist such that $t = xy$ and $t' = yx$.

(ii) a word λ exists such that $t\lambda = \lambda t'$.

In the case of partially commutative monoids, these two conditions are no longer equivalent. We call transposition the relation defined by (i) and conjugacy the one defined by (ii).
Then we show that conjugacy is the transitive closure of transposition. Moreover, we prove that the set of conjugacy factors of t and t' (i.e. the set $\{ \lambda \mid t\lambda = \lambda t' \}$) is a recognizable subset of the free partially commutative monoid.

I.FREE PARTIALLY COMMUTATIVE MONOIDS:

Let A be a finite alphabet and A^* the free monoid it generates. Let $\Theta \subset A\times A$ be a symmetrical and non reflexive relation called concurrency relation. We denote by $\sim$ the congruence in A^* generated by the set of relations $\{ (ab,ba) \mid (a,b) \in \Theta \}$.

The quotient monoid of A^* by $\sim$, denoted by $M(A,\Theta)$ is the <u>free partially commutative monoid</u> over A associated with Θ.
An element of $M(A,\Theta)$, called a <u>trace</u>, consists of all the possible sequential executions of a given set of actions which are consistent with the concurrency relation.
We denote by 1 the empty word of A^* as well as its equivalence class, and by A^+ the semigroup $A^*-\{1\}$. The number of occurrences of $a \in A$ in a word $w \in A^*$ is denoted by $|w|_a$.

Let B be a subalphabet of A, then the projection of A^* into B^* is denoted by Π_B and defined as : $\Pi_B(a)=a$ if $a \in B$ and $\Pi_B(a)=1$ otherwise. By extension we denote by $\Pi_B(t)$ the projection of a trace t. The relations $A \times A - \Theta$ and $B \times B \cap \Theta$ are denoted respectively by $\overline{\Theta}$ and Θ_B.

We call <u>non commutation graph</u> of B the graph denoted by $(B,\overline{\Theta})$, whose vertices are the letters of B and whose edges are the pairs of letters of B that do not commute. We say that B is a <u>clique</u> if $(B,\overline{\Theta})$ is a complete graph, i.e. any two letters of B do not commute. Once for all, we denote by $A_1,\ldots,A_p$ the maximal cliques of A.
We say that the subsets B and C of A are <u>independent</u> if any letter of B commute with any letter of C, i.e. $B \times C \subset \Theta$. We denote by alph (t) the set of letters occurring in t. For any $t,t' \in M(A,\Theta)$ we write $t \mathcal{Z} t'$ if alph (t) and alph (t') are independent.

A subset B of A is said to be <u>connected</u> if the graph $(B,\overline{\Theta})$ is connected. By extension, $t \in M(A,\Theta)$ is connected if alph (t) is connected. Let $C_1,\ldots,C_k$ be the connected components of $(\text{alph}(t),\overline{\Theta})$. Then t can be uniquely written as a product of connected elements t_j of $M(C_j,\Theta_{C_j})$ $(1 \leq j \leq k)$: $t = t_1 \ldots t_k$. $(t_j = \Pi_{C_j}(t))$.

We shall see afterwards that this condition of connectedness often appears when having to solve equations. The previous remark shows that it is not restrictive since we have : $t=t'$ if and only it t and t' have the same connected components $C_1,\ldots,C_k$ and for $j=1,\ldots,k$: $\Pi_{C_j}(t)=\Pi_{C_j}(t')$. Therefore, it suffices to solve the equation for the different projections over the connected components. The original solution of the equation is then obtained as the product of the k connected solutions.

<u>Example 1</u> : $A = \{a,b,c,d,e,f\}$
$\overline{\Theta} = \{(a,b)\ ;\ (b,a)\ ;\ (b,c)\ ;\ (c,b)\ ;\ (a,c)\ ;\ (c,a)\ ;$
$(b,d)\ ;\ (d,b)\ ;\ (d,e)\ ;\ (e,d)\ ;\ (c,e)\ ;\ (e,c)\}$

$(A,\overline{\Theta})$ is the graph :

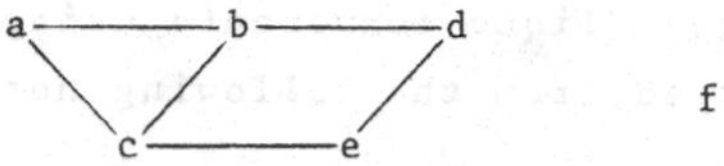

and the maximal cliques are :

$A_1 = \{a,b,c\}$ $\quad A_2 = \{b,d\}$ $\quad A_3 = \{d,e\}$

$A_4 = \{c,e\}$ $\quad A_5 = \{f\}$

Let $B=\{d,e\}$ and $C=\{a,f\}$ then the subsets B and C are independent. The connected components of t =acdaf are $C_1=\{a,c\}$, $C_2=\{d\}$ and $C_3=\{f\}$.

In the sequel, $\Pi_i(u)$ stands for $\Pi_{A_i}(u)$ with $i \in \{1,\dots,p\}$. The following proposition is a modified version of the one established by Cori and Perrin (4). It permits to characterize the elements of $M(A,\Theta)$.

<u>Proposition 1.1.</u> *For any $u,v \in A^*$, $u \sim v$ if and only if for each $1 \le i \le p$: $\quad \Pi_i(u) = \Pi_i(v)$.*

Cori and Métivier (3) have introduced the two following definitions :

Let $F=(w_i)_{i=1,\dots,p}$ be a family of words over the alphabets $(A_i)_{i=1,\dots,p}$. We say that F is <u>reconstructible</u> if there exists a $w \in A^*$ such that for each $1 \le i \le p$: $\Pi_i(w)=w_i$. More generally, F is <u>quasi-reconstructible</u> if it satisfies the weaker condition :

$$\forall i,j \in \{1,\dots,p\}: \quad a \in A_i \cap A_j \Longrightarrow |w_i|_a = |w_j|_a .$$

Now we can state a corollary of proposition 1.1.:

<u>Corollary 1.2.</u> : *$M(A,\Theta)$ is isomorphic to the set of reconstructible families.*

It follows that any free partially commutative monoid can be embedded in a direct product of free monoids. This corollary allows us to write a trace t of $M(A,\Theta)$ as a reconstructible family $(u_1,\dots,u_p)$ $(u_i=\Pi_i(t))$. If $t=(u_1,\dots,u_p)$ and $t'=(v_1,\dots,v_p)$, the independence condition can be written as $t \, Z \, t' \Longleftrightarrow (\forall i=1,\dots,p : u_i \ne 1 \Longrightarrow v_i=1)$.

The method for solving equations in $M(A,\Theta)$, i.e. for determining under which conditions a set of traces satisfy a non trivial relation, is first to consider the traces as families of words in A_i^*. Secondly to solve separately the p equations in the free monoids $A_1^*, A_2^*, \dots, A_p^*$ it defines. And thirdly to construct a total solution of the equation from the p solutions over the clique components using the properties of the reconstructibility deduced from the following notion and results:

Let $F=(w_i)_{i=1,\ldots,p}$ be a quasi-reconstructible family, the <u>graph of occurrences</u> of F denoted by G(F) is defined as follows : The vertices of the directed graph G(F) are the pairs (a,i) with $a \in A_k$ and $1 \leq i \leq |w_k|_a$ and the edges are defined by $(a,i) \longrightarrow (b,j)$ if there exists $k \in \{1,\ldots,p\}$ such that $\{a,b\} \subset A_k$ and the ith occurrence of a in w_k is immediately followed by the jth occurrence of b in w_k.

We can now state the following result:

<u>Proposition 1.3.</u> : *A quasi-reconstructible family F is reconstructible if and only if its graph of occurrences G(F) has no cycle.*

<u>Example 2</u> : Let A and $\overline{\Theta}$ defined as Example 1. The graph of the quasi-reconstructible family F=(bacb, bbd, de, ec) is :

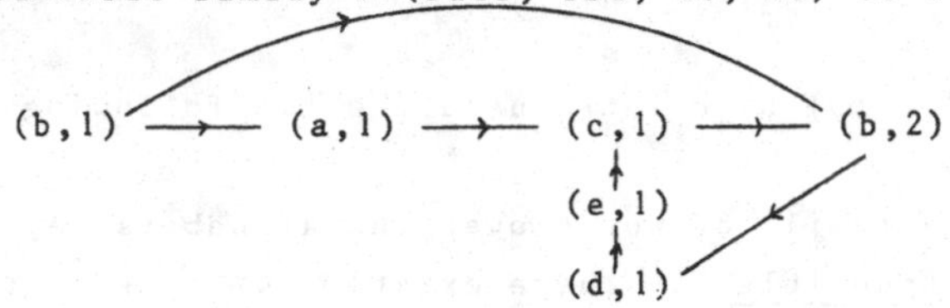

it contains the cycle :

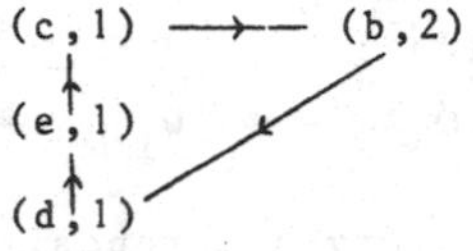

thus the family F is not reconstructible.

The above characterization allows us to show the following properties of the reconstructibility:

<u>Proposition 1.4.</u> : *Given a quasi-reconstructible family $F \in A_1^* \times \ldots \times A_p^*$, then for each family $G \in A_1^* \times \ldots \times A_p^*$, the following conditions are equivalent :*
(i) FG is a reconstructible family.
(ii) F and G are reconstructible families.

<u>Proposition 1.5.</u> : *Let $k \in \mathbb{N}^*$ and $F \in A_1^* \times \ldots \times A_p^*$.*
Then F^k is reconstructible iff F is reconstructible.

II - EQUATIONS IN TWO UNKNOWNS :

We call equation in two unknowns u and v, a pair $e, e' \in \{u,v\}^*$ of words. As usual we write e=e' for such an equation. It is said to be balanced if $|e|_u = |e'|_u$ and $|e|_v = |e'|_v$. The traces t and $t' \in M(A,\Theta)$ satisfy the equation e=e' if this equality holds in $M(A,\Theta)$ when u and v are substituted to t and t' respectively.

The following theorem permits us to solve any equation in two unknowns. Moreover, in the case of an unbalanced equation, it shows that the result obtained in the free monoid (two words satisfying an equation in two unknowns are powers of a common third word) remains true.

Theorem 2.1. : *Let e=e' be an equation in the two unknowns u and v.*

1°) if e=e' is unbalanced then, t and $t' \in M(A,\Theta)$ satisfy the equation iff there exist $w \in M(A,\Theta)$, α, $\beta \in \mathbb{N}$ such that $t=w^\alpha$, $t'=w^\beta$ and $\alpha(|e|_u - |e'|_u) = \beta(|e'|_v - |e|_v)$.

2°) if e=e' is balanced then t and $t' \in M(A,\Theta)$ satisfy the equation iff for each connected components C of t and C' of t' that are not independent, the two following conditions hold :

(i) : C=C'

(ii): $\exists w \in M(C,\Theta_C)$, α, $\beta \in \mathbb{N}$ such that

$$\Pi_C(t) = w^\alpha \text{ and } \Pi_C(t') = w^\beta.$$

As consequences, we can deduce the two following corollaries, obtained by direct methods in (5).

Corollary 2.2. : *For any t, $t' \in M(A,\Theta)$ the following conditions are equivalent :*

(i) : $\exists i,j \in \mathbb{N}^*$ such that $t^i = t'^j$.

(ii): $\exists w \in M(A,\Theta)$, α, $\beta \in \mathbb{N}$ such that $t=w^\alpha$ and $t'=w^\beta$.

An element $t \in M(A,\Theta)$ is primitive if it is not a power of another element ; (i.e. $t \neq 1$ and $t=w^\beta \Longrightarrow \beta=1$). We denote by r(t) the root of t in $M(A,\Theta)$ i.e. the unique primitive element $r(t) \in M(A,\Theta)$, such that $t=r(t)^\alpha$.

For any $t \in M(A,\Theta)$, we denote by C(t) the commutator of t, that is to say the set $\{t' \in M(A,\Theta) \ / \ tt'=t't\}$.

Corollary 2.3. : *Given* $t \in M(A,\Theta)$ *and* $C_1, \dots, C_k$ *its connected components, then* $C(t)=r(t_1)^* \dots r(t_k)^* . B^*$ *where* $t_i = \Pi_{C_i}(t)$ *and* $B \subseteq A$ *is the greatest subalphabet which is independent of alph (t).*

Finally we mention a result concerning an equation in three unknowns :

Lyndon and Schutzenberger have shown that in the free monoid, the equation $u^i v^j = w^k$ with $i,j,k \geq 2$ admits only cyclic solutions (that is: u,v,w are powers of a common word). The following corollary shows that under connectedness hypotheses, this result remains true in $M(A,\Theta)$.

Theorem 2.4. : *Let* w *be a connected trace of* $M(A,\Theta)$. *Then for any* $u, v \in M(A,\Theta)$ *the following conditions are equivalent*

(i) : $\exists i,j,k \geq 2$ *such that* $u^i v^j = w^k$.

(ii): $\exists \alpha, \beta, \gamma \in \mathbb{N}$, $\exists t \in M(A,\Theta)$ *such that* $u=t^\alpha$, $v=t^\beta$ *and* $w=t^\gamma$.

III - CONJUGACY :

We define two relations $\mathcal{T}$ and $\mathcal{C}$ on $M(A,\Theta)$ by setting for each $t, t' \in M(A,\Theta)$:

1°) $t \mathcal{T} t' \iff \exists x,y \in M(A,\Theta)$ such that $t=xy$ and $t'=yx$. The traces t and t' are said to be transposed.

2°) $t \mathcal{C} t' \iff \exists \lambda \in M(A,\Theta)$ such that $t\lambda = \lambda t'$ .The traces t and t' are said to be conjugate, and λ is said to be a conjugacy-factor of (t,t').

Notice that it can be deduced from the results we prove here that $\mathcal{C}$ is an equivalence relation.

If $\Theta = \emptyset$, i.e. if $M(A,\Theta)$ is the free monoid A^* then the relations $\mathcal{T}$ and $\mathcal{C}$ are equal, but it is not the case in general.
Indeed, if $(a,b) \notin \Theta$, $(b,c) \notin \Theta$ and $(a,c) \in \Theta$ then $(abc)(aba) \sim (aba)(cba)$ thus abc and cba are conjugate but they are not transposed. Then we have the result :

Proposition 3.1. : *The following conditions are equivalent :*

(i) : $M(A,\Theta)$ *is a direct product of free monoids (i.e.* $\overline{\Theta}$ *is transitive)*

(ii): $\mathcal{T} = \mathcal{C}$

(iii): $\mathcal{T}$ *is an equivalence relation.*

It is easy to see that two traces t and t' are conjugate (respectively transposed) if and only if they have the same connected components $C_1,\dots,C_k$ and if for each $j=1,\dots,k$: t_j and t'_j are conjugate (respectively transposed) in $M(C_j, \Theta_{C_j})$. Moreover, if $\chi(t,t')$ (respectively $\chi_j(t_j,t'_j)$) designates the set of conjugacy factors of (t,t') (respectively (t_j, t'_j)) belonging to $M(A,\Theta)$ (respectively $M(C_j,\Theta_{C_j})$) then the equality holds :

(1) $\chi(t,t')= \chi_1(t_1,t'_1)\dots \chi_k(t_k,t'_k).\ B^*$ where $B \subseteq A$ is the greatest subalphabet which is independent of alph (t)(=alph (t')).

Moreover we have the following result:

<u>Proposition 3.2.</u> : *For any $t,t' \in M(A,\Theta)$, t and t' are conjugate iff their roots $r(t)$ and $r(t')$ are conjugate and if there exists $\alpha \in \mathbb{N}^*$ such that $t=r(t)^\alpha$ and $t'=r(t')^\alpha$.*

(2) Moreover, the equality : $\chi(t,t')= \chi(r(t),r(t'))$ holds.

The <u>diameter</u> of $(A,\overline{\Theta})$ denoted by d, is the greatest distance between two letters of the same connected component (i.e. it is the length of the largest paths in the graph $(A,\overline{\Theta})$, not entering twice the same node).

Thus, we can state our main theorem which shows in particular that the conjugacy is the transitive closure of the transposition:

<u>Theorem 3.3.</u> : *Let $t,t' \in M(A,\Theta)$. The following conditions are equivalent:*

(i) t and t' are conjugate.

(ii) there exist an integer $0 \le s \le d$ and traces $t_0,t_1,\dots, t_s$ such that: $t=t_0 \top t_1 \top \dots \top t_{s-1} \top t_s=t'$.

(iii) there exist an integer $0 \le s \le d$ and traces $z_0,z_1,\dots,z_s$ such that : $t=z_0z_1\dots z_s$, $t'=z_sz_{s-1}\dots z_0$ and for $0 \le i < j-1 < s$: $z_i\, Z\, z_j$.

Furthermore, in the case of connected and primitive traces t and t' we have:

(3) $\chi(t,t')=t^*(z_0\dots z_{s-1})\dots(z_0z_1)(z_0)$.

<u>Proof:</u> Here we give the outline of the proof.

(iii) $\Longrightarrow$(ii) Let $t_0=(z_0)(z_1\dots z_s)$ then $t_0 \top t_1=(z_1\dots z_s)(z_0)$. Since $z_0\, Z\, z_2\dots z_s$, we have $t_1=(z_1z_0)(z_2\dots z_s) \top t_2=(z_2\dots z_s)(z_1z_0)$.

Repeating this construction, we obtain:

$t_{s-1}=(z_{s-1}\dots z_1z_0)(z_s) \top t_s=z_sz_{s-1}\dots z_1z_0=t'$.

(ii)$\Longrightarrow$(i) Since the transposition is included in the conjugacy, we have $t\, C^s t'$, and thus $t\, C\, t'$ using the transitivity of C.

(i)$\Longrightarrow$(iii) Let $t=(u_1,\ldots,u_p)$, $t'=(v_1,\ldots,v_p)$ and $\lambda=(\lambda_1,\ldots,\lambda_p)$ such that $t\lambda = \lambda t'$. Then for each $1 \leq i \leq p$, we have $u_i\lambda_i=\lambda_i v_i$.
Therefore using the property of conjugacy in free monoids, we prove the existence of integers $k_1,\ldots,k_p$ and words $x_1,y_1 \subset A_1^*,\ldots, x_p,y_p \subset A_p^*$ such that for each i we have: $u_i=x_iy_i$, $v_i=y_ix_i$ and $\lambda_i=(x_iy_i)^{k_i}x_i$.
Let $M=\max k_i$ and $m=\min k_i$. Using the fact that $(\lambda_1,\ldots,\lambda_p)$ is quasi-reconstructible, we can prove that $M-m<d$. Let $s=M-m+1$, for each $0 \leq r \leq s$ and for each $1 \leq i \leq p$ we set:

$$z_{i,r}=\begin{cases} y_i & \text{if } k_i=M-r+1 \\ x_i & \text{if } k_i=M-r \\ 1 & \text{otherwise.} \end{cases}$$

Then we show that for each $0 \leq r \leq s$, the family $(z_{1,r},\ldots,z_{p,r})$ is reconstructible in a trace z_r. And we verify that the traces $z_0,z_1,\ldots,z_s$ satisfy the conditions stated in (iii).□

Actually, knowing the number of transpositions necessary to obtain t from t', we can compute the number of transpositions necessary to obtain t^n from t'^n $(n>0)$.

<u>Proposition 3.4.</u> :*Let t and t' be two conjugate traces. If* $t\,T^s\,t'$ *for some* $0<s\leq d$ *then for each* $n>0$, $t^n\,T^r\,t'^n$ *holds for* $r=\lceil \frac{s}{n} \rceil$ *(where* $\lceil x \rceil$ *is the ceiling of x).*

As a consequence, we have: the n-th powers of two conjugate traces are transposed as soon as n is greater than or equal to the diameter of the non commutation graph.

The relation between the decompositions of two conjugate traces and their powers can been seen as follows:

Let $t=z_0\ldots z_s$ and $t'=z_s\ldots z_0$ be two conjugate traces with for $0 \leq i<j-1<s$: $z_i\,Z\,z_j$.
We consider a new alphabet $B=\{z_0,\ldots,z_s\}$ and a commutation relation ρ defined by: $(B,\overline{\rho})$: z_0——z_1——z_2——...——z_s. The set of all the possible writings of $t^n=(z_0\ldots z_s)^n$ over the alphabet B can be represented by the graph of the reconstructible family : $((z_0z_1)^n,(z_1z_2)^n,\ldots,(z_{s-1}z_s)^n)$ in $M(B,\overline{\rho})$:

<u>For example</u>: if s=7 and n=3 then t^3 and t'^3 are represented by the following graphs :

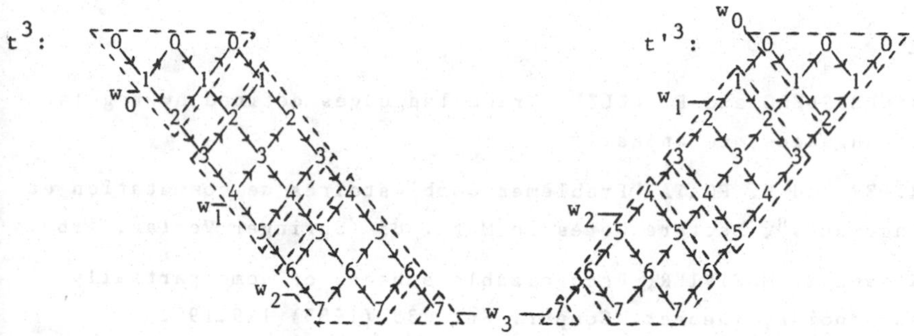

Let w_0, w_1, w_2, w_3 be the traces represented by the groupings indicated in the figure. Then $t^3 = w_0 w_1 w_2 w_3$, $t'^3 = w_3 w_2 w_1 w_0$ with $w_0 \, Z \, w_2 w_3$ and $w_1 \, Z \, w_3$.
We notice that $r=3$ is the ceiling of $\frac{s}{n} = \frac{7}{3}$.

Finally, we may establish a result concerning the recognizability of $\chi(t,t')$. In any monoid M, we say that a subset X of M is recognizable if there exists a finite monoid F and a morphism $f: M \longrightarrow F$ which saturates X, i.e. such that $f^{-1} f(X) = X$. We denote by Rec(M) the family of all recognizable subsets of M.

Cori and Perrin (4) have shown that Rec $(M(A,\Theta))$ is closed under the product and Métivier (9) has proved the following result:

Theorem 3.5. : *Let X be recognizable subset of $M(A,\Theta)$. If for any t belonging to X, t is connected then $X^* \in Rec(M(A,\Theta))$.*

Using the assertions (1),(2),(3) and the above results we show:

Corollary 3.6. : *For any t, $t' \in M(A,\Theta)$, $\chi(t,t')$ is a recognizable subset of $M(A,\Theta)$.*

We can notice that $C(t) = \chi(t,t)$, so we obtain in a different way the result proved in the second paragraph. Moreover, this shows that the commutator of a trace is a recognizable subset of $M(A,\Theta)$.

REFERENCES:

(1) I.J. AALBERSBERG and E. WELZL, Trace languages defined by regular string Languages, to appear.

(2) P. CARTIER and D. FOATA,"Problèmes Combinatoires de commutation et réarrangements", Lecture Notes in Math. 85 (Springer Verlag, 1969)

(3) R. CORI and Y. METIVIER, Recognizable subsets of some partially abelian monoids, Theoret. Comput. Sci. 35 (1985) 179-190.

(4) R. CORI and D. PERRIN, Automates et commutations partielles, Rairo Informat. Theor. 19(1985) 21-32.

(5) C. DUBOC, Some properties of commutation in free partially commutative monoids, Inform. processing letters 20(1985)1-4.

(6) M.P. FLE and G. ROUCAIROL, Maximal Serializability of iterated transactions, Theoret. Comput. Sci. 38(1985) 1-16.

(7) M. LOTHAIRE, "Combinatorics on words" (Addison Wesley, 1983).

(8) A. MAZURKIEWICZ, Concurrent program schemes and their interpretations, DAIMI Rep., PB-78, Aarhus University (1977).

(9) Y. METIVIER, Une condition suffisante de reconnaissabilité dans les monoïdes partiellement commutatifs, To appear.

(10) D. PERRIN, Words over a partially commutative alphabet, Rapport LITP n° 8459 (Paris, 1984).

(11) J.E. PIN, "Variétés de Langages Formels", (Masson, Paris, 1984).

(12) J. SAKAROVITCH, On regular trace languages, to appear.

SEPARATING AND TESTING

Ph. DARONDEAU

IRISA, Campus de Beaulieu
F 35042 RENNES CEDEX

ABSTRACT A class of languages is separable if, for each pair of non identical languages L' and L", there exists some language L such that $L \cap L' = \emptyset \longleftrightarrow L \cap L'' \neq \emptyset$. We give a negative answer to the question of separability for a large variety of classes of infinitary languages, from Alg^{ω} to Σ_1^1. We then prove that there exists for the calculus of communicating systems no notion of testing which can separate every pair of agents which differ by their infinite sequences of visible actions.

1. INTRODUCTION

A process may be defined as a generating device associated with a set of finite or infinite sequences of actions. In the traditional vision, actions of processes are supposed to be autonomous and the generating device operates independently of any environment. Thus, the extension of a process is a language, which is obtained by erasing "invisible" actions from sequences of actions. Processes advocated by R. Milner in his Calculus of Communicating Systems play a more elaborated game, since their actions are no longer autonomous : the generating device exerts some influence on the environment and vice-versa [10]. The extension (i.e. set of observable behaviours) of a process is still a language, but particular environmental conditions are now specified for each word.

We will determine, in those two distinct frameworks, wether processes with different extensions may be distinguished by testing processes.

As concerns autonomous processes, we suggest $|p| \cap |t| \neq \emptyset$ as a criterion of the satisfaction of test t by process p ($|\ \ |$ indicates extensions). We thus raise the question of separability of families of languages, where a family $\mathcal{L}$ is said separable iff for each pair of non identical languages L' and L" in $\mathcal{L}$, there exists some L in $\mathcal{L}$ such that $L \cap L' = \emptyset$ iff $L \cap L'' \neq \emptyset$.

That question has an obvious answer for families of finitary languages and will be asked only after infinitary languages. Even in that case, the separation between L' and L" is immediate when the adherence of L' differs from the adherence of L" [1]. Surprisingly enough, the question of separability has however a negative answer for all the families of infinitary languages that we have examined but the family of the rational. This negative fact holds of most families obtained by the operation of Kleene closure (4). It holds also of Σ_1^1 (11), which leaves little hope to find an adequate way of testing sufficiently general classes of processes.

As concerns communicating processes, we shall investigate the separability of C.C.S. under the basic notion of testing suggested by Hennessy and de Nicola, and also under possible variations of it (7). According to these authors, the testing process executes in parallel with the testee, and either reports success in a finite amount of time or fails to do so. Processes p and q are equivalent if for every test t, each of the assertions "x may satisfy t" and "x must satisfy t" is simultaneously verified or falsified by p and q. Based on this equivalence $\sim$ have been proposed fully abstract models (9) of C.C.S. and S.C.C.S. (7,8). There, the essential function of tests is to offer a criterion of operational nature to judge wether a semantics is correct or not.

Indeed, judgements on the correctness of semantics are based on the intuition that the criterion is adequate. We will give some evidence of the (partial) inadequacy of testing equivalences, by showing that any semantics fully abstract w.r.t. $\sim$ must equate some processes which differ by their infinite sequences of (visible) actions. Our previous results about Σ_1^1 are crucial to the proof of that claim. A possible way to avoid the above mentioned problem is to use implementation preorders in place of testing preorders, as we did for instance in (3).

It may be remarked that any result concerning separability of languages does also concern general tests. Given autonomous processes p and p' which generate languages L and L', every possible pair $\langle w,w'\rangle$ of words $w \in L$ and $w' \in L'$ is produced by their parallel run. Now, if success is attached to identical pairs $\langle w,w\rangle$, then "L' must satisfy L" is false if L' is not a singleton set, and is otherwise equivalent to "L' may satisfy L".

The body of the paper is organized as follows. Section 2 investigates the separation of families of languages. Section 3 extends the results to communicating processes. A short conclusion underlines some of the limitations of algebraic domains for the semantic modelling of concurrency. The detailed proofs of theorems may be found in (2).

2. THE ISSUE OF SEPARABILITY FOR FAMILIES OF LANGUAGES

After some definitions, we examine families of languages produced by the operation of Kleene closure acted upon corresponding families in Chomsky's hierarchy (§2.1). Next, we turn our attention to families of languages involving finitary or infinitary shuffle operations (§2.2). Finally, we consider the question of separability for Σ_1^1 (§2.3).

X is a denumerable alphabet, ε is the neutral element of the free monoïd X^* generated by X, and X^ω is the set $\mathbb{N} \to X$ of the infinite words on X. A class (i.e. set) of languages on X is finitary, resp. infinitary if every language in the class is a subset of X^*, resp. X^ω. In all the sequel, $\mathcal{L}$ resp. $\mathcal{L}$ denotes a class of finitary resp. infinitary languages on X. By way of definition, $\mathcal{L}$ is separable iff for every pair of non identical languages L' and L" in $\mathcal{L}$, there exists some L in $\mathcal{L}$ such that $L \cap L' = \emptyset \Longleftrightarrow L \cap L'' \neq \emptyset$. When such an L exists, we say that (L', L") is a separable pair which is separated by L.

2.1. Kleene closures of AFL's

Given some family $\mathcal{L}$ of finitary languages, a classical way to get a corresponding family $\mathcal{L}$ of infinitary languages is to take the Kleene closure $\mathcal{L}^\omega$ of $\mathcal{L}$, defined as the set of the languages which may be defined by some finite expression $\bigcup_{i=1}^{n} A_i (B_i - \{\varepsilon\})^\omega$ where $A_i, B_i \in \mathcal{L}$. The following theorems answer the question of separability for the hierarchy of families $\mathcal{L}$ obtained this way from the classical AFL's. (Rat resp. Alg denote as usual the families of rational resp. algebraic languages).

<u>Theorem 1</u> Rat^ω is separable.

<u>Proof</u> By the classical theorems of Büchi and Mac Naughton (4), the family of the infinitary rational languages is closed under complementation ▫

<u>Theorem 2</u> If Alg is included in $\mathcal{L}$ then $\mathcal{L}^\omega$ is not separable.

<u>Proof indication</u> Let $E = a^+b$ and $F = \bigcup_{n>0} E^* a^n b E^* a^n b$ (where a,b are letters). If E^ω and F^ω are separated by L, then L does not belong to the Kleene closure of Fin (the class of the finitary languages on X) ▫

2.2. Finitary and infinitary shuffle operations

Two ways are left open to discover some separable families of languages without changing radically their method of formation : one may apply the operation of Kleene closure to finitary families incomparable with Alg, or one may apply variants of the closure operation. We shall explore these two ways.

Conc = $(\cdot, \cup, *, \odot, \circledast)(X \cup \{\varepsilon\})$ is the class of languages produced from ε and letters of X by the rational operators $(\cdot, \cup, *)$ joined to the concurrent operators of shuffle $(\odot)$ and iterated shuffle $(\circledast)$ on $P(X^*)$:

$$A \odot B = \{u_1v_1 \ldots u_nv_n \mid u_i, v_i \in X^*, u_1 \ldots u_n \in A, v_1 \ldots v_n \in B\},$$

$$A^{\circledast} = \bigcup_{i \geq 0} A^{(i)}, \quad A^{(0)} = \{\varepsilon\}, \quad A^{(i+1)} = A^{(i)} \odot A .$$

Properties Alg $\not\subset$ Conc, Conc $\not\subset$ Alg (12,5).

Theorem 3 If Conc is included in $\mathcal{L}$ then $\mathcal{L}^{\omega}$ is not separable.

Proof indication A non-separable pair of languages is given by the following definitions

$$L = (a^*b^*)^* (A^{\omega} \cup B^{\omega} \cup C^{\omega})$$

$$L' = (a^*b^*)^* (A^{\omega} \cup B^{\omega}) \cup ((a \odot b)^{\circledast} \odot (a^+ \cup b^+)) (D^{\omega} \cup E^{\omega}).$$

where we let

$$A = ((ab)^{\circledast} \odot a^+) \quad , \quad B = ((ba)^{\circledast} \odot b^+) ,$$

$$C = (a \odot b)^{\circledast} \quad ,$$

$$D = b(a \odot b)^{\circledast} a \ , \ E = a(a \odot b)^{\circledast} b \qquad \square$$

In the development of the proofs indicated above, the principle is to make use of the following property of (classes of) languages L defined by Kleene closure : if $w \in L$ then there exist infinitely many decompositions u v of w such that $u(v')^{\omega} \in L$ for infinitely many left factors v' of v. To reach separable classes, a possible way out may be to replace the ω-operation on languages by some variant $\circledcirc$ in which the shuffle operation plays the usual role of concatenation. Therefore, we introduce the following operators $\circledcirc : P(X^+) \to P(X^{\omega})$ and $\odot : P(X^*) \times P(X^{\omega}) \to P(X^{\omega})$, respectively called the infinite and infinitary shuffle operators :

$$L^{\textcircled{\omega}} = \{w \in X^{\omega} \mid \exists f : \mathbb{N} \to (\mathbb{N} \to (X \cup \{\varepsilon\})) : f(i) = f_i, \exists g : \mathbb{N} \to \mathbb{N},$$
$$(w = \lim_j (f_{g(0)}(0)\ f_{g(1)}(1) \ldots f_{g(j)}(j))) \ \&$$
$$(\forall i, \forall j, f_i(j) \neq \varepsilon \iff g(j) = i) \ \&$$
$$(\forall i, \lim_j (f_i(0) f_i(1) \ldots f_i(j)) \in L)\},$$

$$A \odot B = \{w \in X^{\omega} \mid \exists f,g : \mathbb{N} \to (X \cup \{\varepsilon\}), \exists h : \mathbb{N} \to \{f,g\} : h(i) = h_i,$$
$$(w = \lim_j (h_0(0)\ h_1(1) \ldots h_j(j))) \ \&$$
$$(\forall i, (h(i) = f \iff f(i) \neq \varepsilon) \ \& \ (h(i) = g \iff g(i) \neq \varepsilon)) \ \&$$
$$(\lim_j (f(0) \ldots f(j)) \in A \ \& \ \lim_j (g(0) \ldots g(j)) \in B)\}.$$

For any $\mathcal{L}$, we define $\mathcal{L}^{\textcircled{\omega}}$ as the family of the languages denoted by finite expressions $\bigcup_{i=1}^{n} A_i\ op_i^1\ (B_i\ op_i^2\ (C_i - \{\varepsilon\})^{\textcircled{\omega}})$, where $\{op_i^1, op_i^2\} = \{.\ , \odot\}$ and $A_i, B_i, C_i \in \mathcal{L}$ for every i.

<u>Theorem 4</u> If Alg is included in $\mathcal{L}$ then $\mathcal{L}^{\textcircled{\omega}}$ is not separable.
<u>Proof indication</u> A non separable pair of languages is given by the following definitions

$$L = (ca^+b)^{\textcircled{\omega}} \cup \{a, b, c\}^*\ ba\{a, b, c\}^{\textcircled{\omega}}$$
$$L' = A \odot (ca^+b)^{\textcircled{\omega}} \cup \{a, b, c\}^*\ ba\{a, b, c\}^{\textcircled{\omega}}$$

where we let

$$A = \bigcup_{n>0} (ca^n b \odot ca^n b). \quad \square$$

<u>2.3. Σ_1^1 as a class of infinitary languages</u>

Let us identify X with the set $\mathbb{N}$ of the natural numbers. Now, an infinitary language on X is a subset of $\mathcal{F}$, the set of the total functions from $\mathbb{N}$ to $\mathbb{N}$ (f is identified with f(0)f(1) ... f(n) ...). In this division, we examine the family of the Σ_1^1 subsets of $\mathcal{F}$ [11]. Let us recall that a set of total functions is in Σ_1^1 iff it may be written $\{f \mid (\exists g)\ (\forall i)\ R(f,g,i)\}$ where R is a relation which is recursive in two function variables (f,g) and one number variable (i). It may be argued that Σ_1^1 is the most complex family of languages for which generating devices may be found, and chapter 3 will shed some light on that issue.

<u>Theorem 5</u> Σ_1^1 is not separable.
<u>Proof indication</u> Let F be the set of the functions f in $\mathcal{F}$ which belong for some i to

the subset of $\mathcal{F}$ with Σ_1^1 - index f(i). Let G be the set of the functions g in $\mathcal{F}$ for which any one of the g(i), $i \in \mathbb{N}$, is the Σ_1^1 - index of a set which intersects F. Define H as the set of the strictly increasing functions in G, and take K as the set of the non minimal elements of H w.r.t. the lexicographic order on words. Then H and K are Σ_1^1 sets of functions, and their symmetric difference is a singleton $\{\check{h}\}$ which is not in Σ_1^1. Now, Σ_1^1 is closed under finite intersections and thus the theorem follows.

Corollary $\Sigma_1^1 \cap P(\{0,1\}^\omega)$ is not separable ◘

Some consequences of theorem 5 may be drawn as regards communicating processes and their effective testing. This is the subject of next section.

3. THE ISSUE OF SEPARABILITY FOR COMMUNICATING PROCESSES

The first division (§3.1) introduces an "effective" version of the calculus of communicating systems. We show that every Σ_1^1 set of infinite words on a finite alphabet is matched by the set of traces of some corresponding process (§3.2). We state our assumptions on tests in §3.3 and use the constructions of §3.2 to prove the non separability of C.C.S. (§3.4).

3.1. An effective version of pure C.C.S.

We refer the reader to (10) for a complete presentation of C.C.S. We consider the pure version of that calculus, with the operational semantics given in (7). However, we forget about the undefined program Ω and extend recursive definitions into systems of recursive definitions (we let $rec_i(x_1,\dots,x_n).(t_1,\dots t_n)$ denote the "solution" in x_i of $x_1 = t_1,\dots, x_n = t_n$). More significantly, we set narrow bounds on the complexity of renaming functions so as to keep the calculus effective. Renaming functions are defined here as total recursive homomorphisms on a set $\Lambda = \Delta \cup \bar{\Delta} \cup \{\perp,\tau\}$ indexed by $(2\mathbb{N} + 2) \cup (2\mathbb{N} + 3) \cup \{0,1\}$, where $\perp$ indicates the undefined action. (We use typically λ resp. μ as variables over $\Delta \cup \bar{\Delta}$ resp. $\Delta \cup \bar{\Delta} \cup \{\tau\}$). The operational semantics is defined as usual by a finite set of axioms and rules of inference. Given programs p,q and action μ, p may perform the action μ and thereupon evolve into q iff $p \xrightarrow{\mu} q$ is provable. A computation is a finite or infinite sequence of transitions $p_i \xrightarrow{\tau} p_{i+1}$. A computation is maximal if it is infinite or can be extended by no transition of the above form.

3.2. Some relations between C.C.S. and $\sum_1^1$

Our first objective is to show that $\sum_1^1$ is a bound of complexity of sets of computations.

Let $\mathcal{E}$ be a maximal computation from the parallel program $p_0|q_0$. A parallel decomposition of $\mathcal{E}$ is any pair

$$\mathcal{E}_1 = (p_0 \xrightarrow{\mu'_1} p_1 \xrightarrow{\mu'_2} \dots p_i \xrightarrow{\mu'_{i+1}} \dots)$$

$$\mathcal{E}_2 = (q_0 \xrightarrow{\mu''_1} q_1 \xrightarrow{\mu''_2} \dots q_i \xrightarrow{\mu''_{i+1}} \dots)$$

from which $\mathcal{E}$ may be deduced back by the logical rules of parallel composition. The elements $\mathcal{E}_1$ and $\mathcal{E}_2$ of the decomposition are open computations. The trace of $\mathcal{E}_1$ is the finite or infinite word $\eta(\mu'_1)\dots\eta(\mu'_i)\dots$, where $\eta(\lambda) = \lambda$ and $\eta(\tau) = \varepsilon$. For the ease of notation, the infinite suffix $(p_n \xrightarrow{\perp})^\omega$ is implicitly appended to the finite computations which end on p_n, and similarly with $\perp^\omega$ for finite traces $\lambda_1 \dots \lambda_n$.

From now on, programs and actions are identified with natural numbers through some appropriate coding functions. This way, $\langle p,\langle\mu,q\rangle\rangle$ expresses the elementary move $p \xrightarrow{\mu} q$ and the open computation $\mathcal{E}_1$ has the functional representation f_1 given by $\pi_1 \circ f_1(i) = p_i$ and $\pi_2 \circ f_1(i) = \mu_i$. (We use $\langle\ \ \rangle$, π_1 and π_2 to denote the pairing, left projection and right projection functions).

<u>Theorem 6</u> The set of open computations from a given C.C.S. program is in $\sum_1^1$, and similarly for the associated set of traces.

<u>Proof indication</u> The operational semantics of C.C.S. is based upon structural inference rules, and all proofs of elementary moves $p \xrightarrow{\mu} p'$ form a recursive set ∎

To prepare the oncoming discussion on tests, we need to establish some relation the other way round between $\sum_1^1$ and C.C.S. . Indeed, we have in mind a very specific form of connection which requires some new definitions.

Let $\mathcal{E}$ be an open computation with functional representation f. We say that $\mathcal{E}$ is maximal iff $\forall i$, $\forall\mu$, $\pi_2 \circ f(i) = \perp \Longleftrightarrow \sim(\pi_2 \circ f(i) \xrightarrow{\mu})$, where $p \xrightarrow{\mu}$ is a shorthand for $(\exists q)\ (p \xrightarrow{\mu} q)$. We say that $\mathcal{E}$ is simple iff it is infinite $(\forall i,\ \pi_2 \circ f(i) \neq \perp)$ and satisfies the following implications for every i and λ :

$$-\ (\pi_1 \circ f(i) \xrightarrow{\lambda}\ ) \Rightarrow (\pi_2 \circ f(i) = \lambda)$$

$- (\pi_2 \circ f(i) = \lambda) \Rightarrow$

$(\exists j)((j<i) \;\&\; (\forall k)((j\leq k \;\&\; k<i) \Rightarrow (\pi_2 \circ f(k) = \tau)))$.

A program p is said simple if all maximal open computations from p are simple.

The idea under these definitions is as follows. In order to establish non separability of C.C.S. under general tests, we wish to lift up the result concerning non separability of Σ_1^1 . So, we intend to derive a pair of non separable processes from a pair of non separable languages. Since communicating processes cannot in general be reduced to their sets of traces, we focus on a particular subclass of processes which offer no form of choice to their environment, so that trace equivalence implies behavioural equivalence. (The second condition ensures that behavioural equivalence is preserved by contexts such as rec x.((   ) | x)).

Theorem 7 For each Σ_1^1 - language L in P $(\{0,1\}^\omega)$, there exists a simple C.C.S. program p_L for which $L \cup \{0,1\}^* \perp^\omega$ is the set of traces of simple computations.

Proof indication Let $L = \{f \mid \exists g \; \forall i \; R(f,g,i)\}$ then it may be assumed w.l.o.g. that R(f,g,i) does not depend upon f(i+j) or g(i+j), j > 0. Then, the main sum-component of p_L iterates the loop

L(i) : choose f(i), choose g(i), check R(f,g,i), and either behave as f(i). L(i+1) if the result is true or else start diverging ∎

3.3. Assumptions on tests

If p and q are programs, a q-test on p is an open computation $\mathcal{E}_q$ which occurs in the parallel decomposition ($\mathcal{E}_p$, $\mathcal{E}_q$) of some maximal computation from p|q. Since open computations have functional representations, a total predicate $\mathcal{C}$(f) of one function variable divides the global set of open computations into a partition {Success, Failures} which may be used as a criterion for tests. The criterion is admissible if $\mathcal{C}$(f) may be obtained from some recursive relation $R(f, i_1, \ldots, i_n)$ by first order quantification. In order to fix the ideas, we show some examples of sensible predicates $\mathcal{C}(q_0 \xrightarrow{\mu_1} q_1 \xrightarrow{\mu_2} \ldots)$: $\exists i, q_i \xrightarrow{\omega}$ - this is roughly the criterion used in (7) - $\forall i, \mu_i \neq \perp \;\&\; (\exists j > i, \mu_j \neq \tau)$ - cooperation criterion -
$\forall i, q_i \xrightarrow{\omega'} \Rightarrow (\exists j > i, q_j \xrightarrow{\omega''})$ - conditional criterion -
$\forall i, \exists j, q_j \xrightarrow{\omega_i}$ - multiple criterion -
Assume that some admissible criterion {Success, Failures} has been fixed, then by way of definition, p may q if some q-test $\mathcal{E}_q$ on p belongs to Success, and p must q if every q-test $\mathcal{E}_q$ on p belongs to Success. Programs p and p' are indistinguishable by test if the assertions C(p) sat q and C(p') sat q are equivalent for any program

q, for any context C( ), for any degree of satisfaction sat $\in$ {may,must}, and for any admissible criterion {Success, Failures}. It may be remarked that the precise notion of testing developped in (7) does not fit exactly into the above frame, since its "must" part involves direct inspection of some divergence properties of the testee which do not influence the testor. However, if p and q are indistinguishable by test in our sense, then a similar property holds certainly for $p|\text{rec } x.\,\tau x$ and $q|\text{rec } x.\,\tau x$ under the assumptions of Hennessy and de Nicola.

3.4. Non separability of C.C.S.

Theorem 8 Some C.C.S. programs which are indistinguishable by test differ by their sets of computation traces.

Proof indication Let H and K be the Σ_1^1 sets used in the proof of theorem 5. Let $\phi(H)$ and $\phi(K)$ be the Σ_1^1 sets obtained by encoding the elements of H and K into $\{0,1\}^\omega$. Let p and q be the simple programs respectively associated by theorem 7 to sets $\phi(H)$ and $\phi(K)$. Then p and q are indistinguishable by test. The full proof of that result uses theorem 6 in conjunction with a strengthened version of theorem 5. The stronger version is stated by the following lemma.

Lemma Given $f : \mathbb{N} \to \mathfrak{F} : i \to f_i$, let $f^\Delta : \mathbb{N} \to \mathbb{N}$ be the infinite sequence $f_0(0)\ f_0(1)\ f_1(0)\ f_0(2)\ f_1(1)\ f_2(0)\ \ldots$. If $F \subset \mathfrak{F}$, let F^Δ be the set of the f^Δ for f ranging over the functions which enumerate subsets of F. Then F^Δ is in Σ_1^1 if F is in Σ_1^1. Moreover, there exist Σ_1^1 sets H and K such that (H,K) and (H^Δ, K^Δ) are inseparable pairs of infinitary languages on a finite alphabet.

4. SOME CONCLUSIONS

In an asynchronous framework, an infinite amount of time is needed to detect the persistent rejection of an action by a process. If refusals can be observed, the same property should be true of infinite sequences of actions. By theorem 7, we know processes which differ by their infinite sequences of actions although their finite behaviours are identical. Hence algebraic domains (where objects are upper bounds of sets of approximants which convey finite properties or better, properties of finite behaviours) are not adequate to construct observational models of reactive programs. More deeply, the notion of improvement ordering which is at the very heart of denotational semantics (13,6) appears here inadequate. Any observational preorder on reactive programs is based on a criterion which allows to decide, given programs p' and p", wether p' cooperates 'more' or 'better' than p" with a possible experimenter program q. A set-theoretic comparison between sets of behaviours of the experimenter program (more) determines an implementation preorder, whereas an improvement preorder rests on the comparison of the qualitative properties of such behaviours (better). Hence, improvement preorders are testing preorders, and they must identify some processes which differ by their infinite sequences of actions.

REFERENCES

(1) BOASSON L., NIVAT M., "Adherences of Languages"
Journal of Computer and System Sciences 20 (1980), 285-309

(2) DARONDEAU Ph., "Une critique de la notion de test de processus fondée sur la non séparabilité de certaines classes de langages"
RR 259 IRISA Rennes (1985)

(3) DARONDEAU Ph., "About Fair Asynchrony"
- à paraître dans T.C.S. -

(4) EILENBERG S., "Automata, languages and Machines"
Vol. A, Academic Press (1974)

(5) GONZALES ALVADARO C.A., "Le Mélange et le Mélange Itératif : les Opérateurs Concurrents"
Thèse de 3ème cycle, Université de Paris VII (1984)

(6) GUESSARIAN I., "Algebraic Semantics"
Springer-Verlag LNCS 99 (1981)

(7) HENNESSY M., DE NICOLA R., "Testing Equivalences for Processes"
Theoretical Computer Science 34 (1984) 83-134

(8) HENNESSY M., "Synchronous and Asynchronous Experiments on Processes"
Information and Control 59 (1983) 36-83

(9) MILNER R., "Fully Abstract Models of Typed Lambda-Calculi"
Theoretical Computer Science 4 (1977) 1-23

(10) MILNER R., "A Calculus of Communicating Systems"
Springer-Verlag LNCS 92 (1980)

(11) ROGERS H., "Theory of Recursive Functions and Effective Computability"
Mc Graw-Hill (1967)

(12) SHAW A.C., "Software Descriptions with Flow Expressions"
IEEE Transactions on Software Engineering 3 (1978) 242-254

(13) STOY J.E., "Denotational Semantics"
M.I.T. Press (1977)

DECOMPOSITION DE FONCTIONS RATIONNELLES

C. CHOFFRUT

UNIVERSITE DE HAUTE NORMANDIE
Faculté des Sciences
BP 67

76130 MONT-SAINT-AIGNAN

M.P SCHUTZENBERGER

UNIVERSITE PARIS 7
UER de Mathématiques et Informatique
2 place Jussieu,
75221 PARIS CEDEX 05

Résumé : On considère une nouvelle classe de fonctions rationnelles d'un monoïde libre dans un autre : les fonctions plurisousséquentielles pour lesquelles il existe une décomposition du domaine de définition en un nombre fini de parties reconnaissables sur chacune desquelles la fonction est sous-séquentielle (c'est à dire grossièrement séquentielle). Nous en donnons une caractérisation qui nous permet de décider si une fonction rationnelle arbitraire est plurisous-séquentielle.

Abstract : We introduce a new family of rational fonctions of a free monoid into another which we call multisubsequential. The domain of these functions can be decomposed into finitely many recognizable subsets in such a way that their restriction to each subset is subsequential (a notion which is close to sequential). We give a characterization of such functions and show that given an arbitrary rational function it is decidable whether it is multisubsequential.

I. Introduction

La théorie des fonctions rationnelles d'un monoïde libre dans un autre est intimement liée à celle des automates finis. A l'origine il était en fait difficile de les distinguer puisque les fonctions rationnelles étaient réalisées par des automates déterministes munis d'une sortie 0 ou 1 suivant que l'état courant est ou non un état final.

C'est Elgot et Mezei qui ont généralisé cette notion initiale de fonctions rationnelles et qui ont défini des objets jouissant de propriétés algébriques remarquables. Ce faisant, ils ont unifié les deux théories au moyen de la notion de partie rationnelle d'un monoïde quelconque. En ce qui concerne les fonctions rationnelles ceci revient à munir un automate non nécessairement déterministe de sorties, obtenant ainsi un transducteur.

Les domaines d'application des fonctions rationnelles sont nombreux. Limitons-nous à une énumération non exhaustive : étude des sous-familles classiques de langages algébriques [Be1], analyseurs lexicaux (bien qu'une étude théorique fasse défaut un bon langage de programmation doit pouvoir être analysé lexicalement par une fonction rationnelle "simple"), additionneurs dans différents systèmes de numération [Be2], combinatoire des mots [Cr] , théorie des codes puisqu'en fait le décodage d'un code est une fonction rationnelle [Ch1] etc...

Il existe cependant une ombre au tableau : les fonctions rationnelles y ont perdu leur simplicité originelle. En effet un transducteur quelconque n'est pas nécessairement équivalent à un transducteur séquentiel (on dirait "déterministe" pour les automates où l'on sait qu'il y a équivalence entre déterministes et non déterministes). En d'autres termes, bien qu'il soit toujours préférable de calculer séquentiellement l'image d'un mot, rien ne garantit, pour une fonction rationnelle donnée, qu'elle puisse être réalisée par un transducteur séquentiel. Il est d'ailleurs symptomatique d'observer que la plupart des fonctions rationnelles non séquentielles qui apparaissent dans la littérature sont "presque" séquentielles (en fait plurisousséquentielles) dans la mesure où l'on peut décomposer leur domaine de définition en un nombre fini de parties reconnaissables sur chacune desquelles la fonction est sous-séquentielle comme par exemple, avec $A=\{a,b\}$, l'application partielle $f:A^* \to A^*$ définie par

$$f(a^n) = \begin{cases} a^n & \text{si } n \text{ est pair} \\ b^n & \text{sinon} \end{cases}$$

Il semblerait donc que les auteurs soient en général réticents à considérer de "vraies" fonctions rationnelles non plurisous-séquentielles. Ceci nous parait justifié par la raison suivante. Au cours du calcul de l'image d'un mot par une fonction rationnelle on est amené à retenir jusqu'à n (n étant le nombre d'états de l'automate sousjacent) préfixes possibles de l'image, alors que pour une fonction séquentielle il existe exactement un préfixe possible : la situation est analogue à celle qui différentie le décodage d'un code quelconque et celui d'un code préfixe. On peut donc se représenter le calcul comme une coopération entre différents processeurs contenant chacun un préfixe dans un registre et échangeant des informations à chaque top d'horloge. En revanche, pour les fonctions plurisousséquentielles, on peut associer à chaque fonction sousséquentielle un processeur mais, et c'est là le point crucial, ils n'ont pas besoin de travailler de manière synchrone puisque chacun fonctionne à son rythme, indépendemment des autres.

Le but de cette communication est de montrer que l'on peut décider si une fonction rationnelle est plurïsous-séquentielle, en en donnant par ailleurs une caractérisation explicite.

II. Fonctions rationnelles

Par relation r d'un ensemble X dans un autre Y, notée $r:X\to Y$, nous entendons une application de X dans l'ensemble des parties de Y. Une telle relation est une fonction si l'image de chaque élément $x\in X$ est un singolet ou l'ensemble vide, c'est-à-dire ssi c'est une application partielle de X dans Y. Nous faisons opérer les relations à droite (x r et non pas r(x)) et nous notons dom $r=\{x\in X|\exists y\in Y \quad y\in xr\}$ le domaine de r.

Soit A un ensemble ou alphabet. On note A^* et A^+ respectivement les monoïdes et semigroupe libres qu'il engendre. Tout élément w de A^* est un mot dont la longueur est notée $|w|$ et l'élément neutre, noté 1, est le mot vide : $A^+=A^*\setminus\{1\}$.

Une relation r d'un monoïde libre A^* dans un autre B^* est rationnelle si son graphe

$$r\,\#\,\{(u,v)\in A^*xB^*\setminus \quad v\in ur\}$$

est une partie rationnelle du monoïde produit A^*xB^*(cf[Ei], p.236).

Le théorème suivant, où pour tout monoïde M, Rat M désigne le semianneau des parties rationnelles de M, caractérise les relations rationnelles, (cf.par ex. [Bel] Thm, 7.1. ou [Ni]).

Théorème 1 :

Soit $r : A^* \to B^*$ une relation. Les conditions suivantes sont équivalentes :

1) r est rationnelle

2) il existe un entier $n > 0$ et un morphisme μ de A^* dans le monoïde multiplicatif des nxn-matrices à entrées dans Rat B^*, un n-vecteur ligne λ et un n-vecteur colonne γ à entrées dans Rat B^* tels que l'on ait pour tout $u \in A^*$:

$$u\,r = \lambda\ u\mu\gamma$$

3) $1r \in$ Rat B^* et il existe un entier $n > 0$ et un morphisme μ de A^+ dans le monoïde multiplicatif des nxn-matrices à entrées dans Rat B^* de telle sorte que pour tout $u \in A^+$ on ait :

$$u\,r = u\mu_{1n} \quad \text{(élément en ligne 1 et colonne n)}$$

Le triplet (λ, μ, γ) ou simplement le morphisme μ dans le cas 3) est appelé transducteur et n est sa dimension. On dit qu'il réalise la relation r.

Les résultats suivants seront utilisés à plusieurs reprises dans la suite de ce travail. Ils découlent de la caractérisation des relations rationnelles par des "bimorphismes" par l'application de propriétés générales sur les parties rationnelles d'un monoïde quelconque (cf. [Be1], Théorème III,3.2).

PROPOSITION 2.

Soit $r : A^* \to B^*$ une relation rationnelle et R Rat B^*. Alors :

$$Rr^{-1} = \{u \in A^* \mid ur \cap R \neq \emptyset\} \in \text{Rat } A^*$$

PROPOSITION 3.

Soit $r : A^* \to B^*$ une relation rationnelle et $R \in$ Rat A^*. Alors la restriction $r_R : A^* \to B^*$ définie par :

$$ur_R = \begin{cases} ur & \text{si } u \in R \\ \emptyset & \text{sinon} \end{cases}$$

est une relation rationnelle.

Particulièrement importante est la famille des fonctions rationnelles c'est à dire des relations rationnelles qui sont des fonctions. On a la propriété de décision suivante, [Sch1,p.245] :

Théorème 4 :

Soit $r : A^* \to B^*$ une relation rationnelle réalisée par un transducteur de dimension n. Alors c'est une fonction ssi pour tout mot $u \in A^*$ de longueur inférieure ou égale à $2n(n-1)+1$, ur contient au plus un mot.

Un cas remarquable est celui des fonctions <u>séquentielles</u> étudiées par Ginsburg et Rose [GiRo], où λ a toutes ses composantes nulles sauf une égale à 1, où les matrices $a\mu$ pour $a \in A$ sont monomiales en ligne (i.e. contiennent au plus un mot par ligne) et où γ à toutes ses entrées égales à 1.

Les fonctions <u>sousséquentielles</u> ont été introduites en [Sch2]. Elles généralisent les fonctions séquentielles en ce sens que γ est alors un vecteur arbitraire à entrées dans $B^* \cup \{\emptyset\}$. L'intérêt de ces fonctions est qu'elles constituent la famille la plus générale de fonctions associées naturellement à des automates déterministes c'est à dire pour lesquelles le calcul de l'image d'un mot se fait séquentiellement, en temps réel.

Comme nous l'avons discuté dans l'introduction, une fonction <u>plurisousséquentielle</u> est une fonction $f : A^* \to B^*$ dont le graphe est union finie de graphes de fonctions sousséquentielles.

Remarquons qu'il existe des fonctions rationnelles qui ne sont pas plurisousséquentielles, par exemple les fonctions de décodage de codes à délai de déchiffrage non borné [Ch1].

Dans la suite toute fonction rationnelle considérée sera définie, comme en 3 du Théorème 1, par un transducteur μ la réalisant. Bien qu'on ne sache pas associer canoniquement un transducteur à une fonction rationnelle on sait cependant construire un transducteur "normalisé" réalisant la même fonction et jouissant de propriétés qui facilitent les énoncés et les preuves des résultats. C'est ce que nous précisons maintenant.

Il est d'abord clair qu'une fonction rationnelle peut toujours être réalisée par un transducteur pour lequel les entrées de $a\mu$ pour chaque $a \in A$ sont dans $B^* \cup \{\emptyset\}$, c'est à dire des singolets ou l'ensemble vide, ce que nous supposerons toujours dorénavant.

D'autre part une fonction est rationnelle (resp. sousséquentielle, plurisousséquentielle) ssi sa restriction à A^+ est elle-même rationnelle (resp. sousséquentielle, plurisousséquentielle). Ceci nous autorise à supposer que le transducteur μ satisfait $n \neq 1$.

On suppose sans perte de généralité que μ est <u>accessible</u> :
pour tout $1 \leq i \leq n$ il existe $u \in A^*$ tel que $u\mu_{1i} \neq \emptyset$
et <u>coaccessible</u> :
pour tout $1 \leq i \leq n$ il existe $u \in A^*$ tel que $u\mu_{in} \neq \emptyset$.
On dit alors qu'il est <u>normalisé</u> (cf.[Bel], Proposition 4,1.1.)

Enfin on suppose que le transducteur est <u>inambigu</u> dans le sens que pour tout couple $1 \leq i,j \leq n$ et tout couple $u,v \in A^*$ il existe un unique $1 \leq k \leq n$ tel que l'on ait :

$$u\mu_{1k} \cdot v\mu_{kj} \neq \emptyset$$

(cf.[Bel], Théorème IV,4.2).

III. Rappel sur les fonctions sousséquentielles

Dans la suite on supposera toute fonction rationnelle donnée par un transducteur μ normalisé et inambigu. Pour nous conformer à la coutume, nous noterons Q et non pas $\{1,\ldots,n\}$ l'ensemble des indices (ou des états) du transducteur, remplaçant ainsi 1 par q_- (état initial) et n par q_+ (état terminal) dans l'énoncé de la condition 3). Enfin $||\mu||$ désignera la longueur maximale des entrées non nulles des matrices $a\mu$ pour $a \in A$.

En ne considérant que les supports on peut définir une action de A^* sur l'ensemble des parties de Q en posant pour tout $u \in A^*$ et $P, P' \subseteq Q$:

$$P.u = P'$$

$$\text{si } P' = \{q' \in Q \mid \exists q \in P \quad u\mu_{qq'} \neq \emptyset\}.$$

Il est clair que la notion de préfixité joue un rôle fondamentale dans l'étude des fonctions séquentielles (qui conservent la préfixité) et sousséquentielles (qui conservent une propriété affaiblie). Etant donné deux mots u,v A^* on note $u < v$ si u est préfixe de v (i.e. v=ux pour un certain $x \in A^*$) et l'on dit que u et v sont incomparables si aucun n'est préfixe de l'autre.

Utilisant la notion de préfixe on peut définir une distance (la distance préfixe) entre deux mots $u,v \in A^*$ en posant :

$$d(u,v) = |u| + |v| - 2|u \wedge v|$$

où $u \wedge v$ désigne le plus long préfixe commun à u et v. Deux mots sont alors d'autant plus proches qu'ils ont un plus long préfixe commun.

On peut alors obtenir une caractérisation des fonctions sousséquentielles en termes de cette distance (cf.[Ch3]) :

Théorème 1 :

Une fonction $f : A^* \to B^*$ est sousséquentielle ssi elle vérifie les deux conditions suivantes :

1) pour toute partie rationnelle $R \in \mathrm{Rat}\, B^*$ on a :

$$Rf^{-1} = \{u \in A^* \mid uf \in R\} \in \mathrm{Rat}\, A^*$$

2) il existe un entier $L > 0$ tel que pour tous $u,v \in \mathrm{dom}\, f$ on ait :

$$d(uf,vf) < Ld(u,v).$$

Par définition, une fonction sous séquentielle peut être réalisée par un transducteur séquentiel c'est à dire mononial au sens du paragraphe antérieur. Ceci n'exclut pas que cette même fonction puisse être réalisée par un transducteur non séquentiel, mais il est alors facile de prévoir que cette "non séquentialité", liée à la notion de branchement définie ci-dessous, sera "bénigne". Ainsi sommes nous amenés à considérer la classification suivante.

Un triplet $(q_1,q,q_2) \in Q'$ est un <u>branchement</u> s'il existe $u \in A^*$ et $x_1,x_2 \in B^*$ tels que l'on ait :

(1) $u\mu_{qq_1}=x_1$ et $u\mu_{qq_2}=x_2$

Ce branchement est <u>faible</u> s'il existe un entier $k > 0$ tel que les égalités (1) entraînent :

(2) $d(x_1,x_2) < k$

Il est <u>fort</u> dans le cas contraire. Enfin il est <u>absolu</u> s'il est fort et si $q=q_1$ ou $q=q_2$.

On peut définir un préordre sur l'ensemble des branchements en disant que (q_1,q,q_2) <u>précède</u> le branchement (q'_1,q,q'_2) s'il existe $v \in A^*$ tel que l'on ait :

$$q'_1 \in q_1.u \quad \text{et} \quad q'_2 \in q_2.u$$

Par conséquent si (q'_1,q,q'_2) est faible alors (q_1,q,q_2) sera lui-même faible.

On montre alors le résultat suivant (cf.[Ch2]) :

<u>Théorème 2.</u>

<u>Soit</u> μ <u>un transducteur réalisant une fonction rationnelle</u> $f : A^* \to B^*$. <u>Alors</u> f <u>est sous-séquentielle ssi tous les branchements de</u> μ <u>sont faibles.</u>

Que cette caractérisation des transducteurs réalisant des fonctions sousséquentielles soit décidable résulte des deux Propositions suivantes.

<u>PROPOSITION 3.</u>

<u>Si</u> (q_1,p,q_2) <u>est un branchement faible, alors on a :</u>

<u>pour tous</u> u,v A* x_1,x_2,y_1,y_2 B* <u>les égalités :</u>

$$u\mu_{pq_1}=x_1 \qquad v\mu_{q_1q_1}=y_1$$

$$u\mu_{pq_2}=x_2 \qquad v\mu_{q_2q_2}=y_2$$

(1) <u>entraînent</u> :

$y_1=y_2=1$ <u>si</u> x_1 <u>et</u> x_2 <u>sont incomparables</u>

$y_1t=ty_2$ <u>si</u> $x_2=x_1t$

$ty_1=y_2t$ <u>si</u> $x_1=x_2t$

Preuve :

Puisque le branchement (q_1,p,q_2) est faible, il existe un entier $k > 0$ tel que l'on ait pour tout $i > 0$:

$$d(x_1y_1^i,x_2y_2^i) < k$$

ce qui entraîne en particulier : $|y_1|=|y_2|$. Sans perte de généralité nous pouvons supposer $y_1\neq 1$ et donc $y_2\neq 1$.

Supposons par exemple $|x_1| \leq |x_2|$. Pour m suffisamment grand les mots $x_1y_1^m$ et $x_2y_2^m$ ont un préfixe commun de longueur $|x_2y_2|$ ce qui entraîne :

$$x_2y_2=x_1y_1^py'_1.$$

où $p > 0$ et $y_1=y_1'y_1''$.

En posant $x_2=x_1t$ et en remarquant que $|y_1|=|y_2|$ entraîne $y_2=y_1''y_1'$ il vient :

$$ty_2=y_1t \text{ où } t=(y_1'y_1'')^{p-1}y_1'$$

ce qui achève la preuve.

■

Nous dirons que le branchement (q_1,p,q_2) satisfait la condition (1) à l'ordre $m > 0$ si celle-ci est vérifie pour tout u,v satisfaisant la condition supplémentaire :

$$|uv| \leq m.$$

On a alors un résultat qui établit la décidabilité du théorème 2.

Proposition 4.

<u>Un branchement</u> (q_1,p,q_2) <u>est faible ssi tous les branchements qui le précédent satisfont la condition</u> (1) <u>à l'ordre</u> n^2+1.

Preuve :

La condition est trivialement nécessaire. Pour montrer qu'elle est suffisante il nous faut introduire la notion suivante :

On dit que u passe par un branchement (r_1,p,r_2) s'il existe une factorisation : u=vw telle que :

$$v\mu_{pr_1} \neq \emptyset \quad w\mu_{r_1q_1} \neq \emptyset$$

$$v\mu_{pr_2} \neq \emptyset \quad w\mu_{r_2q_2} \neq \emptyset.$$

La Proposition découle alors du Lemme :

Lemme 5.

Soit (q_1,p,q_2) un branchement et $u \in A^*$ un mot tel que :

$$u\mu_{pq_1} = x'_1 \in B^* \quad u\mu_{pq_2} = x'_2 \in B^*$$

Si u passe uniquement par des branchements satisfaisant la condition (1) à l'ordre n^2+1 alors on a :

$$d(x'_1,x'_2) \leq n^2 \ ||\mu||$$

Preuve :

Supposons par l'absurde qu'il existe un mot $u \in B^*$ tel que l'on ait :

(2) $\quad d(x'_1,x'_2) > n^2||\mu||.$

Par définition de $||\mu||$ on a donc $|u| > n^2$. Par hypothèse d'inambiguité, les n^2+1 premiers préfixes de u définissent de façon unique autant de paires d'états, donc deux de ces facteurs sont associés à la même paire (r_1,r_2) ce qui revient à dire que l'on peut factoriser u en :

$$u=vhw \qquad h\neq 1 \quad \text{et} \quad |vh| \leq n^2$$

et que l'on a :

$$v\mu_{pr_1}=x_1 \qquad h\mu_{r_1r_1}=y_1 \qquad w\mu_{r_1q_1}=z_1$$

$$v\mu_{pr_2}=x_2 \qquad h\mu_{r_2r_2}=y_2 \qquad w\mu_{r_2q_2}=z_2$$

Puisque le branchement (r_1,p,r_2) satisfait la condition (1) à l'ordre n^2, en raison de la minimalité de $|u|$ on peut sans perte de généralité supposer que l'on a :

$$x_2=x_1t \qquad \text{et} \qquad y_1t=ty_2.$$

Il vient alors :

$$x_2y_2z_2=x_1ty_2z_2=x_1y_1tz_2$$

donc :

$$d(x_1y_1z_1,x_2y_2z_2)=d(z_1,tz_2)=d(z_1,tz_2)=d(x_1z_1,x_2z_2)$$

ce qui contredit la minimalité de u.

■

IV Fonctions pluri-sousséquentielles.

Le but de ce paragraphe est d'établir le résultat suivant qui est de plus décidable en raison de la Proposition III.4.

Théorème 1.

Soit μ un transducteur réalisant une fonction rationnelle $f: A^* \to B^*$. Alors f est plurisousséquentielle ssi μ ne possède aucun branchement absolu.

Preuve :

Condition nécessaire : on utilise une construction inspirée de [Ch2].

Supposons que μ possède un branchement absolu (q_1,q_1,q_2) et posons :

$$u\mu_{q_-q_1}=x\in B^* \qquad w\mu_{q_2q_+}=z\in B^*.$$

Si f était union de N fonctions sousséquentielles il existerait d'après le théorème III.1 un coefficient $L > o$ tel que dans tout ensemble de N+1 mots distincts $t_1,t_2,\dots,t_{N+1}\in \mathrm{dom}\, f$ il en existe deux t_i,t_j $(i < j)$ vérifiant :

$$d(t_if,t_jf) < L\, d(t_i,t_j).$$

C'est cette condition que nous allons nier. Pour cela on considére une suite quelconque $v_1,\dots,v_{N+1}$ de mots de A* vérifiant $\{q_1,q_2\}\in q_1.v_i$ $i=1,\dots,N+1$ et l'on pose :

$$t_i=uv_{N+1}\dots v_iw \qquad i=1,\dots,N+1.$$

On peut alors majorer :

(1) $d(t_if,t_jf) - L\, d(t_i,t_j)$

par

(2) $d(v_j\mu_{q_1q_1},v_j\mu_{q_1q_2}) - \Gamma(v_{j-1},\dots,v_1,z,w)$

où Γ est une fonction ne dépendant pas de v_j. Il suffit alors de déterminer v_j de façon à ce que l'expression (2) soit strictement positive et (1) devient alors :

$$d(t_i f, t_j f) > L\, d(t_i, t_j)$$

obtenant ainsi une contradiction.

Condition suffisante :

Commençons par établir un résultat intéressant en lui-même puisqu'il exprime une propriété de fermeture des fonctions sousséquentielles.

Lemme 2.

Soit $g,h : A^* \to B^*$ des fonctions sousséquentielles et supposons que dom g soit un ensemble préfixe :

$$u, uv \in \text{dom } g \text{ implique } v=1.$$

Alors le produit $gh : A^* \to B^*$ défini par :

$$(uv)gh = ug\ vh$$

est une fonction sousséquentielle.

Preuve :

Le fait que gh soit une fonction résulte du fait que le produit dom g dom h est inambigu (i.e. $u_1,u_2 \in$ dom g, $v_1,v_2 \in$ dom h et $u_1v_1=u_2v_2$ implique $u_1=u_2$ et $v_1=v_2$). De plus cette fonction est rationnelle puisque son graphe est égal au produit des graphes de g et de h. Donc la condition 1) du Théorème III.2 est vérifiée d'après la Proposition II,2.

Soient donc $u,v \in$ dom gh = dom g dom h et $w=u \wedge v$. On considère les factorisations uniques :

$$u=u_1u_2 \qquad v=v_1v_2$$

où $u_1,v_1 \in$ dom g, $u_2,v_2 \in$ dom h.

On peut sans perte de généralité supposer $|u_1| \leq |v_1|$. De plus on a nécessairment $|w| < |u_1|$ car $|u_1| \leq |w|$ implique que u_1 est préfixe propre de v_1. Il vient alors $w=u_1 \wedge v_1$ et par conséquent :

$$d(u_1v_1,u_2v_2)=d(u_1,v_1)+|u_2|+|v_2|.$$

Puisque y est sousséquentielle il existe d'après le théorème III,2 un entier L satisfaisant :

$$d(u_1g,v_1g) \leq L\, d(u_1,v_1).$$

Comme on a d'autre part :

$$d(ugh,vgh) \leq d(u_1g,v_1g)+|u_2h|+|v_2h|$$

il vient :

$$d(ugh,vgh) \leq L\, d(u_1,v_1)+||h||(|u_2|+|v_2|) \leq \max\{||h||,L\}\, d(u,v).$$

Ce qui montre que la condition 2) du Théorème III.2 est vérifiée et achève la preuve.

■

Revenons à la preuve du Théorème et notons Q_1 le sousensemble des états $q_1 \in Q$ pour lesquels il existe $q_2 \in Q$ tel que (q_1, q_-, q_2) soit un branchement fort. Nous nous proposons de décomposer le domaine Y=dom f suivant l'existence d'un état de Q_1 dans les chemins définis par les mots de Y.

Pour cela on pose pour tout $q \in Q_1$:

$$Y_q = \{w \in Y \mid w\mu_{q_-q} \neq \emptyset\}$$

et $$X_q = Y_q - (\bigcup_{q' \in Q_1} Y_{q'})\, A^+.$$

Il est clair que Y_q est reconnaissable ainsi que X_q (X_q est l'ensemble des mots qui définissent un chemin de q_- à q dont aucun état intermédiaire n'appartient à Q_1).

On considère l'ensemble préfixe $X = \bigcup_{q \in Q_1} X_q$ et l'on définit la décomposition (rationnelle) de dom f :

$$Y = \bigcup_{q \in Q_1} X_q Z_q \cup (Y - XA^*)$$

où $Z_q = \{w \in A^* \mid w\mu_{qq_+} \neq \emptyset\}$.

Soit $\alpha : A^* \to B^*$ la restriction de f à $Y-XA^*$ et pour tout $q_1 \in Q_1$ soient β_{q_1} et γ_{q_1} les fonctions définies par :

$$w\beta_{q_1} = w\mu_{q_-q_1} \quad \text{pour tout } w \in X_{q_1}$$

$$w\gamma_{q_1} = w\mu_{q_1q_+} \quad \text{pour tout } w \in A^*.$$

Chacune des fonctions α, β_{q_1} et γ_{q_1} est rationnelle. Pour α et β_{q_1} ceci résulte de la Proposition II,3. Pour γ_{q_1} on remarque plus précisément qu'elle peut être réalisée par le transducteur (q_1, ν, q_+) où ν est obtenu en supprimant dans chaque matrice $a\mu$ ($a \in A$) la ligne et la colonne indicée par q_-. Montrons en effet que q_- n'est pas accessible de q_1. Pour cela soit $q_2 \in Q$ tel que (q_1, q_-, q_2) soit un branchement fort. Si q_- était accessible de q_1 on aurait :

$$w\mu_{q_1q_-} = y \in B^*$$

pour un certain $w \in A^*$. Par hypothèse, le branchement (q_1, q_1, q_2) est faible donc il existe un entier $k > 0$ tel que pour tout $u \in A^*$ vérifiant :

$$u\mu_{q_-q_1} = x_1 \in B^* \quad u\mu_{q_-q_2} = x_2 \in B^*,$$

on ait :

$$d(wu\,\mu_{q_1q_1}, wu\mu_{q_1q_2}) = d(yx_1, yx_2) \leq k$$

d'où $d(x_1,x_2) \leq k$, contrairement à l'hypothèse que (q_1,q_-,q_2) est fort. Par hypothèse de récurrence sur la dimension de ν, la fonction γ_q est donc plurisous- séquentielle. En raison du Lemme précédent il ne reste donc plus qu'à vérifier que α et β_{q_1} sont plurisousséquentielles.

Considérons la fonction α, le cas de la fonction β_{q_1} se traitant par des arguements analogues. D'après la Proposition II,2, la condition 1) du Théorème III, 1 est satisfaite. En ce qui concerne la condition 2), considérons des mots $w,u,v \in A^*$ avec $u \neq v$, tels que

$$wu, wv \in \text{dom } \alpha$$

On a alors :

$$wu\alpha = w\mu_{q_-q_1} \; u\mu_{q_1q_+}$$

$$wv\alpha = w\mu_{q_-q_2} \; u\mu_{q_2q_+}$$

pour certains $q_1, q_2 \in Q$.

Par définition de α, le branchement (q_1,q_-,q_2) est faible ainsi que tous les branchements qui le précèdent. D'après le lemme III,5 on a :

$$d(w\mu_{q_-q_1}, w\mu_{q_-q_2}) \leq n^2 ||\mu||.$$

Mais alors :

$$d(wu\,\alpha, wv\,\alpha) \leq n^2 \; ||\mu|| \; +(|u|+|v|)||\mu||$$

$$(|u|+|v|)\;(n^2+1)\;||\mu|| \leq n^2||\mu|| d(wu,wv)$$

montrant ainsi que la condition 2) est satisfaite, ce qui achève la preuve.

■

V Bibliographie

[Be1] BERSTEL J., "Transductions and Context-Free Languages", Teubner, 1979.

[Be2] BERSTEL J., Fonctions rationnelles et addition, Actes de l'Ecole de Printemps sur la Théorie des Langages, Murol, 1981, p. 177-183.

[Ch1] CHOFFRUT C., Une caractérisation des codes à délai borné par leur fonction de décodage, in Actes de l'Ecole de Printemps sur la Théorie des codes, Jougne, 1979, p. 47-56.

[Ch2] CHOFFRUT C., Une caractérisation des fonctions séquentielles et sous séquentielles, Theoret. Comput. Sci., 5, 1977, p. 325-337.

[Ch3] CHOFFRUT C., A generalisation of Ginsburg and Rose's characterization of g-s-m mappings, Proceedings of the 6 th ICALP Conférence, 1979, p. 88-103.

[Cr] CROCHEMORE M., Optimal factor transducers, Rapport LITP 84-86.

[GiRo] GINSBURG S. & G.F. ROSE, A Characterization of machine mappings, Can. J. of Math., 18, 1966, p. 381-388.

[Ni] NIVAT M., Transductions des Langages de Chamsky, Ann. Inst. Fourier, Grenoble, 18, 1968, p. 339-455.

[Sch1] SCHUTZENBERGER M.P., Sur les relations rationnelles entre monoïdes libres, Thoret. Comput. Sci., 3, 1976, p. 243-259.

[Sch2] SCHUTZENBERGER M.P., Sur une variante des fonctions séquentielles, Theoret. Comput. Sci., 4, 1977, p. 47-57.

LONG UNAVOIDABLE PATTERNS

Ursula Schmidt
LITP, Université Paris VI
Couloir 45-55
4, Place Jussieu
F - 75230 PARIS Cedex 05

Abstract

We examine long unavoidable patterns, unavoidable in the sense of Bean, Ehrenfeucht, McNulty. We prove that there is only one unavoidable pattern of length 2^n-1 on an alphabet with n letters ; this pattern is a "quasi-power" in the sense of Schützenberger. We characterize the unavoidable words of length 2^n-2 and 2^n-3. Finally we show that every unavoidable word sufficiently long has a certain "quasi-power" as a subword.

1. INTRODUCTION

Recently, several papers considered combinatorial properties of words, in connection with the occurrence of subwords of a special form. For example, some papers were devoted to the study of squarefree or overlap-free words [2,3,4,5]. We are interested in a more general problem initiated in 1979 by Bean, Ehrenfeucht, McNulty [1], namely the study of so-called unavoidable patterns.

It is possible to formulate the problem of unavoidable words as follows : We say that a word w divides the word u if there is a non-erasing homomorphism h such that $h(w)$ is a subword of u. w is unavoidable if each infinite set of words on a finite alphabet contains a word which is divisible by w.

Bean, Ehrenfeucht, McNulty [1] proved that the length of the unavoidable words on a given alphabet is bounded, and they provide an algorithm to decide whether a given word is unavoidable. This algorithm allows us to calculate rather quickly all unavoidable words on an alphabet with three and four letters. By considering them closely, one finds that all of them divide the longest unavoidable pattern. So we make the conjecture that on an alphabet with n letters, the unavoidable patterns divide the longest unavoidable pattern, $n \in \mathbb{N}$. The aim of the present article is to prove the conjecture for long unavoidable words.

According to Bean, Ehrenfeucht, McNulty [1], the length of unavoidable words on an alphabet with n letters is bounded by 2^n-1. We show that there exists only one unavoidable pattern of this length : this pattern is a quasi-power in the sense of Schützenberger [6]. Then we give a complete description of the unavoidable patterns of length 2^n-2 and 2^n-3 : this allows us to show that these patterns divide the longest unavoidable pattern. Finally, we describe a property of the unavoidable patterns of a minimum length of 2^n-2^{n-m} that concerns their subwords, $m \leq n$.

We present the main theorems in section 3, which follows the definition section. Section 4 contains the ideas of the proofs of the theorems.

I would like to thank especially Professor Jean Berstel for his help and encouragements.

2. PRELIMINARIES

We denote by $\underline{A}^*$ (resp. $\underline{A}^+$) the free monoid (resp. semi-group) generated by the alphabet A. The elements of A^* and A^+ are called words. We denote the empty word by 1. $|A|$ is the cardinality of the alphabet A. We denote by A_n an alphabet with n letters.

$|w|$ is the length of a word w. We say that w is a subword of the word u, if there are words w_1 and w_2 such that $u = w_1ww_2$. If $w = a_1a_2...a_n$, with $a_i \in A$, $i = 1,...,n$, then $\underline{\tilde{w}} = a_n...a_1$ is the reversal of w.

Let A and E be alphabets. A homomorphism $h : E^* \to A^*$ is non-erasing if $|h(e)| \geq 1$ for each $e \in E$.

Let $w \in E^*$, $u \in A^*$ w divides u if there exists a non-erasing homomorphism $h : E^* \to A^*$ such that $h(w)$ is a subword of u. u avoids w if w doesn't divide u, i.e. if for each subword v of u and each non-erasing homomorphism $h : E^* \to A^*$ we have $h(w) \neq v$. We also call w a pattern.

Let A be an alphabet with n letters. The word w is avoidable on the n letter alphabet if there is an infinite set F of words on A which avoid w. w is avoidable provided there is a finite alphabet A such that w is avoidable on A. Otherwise w is called unavoidable. In other words : w is unavoidable if each infinite set of words on a finite alphabet contains a word which is divisible by w.

An infinite word on A is a mapping $\underline{x} : \mathbb{N} \to A$, denoted by $\underline{x} = x_1x_2 \ldots x_n \ldots, x_i \in A$. So w is avoidable if and only if there exists an infinite word $\underline{x}$ such that $\underline{x}$ avoids w.

Example 1 : $w = a^2$ is avoidable, since there is an infinite squarefree word on a three letter alphabet (Thue [7]).

Example 2 : Let $A = \{a, b, c\}$. w = abacaba is unavoidable according to theorem 1 below.

Definition : A quasi-power of order 0 is an arbitrary nonempty word. A quasi-power of order n+1 is a word of the form uvu with u a quasi-power of order n and v a nonempty word.

Theorem (Schützenberger [6]) : *Let A be a finite alphabet. There exists a sequence (c_n) of integers such that each word of length at least c_n on A contains a subword that is a quasi-power of order n.*

Lemma 2 : *Let $p : A \to A$ be a permutation ; its extension on A^* will also be noted p. Let $w \in A^*$. If w is unavoidable, then $w^\sim$ and $p(w)$ are unavoidable.*

Therefore we may consider avoidable or unavoidable patterns up to permutations and reversal.

3. RESULTS

Bean, Ehrenfeucht, McNulty [1] show that the length of unavoidable words on an alphabet with n letters is bounded by 2^n-1. We can specify the structure and the number of unavoidable patterns of this length.

Let $A_n = \{a_1, \ldots, a_n\}$ be an alphabet with n letters.

Theorem 3 : *There exists exactly one unavoidable pattern on A_n of length 2^n-1 ; this pattern is the quasi-power q_n, inductively defined by*

$$q_1 = a_1$$
$$q_n = q_{n-1}a_nq_{n-1}, \quad n > 1.$$

We can rather easily deal with patterns of length 2^n-2 and 2^n-3. This allows us to establish the following theorem, patterns still being considered up to permutations and reversal :

Theorem 4 : *Let $n \geqslant 3$. There are two unavoidable patterns on A_n of length 2^n-2. There are four unavoidable patterns of length $2^3-3 = 5$ on A_3, and there are seven unavoidable patterns of length 2^n-3 on A_n, $n \geqslant 4$.*

Their structures are characterized as follows :

Let $v_2 = a_1a_2$ and q_n be the pattern of theorem 3. The unavoidable patterns of length $2^{n+1}-2$, $n \geqslant 2$, are

$$v_{n+1} = q_na_{n+1}v_n$$
$$v'_{n+1} = q_na_{n+1}\tilde{v}_n$$

The unavoidable patterns of length 5 on A_3 are

$$x_{3,1} = a_1a_2a_1a_3a_1$$
$$x_{3,2} = a_1a_2a_1a_3a_2$$
$$x_{3,3} = a_1a_2a_3a_1a_2$$
$$x_{3,4} = a_1a_2a_3a_2a_1$$

The unavoidable patterns of length $2^{n+1}-3$, $n \geq 3$, are

$$x_{n+1,1} = q_n a_{n+1} x_{n,1}$$
$$x_{n+1,2} = q_n a_{n+1} \tilde{x}_{n,1}$$
$$x_{n+1,3} = q_n a_{n+1} x_{n,6} \quad \text{where} \quad x_{3,6} = x_{3,4}$$
$$x_{n+1,4} = v_n a_{n+1} v_n$$
$$x_{n+1,5} = v_n a_{n+1} \tilde{v}_n$$
$$x_{n+1,6} = \tilde{v}_n a_{n+1} v_n$$
$$x_{n+1,7} = v'_n a_{n+1} v'_n$$

Proposition : *The words v_n, v'_n and $x_{n,j}$, $j = 1, \ldots 7$, divide q_n, $n \in \mathbb{N}$.*

Theorem 5 : *All unavoidable words of length $\geq 2^n-2^{n-m}$ on A_n contain q_m, $m \leq n$, as a subword. This bound is optimal.*

Let $m = 2$. We may describe in a very detailed manner the unavoidable patterns of maximal length, which do not contain the subword aba, where a, b are arbitrary letters ; let us notice that they are quasi-powers.

Theorem 6 : *There is exactly one unavoidable pattern with length $2^n-2^{n-2}-1$ on A_n, $n \geq 2$, which does not contain the subword aba, where $a, b \in A_n$ are arbitrary letters ; this pattern u_n may be defined inductively by*

$$u_2 = a_1 a_2$$
$$u_n = u_{n-1} a_n u_{n-1}, \quad n \geq 3.$$

Proposition : *The word u_n divides q_n, $n \in \mathbb{N}$.*

By considering the relationship between unavodiable words, we observe that there are words on A_n of which aba is not a subword (a, b arbitrary letters) and that don't divide u_n.

Example : Let $A_4 = \{a, b, c, d\}$. The words abcdbac and abcabdac do not divide abcabdabcab.

Besides, it is not true for $m > 2$ that there exists a unique unavoidable pattern of maximal length which does not contain the subword q_n.

Example with $n = 4$, $m = 3$: there are three unavoidable words of length 13 which do not contain q_3 as a subword :

abacabdabacab, abcabadabcaba and abacabdbacaba.

4. SKETCH OF THE PROOFS

When proving the theorems we use intensively the fact that the length of the unavoidable words is bounded, and the main theorem of Bean, Ehrenfeucht, McNulty [1] (section 3). We first present these theorems.

If a word w is unavoidable, then each infinite set F on a finite alphabet contains a word α_F which is divisible by w. The subwords of w also divide α_F, and so each word u which divides w divides α_F. Therefore we have :

Lemma 7 : *Let u and w be words on finite alphabets. If w is unavoidable and u divides w, then u is unavoidable.*

In particular, all words containing a square are avoidable.

Lemma 8 (Bean, Ehrenfeucht, McNulty [1]) :

Let $w \in A_n^*$, $|w| \geq 2^n$. Then w is avoidable.

Definition : Let A be an alphabet, $a, b \in A$, $w \in A^*$. The relation R_w is defined by

aR_wb if ab is a subword of w.

If there is no ambiguity, we simply note R.

We also write $bR^{-1}a$ for aRb. So we note $aRR^{-1}Rd$, if there are letters b, c such that $aRbR^{-1}cRd$, that is $aRb, bR^{-1}c, cRd$.

We now introduce the notion of bounded and free letters.

<u>Definition</u> : The letter a is <u>bounded</u> for the word w, if there exists $n \in \mathbb{N}$, $n > 0$, such that $a(RR^{-1})^n Ra$. A letter which is not bounded is called a <u>free letter</u>.

<u>Examples</u> :

- a is free in aba
- a is bounded in abcbca.

<u>Definition</u> : Let A be an alphabet, $a \in A$. The projection $\pi_a : A^* \to (A \backslash a)^*$ is defined by

$\pi_a(a) = 1$

$\pi_a(b) = b$ for each $b \in A$, $b \neq a$.

So for $w \in A^*$, $\pi_a(w)$ is the word obtained from w by deleting all occurrences of a.

<u>Lemma 9</u> (Bean, Ehrenfaucht, McNulty [1]) : *If a is free for w and $\pi_a(w)$ is unavoidable, then w is unavoidable.*

<u>Lemma 10</u> : *If the word u is obtained from w by identification of two letters occurring in w and u is unavoidable, then w is unavoidable.*

This lemma is a consequence of lemma 7.

<u>Definition</u> : A word w <u>reduces</u> to u, if there are words $v_1, v_2, \ldots, v_r$ such that $w = v_1$, $u = v_r$ and v_{i+1} is obtained from v_i either by identification of two letters occurring in v_i or by deleting a free letter of v_i, $1 \leq i \leq r-1$.

<u>Theorem 11</u> (Bean, Ehrenfeucht, McNulty [1]) : *The word w is unavoidable if and only if it reduces to a word of length one.*

The following detailed version is much more useful :

<u>Theorem 11'</u> : *The word w is unavoidable if and only if there are words $v_1, v_2, \ldots, v_r$ such that $w = v_1$, $|v_r| = 1$, v_i is unavoidable and v_i is obtained from v_{i-1} either by identification of two letters occurring in v_{i-1} or by deleting all occurrences of a free letter of v_{i-1}, $2 \leq i \leq r$.*

We call $(v_i)_{1 \leq i \leq r}$ <u>the sequence of reduced words associated to</u> w.

Lemma 14 : *If w is unavoidable and a is a letter not occurring in w, then $w' = waw$ is unavoidable.*

The proof themselves of the statements of section 3 are made by induction on the cardinality of the alphabet.

To start with theorem 3, we have to prove that q_n is unique. For this, we show that the word w_{i+1} of the sequence $(w_i)_{1 \le i \le r}$ of reduced words associated to q_n is obtained from w_i by deleting all occurrences of the free letter a_i, $1 \le i \le n-1$; that is, the sequence is unique and there exists a permutation p_i such that $w_i = p(q_{n-i+1})$, $1 \le i \le n$. We use mainly the relation of neighbourhood R_w, the theorem of Thue about the avoidability of words containing a square and lemma 8.

Concerning theorem 4, there are eight possibilities (up to permutation and reversal) to form unavoidable words of length $2^{n+1}-2$, for example

$$w_1 = q_n a_{n+1} v_n \qquad w_3 = q_n a_{n+1} p(v_n)$$
$$w_2 = q_n a_{n+1} \tilde{v_n} \qquad w_4 = q_n a_{n+1} v'_n$$

where p is an arbitrary permutation.

w_1 and w_2 are unavoidable because they divide q_{n+1}. Then we show that $w_3, \ldots, w_8$ are avoidable if p is not the identity. For this, we use mainly the uniqueness of q_n and of the sequence of reduced words associated to q_n.

We use similar arguments for the words of length 2^n-3.

Proof of theorem 5 : Suppose that the theorem is true for all integers less or equal to n.

Let $w \in A_{n+1}^*$ be an unavoidable word. It follows from theorem 11 that there is a letter $a \in A_{n+1}$ and unavoidable words $w', w'' \in (A_{n+1} \setminus a)^*$ such that $w = w'aw''$. Suppose that w does not contain q_m as a subword. Then neither w' nor w'' contain q_m as a subword. By hypothesis of induction, we have

$$|w'|, |w''| \le 2^n - 2^{n-m} - 1.$$

Hence, $|w| \leq 2 \cdot (2^n - 2^{n-m} - 1) + 1 = 2^{n+1} - 2^{n+1-m} - 1$.

The interesting part of <u>theorem 6</u> is the uniqueness of u_n. We have two possibilities to find w_2 of the sequence $(w_i)_{1 \leq i \leq n}$ of reduced words associated to u_n : we may delete all occurrences of a_1 or those of a_2. These two cases lead us to a permutation of q_{n-1}, which yields the uniqueness of u_n.

BIBLIOGRAPHIE

[1] Bean D.R., Ehrenfeucht A., McNulty G.F., Avoidable patterns in strings of symbols, Pacific J. Math. 85 (1979), 261-294.

[2] Berstel J., Some recent results on squarefree words, STACS 84, Springer Lecture Notes in Computer Science, Vol. 166 (1984), 14-25.

[3] Main M.G., Lorentz R.J., An O(n log n) Algorithm for Finding All Repetitions in a String, J. Algorithms 5 (1984), 422-432.

[4] Lothaire M., Combinatorics on Words, Addison-Wesley 1983.

[5] Restivo A., Salemi S., On Weakly Square-free Words, Bull. EATCS 21 (1983), 49-56.

[6] Schützenberger, M.P., On a Special Class of Recurrent Events, Annals Math. Stat. 32 (1961), 1201-1213.

[7] Thue A., Uber unendliche Zeichenreihen, Norske Vid. Selsk. Skr., I. Mat. Nat. Kl., Christiania, 7 (1906), 1-22.

[8] Thue A., Uber die gegenseitige Lage gleicher Teile gewisser Zeichenreihen, Norske Vid. Selsk. Skr., I. Mat. Nat. Kl., Christiania, 1 (1912), 1-67.

ABSTRACT IMPLEMENTATIONS AND CORRECTNESS PROOFS

Gilles BERNOT, Michel BIDOIT, Christine CHOPPY

Laboratoire de Recherche en Informatique
Bât 490, Université PARIS-SUD
F-91405 ORSAY CEDEX
FRANCE

ABSTRACT

In this paper, we present a new semantics for the implementation of abstract data types. This semantics leads to a simple, exhaustive description of the abstract implementation correctness criteria. These correctness criteria are expressed in terms of ***sufficient completeness*** and ***hierarchical consistency***. Thus, correctness proofs of abstract implementations can always be handled using classical tools such as ***theorem proving*** methods, ***structural induction*** methods or ***syntactical methods*** (e.g. fair presentations). The main idea of our approach is the use of intermediate "concrete sorts", which synthesize the available values used by implementation. Moreover, we show that the ***composition*** of several correct abstract implementations is always correct. This provides a formal foundation for a methodology of program development by stepwise refinement.

1. INTRODUCTION

For about ten years [LZ 75, Gut 75, ADJ 76], the formalism of abstract data types has been considered a major tool for writing hierarchical and modular specifications. Algebraic specifications provide the user with legible and relevant properties concerning the specified data structure. In particular, an abstract specification does not necessarily reflect the "concrete" implementation of the described data structure. But then, we have often to prove that the concrete implementation is *correct* according to our abstract specification. The following example shows the difference between "*abstract*" and "*concrete*" specifications.

Example 1

Let us specify the stacks of natural numbers. *STACK(NAT)* is specified as follows :

$$pop(empty) = empty$$
$$pop(push(n,X)) = X$$
$$top(empty) = 0$$
$$top(push(n,X)) = n$$

But this data structure is often implemented by means of arrays. A stack is then characterized by an array, which contains the elements of the stack, and an integer, which is the height of the stack :

$$\begin{aligned} empty &= \langle t,0\rangle \\ push(n,\langle t,i\rangle) &= \langle t[i]{:=}n, succ(i)\rangle \\ pop(\langle t,0\rangle) &= \langle t,0\rangle \\ pop(\langle t,succ(i)\rangle) &= \langle t,i\rangle \\ top(\langle t,0\rangle) &= 0 \\ top(\langle t,succ(i)\rangle) &= t[i] \end{aligned}$$

The first element pushed onto the stack is then $t[0]$; and the index i points to the place where the next element will be pushed.

Our problem is to prove that the second set of axioms ***simulates*** the data structure described by the first one. Correctness proofs of abstract implementations can be done by using the notions of ***representation invariants*** and ***equality representation*** [GHM 76, Gau 80]. For instance, the equality representation of Example 1 can be stated by :

$$\langle t,i\rangle = \langle t',i'\rangle \;\; \textit{iff} \;\; i=i' \;\; \textit{and} \;\; t[j]=t'[j] \;\; \textit{for all} \;\; j=0..i$$

Unfortunately, this equality representation must be specified by the user, and nothing proves that it is correct. In particular, if we specify an equality representation where "everything is true", then every implementation will be correct. Since 1980, several works have formalized the notion of ***simulation*** [EKP 80, EKMP 80, SW 82] ; all these works give ***pure semantical*** correctness criteria (such as existence of a morphism between two algebras). Unfortunately, pure semantical correctness criteria do not provide the specifier with ***theorem proving*** methods or ***structural induction*** methods. It is therefore necessary to complete the abstract data type framework with an abstract implementation formalism which is able to provide the user with "simple" correctness proof criteria. These criteria are mainly ***sufficient completeness*** and ***hierarchical consistency***.

In this paper, we present a new formalism of abstract implementation. This formalism leads in a natural way to an exhaustive description of the abstract implementation correctness criteria. These correctness criteria can be checked via classical methods since they are expressed in terms of sufficient completeness and hierarchical consistency. This approach is especially powerful, since it is then always possible to prove the correctness of an implementation via theorem proving methods. Moreover, we prove that our formalism is compatible with ***enrichment*** and that the ***composition*** of two correct implementations always gives a correct result. Our formalism allows use of ***positive conditional axioms***. We will show that this feature imposes an explicit specification of the equality representation, but that it also facilitates the specification process. In particular our abstract implementation formalism can easily be extended to the algebraic data types with exception handling features [Ber 85].

The next section explains the classical problems related to abstract implementation. Section 3 describes the main ideas of our formalism which solve these problems. Sections 4 through 6 describe our abstract implementation formalism. In Section 7, we show how correctness proofs of abstract implementation can be handled. And finally, we prove that abstract implementations cope with ***enrichment*** (Section 8), and ***composition*** (Section 9). We assume that the reader is familiar with elementary results of category theory and abstract data type theory.

2. PROBLEMS RAISED BY ABSTRACT IMPLEMENTATION

Abstract implementations can be specified in two main ways : with an ***abstraction*** function, or with a ***representation*** function.

2.1. Abstraction

The abstraction takes already implemented objects (e.g. arrays and natural numbers), and returns "abstract" objects (e.g. stacks). This is done by means of an ***abstraction operation*** (e.g. *A: ARRAY NAT → STACK*). For instance, we obtain the axioms of the implementation of stacks by substituting *A(t,i)* for <t,i> in Example 1. Another example is the following :

Example 2
Natural numbers can be implemented by means of integers as follows :

$$
\begin{aligned}
0_{\mathbb{N}} &= A(0_{\mathbb{Z}}) \\
succ_{\mathbb{N}}(A(z)) &= A(succ_{\mathbb{Z}}(z)) \\
eq?_{\mathbb{N}}(A(z),A(z')) &= eq?_{\mathbb{Z}}(z,z')
\end{aligned}
$$

where *A: INT → NAT* is the abstraction operation.

Unfortunately, abstraction operations create too many abstract objects. For instance, *A(create,4)* does not implement any stack, since if the height of a stack is equal to 4, then the four first ranges of the corresponding array must be initialized. In the same way, *A(-1)* does not implement any natural number.
As shown in [EKMP 80], this fact prevents the specifier from carrying out simple correctness proofs by theorem proving methods. For instance, one of the proofs needed by implementation is the consistency of the implementation. This means that two distinct abstract objects must be implemented by two distinct concrete objects. The only formal concept of abstract data types which can handle such a condition is ***hierarchical consistency***. Thus, it is necessary to put together the specification of our implementation (Example 2) and the abstract specification to be implemented (*NAT*). Then, we obtain a specification that contains both the abstract implementation and the specification to be implemented, and we can check whether this specification is hierarchically consistent over *NAT*. *NAT* is specified as follows :

$$
\begin{aligned}
eq?_{\mathbb{N}}(0_{\mathbb{N}},0_{\mathbb{N}}) &= True \\
eq?_{\mathbb{N}}(0_{\mathbb{N}},succ_{\mathbb{N}}(m)) &= False \\
eq?_{\mathbb{N}}(succ_{\mathbb{N}}(n),0_{\mathbb{N}}) &= False \\
eq?_{\mathbb{N}}(succ_{\mathbb{N}}(n),succ_{\mathbb{N}}(m)) &= eq?_{\mathbb{N}}(n,m)
\end{aligned}
$$

But then, we obtain : $True = eq?_{\mathbb{N}}(0_{\mathbb{N}},0_{\mathbb{N}}) = eq?_{\mathbb{N}}(0_{\mathbb{N}},succ_{\mathbb{N}}(A(-1))) = False$. Consequently, we cannot prove the consistency of our implementation this way.

2.2. Representation

The aim of a representation is to provide a composition of already implemented operations (e.g. those of *NAT* and *ARRAY*) for every operation to be implemented (e.g. ***empty, push, pop, top***). For instance, the representation associated with Example 1 is specified as follows :

$$\begin{aligned}
\rho(empty) &= \langle t,0\rangle \\
\rho(push(n,\langle t,i\rangle)) &= \langle t[i]:=n, succ(i)\rangle \\
\rho(pop(\langle t,0\rangle)) &= \langle t,0\rangle \\
\rho(pop(\langle t,succ(i)\rangle)) &= \langle t,i\rangle \\
\rho(top(\langle t,0\rangle)) &= 0 \\
\rho(top(\langle t,succ(i)\rangle)) &= t[i]
\end{aligned}$$

where ρ is the ***representation*** function.
Since representation only gives a representation for each operation to be implemented, it should not create undesirable abstract values. Unfortunately, it is very difficult to give an algebraic meaning to such axioms. This is due to the fact that "$\langle\_,\_\rangle$" has no real algebraic definition. If we consider $\langle\_,\_\rangle$ as an operation, then its arity is necessarily : $\langle\,,\,\rangle$: *ARRAY NAT* → *STACK* because it takes an array and a natural number, and returns a stack (as we apply *pop* to $\langle t,i\rangle$). Consequently, the arity of $\langle\_,\_\rangle$ is the same as the arity of the abstraction operation. Thus, the function ρ is useless (equal to the identity), since the operation $\langle\,,\,\rangle$ can simply be used as an abstraction operation, which simplifies the specification of abstract implementation. Nevertheless, we will show how our formalism uses both ρ and A, by means of an intermediate "product sort".

2.3. Presentations and implementations

Assume that the *STACK* data structure is already implemented by means of *ARRAY* and *NAT*. The user of this data structure will probably specify a presentation over the *STACK* specification (presentations over *STACK* can be viewed as abstract programs). But the user should never have to know how the implementation is done. In other words, (s)he knows the abstract specification of *STACK*, but not the specification of the implementation. Thus, every proof concerning this enrichment is done w.r.t. the abstract specification of *STACK*, but not w.r.t. the abstract implementation. Nothing proves that the composition of our implementation and the new enrichment gives the expected results. A particular subproblem of this is the composition of several implementations. All correctness proofs of the second implementation are handled w.r.t. to the abstract specification of the first implemented data structure, but they are not done w.r.t. to the concrete specification of the first implementation. In our framework, an enrichment of an abstract implementation always gives the expected result. This feature was not provided for in any of the works previously put forward.

In order to achieve this goal, we need an ***explicit*** specification of the equality representation in the implementation : when we enrich the implementation of *STACK*, the associated presentation will probably contain some axioms of the form :

$$X = Y \quad \Longrightarrow \quad \ldots$$

We may have : $X = empty$ and $Y = pop(push(x,empty))$. The implementations of X and Y are then $\langle create, 0\rangle$ and $\langle create[0]:=x, 0\rangle$. If the designer of the implementation says nothing about "***when two distinct pairs implement the same stack***", our enrichment viewed through the implementation will not be correct, since several occurrences of these axioms are not taken into account. Thus, it is necessary to specify the ***equality representation*** in the implementation, in order to handle conditional axioms. We will show that equality representation is also a useful tool for correctness proofs.

3. PRESENTATION OF OUR FORMALISM

Our situation is described as follows :

- The already implemented data structure (e.g. *ARRAY* and *NAT*) is specified by $\mathbf{SPEC_0} = <\mathbf{S_0},\Sigma_0,\mathbf{A_0}>$, where $\mathbf{S_0}$ is a set of sorts, Σ_0 is a set of operations with arity in $\mathbf{S_0}$, and $\mathbf{A_0}$ is a set of ***positive conditional*** axioms over the signature $<\mathbf{S_0},\Sigma_0>$. $\mathbf{SPEC_0}$ is called the ***resident*** specification.
- We want to implement an enrichment (e.g. *STACK*) of the already implemented data structure. This enrichment is described by a specification $\mathbf{SPEC_1} = <\mathbf{S_1},\Sigma_1,\mathbf{A_1}>$ which contains $\mathbf{SPEC_0}$, and is persistent over $\mathbf{SPEC_0}$. $\mathbf{SPEC_1}$ is the ***abstract specification*** of the data structure obtained after the implementation is done (*STACK+ARRAY+NAT*).

Our implementation will be made in five steps :

- The first step describes the representation. For each (abstract) sort of $\mathbf{SPEC_1}$ (e.g. *STACK*), there is a ***concrete*** sort which represents it ($\overline{STACK}$) ; $\overline{STACK}$ will be the product sort "Array×Natural". For each (abstract) operation of $\mathbf{SPEC_1}$ (e.g. ***empty***, ***push***, ***pop***, ***top***), there is a ***concrete*** operation which is its ***actual implementation*** ($\overline{empty}$, $\overline{push}$, $\overline{pop}$, $\overline{top}$). These concrete operations work on the concrete sorts (e.g. $\overline{STACK}$) instead of working on the abstract sorts to be implemented (*STACK*).
- The second step synthesizes the ***concrete values*** used by implementation. These concrete values are synthesized by means of abstraction operations. For instance, A_{STACK}: *ARRAY NAT* → $\overline{STACK}$ is the abstraction operation that synthesizes the product sort $\overline{STACK}$ (*ARRAY*×*NAT*), associated with *STACK* ∈ $\mathbf{S_1}$.
- The third step is only a convenient (hidden) enrichment of the previously synthesized data structure. This ***hidden component*** of the implementation was first introduced in [EKP 80]. It allows us to add hidden operations which are useful to specify the implementation. For instance, if the resident specification of integers (Example 2) does not contain the operation $eq?_{\mathbf{Z}}$, then it is very useful to define it in the hidden component before specifying the main part of the implementation.
- The fourth step recursively specifies the actual implementation of the concrete operations, on the concrete sorts. This step is handled by means of (conditional) axioms, as in previous examples.
- The last step specifies the equality representation. It will be specified by means of a set of (conditional) axioms. Thus, our last step specifies the implementation of the ***classes*** (or equivalently ***values***) to be implemented.

This approach can be pictured as follows :

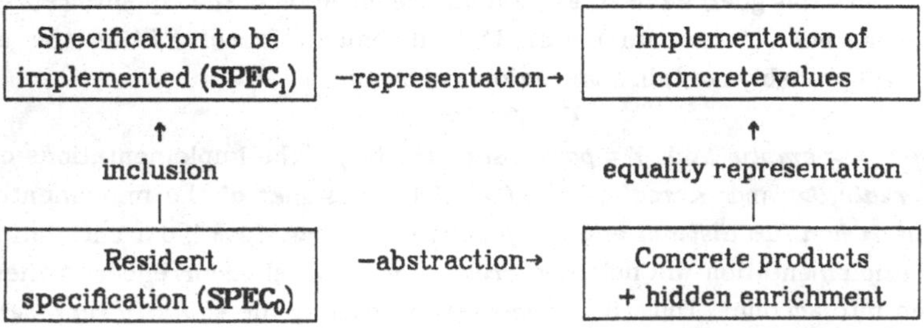

Our abstract implementation is described on three different levels :

- the *formal definition* only contains the information which the specifier must provide in order to define the implementation
- the *associated syntax* is automatically deduced from the formal definition ; it gives an algebraic specification for the implementation
- the *associated semantics* is automatically deduced from the syntax ; it describes the models (algebras) of the implementation.

The distinction between these three levels was first introduced by [EKP 80]. This distinction has been shown to be a firm basis to handle correctness proofs for implementations.

4. FORMAL DEFINITION

Definition 1

We define an *abstract implementation*, denoted by **IMPL**, as a tuple :

$$\mathbf{IMPL} = \langle \rho , \Sigma_{ABS} , \mathrm{H} , \mathrm{A}_{OP} , \mathrm{A}_{EQ} \rangle$$

where :

- ρ is the signature isomorphism defined as follows :
  - for each abstract sort to be implemented, $s \in \mathrm{S}_1$, there is an associated "concrete sort", $\bar{s}$. We denote the set of concrete sorts by S_{ABS} (since it will be synthesized by the abstraction operations [*]). Thus, S_{ABS} is a copy of S_1.
  - for each operation to be implemented ($\in \Sigma_1$), $op: s_1 \cdots s_n \rightarrow s_{n+1}$, there is a "concrete operation", $\overline{op}: \overline{s_1} \cdots \overline{s_n} \rightarrow \overline{s_{n+1}}$, where $\overline{s_i}$ is the concrete sort associated with s_i. We denote the set of concrete operations by Σ_{OP}.

  ρ is the signature isomorphism from $\langle \mathrm{S}_1,\Sigma_1\rangle$ to $\langle \mathrm{S}_{ABS},\Sigma_{OP}\rangle$. ρ is called *representation signature isomorphism*, or simply *representation*, since it gives the actual representation of each sort (resp. operation) to be implemented. For instance, ρ sends the sort *NAT* to $\overline{NAT}$, *STACK* to $\overline{STACK}$, *push: NAT STACK* → *STACK* to $\overline{push}$: $\overline{NAT}$ $\overline{STACK}$ → $\overline{STACK}$, and so on.
- Σ_{ABS} is the set of *abstraction operations* : for each sort to be implemented, $s \in \mathrm{S}_1$, there is one abstraction operation, $A_s: r_1 \cdots r_m \rightarrow \bar{s}$, where all the r_i are sorts in S_0 . For instance, the abstraction operation associated with the sort *STACK* is : A_{STACK}: *ARRAY NAT* → $\overline{STACK}$; the abstraction operation associated with *NAT* is a copy operation : A_{NAT}: *NAT* → $\overline{NAT}$.
- H is the *hidden component* of **IMPL**. $\mathrm{H} = \langle \mathrm{S_H},\Sigma_\mathrm{H},\mathrm{A_H}\rangle$ is a presentation over $\mathbf{ABS} = \mathbf{SPEC}_0+\langle \mathrm{S}_{ABS},\Sigma_{ABS},\phi\rangle$, which enriches the concrete data structure in order to facilitate the implementation. In our *STACK* by *ARRAY* example, H is empty.
- A_{OP} is a set of positive conditional axioms over the signature $\langle \mathrm{S}_0+\mathrm{S_H}+\mathrm{S}_{ABS},\Sigma_0+\Sigma_\mathrm{H}+\Sigma_{ABS}+\Sigma_{OP}\rangle$. It describes the actual implementation of the concrete operations $\overline{op}$. A_{OP} is the set of operation implementing axioms. These axioms are those specified for abstraction :

$$\overline{empty} = A_{STACK}(t,0)$$
$$\overline{push}(A_{NAT}(n),A_{STACK}(t,i)) = A_{STACK}(t[i]:=n,succ(i))$$

[*] in our formalism, *abstraction* functions return *concrete* values (!).

$$\overline{pop}(A_{STACK}(t,0)) = A_{STACK}(t,0)$$
$$\overline{pop}(A_{STACK}(t,succ(i))) = A_{STACK}(t,i)$$
$$\overline{top}(A_{STACK}(t,0)) = A_{NAT}(0)$$
$$\overline{top}(A_{STACK}(t,succ(i))) = A_{NAT}(t[i])$$

- $\mathbf{A}_{EQ}$ is a set of positive conditional axioms over the same signature. It defines the ***equality representation***. For instance, the equality representation of our *STACK* by *ARRAY* example can be specified as follows [*] :

$$A_{STACK}(t,0) = A_{STACK}(t',0)$$
$$A_{STACK}(t,i)=A_{STACK}(t',i) \wedge t[i]=t'[i] \implies A_{STACK}(t,succi)=A_{STACK}(t',succi)$$

5. ASSOCIATED SYNTAX

The syntax associated with the formal definition of an abstract implementation is defined as follows :

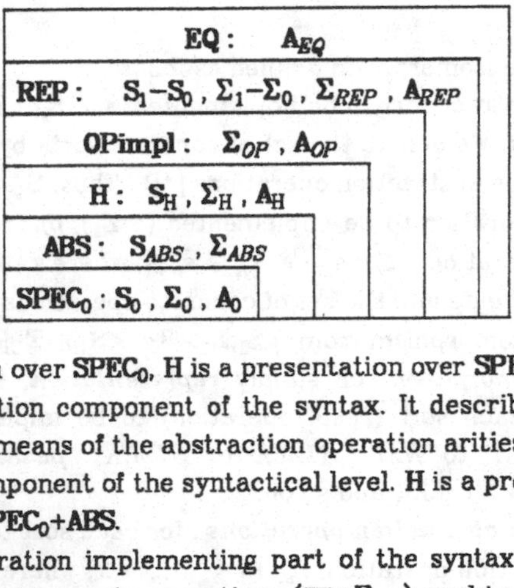

where **ABS** is a presentation over $\mathbf{SPEC_0}$, H is a presentation over $\mathbf{SPEC_0}$+**ABS**, and so on.

- **ABS** is the abstraction component of the syntax. It describes the synthesis of the concrete sorts $\bar{s}$, by means of the abstraction operation arities ($A_s: r_1 \cdots r_n \to \bar{s}$).
- **H** is the hidden component of the syntactical level. **H** is a presentation over the concrete specification $\mathbf{SPEC_0}$+**ABS**.
- **OPimpl** is the operation implementing part of the syntax. It specifies the actual implementation of the concrete operations ($\overline{op} \in \Sigma_{OP}$) working on the concrete sorts, by means of $\mathbf{A}_{OP}$.
- **REP** is the representation component. It ***explicitly*** specifies (in the syntax) the effect of the representation signature isomorphism. We define $\mathbf{\Sigma}_{REP}$ and $\mathbf{A}_{REP}$ below.
- **EQ** is the equality representation part of the syntax. It specifies when two distinct availables values (concrete values) represent the same abstract value.

H, S_{ABS}, Σ_{ABS}, Σ_{OP}, A_{OP} and A_{EQ} are defined in Section 4. $\mathbf{\Sigma}_{REP}$ and $\mathbf{A}_{REP}$ are defined as follows :

- $\mathbf{\Sigma}_{REP}$ is the set of ***representation operations***. For each abstract sort, $s \in \mathbf{S}_1$, there is one representation operation : $\overline{\rho_s}: s \to \bar{s}$.
- $\mathbf{A}_{REP}$ is the set of axioms which state that $\overline{\rho_s}$ extends the representation signature isomorphism ρ. This means that for all $\mathbf{\Sigma}_1$-terms, t, of sort s, $\overline{\rho_s}(t)$ is equal to the term

[*] In fact, $\mathbf{A}_{EQ}$ can be empty in this example, since $\mathbf{A}_{OP}$ already implies our two axioms. But this is particular to our example.

deduced from t via ρ. Thus, for each operation to be implemented, $op \in \Sigma_1$, A_{REP} contains the following axiom :

$$\overline{\rho_s}(op(x_1, \ldots, x_n)) = \rho(op)(\overline{\rho_{s_i}}(x_i), \ldots, \overline{\rho_{s_n}}(x_n)) \quad [*]$$

where s is the target sort of op, and s_i is the sort of x_i.

Moreover, A_{REP} contains the following axiom for each abstract sort, $s \in S_1$:

$$\overline{\rho_s}(x) = \overline{\rho_s}(y) \implies x = y.$$

This axiom is explained as follows : our goal is to specify the data structure obtained after the implementation is done. If two terms to be implemented, x and y, are represented by the same concrete values, then it is impossible to distinguish x from y. Thus their values are equal in the resulting data structure.

Example 3

In the *STACK* by *ARRAY* example, A_{REP} is deduced from the signature isomorphism ρ as follows :

$$\overline{\rho_{STACK}}(empty) = \overline{empty}$$
$$\overline{\rho_{STACK}}(push(x,X)) = \overline{push}(\overline{\rho_{NAT}}(x), \overline{\rho_{STACK}}(X))$$
$$\overline{\rho_{STACK}}(pop(X)) = \overline{pop}(\overline{\rho_{STACK}}(X))$$
$$\ldots etc \ldots$$
$$\overline{\rho_{STACK}}(X) = \overline{\rho_{STACK}}(Y) \implies X = Y$$
$$\overline{\rho_{NAT}}(m) = \overline{\rho_{NAT}}(n) \implies m = n$$
$$\overline{\rho_{ARRAY}}(t) = \overline{\rho_{ARRAY}}(t') \implies t = t'$$

6. ASSOCIATED SEMANTICS

The semantics of our abstract implementation is the composition of two functors :

$$\begin{array}{ccccc} Alg(SPEC_0) & -F_{ABS+H+OPimpl+REP+EQ}\rightarrow & Alg(EQ) & -U_{<S_1,\Sigma_1>}\rightarrow & Alg(<S_1,\Sigma_1>) \\ T_{SPEC_0} & \vdash F_{ABS+H+OPimpl+REP+EQ}\rightarrow & T_{EQ} & \vdash U_{<S_1,\Sigma_1>}\rightarrow & SEM_{IMPL} \end{array}$$

where $F_{ABS+H+OPimpl+REP+EQ}$ is the usual synthesis functor associated with the presentation ABS+H+OPimpl+REP+EQ over $SPEC_0$; and $U_{<S_1,\Sigma_1>}$ is the usual forgetful functor.

More precisely, the intuitive meaning of this semantics can be divided as follows :

- T_{SPEC_0} describes the (abstract) resident data structure.
- T_{ABS} describes the concrete data structure synthesized from the resident one by means of the abstraction operations. T_{ABS} is the *available* structure which our abstract implementation can use.
- T_H describes the hidden enrichment of the concrete data structure and the resident abstract data structure.
- T_{OPimpl} handles the concrete implementation of the concrete operations ($\overline{op}$) over the previously synthesized concrete sorts.
- T_{REP} is the implementation of the abstract ground terms to be implemented. It contains both the abstract operations (op), and their concrete implementation ($\overline{op}$). The correspondance between op and $\overline{op}$ is made via the representation operations $\overline{\rho_s}$.

---

[*] $\rho(op)$ is equal to $\overline{op}$.

- T_{EQ} handles the *identification* of the concrete terms which represent the same abstract value.
- Notice that T_{EQ} contains all the sorts and operations used in our implementation. Thus, it is necessary to remove the hidden sorts and operations, the intermediate concrete sorts, the abstraction operations, and the concrete operations $\overline{op}$. This is done by means of a forgetful functor, and the ***semantical result*** is a Σ_1-algebra, denoted by SEM_{IMPL}. Thus, SEM_{IMPL} is the "user view" of the implementation, since the user must not use the specific operations and sorts of the implementation.

7. CORRECTNESS PROOFS

The above semantics leads, in a natural way, to define abstract implementation correctness as follows : an abstract implementation is ***correct*** iff each operation to be implemented has a (complete) concrete representation, and the semantical result (SEM_{IMPL}) is isomorphic to the initial algebra to be implemented (T_{SPEC_1}). These criteria are handled in four steps. The complete implementation of all operations to be implemented is called ***operation-completeness***. The isomorphism between SEM_{IMPL} and T_{SPEC_1} is divided into three conditions. SEM_{IMPL} must be finitely generated over Σ_1 ; this condition is the ***data protection***. SEM_{IMPL} must be a **SPEC**$_1$-algebra ; this condition is the ***validity*** of **IMPL**. SEM_{IMPL} must be an initial **SPEC**$_1$-algebra ; this condition is the ***consistency*** of **IMPL**.

7.1. Operation completeness

Operation completeness was first introduced by [EKP 80]. The fact that all abstract operations have a concrete implementation means that all Σ_1-terms have an "available" representation. Thus, operation completeness is defined as follows :

Definition 2
IMPL is *op-complete* iff for all terms $t \in T_{\Sigma_1}$, there is $\alpha \in T_{ABS}$ such that $\overline{p_s}(t)=\alpha$ in T_{REP}
Notice that op-completeness must be tested without any consideration of the equality representation. Thus, it is defined in T_{REP} and not in T_{EQ}.

Op-completeness can be directly proved by structural induction. Moreover, we have the following theorem :

Theorem 1
If **OPimpl** is sufficiently complete over **ABS**, then **IMPL** is op-complete.

Proof : Since **REP** is always sufficiently complete over **OPimpl** (fair presentation, [Bid 82]), (**REP**+**OPimpl**) is also sufficiently complete over **ABS**. But the sufficient completeness of **REP** over **ABS** means that for each $(\Sigma_1+\Sigma_H+\Sigma_{ABS}+\Sigma_{OP}+\Sigma_{REP})$-term, r, whose sort belongs to $(S_0+S_H+S_{ABS})$, there is $\alpha \in T_{ABS}$ such that $r=\alpha$ in T_{REP}. In particular, this holds for all terms of the form $\overline{p_s}(t)$, as needed. ▫

Example 4
We prove that our implementation of *STACK* by *ARRAY* is op-complete, by structural induction.

- $\overline{\rho_{STACK}(empty)}$ is equal to $\overline{empty}$, which is equal to $\alpha = A_{STACK}(create, 0)$
- if x and X have concrete representations ($x = \alpha_1$ and $\overline{\rho_{STACK}(X)} = \alpha_2 = A_{STACK}(t, i)$), then $\overline{\rho_{STACK}(push(x, X))}$ do too :

$$\overline{\rho_{STACK}(push(x,X))} = \overline{push}(\alpha_1, A_{STACK}(t,i)) = A_{STACK}(t[i]:=\alpha_1, succ(i)) .$$

- similar reasoning applies for *pop* and *top*.

7.2. Data protection

Theorem 2

If **H** is sufficiently complete over $\mathbf{SPEC_0}$, then $SEM_{\mathbf{IMPL}}$ is finitely generated over Σ_1.

Proof : The syntax of our abstract implementation does not contain any operations with target sort in $\mathbf{S_1} - \mathbf{S_0}$, except those of Σ_1. Thus, $SEM_{\mathbf{IMPL}}$ is always finitely generated w.r.t. the sorts of $\mathbf{S_1} - \mathbf{S_0}$. It suffices to prove that $SEM_{\mathbf{IMPL}}$ is finitely generated w.r.t. the sorts of $\mathbf{S_0}$. Consequently, Theorem 2 results from the fact that our abstract implementation syntax does not contain any operation with target sort in $\mathbf{S_0}$, except those of Σ_1 and $\Sigma_{\mathbf{H}}$. ▫

Definition 3

IMPL is ***data protected*** iff **H** is sufficiently complete over $\mathbf{SPEC_0}$. This means that the resident (abstract) sorts are protected through **IMPL**.

Data protection is then not difficult to prove, since it can be proved by structural induction or via syntactical tools (such as ***fair presentations***, [Bid 82]). Our *STACK* by *ARRAY* example is clearly data protected, as **H** is empty.

7.3. Validity

Definition 4

IMPL is a *valid* abstract implementation iff for all Σ_1-terms, t and t', we have :

$$\text{if } t=t' \text{ in } T_{\mathbf{SPEC_1}} \text{ then } t=t' \text{ in } SEM_{\mathbf{IMPL}}.$$

Theorem 3

If **IMPL** is data protected then the following conditions are equivalent :

- **IMPL** is a valid abstract implementation
- there is a Σ_1-morphism from $T_{\mathbf{SPEC_1}}$ to $SEM_{\mathbf{IMPL}}$
- $SEM_{\mathbf{IMPL}}$ validates the axioms of $\mathbf{A_1} = \mathbf{A_0} + \mathbf{A}$
- $SEM_{\mathbf{IMPL}}$ validates the axioms of **A**
- $T_{\mathbf{EQ}}$ validates the axioms of **A**
- **ID** is hierarchically consistent over **EQ**

where **ID** is the presentation over **EQ** which contains the set of axioms **A**. Thus, **ID** contains all the specifications involved in our formalism (both the syntax of **IMPL** and $\mathbf{SPEC_1}$).

Proof : given in Appendix.

The main result is the equivalence between the validity of **IMPL** and the consistency of **ID** over **EQ**. This feature is entirely due to our intermediate product sorts and the equality representation explicitly specified via $\mathbf{A}_{EQ}$. This result facilitates the validity proofs, since then, they can always be handled by theorem proving methods.

Example 5
The validity of our abstract implementation of *STACK* is shown by proving that each *STACK*-axiom is a theorem of the syntax of **IMPL**. We prove here that *pop(push(x,X))* is equal to *X* in $T_{\mathbf{EQ}}$. Other axioms of *STACK* are proved in a straightforward manner, following the same method.
Since $\mathbf{A}_{REP}$ contains the axiom $\overline{\rho_{STACK}}(X)=\overline{\rho_{STACK}}(Y) \implies X=Y$, and since our implementation is op-complete, it suffices to show that $\overline{pop}(\overline{push}(x,A_{STACK}(t,i)))$ is equal to $A_{STACK}(t,i)$ in $T_{\mathbf{EQ}}$. From $\mathbf{A}_{OP}$, it results that $\overline{pop}(\overline{push}(x,A_{STACK}(t,i))) = A_{STACK}(t[i]:=x,i)$. Moreover, from the equality representation ($\mathbf{A}_{EQ}$), it results that $A_{STACK}(t[i]:=x,i) = A_{STACK}(t,i)$, which ends our proof.

7.4. Consistency

Definition 5
IMPL is *consistent* iff for all Σ_1-terms, t and t', we have :

$$\text{if } t=t' \text{ in } SEM_{\mathbf{IMPL}}, \text{ then } t=t' \text{ in } T_{\mathbf{SPEC}_1}.$$

Theorem 4
If **IMPL** is data protected and valid, then the following conditions are equivalent :

- for all t and t' in T_{Σ_1}, if $t=t'$ in $T_{\mathbf{EQ}}$ then $t=t'$ in $T_{\mathbf{SPEC}_1}$
- **IMPL** is consistent
- the initial morphism from $T_{\mathbf{SPEC}_1}$ to $SEM_{\mathbf{IMPL}}$ is a monomorphism
- $SEM_{\mathbf{IMPL}}$ is an initial $\mathbf{SPEC}_1$-algebra
- the initial morphism from $T_{\mathbf{SPEC}_1}$ to $U_{\mathbf{S}_1}(T_{\mathbf{ID}})$ is a monomorphism
- **ID** is hierarchically consistent over $\mathbf{SPEC}_1$

Proof : given in Appendix.

For the same reasons as Theorem 3, Theorem 4 facilitates the consistency proofs, since they can always be handled by theorem proving methods.

Example 6
The only axioms that can destroy the consistency of **ID** over $\mathbf{SPEC}_1$ are the axioms whose sort is in $\mathbf{S}_1$. These axioms are :

$$\overline{\rho_{STACK}}(X) = \overline{\rho_{STACK}}(Y) \implies X = Y$$
$$\overline{\rho_{NAT}}(m) = \overline{\rho_{NAT}}(n) \implies m = n$$
$$\overline{\rho_{ARRAY}}(t) = \overline{\rho_{ARRAY}}(t') \implies t = t'$$

These axioms lead to show that two abstract terms represented by the same concrete value (in $T_{\mathbf{EQ}}$), are equal. Thus, we must consider each axiom of $\mathbf{A}_{OP}\cup\mathbf{A}_{REP}\cup\mathbf{A}_{EQ}$, and prove that it does not create inconsistencies. Let us consider, for instance, the axiom

$$\overline{push}(A_{NAT}(x),A_{STACK}(t,i)) \;=\; A_{STACK}(t[i]:=x,succ(i))\,.$$

Since we work in the stack *values* (not in the stack ground terms), we can handle our proofs w.r.t. the normal forms of *STACK*. It is possible to prove, by structural induction, that $A_{STACK}(t,i)$ represents the stack $push(t[i\text{-}1],push(\ldots,push(t[0],empty)..))$. Then, our proof is clear, as $\overline{push}(x,\overline{\rho_{STACK}}(X))$ represents *push(x,X)*. Other axioms are handled in a similar manner, by using the normal forms.

Definition 6
IMPL is *correct* iff it is both op-complete, data protected, valid and consistent.

8. ABSTRACT IMPLEMENTATIONS AND ENRICHMENTS

Let $\mathbf{SPEC}_1$ be a specification implemented via **IMPL**. Let P be a presentation over $\mathbf{SPEC}_1$. We have shown (Section 2.3) that every proof concerning P is done w.r.t. $\mathbf{SPEC}_1$, but not w.r.t. the syntax of **IMPL**. The "concrete" implementation of P+$\mathbf{SPEC}_1$ is not specified by P+$\mathbf{SPEC}_1$. It is specified by P+**EQ**, where **EQ** is the whole syntax of the implementation of $\mathbf{SPEC}_1$. The following theorem proves that the user view of the concrete specification P+**EQ** is isomorphic to the data structure specified by P+$\mathbf{SPEC}_1$.

Theorem 5
If **IMPL** is a correct abstract implementation of $\mathbf{SPEC}_1$, then for all persistent presentations, P, over $\mathbf{SPEC}_1$, we have :

$$U_{<\Sigma_1+\Sigma_P>}(T_{\mathbf{EQ}+\mathbf{P}}) = T_{\mathbf{SPEC}_1+\mathbf{P}}$$

Proof : given in Appendix.

This theorem proves that the presentation P, pushed together with the abstract implementation of $\mathbf{SPEC}_1$, always provides the user with the expected results.

9. COMPOSITION OF ABSTRACT IMPLEMENTATIONS

When we implement $\mathbf{SPEC}_1$ by means of $\mathbf{SPEC}_0$, the resident specification $\mathbf{SPEC}_0$ is often already implemented by means of a lower level specification. But all our correctness proofs are done w.r.t. the specification $\mathbf{SPEC}_0$, not w.r.t. the specification of the implementation of $\mathbf{SPEC}_0$. We prove in this section that the composition of two correct implementations always gives correct results. This feature is not provided in any work already put forward. The formalism of [SW 82] provides correct "vertical compositions", but these vertical compositions do not solve our problem : all upper level implementation operations must be implemented by the lower level implementation. This results in a large amount of operations to be implemented by the lowest level implementation ; moreover, this implies that all the lower level implementations must be redefined each time we add a new implementation. Such a composition is incompatible with modular, structured implementation.
The following theorem proves that the user view, obtained by pushing two correct abstract implementations together, is always correct.

Theorem 6
Let $\mathbf{IMPL}_2$ be an abstract implementation of $\mathbf{SPEC}_2$ by means of $\mathbf{SPEC}_1$. Let $\mathbf{IMPL}_1$ be an abstract implementation of $\mathbf{SPEC}_1$ by means of $\mathbf{SPEC}_0$. Consider the specification **IMPL**(1,2) obtained from the syntax of $\mathbf{IMPL}_2$ by substituting the syntax of $\mathbf{IMPL}_1$ for $\mathbf{SPEC}_1$.

$$\mathbf{IMPL}(1,2) = \mathbf{SPEC}_0 + (\mathbf{H}_1+\mathbf{ABS}_1+\ldots+\mathbf{EQ}_1) + (\mathbf{H}_2+\mathbf{ABS}_2+\ldots+\mathbf{EQ}_2)$$

If $\mathbf{IMPL}_1$ and $\mathbf{IMPL}_2$ are both correct, then we have :

$$U_{<S_2,\Sigma_2>}(T_{\mathbf{IMPL}(1,2)}) = T_{\mathbf{SPEC}_2}$$

Proof : , Since **IMPL**$_2$ is correct, ($\mathbf{H}_2$+...+$\mathbf{EQ}_2$) is persistent over $\mathbf{SPEC}_1$. Thus, Theorem 5 proves that $U_{\mathbf{SPEC}_1+..+\mathbf{EQ}_2}(T_{\mathbf{IMPL}(1,2)}) = T_{\mathbf{EQ}_2}$.
In particular, $U_{<\mathbf{S}_2,\Sigma_2>}(T_{\mathbf{IMPL}(1,2)}) = U_{<\mathbf{S}_2,\Sigma_2>}(T_{\mathbf{EQ}_2}) = SEM_{\mathbf{IMPL}_2}$. Moreover, the correctness of **IMPL**$_2$ implies that $SEM_{\mathbf{IMPL}_2} = T_{\mathbf{SPEC}_2}$, which ends our proof. ▫

This theorem can easily be extended to every (finite) number of implementations. Thus, it is possible to handle structured and modular abstract implementations. This provides a formal foundation for a methodology of program development by stepwise refinement.

10. CONCLUSION

The abstract implementation formalism described in this paper relies on three main ideas :

- Abstract implementation is done by means of intermediate concrete values, which are distinct from the abstract values to be implemented. These concrete sorts are synthesized by means of ***abstraction operations.***
- The correspondance between the abstract sorts or operations to be implemented and the concrete sorts or operations is specified by means of a ***representation signature isomorphism.***
- The ***equality representation*** is explicitly introduced into the abstract implementation, in order to handle conditional axioms.

The main results of this abstract implementation formalism are the following :

- It allows use of ***positive conditional axioms***, which facilitates the specifications and increases the class of models taken into account.
- All correctness proof criteria for abstract implementation are "simple" ones (sufficient completeness, hierarchical consistency or fair presentations). This feature provides the specifier with ***theorem proving*** methods, ***structural induction*** methods or ***syntactical*** criteria.
- Abstract implementations cope with the notion of ***enrichment.***
- The ***composition*** of several correct implementations always gives correct results. Thus, abstract implementations can be specified in a modular and structured way.

As a last remark, we want to emphasize the fact that the semantics of our abstract implementation is a functorial one. Thus it is not difficult to include the notion of ***parameterization*** into our formalism, since parameterization mainly relies on synthesis functors and pushouts (see [ADJ 80]).

ACKNOWLEDGEMENTS

This work is partially supported by CNRS GRECO de Programmation, ESPRIT Project METEOR and FOR-ME-TOO.

11. APPENDIX

This appendix contains the technical proofs omitted in the body of the article. The results being proved are restated for convenience of reference.

11.1. Proof of Theorem 3

Theorem 3

If **IMPL** is data protected then the following conditions are equivalent :

1) **IMPL** is a valid abstract implementation
2) there is a Σ_1-morphism from T_{SPEC_1} to SEM_{IMPL}
3) SEM_{IMPL} validates the axioms of $\mathbf{A_1} = \mathbf{A_0}+\mathbf{A}$
4) SEM_{IMPL} validates the axioms of **A**
5) T_{EQ} validates the axioms of **A**
6) **ID** is hierarchically consistent over **EQ**

where **ID**=**EQ**+<**A**>.

Proof :

[1 ⟺ 2] is clear : since T_{SPEC_1} is finitely generated over Σ_1, there is a morphism from T_{SPEC_1} to SEM_{IMPL} if and only if two Σ_1-terms equal in T_{SPEC_1} are also equal in SEM_{IMPL}.

[2 ⟺ 3] results from the facts that SEM_{IMPL} is finitely generated over Σ_1 and that T_{SPEC_1} is initial in $\mathbf{SPEC_1}$. Thus, there is a morphism from T_{SPEC_1} to SEM_{IMPL} if and only if SEM_{IMPL} is a **SPEC**-algebra (i.e. SEM_{IMPL} validates $\mathbf{A_1}$).

[3 ⟺ 4] results from the fact that **EQ** contains $\mathbf{A_0}$. Thus, SEM_{IMPL} always validates $\mathbf{A_0}$.

[4 ⟺ 5] results from the fact that the axioms of **A** only concern the signature $<S_1,\Sigma_1>$, and $SEM_{IMPL} = U_{<S_1,\Sigma_1>}(T_{EQ})$.

[5 ⟺ 6] results from the fact that **ID** does not add new operations to **EQ** (**EQ**=**ID**−**A**). Thus, **ID** is hierarchically consistent over **EQ** if and only if T_{EQ} already validates the axioms of **A** ▫

11.2. Proof of Theorem 4

Theorem 4

If **IMPL** is data protected and valid, then the following conditions are equivalent :

1) for all t and t' in T_{Σ_1}, if $t=t'$ in T_{EQ} then $t=t'$ in T_{SPEC_1}
2) **IMPL** is consistent
3) the initial morphism from T_{SPEC_1} to SEM_{IMPL} is a monomorphism
4) SEM_{IMPL} is an initial $\mathbf{SPEC_1}$-algebra
5) the initial morphism from T_{SPEC_1} to $U_{S_1}(T_{ID})$ is a monomorphism
6) **ID** is hierarchically consistent over $\mathbf{SPEC_1}$

Proof :

[1 ⟺ 2] results from the fact that SEM_{IMPL} is equal to the part of T_{EQ} concerning the signature $<S_1,\Sigma_1>$.

[2 ⟺ 3] results from the fact that T_{SPEC_1} is finitely generated over Σ_1, and from Definition 5. Notice that the initial morphism $T_{SPEC_1} \to SEM_{IMPL}$ exists, from Theorem 3.

[3 ⟺ 4] results from the fact that SEM_{IMPL} is finitely generated over Σ_1.

[3 ⟺ 5] results from $SEM_{IMPL} = U_{S_1}(T_{EQ})$, and from $T_{EQ} = T_{ID}$ (Theorem 3).

[5 ⟺ 6] is clear since the initial morphism $T_{SPEC_1} \to U_{S_1}(T_{ID})$ is the unit of adjunction associated with the presentation **ID** over $\mathbf{SPEC_1}$. ▫

11.3. Proof of Theorem 5

Theorem 5
If **IMPL** is a correct abstract implementation of $\mathbf{SPEC}_1$, then for all persistent presentations, P, over $\mathbf{SPEC}_1$, we have :

$$U_{<\Sigma_1+\Sigma_P>}(T_{\mathbf{EQ+P}}) = T_{\mathbf{SPEC}_1+\mathbf{P}}$$

Proof : We recall the following classical lemma :

Lemma If P_a and P_b are two *persistent* presentations over a specification **SP** such that $<S_a,\Sigma_a> \cap <S_b,\Sigma_b>$ is empty, then P_b is still a persistent presentation over $(P_a+\mathbf{SP})$.
(proved in [Ber 85] with positive conditional axioms)

The correctness of **IMPL** implies that **ID** is persistent over $\mathbf{SPEC}_1$. Thus, our lemma proves that $T_{\mathbf{SPEC}_1+\mathbf{P}}$ is isomorphic to $U_{<\Sigma_1+\Sigma_P>}(T_{\mathbf{ID+P}})$.
Moreover, since P is sufficiently complete over the S_1 part of $T_{\mathbf{ID+P}}$, Theorem 3 proves that $T_{\mathbf{EQ+P}}$ is isomorphic to $T_{\mathbf{ID+P}}$. Consequently, $U_{<\Sigma_1+\Sigma_P>}(T_{\mathbf{EQ+P}})$ is isomorphic to $T_{\mathbf{SPEC}_1+\mathbf{P}}$, as needed. □

12. REFERENCES

[ADJ 76] Goguen J., Thatcher J., Wagner E. : "An initial algebra approach to the specification, correctness, and implementation of abstract data types", Current Trends in Programming Methodology, Vol.4, Yeh Ed. Prentice Hall, 1978 (also IBM Report RC 6487, Oct. 1976).

[ADJ 80] Ehrig H., Kreowski H., Thatcher J., Wagner J., Wright J. : "Parameterized data types in algebraic specification langages", Proc. 7th ICALP, July 1980.

[Ber 85] Bernot G. : "Une sémantique algébrique pour une spécification différenciée des exceptions et des erreurs : application à l'implémentation et aux primitives de structuration des spécifications formelles", Thèse de troisième cycle, Université de Paris-Sud, Orsay, 1985.

[Bid 82] Bidoit M. : "Algebraic data types: structured specifications and fair presentations", Proc. of AFCET Symposium on Mathematics for Computer Science, Paris, March 1982.

[EKMP 80] Ehrig H., Kreowski H., Mahr B., Padawitz P. : "Algebraic implementation of abstract data types", Theoretical Computer Science, Oct. 1980.

[EKP 80] Ehrig H., Kreowski H., Padawitz P. : "Algebraic implementation of abstract data types: concept, syntax, semantics and correctness", Proc. ICALP, Springer-Verlag LNCS 85, 1980.

[Gau 80] Gaudel M.C. : "Génération et preuve de compilateurs basée sur une sémantique formelle des langages de programmation", Thèse d'état, Nancy, 1980.

[GHM 78] Guttag J.V., Horowitz E., Musser D.R. : "Abstract data types and software validation", C.A.C.M., Vol 21, n.12, 1978. (also USG ISI Report 76-48).

[Gut 75] Guttag J.V. : "The specification and application to programming", Ph.D. Thesis, University of Toronto, 1975.

[LZ 75] Liskov B., Zilles S. : "Specification techniques for data abstractions", IEEE Transactions on Software Engineering, Vol.SE-1 N 1, March 1975.

[SW 82] Sanella D., Wirsing M. : "Implementation of parameterized specifications", Report CSR-103-82, Department of Computer Science, University of Edinburgh.

Strictness and Serializability

Udo Kelter
Universität Dortmund, Fachbereich Informatik 4
Postfach 500500, 4600 Dortmund 50, W. Germany

Abstract: In the theory of concurrency control several notions of the correctness of logs have been developed, particularly final-state-, view-, and conflict-preserving-serializability. SR, VSR, and CPSR are the respective sets of logs. In each case a strict variant can be defined. The respective sets are SSR, SVSR, and SCPSR. While SSR has already been investigated, this is not the case for SVSR and SCPSR. In this paper we will show the following:

- SCPSR = W2PL, W2PL being the class of weakly two-phase locked logs.
- Implications between the notions of correctness (or inclusions of sets) are as follows (A → B reads as A $\subseteq$ B):

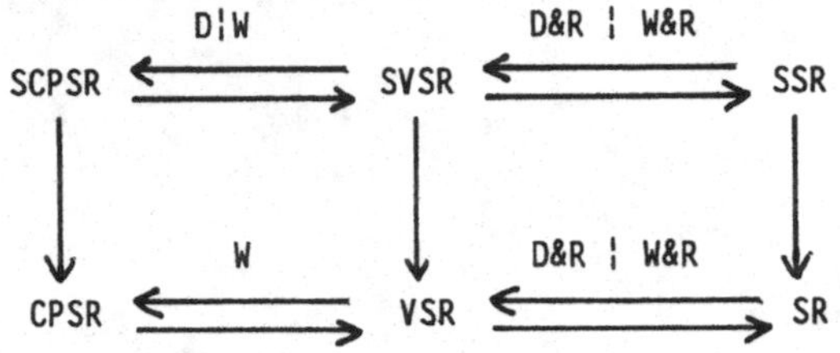

The labels indicate conditions when the inclusions hold; the abbreviations used are (& = and, ¦ = or):

D : dead values do not occur

W : every transaction reads an object before writing it

R : read-only transactions do not occur

None of these conditions can be dropped; this contradicts two claims made in the relevant literature ([P79], [BSW79]).

1. Introduction and Review of Earlier Work

When a database is accessed by interleaved transactions certain anomalies may occur, e.g. the database may become inconsistent or a transaction may read inconsistent data. The basic problem of concurrency control is to avoid such anomalies.

Basic Notations

In the theory of concurrency control formal models are used to investigate interleaved transactions. In this paper we will use the two-step-model of [P79] (but our results also apply to the n-step-model, as used e.g. in [Y84]).

Let $T_1,\ldots,T_n$ be a set of transactions. We assume that the execution of T_i consists of an atomic event R_i and a later atomic event W_i. R_i indicates that a finite set of objects (i.e. data base entities) **readset$_i$**, is read, W_i indicates that a finite set of objects, **writeset$_i$**, is written.

A transaction T_i with writeset$_i$ = Ø is called a **read-only transaction**.

A log represents one possible interleaved execution of all transactions. Thus a **log** l is a sequence containing all R_i and W_i with R_i --> W_i, where --> denotes "precedes" in l. Logs are denoted as words: $R_i[\ldots]$ ($W_i[\ldots]$) denotes the atomic event: transaction T_i reads (writes) objects ... .

A log in which transactions do not overlap is called **serial**. **S** is the set of all serial logs.

Serializability

A log is considered "correct" or admissible if anomalies do not occur. Serial logs are always considered correct. In the theory of concurrency control several notions of the correctness of non-serial logs have been developed (see [BSW79], [C81], [K85], [P79], [S82], [Y84]), particularly variants of serializability. A log is called

- **final-state-serializable**, in short **fs-serializable**,
- **view-serializable**, in short **v-serializable**, or
- **conflict-preserving-serializable**, in short **cp-serializable**

iff it is fs-, v-, or cp-equivalent to a serial one, respectively.

The related classes of logs are **SR**, **VSR**, and **CPSR**, respectively.

Two logs are

- **fs-equivalent** if both produce the same final state, irrespective of the interpretation. An **interpretation** specifies the actual computation performed by the transactions and initial contents of all objects.
- **v-equivalent** if both provide each transaction with the same **view**, i.e. the same input data, in both logs, and produce the same final state, irrespective of the interpretation.

- **cp-equivalent** if any pair of conflicting events appear in the same order in both logs. Two events are in **conflict** if both use an object and at least one event writes this object. (More detailed presentations of these standard notions can be found e.g. in [P79], [BSW79], [K85].)

Thus, serializability refers always to an equivalence of logs.

Strictness

A serial log which is equivalent to a serializable one denotes the logical sequence in which the transactions occur atomically from the user's point of view. Sometimes a strange effect occurs: a log can only be **serialized**, i.e. transformed into an equivalent serial one, if two non-overlapping transactions are changed in order; we call this a **reversal**. The classic example is:

$l_1 = R_1[v]\ R_2[v,w]\ W_1[v]\ R_3[w,x]\ W_2[w]\ W_3[x]$

The only fs-equivalent serial log is $T_3\ T_2\ T_1$; thus T_1 and T_3 must be reversed. If both are started by the same user then their logical order is just the contrary to what the user has in mind. This behavior is abnormal for the user and should be avoided, i.e. logs should be serializable without reversals. Thus we define: A log is **strictly fs-**, **v-**, or **cp-serializable** iff it is fs-, v-, or cp-equivalent to some serial log without reversals. The related sets of logs are **SSR**, **SVSR**, and **SCPSR**.

Relations between variants of serializability

It is well known that cp-equivalence implies v-equivalence and that v-equivalence implies fs-equivalence. We have immediately the following inclusions of sets ($A \longrightarrow B$ reads as $A \subseteq B$):

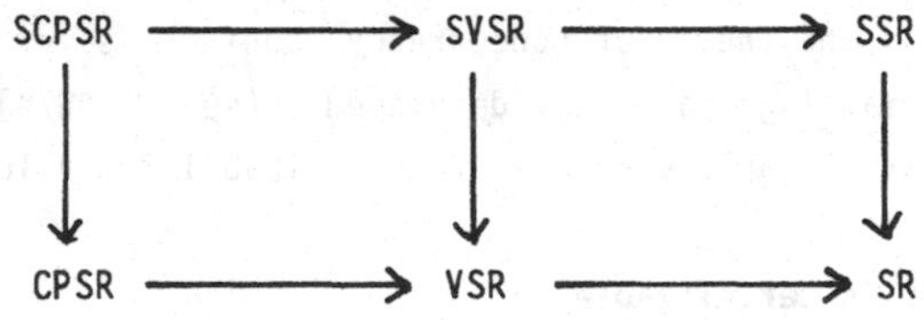

In general, all of these inclusions are proper. This can be seen with the following examples:

- l_1 is in CPSR, VSR, and SR, but not in SSR, SVSR, or SCPSR.
- $l_2 = R_1[x]\ R_2[y]\ W_2[x]\ W_1[y]\ R_3[y]\ W_3[x]$ is in SR and SSR, but not in VSR or SVSR.
- $l_3 = R_1[x]\ R_2\ W_2[y]\ R_3[y]\ W_3[x]\ W_1[y]\ R_4\ W_4[y]$ is in VSR and SVSR, but not in CPSR or SCPSR.

The most important reason why fs-equivalence (or fs-serializability) does not imply the other variants is the occurrence of so-called dead values. A value, contained in some object, is called **dead** in a log, if it does not contribute to the final state of all objects after this log. Otherwise it is called **live** in this log. In l_2, for example, W_2 writes a dead value into x.

A sufficient condition for the absence of dead values in fs-serializable logs is that no transaction writes an object without having read it before (see lemma 2 below).

Results of this Paper and Review of Earlier Work

The main findings presented in this paper are sufficient conditions for further inclusions of sets or, in other words, implications between the notions of correctness:

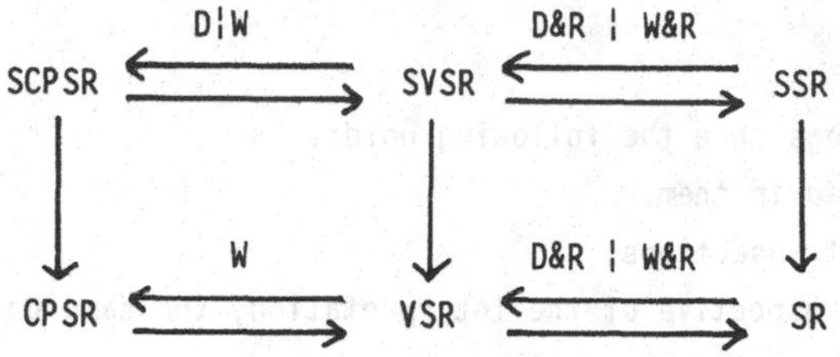

The labels indicate sufficient conditions under which the inclusions hold; abbreviations are (& = and, ¦ = or):

D : dead values do not occur

W : every transaction reads an object before writing it

R : read-only transactions do not occur

None of these conditions can be dropped; this falsifies two contrary claims in the relevant literature, namely

- theorem $W2PL_4$ in [BSW79]: This theorem claims that condition D alone implies SSR $\subseteq$ W2PL (= SCPSR). A counter-example is:

$$l_4 = R_1[x,y]\ R_2[x,z]\ W_2[x,z]\ R_3[y,z]\ W_1[y]\ W_3$$

- theorem 8 in [P79]: This theorem claims that condition W alone implies SR = CPSR, furthermore, figure 9 in [P79] indicates that SSR = SCPSR. Again, l_4 is a counter-example.

The rest of this paper is organized as follows: Section 2 presents some basic results about liveness. Sections 3 and 4 consider the consequences of condition D and W, respectively. Section 5 shows that W2PL = SCPSR, and section 6 discusses the results.

2. Liveness

The notions of deadness and liveness of values have already been defined informally above. In this section we will present some basic results concerning liveness.

A value has been called live in a log l if it contributes to the final state after l. More precisely, a value written by some transaction is called **live** in l if it remains unchanged for the rest of l or if it is read by some transaction which writes at least one live value; such a transaction is also called live.

Because live values contribute to the final state two fs-equivalent logs must have the same "live parts"; this can be shown formally with the help of Herbrand interpretations (see [K85]):

Lemma 1: If l, l' are fs-equivalent logs then the following holds:

a) The same live values are produced in them.

b) They have the same set of live transactions.

c) Each live transaction reads, irrespective of the interpretation, the same data in l and l'.

The converse of lemma 1 does not hold, a counter-example is the pair of serial logs:

$l_5 = R_1[x]\ W_1[y]\ R_2[y]\ W_2[z]\ R_3[u]\ W_3[y]\ R_4[y]\ W_4[v]$

$l_6 = R_3[u]\ W_3[y]\ R_4[y]\ W_4[v]\ R_1[x]\ W_1[y]\ R_2[y]\ W_2[z]$

Lemma 2: Assume that $writeset_i \subseteq readset_i$ for all i, $1 \leq i \leq n$, l in SR. Then no dead values are produced in l.

Proof: immediately from lemma 1.

3. Logs Without Dead Values

Dead values are the main reason why fs-equivalence (or fs-serializability) does not imply the other variants. In this section we investigate whether the variants of serializability coincide when dead values are absent.

Theorem 1: If no dead values occur in SVSR then SVSR = SCPSR.

Proof: obviously it suffices to show the following: if l is in SR, l' in S, both without dead values and without reversals, then their view-equivalence implies their cp-equivalence.

Assume the contrary, i.e. two conflicting events appear in different order in l and l'. From the view-equivalence we can derive (using Herbrand interpretations) that the "reads-from"-structure (see [P79], [K85]) is the same in l and l'. Then one of three cases must hold:

1) Some W_i and W_j are the reversed conflicting events, and x in $writeset_i \cap writeset_j$. The value T_j which writes into x in l' is live by assumption. It cannot be the final content of x; thus some read-event R_k reading x from W_j in l' (and l) must exist, so that

in l: R_i ---> W_i ---------------------------> W_j ----> R_k

in l': W_j ----> R_k --> W_k ----> R_i --> W_i

But then T_i and T_k are reversed. This contradicts the strictness assumption.

2) Some R_i and W_j are the events in question, x causes the conflict, and R_i ---> W_j in l. The equality of the "reads-from"-structure implies that R_i cannot read x from W_j in l', and that some W_k must exist so that:

in l: W_k ----> R_i ------------> W_j

in l': W_j ----> W_k ----> R_i

W_j and W_k both write x, hence are in conflict, and appear in different order in l and l'. But this is impossible as shown in case 1.

3) The assumption W_j ---> R_i leads essentially to the same situation and the same contradiction as case 2.

Corollary 1: If dead values or read-only transactions do not occur in SR then SR = VSR and SSR = SVSR.

Proof: The assumptions imply that dead transactions do not occur in SR. Then lemma 1 shows that fs-equivalence implies view-equivalence.

Even under the assumptions of corollary 1 we do not have CPSR = VSR. A counter-example is:

$l_7 = R_1[y]\ R_3\ W_3[x]\ R_4[x]\ W_4[y]\ W_1[x]\ R_2[x]\ W_2[z]\ R_5\ W_5[x]$

4. Logs Without Erasures

If $writeset_i \not\subseteq readset_i$, x in $writeset_i \setminus readset_i$, then T_i writes x without having read the old content of x. Thus the old value is erased, it is dead, but this happened intentionally and is not an anomaly due to parallelism. Erasures cannot be avoided by a scheduling mechanism, but the user can do so. The implications of their absence will be investigated in this section.

Corollary 2: If $writeset_i \subseteq readset_i$ for all i, $1 \le i \le n$, then SCPSR = SVSR.
Proof: immediately from lemma 2 and theorem 1.

Theorem 2: If $writeset_i \subseteq readset_i$ for all i, $1 \le i \le n$, then VSR = CPSR.

The proof of theorem 2 will be prepared with lemmata 3, 4, and 5. We have to introduce another equivalence before: l,l' are **sequence-of-contents equivalent** (in short: **sc-equivalent**) iff for any object x the sequence of contents l writes into x is the same one which l' writes into x.

Lemma 3: Assume $writeset_i \subseteq readset_i$ for all i, $1 \le i \le n$, l,l' in SR, l,l' fs-equivalent. Then l and l' are sc-equivalent.
Proof: First, we prove the claim for the case that l' in S.

Let x be an object. By lemma 2 any value written into x is live; the transaction which writes this value is live and, by lemma 1, reads the same values in l and l', and thereby writes the same value into x. Thus the <u>set</u> of values written into x is the same in l and l', irrespective of the interpretation.

Now assume a Herbrand interpretation. Because l' is serial the final value written into x by l' enables us to reconstruct the sequence of contents written into x by l'. Each content of x depends on all earlier ones, so this final content of x cannot be produced unless all transactions writing x are executed serially in the order given by l'. Thus l must produce the same sequence of contents in x as l'.

The restriction l' in S remains to be removed. If l' in SR \ S, we can find a serial l_s which is fs-equivalent to both l and l'. Then l_s is sc-equivalent to l and l' too, and by transitivity l and l' are sc-equivalent.

Lemma 4: Assume $writeset_i \subseteq readset_i$ for all i, $1 \le i \le n$, l,l' in SR, without read-only transactions, and fs-equivalent. Then l and l' are sc-equivalent.
Proof: From lemma 3 we know that l and l' are sc-equivalent. Assume that two conflicting events appear in different order in l and l', and assume furthermore a Herbrand interpretation.

1) Assume that W_i and W_j are the reversed events. This leads to an immediate

contradiction to the sc-equivalence of l and l'.

2) Assume that W_i and R_j are the reversed events. R_j does not read the same content of x in l and l'. As T_j is not a read-only transaction, W_j writes different values into some variable in l and l'. This contradicts sc-equivalence of l and l'.

Lemma 5: Assume $writeset_i \subseteq readset_i$ for all i, $1 \leq i \leq n$, l in VSR, l_s in S, l,l_s view-equivalent. Then l and l_s are cp-equivalent.

Proof: Let l' and l_s' be the result of deleting all read-only transactions from l and l_s. l' and l_s' are view-equivalent, too. By lemma 4, l' and l_s' are in fact cp-equivalent. Thus all pairs of conflicting events which belong to non-read-only transactions appear in the same order in l and l_s.

Now, assume two conflicting events which appear in different order in l and l_s. It has just been shown that it cannot be true that both events belong to non-read-only transactions. Thus one event belongs to a read-only transaction, and must be a read-event, say R_i. The other event must be a write-event, say W_j. Let x cause the conflict between R_i and W_j. Under a Herbrand interpretation W_j writes a value into x which is different from the initial value of x and from any value written by any other transaction. Hence R_i does not read the same data in l and l_s. But this contradicts the hypothesis that l and l_s are view-equivalent.

Proof of theorem 2: immediately from lemma 5.

Corollary 3: If $writeset_i \subseteq readset_i$ for all i, $1 \leq i \leq n$, and read-only transactions do not occur, then SR = VSR = CPSR and SSR = SVSR = SCPSR.

Proof: immediately from lemma 4.

5. Weakly Two-Phase Locked Logs

Although the class SCPSR is new this subset of L is, in fact, well known as W2PL (in [BSW79] or Q in [P79]), the set of weakly two-phase locked logs.

A log is **weakly two-phase locked** iff we can choose a point of time S_i for every T_i in l (so-called **serializability points**) such that for all i,j, $1 \leq i,j \leq n$: R_i ---> S_i ---> W_i and if S_i ---> S_j then

1) R_j ---> W_i ==> $readset_j \cap writeset_i = \emptyset$ and
2) W_j ---> W_i ==> $writeset_j \cap writeset_i = \emptyset$.

W2PL is the set of weakly two-phase locked logs.

Theorem 3: W2PL = SCPSR.

Proof:

1) W2PL $\subseteq$ SCPSR: The serializability points S_i of a log l indicate that both events of each transaction can be shifted towards their serializability point without causing a conflicting pair of events to be changed in order. Thus the effect of each transaction T_i remains the same as if it were atomically executed at the time S_i or, in other words, l is cp-equivalent to a serial log in which all transactions are ordered according to their serializability points.

The order of non-overlapping transactions is not reversed because the serializability points lie "inside" the transactions. We can conclude immediately that a weakly two-phase locked log is strictly cp-serializable.

2) SCPSR $\subseteq$ W2PL: Assume that l,l' are cp-equivalent without reversals, l' in S. Renumber all transactions so that $T_1,\ldots,T_n$ is the order of them in l'.

At first we show that one can choose points of time S_1 ---> S_2 ---> ... ---> S_n in l with R_i ---> S_i ---> W_i for all i. Whenever T_i lies before T_j in l' we must achieve to choose S_i ---> S_j. We have this possibility exactly if R_i ---> W_j in l. If W_i ---> R_j then R_i ---> W_j; otherwise we cannot have W_j ---> R_i in l because then the transactions T_i and T_j do not overlap in l, but their order is not the same as in l'. So R_i ---> W_j and the existence of the S_i's is proved.

Next we show that any such choice yields indeed a set of serializability points. Assume that S_i ---> S_j in l. We then have further:

in l: R_i ---> S_i ---> S_j ---> W_i

in l': R_i ---> W_i ---> R_j ---> W_j

We have to show that:

1) R_j ---> W_i in l ==> $readset_j \cap writeset_i = \emptyset$ and

2) W_j ---> W_i in l ==> $writeset_j \cap writeset_i = \emptyset$.

Under the assumptions in 1 and 2 the two events in question appear in different order in l and l', respectively. cp-equivalence of l and l' then implies that these pairs of events cannot be in conflict.

6. Discussion

A summary of the inclusions has already been given in the introduction. The conditions mentioned for the non-trivial inclusions are "necessary" in the sense that they cannot be dropped.

The conditions which are necessary to make VSR = CPSR are weaker than the ones to make SR = VSR. Thus VSR is, in a certain sense, closer to CPSR than to SR. The same observation can be made with the strict variants.

It should be noted that the conditions necessary for the equality of the strict forms of serializability are weaker than in the case of the non-strict forms. (A similar effect is reported in [S82] with regard to the decidability of SR and SSR.) Thus strictness is not "orthogonal" to the basic notions of the correctness of logs.

The property of strictness is granted by most of the realistic concurrency control mechanisms. The widely used two-phase locking protocol corresponds to a proper subset 2PL of W2PL (see [K85], [P79]). Mechanisms based on the restart of transactions (namely time-stamp and optimistic mechanisms) may reverse the order of transactions, but only internally; the user is not aware of these internal reversals.

The r/a/c-protocol (of [BHR80]) is a rare exception of a mechanism which allows for reversals and another similar effect which a user can realize (see [BHR80], section 5.2 "A strange situation"). This protocol combines locking and restarting to guarantee the correctness of logs. In many real applications the property of strictness can, in fact, be sacrificed in order to achieve higher parallelism.

References

[BHR80] Bayer, R.; Heller, H.; Reiser, A.: Parallelism and recovery in database systems; ACM-TDS 5:2, p.139-156; 1980/06

[BSW79] Bernstein, P.A.; Shipman, D.W.; Wong, W.S.: Formal aspects of serializability in database concurrency control; IEEE-TSE SE-5:3, p.203-216; 1979/05

[C81] Casanova, M.A.: The concurrency control problem for database systems; Springer, LNiCS 116, 175p; 1981

[K85] Kelter, U.: Parallele Transaktionen in Datenbanksystemen; B.I. Wissenschaftsverlag, Reihe Informatik/51, 201p; 1985/08

[P79] Papadimitriou, C.H.: The serializability of concurrent database updates; JACM 26:4, p.631-653; 1979/10

[S82] Sethi, R.: Useless actions make a difference: strict serializability of database updates; JACM 29:2, p.394-403; 1982/04

[Y84] Yannakakis, M.: Serializability by locking; JACM 31:2, p.227-244; 1984/04

TOWARDS SPECIFICATION AND PROOF OF ASYNCHRONOUS SYSTEMS

GAMATIE B.
IRISA/INRIA Campus de beaulieu
35042 RENNES CEDEX (FCE)

Abstract

A communication based language is presented .It allows to specify asynchronous systems of processes. Together with this language, we define an equivalence relation which is a congruence, merging both notions of complexity of accepted languages and of nondeterminism. This equivalence is generated by a preorder relation which allows to provide the processes set with a fully defined (and convergent) minimal element. It is also characterized by an axiom set that we prove to be sound and complete.

Key-words: *Asynchronous systems, nondeterminism , process interface , equivalence and congruence of processes , least process .*

I-INTRODUCTION

Recently ,several papers have been published, aiming in defining and formalizing the concept of process: [ARN82, AUS84, DAR83, HOA81, HEN85, HEN83, KAH77, MIL80...] . This is essentially due to the fact that newly proposed languages integrate such notions as explicit communications and parallelism. And in fact a process can intuitively be seen as an abstract machine which can perform actions compounded of basic operations concurrently with other processes. More precisely we consider that *the only actions a process can perform are communication ones*. However the communicated items may be either data values or control signals, and they may be addressed either to another process (the communication is then said to be external) or to some subcomponent of the process (in this case the communication is said to be internal). So, considering that these (communication) actions can be formally represented by relations over the set of processes(two processes t and t' are related by such a relation if t represents the state of the process before the action while t' represents that after the action), we argue that a process is an object whose (operational) semantics can be entirely specified using exclusively communication actions and relations parametrized by these actions. Moreover since operational semantics specifies all possible operations an object can perform, together with all the state changes that result, the previous point means that *process state changes result exclusively from communication action performance* .

Now considering a set of processes , it is in general, said to be asynchronous if it is "insensible" to time considerations, in constrast with synchronous ones where time dependancies are a crucial question. And relating these notions to processes semantics usally amounts to neglect all internal communication occurences while specifying process behaviour. For instance, in models for C.C.S. based languages, this leads to set the equivalence of t and τt where τ represents internal actions, t a process and τt a process which first performs an internal action and then behaves like t. However this equivalence is not valid in all contexts, particulary in nondeterministic ones. As for us, we define an asynchronous system as a set of processes where the inactivity of any one among them doesn't induce the inactivity of all the system in constrast with synchronous one where the "death" of any component induces the "death" of the whole system . And we *relate this notion to process states by allowing an asynchronous process to remain idle (in fact to perform a null action which is not the internal one) during a finite amount of time without changing its state* . Formally this implies that our composition operation of actions will admit as neutral element not the internal action but the null one .

Relying upon these ideas we define structures for expressing asynchronous parallel algorithms (in fact these structures allowed us to define certain class of both synchronous and asynchronous applications : see [GAM84]) . In our approach, as stated earlier, a process can change its state exclusively by performing communication actions so as its operational semantics could be always definable using communication relations exclusively. As a consequence , our processes are objects which are fully defined from an operational point of view; so general form of recursivity which allows to specify undefined objects (hint for instance that specified by expression recx.x) is not be considered in our framework. As a counterpart, we introduce a "guarded parallel itteration" operation which allows to define infinite processes using communication actions(which may be either internal or external).

This rather original position quickly leads us to problems of finding appropriate relations between systems of processes that is finding an adequate equivalence relation over the set of processes . In fact this important question has been emphasized by all the proposals of models for processes; moreover the proposed equivalences have been in general axiomatized leading to processes calculi(hint for instance the well known C.C.S. calculus[MIL80]) unfortunatly these results do not fit our approach.

Most of authors now agree to say that two processes are equivalent if no external communication(or interaction with the environment) allow to distinguish one from the other. And two processes are said to be congruent if any one can be replaced by the other in any context without observable differences. *Our opinion is that a "real" processes equivalence must be a congruence* since it relies on communication actions which happen to be the only means a process has to interact with its environment. Unfortunately this is not so general:Obviously identity of accepted languages cannot constitute an equivalence relation for processes in general (as this was the case for sequential deterministic machines) since then it would not be possible to capture such notions as deadlocks ([MIL80,HEN83]). Relying upon this fact , observational equivalence was proposed [MIL80,HEN85] so as to take into account all the different states reached by processes during observation. This equivalence,and all those based on the the notion of bisimulation [AUS84], have been shown too discriminative [DAR82,HEN83] because they sometimes differentiate processes whose internal activities have the same external effects. Moreover this equivalence is not a congruence. However the congruence it contains has been axiomatized, leading to C.C.S. calculus . Later on other equivalences have been proposed in order to deal with these internally different but externally non differentiable processes: [DAR82,DAR83, HOA81,HEN83] unfortunately they are also not preserved by all process operations in general (in particular considering the case of nondeterministic composition in languages where internal actions can be explicitly specified).

In this paper we define a preorder over the set of processes,which is based on (pre)order relations we provide with the action set, and on the notion of *terms interface* ; our preorder relies on two fundamental intuitions:

1) *The more you can do, the greater you are* that is processes will be compared relying first on their accepted languages . And 2) *The less the environment can influence your decisions, the greater you are* that is nondeterminism (evaluated as the ability of interaction the environment is offered by processes) will also be taken into account . More precisely we use the notion of interface (which contains all possible actions the process can immediately be embeded into) in order to evaluate nondeterminism, since any possible interaction with any other process, has obviously an element of the interface as prefix . Fortunately the equivalence generated by this preorder is actually a congruence relation for our specification language. It is presented in chapter III, and a sound and complete characterization is provided in chapter IV. Right now, in chapter II, we introduce our language called Concurrently Functioning Agents, its syntax and semantics .

II-THE LANGUAGE

As stated earlier,the language we consider here relies heavily on the ideas of communication already used in other process language approaches: Milner's C.C.S.[MIL80],Hoare's C.S.P.[HOA78]...Actually our approach is essentially characterized by the fact that a process cannot change its state without performing communication actions (which are the only operations it can perform) so that our processes are object which are always operationally fully defined (considering operational semantics which are exclusively based on communication relations). In fact these communication actions may be either internal or external and may also be composed of several (but finite anyway) basic events (to be performed simultaneously) ,provided they are compatible.We also assume that they only involve pure signals. Let's now formally introduce these notions .

1) *The action set*

First of all we assume the existence of the following set:
$\Lambda = \cup \{< \Lambda \times N > \}$ a set of numbered communication ports; for each integer i, $<\Lambda \times \{i\}>$contains all ports of number (or level) i. (N represents the set of positive integers) .

definition 1.1 : let A denote the set { $<\Lambda \times \{?\}>\} \cup \{<\Lambda \times \{!\}>\} \cup \{\tau\}$; we provide A with a binary, symetric and transitive relation called *compatibility relation* and denoted "#" s.t. $\forall\alpha$ in A $\tau \# \alpha$ .Now an action is any subset a of A s.t. $\forall \alpha,\beta$ in a, $\alpha\#\beta$.Obviously the empty set is an action; we denote it γ .The set of all actions is denoted $A = A_0 \cup \{\gamma\} = A_+ \cup \{\tau,\gamma\}$ Similary for any subset of actions E we let $E_+ = E/\{\tau,\gamma\}$.

Note that the compatibility relation is an immediate generalization of the predicates, usually assumed while defining actions . For example the action set introduced in C.C.S is obtained by first restricting event subsets to singletons, and allowing external actions to be compatible iff they use the same port,but have different directions (import versus export).

definition1.2 : we extend the previous compatibility relation to actions and denote it the same way: a#b iff $\forall \alpha,\beta \in a\cup b$, $\alpha\#\beta$ .We now provide *A* with a composition relation which allow to define new actions given existing ones: $\forall$ a,b in *A* , ab (=$a\cup b$) is an action which we set equal to γ if $\neg(a\#b)$.Obviously this composition operation admits γ as neutral element (one immediately verify that $\gamma\#a$ $\forall$ a in *A*).

Setting : henceforth we let $\mathbf{A}=<\Lambda\times\{?\}>$ and $\bar{\mathbf{A}}=<\Lambda\times\{!\}>$ s.t. $A_+=\mathbf{A}\cup\bar{\mathbf{A}}$; intuitively

$\bar{A}$ contains sending actions and **A** receiving ones and we let the compatibility relation embody the usual C.C.S complementarity relation: a#b iff a∈ $A\cup\{\tau,\gamma\}$, b∈$\bar{A}\cup\{\tau,\gamma\}$ and they don't use different ports(if they use any). Finally we set: if a and b are in A_+ then ab=τ if a#b, otherwise ab=γ.
Note that altought γ has been found to be the neutral element of composition, within the subset of non null actions (≠ γ) τ acts also as neutral element ie: ∀ a ≠γ, aτ=a .

2) *Syntax*

definition2.1 : we let Ψ be a set of mappings over Λ which we generalize to the set of actions s.t. given φ in Ψ and a in A then

i) φ(a) =τ iff a=τ
ii) φ(a)=γ iff a=γ or φ(λ) is undefined where λ is the port used in a
iii) φ(<λ,?>) = <φ(λ),?> and φ(<λ,!>) = <φ(λ),!> if φ(λ) is defined .

Now C.F.A. terms are those of the word algebra W_Σ generated by the following signature Σ . (Σ_i contains all i-ary operators) :

$\Sigma_0=$ {nil}

$\Sigma_1=$ {a: | a∈ A_+ } ∪ { a→| a∈ A_+} ∪ { [φ] | φ∈ Ψ }

$\Sigma_2=$ { + , ‖ } and $\Sigma_i = \emptyset$ for 3≤i .

Operators"a:" and "a→"are prefixed, [φ] is postfixed and "+" and "‖" are infixed. Note that we don't use the internal action in the set of operators Σ_1 of our signature . This is essentially because we consider that τ represents the behaviour of parts of the system, whose activity one does not want to be aware of; simultaneously we assume that what is internal or external is uniquely a matter of taste. That's why our internal actions only result from composition of compatible external actions. Now Ψ elements allow in some sense to change the level of abstraction from which one is observing a system , and thus may mask some parts of that system, enforcing then internal actions occurrences. We'll formalize these notions while defining the operational semantics of our language. Before, let's pursue this informal presentation and examine intuitively what Σ's operators are intended to do :
NIL operator (nil) , *guarding* (a:), *sum* (+) and *renaming* ([φ]) are quite similar to those used in C.C.S and by some extend can be immediately expressed in C.S.P.
for example the term ((a:nil)+(b:nil))[φ] where φ(a)=a and φ(b)=γ , represents a process which can perform an a-action and "die" , but it may never perform b-action since the renaming inhibits this action.
Operator "‖" represents usual *asynchronous parallel composition* :t‖t' denotes a process composed of two subcomponents which can proceed concurrently and communicate . The communication is constrained by the usage of the same port, and a term may remain iddle (for only a finite delay) though it might perform some action .Note also that the parallelism (ie: the simultaneity of actions performance) is based not on complementarity, but on compatibility which is a more general notion .
for example ((a:nil+b:nil) ‖ $\bar{b}$:c:nil)[φ] (where φ(a)=a , φ(b)= φ($\bar{b}$)=γ and φ(c)=c and a#c , b#$\bar{b}$ but not(a#$\bar{b}$)) represents a term which can either perform action a and die or decide "internally" to perform action c and die .

Operator "a→" (***guarded parallel itteration***) has no counterpart neither in C.C.S. nor in C.S.P. It allows to generate an infinity of terms which proceed concurrently. However this process of terms generating may be completely controled by the environment: a new term is generated if and only if the "guard" a is "passed". Therefore gpi allows to perform infinite sequences of actions.

For example : the term : $(<\alpha,0>! \to \text{nil})$ can perform the infinite sequence $<\alpha,0>!.<\alpha,1>!.<\alpha,2>!...<\alpha,n>!...$ where $<\alpha,i>$ represents port α at level i .*In fact each newly generated term has all its ports' number incremented by one*. This allows to distinguish the different instances of generated terms. However if necessary this distinction can be erased using renamings; for instance, if we denote ψ_0 the renaming that changes all ports number to zero ie: $\forall <\alpha,i>$ in Λ, $\psi_0(<\alpha,i>) = <\alpha,0>$ then the term $(<\alpha,0>! \to \text{nil})[\psi_0]$ realises the behaviour of a constant operator (ie: it is always able to send the same item via port $<\alpha,0>$) .

3) Operational semantics

The semantics of C.F.A. terms relies essentially on two notions: first that of *interface* which contains the actions the term can immediately perform(including internal ones) and that of *communication relations* which are binary relations parametrized by actions. The semantics is given by means of conditional rules (à la Plotkin [PLO81]).

Definition3.1 : let I be a total mapping of C.F.A. into the set of finite subsets of non null actions . I(t) denotes the interface of term t and is s.t. if R_a is the communication relation involved in action a then $(\exists t' \in \text{C.F.A.}: t\, R_a\, t' \wedge a \neq \gamma) \Leftrightarrow a \in I(t)$.

Definition 3.2 :let $\xrightarrow{a}$ denote the communication relation parametrized with action a . We generalize such a relation to sequence of actions and denote $t \xrightarrow{s}{}^{*}$ (where s is a sequence of actions) s.t. :

1) $t \xrightarrow{\varepsilon}{}^{*} t$ and $(t \xrightarrow{\varepsilon}{}^{*} t' \Leftrightarrow t \equiv t'\ \forall t)$

2) $t \xrightarrow{sa}{}^{*} t_1 \Leftrightarrow \exists t' : t \xrightarrow{s}{}^{*} t'$ and $t' \xrightarrow{a} t_1$.

The operational semantics of C.F.A. is now defined by the following rules:

R_0) $t \xrightarrow{\gamma} t$ and $(t \xrightarrow{\gamma} t') \Rightarrow (t' \equiv t)\ \forall t, t' \in \text{C.F.A.}$,
$I(\text{nil}) = \emptyset$

R_1) $I(a{:}t) = \{a\}$, $a{:}t \xrightarrow{a} t$

R_2) $I(t_1+t_2) = I(t_1) \cup I(t_2)$, $t_1 \xrightarrow{a} t'_1,\ a \neq \gamma \Rightarrow t_1+t_2 \xrightarrow{a} t'_1,\ t_2+t_1 \xrightarrow{a} t'_1$

R_3) $I(t[\varphi]) = \{\varphi(a) \mid a \in I(t) \wedge \varphi(a) \neq \gamma\}$, $t \xrightarrow{a} t' \wedge \varphi(a) \neq \gamma \Rightarrow t[\varphi] \xrightarrow{\varphi(a)} t'[\varphi]$

R_4) $I(t_1 \| t_2) = I(t_1) \cup I(t_2) \cup \{ab \mid a\#b, <a,b> \in (I(t_1) \times I(t_2) \cup I(t_2) \times I(t_1))\}$

$t_1 \xrightarrow{a} t'_1,\ t_2 \xrightarrow{b} t'_2,\ a\#b \Rightarrow (t_1 \| t_2) \xrightarrow{ab} (t'_1 \| t'_2),\ (t_2 \| t_1) \xrightarrow{ab} (t'_2 \| t'_1)$.

R_5) $I(a \to t) = \{a\}$, $(a \to t) \xrightarrow{a} ((a \to t) \| t)[\psi^1]$ where $\forall <\alpha,i> \in \Lambda, \psi^1(<\alpha,i>) = <\alpha,i+1>$

III- EQUIVALENCE AND CONGRUENCE OF C.F.A. TERMS

In this section we define an equivalence relation over C.F.A. terms. As stated earlier this equivalence is generated by a preorder, so that two terms could be related even if they do not behave in exactly the same way, but if one among them "approximates" the other. More over we impose that two equivalent terms be interchangeable in any context without visible differences. Actually our equivalence merges both notions of process accepted language and nondeterminism . And it heavilly relies on term interfaces and on restricted communication relations which encompass the fact that internal communications should be neglected under certain circumstances, so as the declared differences between terms be those which are actually visible . Thus while comparing terms, we consider that internal moves which do not affect "external" behaviour must be ignored and we set that (finite) sequences of internal moves cannot be differentiated from a single internal move . Intuitively , *two terms are said to be equivalent if and only if they may perform the same computations, and offer their environment the same abilities of interaction after each step of computation* .Let's now formally introduce these notions:

definition :given an action a, $\overset{a}{\Longrightarrow}$ denotes a binary relation over C.F.A. called basic *a-observation relation* and is s.t. $\overset{a}{\Longrightarrow} = \overset{\tau^*}{\longrightarrow}\overset{a}{\longrightarrow}\overset{\tau^*}{\longrightarrow}$. This relation is extended to sequences of actions and denoted $\overset{s}{\Longrightarrow}$ s.t. :

i) $\overset{\varepsilon}{\Longrightarrow} = \overset{\tau^*}{\longrightarrow}$, ii) $\overset{sa}{\Longrightarrow} = \overset{s}{\Longrightarrow}\overset{a}{\Longrightarrow}$ where ε denotes the empty sequence

These relations allow to mask certain internal actions during computation and deal with our requirement to neglect some internal actions under particular circumstances. Now in order to be able to formally evaluate nondeterminism, we provide the action set with the following relations:

1) Ordering the action set

definition1 we let < denote a binary relation over the action set s.t. $\forall a \in A$, $\gamma < a < a < \tau$.

This relation is obviously an order relation over *A* . We now extend it to the set of subsets of actions:

definition2 given two subsets E and E' of actions , E is said to be less than E' (we denote $E' \le E$) iff $\forall a \in E, \exists b \in E' \mid a < b$.

proposition1.1 relation $\le$ is a preorder relation in the set of subsets of actions and more over , given two actions subset X and Y ,the following hold :

i) $\emptyset \le X \le Y \cup \{\tau\}$

ii) $(X \le Y \wedge \tau \in X) \Rightarrow \tau \in Y$

iii) $Y \supset X \Rightarrow X \le Y$

proof immediate .

The intuitive meaning of relation ≤ is the following : suppose that subsets E and E' represent the possible actions two processes p and p' can respectively perform in given states, then E≤E' means that if p can proceed "by itself" during the next step of its computation, so can do p' and moreover if p cannot neglect the environment during next step, then any action it can perform can also be performed by p' ; thus relation ≤ is exactely what we need in order to compare different potentialities of interaction , different processes in specific states offer the environment .
Before going on to define our equivalence, let's introduce a relation which will be usefull later on: the divergence predicate

2) *Divergence predicate*

definition2.1 a term t is said to be *divergent* iff it verifies the following predicate (denoted in postfixed notation) $X\uparrow \Leftrightarrow \exists X' \mid X \xrightarrow{\tau} X' \wedge X'\uparrow$. That is t can perform an infinite sequence of internal actions.

For example the following terms:
i) $((a\to t) \| t')[\varphi]$ s.t. $\exists b \in I(t) \cap I(t') \wedge ab=\tau \wedge \varphi(a)=\gamma$
ii) $(t \| t')$ where $t\uparrow \vee t'\uparrow$ iii) $(t + t')$ where $t\uparrow \vee t'\uparrow$
iv) $t[\varphi]$ where $t\uparrow$ v) $((a:t) \| t')$ s.t. $\exists b \in I(t') \mid ab=\tau \wedge t\uparrow$
are divergent terms .

definition 2.2 a term t is said to be s-divergent (we denote $t\uparrow s$) where s is a sequence of external actions iff there exists a term t' s.t. $t \overset{s}{\Rightarrow} t' \wedge t'\uparrow$
We now define the preorder which generates our equivalence .

3) *Ordering terms*

Our preorder relation essentially relies on two notions: first that of accepted language. Given two related terms, *the greater one admits at least the same language as the least one* (we use the notion of accepted language in its usual sense). Secondly the preorder encompasses the notion of nondeterminism: if *process t is greater than process t' then t' is at least as deterministics as t* , in the sens that while accepting a sequence , that both can accept, the influence (if there exists any) of the environment is greater while using the least one than the greater one . In fact this relation is a less restrictive version of that used in [GAM85] and allows to merge in a single relation both safety and implementation:*the safest process which implements language σ is the least one if it exists ,among all those whose accepted language includes σ* .
definition3.1 : given two terms ,say t_1 and t_2 ,then t_1 is said to be less than t_2 (we denote $t_1 < t_2$) iff

1) $I(t_1) \le I(t_2)$
2) $\forall s \in A_+^*$, $(t_1 \overset{s}{\Rightarrow}) \Rightarrow (t_2 \overset{s}{\Rightarrow})$ ∧
   a) $t_1\uparrow s \Rightarrow t_2\uparrow s$
   b) $(t_2 \overset{s}{\Rightarrow} t'_2 \Rightarrow t'_2 \overset{a}{\Rightarrow}) \Rightarrow (t_1 \overset{s}{\Rightarrow} t'_1 \Rightarrow t'_1 \overset{a}{\Rightarrow}) \vee (t_1 \overset{sa}{\not\Rightarrow})$
   ($t \overset{s}{\Rightarrow}$ means $\exists t'$ s.t. $t \overset{s}{\Rightarrow} t'$)

Informally, $t_1 < t_2$ iff any string that t_1 may accept may also be accepted by t_2 and moreover any string that t_2 must accept, must also be accepted by t_1, provided it may accept it . Here we use notions may and must with their meanings of [HEN83]. That is : t may accept s iff $t =^s\Rightarrow$ and t must accept a after having accepted s iff $\forall t' : t =^s\Rightarrow t'$, $t' =^a\Rightarrow$ .Notice that if t is s-divergent,then it must not accept anything after s .

Examples

A) **nil < t for any t in C.F.A.**

proof : 1) $I(nil) = \emptyset \leq I(t) \quad \forall t$

2) $\forall s \in A^*_+$, $nil =^s\Rightarrow \Leftrightarrow s = \varepsilon$ and not$(nil\uparrow\varepsilon)$ the result follows since $\forall t$, $t =^\varepsilon\Rightarrow t$ and nil cannot be externally rewriten .

This example states that the language accepted by nil is also accepted by any other term (nil accepts the language reduced to the empty sequence); moreover, while accepting this language, nil is at least as deterministic as any other process . That is, the safest term for recognizing the empty string is nil .

B) **a:nil < a:nil + b:nil**

proof : 1) $I(a{:}nil) = \{a\} \leq \{a,b\} = I(a{:}nil+b{:}nil)$

2) by definition of "+" , $a{:}nil =^s\Rightarrow t \Rightarrow a{:}nil + b{:}nil =^s\Rightarrow t$.

This example is an instance of a more general statemant we'll prove later : summing any process with t , deliver a process greater than t. this can be intuitively justified by noting that sum operator allows to both increase the accepted language and decrease the influence of environment while accepting this language.

C) **a:nil < ((α:a:nil) ‖ β:nil) [φ] where** $\varphi(\alpha) = \varphi(\beta) = \gamma$ **and** $\alpha\beta = \tau$ **and** $\varphi(a) = a$.

proof : let's denote p and q the left and right side(respectively) of sign <; then 1) $I(p) = \{a\} \leq \{\tau\} = I(q)$.

2) $(p =^s\Rightarrow p') \Rightarrow (q =^s\Rightarrow p'[\varphi])$ by definition and moreover p is fully deterministic .

We have here a particular form of a more general law which we'll state later : $t < \tau t$. Intuitively one can convince oneself of the validity of this law by noting that t and τt accept exactely the same language, but one can easily exhibit an environment which has more influence on t than on τt (hint think to nondeterministic environments).

For relation "<" to generate an equivalence relation, it must enjoy certain properties; we state them in the following

proposition 3.1 : relation "<" is a preorder relation over C.F.A. that is for any terms t,t' and t" the following holds :

a) $t < t$

b) $(t < t' \wedge t' < t") \Rightarrow (t < t")$

proof immediate .

Now in order "<" to generate a congruence over C.F.A. , it must enjoy some other properties with regard to Σ's operators . It is well known that preorders preserved by all operators of a signature generate congruence over the word algebra generated by this signature. Actually "<" is not preserved by all Σ's operators; however because of its structure, the equivalence it generates is still a congruence relation .

proposition 3.2 : let p , p', q and q' be C.F.A. terms s.t. $p<p'$ and $q<q'$ then the following holds:

1) $a{:}p < a{:}p' \quad \forall a \in A_+$
2) $p[\varphi] < p'[\varphi] \quad \forall \varphi \in \Psi$
3) $a \to p < a \to p' \quad \forall a \in A_+$

moreover if $\{ s \in A_+^* : p=^{s}\Rightarrow \wedge\ q=^{s}\Rightarrow \} \supset \{s \in A_+^* : (p'=^{s}\Rightarrow \wedge\ q'=^{s}\Rightarrow) \wedge (p=^{s}\Rightarrow \vee\ q=^{s}\Rightarrow)\}$ (let's denote P3.2 this condition) then

4) $p + q < p' + q'$
5) $p \parallel q < p' \parallel q'$

So this proposition shows that relation "<" is not a precongruence , but it also introduces a necessary and sufficient condition for "<" to actually be a precongruence. Note that condition P3.2 is a rather complex one and we'll in general use the following simpler but also stronger form :
lemma3.1 : if p ,p' ,q and q' are such that p and p' (resp. q and q') accept the same language, then p , p' , q and q' verify condition P3.2 .

4) *The equivalence relation*

definition4.1 : two terms t and t' are said to be equivalent , we denote $t \approx t'$ iff $t < t' \wedge t' < t$.
Example : $\mathbf{nil} \approx \mathbf{nil[\varphi]} \quad \forall \varphi \in \Psi$
proof : i) $nil < nil[\varphi]$ has been shown in example A) of previous section
ii) $nil[\varphi] < nil$ since $I(nil[\varphi]) = \varnothing \leq I(nil) = \varnothing$ and $(nil[\varphi]=^{s}\Rightarrow t' \Rightarrow t' \equiv nil[\varphi])$ and not$(nil[\varphi] \uparrow \varepsilon)$ and nil "must" not any action.
lemma : $\forall\, t , t' \in$ C.F.A. , $t \approx t' \Rightarrow \forall s \in A_+^*\ \ t=^{s}\Rightarrow\ \Leftrightarrow t'=^{s}\Rightarrow$.
proof : immediate .

Theorem 1 : relation " ≈" is a congruence over C.F.A.
proof : immediate using previous lemma , proposition3.2 and lemma 3.1 .

This result is an important one among those which differentiate our equivalence from, for example testing equivalence or those based on bisimulation , which are not preserved by sum operator .
Now to sum up, we define an equivalence relation over C.F.A. which first encompasses our intuitions about processes behaviour and moreover, happens to be a congruence relation. So we get the means for discussing whether or not two processes can be interchangeable in any context . However it may be sometimes difficult to directly deal with the definition of the equivalence, since one must then , examine all the accepted language, and in the case of infinite processes , it is infinite too. So we need another mechanism in order to finitely carry out properties about these infinite objects .

IV- AXIOMATIZATION OF THE CONGRUENCE

In this section we provide a system of (in)equalities between C.F.A. terms which allows to relate two given terms. Our system relies on mathematical induction rules [KLE71] and is proved to be sound and complete with regard to preorder "<" . Actually this proof relies on an alternative characterization of relations "≈" and "<" .

1) *Alternative characterization of "<"*

definition1.1 : given an integer n, we let $<_n$ denote a binary relation over C.F.A. s.t. $\forall t, t'$ $t <_n t'$ iff :

1) $I(t) \leq I(t')$
2) $\forall s \in A_+^n$, $t{=}^s{\Rightarrow}$ $\Rightarrow$ $t'{=}^s{\Rightarrow}$ $\wedge$
   a) $t\uparrow s \Rightarrow t'\uparrow s$
   b) $(t' {=}^s{\Rightarrow} t'_1 \Rightarrow t'_1{=}^a{\Rightarrow}) \Rightarrow ((t{=}^s{\Rightarrow} t_1 \Rightarrow t_1{=}^a{\Rightarrow}) \vee (t1 \neq^{sa}\Rightarrow))$.

In previous definition, A_+^n denotes the set of sequence of elements whose length is less (or equal)than n . Relations $<_n$ look very similar to < except that $<_n$ is only concerned with experiments of length n (at most). The intuitive meaning of these relations is the following:if we use the usual tree representation for processes , then "$<_n$" compare the n first levels and examine the leaves going out of level n . *This constitutes the fundamental difference from the principle supporting Milner's recursive equivalence which is not concerned with interfaces at level n .*

proposition1.1 : relation $<_n$ is a preorder relation over C.F.A. for any integer n.
proof : quite similar to that of < .

proposition1.2 : $\forall n$, $<_{n-1} \supset <_n$ ie: $t <_n t' \Rightarrow t <_{n-1} t'$.
proof : immediate , noticing that $A_+^n \supset A_+^{n-1}$.

This proposition states that relations "$<_n$" constitute a chain and allows to relate relation "< " with "$<_n$" .

proposition 1.3 : "<" is the least upper bound of the set of relations "$<_n$" ie: $< = \cap_n <_n$.

proof : notice that $\forall n$, $A_+^* \supset A_+^n$ and $A_+^* = \cup_n A_+^n$.

2) *The axiom set*

Henceforth relations "$\leq_n$ and $\leq$" stand for preorder relations which generate equivalences " $=_n$ and =" respectively . So our system is intended to be used in conjunction with the following rules : let t and t' be C.F.A. terms and n an integer then :

(R_0) $t \leq_n t' \Rightarrow t \leq_{n-1} t'$

(R_1) $t \leq_n t$

(R_2) $t \leq_n t' \wedge t' \leq_n t'' \Rightarrow t \leq_n t''$

(R_3) $t \leq_n t' \wedge t' \leq_n t \Leftrightarrow t =_n t'$

(R_4) $t \leq_n t_1 \wedge t' \leq_n t'_1 \Rightarrow$

i) $a{:}t \leq_n a{:}t_1$

ii) if $\{s \in A_+^n : t{=}^s{\Rightarrow} \wedge t'{=}^s{\Rightarrow}\} \supset \{s \in A_+^n : (t_1{=}^s{\Rightarrow} \wedge t'_1{=}^s{\Rightarrow}) \vee (t{=}^s{\Rightarrow} \vee t'{=}^s{\Rightarrow})\}$ then $t+t' \leq_n t_1+t'_1$

We let " Ω" denote the fully divergent term of C.F.A. ie: $\forall n$, $\Omega \text{-}\tau^n\rightarrow_* \Omega$. Our system (called S_0) is the following:

$A_0)$ $\quad nil \leq_n X$

$A_1)$ $\quad X+Y =_n Y+X$

$A_2)$ $\quad X+(Y+Z) =_n (X+Y)+Z$

$A_3)$ $\quad X+nil =_n X$

$A_4)$ $\quad X+X =_n X$

$A_5)$ $\quad a{:}X+a{:}Y =_n a{:}(\tau{:}X+\tau{:}Y)$

$A_6)$ $\quad X+\tau{:}Y =_n \tau{:}(X+Y)$ if $I(Y) \supset I(X) \vee \tau \in I(Y)$

$\quad\quad =_n \tau{:}(X+Y) + \tau{:}Y$ anyway

$A_7)$ $\quad$ if $X \equiv \Sigma_{a\in L}\, a{:}X_a$ and $Y \equiv \Sigma_{b\in L'}\, b{:}Y_b$ then

$\quad X||Y =_n \Sigma_{a\in L}\, a{:}(X_a||Y) + \Sigma_{b\in L'}\, b{:}(X||Y_b) + \Sigma_{a\#b}\, ab{:}(X_a||Y_b)$

$A_8)$ $\quad (a{:}X)[\varphi] =_n \varphi(a){:}X[\varphi]$ if $\varphi(a)\neq\gamma$, nil otherwise

$A_9)$ $\quad (X+Y)[\varphi] =_n X[\varphi] + Y[\varphi]$

$A_{10})$ $\quad nil[\varphi] =_n nil$

$A_{11})$ $\quad a\rightarrow X =_n a{:}((a\rightarrow X)||X)[\psi^1]$

$A_{12})$ $\quad \Omega + X =_n \Omega + \tau{:}X$ if $I(X)\neq\emptyset$

$A_{13})$ $\quad X \leq_n \tau{:}X$ and $\tau{:}X \leq_n X$ if $\tau \in I(X)$

$A_{14})$ $\quad X \leq_n X+Y$

Interfaces of terms are inductively defined as stated in section II.3). Notation $\Sigma_{a\in L}\ a{:}X_a$ stands for $a_1{:}X_1+a_2{:}X_2+\ldots+a_n{:}X_n$ if $L=\{a_1,a_2,\ldots,a_n\}$, ψ^1 is the already defined renaming, $\equiv$ denotes syntactical identity and $\tau{:}X$ is put for terms like $(\alpha{:}X \parallel \beta{:}nil)[\varphi]$ where $\alpha\#\beta$ and $\varphi(\alpha)=\varphi(\beta)=\gamma$, and φ preserves any action of X .

Most of these axioms are those usally proposed when axiomatizing congruence of C.C.S. based languages . For example the four first ones allow to make the set of processes, together with sum operator , into an abelian monoid, nil being the neutral element .However there exists some significant differences which we note in the followings:

i) Usually proof systems do not use the notion of interface; but here this notion allows us to define a more refined form of those laws that are generally presented as τ-laws (for instance A_{5-6} and A_{13})

ii) Axiom A_{13} in its totality has no counterpart: it depart from the famous $\tau{:}X=X$ and considering preorders which allow $\tau X \leq X$ then it allows our preorder to be more finer .

iii) Axiom A_0 is usually absent from proof systems, since in general the other approaches set Ω to be the least process . Notice also that A_{14} does no hold in general in other approaches .

Now S_0 axioms are rather basic ones ; and more complex derived ones can be deduced from our system. We propose some useful ones in the following:

proposition2.1 : given system S_0 , the following hold :

d1) $a:\tau:X =_n a:X$

d2) $a:X + a:(Y+Z) =_n a:X + a:(X+Y) + a:(X+Z) + a:(X+Y+Z)$

d3) $X + \tau:X =_n \tau:X$

d4) $X + \tau:(X+Y) =_n \tau:(X+Y)$

d5) $a:X + a:Y + a:(X+Y) =_n a:X + a:Y$.

Recall that we are looking for mechanisms which will allow us to discuss about terms equivalence, without directly dealing with the definition of our relations. Fortunatly system S_0 has properties which allow this:

Theorem 2 :system S_0 together with rules R_0-R_4 is sound and complete for relations $<_n$ over C.F.A. .

Now the axiomatization of relation "<" becomes quite easy . Before that let's augment our rules R_0-R_4 with the following two :

R_5) $\forall n, t[>n] \leq t$

R6) $(t \leq_0 t' \wedge (t \leq_n t' \Rightarrow t \leq_{n+1} t')) \Rightarrow t \leq t'$

where $(t[>n] =^s\Rightarrow t'[>m]) \Leftrightarrow (t =^s\Rightarrow t' \wedge |s| = n-m)$

Here, we allow some kind of renaming which restricts strings accepted by a process s.t. their length be bounded . Rule R_6) relates relations $\leq_n$ and $\leq$, allowing a mathematical induction to be used while relating terms .

Theorem 3 : System S_0 together with rules R_0-R_6 is sound and complete for relation < over C.F.A. ie: $\forall$ t,t' $\in$ C.F.A. , $t \leq t' \Leftrightarrow t < t'$.

The proof of these results heavily relies on existence, for C.F.A. terms, of normal forms, based on convex sets of finite sets of external actions . The interested reader may refer to [GAM85'] .

V- SOME CONCLUSIONS

In this paper,we defined a communication based language which allows to express parallel agents in an asynchronous framework. Our approach relies entirely on intuitions we have about process behaviour :

1) in our opinion, a process can be seen as an abstract computation station, with its own clock, and which is only capable of performing communication actions; these actions may be either external ie they require participation of some other process, or internal ie: they only involve subcomponents of the process .

2) we define asynchrony as the ability a process has to perform a finite sequence of null actions (i.e: not to communicate) without changing its state. That is, in our case the neutral element of composition of actions is no more the internal one, but the absence of actions . And in fact internal actions are actually "real" actions, restricted in such a way that they do not involve participation of the environment.

3) as a consequence of the first point, a process, in our approach, cannot change its state without communicating. So in our language any recursive expression constructed from process variables does not necessarely denote a process expression. For instance, we do not have an undefined process in our

formalism. As a counter part, we introduce some kind of iteration which allows to generate different (possibly infinite) instances of the same process; however any new generation activity is preceded by a "guard passing" .

All these points make our approach rather original, and as a consequence, discard the possibility of immediately applying the results till now proposed in order to formalize process behaviour .

we then define an equivalence relation which, fortunatly turns out to be a congruence relation over our language . *This equivalence is generated by a preorder which relies on an ordering we provide with the action set and on the notion of term interface , and which allows to merge in a single relation both notions of complexity of accepted language, and of nondeterminism : the least process within a set of processes, accepts as language the intersection of their accepted languages and is at least as deterministic as any one among them* . As an important consequence, we prove nil to be the least process , show that sum increases processes and depart from the famous $\tau t=t$ law . Moreover, we provide a set of axioms, together with mathemetical induction rule , that we proved to be sound and complete for our relations .

This language allows us to express certain class of parallel systems and we have used it in a previous paper [GAM84] to specify "data-flow" and "reduction" applications . In fact our approach together with the equivalence and the preorder we provide with processes, seems quite well suited for the parallel interpretation of functional expressions . Another quite interesting direction, we undertake now, is to provide a model of asynchronous processes, based on these ideas .

REFERENCES

AUS84: AUSTRY D. , BOUDOL G. - Algèbre de processus et synchronisation TCS 30,1 (pp . 91-131) -1984 -

ARN82: ARNOLD A. , NIVAT M. - Comportement de processus Colloque AFCET : les mathematiques de l'informatique -1982-

BRO83: BROOKES S. D. - A model for communicating sequential processe Phd thesis Oxford University -1983 -

DAR82: DARONDEAU Ph. - An enlarged definition and complete axiomatization of observational congruence of finite processes LNCS 137 -1982-

DAR83: DARONDEAU Ph. , KOTT L. - On the observational semantics of fair asynchro Proc ICALP 83, LNCS 154 -1983 -

GAM84: GAMATIE B. -Systèmes de processus communicants et interprétation parallèle de languages fonctionnels IR n° 320 INRIA -1984-

GAM85: GAMATIE B. -Observational congruence of nondeterministic and communicating finite processes in asynchronous systems IR . n° 254 IRISA -1985-

GAM85': GAMATIE B. - Towards specicication and proof of asynchronous systems IR. IRISA -1985-

KAH77: KAHN G., MC QUEEN D.B. - Coroutines and networks of parallel processes Gilchrist B. (Ed.) Information processing Amsterdam -1977-

KLE71: KLEENE S.C. -Introduction to metamathematics (Ed.) De Bruijn N.G., De Groot J., Zaanen A.C. -1971-

HOA78: HOARE C.A.R. -Communicating sequential processes CACM 21, vol 8 -1978-

HOA81: HOARE C.A.R. , BROOKES S.D. , ROSCOE A.W. - A theory of communicating processes PRG-16 Oxford University-1981-

HEN85: HENNESSY M., MILNER R. - Algebraic laws for nondeterminism and concurrency JACM 32 ,1 -1985-

HEN85: HENNESSY M. , DE NICOLA R. - Testing equivalence for processes Proc ICALP 83, LNCS 154 -1983-

MIL80: MILNER R. - A calculus of communicating systems LNCS 92 -1980-

PLO81: PLOTKIN G. - A structural approach to operational semantics DAIMI FN -19 Comp. Sc. Dept. Aarhus University -1981-

Monotone Boolean Formulas, Distributive Lattices, and the Complexities of Logics, Algebraic Structures, and Computation Structures (Preliminary Report)

H.B. Hunt, III
and
R.E. Stearns

(Research supported in part by NSF Grants No. DCR 84-03014 and DCR 83-03932.)

Computer Science Department
State University of New York at Albany
Albany, New York 12222, USA

Abstract

We refine and significantly extend the known results on the complexities of the Satisfiability, Tautology, Equivalence, and $\leq$-Problems for classes of Boolean formulas. Results are presented on the relationships between the number of repetitions of variables occurring in formulas and the complexities of decision problems for the formulas. Results are also presented on the complexities of very simple monotone Boolean formulas and of implication.

A variety of applications of these results are presented to a number of logics studied in the literature, to computational probability and counting, to algebraic structures, and to program schemes and Binary Decision Diagrams.

Assuming **P** $\neq$ **NP**, a number of the results are "best" possible or are close to "best" possible.

1. Introduction

We refine and significantly extend the known results on the complexities of the Satisfiability, Tautology, Equivalence, and $\leq$-Problems for classes of Boolean formulas [Co, GJ, Go, BHR, To]. Special emphasis is placed upon these problems for very simple monotone Boolean formulas. Applications of these results are presented to a number of logics studied in the literature [He, HB, Kl, LL, Me, Po, Ra, RaS], to computational probability and counting [Fe, PMcC, Va], to algebraic structures, and to program schemes and Binary Decision Diagonals [Ak1, Ak2, Ma, Mo, FHS]. Assuming **P** $\neq$ **NP**, a number of these results are "best" possible or are close to "best" possible.

We emphasize monotone Boolean formulas and distributive lattices, rather than Boolean formulas with occurrences of *not* and Boolean algebras. Doing this enables us to obtain lower bounds on the complexities of the Generalized Tautology Problem [defined below] for many of the lattice theoretical models of propositional calculi studied in the literature. As immediate corollaries, **coNP**-hard lower bounds are obtained on the Logical Validity Problems for the propositional calculi of classical two-valued logic [Me], positive logic [HB], intuitionistic logic [He, Kl], the modal logic S_4 [LL], and the multiple-valued logics of Post [Po]. For each of these propositional calculi, we show that the Logical Validity Problem is **coNP**-complete for formulas involving only the operators *or* and *and* and a **single** occurrence of the operator $\Rightarrow$ (i.e. implication) in which no variable occurs more than twice. We also show that that the Tautology Problem for Boolean formulas involving only the operator $\Rightarrow$ is **coNP**-complete. One immediate corollary that the set of theorems of the propositional calculus of classical implicative logic [Ra] is **coNP**-complete.

We also emphasize Boolean and monotone Boolean formulas without repeated variables or in which no variable occurs more than two or three times. This enables us to obtain hardness results for formulas that are easily, provably, minimal. For example, we show that the $\leq$-Problem is **coNP**-complete for monotone Boolean formulas without repeated variables. Each such formulas is easily seen to be minimal. Applications of this result are presented to computational probability and counting and to program schemes and Binary Decision Diagrams. One important corollary is that the problems of computing the probabilities of a joint event $\{e_1 \text{ and } e_2\}$ and of a conditional event $\{e_1 \mid e_2\}$ become "hard" almost immediately, when the events $\{e_1\}$ and $\{e_2\}$ are **not** statistically independent. Moreover, this is true when the probabilities of the events $\{e_1\}$ and $\{e_2\}$ are easily computable deterministically in polynomial time. In contrast, we also show that the Equivalence Problem for Boolean formulas involving only the operators *and, or, not,* and $\Rightarrow$ without repeated variables is decidable deterministically in polynomial time.

By an *algebraic structure S,* we mean a nonempty set S (called the *domain* of *S*), together with operations on S of various arities [MacLB]. By a *nondegenerate* structure, we mean an algebraic structure whose domain has at least two elements. The decision problems for algebraic structures considered here include --

1. the *Equivalence Problem,* i.e. the problems of determining if two formulas on the structure denote the same function, and
2. the *$\leq$-Problem,* i.e. the problem of determining, for formulas F and G on a partially ordered structure, if $F \leq G$.

Additional problems for lattices and Binary Decision Diagrams considered here include --

3. the *Generalized Tautology Problem,* i.e. the problem of determining, for a formula or diagram F and a constant *c*, if the function denoted by F equals *c*, and
4. the *Computational Probability Problem,* i.e. the problem of computing, given a formula, circuit, or diagram F, a constant *c*, and a probability distribution *p*, the value of $p\{F=c\}$.

The definitions of the complexity classes, **P, NP, coNP, #P,** and **RP** are standard. Most of the hardness results presented here follow from the next proposition from [Co,GJ] (Part 1) and [BHR] (Part 2).

Proposition 1.1.

1. The Satisfiability Problem for CNF Boolean formulas with no more than three literals per clause is **NP**-complete.

2. The Equivalence Problem for monotone Boolean formulas F and G such that $F \leq G$ is **coNP**-complete.

Finally, let F be a formula on an algebraic structure with domain S. Let **v** be an assignment of values from S to the variables of F. We denote the value taken on by F under **v** by **v**[F].

2. On the Complexities of Boolean and Monotone Boolean Formulas

We refine and significantly extend the known results on the complexities of the Satisfiability, Tautology, Equivalence, and $\leq$-Problems for Boolean and monotone Boolean formulas.

Theorem 2.1. The following problems are **coNP**-complete:

1. the Tautology Problem for Boolean formulas $(F \Rightarrow G)$, where F and G are monotone Boolean formulas;
2. the Tautology Problem for Boolean formulas involving only the operators *or*, *and* and $\Rightarrow$ in which no variable occurs more than three times;
3. [GJ] the Tautology Problem for DNF Boolean formulas in which no variable occurs more than three;
4. the Tautology Problem for Boolean formulas f, that consist of monotone Boolean combinations of literals, such that each variable of f occurs exactly once complemented and exactly once uncomplemented;
5. the $\leq$-Problem for monotone Boolean formulas F and G such that no variable occurs more than once in F and more than once in G;
6. the Equivalence Problem for monotone Boolean formulas F and G such that $F \leq G$ and such that no variable occurs more than two times in F and more than one time in G; and
7. the Tautology Problem for Boolean formulas of the form $(F \Rightarrow G)$, where F and G are monotone Boolean formulas such that no variable occurs more than one time in F and more than one time in G.

[We include 3 of Theorem 2.1 to simplify the proof of Part 4 of Theorem 2.1.]

Proof. Detailed proofs appear in [HS1]. We only outline the proofs that $1 \Rightarrow 2$, $1 \Rightarrow 3$, $3 \Rightarrow 4$, and $4 \Rightarrow 5$.

Proof of $1 \Rightarrow 2$. By 1 the set of tautological Boolean formulas involving only the operators *or*, *and*, and $\Rightarrow$ is **coNP**-hard. Let g be such a formula. Let $x_1, \ldots,$ and x_N be the variables of g. Let $i_1, \ldots,$ and i_N be the numbers of occurrences of $x_1, \ldots,$ and x_N, respectively, in g. Let $x_{1,1},\ldots,x_{1,i_1},\ldots,x_{N,1}, \ldots,$ and x_{N,i_N} be distinct variables other than $x_1, \ldots,$ and x_N. Let g' be the formula that results from g by replacing, for $1 \leq j \leq N$ and $1 \leq k \leq i_j$, the k-th occurrence of x_j in g by $x_{j,k}$. Let $F(x_{1,1},\ldots,x_{N,i_N})$ be the formula

$$[[x_{1,1} \Rightarrow x_{1,2}] \textit{ and } \cdots \textit{ and } [x_{1,i_1} \Rightarrow x_{1,1}]] \textit{ and } \cdots \textit{ and}$$

$$[[x_{N,1} \Rightarrow x_{N,2}] \textit{ and } \cdots \textit{ and } [x_{N,i_N} \Rightarrow x_{N,1}]].$$

Let h be the formula $[F(x_{1,1},\ldots,x_{N,i_N}) \Rightarrow g']$. Then, no variable occurs more than three times in h; and h is a tautology if and only if g is a tautology.

Proof of $1 \Rightarrow 3$. The proof closely follows that of $1 \Rightarrow 2$ except that g is now a DNF Boolean formula. Let $x_1,\ldots,x_N,x_{1,1},\ldots,x_{N,i_N}$, g', $F(x_{1,1},\ldots,x_{N,i_N})$, and h be as in the proof of $1 \Rightarrow 2$. Let $F'(x_{1,1},\ldots,x_{N,i_N})$ be the formula

$$[[(x_{1,1} \textit{ and } (\textit{not } x_{1,2})) \textit{ or } \cdots \textit{ or } (x_{1,i_1} \textit{ and } (\textit{not } x_{1,1})) \textit{ or } \cdots \textit{ or }$$
$$[(x_{N,1} \textit{ and } (\textit{not } x_{N,2})) \textit{ or } \cdots \textit{ or } (x_{N,i_N} \textit{ and } (\textit{not } x_{N,1}))]]].$$

Let h' be the DNF Boolean formula $F'(x_{1,1},\ldots,x_{N,i_N})$ *or* g'. Then, h' is a tautology if and only if g is a tautology.

Proof of $3 \Rightarrow 4$. Let $F(x_1,\ldots,x_n)$ be a DNF Boolean formula in which no variable occurs more than three times. Since F is a monotone Boolean combination of literals, we can assume that each variable in F occurs at least once uncomplemented and at least once complemented. We can also assume that each variable that occurs three times in F occurs exactly two times uncomplemented and exactly one time complemented. Let F' be the formula that results from F as follows. For each variable x_i occurring three times in F, let x_{i1} and x_{i2} be two new variables. Replace the first uncomplemented occurrence of x_i by x_{i1}; replace the second uncomplemented occurrence of x_i by x_{i2}; and replace the complemented occurrence of x_i by $(\overline{x_{i1}} \textit{ or } \overline{x_{i2}})$. Then, F' is a monotone Boolean combination of literals such that each variable in F' occurs exactly once uncomplemented and exactly once complemented. Moreover, F is a tautology if and only if F' is a tautology.

To see this, it suffices to consider assignments v of values to the variables such that, for some i, $v[x_{i1}] \neq v[x_{i2}]$. In which case, $v[\overline{x_{i1}} \textit{ or } \overline{x_{i2}}] = 1$ for each such i. Let w be an assignment to the variables such that w is the same as v except that, for all such i, $w[x_{i1}] = w[x_{i2}] = 0$. Since F' is a monotone Boolean combination of literals, $v[F'] \geq w[F']$. Thus if F is a tautology, for all assignments v of values to the variables such that $v[x_{i1}] \neq v[x_{i2}]$ for some i, $v[F'] = 1$.

Proof of $4 \Rightarrow 5$. Let f be a monotone Boolean combination of literals such that each variable in f occurs exactly once uncomplemented and exactly once complemented. Let $x_1, \ldots,$ and x_n be the variables of f. Let $y_1, \ldots,$ and y_n be distinct variables other than $x_1, \ldots,$ and x_n. Let f' be the monotone Boolean formula that results from f by replacing, for $1 \leq i \leq n$, the occurrence of *not* x_i in f by y_i. Let F_n be the formula $(x_1 \textit{ or } y_1) \textit{ and } \cdots \textit{ and } (x_n \textit{ or } y_n)$. Then, f is a tautology if and only if $F_N \leq f'$.

This follows by noting that the following are equivalent:

i. f is a tautology;

ii. for all assignments v of values to the variables such that, for $1 \leq i \leq n$, exactly one of $v[x_i]$ and $v[y_i]$ equals 1, $v[f'] = 1$;

iii. for all assignments v values to the variables such that, for $1 \leq i \leq n$, at least one of $v[x_i]$ and $v[y_i]$ equals 1, $v[f'] = 1$;

iv. for all assignments v of values to the variables such that $v[F_n] = 1$, $v[f'] = 1$; and

v. $F_n \leq f'$. □

Theorem 2.2. The following problems are *NP*-complete:

1. the Satisfiability Problem for Boolean formulas (F *and* (*not* G)), where F and G are monotone Boolean formulas such that no variable occurs more than once in F and more than once in G;
2. the Satisfiability Problem for Boolean formulas f, that are monotone Boolean combinations of literals, such that each variable of f occurs exactly once uncomplemented and exactly once uncomplemented; and
3. the Satisfiability Problem for CNF Boolean formulas such that
   i. no clause of f contains more than three literals,
   ii. no variable of f occurs more than three times, and
   iii. no clause of f contains occurrences of both uncomplemented and complemented literals.

Proof. 1 and 2 follow from Theorem 2.1 by duality. A detailed proof of 3 can be found in [HS1]. An outline of this proof appears in the appendix. □

Theorem 2.3. The Tautology Problem is **coNP**-complete for Boolean formulas involving only the operator $\Rightarrow$. Moreover, the Tautology Problem is **coNP**-complete for such formulas in which no variable occurs more than three times.

Proof. A detailed proof appears in [HS1]. A sketch of the proof for such formulas with arbitrary repetitions of variables appears in the appendix. □

Direct analogues of Theorem 2.3 hold for the propositional calculi of classical implicative logic [Ra], of intuitionistic logic [He, Kl], and of the modal logic S_4 [LL], and for each nondegenerate implication algebra [Ab, Ra]. Moreover, the method of eliminating Boolean operators in the proof of Theorem 2.3 can also be applied to the formulas of any first-order logical theory. Here, we only consider the propositional calculus of classical implicative logic, defined in [Ra].

Corollary 2.4. The set of theorems of the propositional calculus of classical implication is **coNP**-complete.

Proof. The set of such theorems is precisely the set of tautological Boolean formulas involving only the operator $\Rightarrow$ [Ra]. □

Theorem 2.5. The Equivalence Problem for Boolean formulas without repeated variables involving only the operators *and*, *or* *not*, $\Rightarrow$, | (nand), and ↓ (nor) is decidable deterministically in polynomial time.

Proof. A detailed proof appears in [HS1]. An outline of the proof appears in the appendix. □

Theorem 2.5, Observation 2.5.2 in the appendix, and the following result from [To]

> the Satisfiability Problem for CNF Boolean formulas in which no variable occurs more than twice is decidable deterministically in polynomial time

show that the results of Theorems 2.1, 2.2, and 2.3 are "best" possible or are close to "best" possible, unless P = NP.

3. Applications

We sketch direct applications of the results of Section 2 to logics, computational probability and counting, algebraic structures, and program schemes and Binary Decision Diagrams.

3.1. Applications to Logics

Analogues of the Tautology and Satisfiability Problems are **coNP**- and **NP**-complete, respectively, for very simple formulas on many different kinds of distributive lattices including the lattice-theoretical models of propositional calculi studied in the literature [Ra, RaS]. These lower bounds for lattices imply that --

3.1a. any reasonable propositional calculus with a reasonable implication operator has a **coNP**-hard Logical Validity Problem, and

3.1b. any reasonable propositional calculus with a reasonable negation operator has an **NP**-hard Logical Satisfiability Problem. (By the Logical Satisfiability Problem, we mean the problem of determining if a formula can take on the value **True** in each model of the logic.)

By a reasonable propositional calculus, we mean a propositional calculus, each of whose models is a distributive lattice with a maximal element **1** (called **True**). By a reasonable implication operator $\Rightarrow$, we mean that the operator $\Rightarrow$ is binary and that $a \Rightarrow b = \mathbf{1}$ if and only if $a \leq b$. By a reasonable negation operator $\sim$, we mean that the operator $\sim$ is unary and that $\sim\mathbf{1} \neq \mathbf{1}$ and $\exists$ b for which $\sim b = \mathbf{1}$.

A detailed discussion of these results appears in [HS1]. Here, we only briefly sketch the results obtained for Generalized Tautology Problems for lattices and for Logical Validity Problems for propositional calculi.

Theorem 3.1.1. Let $S = (S, \vee, \wedge, \Rightarrow, \mathbf{1})$ be an algebraic structure such that

i. $T = (S, \vee, \wedge)$ is a nondegenerate distributive lattice;

ii. $\mathbf{1} \in S$ is a maximal under $\leq$; and

iii. the operator $\Rightarrow$ is binary such that $x \Rightarrow y = \mathbf{1}$ if and only if $x \leq y$.

Then, the Generalized Tautology Problem for S is **coNP**-complete for formulas $(F \Rightarrow G)$ and the constant **1**, where F and G involve only the operators $\vee$ and $\wedge$ and such that no variable occurs more than once in F and more than once in G.

Proof. $(F \Rightarrow G) = \mathbf{1}$ on S if and only if $F \leq G$ on S if and only if $F \leq G$ on the two element distributive lattice. By Part 5 of Theorem 2.1, this last problem is **coNP**-complete. □

Theorem 3.1.2. Let L be the propositional calculus of classical two-valued logic [Me], positive logic [HB], intuitionistic logic [He, Kl], minimal logic [Ra], positive logic with semi-negation [Ra], constructive logic with strong negation [Ra], the modal logic S_4 [LL], and for $m \geq 2$ the m-valued logic of Post [Po]. Then, the Logical Validity Problem is **coNP**-complete for formulas $(F \Rightarrow G)$ on **L**, where F and G involve only the operators $\bigvee$ and $\bigwedge$ and such that no variable occurs more than once in F and more than once in G.

Proof. For each such **L**, each nondegenerate model of **L** satisfies the conditions of Theorem 3.1.1. Moreover for each such formula $(F \Rightarrow G)$ on **L**, $(F \Rightarrow G)$ is logically valid if and only if $(F \Rightarrow G) = \mathbf{1}$ on each model of **L** [Ra]. But this is true if and only if $F \leq G$ on the two element distributive lattice. □

3.2. Applications to Computational Probability and Counting

Def. 3.2.1. Let $n \geq 1$. Let $c_1, \ldots,$ and $c_n \in \{0,1\}$. Let E_n be the event space consisting of all finite unions of events e of the form $e = \{\bigwedge_{i=1}^{n} x_i = c_i\}$. We call such events e *atomic events*. Let p be a probability distribution on E_n such that, for all $d_1,\ldots,d_n \in \{0,1\}$, the events $\{x_1 = d_1\}, \ldots,$ and $\{x_n = d_n\}$ are statistically independent. Then, we say that p is an *independent distribution*. Otherwise, we say that p is a *dependent distribution*.

Let p be an independent distribution; and let $F(x_1,\ldots,x_n)$ be a Boolean formula without repeated variables. Then, a straight-line program, that computes $p\{F=1\}$ in terms of the values of $p\{x_i = 1\}$ $(1 \leq i \leq n)$ can be computed deterministically in polynomial time in F [ACHM]. Part 5 of Theorem 2.1 shows that the problems of computing the values of $p\{F=1 \text{ and } G=1\}$, $p\{F=1 \text{ or } G=1\}$, and $p\{F=1 \mid G=1\}$ are $(\mathbf{NP} \cup \mathbf{coNP})$-hard, where

i. F and G are monotone Boolean formulas in which no variable is repeated more than once in F and more than once in G, and

ii. p is an independent distribution such that, for all events e in E_i, $p\{e\}=0$ implies $e = \emptyset$.

3.3. Applications to Program Schemes and Binary Decision Diagrams

The *Executability Problem* or *EP* for a class C of program schemes is the problem of determining, given a scheme S in C and a label λ of S, if there exists an interpretation I of S such that the statement labeled by λ in S is executed during the computation of S under I. In [CHS] the EP was shown to be **NP**-complete for the class Sw of monadic single variable program schemes without loops consisting only of predicate tests and Halt statements. Part 4 of Theorem 2.1 implies the significantly stronger result that the EP is still **NP**-complete for the class of programs schemes in S in Sw such that no predicate test occurs more than two times in S. One immediate corollary is the following:

Theorem 3.3.1. The computational identity, isomorphism, strong equivalence, weak equivalence, containment, totality, and divergence problems or their negations are *coNP*-complete for the class of monadic single variable program schemes S such that no predicate test occurs more than two times in S.

Any monadic single variable program scheme in which no predicate test occurs more than once is *free*. Thus, Part 5 of Theorem 2.1 yields a simple immediate and direct proof of the following theorem from [FHS]:

Theorem 3.3.2. The weak equivalence and containment problems for the free monadic single variable program schemes are *coNP*-complete.

Proof sketch. Let F and G be monotone Boolean formulas, each without repeated variables. As show in Figure 1, the monadic single variable program schemes S_F and S_G can be constructed from F and G, respectively, deterministically in polynomial time. Since no variable is repeated in F or is repeated in G, no predicate test occurs more than once in S_F and more than once in S_G. Let S_F' and S_G' be the free monadic single variable program schemes in Figure 2. Then, it is easily seen that the following statements are equivalent:

1. $F \leq G$;
2. for any interpretation I such that the statement labeled A in S_F' is executed during the computation of S_F' under I, the statement labeled A in S_G' is executed during the computation of S_G' under I;
3. S_F' is weakly equivalent to S_G'; and
4. S_F' is contained by S_G'. □

Each monadic single variable program scheme in *Sw* can also be viewed as a Binary Decision Diagram [Ak1, Mo], henceforth abbreviated BDD. A number of complexity results for BDDs can be read-off from Theorems 3.3.1 and 3.3.2 and their proofs. For example, we have shown the following:

Theorem 3.3.3.

1. The Tautology, Satisfiability, and Equivalence Problems are **coNP**-complete for BDDs in which no variable occurs more than two times.
2. The $\leq$-Problem is **coNP**-complete for BDDs in which no variable occurs more than one time.
3. There exists a deterministic or there exists a nondeterministic polynomially time-bounded algorithm to convert a BDD, in which no variable occurs more than two times, into an equivalent BDD, in which no variable occurs more than one time along any path, only if **P** = **NP** or only if **NP** = **coNP**, respectively.

Finally, let $F(x_1,...,x_n)$ be a Boolean formula denoted by a BDD D_F in which no variable occurs more than one time along any path. A straight-line program, to compute the value of $p\,\{F{=}1\}$ from the values of $p\,\{x_i{=}1\}$ $1 \leq i \leq n$ for any independent probability distribution p, can be constructed from D_F deterministically in polynomial time [CH]. Let F and G be two such formulas. Let p_F and p_G be the associated straight-line programs computed from BDDs D_F and D_G. Then, p_F and p_G are equivalent for all assignments of values from $\{x \text{ is a real} \mid 0 \leq x \leq 1\}$ to their variables if and only if F=G if and only if p_F and p_G are equivalent for all assignments of values from the reals to their variables. Using the *RP* algorithm in [IM] for the Inequivalence Problem for straight-line programs on infinite integer domains, we obtain an alternative proof for the following theorem from [BCW]:

Theorem 3.3.4. There are *RP* algorithms for the Inequivalence Problem for BDDs in which no variable occurs more than once along a path and for the Strong Equivalence Problem [Ma] for free monadic single variable program schemes.

3.4. Applications to Algebraic Structures

Part 2 of Proposition 1.1 and Theorem 2.1 can be used to obtain a number of new results on the complexities of decision problems for a variety of algebraic structures besides lattices. For example, we have shown the following:

Theorem 3.4.1. Let $S = (S,+,-,\cdot,\mathbf{0},\mathbf{1})$ be a nondegenerate ring with a multiplicative identity **1**. Then, the problem of determining if a system of simultaneous quadratic equations on S has a solution is **NP**-hard for systems such that

1. the only constant symbols appearing in the system are **0** and **1**, and
2. the system has a solution if and only if it has a $\{\mathbf{0},\mathbf{1}\}$-valued solution.

Theorem 3.4.2. Let F be a finite field. Then, the Equivalence Problem for formulas on F involving only variables, parenthesis, +,−,·, and exponentiation by constants in which no variable occurs more than two times is *coNP*-complete. (For such formulas, we say that x appears once in the subformula x^c.) The Equivalence Problem for formulas on the finite field *Z*, involving only variables, parentheses, +,−, and · in which no variable occurs more than two times is *coNP*-complete.

4. References

[Ab] J.C. Abbott, *Sets, Lattices, and Boolean Algebras,* Allyn and Bacon, Boston, Mass., 1969.

[Ak1] S.B. Akers, Binary decision diagrams, *IEEE Trans. on Computers,* vol. C-27, 1978, pp. 509-516.

[Ak2] S.B. Akers, A procedure for functional design verification, *Digest of 10-th International Symp. on Fault Tolerant Computing,* 1980, pp. 65-67.

[ACHM] D.N. Arden, S. Chakravarty, H.B. Hunt III, and R.M. Murray, Computational probability with application to fault detection, Technical Report 84-17, Department of Computer Science, SUNY Albany, Albany, New York, 1984.

[Bi] G. Birkhoff, *Lattice Theory,* (3rd Edition), Am. Math. Soc., Providence, R.I., 1967.

[BCW] M. Blum, A.K. Chandra, and M.N. Wegman, Equivalence of free Boolean graphs can be decided probabilistically in polynomial time, *Information Processing Letters* 10, 1980, pp. 80-82.

[BHR] P.A. Bloniarz, H.B. Hunt III, and D.J. Rosenkrantz, Algebraic structures with hard equivalence and minimization problems, *J. ACM,* 31, 1984, pp. 879-904.

[CH] S.K. Chakravarti and H.B. Hunt III, Binary decision diagrams, unpublished manuscript.

[CHS] R.L. Constable, H.B. Hunt III, and S. Sahni, On the computational complexity of scheme equivalence, *Proc. 8-th Annual Princeton Conference of Information Sciences and Systems,* Princeton, N.J., 1974. Also appears as -- H.B.Hunt III, R.L. Constable, and S. Sahni, On the computational complexity of program scheme equivalence, *SICOMP* 9, 1980, pp. 349-416.

[Co] S.A. Cook, The complexity of theorem-proving procedures, *Proc. Third Annual ACM Symp. on Theory of Computing,* 1971, pp. 151-158.

[Fe] W. Feller, *An Introduction to Probability Theory and its Applications* Vol. 1 (3rd Edition), John Wiley and Sons, New York, 1968.

[FHS] S. Fortune, J. Hopcroft, and E.M. Schmidt, The complexity of equivalence and containment for free single variable program schemes, Technical Report TR 77-310, Department of Computer Science, Cornell University, Ithaca, New York, 1977.

[GJ] M.R. Garey and D.S. Johnson, *Computers and Intractability: A Guide to the Theory of NP-Completeness,* W.H. Freeman, San Francisco, Ca., 1979.

[Go] E.M. Gold, Complexity of automaton identification from given data, *Inf. and Control* 37, 1978, pp. 302-320.

[He] A. Heyting, *Intuitionism,* North-Holland, Amsterdam, 1959.

[HB] D. Hibert and P. Bernays, *Grundlagen der Mathematik,* vol. 1, Springer, Berlin, 1934.

[HS1] H.B. Hunt III and R.E. Stearns, Distributive lattices, and the complexity of logics and probability, submitted for publication.

[HS2] H.B. Hunt III and R.E. Stearns, Nonlinear algebra for rings is "hard", submitted for publication.

[IM] O.H. Ibarra and S. Moran, Probabilistic algorithms for deciding equivalence of straight-line programs, *JACM* 30, 1983, pp. 217-228.

[Kl] S.C. Kleene, *Introduction to Metamathematics,* D. VanNostrand Co., Inc., Princeton, N.J., 1950.

[LL] C.I. Lewis and C.H. Langford, *Symbolic Logic,* New York, 1932.

[MacLB] S. MacLane and G. Birkhoff, *Algebra,* MacMillan, New York, 1967.

[Ma] Z. Manna, *Mathematical Theory of Computation,* McGraw-Hill, ew York, 1974.

[Me] E. Mendelson, *Introduction to Mathematical Logic* (2nd edition), D. VanNostrand, New York, 1979.

[Mo] B.M.E. Moret, Decision trees and diagrams, *Computing Surveys* 14, 1982, pp. 593-623.

[PMcC] K.P. Parker and E.J. McCluskey, Probabilistic treatment of general combinational networks, *IEEE Trans. on Computers,* 24, 1975, pp. 668-670.

[Po] E.L. Post, Introduction to a general theory of elementary propositions, *Amer. J. Math.,* 43, 1921, pp. 165-185.

[Ra] H. Rasiowa, *An Algebraic Approach to Non-Classical Logics,* North-Holland, Amsterdam, 1974.

[RaS] H. Rasiowa and R. Sikorski, *The Mathematics of Meta-mathematics,* Panstwowe Wydawnictwo Naukowe, Warzawa, 1963.

[To] C.A. Tovey, A simplified NP-complete satisfiability problem, *Discrete Applied Mathematics* 8, 1984, pp. 85-89.

[Va] L.G. Valiant, The complexity of enumeration and reliability problems, *SIAM J. Comput.* 8, 1979, pp. 410-421.

Appendix: Selected Proof Sketches

I. **Proof sketch** of Theorem 2.2. Let $f(x_1,...,x_n)$ be a CNF Boolean formula such that

a. no variable occurs more than three times in f, and

b. each variable in f occurs both complemented and uncomplemented.

By Part 2 of the theorem, the Satisfiability Problem for such CNF formulas is **NP**-complete. Let $y_1, \ldots,$ and y_n be distinct variables other than $x_1, \ldots,$ and x_n. Let f' be the result of replacing, for $1 \leq i \leq n$, y_i for the occurrence(s) of *not* x_i in f. Let f'' be [f' *and* $(\overline{x_1}$ *or* $\overline{y_1})$ *and* $\cdots$ *and* $(\overline{x_n}$ *or* $\overline{y_n})$]. Then, f'' is in CNF and satisfies conditions i, ii, and iii. Moreover, f is satisfiable if and only if f'' is satisfiable.

II. **Proof sketch** of Theorem 2.3. Let f be a DNF Boolean formula.

Step 1. Replace each occurrence of the operators *or* and *and* in f using the identities A *or* B = (*not* A) $\Rightarrow$ B and A *and* B = *not* (A $\Rightarrow$ (*not* B)). Let f_1 be the resulting Boolean formula.

Step 2. Let y be a variable not occurring in f. Replace each occurrence of the operator *not* in f_1 recursively as follows. Each subformula (*not* g) is replaced by (g $\Rightarrow$ y).

Step 3. Let f_3 be the formula $((f_2 \Rightarrow y) \Rightarrow y)$.

Then, f is a tautology if and only if f_3 is a tautology. □

III. **Proof sketch** of Theorem 2.5. Recalling the identities A $\Rightarrow$ B = (*not* A) *or* B, *A* | *B* = *not* (A *and* B), and A $\downarrow$ B = *not* (A *or* B), it suffices to consider Boolean formulas F and G without repeated variables involving only the operators *or*, *and*, and *not*. By repeated application of DeMorgan's Laws, it suffices to consider such Boolean formulas F and G such that the argument of each *not* in F or in G is a variable.

Let F and G be such Boolean formulas. We show that F=G if and only if F and G are identical up to commutativity and associativity of *and* and of *or*. The proof consists of several observations and lemmas. First, we need some notation.

Let **E**[F] be an *or, and, not* -formula that results from F by repeated application of the distributive laws until no further application is possible. Thus, **E**[F] is of the form t_1 *or* $\cdots$ *or* t_k $(k \geq 1)$, where each t_j is of the form l_{j1} *and* $\cdots$ *and* l_{jl} $(l \geq 1)$ and each l_{ji} is a literal. The subformulas $t_1,...,t_k$ are called the *terms* of **E**[F]. For each term t, **Var**[t] is the set of all variables occurring in t.

Obs. 2.5.1. Let x be a variable occurring in F. Then, x occurs uncomplemented in F if and only if x occurs uncomplemented in each term of **E**[F] in which it occurs.

Obs. 2.5.2. The formula F is neither unsatisfiable nor a tautology.

Lemma 2.5.3. Let t and s be terms of some **E**[F]. Then, $t \leq s$ if and only if t=s if and only if the set of literals occurring in t equals the set of literals occurring in s if and only if **Var**[t] = **Var**[s].

Lemma 2.5.4. Let t be a term of some **E**[F]. Then, there exists an assignment **w** of values from {0,1} to the variables such that **w**[t]=1 and such that **w**[s]=0 for all other terms of **E**[F] such that $s \not\equiv t$.

Proof. By 2.5.1 and 2.5.3 for each such term s, there exists a variable x ∈ **Var**[s] - **Var**[t].

Lemma 2.5.5. If F≡G, then every variable occurring in F occurs in G and every variable occurring in G occurs in F.

Proof. The proof follows from Obs. 2.5.1 and Lemma 2.5.4.

Lemma 2.5.6. Let F and G be as above. Suppose F is of the form t_1 *or* ⋯ *or* t_k ($k \geq 1$), where each term t_i is a variable, negated variable, or t_i' s principal connective is ***and***. Suppose G is of the form s_1 ***and*** ⋯ ***and*** s_l ($l \geq 1$), where each term s_j is a variable, negated variable, or s_j' s principal connective is ***or***. If F≡G, then k=1 or l=1.

Proof. Suppose k>1 and F≡G. Let x ∈ **Var**[t_1]. Let y be a variable occurring in F such that

$$y \notin \mathrm{Var}[t_1] \text{ and } \exists j \text{ with } x,y \in \mathrm{Var}[s_j].$$

If no such x and y exist, then l=1. Without loss of generality, we assume that both x and y occur uncomplemented in F. Then, there is a term σ of any E[G] such that x,y ∈ Var[σ]. By Lemma 2.5.4, there is an assignment **w** of values form {0,1} to the variables such that

$$\mathbf{w}[\sigma] = 1 \text{ but } \mathbf{w}[\tau] = 0 \text{ for all other terms } \tau \text{ of E[G]}.$$

Since F≡G by assumption, **w**[F]=1. But **w**[F]=1 iff ∃i, $1 \leq i \leq k$, such that

$$\mathbf{w} \mid_{\mathrm{Var}[t_1]} [t_1] = 1, \ldots, \text{ or } \mathbf{w} \mid_{\mathrm{Var}[t_k]} [t_k] = 1.$$

Let k_0 be such an i. Let **w**' be the assignment of values from {0,1} to the variables such that

i. for all z ∉ **Var**[σ], **w**' [z] = w[z];

ii. for all z ∈ **Var**[t_{k_0}], **w**' [z] = w[z]; and

iii. **w**' [l] = 0 for all other literals in σ.

Since x ∈ **Var**[t_1] and y ∉ **Var**[t_1], there is at least one literal (namely, x or y) satisfying iii, whose value is not forced by i or ii. Then, $\mathbf{w}[F] = 1 = \mathbf{w} \mid_{\mathrm{Var}[t_{k_0}]} [t_{k_0}] = \mathbf{w}'[F]$. But, $\mathbf{w}'[G] = 0$, a contradiction.

Lemma 2.5.7. Let F and G be as above. Suppose that F is of the form t_1 *or* ⋯ *or* t_k ($k \geq 2$), where each t_i is either a variable, a negated variable, or t_i' s principal connective is ***and***. Suppose that G is of the form s_1 *or* ⋯ *or* s_l ($l \geq 2$), where each s_j is either a variable, a negated variable, or s_j' s principal connective is ***and***. If F≡G, then k=l and ∃a bijection σ: {1,...,k} → {1,...,k} such that, for $1 \leq i \leq k$, $t_i = s_{\sigma(i)}$.

Lemma 2.5.8. The Dual of Lemma 2.5.7.

By 2.5.1 - 2.5.8, two such formulas F and G are equivalent iff they are identical up to commutativity and associativity of ***and*** and of ***or***. But this can easily be determined deterministically in polynomial time by recursive application of Lemmas 2.5.7 and 2.5.8.

Figure 1. The Construction of the Scheme S_F.

S_{x_i} is

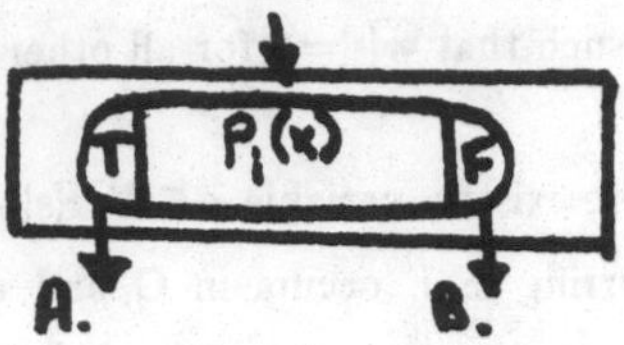

$S_{(F_1 \text{ or } F_2)}$ is

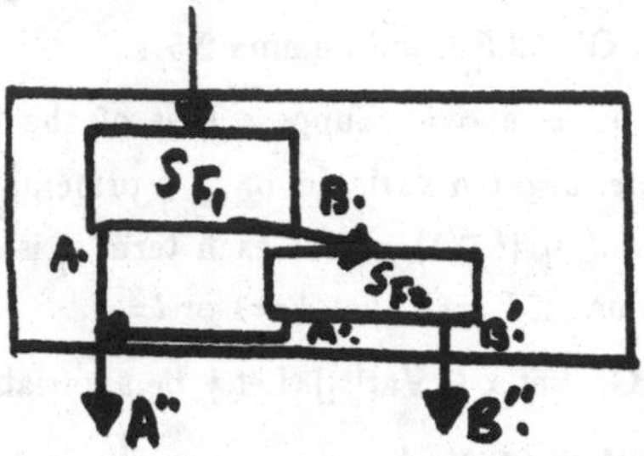

$S_{(F_1 \text{ and } F_2)}$ is

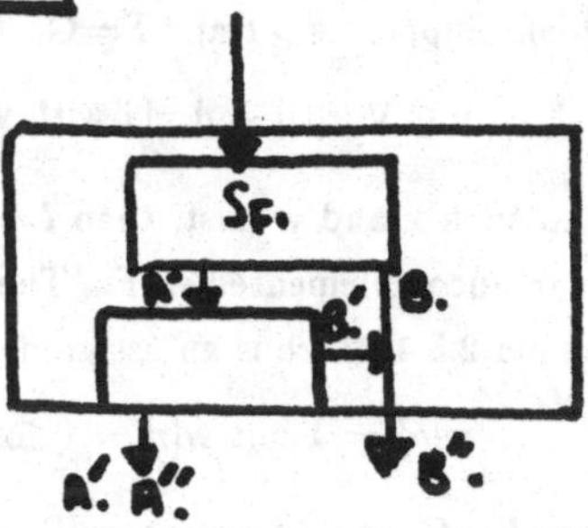

Figure 2. The Schemes S_F' and S_G'.

S_F' :

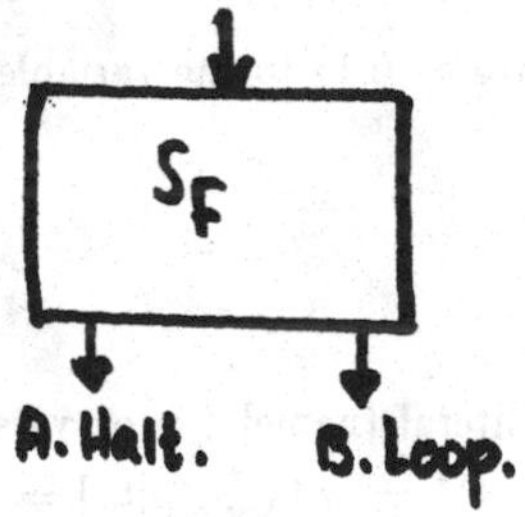

S_G' :

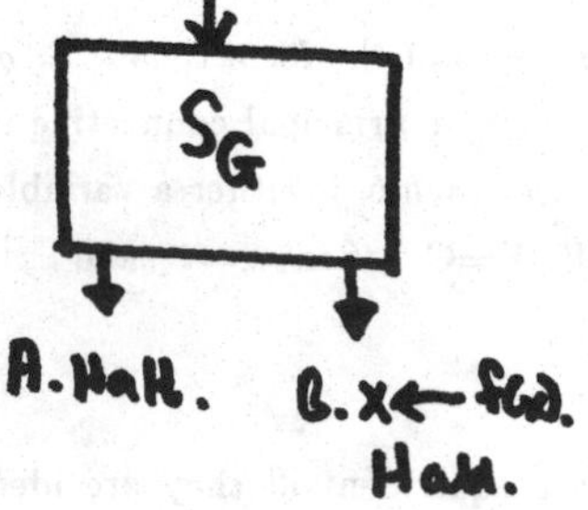

CONCURRENT CONCISENESS OF DEGREE, PROBABILISTIC, NONDETERMINISTIC AND DETERMINISTIC FINITE AUTOMATA* - Extended Abstract -

C.M.R. Kintala
AT&T Bell Laboratories
Murray Hill, N. J.
U.S.A.

Detlef Wotschke
J. W. Goethe-Universität
Fachbereich Informatik
6000 Frankfurt/Main
West-Germany

Abstract

The conciseness of degree automata (nondeterministic finite automata with a specified acceptance degree) and probabilistic automata over both nondeterministic and deterministic finite automata is investigated. In particular, we exhibit a class of languages for which degree automata are at least polynomially more concise than the equivalent nondeterministic automata. We show that there is no function which bounds the conciseness of probabilistic automata with isolated cut-points over nondeterministic or degree automata. The *concurrent conciseness* of probabilistic automata and degree automata over nondeterministic and deterministic automata is also studied.

1. Introduction

In their paper on economies of description by automata, Meyer and Fischer [5] have exhibited a class of languages $\{A_n | n \geq 1\}$ such that, for each n, there is a n-state nondeterministic finite automaton accepting A_n but for which the equivalent minimal deterministic finite automaton has 2^n states. Thus, for certain classes of languages, nondeterministic finite automata, NFA, provide 2^n-concise descriptions over deterministic automata, DFA. Schmidt [8] proved the $2^{c_1 \cdot \sqrt{n}}$-conciseness of NFA over unambiguous finite automata, UFA. The conciseness of degree automata, DA [9] (NFA with a specified acceptance degree), and probabilistic automata, PA [6], is investigated in this paper.

* This work was supported in part by the National Science Foundation under Grant No. MCS76-10076A01 and by "Deutsche Forschungsgemeinschaft" under Grant No. Wo334/1-1 while the second author was visiting the Pennsylvania State University.

After the preliminaries and definitions in Section 2, we prove the polynomial-conciseness of DA over NFA in Section 3. Since any degree-automaton with n-states is equivalent to a deterministic automaton with at most 2^n states, we observe from this conciseness result that degree automata are a 'natural' extension of nondeterministic automata, at least from the standpoint of conciseness. In Section 4, we study the conciseness of PA and show that there is no function which bounds the conciseness of PA with isolated cutpoints over DA or NFA.

In Section 5, we will introduce the concept of *concurrent conciseness*. Concurrent conciseness is an important generalization of 'simple' conciseness for the following reasons. Assume that we have three classes of automata C_1, C_2 and C_3. One is often able to prove the conciseness of C_2 over C_1, using a sequence of languages $\{A_n\}$, and the conciseness of C_3 over C_2, using a sequence of languages $\{B_n\}$. The problem is that $\{A_n\}$ and $\{B_n\}$ have often very little in common since $\{A_n\}$ exploits the advantages of C_2 over C_1 and $\{B_n\}$ exploits the advantages of C_3 over C_2. Concurrent conciseness addresses the question whether there is *one* sequence of languages which concurrently establishes the conciseness of C_2 over C_1 and that of C_3 over C_2. We will, in Sections 5 and 6, prove results on concurrent conciseness between the following classes of automata: PA, DA, NFA and DFA. In Section 7, we will summarize, in the form of a table, the upper and worst-case lower bounds for the conciseness of the classes of automata discussed in this paper.

Our results are also interesting in light of the observations that probabilistic algorithms provide 'fast methods' to solve some 'seemingly intractable' problems with a large degree of confidence in their answers [7]. Likewise, our results dealing with the *descriptional* complexity of probabilistic and degree automata constitute the logical counterpart to the results on the *computational* complexity of these machines [1,2,3].

2. Preliminaries

We assume that the reader is familiar with the standard definitions of a *nondeterministic finite automaton*, *nfa*, $M = (Q,\Sigma,\delta,q_0,F)$, a configuration (q,x) of M for $q \in Q$ and $x \in \Sigma^*$, and the language $T(M)$ accepted by M. M is a *deterministic finite automaton*, dfa, if for all $q \in Q$ and $a \in \Sigma$, $\delta(q,a)$ contains at most one element. Note that we do not require the deterministic automata to be completely specified. M is said to be an *unambiguous finite automaton*, *ufa*, if no word is accepted in more than one way.

<u>Definition</u>: A class of automata C_1 is said to be <u>f-concise</u> over another class C_2 if and only if there is an infinite sequence of languages $\{L_n\}$ such that

(i) for all n, there is a n-state automaton M_n in C_1 accepting L_n

and

(ii) for almost all n, every M in C_2 accepting L_n must have at least f(n) states.

We denote this property by $C_1\text{-}f(n)\rightarrow C_2$. It is already known that

(i) $NFA\text{-}2^n\rightarrow DFA$ [5]

and

(ii) $NFA\text{-}2^{c_1\cdot\sqrt{n}}\rightarrow UFA$ [8] and $UFA\text{-}2^{n-1}\rightarrow DFA$ [5].

We say that C_1 is <u>f,g-concurrently concise</u> over C_2 and C_3, denoted by $C_1\text{-}f(n)\rightarrow C_2\text{-}g(n)\rightarrow C_3$, for some f(n) and g(n), if C_1 is f-concise over C_2 for some sequence of languages and C_2 is g-concise over C_3 for the *same* sequence of languages.

A *degree automaton*, *da*, is a nondeterministic automaton with a specified acceptance degree d, $0\leq d\leq 1$. The language accepted by such a *da* M with degree d is $T(M,d) = \{w \mid |\delta_M(q_0,w)\cap F|/|\delta_M(q_0,w)|>d\}$[1]. Observe that from the point of view of the classes of languages, the degrees *d* need only be rational. Every *nfa* is a *da* with degree 0. Such degree automata and degree languages have been studied with respect to general classes of automata by Wotschke [9]. As was shown there, degree automata for any 'reasonable' class of nondeterministic automata characterize at least all the languages defined by the underlying class of nondeterministic automata and at most their Boolean closure. This means that for the regular case, finite degree automata accept exactly the regular languages. We will show in the next section that DA are at least polynomially-concise over NFA. On the other hand, using a modified subset-construction, we will show that for every *da* with *n* states there exists a *dfa* with at most 2^n states. So DA are a 'natural' extension of NFA.

1 For a finite set S, |S| denotes the number of elements of S

A *probabilistic automaton*, *pa*, is a nondeterministic finite automaton whose transitions are associated with probabilities. Informally, a word w is accepted by such a *pa* M with a *cutpoint* λ, $0 \leq \lambda < 1$, if and only if on input w, starting at the specified initial state, the probability of reaching a final state is greater than λ. Formally, a probabilistic automaton is a pair (M,λ) where λ is cutpoint, $0 \leq \lambda < 1$, and M is a 5-tuple $(Q,\Sigma,\{A(a)|a\in\Sigma\},q_0,F)$ where $Q=\{q_0,q_1,\ldots,q_{k-1}\}$ is a set of k states, Σ is a finite alphabet, $F \subseteq Q$ is the set of final states and $A(a)$ is a stochastic matrix of order k associated with a (a stochastic matrix of order k is a matrix $[a_{ij}]$ of size $k \times k$ such that $0 \leq a_{ij} \leq 1$ and $\sum_j a_{ij} = 1$ for all i.). If $x \in \Sigma^*$ such that $x = a_1 a_2 \ldots a_n$, then $A(x) = A(a_1)(a_2)\ldots A(a_n)$. Suppose $A(x)=[a_{ij}(x)]$. Then $a_{ij}(x)$ is the probability that the automaton, being in state q_i, will go to state q_j on input x. If $F = \{q_{i_1},\ldots,q_{i_s}\}$, let U_F denote the column vector of size k containing 1's at the positions $i_1,\ldots,i_s$ and 0's elsewhere. Let U_0 denote the unit-row vector [1 0 0..0] of size k. Then, for all $x \in \Sigma^*$, define $P_M(x)=U_0 A(x) U_F$. $P_M(x)$ is the probability that M will reach a final state on the string x starting at state q_0. The language accepted by such a *pa* (M,λ) is $T(M,\lambda) = \{w | P_M(w) > \lambda\}$. The following example from Paz [6] plays a central role in the theory of probabilistic automata and will yield the first conciseness result:

Example: Let $M = (\{q_0,q_1\},\{0,1\},\{A(0),A(1)\},q_0,\{q_1\})$ where $A(0)=\begin{vmatrix} 1 & 0 \\ \frac{1}{2} & \frac{1}{2} \end{vmatrix}$ and $A(1) = \begin{vmatrix} \frac{1}{2} & \frac{1}{2} \\ 0 & 1 \end{vmatrix}$.

In the above example, it is easy to see that for $x = a_1 \ldots a_k, P_M(x) = .a_k \ldots a_1$ in binary representation. So if $0<\lambda_1<\lambda_2<1$, then $T(M,\lambda_1) \neq T(M,\lambda_2)$. Since there are nondenumerably many such λ, this example shows the existence of a *pa* accepting nonregular sets.

Paz also shows that, for the above M, $T(M,\lambda)$ is regular if and only if λ is a rational number. Hence this example shows the existence of an infinite sequence of 2-state *pa's* for which the number of states in the equivalent *dfa* (or *nfa*) is not bounded. In light of the fact that PA accept non-regular languages, this result might not be too surprising. However, Rabin [6] has shown that PA with isolated cutpoints accept all and only the regular sets. More specifically, let (M,λ) be a *pa*. For a given $\epsilon>0$, the cutpoint λ is ϵ-isolated with respect to M if $|P_M(x)-\lambda| \geq \epsilon$ for all $x \in \Sigma^*$. Rabin proved the following:

If λ is an ϵ-isolated cutpoint for a *pa* (M,λ), then there exists a *dfa* N such that $T(M,\lambda) = T(N)$. Moreover, if M has m states, then N can be chosen to have n states where $n \leq (1+\frac{1}{2\epsilon})^{m-1}$.

We will exhibit, in Section 4, an infinite sequence of languages for which there exist 2-state *pa's* with isolated cutpoints, but for which the smallest equivalent *nfa's* have no bound on their size. This implies that the 'isolation gap', ϵ, in Rabin's theorem is a quantity which plays an essential role in determining the upper bound for converting a *pa* with an isolated cutpoint into a *dfa*. Observe also that the examples used by Paz do not have isolated cutpoints. We will investigate the concurrent conciseness of DA over NFA and DFA in Section 5, and that of PA over NFA and DFA in Section 6.

3. Conciseness of Degree Automata

For each $n>1$, define a language B_n over the alphabet $\{a,b,c,r\}$ as:

$B_n = \{w \mid w = w_0 r w_1 r w_2 \ldots w_{k-1} r w_k$ for *some* $k\geq 0$;
for *each* $0\leq i\leq k$, *the following holds:*
(i) $w_i \in \{a,b,c\}^*$,
(ii) if $w_i = xyz$ for *some* y, $|y| = n$,
then $y = uav$ and $y = u'bv'$ for *some* $u,v,u',v'\}$.

Intuitively, in each w_i of w as above, every substring of length n must contain at least one occurrence of 'a' and at least one occurrence of 'b'. The symbol 'r' acts like a 'reset character'.

Lemma 3.1: B_n can be accepted by an n^2+1-state *dfa*.
For the proof, the reader is referred to [4].

Since a and b are two distinct symbols in the above language, we expect that any finite automaton, deterministic or not, must internally keep two separate counters for the non-a and non-b characters, each counter capable of counting at least n different values. The following lemma is a formal counterpart to that intuition.

Lemma 3.2: Any nondeterministic automaton accepting B_n must have at least n^2 states.

Proof: Suppose N is a *nfa* accepting B_n. We shall construct a fixed string $w\in B_n$ and exhibit n^2 different positions in w in such a way that any *nfa* correctly accepting B_n must be in distinct states at those positions during an accepting computation on w. Otherwise, if at any two of these positions the *nfa* is in the same state then we can either repeat the subword between these two states or we can delete it, producing, in both instances, a word which would be accepted by the *nfa* but which, in at least one instance, is not in B_n. For each possible pair (i,j), $0\leq i, j\leq n-1$, define w_{ij} and v_{ij} as below:

case (i) $i>j: w_{ij} = c^{i-j-1}bc^{j}$ and $v_{ij} = c^{n-i-1}ac^{i-j-1}r$

case (ii) $j>i: w_{ij} = c^{j-i-1}ac^{i}$ and $v_{ij} = c^{n-j-1}bc^{j-i-1}r$

case (iii) $i=j: w_{ij} = c^{i}$ and $v_{ij} = c^{n-i-1}r$.

Let $w = \prod_{i=0}^{n-1}\prod_{j=0}^{n-1} w_{ij}v_{ij}$, where Π denotes the iterated concatenation of the strings defined over the specified indices. The idea is to force the machine N to go to a state equivalent to state (i,j) of the *dfa* M_n after reading w_{ij} from w, for all possible i,j. The strings v_{ij} are so designed that in $w_{ij}v_{ij}$ the number of non-a characters before the next occurrence of a (or the reset character) is exactly $n-1$, and similarly for b. Observe that w is in B_n and hence there is an accepting computation of N on w. Consider one such computation. Let q_{ij} be the state of N after reading the initial substring of w up to and including w_{ij} in the accepting computation being considered. We will show that all these q_{ij} are distinct. This implies that, since there are n^2 possible such q_{ij}, N must have at least n^2 states. In the remainder of the proof, we will show that these q_{ij} are distinct, i.e. $(g,h)\neq(i,j) \Rightarrow q_{gh}\neq q_{ij}$.

Suppose there exist (g,h) and (i,j) such that the above claim is false. Without loss of generality, decompose w such that $w = xw_{gh}v_{gh}yw_{ij}v_{ij}z$ for some $x,y,z \in \{a,b,c,r\}^*$. Since $q_{gh} = q_{ij}$, by assumption, both $w' = xw_{gh}v_{ij}z$ and $w''=xw_{gh}(v_{gh}yw_{ij})^2v_{ij}z$ must be accepted by N. However, we claim that either w' or w'' does not belong to B_n, since, as the reader can easily verify,

(1) in the string $w_{gh}v_{ij}$, the number of non-a (non-b) characters before an occurence of a (b), or the reset character r, is $n-1+g-i$ ($n-1+h-j$, respectively), and

(2) in the string $w_{ij}v_{gh}$, the number of non-a (non-b) characters before an occurrence of a (b), or the reset character r, is $n-1+i-g$ ($n-1+j-h$, respectively).

Since $(g,h)\neq(i,j)$, one of the following expressions $g-i, i-g, h-j$ or $j-h$ must be greater than zero. So $w_{gh}v_{ij}$ or $w_{ij}v_{gh}$ cannot be a substring in any string belonging to B_n and hence w' or w'' is not in B_n, but both are accepted by N, a contradiction. □

However, the following lemma shows that there exists a considerably more concise *da* accepting B_n.

<u>Lemma 3.3</u>: B_n can be accepted by a $2n+2$-state degree automaton with an acceptance degree of $\frac{1}{2}$.

<u>Proof</u>: The reader can verify that the following $2n+2$-state degree automaton S_n accepts B_n.

$S_n = (Q, \Sigma, \delta, q_0, F)$ where
$Q = \{q_0, a_0, \ldots, a_{n-1}, b_0, \ldots, b_{n-1}, TRAP\}$, $\Sigma = \{a,b,c,r\}$, $F = Q-\{TRAP\}$,
and δ is defined as:

$$\begin{aligned}
\delta\,(q_0,r) &= \{q_0\}\\
\delta\,(q_0,a) &= \{a_0,b_1\}\\
\delta\,(q_0,b) &= \{a_1,b_0\}\\
\delta\,(q_0,c) &= \{a_1,b_1\}\\
\delta\,(a_i,\sigma) &= \{a_{i+1}\} \text{ for } i = 0,\ldots,n-2;\ \sigma\in\{b,c\}\\
\delta\,(a_i,\sigma) &= \{a_0\} \text{ for } i = 0,\ldots,n-1;\ \sigma\in\{a,r\}\\
\delta\,(a_{n-1},\sigma) &= \{TRAP\} \text{ for } \sigma\in\{b,\sigma\}\\
\delta\,(b_i,\sigma) &= \{b_{i+1}\} \text{ for } i = 0,\ldots,n-2;\ \sigma\in\{a,c\}\\
\delta\,(b_i,\sigma) &= \{b_0\} \text{ for } i = 0,\ldots,n-1;\ \sigma\in\{b,r\}\\
\delta\,(b_{n-1},\sigma) &= \{\text{TRAP}\} \text{ for } \sigma\in\{a,c\}\\
\delta\,(\text{TRAP},\sigma) &= \{\text{TRAP}\} \text{ for } \sigma\in\Sigma.
\end{aligned}$$

Acceptance degree: $d = \frac{1}{2}$.

Informally, states $b_0, b_1, \ldots, b_{n-1}$ of the above automaton accept strings in which every substring of length n has an occurrence of b or r and, similarly, states $a_0, a_1, \ldots, a_{n-1}$ accept strings in which every substring of length n has an occurrence of a or r. A straightforward combination of these two parts gives rise to a nondeterministic machine (i.e. a degree automaton with acceptance degree 0) accepting the union of these two sets. However, the combined machine with an acceptance degree $\frac{1}{2}$ will accept the intersection of those two sets which is equal to B_n. This is because every string ends up in at most two accepting states. □

The above *da* together with Lemma 3.2 proves the following theorem on conciseness of DA over NFA.

Theorem 3.4: DA-$c \cdot n^2$→NFA, where $c \cong \frac{1}{2}$.

The construction in Lemma 3.3 leads to the following generalization which we claim without proof.

Lemma 3.5: Let $M_1 \ldots, M_k$ be k *dfas* with $n_1, \ldots, n_k$ states respectively. Then there exists a *da* M' with $\sum_{i=1}^{k} n_i + 2$ states such that $T(M', \lambda) = \bigcap_{i=1}^{k} T(M_i)$ for any λ with $\frac{k-1}{k} < \lambda < 1$.

Likewise, the definition of the languages $\{B_n\}$ can be generalized to prove the following:

Lemma 3.6: There exist k *dfa's* $M_1, \ldots, M_k$ with n states each, such that every *nfa* M' with $T(M') = \bigcap_{i=1}^{k} T(M_i)$ needs at least n^k states.

The previous two lemmas together lead to the following generalization of Theorem 3.4:

Theorem 3.7: DA-$c.n^k$→NFA, where c is $\cong \frac{1}{k}$.

Since DA can be at least polynomially concise over NFA, the immediate question that arises is whether DA can be more than exponentially concise over DFA. The following theorem answers this question in the negative.

Theorem 3.8: For any *da* with n states, there exists an equivalent *dfa* with at most 2^n states.

Proof: see [4].

Observe that the acceptance degree in the entire sequence of *da's* for $\{B_n\}$ in Lemma 3.3 and for the one in Lemma 3.5 is a constant. Thus the acceptance degree, in terms of size, is only an additive constant. One therefore could *not* argue that the real reason for DA being so much more concise than NFA is that substantial, and growing along the sequence, information is encoded into the acceptance degrees. The observations in this section make us believe that finite degree automata are a 'natural' generalization of nondeterministic finite automata.

4. Conciseness of Probabilistic Automata

For $n \geq 2$, let $C_n = \{w \mid w \in \{a,b\}^*$ *and w has at most n occurrences of a*$\}$.

Lemma 4.1: There is a 2-state *pa* T_n which accepts C_n with an isolated cutpoint of $\frac{1}{2}$.

Proof: see [4].

The isolation gap ϵ_n in the previous lemma becomes smaller with increasing n, and the transition probabilities depend on n whereas the cutpoint is a constant. On the other hand, there exists a 2-state *pa* for C_n with constant transition probabilities and where the cutpoint λ depends on n. For details the reader is referred to [4]. In this automaton, both the cutpoint and the isolation gap become smaller with increasing n. It would be interesting to study the trade-offs between the representation lengths of the cutpoints and transition probabilities in general. It is easy to construct a $(n+1)$-state *dfa* accepting C_n.

Lemma 4.2: Every *nfa* accepting C_n must have at least $n+1$ states.

Proof: See [4].

Lemma 4.3: Every *da* accepting C_n must have at least $log(n+1)$ states.

Proof: See [4].

Remark: It is not clear whether there exists a *da* with only $\lceil log(n+1) \rceil$ states accepting C_n.
The above three lemmas prove the following:

Theorem 4.4: There is no function $f(n)$ which can bound the conciseness of PA over DA and also that of PA over NFA, even when the PA are restricted to having only isolated cutpoints.

The reader will notice that the unbounded conciseness of PA over DA and over NFA results from the fact that substantial and increasing information can be encoded into the cutpoints or the transition probabilities in PA. In contrast, this encoding was not necessary for showing the conciseness of DA over NFA in Section 3.

5. Concurrent Conciseness of Degree Automata

We study the concurrent conciseness of DA over NFA and DFA in this section. The main observation is that if a sequence $\{B_n\}$ establishes the conciseness of DA over NFA and if another sequence $\{D_n\}$ establishes the conciseness of NFA over DFA, then a marked union of those two sequences is a 'candidate' for establishing the concurrent conciseness of DA over NFA and DFA. For $n,m \geq 2$, let $E_{n,m} = d_1B_n \cup d_2D_m$ where d_1 and d_2 are two new symbols, B_n is as defined in Section 3, and $D_m = \{w | w \in \{0,1\}^*1\{0,1\}^{m-1}\}$.
Lemma 3.3 provides a $2n+2$-state *da* S_n with acceptance degree ½ for B_n. One can construct a *da* R_m with $2m+3$ states and acceptance degree ½ for D_m as follows:

$R_m = (Q,\{0,1\},\delta, r_o,F)$ where
$Q = \{r_0,r_1,\ldots,r_m,r_{m+1},\ldots,r_{2m+1}, TRAP\}$, $F=\{r_m,r_{m+1},\ldots,r_{2m+1}\}$,

and δ is defined as

$\delta(r_0,0) = \{r_0\}$, $\delta(r_0,1) = \{r_0,r_1\}$
$\delta(r_i,\sigma) = \{r_{i+1}\}$ for $i = 1,n\S\ldots,m-2$; $\sigma\in\{0,1\}$
$\delta(r_{m-1},\sigma) = \{r_m,r_{m+1},\ldots,r_{2m+1}\}$; $\sigma\in\{0,1\}$
$\delta(r_i,\sigma) = \{TRAP\}$ for $i = m,m+1,\ldots,2m+1$; $\sigma\in\{0,1\}$
$\delta(TRAP,\sigma) = \{TRAP\}$ for $\sigma\in\{0,1\}$.

Observe that, for all $w \in D_m$, $\delta_{R_m}(q_0,w) \cap F = F$ and, for all $w \notin D_m$, $\delta_{R_m}(q_0,w) \cap F = \emptyset$.

Since, for all $w \in D_m$, $\dfrac{|\delta_{R_m}(q_0,w) \cap F|}{|\delta_{R_m}(q_0,w)|} \geq \dfrac{|F|}{|Q|} = \dfrac{m+2}{2m+3} > \frac{1}{2}$, $T(R_m,\frac{1}{2}) = D_m$.

Combining S_n and R_m by creating a new starting state for the first transition on the symbols d_1 or d_2 and by merging the *TRAP* states of these two machines, we can construct a *da*, $P_{n,m}$, for $E_{n,m}$. For details the reader is referred to [4]. $P_{n,m}$ has $2n+2m+5$ states and its acceptance degree is $\frac{1}{2}$.

Lemma 5.1: $P_{n,m}$ accepts $E_{n,m}$ correctly.

Proof: See [4].

We thus have a $(2n+2m+5)$-state *da* $P_{n,m}$ for $E_{n,m}$. Using the construction in Lemma 3.1, it is possible to construct a (n^2+m+3)-state *nfa* to accept $E_{n,m}$. Lemma 3.2 has shown that any *nfa* accepting B_n must have at least n^2 states.

Lemma 5.2: Every *nfa* accepting D_m must have at least $m+1$ states.

Proof: See [4].

Lemma 5.3: Any completely specified *nfa* accepting $E_{n,m}$ must have at least n^2+m+1 states.

Proof: See [4].

It is also easy to construct a (n^2+2^m+2)-state *dfa* accepting $E_{n,m}$. Lemma 3.2 shows also that any *dfa* accepting B_n must have at least n^2 states. It is easy to show that any *dfa* accepting D_m must have at least 2^m states.

Lemma 5.4: Any *dfa* accepting $E_{n,m}$ must have at least (n^2+2^m) states.

Proof: Analogous to the proof of the previous lemma. □

Combining Lemmas 5.3 and 5.4, we have the following theorem on concurrent conciseness of DA over NFA and DFA.

Theorem 5.5: There are constants, c_1, c_2 and c_3, and a sequence of languages E'_n $n\geq 2$, such that

(i) there is a *da* accepting E'_n having only $c_1\cdot n$ states,

(ii) there is a *nfa* accepting E'_n having $c_2\cdot n^2$ states, and every *nfa* accepting E'_n must have at least n^2+n+1 states

and

(iii) there is a *dfa* accepting E'_n having $c_3\cdot 2^n$ states, and every *dfa* accepting E'_n must have at least 2^n+n^2 states.

Proof: Choose $E'_n = E_{n,n}$ where $E_{n,m}$ is as defined earlier. □

A generalization of the above theorem establishes the concurrent conciseness of DA over NFA and DFA: for each $k\geq 2$, there exist constants, c_1 and c_2, and a sequence of languages for which

$$\text{DA}-c_1\cdot n^k \rightarrow \text{NFA}-2^{c_2\cdot n^{\frac{1}{k}}} \rightarrow \text{DFA}$$

6. Concurrent Conciseness of Probabilistic Automata

We shall establish the concurrent conciseness of probabilistic automata with isolated cutpoints over NFA and DFA. To do this, we attempted at first to modify the proofs in the previous section in a straightforward manner without success. This reinforced our observation in Section 4 that the cutpoints in probabilistic automata play a subtle and crucial role. We change the language D_m, used in the previous section, to establish the concurrent conciseness in this section. For $n,m\geq 2$, let $F_{n,m} = cC_n \cup dD'_m$ where c and d are new symbols, C_n is as defined in Section 4, and

$D'_m = \{w1x \mid w,x\in\{0,1\}^*;\ w \text{ has at most } (m-1)\ 1\text{'s and } |x|=m-1\}$.

A 2-state *pa*, T_n, for C_n is given in Lemma 4.1. As is shown in [4] , one can construct a $(2m+1)$-state *pa* R'_m for D'_m. As cutpoint we choose $\delta=0$ which is isolated. Combing T_n and R'_m, we can construct a *pa*, $U_{n,m}$, for $F_{n,m}$, where the isolated cutpoint for $U_{n,m}$ is $\frac{1}{2}$. $U_{n,m}$ has $2m+4$ states including a *'TRAP'* state for the unspecified transitions.

Lemma 6.1: $U_{n,m}$ correctly accepts $F_{n,m}$.

For the proof, the reader is referred to [4].

We thus have a $(2m+4)$-state *pa* $U_{n,m}$ for $F_{n,m}$. It is easy to construct a $(n+2m+3)$-state *nfa* to accept $F_{n,m}$. Lemma 4.2 has shown that any *nfa* accepting C_n must have at least $(n+1)$ states.

Lemma 6.2.: Every *nfa* accepting D'_m must have at least $2m$ states.

Proof: See [4].

Lemma 6.3: Any completely specified *nfa* accepting $F_{n,m}$ must have at least $n+2m+1$ states.

Proof: See [4].

D'_m can be accepted by the $2^m\cdot(m+1)$-state *dfa* $M = (Q,\{0,1\}\delta,q_0,\lambda,F\subset Q)$ where

$Q = \{q_{i,x} \mid 0\leq i\leq m-1; x\in\{0,1\}^*; |x|\leq m;$ and if $|x|<m$ then $i=0\}\cup\{TRAP\}$,

$F = \{q_{i,x} \mid |x|=m$ and $x=1u$ for some $u\}$

and δ is defined as follows:

for all x with $|x|<m$ and for all $a\in\{0,1\}$: $\delta(q_{0,x},a) = q_{0,xa}$;

for all x with $|x|=m$ and for all $a\in\{0,1\}$: if $x=1u$ for some u then,

if $i+1\leq m-1$, $\delta(q_{i,1u},a) = q_{i+1,ua}$ and $\delta(q_{i,1u},a) = TRAP$ otherwise,

if $x=0u$ for some u then $\delta(q_{i,0u},a) = q_{i,ua}$.

Using this machine, it is easy to construct a $(n+2^m\cdot(m+1)+2)$-state *dfa* accepting $F_{n,m}$. Lemma 4.2 shows also that any *dfa* accepting C_n must have at least $n+1$ states.

Lemma 6.4: Any *dfa* accepting D'_m must have at least 2^m states.

Proof: Suppose that D is a *dfa* accepting D'_m. Consider any two strings $u,v \in \{0,1\}^*$ such that $|u| = |v| = m$ and $u \neq v$. We claim that $\delta(q_0,u) \neq \delta(q_0,v)$. Otherwise, if $\delta(q_0,u) = \delta(q_0,v)$, let $u = w1x$ and $v = w'0x$ for some w, w' and x. The words w and w' have at most $(m-1)$ 1's. Then consider the two strings $u0^k$ and $v0^k$ where $k = m-1-|x|$. $u0^k$ is in D'_m by definition and hence should be accepted by D. Then, by the assumption in this proof, $v0^k$ will also be accepted by D leading to a contradiction because $v0^k$ is not in D'_m. Since there are 2^m such strings of length m, D must have at least 2^m states. □

Lemma 6.5: Any *dfa* accepting $F_{n,m}$ must have at least $(n+2^m+1)$ states.

Proof: Analogous to the proof of Lemma 6.3. □

Combining Lemmas 6.3 and 6.5, we have the following theorem on concurrent conciseness of PA with isolated cutpoints over NFA and DFA.

Theorem 6.6: For any monotonically increasing function $g(n)$ such that $n \leq g(n) << 2^n$, there are constants, c_1, c_2, c'_2, c_3, c'_3, and a sequence of languages $F'_n, n \geq 2$, such that

(i) there is a *pa*, with an isolated cutpoint, accepting F'_n having only $c_1 \cdot n$ states,

(ii) there is a *nfa* accepting F'_n having $c_2 \cdot g(n)$ states, and every *nfa* accepting F'_n must have at least $c'_2 \cdot g(n)$ states

and

(iii) there is a *dfa* accepting F'_n having $c_3 \cdot n \cdot 2^n$ states and every *dfa* accepting F'_n must have at least $c'_3 \cdot 2^n$ states.

Proof: Choose $F'_n = F_{g(n),n}$ where $F_{n,m}$ is as defined earlier. □

The above theorem establishes the following concurrent conciseness of PA with isolated cutpoints over NFA and DFA: For $g(n)$ as defined before, there are constants c_1 and c_2 such that

$$\text{PA-}c_1 \cdot g(n) \rightarrow \text{NFA-}2^{c_2 \cdot g^{-1}(n)} \rightarrow \text{DFA}.$$

By taking a marked union of B_n, C_m and D'_p, it is possible to prove the following stronger result on concurrent conciseness.

Theorem 6.7: For a given $k \geq 2$ and any monotonically increasing function $g(n) \geq n$ such that $g(n) << n^k$, there exist constants c_1, c_2 and c_3 such that

$$\text{PA-}c_1 \cdot g(n) \rightarrow \text{DA-}c_2 \cdot (g^{-1}(n))^k \rightarrow \text{NFA-}2^{c_3 \cdot (g^{-1}(n))^{\frac{1}{k}}} \rightarrow \text{DFA}.$$

7. Summary

We summarize our results from Sections 3 and 4 and the related results from the literature by the matrix in Figure 7.1. The *upper* triangle of the matrix represents *upper* bounds, the *lower* triangle of the matrix represents *lower* bounds. Specifically, the entry $[i,j]$, for $j>i$, contains the upper bound for converting a device in class i to a device in class j; and the entry $[i,j]$, for $i>j$, contains the worst-case lower bound for converting a device in class j to a device in class i.

	PA	*PA*(isol)	*DA*	*NFA*	*UFA*	*DFA*
PA	-	?	unbounded	unbounded	unbounded	unbounded
PA(isol)	?	-	$\leq(1+\frac{1}{2\epsilon})^{n-1}$!	$\leq(1+\frac{1}{2\epsilon})^{n-1}$!	$\leq(1+\frac{1}{2\epsilon})^{n-1}$!	$\leq(1+\frac{1}{2\epsilon})^{n-1}$
DA	$f(n)$	$f(n)$	-	$\leq 2^n$!	$\leq 2^n$!	$\leq 2^n$
NFA	$f(n)$	$f(n)$	$\geq c.n^k$	-	$\leq 2^n$!	$\leq 2^n$
UFA	$f(n)$	$f(n)$	$\geq 2^{c.\sqrt{n}}$	$\geq 2^{c.\sqrt{n}}$	-	$\leq 2^n$
DFA	$f(n)$	$f(n)$	$\geq 2^n$!	$\geq 2^n$	$\geq 2^{n-1}$	-

<u>Figure 7.1</u>: *PA*(isol) represents *PA* with isolated cutpoints. $f(n)$ represents any arbitrary function. The isolation gap is denoted by ϵ, c is a constant and k is an arbitrary positive integer.

With the exception of PA with isolated cutpoints, this matrix is based on the obvious, implicit hierarchy. A device of a class further to the right or further below is also a device (or can be trivially transformed into, by adding at most one state) of a class further to the left or further to the top. For example, every *ufa* is also a *nfa*, every *nfa* can be easily transformed into a *pa*. Since PA with isolated cutpoints do not fit into this pattern, the corresponding row and column are set off by double-lines against the others.

Therefore, while excluding PA with isolated cutpoints, we obtain the following 'propagation mechanism' for the upper and lower bound results: *upper* bounds propagate from *right to left* along a row and from *top to bottom* along a column in the upper triangle of the matrix, and likewise for the lower bounds in the lower triangle of the matrix. An entry in the matrix without an exclamation mark represents a bound explicitly proved for that case. An entry with an exclamation mark represents a bound derived via the 'propagation mechanism'. An entry consisting of a question mark indicates that no bound is known yet.

The reader will notice some apparent contradictions between several pairs of entries; for example between the lower bound in [NFA,PA(*isol*)] and the upper bound in [PA(*isol*),NFA]. These contradictions can be easily resolved by observing that the lower bounds are functions of n alone, whereas the upper bounds in those pairs are functions of n and ϵ, the isolation gap. This observation also suggests the study of the trade-offs between the transition probabilities, the cutpoints and the isolation gaps, about all of which very little is known so far.

Summarizing our results from Sections 5 and 6 on Concurrent Conciseness, we observe that for many classes of automata C_1, C_2 and C_3 in 'ascending' order (i.e. C_{i+1} is at least as concise as C_i) the following holds: even though it is not possible to widen the conciseness gap between C_3 and C_1, one can, within the overall bounds, *arbitrarily* increase (decrease) the trade-off between C_2 and C_1 and, at the same time, decrease (increase) the trade-off between C_3 and C_2 such that the two trade-offs add up to roughly the total trade-off between C_3 and C_1.

References

[1] Freivalds, R.: "Probabilistic machines can use less running time", IFIP77, North-Holland, Amsterdam, 1977, pp 839-842.

[2] Gill, J. III: "Computational Complexity of Probabilistic Turing Machines", SIAM *J. of Computing*, Vol. 6, No. 4, 1977, pp 675-695.

[3] Gill, J. III, H. Hunt, and J. Simon: "Deterministic Simulation of Probabilistic Turing Machine Transducers", *Theoretical Computer Science*, Vol. 12, No. 3, 1980, pp 333-338.

[4] Kintala, C.M.R. and D. Wotschke: "Concurrent Conciseness of Degree, Probabilistic, Nondeterministic and Deterministic Finite Automata", *Technical Report*, 1985.

[5] Meyer, A.R. and M.J. Fischer: "Economy of Description by Automata, Grammars and Formal Systems", *Proc. of the 12th IEEE Symp. on Switching and Automata Theory*, 1971, pp 188-190.

[6] Paz, A.: "Introduction to Probabilistic Automata", Academic Press, 1971.

[7] Rabin, M.O.: "Probabilistic Algorithms", in J. Traub, Ed., *Algorithms and Complexity: New Directions and Recent Results*, Academic Press, 1976, pp 21-39.

[8] Schmidt, E.M.: "Succinctness of Descriptions of Context-free, Regular, and Finite Languages", Ph. D. Dissertation, Cornell

University, 1977.

[9] Wotschke, D.: "Degree Languages: A New Concept of Acceptance", *J. of Computer and System Sciences*, Vol. 14, No. 2, 1977, pp 187-199.

LOGSPACE HIERARCHIES, POLYNOMIAL TIME AND THE COMPLEXITY OF FAIRNESS PROBLEMS CONCERNING ω-MACHINES

Louis E. Rosier and Hsu-Chun Yen
Department of Computer Sciences
University of Texas at Austin
Austin, TX 78712

1. Introduction

One of the more fundamental tools used in categorizing the complexity of decision problems is the notion of completeness. Most notable, of course, is the class of problems which are NP-complete. See e.g. [6, 10, 16]. Other complexity classes for which abundant numbers of complete problems are known include NLOGSPACE, PTIME, and PSPACE. See e.g. [10, 13-15]. More recently certain natural problems have been shown to be complete for certain complexity classes which are "between" NP and PSPACE. Recent advances here include [1, 23, 24], which tend to consider problems which are complete for various levels of the Polynomial-time Hierarchy [28]. One could also consider the analogous complexity classes for space hierarchies which fall "between" NLOGSPACE and PTIME. Appropriate consideration here then might focus on the *logspace oracle hierarchy* and the *logspace alternation hierarchy* (which is contained in the second level of the logspace oracle hierarchy), which were introduced in [2] and [27].[1] Both of these hierarchies are contained in PTIME ∩ DSPACE($\log^2 n$). Other complexity classes "below" PTIME for which complete problems are known can be found in [5, 20, 25].

In this paper, we define a *restricted logspace oracle hierarchy* (which as we shall later see turns out to be essentially equivalent to the logspace alternation hierarchy of [2]) which is also contained within the second level of the logspace oracle hierarchy. Our restrictions have to do with fixing the number of oracle calls allowed during a computation. We then examine problems concerning various types of "fair" computations with respect to *ω-Finite State Machines* (ω-FSM's), *ω-One Counter Machines* (ω-1CM's) and networks of *Communicating Finite State Machines* (CFSM's). In particular, we consider the non-emptiness problem for ω-FSM's and ω-1CM's where acceptance is defined as in [4, 18] (other acceptance criteria are also considered), but with a fairness constraint imposed on accepting computations. (For a discussion about various types of fairness see e.g. [11, 19].) We consider the problem for seven different types of acceptance criteria and two different types of fairness. (A summary of the derived complexities can be found in Tables 4.1 and 4.2.) Our results yield problems that are complete for NLOGSPACE, the second level of the restricted logspace oracle hierarchy, the third level of the restricted logspace oracle hierarchy, and PTIME. These results, we feel, are interesting for the following reasons:

i. As far as we know, these are the first natural problems which have been shown to be complete for nontrivial levels of the logspace alternation hierarchy of [2].

ii. The problems are also of independent interest. In fact, the non-emptiness problem (with fairness constraints) for ω-machines has been shown to have immediate applications to the verification of concurrent finite-state programs. (See e.g. [29].)

iii. The results can also be used to show that the canonical form model checking problem of [8]

---

[1] These were referred to, in [27], as the log n space "oracle hierarchy" and log n space "alternation hierarchy", respectively.

(see also [21]) is PTIME-complete; and that certain liveness questions [3] concerning networks of CFSM's are either PTIME-hard or complete for the third level of the restricted logspace oracle hierarchy.

Related complexity results concerning questions about fair computations can be found in [7, 8, 9, 21, 29]; while completeness results concerning complexity classes "between" DLOGSPACE and NLOGSPACE can be found in [20]. See also [25].

In what follows, we assume the reader is familiar with the basic tenets of automata and complexity theory. Relevant sources would include [10, 13]. The basic computational model used in this paper is the *nondeterministic offline multitape Turing machine* (NTM). Since this paper concerns itself with many different problems the relevant definitions are introduced in the text as they are needed. For brevity, we sometimes use the terms DL and NL to denote the complexity classes DLOGSPACE and NLOGSPACE, respectively. All completeness classes mentioned in this paper are with respect to deterministic logspace (many-to-one) reductions.

The remainder of the paper is organized as follows. In section 2, we define the restricted logspace oracle hierarchy and in section 3, we illustrate some useful graph problems that are complete for certain levels within this hierarchy. Section 4 concerns itself with the complexity of the non-emptiness problem with respect to ω-FSM's and ω-1CM's. The last section seeks to apply our results to problems considered in [8] and [3].

2. The Restricted Logspace Oracle Hierarchy

In [27], the logspace oracle hierarchy which fell between NSPACE(log n) and PTIME $\cap$ DSPACE($\log^2 n$) was defined. Our intention, in this section, is to see what happens to this hierarchy when constraints are imposed on the OTM's restricting the number of allowable oracle calls made during the course of a computation. In particular, we focus on the case where at most one oracle call is allowed during the course of a computation. What happens is that we obtain a new hierarchy - which we call the restricted logspace oracle hierarchy. We then show that the restricted logspace oracle hierarchy coincides with the logspace alternation hierarchy[2], which was also discussed in [27]. This characterization is potentially useful because when considering problems related to this hierarchy it allows us to provide the analysis using either computational model. Furthermore, this hierarchy has the following interesting property:

> As pointed out in [27], the restricted logspace oracle hierarchy (or the logspace alternation hierarchy), unlike its polynomial time analog, is clearly contained within the second level of the logspace oracle hierarchy.

In subsequent sections, we show that some natural problems concerning the notion of fair computations are complete for certain levels in this hierarchy. This study, we feel, is of interest because it allows us to have more insight into the question whether the inclusion in "NSPACE(log n) $\subseteq$ PTIME" is proper. Results concerning relativized logspace have received broad attention in recent years[17, 22, 27]. Unlike the case with the polynomial-time hierarchy[1, 23], however, little has been done in actually "pigeonholing" natural problems into the logspace hierarchies. The main contribution of this paper will be exactly that; and thus, in some sense, we examine this portion of sublinear space from the problem-oriented point of view.

Informally, an *oracle Turing machine* (OTM, for short) M is a nondeterministic offline multitape Turing machine with an additional write-only tape called a *query tape* and three distinguished states called *query*, *yes* and *no states*. In addition, a set A, called the *oracle set* is always related to the computation of the OTM M. For convenience, we use $L(M^A)$ to denote the language accepted by the OTM M using A as its oracle set (denoted by M^A). The computation of an OTM is similar to that of an ordinary NTM except when visiting the query states. When in a query state, if the string on the query tape is in the oracle set, then the machine enters the yes state; otherwise, it enters the no state. Moreover, the contents of the query tape will be erased immediately upon entering the yes or no state. The machine can write a symbol on the query tape in every state except the query state. We define X^Y to be the complexity class such that for each language L in X^Y, L can be recognized by an OTM M with oracle set A where M operates within the complexity constraints of X and A is in Y.

In order to study the space hierarchy below PTIME, it is natural to define classes like DL^{NL}, NL^{NL},..., etc. Unfortunately, this kind of definition does not seem to be of great interest because when the OTM's are defined as above one obtains $NL^{NL}=NL^{DL}=NP$. That is, the logspace hierarchy jumps into the polynomial-time hierarchy on the second level. As pointed out in [17, 27], this phenomenon occurs because nondeterminism when combined with the ability to write long strings on the query tape, interacts in such a way that the machine's power is boosted dramatically. To limit the undesired boost in the power of the OTM's, [27] required that only strings of logarithmic length could be written on the query tape. However, the query machine was also, in a sense, allowed read access to the input of the oracle machine. More precisely, the string that appears on the query tape at any instance will be of the form x#y, where x (which cannot be altered by the OTM) is a copy of the OTM's input tape, and |y| is O(log|x|). One may consider the string x# to always be on the query tape (i.e., it will not be erased), and only the y part to be alterable during the course of a computation. In this paper, we consider only OTM's of this sort. Using such OTM's, a hierarchy, similar to the polynomial time hierarchy, was defined in [27] as follows: $\Sigma_0^L = DL$, $\Sigma_{k+1}^L = NL^{\Sigma_k^L}$, $\Delta_{k+1}^L = DL^{\Sigma_k^L}$. The following theorem was shown in [27].

Theorem 2.1: $\cup_k \Sigma_k^L \subseteq PTIME \cap DSPACE(\log^2 n)$.

An interesting question now arises when one also restricts the number of oracle calls allowed during the course of a computation. Intuitively, the power of an OTM seems to be enhanced as it is allowed to make more oracle calls. We define the hierarchies $\Sigma_k^{L[1]}$ and $\Delta_k^{L[1]}$ to be the classes where, in each level the OTM, during the course of its computation, is allowed to consult the oracle at most once.

In [2], the alternation logspace hierarchy was introduced based on the model of *alternating Turing machines* (ATM's). Basically the concept of alternation is a generalization of nondeterminism in a way that allows existential and universal quantifiers to alternate during the course of a computation. Four kinds of states exist in an ATM; namely existential, universal, accepting and rejecting states. A universal state can lead to acceptance iff all successors lead to acceptance. On the other hand, an existential state leads to acceptance iff there exists a successor that leads to acceptance. Details can be found in [2]. The complexity classes of languages accepted by time (space) bounded ATM's were also defined in [2]. In particular, $A\Sigma_k^L$ was defined to be the set of languages accepted by log n space-bounded ATM's in which the starting state was an existential state and the machine was constrainted to make at most k-1 alternations during the course of a computation. In what follows, we show that the $A\Sigma_k^L$ hierarchy coincides with the restricted logspace hierarchy $\Sigma_k^{L[1]}$ defined earlier. This characterization proves useful in later sections as both computational models are used in deriving completeness results for various levels of this hierarchy.

By induction one can now show the following theorem. (See [26].)

Theorem 2.2: $\Sigma_k^{L[1]} \equiv A\Sigma_k^L$

In [27], it has been shown that $\cup_k A\Sigma_k^L \subseteq DL^{NL}$. Using Theorem 2.2, we then have that the restricted logspace oracle hierarchy is contained in DL^{NL}.

3. Some Complete Problems

In this section, we introduce some easy graph problems that are complete for $NL^{NL[1]}$. These problems are useful, in the sense, that they will later be used in Sections 4 and 5 as a vehicle to analyze the complexity of problems concerning ω-machines and networks of CFSM's. In what follows, we define the notion of liveness for a graph, and then we show that the problem to decide whether a node in a graph is "not" live is complete for $NL^{NL[1]}$. First, however, the following definitions are required.

An *I-graph* G (or simply a graph if the initial node is clear and understood) consists of a directed graph G=(V,E), where V and E represent the sets of nodes and edges respectively, and there is a unique distinguished node $v_0 \in V$ called the initial node. For two nodes p and q in V, q is said to be *reachable* from p (denoted by $p \overset{*}{\to} q$) iff there exists a sequence of nodes $s_0,s_1,\ldots,s_k$ such that $s_0=p$, $s_k=q$ and for each i, $0 \leq i \leq k-1$, $s_i \in V$ and the edge (s_i, s_{i+1}) is in E. We use $p \overset{+}{\to} q$ to denote the case when $k \neq 0$. Similarly, an *infinite path* is an infinite sequence of nodes $s_0,s_1,\ldots,s_n,\ldots$ such that $s_0=v_0$ (the initial node) and for every i, $s_i \in V$ and the edge (s_i, s_{i+1}) is in E. An infinite path P is said to be *strongly fair* iff for every node v that occurs infinitely often in P, it is the case that <u>all</u> outgoing edges of v have been traversed infinitely often in P. A node u is said to be *weakly live* iff on every <u>strongly</u> fair path, u occurs infinitely often. A subgraph G'=(V',E') of G is called an *Isolated Reachable Component* (IRC, for short), if G' satisfies the following conditions:

1. $\exists\, v \in V'$, $v_0 \overset{*}{\to} v$ in G.

2. $\forall\, v,w \in V'$, $v \overset{+}{\to} w$ and $w \overset{*}{\to} v$.

3. $\forall\, v \in V'$ and $w \in V$, $v \overset{*}{\to} w$ in G implies $w \in V'$.

The first condition indicates that the IRC G' is reachable from v_0. The second condition guarantees that G' is strongly connected. The third condition indicates that no node in V-V' can be reached from any node in V'. (The reader can therefore think of G' as sort of a black hole.) The following lemma provides a way to test whether a node in a graph is weakly live. The proof is quite easy and hence will be left to the reader.

Lemma 3.1: Given an I-graph G and a node u, u is not weakly live iff there exists an IRC G' that does not contain u.

Theorem 3.1: The language L_1={(G,u)|G is an I-graph, u is a node in G, and u is not <u>weakly</u> live} is $NL^{NL[1]}$-complete.

Proof. Let u_0 be the initial node of the I-graph G. First, we show that L_1 is in $NL^{NL[1]}$. To do this, we construct a new graph G' from G by adding an edge from every deadend node (i.e., nodes without outgoing edges) to the node u, and an edge from u to the initial node u_0 of G. It should be reasonably easy to see that, every IRC not containing u in G is also an IRC not containing u in G'. The converse may not be true. This will be the case only if u is not reachable in G, and from u an IRC is reachable in G' that was not reachable in G. In either case, by Lemma 3.1 we have that u is not weakly live in G iff there is an IRC C in G' (which is also reachable in G) such that u is not in C. Note that the transformation from G to G' requires only deterministic logspace.

Since G' has no deadend nodes, u is not weakly live in G iff the following things are true:

1. $\exists$ v $\in$ G, $u_0 \overset{*}{\to}$ v in G, and

2. $\neg$(v $\overset{*}{\to}$ u) in G'.

Let A={(G,u,v)| u,v are either not nodes in the graph G or v$\overset{*}{\to}$u in the graph G'}, where G' is the graph obtained from G as indicated above. Clearly A is in NL. Then we can construct an OTM M using A as its oracle set such that $L(M^A)=L_1$. Basically, M nondeterministically chooses a node v in G and writes v on the query tape. M then nondeterministically verifies that $u_0\overset{*}{\to}$v in G. If M is unable to do so the input is rejected; otherwise, M consults its oracle and accepts the input only if the response is "no". Thus, an input (G,u) will be accepted iff 1 and 2 above are true. Hence, L_1 is in $NL^{NL[1]}$.

In what follows, we show that L_1 is $NL^{NL[1]}$-hard. Let M be an O(log n) space bounded OTM that makes at most one oracle call during the course of any computation. Let A be in NL. Without loss of generality, we assume that A={(G,u,v)|u and v are nodes in G and u$\overset{*}{\to}$v in G}—the directed graph reachability problem. We also assume that M behaves in such a way that the last step of any computation is the oracle call and M accepts its input only when it receives a negative oracle response. We now show how to construct an I-graph G containing a node u (depending on M, A, and x), in deterministic log space, such that M accepts x iff u is not weakly live in G.

Let T be a NTM that accepts A and operates in O(log n) space. A configuration of M (on input x), as defined in Section 2, is a 4-tuple c=(q,i,z,w), where q is the current state of M, i is the input head position, and z and w are contents of the tape and query tape respectively. (z includes the tape head position as well.) A configuration of T (on some input y) is a 3-tuple (q,i,z), where each term is the same as above. We construct a graph $G_{M,x}$ such that each node represents a configuration of M on x, and each edge denotes the corresponding transition. Let the initial configuration of M on x be the initial node of $G_{M,x}$. Similarly, we define $G_{T,y}$ to be the computation graph of T on y. Note that since M operates in O(log n) space, the size of $G_{M,x}$ is polynomially related to the size x. Now, the graph G can be built as follows. G will contain $G_{M,x}$ (as a subgraph) and a new node q'. Furthermore, for each query configuration c=(q,i,z,w), we add an edge from c to the initial node of $G_{T,w}$. In addition, from every accepting node in $G_{T,w}$ we add an edge to the node q', and for every non-accepting node we add an edge to the initial node of $G_{T,w}$. Lastly, we add an edge from every node of $G_{M,x}$ to c_0 - the initial node of $G_{M,x}$, from c_0 to q' and from q' to c_0. See Figure 3.1. Note that since the string w is always of length logarithmic in x (the input of M), the size of each $G_{T,w}$ will be polynomially related to the size of x. Therefore, the size of the whole graph G is polynomial in the size of x. This implies that the above construction can be done in deterministic log space.

Now, we claim that M accepts x iff the node q' is not weakly live. To see this, we first note that M accepts x iff for some reachable query configuration (q,i,z,w) in G, an accepting state is not reachable in $G_{T,w}$. This is true iff the node q' is not reachable from the initial node of $G_{T,w}$, which in turn is true iff there exists some IRC in $G_{T,w}$ not containing q'. Thus, we have that L_1 is $NL^{NL[1]}$-hard. □

From Theorem 3.1 we can easily derive:

Theorem 3.2: The language L_2={G| G has an IRC} is complete for $NL^{NL[1]}$.

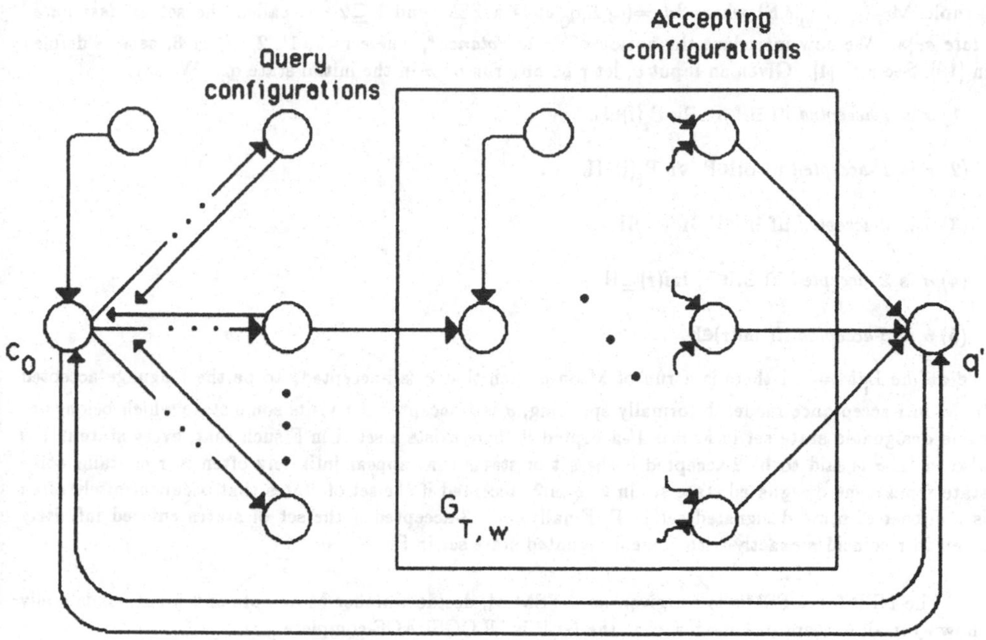

Figure 3.1 The I-graph G.

4. ω-Machines With Fairness Constraints

Our main concern in this section is to define ω-machines where acceptance is defined as in [4, 18] but with the additional criteria that all accepting computations satisfy some fairness constaint. Then we investigate the complexity of the *Non-Emptiness Problem* (NEP) for such machines.

4.1 ω-finite state machines

A *nondeterministic finite state machine* (FSM) M is a 4-tuple (Q,Σ,q_0,δ) where Q is the finite set of states, Σ is the finite set of input symbols, q_0 is the initial state, and δ: $Q \times \Sigma \rightarrow 2^Q$ is the transition function. Let Σ^ω denote the set of infinite strings over Σ. Let $\sigma=a_1,a_2,\ldots$ be an infinite sequence of input symbols, i.e., an element in Σ^ω. A ***run*** r on σ in the state q is an infinite sequence of states $q_1,q_2,\ldots$ such that $q_1=q$ and for every $1\leq i$, $q_{i+1}\in\delta(q_i,a_i)$. For a run $r=q_1,q_2,\ldots$, we define $P_r(i)=q_i$, i.e., the i-th state in the sequence. Let q be a state, we use $\#_r(q)$ to denote the number of occurrences of q in the run r. Let $\#_r(q)=\infty$ iff q occurs infinitely often in r. We also define $\mathrm{Inf}(r)=\{q \mid \#_r(q)=\infty\}$. In other words, Inf(r) is the set of states that occur infinitely often in r. An ω-FSM is a

5-tuple $M=(Q,\Sigma,q_0,\delta,F)$ where $M_1=(Q,\Sigma,q_0,\delta)$ is a FSM and $F\subseteq 2^Q$ is called the set of *designated state sets*. We now introduce the notion of "*i-acceptance*", where i=1, 1', 2, 2', or 3, as was defined in [18]. See also [4]. Given an input σ, let r be *any* run on σ in the initial state q_0. We say:

(1) σ is *1-accepted* iff $\exists H\in F$, $\exists i$, $P_r(i)\in H$.

(2) σ is *1'-accepted* iff $\exists H\in F$, $\forall i$, $P_r(i)\in H$.

(3) σ is *2-accepted* iff $\exists H\in F$, $Inf(r)\cap H\neq\phi$.

(4) σ is *2'-accepted* iff $\exists H\in F$, $Inf(r)\subseteq H$.

(5) σ is *3-accepted* iff $Inf(r)\in F$.

We define $L_i(M)=\{\sigma|$ there is a run of M on σ such that σ is i-accepted$\}$ to be the language accepted by M in i-acceptance mode. Informally speaking, σ is 1-accepted if r visits some state which belongs to some designated state set in F. σ is 1'-accepted if there exists a set H in F such that, every state in r is also in H. σ is said to be 2-accepted if the set of states that appear infinitely often in r contains some state from some designated state set in F. σ is 2'-accepted if the set of states that occur infinitely often is a subset of some designated set in F. Finally, σ is 3-accepted if the set of states entered infinitely often in r coincides exactly with some designated state set in F.

The NEP for ω-FSM's is to, given an ω-FSM M, decide whether M accepts any input. It is easily shown for all i-acceptance modes, that the NEP is NLOGSPACE-complete.

In what follows, we introduce the notion of *fair acceptance* for ω-FSM's. Let $M=(Q,\Sigma,q_0,\delta,F)$ be an ω-FSM. Let r $(=q_0,q_1,\ldots)$ be a run over the input σ $(=a_0,a_1,\ldots)$. With respect to r and σ, we can define an infinite sequence of transitions E: $e_0,e_1,\ldots$ such that, e_i is the transition $(q_i,a_i)\rightarrow q_{i+1}$. The run r is said to be *strongly fair* iff for every state q such that $\#_r(q)=\infty$, every outgoing transition of q must occur infinitely often in E. The run r is said to be *fair* if for each e: $(q,a)\rightarrow q'$, e occurs infinitely often in E, then every transition $(q,a)\rightarrow q''$, where $q''\in\delta(q,a)$, must also occur infinitely often. Note that with comparison to a strongly fair run, a fair run only requires that, those transitions that have been "enabled" infinitely often must be executed infinitely often as well. We then define the language of fair (strongly fair) i-acceptance by an ω-FSM M to be $L_i^f(M)=\{\sigma|$ there exists a fair run r on σ such that, σ is i-accepted$\}$ ($L_i^{sf}(M)=\{\sigma|$ there exists a strongly fair run r on σ such that, σ is i-accepted$\}$). The fair (strongly fair) NEP will be to, given an ω-FSM M, determine whether $L_i^f(M)\neq\phi$ ($L_i^{sf}(M)\neq\phi$).

Our first theorem concerns only 3-acceptance.

Theorem 4.1: Given an ω-FSM M, the fair (or strongly fair) NEP, i.e., "Is $L_3^f(M)\neq\phi$ (or $L_3^{sf}(M)\neq\phi$)?", is NLOGSPACE-complete.

This theorem tells us that, type 3-acceptance is, in some sense, easier to analyze than other types of acceptance. In the remainder of this section, we only consider type 1, 1', 2, and 2'-acceptance modes. First, we show that given an ω-FSM M, the fair NEP, i.e., "Is $L_i^f(M)\neq\phi$, where i=1, 1', 2, or 2'", is PTIME-hard. To show this, we reduce the path system problem, which is well-known to be PTIME-complete[14], to the fair NEP for ω-FSM's. In Section 5, we will further see that the model of fair ω-machines can be modelled by using the so-called Fair Computation Tree Logic. Furthermore, the fair NEP can be reduced to the canonical form model checking problem for that kind of logic, which is known to be solvable in PTIME[8]. Consequently, we have the following result:

Theorem 4.2: The fair NEP for ω-FSM's (for acceptance modes 1, 1', 2 and 2') is PTIME-complete.

The proof of hardness in the above lemma required that the constructed ω-FSM have two distinct input symbols. See [26]. An interesting question arises if we restrict the problem to ω-FSM's over a single letter input alphabet. In this case, it turns out that the aforementional problems are $NL^{NL[1]}$-complete.

Theorem 4.3: For ω-FSM's over a 1-letter alphabet, the fair (for acceptance modes 1, 1' and 2') NEP is $NL^{NL[1]}$-complete.

Proof. Notice that a fair run for an ω-FSM over a 1-letter alphabet is a strongly fair run, and vice versa. Based on this observation, we first show that the fair NEP is $NL^{NL[1]}$-hard. To show this, we reduce the problem L_2 mentioned in Section 3 (the problem, given an I-graph G=(V,E), to determine if G contains an IRC), to the fair NEP for ω-FSM's. Such a reduction can easily be derived for acceptance modes 1, 1', 2 and 2'.

Next, we show that the fair NEP is doable in $NL^{NL[1]}$. Consider an ω-FSM $M=(Q,\{a\},q_0,\delta,\{H_1,H_2,...,H_k\})$. We first construct M' from M by adding a new state q' and transitions from every deadend state (a state with no outgoing transitions) to q'. (This is similar to the construction used in the proof of Theorem 3.1.) In the subsequent discussion, we consider the FSM's M and M' as I-graphs with q_0 as the initial node. The edges, of course, are defined by the transitions. In what follows, we construct an OTM M^i and an oracle set A^i, for each i, such that M^i will accept exactly those machines M where $L_i^f(M)\neq\phi$. Each M^i is similar to the OTM constructed in Theorem 3.1. However, for different accepting modes, additional checking steps are required. Let $A^1=\{(M,i,u)|$ one of the following is true:

- M is not an ω-FSM,
- i does not represent the index of one of M's designated state sets,
- u is not a state in M, or
- $u\overset{*}{\rightarrow}q'$ in M'}.

Let
$A^{1'}=A^{2'}=\{(M,i,u)|$ one of the following is true:

- M is not an ω-FSM,
- i does not represent the index of one of M's designated state sets,
- u is not a state in M, or
- $\exists\ w\notin H_i\ u\overset{*}{\rightarrow}w$ in M'}.

These sets can easily be seen to be in NL. Intuitively speaking, (M,i,u) is not in A^1 if u can not reach the deadend node q' in M', and hence u can reach some IRC of M. Similarly, (M,i,u) is not in $A^{1'}$ ($A^{2'}$)

if u can reach some IRC of M and the set of states in that IRC is a subset of H_i. Now, M^n (n=1, 1', 2') on input M operates as follows:

1. M^n guesses a value i, $1 \leq i \leq k$.

2. M^n nondeterministically traverses the state graph of M until some state say u (chosen nondeterministically) is visited. If n=1 (1') some (each) state visited must be in H_i; if n=2' u must be in H_i.

3. M^n then accepts iff $(M,i,u) \notin A^n$.

The reader can now verify that M^n accepts M iff $L^f_n(M) \neq \phi$. Notice that each OTM mentioned above requires only log space for its working tape, writes only strings of logarithmic length on the query tape, and consults its oracle only once. The theorem then follows. □

The following corollary is immediate:

Corollary 4.1: The strongly fair NEP for ω-FSM's (for acceptance modes 1, 1' and 2') is $NL^{NL[1]}$-complete.

Theorem 4.3 (and Corollary 4.1) do not hold for 2-acceptance. We prove, in subsection 4.3, that the analogous problems for 2-acceptance are complete for $NL^{NL[1]^{NL[1]}}$.

4.2 ω-one counter machines

An ω-1CM is a 7-tuple $M=(Q,\Sigma,\Upsilon,q_0,\delta,Z_0,F)$, where Q is the set of states, Σ is the input alphabet, $\Upsilon=\{Z_0,B\}$ is the stack alphabet, q_0 is the initial state, δ: $Q\times\Sigma\times\Upsilon\rightarrow 2^{Q\times\{-1,0,+1\}}$ is the transition function, Z_0 is the bottom-of-stack marker (Z_0 can neither be written nor erased), and F ($\subseteq 2^Q$) is the set of designated state sets. Roughly speaking, ω-1CM's operate in a similar way as conventional 1CM's except that, we are interested in those inputs over Σ^ω, instead of Σ^*. The actions of the ω-1CM depend on the current input symbol, the internal state of the machine, and the status of the counter: positive or zero (i.e., whether there are zero or a positive number of B's currently on the stack). The definition of strongly fair i-acceptance for ω-1CM's is exactly the same as that for ω-FSM's. However, for the definition of fair acceptance, the notion of when a transition is "enabled" is essential. We define a configuration of an ω-1CM to be a 3-tuple (q,i,h) where q is the current state of the machine, i is the current input head position, and h is the value of the counter (i.e., the number of B's currently on the stack). Let c_1 and c_2 be two configurations. We use $c_1 \rightarrow c_2$ to denote that c_1 can lead to c_2 in one computational step. (The input is not important here, and hence is not explicitly shown.) Let $c_1 \xrightarrow{*} c_2$ represent the reflexive transitive closure of the "→" relation. Let $c_0=(q_0,0,0)$ denote the initial configuration. A transition is said to be enabled in a configuration iff the move defined by the transition can be taken. An infinite computation path (i.e., an infinite sequence of configurations beginning with c_0 such that each subsequent configuration follows from its predecessor) is said to be a fair run iff every transition that is enabled infinitely often is executed infinitely often. Based on this notion, fair i-acceptance can then be defined similarly to that for ω-FSM's.

It is easily shown, for all i-acceptance modes, that the NEP is NLOGSPACE-complete. Similar ideas as those used in Theorem 4.1 and [12] can be combined to show that the ω-1CM fair (strongly fair) NEP for 3-acceptance is also NLOGSPACE-complete. Hence, once again we only consider acceptance modes 1, 1', 2 and 2'. Since ω-FSM's are just special cases of ω-1CM's, the fair NEP for ω-1CM's is at least PTIME-hard. In what follows, we focus on those ω-1CM's over 1-letter input alphabets. First we show:

Lemma 4.2: Given an ω-1CM M over a 1-letter alphabet, the fair NEP is PTIME-hard.

An upper bound for this problem is provided in section 5. Lastly, we have:

Theorem 4.4: The strongly fair (for acceptance modes 1, 1', 2 and 2') NEP for ω-1CM's is $NL^{NL[1]^{NL[1]}}$-complete.

Proof. The proof of this result is somewhat lengthy; hence only the general idea is presented here. The details can be found in [26]. We show how to construct OTM's M^n (that make at most one oracle call during the course of a computation) and oracle sets A^n (in $NL^{NL[1]}$), n=1, 1', 2, 2', such that M^n using the oracle A^n accepts an ω-1CM W iff $L_i^{sf}(W) \neq \phi$. The hardness holds even if we restrict the problem to 1-letter alphabets. As we know from Theorem 3.2, the restricted logspace oracle hierarchy is the same as the logspace alternation hierarchy. Lastly, we show that the problem is hard for $A\Sigma_3^L$, the class of logspace ATM's using at most two alternations. □

4.3 Extensions for other acceptance modes

Other acceptance modes for ω-machines have also been studied in the literature. See e.g. [7, 8, 29]. The emptiness problem for certain classes of ω-machines (where acceptance depends on a fairness constraint) was considered in [29] and was shown to have immediate applications to the verification of concurrent programs. See also [7, 8]. In [8] three modes of acceptance were considered: Buchi acceptance, pairs acceptance and complemented pairs acceptance. (Buchi acceptance and complemented pairs acceptance were also considered in [29]; there however the latter was called Streett acceptance.) Now Buchi acceptance is the same as 2-acceptance and hence has already been defined and partially discussed. The remainder of this subsection is concerned with the fair (strongly fair) NEP for ω-FSM's and ω-1CM's where acceptance is defined with respect to Buchi, pairs and complemented pairs acceptance.

We now give a definition for pairs and complemented pairs acceptance. Now ω-machines are defined as before, except that F is now a subset of $2^Q \times 2^Q$. Given an input σ, let r be any run on σ in the initial state q_0.

(6) pairs acceptance: σ is pairs accepted iff ∃ (A,B)∈F such that $Inf(r) \cap A = \phi$ and $Inf(r) \cap B \neq \phi$.

(7) complemented pairs acceptance: σ is c-pairs accepted iff ∀ (A,B)∈F $Inf(r) \cap A \neq \phi \Rightarrow Inf(r) \cap B \neq \phi$.

For these two acceptance modes similar PTIME-hardness and completeness results hold; i.e., Theorem 4.2 and Lemma 4.2 hold. Also, Theorem 4.4 holds for these two acceptance modes as does the lower bound of Theorem 4.3 (and Corollary 4.1). A contrasting result is :

Theorem 4.5:

(a) The fair (Buchi acceptance, pairs acceptance, c-pairs acceptance) NEP, for ω-FSM's over a 1-letter alphabet, is $NL^{NL[1]^{NL[1]}}$-complete.

(b) The strongly fair (Buchi acceptance, pairs acceptance, c-pairs acceptance) NEP, for ω-FSM's, is $NL^{NL[1]^{NL[1]}}$-complete.

The proof of this theorem is very similar to the proof of Theorem 4.4.

A summary of the complexity results broken down by acceptance type, fairness type and machine type is shown in Tables 4.1 and 4.2; where the abbreviation Ψ-C denotes that the problem is complete for the complexity class Ψ.

5. Applications to Related Problems

In this section, we use the results obtained earlier and apply them to some problems which were considered previously in [3] and [8].

In [3], liveness problems concerning networks of CFSM's were considered. A CFSM M is a directed labelled graph with two types of edges, namely *sending* and *receiving* edges. A sending (receiving) edge is labelled *send(g)* (*receive(g)*), for some message g in a finite set G of messages. One of the nodes in M is called the *initial node*. A *network* of CFSM's consists of two or more CFSM's where each pair of machines communicate by sending (or receiving) messages via one-directional, error-free, unbounded, FIFO channels. Let M and N be two CFSM's over the same message set G. We use (M,N) to denote the network of M and N. A *state* of (M,N) is a 4-tuple [v,w,x,y] where v and w are nodes in M and N respectively, and x and y are two strings over the message set G. Informally, the state [v,w,x,y] means that the executions of M and N have reached nodes v and w respectively, while the input channels of M and N contain the message strings x and y respectively. We define the *initial state* of (M,N) to be $[v_0,w_0,E,E]$, where v_0 and w_0 are initial nodes of M and N, respectively, and E is the null string. See [3] for more detailed definitions.

A *computation path* (or *path*, for short) of (M,N) is a infinite sequence of states l: $s_0,s_1,...$ such that s_0 is the initial state of (M,N) and each s_{i+1} follows s_i by executing one move (i.e., traversing one edge) of M or N. (See [3] for a more precise definition of "follow".) A path l of a network (M,N) is called *strongly fair* iff, for any node u in M or N, if u occurs infinitely often in l then all of its outgoing edges must be executed infinitely often in l. A path l is called *fair* iff for any node u in M (or N) that occurs infinitely often in l, the following two conditions are satisfied:

1. Each outgoing sending edge of u must be executed infinitely often in l.

2. If a state of the form $[u,w_i,x_i,y_i]$ ($[v_i,u,x_i,y_i]$) occurs infinitely often in l, and g is the head message in x_i (y_i), and if u has an outgoing edge e with label receive(g), then the edge e must be executed infinitely often in l.

A node u in M or N is said to be *live* (*weakly live*) iff u occurs infinitely often in every *fair* (*strongly fair*) path of (M,N). Given a network (M,N) and a node u in M or N, the liveness (weak liveness) problem is to determine if u is live (weakly live). For certain restricted classes of CFSM networks, the liveness (weak liveness) problem becomes decidable. Among them, the following two classes of networks:

1. C_1: networks of two CFSM's whose communication is known to be bounded by some constant k in one channel, and

2. C_2: networks of two CFSM's in which one machine sends only one type of message,

were considered in [3]. There it was shown for both C_1 and C_2 that the problem of deciding whether a node was not live (weakly live) is NLOGSPACE-hard. Also, weak liveness was shown to be decidable

	fair	s-fair	fair(1-letter)
1	PTIME-C	$NL^{NL[1]}$-C	$NL^{NL[1]}$-C
1'	PTIME-C	$NL^{NL[1]}$-C	$NL^{NL[1]}$-C
2	PTIME-C	$NL^{NL[1]^{NL[1]}}$-C	$NL^{NL[1]^{NL[1]}}$-C
2'	PTIME-C	$NL^{NL[1]}$-C	$NL^{NL[1]}$-C
3	NL-C	NL-C	NL-C
pair	PTIME-C	$NL^{NL[1]^{NL[1]}}$-C	$NL^{NL[1]^{NL[1]}}$-C
c-pr	PTIME-C	$NL^{NL[1]^{NL[1]}}$-C	$NL^{NL[1]^{NL[1]}}$-C

Table 4.1 The complexity of the fair non-emptiness problem for ω-FSM's.

	fair	s-fair	fair(1-letter)
1	PTIME-C	$NL^{NL[1]^{NL[1]}}$-C	PTIME-C
1'	PTIME-C	$NL^{NL[1]^{NL[1]}}$-C	PTIME-C
2	PTIME-C	$NL^{NL[1]^{NL[1]}}$-C	PTIME-C
2'	PTIME-C	$NL^{NL[1]^{NL[1]}}$-C	PTIME-C
3	NL-C	NL-C	NL-C
pair	PTIME-C	$NL^{NL[1]^{NL[1]}}$-C	PTIME-C
c-pr	PTIME-C	$NL^{NL[1]^{NL[1]}}$-C	PTIME-C

Table 4.2 The complexity of the fair non-emptiness problem for ω-1CM's.

in PTIME. Here, we derive some sharper results for these network classes. For example, we show:

Theorem 5.1: Given a network (M,N) in class C_1 (C_2) and a node u in M or N, the question "Is u not live?" is PTIME-hard.

Theorem 5.2: For classes C_1 and C_2 networks, given a node u to determine whether u is not weakly live is $NL^{NL[1]^{NL[1]}}$-complete.

The second part of this section is devoted to applying our previous results to the Fair Model Checking Problem (FMCP) for Fair Computation Tree Logic (FCTL), which was considered in [8]. In [8], the authors show that the FMCP is, in general, NP-complete. But the canonical form FMCP is shown to be doable in PTIME (actually linear time). However, no lower bound is given for this restricted class. In what follows, we show that the canonical form FMCP is PTIME-hard, and thus PTIME-complete. Before proceeding, some preliminaries are required. Further details can be found in [8].

A structure M=(S,R,L) is a labelled transition graph where S is a finite set of states, R ($\subseteq S \times S$) is a binary relation representing the possible transitions between states, and L is a labelling which assigns each state to a set of atomic transitions (i.e., those propositions which are true at that state). A fairness constraint Φ_0 is constructed from the propositions $\overset{\infty}{F} p$ ("infinitely often p") and $\overset{\infty}{G} p$ ("almost always p") using the standard boolean operators. p can be any boolean formula constructed from the atomic propositions. For a structure M and an infinite path x= $x_0, x_1, \ldots$, the $\models$ relation is defined inductively as follows: (Let $x^i = x_i, x_{i+1} \ldots$)

1. M,x $\models$ P iff the atomic proposition P is true at x_0.

2. M,x $\models \neg p$ iff not(M,x $\models$ p).

3. M,x $\models p \wedge q$ iff M,x $\models$ p and M,x $\models$ q.

4. M,x $\models \overset{\infty}{F} p$ iff there exists infinite many $i \geq 0$ such that $M,x^i \models p$.

5. M,x $\models \overset{\infty}{G} p$ iff $\exists i \geq 0 (\forall j \geq i, M,x^j \models p)$.

Given a structure M=(S,R,L) and a fairness constraint Φ_0, the Fair State Problem (FSP) is to determine for each state s in S, whether there exists a path (in M) x starting at s such that M,x $\models \Phi_0$. Note that the FSP is a special case of the FMCP. In [8], it has been shown that the FMCP can be efficiently reduced to the FSP. There it is shown that, in general, the FSP is NP-complete. However, when Φ_0 is in the canonical form $\wedge_{i=1}^{k} (\overset{\infty}{G} p_i \vee \overset{\infty}{F} q_i)$, the FSP can be solved in linear time. In what follows, we reduce the fair NEP for ω-FSM's under 2-acceptance to the canonical form FSP. Since the former problem is known to be PTIME-complete, therefore the canonical form FSP is PTIME-hard (and hence so is the canonical form FMCP).

Lemma 5.1: The fair NEP for ω-FSM's under 2-acceptance can be reduced to the canonical form FSP by a deterministic log space reduction.

Hence, we obtain:

Theorem 5.3: The canonical form FMCP is PTIME-complete.

We also show that the fair NEP (for acceptance modes 1, 1', 2 and 2') for ω-1CM's can be reduced to the canonical form FSP. Hence, using Lemma 4.2 we obtain:

Theorem 5.4: The fair NEP (for acceptance modes 1, 1', 2 and 2') for ω-1CM's is PTIME-complete.

References

[1] Bentley, J., Ottmann, T. and Widmayer, P., The complexity of manipulating hierarchically defined sets of rectangles, *Advances in Computing Research*, JAI Press Inc., Vol. 1, 1983, pp. 127-158.

[2] Chandra, A., Kozen, D. and Stockmeyer, L., Alternation, *JACM*, Vol. 28, No. 1, January 1981, pp. 114-133.

[3] Chang, C., Gouda, M. and Rosier, L., Deciding liveness for special classes of communicating finite state machines, *Proc. of the 22nd Annual Allerton Conf. on Communication, Control, and Computing*, 1984, pp. 931-939.

[4] Cohen, R. and Gold, A., Theory of ω-languages. I: Characterizations of ω-Context-Free languages, *J. of Computer and System Sciences*, 15, 1977, pp. 169-184.

[5] Cook, S., The classification of problems which have fast parallel algorithms, *Fundamentals of Computation Theory*, LNCS 158, 1983, pp. 78-93.

[6] Cook, S., The complexity of theorem proving procedures, *Proc. of the 3rd Annual ACM Symp. on Theory of Computing*, 1971, pp. 151-158.

[7] Emerson, E. and Lei, C., Modalities for model checking: branching time strikes back, *Proc. of the 12th Annual ACM Symp. on Principles of Programming Languages*, 1985, pp. 84-95.

[8] Emerson, E. and Lei, C., Temporal model checking under generalized fairness constraints, *Proc. of the 18th Annual Hawaii Int. Conf. on System Sciences*, 1985, pp. 277-288.

[9] Fischer, M. and Paterson, M., Storage requirements for fair scheduling, *Information Processing Letters*, 17, 1983, pp. 249-250.

[10] Garey, M. and Johnson, D., "Computers and Intractability: A Guide to the Theory of NP-Completeness", W. H. Freeman and Company, San Francisco, 1979.

[11] Gouda, M. and Chang, C., A technique for proving liveness of communicating finite state machines with examples, *Proc. of the 3rd Annual ACM Symp. on Principles of Distributed Computing*, 1984, pp. 38-49.

[12] Gouda, M. and Rosier, L., On deciding progress for a class of communication protocols, *Proc. of the 18th Annual Conf. on Information Sciences and Systems*, Princeton Univ., 1984, pp. 663-667.

[13] Hopcroft, J. and Ullman, J., "Introduction to Automata Theory, Languages, and Computation", Addison-Wesley, Reading, Mass., 1979.

[14] Jones, N. and Laaser, W., Complete problems for deterministic polynomial time, *Theoretical Computer Science*, 3, 1977, pp. 105-117.

[15] Jones, N., Lien, E. and Laaser, W., New problems complete for nondeterministic log space, *Mathematical Systems Theory*, 10, 1976, pp. 1-17.

[16] Karp, R., Reducibility among combinatorial problems, in *Complexity of Computer Computations*, edited by R. E. Miller and J. Thatcher, Plenum Press, New York, 1972, pp. 85-104.

[17] Ladner, R. and Lynch, N., Relativization of questions about log space computability, *Mathematical Systems Theory*, 10, 1976, pp. 19-32.

[18] Landweber, L., Decision Problems for ω-automata, *Mathematical Systems Theory*, 3, 1969, pp. 376-384.

[19] Lehmann, D., Pnueli, A and Stavi, J., Impartiality, justice and fairness: The ethics of concurrent termination, *Automata, Languages and Programming*, LNCS 115, 1981, pp. 264-277.

[20] Lewis, H. and Papadimitriou, C., Symmetric space-bounded computation, *Automata, Languages and Programming*, LNCS 85, 1980, pp. 374-384.

[21] Lichtenstein, O. and Pnueli, A., Checking that finite state concurrent programs satisfy their linear specification, *Proc. of the 12th Annual ACM Symp. on Principles of Programming Languages*, 1985, pp. 97-107.

[22] Lynch, N., Log space machines with multiple oracle tapes, *Theoretical Computer Science*, 6, 1978, pp. 25-39.

[23] Papadimitriou, C., On the complexity of unique solutions, *JACM*, Vol. 31, No. 2, April 1984, pp. 392-400.

[24] Papadimitriou, C. and Yannakakis, M., The complexity of facets (and some facets of complexity), *J. of Computer and System Sciences*, 28, 1984, pp. 244-259.

[25] Reif, J., Symmetric complementation, *JACM*, Vol. 31, No. 2, April 1984, pp. 401-421.

[26] Rosier, L. and Yen, H., Logspace hierarchies, polynomial time and the complexity of fairness problems concerning ω-machines, Univ. of Texas at Austin, Dept. of Computer Sciences, Tech. Report No. 85-08, May 1985.

[27] Ruzzo, W., Simon, J. and Tompa, M., Space-bounded hierarchies and probabilistic computations, *J. of Computer and System Sciences*, 28, 1984, pp. 216-230.

[28] Stockmeyer, L., The polynomial-time hierarchy, *Theoretical Computer Science*, 3, 1977, pp. 1-22.

[29] Vardi, M., Automatic verification of probabilistic concurrent finite-state programs, *Proc. of the 26th Annual Symposium on Foundations of Computer Science*, 1985, pp. 327-338.

On Sparse Oracles Separating Feasible Complexity Classes

Juris Hartmanis*
Lane Hemachandra†

Department of Computer Science
Cornell University

ABSTRACT

This note clarifies which oracles separate NP from P and which do not. In essence, we are changing our research paradigm from the study of which problems can be relativized in two conflicting ways to the study and characterization of the class of oracles achieving a specified relativization. Results of this type have the potential to yield deeper insights into the nature of relativization problems and focus our attention on new and interesting classes of languages.

A complete and transparent characterization of oracles that separate NP from P would resolve the long-standing P=?NP question. In this note, we settle a central case. We fully characterize the sparse oracles separating NP from P in worlds where P=NP. We display related results about coNP, E, NE, coNE, and PSPACE.

*Research supported by NSF grant DCR-8301766.

†Research supported by a Fannie and John Hertz Foundation Fellowship and NSF grant DCR-8301766.

1 Introduction and Overview

Structural questions about feasible complexity classes, such as P=?NP, are usually first analyzed in relativized worlds. Researchers prove that, in appropriately relativized worlds, both a statement and its converse can be made to hold. This is interpreted as strong evidence that current proof techniques lack the power to resolve the question.[1]

In this note, we propose a new approach to structural questions that is both richer and more challenging than simply finding oracles relativizing a question in conflicting ways. We suggest, instead, characterizing the class of oracles achieving a specified relativization of the question.

Consider the ubiquitous P=?NP question. It is well known that this problem can be relativized both ways [1]. A complete and transparent characterization of oracles collapsing NP into P would resolve the P=?NP question. Leaving this to the interested reader, we instead find a complete classification for a central case. In worlds where P = NP, we completely characterize the sparse[2] oracles separating NP from P.

Theorem 1.1 *If* $\mathrm{P}^A = \mathrm{NP}^A$ *and* S *is sparse, then* $[\mathrm{P}^{A,S} = \mathrm{NP}^{A,S} \Longleftrightarrow S$ *is* $\mathrm{P}^{A,S}$*-printable*$]$.

Whimsically phrased, this theorem says that the ability of a set to fool the P mechanism while remaining faithful to the NP mechanism depends on the complexity of the set's internal information organization (and not, for example, on the classical complexity of the set).

Next we dissect the theorem, strengthening each direction. While doing this, we note that many complexity properties of sparse sets degenerate into equivalence in worlds where P = NP. Here we have equivalent characterizations via classical uniform complexity, non-uniform complexity, and time-bounded Kolmogorov complexity.

Theorem 1.2

1. *If* P = NP *and* T *is self-encodable*[3], *then* $\mathrm{P}^T = \mathrm{NP}^T$.
2. *[8] If* S *is sparse and* S *is not* P^S*-printable, then* $E^S \neq NE^S$.

Theorem 1.3 *If* P = NP *and* S *is sparse, the following are equivalent:* [4]

1. S *is* P^S*-printable (self-printable).*
2. S *is self-encodable.*
3. $\mathrm{P}^S = \mathrm{NP}^S$.
4. $\mathrm{E}^S = \mathrm{NE}^S$.
5. $S \in \mathrm{PH}//\mathrm{poly}$.
6. $(\exists c)(S \subseteq K^S[c \log n, n^c + c])$.

Finally, we note that the same techniques can be applied to many other classes. We state theorems for coNP, E, NE, coNE, PSPACE, and even the polynomial hierarchy. For example, in worlds where coNP = NP, we completely characterize the sparse sets separating coNP and NP. Interestingly, we note that oracles from the advice hierarchy [14] have no effect on the structure of the polynomial hierarchy. This gives strong evidence that PSPACE is not in the advice hierarchy.

---

[1] Some recent results present exceptions to this truism [5][7].

[2] A set S is *sparse* iff $(\exists \text{ polynomial } p(\cdot))(\forall i)[|S \cap (\Sigma + \epsilon)^i| \leq p(i)]$.

[3] Self-encodability is discussed later in this paper. A set S is self-encodable iff there are polynomial time machines H and J so $S = \{x \mid H(x, J^S(1^{|x|}))\text{accepts}\}$.

Intuitively, a set is self-encodable if, given the set, one can quickly distill enough information to allow quick answers to future membership queries. That is, we can make a crib sheet.

[4] Definitions are stated in the body of this paper.

Theorem 1.4

1. *If* coNP^A = NP^A *and S is a sparse set, then* [coNP^{A,S} = NP^{A,S} $\Longleftrightarrow$ *S is* NP^{A,S}*-printable*].
2. *If* P^A = PSPACE^A *and S is a sparse set, then* [P^{A,S} = PSPACE^{A,S} $\Longleftrightarrow$ *S is* P^{A,S}*-printable*].

Theorem 1.5 *If T is in the advice hierarchy then* [PH *collapses* $\Longleftrightarrow$ PH^T *collapses*].

Corollary 1.6 *If* PSPACE *is in the advice hierarchy, then* PH *collapses.*

2 Basic Result

We prove, in worlds where P = NP, that the sparse sets separating NP from P are exactly those that are not *self-printable.* The internal organization of these sets is so complex that even given the set as an oracle, no polynomial time machine can hunt down the strings in the set.

Definition 2.1

1. *A set T is* P^S-printable *iff there is a polynomial time function f so* $f^S(1^n) = (\Sigma + \epsilon)^n \cap T$.
2. *A set T is* self-printable *iff T is* P^T*-printable.*

Theorem 2.2

- *If* P = NP *and S is sparse, then* [P^S = NP^S $\Longleftrightarrow$ *S is* P^S*-printable*].
- *(Relativized Version) If* P^A = NP^A *and S is sparse, then* [P^{A,S} = NP^{A,S} $\Longleftrightarrow$ *S is* P^{A,S}*-printable*].

Proof of Theorem 2.2

$\Rightarrow$ Suppose S is sparse and P^S = NP^S. Let $L_{\text{search}} = \{(a,b) \mid$ there is a string in S lexicographically between a and $b\}$. L_{search} is in NP^S, so by assumption, $L_{\text{search}} \in$ P^S. Since S is sparse, it is easy to see that, using binary search repeatedly to find the smallest new element of S, we can P$^{L_{\text{search}}}$-print S. Thus, S is P^S-printable.

$\Leftarrow$ Suppose S is P^S-printable and P = NP. Let $L \in$ NP^S, say $L = L(N^S)$ running in NTIME[$p(n)$]. Consider the set $U = \{x\#T \mid T$ is a set of strings and $N^T(x)$ accepts$\}$. U is in NP. Thus by assumption U is in P. Since S is P^S-printable, we can build a P^S machine that, on input x, first finds $(\Sigma + \epsilon)^{p(|x|)} \cap S$, and then asks if $x\#((\Sigma + \epsilon)^{p(|x|)} \cap S)$ is in U. It accepts if so, otherwise it rejects. Thus $L \in$ P^S. Since L was an arbitrary NP^S language, P^S = NP^S. ♠

Interestingly, the characterization of Theorem 2.2 is not one of classical (uniform) complexity. Indeed, many uncomputable sets S are P^S-printable. The theorem states that the P = NP question crucially depends on the complexity of the organization of S, a non-uniform property.

We proved our theorem in a simple form. In the following section we dissect and strengthen our theorem, and explore the behavior of sparse self-printable sets in worlds where P = NP.

3 Self-encodability

The previous section focused on self-printability. Self-printability is a valuable tool in discussions of sparse sets, but only sparse sets can be self-printable. Nonetheless, we'd like to be able to prove theorems about sets that have "sparse information," even if they are dense.

Definition 3.1 *A set S is* self-encodable *iff there are polynomial time machines H and J so that* $S = \{x \mid H(x, J^S(1^{|x|}))$ accepts$\}$.

Definition 3.2

1. *C/poly = $\{S \mid \exists f$ so $\lambda y.|f(1^{|y|})|$ is in* P *and $D_{S,f} \cap C \neq \emptyset\}$, where $D_{S,f} = \{T \mid (\forall x)[x\#f(1^{|x|}) \in T \iff x \in S]$.*
2. *$C//G = \{S \mid S$ is in C/poly with f computable in $G^S\}$.*
   Note: S is self-encodable $\iff S \in$ P//poly.

Though we give a machine-based definition of self-encodability, the motivation for self-encodability lies in the non-uniform complexity classes of Karp and Lipton [10]. Definition 3.2, part 2, notes this connection.

The Karp-Lipton classes of Definition 3.2, part 1, contain sets that are easy to recognize, *given a (perhaps uncomputable) advice string dependent only on the length of the input string.* For example, P/poly is the class of all sets S so that there is an advice function f (whose output *size* is polynomial in the size of its input) for which "$x\#f(1^{|x|}) \in S$?" is answerable in P. Self-encodability reflects the added property that a set's advice function can be easily computed, given the set.

Loosely put, a self-encodable set is one for which, given the set on loan, we can quickly distill a small 'crib sheet' with which we can quickly answer membership questions even when the set is taken away. Self-encodability has less to do with the classical complexity of the set than with the fact that the set's organization is internally systematic. Indeed, though there are uncomputable self-encodable sets, there are also non-self-encodable sets in TIME[$n^{\log n}$].

Using self-encodability, the flavor of Theorem 2.2 applies even to non-sparse sets. Theorem 3.3 is a broad generalization of a theorem of [2] that applies only to tally sets.

Theorem 3.3 *If* P = NP *and S is self-encodable, then* $\mathrm{P}^S = \mathrm{NP}^S$.

Proof of Theorem 3.3 Let $L \in \mathrm{NP}^S$, say $L = L(N^S)$ running in NTIME[$p(n)$]. Let H and J be the machines of Definition 3.1 that certify S's self-encodability. Consider the set

$U = \{x\#y \mid y = y_0, \ldots, y_{p(|x|)}$ and if we simulate $N(x)$, answering oracle queries of the form "$z \in S$?" by running $H(z, y_{|z|})$, N accepts$\}$.

U is in NP so by assumption U is in P. Thus there is a machine in P^S that on input x computes $y = J^S(1^0), \ldots, J^S(1^{p(|x|)})$ and then answers the P question: "$x\#y \in U$." Thus $\mathrm{P}^S = \mathrm{NP}^S$. ♠

Finally, Theorem 3.6 shows that in worlds where P = NP many properties become equivalent on sparse sets.

Definition 3.4 *The time-bounded Kolmogorov class [6][12] $K^S[f(n), g(n)]$ is defined by: $x \in K^S[f(n), g(n)]$ $\iff$ there is a string y of length at most $f(|x|)$ for which $M^S_{\text{universal}}(y)$ computes output x in at most $g(|x|)$ steps.*

Lemma 3.5 *S is* P^S*-printable* $\iff (\exists c)(S \subseteq K^S[c \log n, n^c + c])$. *This says that strings in self-printable sets have short names: their position in the set; strings in the Kolmogorov class can be self-printed by brute force.*

Theorem 3.6 *If* P = NP *and S is sparse, the following are equivalent:*

1. *S is* P^S*-printable (self-printable).*
2. *S is self-encodable.*
3. $\mathrm{P}^S = \mathrm{NP}^S$.
4. $\mathrm{E}^S = \mathrm{NE}^S$.
5. $S \in$ PH//poly.
6. $(\exists c)(S \subseteq K^S[c \log n, n^c + c])$.

Proof of Theorem 3.6 1≡6 by Lemma 3.5. Clearly 3 ⇒ 4 and 1 ⇒ 2. 4 ⇒ 3, in a fashion similar to the left to right direction of Theorem 2.2, as shown in [8]. Self-encodability, viewed as P//poly, is easily seen to be PH//poly when P = NP, so 5 ≡ 2. Finally, 2 ⇒ 3 by Theorem 3.3 and 3 ⇒ 1 by Theorem 2.2. ♠

Figure 1 summarizes our classification of the effects of nonuniform oracles. We use, in addition to the results already stated, the simple fact that: If S is in P//NPF but S is not self-encodable, then $P^S \neq NP^S$.

4 Generalizations

The thrust of this paper is to encourage the characterization of oracles achieving specified relativizations. We've characterized sparse sets separating NP from P in worlds where P = NP. The same techniques apply to a wide variety of classes. For sparse sets, we characterize sets separating coNP and NP in worlds where NP = coNP, and sets separating PSPACE from P in worlds where P = PSPACE.

Theorem 4.1

1. *If* $coNP^A = NP^A$ *and S is a sparse set, then* $[coNP^{A,S} = NP^{A,S} \iff S$ *is* $NP^{A,S}$*-printable*$]$.
2. *If* $P^A = PSPACE^A$ *and S is a sparse set, then* $[P^{A,S} = PSPACE^{A,S} \iff S$ *is* $P^{A,S}$*-printable*$]$.

Underlying these theorems are lemmas on the effects of oracle queries. We state these lemmas, and some related ones for exponential time classes. Some of the conditions involved are delicate, requiring certain functions to be total and restricting the allowed query lengths of oracle machines. However, the proofs, included in Appendix A, are in spirit the same as the proof of Theorem 3.3. Figure 2 summarizes our results of this type.

Theorem 4.2 [5]

1. $NP = coNP \iff (\forall T \in PH//NPF_{total})[NP^T = coNP^T]$.
2. $P = PSPACE \iff (\forall T \in P//poly)[P^T = PSPACE^T]$.
3. $E = NE \iff (\forall T \in P/(poly, EF_P))[E_P^T = NE_P^T]$.
4. $NE = coNE \iff (\forall T \in P/(poly, NEF_{P,total}))[NE_P^T = coNE_P^T]$.

Corollary 4.3

1. *If* $coNP = NP$ *and S is* NP^S*-printable, then* $NP^S = coNP^S$.
2. *If* $P = PSPACE$ *and S is* P^S*-printable, then* $P^S = PSPACE^S$.

5 The Polynomial Hierarchy and Compressible Sets

Just as Theorem 3.3 broadens results from tally sets to self-encodable sets, so also can we broaden many results from sparse sets to the advice hierarchy [14]. The advice hierarchy, PH/poly in the Karp-Lipton notation of Definition 1, is the class of all sets recognizable within the polynomial hierarchy, given a polynomial sized amount of (sorcerously obtained) advice dependent only on the length of the input.

A detailed combination of the techniques of this paper and the methods of [2] shows that an oracle from the advice hierarchy collapses its relativized polynomial hierarchy if and only if the unrelativized polynomial hierarchy collapses. (This was previously known only for the special case of sparse sets, which are all contained in P/poly.) As a consequence, if PSPACE is contained in the advice hierarchy, then the polynomial hierarchy collapses (and, indeed, by employing the techniques of [10], PSPACE=PH).

[5] Notations defined in Figure 2.

Theorem 5.1 *If* T *is in the advice hierarchy, then* [PH *collapses* $\Longleftrightarrow$ PH^T *collapses*].

Proof of Theorem 5.1 Appendix B.

Corollary 5.2 *If* PSPACE *is in the advice hierarchy, then* PH *collapses.*

6 Conclusions

Self-encodability largely characterizes the oracle set organizations that allow the NP mechanism no more power than the P mechanism. For sparse sets in worlds where P = NP, this characterization is complete. Thus, our suggested research paradigm of classifying oracles that achieve a specified relativization has rewarded us with deeper insight into the linkage between the relativized and unrelativized structure of the polynomial hierarchy.

A Appendix:

Proof of Theorem 4.2

$\Longleftarrow$ directions: Simply set $T = \emptyset$.
$\Longrightarrow$ directions:

1. Assume NP = coNP and $T \in$ PH//NPF$_{\text{total}}$. We must show $\text{NP}^T = \text{coNP}^T$.

   (a) First we show that $\text{NP}^T \subseteq \text{coNP}^T$. Let L be any NP^T language. We will show that L is in coNP^T.

   Since T is in PH//NPF$_{\text{total}}$, there is a machine M_T in the polynomial hierarchy (and thus in NP) and an NP function f, well-defined on all inputs, so x is in T if and only if $M(x\#f^T(1^{|x|}))$ accepts.

   Let N_L^T accept L and w.l.o.g. run in Ntime$[n^i + i]$. Let's define two useful sets.
   $R = \{x\#z \mid M(x\#z) \text{ accepts}\}$
   $S_\star = \{x\#y_{|x|^i+i}\#y_{|x|^i+i-1}\# \cdots \#y_0 \mid N_L^R(x) \text{ accepts }\}$

   R is in NP (=coNP), so $S_\star$ is in $\text{NP}^R \subseteq \Sigma_2 \subseteq$ coNP. $S_\star$ says: using y as a collection of advice strings for T, we think that $N_L^T(x)$ accepts.

   Now, consider the coNP machine that (on input x) on each computation path tries to guess a function-computing path[6] of $f(1^0)$ and $f(1^1)\ldots$ and $f(1^{|x|^i+i})$. On a coNP path that fails to compute one of the advice strings (i.e., which has guessed some non-function-computing path), accept out of hand. On paths that do compute all the advice functions, $y = y_{|x|^i+i}\#y_{|x|^i+i-1}\#$-$\ldots\#y_0$, accept if and only if $x\#y$ is in $S_\star$. Since $T \in$ PH//NPF$_{\text{total}}$, some path will know the advice, so we'll accept if and only if x is in L. Thus $\text{NP}^T \subseteq \text{coNP}^T$.

   (b) The proof that $\text{coNP}^T \subseteq \text{NP}^T$ is similar.

2. P = PSPACE $\wedge\, T \in$ P//poly $\Longrightarrow$ $\text{P}^T = \text{PSPACE}^T$, just as in Theorem 3.3. Crucially, note that we are using the standard model of relativized PSPACE [4]; there is a polynomial bound on the lengths of oracle queries.

3. It suffices to show: E = NE $\wedge\, T \in$ P/(poly, EF_P) $\Longrightarrow$ $\text{E}_\text{P}^T = \text{NE}_\text{P}^T$. Since $T \in$ P/(poly, EF_P), there is a polynomial time machine M and an exponential time function f with a polynomial bound on its query lengths and output size for which:

$$x \in T \Longleftrightarrow M(x, f^T(1^{|x|})) \text{ accepts.}$$

   Now let A be an arbitrary language in NE_P^T. Thus $A = L(N^T)$ for some NE machine N that on input x queries strings at most polynomially longer that x (say at most length $q(|x|)$). The following scheme shows that A is in fact in E_P^T.

   (a) On input x, compute $y = f^T(1)\# \cdots \#f^T(1^{q(|x|)})$.
   (b) Ask if $x\#y \in B$, where
   $B = \{a\#b \mid b = b_1, \ldots, b_{q(|x|)} \text{ and } N^{C_b}(a) \text{ accepts}\}$.
   $C_b = \{z \mid M(z, b_{|z|}) \text{ accepts}\}$.

   These two steps can easily be done by a E_P^T machine, since $B \in$ NE so $B \in$ E.

4. Combine the method of parts 1 and 3 above.

[6] Recall, for our total NP function, at least one computation path computes the function value, and all paths that compute a value ("function-computing paths") compute the same value.

B Appendix:

Proof of Theorem 5.1

Here we prove Theorem 5.1 of Section 5. For sparse oracles, this theorem couples the collapse of the relativized and unrelativized polynomial hierarchies. Our supporting lemmas go further. They link the extent of these collapses, as described below in Fact B.4. When either the unrelativized or relativized polynomial hierarchy collapses, the other can never extend too much farther.

Theorem B.1 *If T is in the advice hierarchy, then* [PH*collapses if and only if* PH^T *collapses*].

Proof of Theorem B.1 The theorem follows from the two lemmas below. ♠

Lemma B.2 *If $T \in \mathrm{PH/poly}$ and $(\exists k)[\mathrm{PH} \subseteq \Sigma_k^T]$, then the polynomial hierarchy collapses.*

Lemma B.3 *If $T \in \mathrm{PH/poly}$ and the polynomial hierarchy collapses, then PH^T collapses.*

Corollary B.4

1. *Suppose $\mathrm{PH} = \Sigma_k$. For all sets T in the advice hierarchy, $\mathrm{PH}^T = \Sigma_{k+2}$.*
2. *(a) Let T be in the advice hierarchy with $T \in \Sigma_m/\mathrm{poly}$. If $\mathrm{PH}^T = \Sigma_l^T$, then $\Sigma_{l+k+2} = PH$.*
   (b) If T is in the advice hierarchy and $PH^T = \Sigma_l^T$, then $PH = \Sigma_{2l+2}$.

Proof of Corollary B.4: These facts follow, respectively, from the proofs of Lemmas B.2 and B.3. ♠

Sublemma B.5 $(\forall T \in \Sigma_m/\mathrm{poly})(\forall A)$[*If A is self-reducible*[7] *and* $(\exists k \geq 1)[A \in \Sigma_k^T]$, *then A is in* Σ_{k+m+1}.]

Proof of Lemma B.2 B_i, the standard Σ_i complete set of [13], is self-reducible. So by our hypothesis, B_i is in $\mathrm{PH} \subseteq \Sigma_k^T$. Thus, by Sublemma B.5, $B_i \in \Sigma_{k+3+c_T}$. Since this membership holds for all i, the polynomial hierarchy is contained in Σ_{k+3+c_T}. ♠

Proof of Sublemma B.5

Fix $T \in \Sigma_m/\mathrm{poly}$ and A self-reducible. There are strings $\{w_i\}$, a Σ_m machine M_T, and a polynomial $r(\cdot)$ with $|w_i| \leq r(i)$ so that

$$(\forall z)[z \in T \iff M_T(z, w_{|z|}) \text{ accepts}].$$

Also, there is a polynomial time machine M_{self} that on input of size n queries strings of length at most $n-1$ for which $(\forall z)[z \in A \iff M_A^A(z) \text{ accepts}]$. Since $A \in \Sigma_k^T$, there is a Σ_k^T machine M_k accepting A.

Our plan is as follows.

1. On input x we guess some advice strings (y).
2. Each guess y will, via M_T, define a set T_y.
3. For each T_y, we check if it has the agreeable behavior that, if it is used as T, M_{self} and M_A agree up to length $|x|$. Later we note that this implies that they both compute A correctly.
4. For T_y that survived the above test, we use T_y to test if x is in A.

Now let's go through each step in detail. In effect, we are describing the code of a Σ_{k+m+2} machine accepting A.

---

[7] A set A is self-reducible [2][9] if $[x \in A \iff M^{A|(|x|-1)}(x) \text{ accepts}]$ for some polynomial time machine M. $A|k$ denotes A restricted to strings of length at most k.

Step 1 On input of size z, f queries strings at most polynomially longer than $|z|$, say $q(|z|)$. On input x, we immediately guess all advice strings $y = y_0\# \cdots \# y_{q(|x|)}$ for which $(\forall i \leq q(|x|))[|y_i| \leq r(i)]$.

Step 2 Each guess y defines a set T_y. T_y is what T is if the advice strings y are assumed to be the advice strings of T. Similarly, y defines a guess for A.

$T_y = \{z \mid M_T(z, y_{|z|}) \text{ accepts}\}$
$A_y = \{z \mid M_A^{T_y}(z, y_{|z|}) \text{ accepts}\}$

Step 3 Given a guess y, we are interested in if T_y allows us to correctly recreate A. Crucially, note that if $(*)$ holds,

$$(\forall z \ni |z| \leq |x|)[M_{\text{self}}^{A_y}(z) \text{ accepts} \iff z \in A_y] \quad (*)$$

then we can conclude that $M_{\text{self}}^{A_y}$ computes A for strings of length at most $|x|$. This conclusion holds by straightforward induction, using the fact that our machine M_{self} queries only strings shorter than its input.

Now we simply check condition $(*)$ for our current y. If it holds, this path goes on to Step 4. Otherwise, this path rejects.

Let's note two facts. First, at least one path will go on to Step 4- the path that guesses the actual advice strings of T. Secondly, many paths with different T_y's may go on to Step 4. The fact that the paths have different guesses of T does not trouble us; each path has a guess of T that correctly aids membership testing in A.

Step 4 On the current path, accept if and only if $M_A^{T_y}(x)$ accepts.

We sketch the cost of the above procedure.

$T_y \in \Sigma_m$.
$A_y \in \Sigma_k^{T_y} \subseteq \Sigma_{k+m}$.
$H_y = \{z \mid M_{\text{self}}^{A_y}(z) \text{ accepts}\} \in \mathrm{P}^{A_y} \subseteq \Delta_{k+m+1}$

So testing condition $(*)$ of Step 3 is of the form $\forall_{\text{polynomiallybounded}}[\Delta_{k+m+1} \iff \Sigma_{k+m}]$. This can be done in Π_{k+m+1}. Taking into account the nondeterministic initial guess of Step 1, the whole algorithm runs in $\Sigma_1^{\Pi_{k+m+1}} \subseteq \Sigma_{k+m+2}$. ♠

Proof of Lemma B.3

Suppose PH $= \Sigma_r$ and $T \in$ PH/poly. Let $Y \in \mathrm{PH}^T$. We show that $Y \in \Sigma_{r+2}^T$, thus $PH^T = \Sigma_{r+2}^T$.

Since T is in PH/poly, there are strings $\{y_i\}$, a PH machine M_T, and a polynomial $q(\cdot)$ with $|y_i| \leq q(i)$ so that

$$(\forall z)[z \in T \iff M_T(z, y_{|z|}) \text{ accepts}].$$

Since $Y \in \mathrm{PH}^T$, there is a PH^T machine M_Y, with each computation path having at most polynomially many steps, say $p(\cdot)$, so $Y = L(M_Y)$.

Let

$L_1 = \{< x, y > \mid y = y_0\# \cdots \# y_{p(|x|)} \text{ and } M_Y^{A_y}(x) \text{ accepts}\}$
$A_y = \{z \mid M_T(z, y_{|z|}) \text{ accepts}\}$.

That is, check if $x \in Y$ assuming that the advice strings y are correct advice strings for T.

Now $L_1 \in$ PH so $L_1 \in \Sigma_r$. So, ***if we can find good advice strings***, we can use L_1 to check membership in Y. The set below defines good advice strings.

$L_2^T =$
$\{ < l, w > \mid w$ is a good advice string of length l for $T\} =$
$\{ < l, w > \mid (\forall x)[|x| = l \Longrightarrow [x \in T \Longleftrightarrow M_T(x, w)$ accepts$]]\}$.

L_2^T is easily in $\Pi_1^{\Sigma_r \oplus T} \subseteq \Pi_{r+1}^T$.

Our Σ_{r+2}^T machine for Y runs as follows on input x. It guesses many advice strings, then checks to find good advice strings, and finally feeds the good strings to L_1.

{Nondeterministically guess advice strings $y = y_0, \ldots, y_{p(|x|)}$.

/* Now there are many computation paths*/

If $(\exists i)[0 \leq i \leq p(|x|) \wedge < i, y_i > \notin L_2^T]$ reject on this path.

/* At this point, we know the advice strings are good*/
/* At least one path will survive to this point since T is in the advice hierarchy */

Accept on this path if and only if $< x, y > \in L_1$.
}

The above program runs in $\mathrm{NP}^{L_2^T \oplus L_1} \subseteq \mathrm{NP}^{\Pi_{r+1}^T \oplus \Sigma_r} \subseteq \Sigma_{r+2}^T$. ♠

References

[1] T. Baker, J. Gill, and R. Solovay, "Relativizations of the *P=?NP* Question," *SIAM Journal on Computing*, 1975, pp. 431-442.

[2] J. Balcázar, R. Book, T. Long, U. Schöning, and A. Selman, "Sparse Oracles and Uniform Complexity Classes," *FOCS 1984*, pp. 308-313.

[3] A. Chandra, D. Kozen, and L. Stockmeyer, "Alternation," *JACM*, V. 26, #1, 1981.

[4] M. Furst, J. Saxe, and M. Sipser, "Parity, Circuits, and the Polynomial-Time Hierarchy," *FOCS 1981*, pp. 260-270.

[5] W. Gasrarch, "Recursion Theoretic Techniques in Complexity Theory and Combinatorics," Center for Research in Computing and Technology Report TR-09-85, Harvard University, May 1985.

[6] J. Hartmanis, "Generalized Kolmogorov Complexity and the Structure of Feasible Computations," Cornell Department of Computer Scince Technical Report TR 83-573, September 1983.

[7] J. Hartmanis, to appear in EATCS Bulletin.

[8] J. Hartmanis and Y. Yesha, "Computation Times of NP Sets of Different Densities," *Theoretical Computer Science*, V. 34, 1984, pp. 17-32.

[9] K-I. Ko, "On Self-reducibility and Weak P-Selectivity," *Journal of Computer and System Sciences*, V. 26, 1983, pp. 209-221.

[10] R. Karp and R. Lipton, "Some Connections Between Nonuniform and Uniform Complexity Classes," *STOC 1980*, pp. 302-309.

[11] S. Mahaney "Sparse Complete Sets for NP: Solution of a Conjecture of Berman and Hartmanis," *FOCS 1980*, pp. 54-60.

[12] M. Sipser, "A Complexity Theoretic Approach to Randomness," *STOC 1983*, pp. 330-335.

[13] C. Wrathall, "Complete Sets and the Polynomial-time Hierarchy," *Theoretical Computer Science*, V. 3, 1977, pp. 23-33.

[14] C. Yap, "Some Consequences of Non-uniform Conditions on Uniform Classes," *Theoretical Computer Science*, V. 26, 1983, pp.287-300.

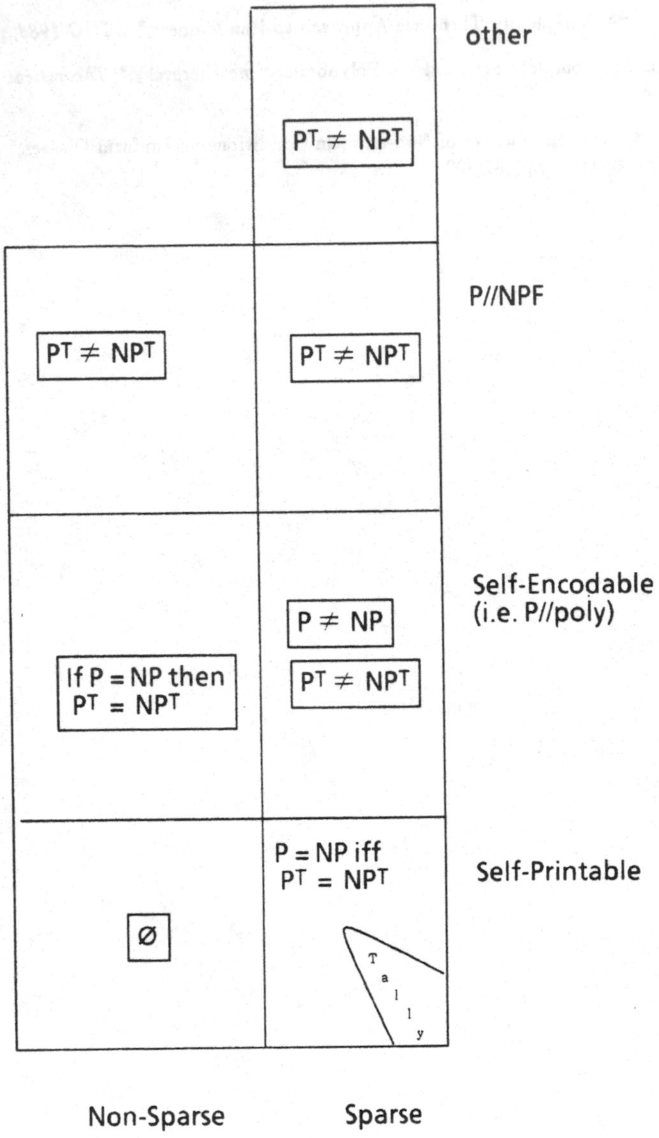

Figure 1

The Effects of Nonuniform Oracles

Each box lists the conclusions that can be drawn if there is a set T in that box. For example, for every sparse set T that is self-encodable but not self-printable, $P^T \neq NP^T$. Indeed, if any such set T exists then $P \neq NP$.

$Q \Leftrightarrow (\forall S \in C)[R]$		
Q	C	R
P = NP	PH//poly	$P^S = NP^S$
NP = coNP	$PH//NPF_{total}$	$NP^S = coNP^S$
P = PSPACE	PSPACE//poly	$P^S = PSPACE^S$
E = NE	$P/(poly, EF_p)$	$E_p{}^S = NE_p{}^S$
NE = coNE	$P/(poly, NEF_{P,total})$	$NE_p{}^S = coNE_p{}^S$
PH collapses	PH/poly	PH^S collapses

Figure 2

An NP function maps from Σ^* to $\Sigma^* \cup$ **undef**. It takes value **undef** if each computation path declares itself unable to compute the function. It computes value y if every path that computes some value computes y, and at least one path computes y. For a valid NP function, we require that one of these two possibilities occurs for each input.

NPF_{total} is the class of NP functions (as defined in this section) that never take on the value **undef**. That is, they are the total functions computable in NP. E(NE), exponential time, is $\bigcup_{c>0} Time[2^{cn}]$ ($\bigcup_{c>0} Ntime[2^{cn}]$). EF is the class of functions computable in deterministic exponential time. NEF_{total} is the class of NE functions that never take on the value **undef**. E_p (NE_p) is the class of languages recognized by a deterministic (nondeterministic) exponential time machine that only queries its oracle about strings of length at most polynomial in the input size.

We say $S \in C/(F,G)$ if S is in C/F, and S has an advice function computable in G^S.

ON GENERALIZED KOLMOGOROV COMPLEXITY†

José L. Balcázar

Facultat d'Informàtica
Universitat Politècnica de Barcelona
Jordi Girona Salgado, 31
08034 Barcelona, Spain

Ronald V. Book

Department of Mathematics
University of California
Santa Barbara, Ca. 93106, U.S.A.
and
Mathematical Sciences Research Inst.
1000 Centennial Drive
Berkeley, Ca. 94720, U.S.A.

Section 1

The idea of the "Kolmogorov complexity" of finite strings provides a definition of the notion of the "degree of randomness" of a string. Informally, the Kolmogorov complexity of a finite string is the length of the shortest program that will generate the string; intuitively, it is a measure of the amount of information that the string contains. A string is considered to be "random" if the length of the shortest problem that generates the string is the same as that of the string itself. This concept has been studied extensively and has been used in a number of applications in computer science. Introduced by Kolmogorov [11] and by Chaitin [4,5], the notion of Kolmogorov complexity has been used by a number of different authors in the context of computational complexity theory ([6,8,15,19]). A modification of the original idea has also been developed: consider not only the length of a program but also, and simultaneously, the running time of the program. This modification has been used by Ko [8] and by Sipser [19] and, more recently, by Hartmanis [7].

Hartmanis considered the notion of "a generalized, two-parameter Kolmogorov complexity measure for finite strings which measures *how far* and *how fast* a string can be compressed." Given a universal Turing machine U and functions G and g, a string x is in the <u>generalized Kolmogorov class</u> $K_U[g(|x|), G(|x|)]$ if there is a string y of length at most $g(|x|)$ with the property that U will generate x on input y in at most $G(|x|)$ steps. Thus, again quoting Hartmanis,

†This research was supported in part by the National Science Foundation under Grant No. DCR83-12472.

this new approach "measures the amount of randomness detectable in a given time." We modify the notion introduced by Hartmanis in order to consider sets of strings of "small generalized Kolmogorov complexity." Set A has small generalized Kolmogorov complexity if there exist constants c and k and a set B such that for every $x \in B$, x is in $K[c \cdot \log|x|, |x|^k]$ and A is a finite extension of B.

The purpose of the present paper is to investigate how the class of sets with small generalized Kolmogorov complexity is related to other classes that have received attention in the study of structural properties of complexity classes and complexity-bounded reducibilities. More specifically, we are concerned with the comparison of the class of sets with small generalized Kolmogorov complexity to the class of tally sets. We establish a precise connection between these two classes by showing that a set has small generalized Kolmogorov complexity if and only if it is "semi-isomorphic" to a tally set. We are also concerned with the comparison of the class of sets with small generalized Kolmogorov complexity to the class of sets with polynomial-size circuits. We show that every set with small generalized Kolmogorov complexity has a representation in terms of polynomial-size circuits of a restricted type. In addition, we consider the question of whether sets with small generalized Kolmogorov complexity are "low" in terms of the concept studied by Schöning [17] and others. We answer this question by showing that this class is a proper subset of the extended low class EL_1 defined by Balcázar, Book, and Schöning [2]; if a set A has small generalized Kolmogorov complexity, then $P(A) \subseteq NP(A) \subseteq P(K \oplus A)$, where K is any set that is NP-complete. Hence, for every integer $n \geq 0$, the polynomial-time hierarchy collapses to Σ_n^P if and only if for all sets A with small generalized Kolmogorov complexity, $\Sigma_n^P(A) = \Sigma_{n+1}^P(A)$.

Thus, sets with small generalized Kolmogorov complexity are not very powerful in terms of the information their strings encode. They are closely related to tally sets. Their characteristic functions can be computed by polynomial-size circuits of a restricted type. They do not have a great deal of power as oracle sets since they lie at the bottom level of the "extended low" hierarchy. In addition, we can show that other properties of the class of sets with small generalized Kolmogorov complexity (as exhibited by Hartmanis [7]) are corollaries of stronger results on classes of sets with "lowness properties."

For the most part our notation is standard. We assume the existence of a set of pairing functions that are computable in polynomial time and denote the application of a pairing function to the pair x, y by $\langle x,y \rangle$. The length of string w is denoted by $|w|$.

We denote the collection of sets with small generalized Kolmogorov complexity by K[log,poly]. Thus, $A \in K[\log,\text{poly}]$ if and only if there exists a set B with the following properties:

(i) A is a finite extension of B;

(ii) there exist a universal Turing machine U and constants c and k such that for every $x \in B$ there exists a string y, where y has length at most $c \cdot \log|x|$, with the property that U will generate x on input y in at most $|x|^k$ steps.

Section 2

Returning to the idea that generalized Kolmogorov complexity is a measure of "*how far* a given string can be compressed and *how easily* it can be recomputed from the shortened description," we ask whether every set with small generalized Kolmogorov complexity has a representation similar to that of sets with small size. In particular, we are interested in the relationship between sets with small generalized Kolmogorov complexity and tally sets. The first result makes precise the relation between sets in K[log,poly] and tally sets.

A polynomial semi-isomorphism from set A to set B is a function f computable in polynomial time with the properties that:

(i) f witnesses the fact that $A \leq_m^P B$;

(ii) the restriction of f to A is a polynomially invertible bijection between A and B.

Observe that if f is a polynomial semi-isomorphism from A to B then there is a reduction from B to A obtained by computing the inverse of the bijection and giving as output a fixed string not in A if it is undefined. Further, the new reduction obtained in this way is again a polynomial semi-isomorphism.

Theorem 1. For every set A, A is in K[log,poly] if and only if there is a tally set $T \subseteq \{0\}^*$ such that A is polynomially semi-isomorphic to T.

It should be noted that there are sparse sets not in K[log,poly].

Section 3

Now that we know how sets with small generalized Kolmogorov complexity relate to tally sets we can compare sets of this type with sets with polynomial-size circuits.

A set A has self-producible circuits [9] if there exists a polynomial length-bounded function $h : \{0\}^* \rightarrow \{0,1\}^*$ and a set B in

P such that the following conditions hold:

(i) for every $x \in \{0,1\}^*$, $x \in A$ if and only if $\langle x, h(0^{|x|})\rangle \in B$;

(ii) the function h can be computed relative to A by a deterministic polynomial time-bounded oracle transducer.

Observe that clause (i) simply says that A is in P/poly, that is, A has polynomial-size circuits, or, equivalently, there is a sparse set S such that $A \in P(S)$. Clause (ii) makes a finer distinction.

Ko [9] has shown that tally sets have self-producible circuits as do left cuts.

Theorem 2. A set A has self-producible circuits if and only if there is a tally set T such that $P(A) = P(T)$, i.e., $A \equiv_T^P T$.

Corollary. Every set in K[log,poly] has self-producible circuits.

Recall that for any set A, DEXT(A) is the class of sets accepted relative to A by deterministic oracle machines that operate within time 2^{cn} for some $c > 0$.

Corollary. If A has self-producible circuits and DEXT(A) = DEXT, then A is in P.

Section 4

Schöning [16] developed the notion of sets being "low" or "high" with respect to the class NP. Intuitively, a set is low if it provides a small amount of information when used as an oracle set; for example, a tally set is low. A set is high if it provides a large amount of information when used as an oracle set; for example, a set that is NP-complete is high. While Schöning considered only sets in NP, Balcázar, Book, and Schöning [2] generalized his work (see also Ko and Schöning [10]) to develop a notion of "lowness" with respect to the classes in the polynomial-time hierarchy, and this is the notion that appears to be of most interest here. A set A is extended low if for some k, $\Sigma_k^P(A) \subseteq \Sigma_{k-1}^P(K \oplus A)$, where K is any NP-complete set; we denote this by writing $A \in EL_k$.

It is reasonable to think that a set with small complexity must be low. We prove that this is true by showing that for every set A in K[log,poly], A is in EL_1. This means that every set in K[log,poly] is in the bottom level of the extended-low hierarchy developed in [2].

Recall that a set A is in EL_1 if and only if $NP(A) \subseteq P(K \oplus A)$.

Theorem 3. If a set A has self-producible circuits, then A is in EL_1. Hence, every set in K[log,poly] is in EL_1.

It is easy to see that for every n, $EL_n \subseteq EL_{n+1}$. Further, it follows from the definition of extended lowness that for every n, $\Sigma_n = \Sigma^P_{n+1}$ if and only if for every set A in EL_{n+1}, $\Sigma^P_n(A) = \Sigma^P_{n+1}(A)$.

Theorem 4. For every n, the polynomial-time hierarchy collapses to Σ^P_n if and only if for every set $A \in$ K[log,poly], $\Sigma^P_n(A) = \Sigma^P_{n+1}(A)$.

Corollary [7]. P = NP if and only if for every set A in K[log,poly], P(A) = NP(A)

Section 5

As part of a study of "positive relativizations" of the P =? NP problem, Book, Long, and Selman [3] studied oracle machines that have limited access to the oracle sets. For any set A, let $NP_B(A)$ be the class of sets L whose membership in NP(A) is witnessed by a nondeterministic polynomial time-bounded oracle machine M such that for some polynomial q and all inputs x to M, the size of the set $\{y \mid$ in some computation of machine M on input x relative to A, M queries the oracle about y's membership in A$\}$ is bounded by $q(|x|)$. Book, Long, and Selman showed that for every set A, $P(A) \subseteq NP_B(A) \subseteq P(A \oplus SAT)$, and that P = NP if and only if for every set A, $P(A) = NP_B(A)$.

We are interested in comparing the power of oracle machines with limited access to the oracle set (as in the positive relativization of Book, Long, and Selman) with the power of unrestricted oracle machines that operate relative to oracle sets that have small Kolmogorov complexity. It is clear that for every set A, $A \in NP_B(A)$, but Long [13] has shown that there is a sparse set S such that $NP_B(S) \neq NP(S)$. In addition, Long has shown that $\cup\{NP_B(S) \mid S$ is sparse$\} = \cup\{NP(S) \mid S$ is sparse$\}$ but there is a recursive set R that is not in $\cup\{NP(S) \mid S$ is sparse$\}$. Thus, the fact that every set in K[log,poly] is sparse does not help. Our result is about sets that are "self-p-printable."

For any A, let $enum_A$ be the function that for each string 0^n has value a string encoding the set of all strings x in A such that x has length at most n. A set A is <u>self-p-printable</u> if there is a deterministic polynomial time-bounded oracle transducer that computes relative to A the function $enum_A$.

It is clear that every tally set is self-p-printable. Since sets in K[log,poly] are closely related to tally sets (by Theorem 1), the next result is not surprising.

Theorem 5. Every set A in K[log,poly] is self-p-printable.

Corollary. Every set that is self-p-printable, hence, every set in K[log,poly], is sparse.

It is clear that every set that is self-p-printable is in EL_1.

Theorem 6. If a set A is self-p-printable then $NP_B(A) = NP(A)$.

Corollary. If a set A is in K[log,poly], then $NP_B(A) = NP(A)$.

It would be of interest to characterize the class of sets A with the property that $NP_B(A) = NP(A)$.

References

1. J. Balcázar, R. Book, and U. Schöning, On bounded query machines, Theoret. Comput. Sci., to appear.

2. J. Balcázar, R. Book, and U. Schöning, Sparse sets, lowness, and highness, SIAM J. Computing, to appear. Also see Mathematical Foundations of Computer Science - 1984, Lecture Notes in Computer Science 176 (1984), 185-193.

3. R. Book, T. Long, and A. Selman, Quantitative relativizations of complexity classes, SIAM J. Computing 13 (1984), 461-487.

4. G. Chaitin, On the length of programs for computing finite binary sequences, J. Assoc. Comput. Mach. 13 (1966), 547-569.

5. G. Chaitin, Information-theoretic limitations of formal systems, J. Assoc. Comput. Mach. 21 (1974), 403-424.

6. G. Chaitin, A theory of program size formally identical to information theory, J. Assoc. Comput. Mach. 22 (1975), 329-340.

7. J. Hartmanis, Generalized Kolmogorov complexity and the structure of feasible computations, Proc. 24th IEEE Symp. Foundations of Computer Science, 1983, 439-445.

8. K. Ko, Resource-bounded program-size complexity and pseudo-random sequences, Technical Report, University of Houston.

9. K. Ko, Continuous optimization problems and a polynomial hierarchy of real functions, J. Complexity, to appear.

10. K. Ko and U. Schöning, On circuit-size complexity and the low hierarchy in NP, SIAM J. Computing 14 (1985), 41-51.

11. A. Kolmogorov, Three approaches for defining the concept of information quality, Prob. Info. Trans. 1 (1965), 1-7.

12. R. Ladner, The circuit value problem is log space complete for P, SIGACT News 7 (1975), 18-20.

13. T. Long, On restricting the size of oracles compared with restricting access to oracles, SIAM J. Computing 14 (1985), 585-597.

14. T. Long and A. Selman, Relativizing complexity classes with sparse oracles, J. Assoc. Comput. Mach., to appear.

15. W. Paul, J. Seiferas, and J. Simon, An information-theoretic approach to time bounds for on-line computation, Proc. 12th ACM Symp. Theory of Computing, 1980, 357-367.

16. U. Schöning, a low- and a high-hierarchy in NP, J. Comput. Syst. Sci. 27 (1983), 14-28.

17. U. Schöning, Habilitationsschrift, Institut für Informatik, Universität Stuttgart, 1985.

18. A. Selman, Xu Mei-rui, and R. Book, Positive relativizations of complexity classes, SIAM J. Computing 12 (1983), 565-579.

19. M. Sipser, A complexity theoretic approach to randomness, Proc. 15th ACM Symp. Theory of Computing, 1983, 330-335.

Area-time Optimal Division for $T = \Omega((\log n)^{1+\epsilon})$

K. Mehlhorn* and F.P. Preparata**

* Fachbereich 10, Informatik, Universität des Saarlandes, 6600, Saarbrücken, West Germany.

** Coordinated Science Laboratory, University of Illinois, Urbana, IL 61801.

This work was supported by the DFG, SFB 124, TP B2, VLSI Entwurf und Parallelität, and by NSF Grant ECS-84-10902.

A family of area-time (AT^2) optimal networks for the computation of the inverse of an n-bit number (referred to here as "dividers") has been proposed some time ago by Mehlhorn [1]. A network of this type can be constructed for each computation time T in the range $[\Omega(\log^2 n), O(\sqrt{n})]$. Since then considerable progress has been made in the design of faster dividers [2], culminating in the result of Beame-Cook-Hoover [3] illustrating an $O(\log n)$-time divider (i.e. , a time-optimal network in the hypothesis of bounded-fan-in components). However the Beame-Cook- Hoover network (referred to here as the BCH network) does not achieve area optimality. Thus, it is natural to ask the question of the existence of area-time optimal dividers for $T = o(\log^2 n)$. This paper provides an affirmature answer for $T \in [\Omega((\log n)^{1+\epsilon}), O(\log^2 n)]$ for any positive constant $\epsilon \leq 1$. It must be pointed out that the proposed networks are so complicated - notwithstanding their area-time-optimality - that they are exclusively of theoretical interest.

The network (see Figure 1) consists of $\lceil J \rceil + 2$ cascaded modules, where $J \simeq 1/\epsilon$. The first J modules are modified dividers of the BCH type, computing a sequence of approximations of the inverse with increasing numbers of bits $l_1 \leq l_2 \leq \ldots \leq l_J < n$.

The last two modules are designed to complete the build-up of the result size from l_J to n bits by implementing the Newton approximation method, which, at each iteration doubles the length of the result. This is carried out in two phases, respectively executed by the "fast" and "slow" approximators. The fast approximator basically consists of a single area-time optimal fastest multiplier, used to execute the initial iterations; the slow approximator is instead a cascade of affordably slow multipliers, each executing one of the final iterations. Both approximators execute $O(\log \log n)$ iteration steps. Note that the cascade of the two Newton approximators structurally coincides with Mehlhorn's divider [1].

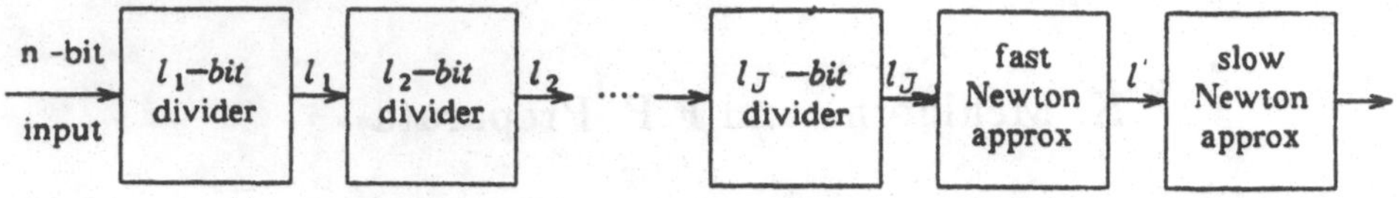

Abb. 1. Block structure of the divider

The paper is organized as follows. In section 2 we present a more efficient implementation of the BCH method leading to a circuit referred to as "modified BCH divider". In Section 3 we discuss an alternative method for the computation of the inverse, which uses the modified BCH method as a subroutine. Finally, in Section 4 we illustrate the combination of the previous techniques with the Newton approximation, to yield our proposed network, while Section 5 contains a few closing remarks.

2. An efficient implementation of the BCH method.

In this section we first describe (a variant of) the BCH method [3] and then modify it so as to reduce its area requirement.

The original BCH method computes the inverse of an n-bit number x by adding the first n powers of $u = 1 - x$ and truncating the n^2-bit result to its leading n-bits. Each power of u is computed individually and the n powers are subsequently added together; so we just consider the computation of u^n. The approach consists of taking the "logarithm" of u, multiplying it by n, and then taking the "antilogarithm".

Since taking logarithms of large numbers is very hard, the method resorts to a modular representation and works as follows:

Algorithm INVERSE1(x)

Input: an n-bit number x in the range $[1/2, 1)$. Given are primes $p_1, \ldots, p_m$ such that

$$\prod_{j=1}^{m} p_j \geq 2^{(n^2)} \quad \text{(Note that } m \simeq n^2/\log n\text{)}$$

(n is assumed to be a power of two)

Output: an $(n+2)$-bit number v in the range $(1,2]$, so that $v \times x = 1 + \delta$ with $\delta < 2^{-n-1}$ (v is given by the first $n+2$ bits of $\sum_{i=0}^{n-1}(1-x)^i$)

(1) **begin** $u := (1-x)2^n$;(* u is an integer *)
(2) **for** $j, 1 \leq j \leq m$
(3) **pardo** $b_j := u mod p_j$;
(4) compute r_j so that $a_j^{r_j} = b_j$, where
a_j is a generator of the multiplicative group of $\mathbf{Z}^*{}_{p_j}$;
(5) **for** $l = 0$ **to** $\log n - 1$
(6) **do** $m_j^{(l)} := a_j^{r_j 2^l mod(p_j - 1)}$ (* $m_j^{(l)} = u^{2^l} mod p_j$ *)
(7) **od**;
(8) $v_j := \prod_{l=0}^{\log n - 1}(m_j^{(l)} + 2^{n2^l}) mod p_j$
(* $v_j = 2^{n(n-1)} \cdot \sum_{t=0}^{n-1}(u/2^n)^t \quad mod p_j$ *)
(9) $V_j := v_j M_j mod(p_1 \ldots p_m)$
(* first step of Chinese remaindering *)
(10) **odpar**;
(11) $v := \sum_{j=1}^{m} V_j mod(p_1 \ldots p_m)$; (* second step of Chinese remaindering *)
(12) $v :=$ truncate v to the first $m+2$ bits and set
point after the second bit from the left
(13) **end**

Let us next describe the different steps of this algorithm in more detail. In this description we will make frequent use of the following two facts.

1) One can multiply two k-bit integers in time T and area A where $AT^2 = O(k^2)$ and $T \in [\Omega(\log k), O(\sqrt{k})]$. This is the result of [6].

2) One can add m k-bit integers in time $O(\log m + \log k)$ and area $O(km \cdot \log m)$. This can be achieved by expressing the m integers in redundant representation (see, e.g. [4,5,6]) and then adding them in a tree-like fashion. The tree has depth $O(\log m)$ and requires area $O(m \log m)$ for every bit position. Each level of the tree introduces a delay of just $O(1)$ thanks to the redundant number representation.

We are now ready to describe the circuit in more detail. We start with the parallel loop, lines 2-10.

Line 3: This line is easily executed in time $O(\log n)$ and area $O(n(\log n)^2)$ for each p_j by expressing u by its binary expansion $u = \sum_{t=0}^{n-1} u_t 2^t, u_t \in \{0,1\}$, storing the numbers $2^t mod p_j$ in a table and performing the required additions in redundant number representation. We leave the details of this step to the reader.

Line 4: Step 4 is realized by a table-look-up, i.e. by a loop-up in a table which gives the value of r_j for each possible value of b_j. Since p_j can certainly be expressed using $2\log n$ bits this table has n^2 extries of $2\log n$ bits each. We realize this table by $2\log n$ H-trees each requiring area $O(n^2)$. Thus the total area is $O(n^2 \log n)$ for each p_j, and a table-loop-up takes time $O(\log n)$.

Note that the $2\log n$ slices of the table are accessed in parallel. Also note that this circuit is pipelinable, (its period is $O(1)$ in technical terms) and therefore $O(\log n)$ look-ups can also be performed in time $O(\log n)$ using the same area. This observation is important for step 6.

Line 5,6,7: Consider a fixed l first. We first compute

$$R_j^{(l)} = r_j 2^l mod(p_j - 1)$$

as outlined in line 3. Note that the l-place shift does not have to be executed explicitly; it only determines which powers of two need to be looked-up. The computation of $R_j^{(l)}$ takes time $O(\log n)$ and area $O(n(\log n)^2)$. We perform this computation in parallel for all l, $0 \leq l \leq \log n - 1$.

The integer $m_j^{(l)}$ is computed from $R_j^{(l)}$ by look-up in a table of "antilogarithms". The $\log n$ look-ups are pipelined and take time $O(\log n)$ and area $O(n^2 \log n)$ for each p_j, (refer to the description of line 3).

Finally note that $m_j^{(l)} = a_j^{r_j 2^l mod(p_j-1)} = b_j^{2^l} mod p_j = u^{2^l} mod p_j$.

Line 8: We use a tree of multipliers. This tree has depth $O(\log\log n)$ and has $\log n$ nodes. Each node contains a circuit multiplying two $2\log n$ bit numbers and reducing the result $mod p_j$ in time $O(\log\log n)$ and area $O((\log n)^2)$. This shows that step 8 takes time $(\log n)$ and area $O(n)$. Both estimates are very generous.

Finally note that

$$\prod_{l=0}^{\log n-1} (2^{n2^l} + m_j^{(l)}) = \prod_{l=0}^{\log n-1} (2^{n2^l} + u^{(2^l)}) = 2^{n(n-1)} \cdot \sum_{t=0}^{n-1} (u/2^n)^t$$

Line 9: Let $M_j = [(p_1 \dots p_m)/p_j]^{p_j-1}(mod p_1 \dots p_m)$. Then M_j is the coefficient of v_j required for Chinese remaindering [7]. The number M_j is precomputed and stored in a register of length $O(n^2)$. We multiply v_j by M_j by dividing M_j into $n^2/\log n$ pieces of length $O(\log n)$, performing $n^2/\log n$ multiplications in parallel and then summing the results. This can certainly be done in time $O(\log n)$ and area $O(n^2 \log n)$. Also the reduction $mod(p_1 \dots p_m)$ can be done in that area and time.

Summary: Line (3) to (9) take time $O(\log n)$ and area $O(n^2 \log n)$ for each p_j. Since u^n has n^2 bits we have $m = \Theta(n^2/\log n)$ and each modulus is representable in $2\log n$ bits. We realize loop (2) to (10) by having a module for each modulus and hence the loop takes time $O(\log n)$ and area $O(n^4)$.

Line 11: In Line 11 we add m numbers of n^2 bits each. This takes time $O(\log n)$ and area $O(m \log m \cdot n^2) = O(n^4)$.

Lemma 1. There exists a circuit which computes the n-bit inverse of an n-bit number in time $O(\log n)$ and area $O(n^4)$.

Proof: Immediate from the discussion above. ∎

The enormous space requirement of the method sketched above is essentially due to the fact that the powers of u are computed with $\Theta(n^2)$ bits of precision. However, only the leading $n + \log n$ bits are truly needed for the computation of v. This observation is the key to the "modified" BCH method, to be described next. In the modified method we compute the powers of an l-bit integer u in m rounds (this m has nothing to do with the m in algorithm INVERSE1), where m is a design parameter to be selected. In each round we compute the sum of $s = (l)^{1/m}$ consecutive powers using the method of Lemma 1. We call s the *depth* of the method. This takes time $O(\log l)$ and area $O((ls)^2)$ and yields a result of $O(ls)$ bits. The space requirement results from the fact that only $ls/\log(ls)$ different prime moduli, each of length $2\log(ls)$ bits, must be used. We truncate this result to $l + \lceil \log 12m \rceil$ bits and start the next round. The details are as follows.

Algorithm INVERSE2(x)

Input: an l-bit number $x \in [1/2, 1)$ and an integer $s = (l)^{1/m}$.
Output: an $(l+2)$-bit number $v \in (1, 2]$

begin $u_o := 1 - x$;
  for $i = 0$ **to** $m - 1$ **do**
    begin
    $\sigma_i := \sum_{j=0}^{s-1} u_i^j$
    $u_{i+1} :=$ truncate u_i^s to $q = l + \lceil \log 12m \rceil$ bits right of point;
    end;
  $v :=$truncate $\sigma_0\sigma_1 \ldots \sigma_{m-1}$ to l bits right of point;
end.

To prove the correctness of this algorithm we must show that v gives the $(l+2)$ leading bits of $1/(1-u)$ (of which the rightmost l bits represent the fractional part). To this end, we must show that the error of the approximation is $< 2^{-l}$.

For any variable a used by the above algorithm let $\tilde{a}$ denote the corresponding exact value (note that, since all numbers are nonnegative, the truncation mechanism gives $\tilde{a} \geq a$), and $\delta(a)$ the absolute error on a, such that $a = \tilde{a} - \delta(a)$. Recall also that $\delta(a \cdot b) < \delta(a)\tilde{b} + \delta(b)\,\tilde{a}$ and that $\delta(a+b) = \delta(a) + \delta(b)$. Using these relationships, we readily have

$$\delta(\sigma_0 \ldots \sigma_{m-1}) < \tilde{\sigma}_0 \ldots \tilde{\sigma}_{m-1} \left(\frac{\delta(\sigma_0)}{\tilde{\sigma}_0} + \ldots + \frac{\delta(\sigma_{m-1})}{\sigma_{m-1}} \right)$$

Since $\tilde{\sigma}_0 \ldots \tilde{\sigma}_{m-1} < 3$ and $\tilde{\sigma}_i > 1 (i = 0, \ldots, m-1)$, we obtain

$$\delta(\sigma_0 \dots \sigma_{m-1}) < 3(\delta(\sigma_0) + \dots + \delta(\sigma_{m-1})).$$

From $\tilde{\sigma}_i = \sum_{j=0}^{s-1} \tilde{u}_i^j$ we have

$$\delta(\sigma_i) = \sum_{j=0}^{-1} \delta(u_i^j) < \sum_{j=0}^{s-1} j\tilde{u}_i^{j-1}\delta(u_i) < \delta(u_i)/(1-\tilde{u}_i)^2 < 4\delta(u_i)$$

since $\tilde{u}_i < 1/2$ for $i = 1, \dots, m-1$. (Obviously $\delta(u_0) = 0$.)

Thus $\delta(\sigma_0 \dots \sigma_{m-1}) < 12m \max \delta(u_i)$ and the condition

$$12m \max \delta(u_i) < 2^{-l}$$

ensures the correctness of the method. We claim that $\delta(u_i) < 2^{-q}$ as a result of truncating to q bits right of the point. Indeed $\delta(u_1) < 2^{-q}$, trivially. For $i \geq 1$, assuming $\delta(u_i) < 2^{-q}$, let $u_{i+1}^* = u_i^s$ (before the truncation). Then

$$\delta(u_{i+1}^*) < s\tilde{u}_i^{s-1}\delta(u_i) < \frac{s}{2^{s-1}}\delta(u_i)$$

since $u_i < 1/2$ for $i > 1$. If we assume $s \geq 2$, then $\delta(u_{i+1}^*) < 2^{-q}$, which shows that its q bits to the right of the point are correct. Thus, the prescribed truncation yields $\delta(u_{i+1}) < 2^{-q}$, and the induction step is complete. In conclusion, we choose

$$q \geq l + \log 12m$$

(Note that for any choice of s, $\lceil \log 12m \rceil < 4 + \log\log l$ by the definition of m.)

Noting that $m \cdot O(\log l) = O(\log l / \log s)$, we have:

Lemma 2. For any $2 \leq s \leq l$ there exists a circuit computing the l-bit inverse of an l-bit number in time $O(\log^2 l / \log s)$ and with area $O((ls)^2)$.

The AT^2-performance of the above circuit is given by

$$AT^2 = O\left(l^2 \log^4 l \cdot \frac{s^2}{\log^2 s}\right) \tag{1}$$

By choosing the depth s as $s = l^\epsilon (\epsilon > 8)$, the resulting circuit achieves $T = O((1/\epsilon)\log l)$ and $AT^2 = O(l^{2(1+\epsilon)})$, i.e. it is a moderately AT^2- suboptimal divider still achieving $T = O(\log l)$, for fixed ϵ. We are aware that this result had been previously obtained by F. T. Leighton [8], presumably by a similar argument.

3. An Accelerating Technique

We now describe an alternative approach to the computation of the inverse of an l-bit number, which capitalizes on the presence of leading zeros in the representation of the number to be inverted. This method is best described for an l-bit integer $x \in [1, 2)$.

The number $x \in [1,2)$ can be written as

$$x = x_1 + 2^{-l_1} w$$

where x_1 is an l_1-bit number (the leading l_1 bits of x) and w is an $(l - l_1)$-bit number (the trailing $l - l_1$ bits of x). Then $x_1 \in [1, 2)$ and $2^{-l_1} w \in [0, 2)$. Let v_1 be an l_1-bit approximation to x_1 (i.e. $x_1 v_1 = 1 + \eta, \eta < 2^{-l_1}$). Then

$$v_1 x = v_1 x_1 + v_1 w 2^{-l_1} = 1 + \eta + v_1 w 2^{-l_1},$$

that is, $v_1 x$ has at least $l_1 - 1$ consecutive 0's immediately to the right of the point. Define

$$y = v_1 x$$

Then, if v_2 denotes an approximation of $1/y$, we have $v_1 v_2 \simeq 1/x$. Also, if $v_2 y = 1 + \eta'$ then $v_1 v_2 x = 1 + \eta'$, i.e. $v_1 v_2$ is an approximation of $1/x$ of precision η'. The process can be iterated for the computation of the inverse of y, thereby obtaining

$$1/x \simeq v_1 v_2 \ldots v_k$$

This leads to the following algorithm:

Algorithm INVERSE3(x)

Input: an l-bit number $x \in [1, 2)$, and an integer sequence $l_1 < l_2 < \ldots < l_k = l$.
Output: an l-bit number $v \in (1/2, 1]$, such that $vx = 1 + \epsilon, \epsilon < 2^{-l}$

(1) **begin** $z := x$
(2) **for** $i = 1$ **to** k **do**
(3) **begin** $x_i :=$ leftmost l_i bits of z_i;
(4) $v_i := (l_i + 1)$-bit inverse of x_i;
(5) $z_{i+1} := z_i v_i$

end;

(6) $v := v_1 v_2 \dots v_k$

end

The correctness of the method follows from the fact that $\delta(v) = \tilde{v}_1 \dots \tilde{v}_{k-1} \cdot \delta(v_k) < 2 \cdot 2^{-l-1} = 2^{-l}$.

Step 4 is the crucial action in the above algorithm. To analyze its performance, we need the following result.

Lemma 3. If an l-bit number $x \in [1,2)$ has $l_1 - 1$ zeros immediately to the right of the point, the l-bit inverse of x can be computed in time $T = O(\log(l/l_1) \cdot \log l / \log s)$ and area $A = O((ls)^2)$, for any $2 \leq s < l/l_1$. (Note that this result subsumes Lemma 2 for $l_1 = 1$.)

Proof: Indeed $u = 1 - x$ is a (negative) number with l_1 zeros immediately to the right of the point. This implies that $u^{\lceil l/l_1 \rceil} < 2^{-l}$, so that only the first $\lceil l/l_1 \rceil$ consecutive powers of u need to be computed. ∎

The numbers $x_i, i = 1, \dots, k$, used in Step 4 meet the conditions of Lemma 3, since $1 - z_i v_i$ is a (negative) number with l_i leading zeros. Step 4 is therefore carried out by applying Algorithm INVERSE2 so that the i-th iteration is characterized by length l_i and depth s_i. An implementation of this accelerating technique is therefore completely specified by the two sequences:

$$l_1, l_2, \dots, l_k$$

and

$$s_1, s_2, \dots, s_k,$$

Before closing this section we note that Step 5 involves a multiplication of $(l_i + 1)$-bit numbers at the i-th step; thus this operation is no more complex than the execution of the homologous Step 4, and will not be further mentioned in this discussion.

4. The Divider Network

We have all the premises to illustrate in detail the structure of the divider sketched in Figure 1.

The first J stages are collectively designed to implement the accelerating technique; each module implements the modified BCH algorithm. For $i = 1, 2, \dots, J$, let l_i be the (output) operand length, s_i the depth, $A_{1,i}$ the area, and $T_{1,i}$ the time of the i-th module. We seek a solution where all such modules have identical area (i.e. $A_{1,i} = A'$ for $i = 1, \ldots, J$) and identical computation time, equal to the target time (i.e. , $T_{1,i} = \theta((\log n)^{1+\epsilon}), i = 1, \ldots, J$). By the requirement of optimality, we have

$$\sqrt{A_{1,i}} = \frac{n}{T_{1,i}} = \frac{n}{(\log n)^{1+\epsilon}} \tag{2}$$

We also choose:

$$l_i = \frac{n}{(\log n)^{1+\epsilon} s_i}, \tag{3}$$

$$s_i = \left(\frac{n}{(\log n)^{1+\epsilon}} \right)^{1/2(\log n)^{\epsilon(i-1)}} \qquad (i = 1, \ldots, J), \tag{4}$$

The parameter J is chosen as the largest value of i for which $s_i > 2$, and is readily found to be $\Theta(1/\epsilon)$. Since the area of the i-th module is $\theta((l_i s_i)^2)$, condition (2) is obviously verified. Next note that $\log l_i = O(\log n), i = 1, \ldots, J$. From Lemma 3 we therefore infer for $i = 2, \ldots, J$

$$\begin{aligned}
T_{1,i} &= O(\log \frac{l_i}{l_{i-1}} \cdot \frac{\log l_i}{\log s_i}) \\
&= O(\log \frac{s_{i-1}}{s_i} \cdot \frac{\log l_i}{\log s_i}) \qquad \text{since} \quad l_i s_i = l_{i-1} s_{i-1} \\
&= O(\log l_i \cdot \frac{\log s_{i-1}}{\log s_i}) \qquad \text{since} \quad s_i \geq 1 \\
&= O(\log n \cdot \frac{2(\log n)^{\epsilon(i-1)}}{2(\log n)^{\epsilon(i-2)}}) \\
&= O((\log n)^{1+\epsilon})
\end{aligned}$$

thus verifying the objective for the computation time.

With these choices, each module of the chain is AT^2-optimal, and the global computation time is $c_1(1/\epsilon)(\log n)^{1+\epsilon} = \theta((\log n)^{1+\epsilon})$, for some constant c_1. The value of l_J, the number of bits of the result, is approximately

$$l_J = \frac{n}{(\log n)^{1+\epsilon} \cdot 2}.$$

since $s_J \simeq 2$.

This value l_J represents the length of the operand supplied to the cascade of the two Newton approximators, to be described next.

Starting with the downstream approximator, we recall (see figure 2) that this module is in turn the cascade of p submodules (p is an integer to be defined shortly), where the i-th submodule has area and time $A_{3,i}$ and $T_{3,i}$, respectively, and

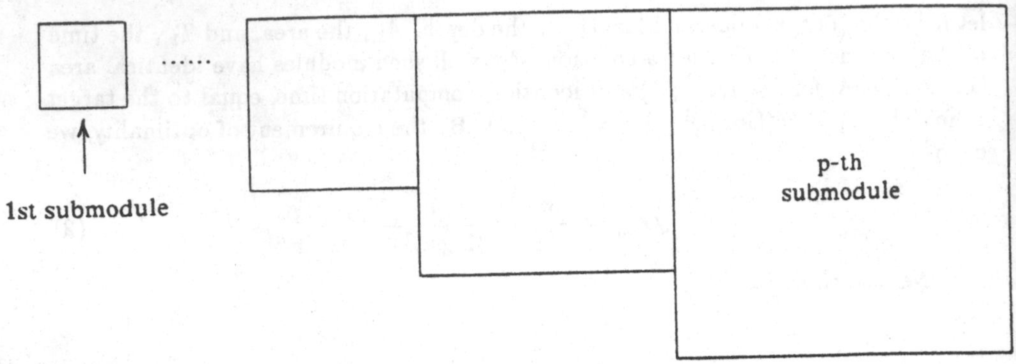

Abb. 2. The module structure of the slow "Newton approximator".

$$A_{3,i} = 2A_{3,i-1}, \quad T_{3,i} = \sqrt{2}T_{3,i-1} \quad i = 2, 3, \ldots, p.$$

With this choice (originally proposed in [1]), the global area and time of the slow approximator are respectively proportional to the area $A_{3,p}$ and time $T_{3,p}$ of the p-th (last) submodule. Since we are aiming for an AT^2-optimal network with computation time $O(T)$, we must have

$$A_{3,p}T_{3,p}^2 = O(n^2)$$

and

$$T_{3,p} = T.$$

This condition enables us to specify the parameter p. Indeed, the speed of the submodules increases as we proceed upstreams (by decreasing submodule index), and each submodule must satisfy the condition that its multiplication time is at least logarithmic in the operand length. Since the operand length is halved in going from index i to index $i-1$ (due to the mechanism of the Newton approximation), and the most stringent condition occurs for $i = 1$, we have

$$\frac{T}{(\sqrt{2})^p} \geq \log(\frac{n}{2^p}),$$

which is certainly satisfied if we select p as follows:

$$p = 2\log\left(\frac{T}{\log n}\right) = 2\epsilon \log\log n. \tag{5}$$

Finally we turn our attention to the "fast approximator". This module receives an approximation of length $l_{1/\epsilon} = n/(\log n)^{1+\epsilon} \cdot 2$ and delivers an approximation of length $n/(\log n)^{2\epsilon}$. Thus, this module must execute $(1-\epsilon)\log\log n + 1$ iteration steps, each of them within time $\theta(\log n)$. The module essentially consists of a "fastest" multiplier of numbers of length $n/(\log n)^{2\epsilon}$, and can be realized with area A_2 such that $A_2(\log n)^2 = \Theta((n/2^p)^2)$, i.e. , $A_2 = \Theta((n/(\log n)^{1+2\epsilon})^2)$. Thus, the resulting AT^2-measure for this module is

$$A_2T^2 = \Theta((\frac{n}{(\log n)^{1+2\epsilon}} \log n \cdot (1-\epsilon)\log\log n)^2) = O(n^2)$$

and the optimality condition is clearly satisfied.

Since each of the three major units of our divider - the chain of modified BCH dividers, the fast Newton approximator and the slow Newton approximator - has area $O((n/(\log n)^{1+\epsilon})^2)$ and time $O((\log n)^{1+\epsilon})$, we conclude with the following result:

Theorem 1 For any fixed $1 \geq \epsilon > 0$, the n-bit inverse of an n-bit number can be calculated with optimal AT^2-performance for any $T \in [\Omega((\log n)^{1+\epsilon}), O((\log n)^2)]$.

5. Conclusion.

We constructed an AT^2-optimal divider with computation time $(\log n)^{1+\epsilon}$ for any $\epsilon > 0$. The reader may wonder whether one can choose ϵ as a decreasing function of n (tending to zero as n goes to infinity). This is indeed the case if the construction is slightly modified. In the construction as it is now we use a chain of modified BCH dividers each with the same area and speed. Thus both area and time grow as $1/\epsilon$ and hence AT^2 grows (at least) as $(1/\epsilon)^3$.

If ϵ is chosen as a function of n, then this simple chain of equally sized modules does not suffice. Rather one has to use a chain of increasingly larger (and slower) modules as we did for the Newton iteration. Omitting the tedious and not particular illuminating details we have:

Theorem 2. There is an AT^2-optimal divider for n-bit integers for any $T \in [\Omega(\log n \cdot 2^{(\log\log n)^{3/4}}), O((\log n)^2)]$.

Note that $2^{(\log\log n)^{3/4}} = O((\log n)^\epsilon)$ for any $\epsilon > 0$.

References

[1] K. Mehlhorn: "AT^2-optimal VLSI Integer Division and Integer Square Rooting", *Integration*, 2, 163-167, 1984.

[2] J. Reif: "Logarithmic Depth Circuits for Algebraic Functions", 24th FOCS, 138-145, 1983.

[3] P.W. Beame, S.A. Cook, H.J. Hoover: "Log Depth Circuits for Division and Related Problems", 24th FOCS, 1-6, 1984.

[4] W.K. Luk, J. Vuillemin: "Recursive Implementation of Optimal Time VLSI Integer Multipliers", VLSI 83, Trondheim, Norway, 1983.

[5] O. Spaniol: "Arithmetik in Rechenanlagen", Teubner Verlag, Stuttgart, 1976.

[6] K. Mehlhorn, F.P. Preparata: "AT^2-optimal VLSI Integer Multiplier with Minimum Computation Time", *Information and Control*, 58, 1-3, 137-156, 1983.

[7] D.E. Knuth: "The Art of Computer Programming", Vol. 2: Seminumerical Algorithms, Addison-Wesley, Reading, Mass. 1981, 2d ed.

[8] F.T. Leighton, personal communication, May 1985.

A TIME-SPACE TRADEOFF FOR ELEMENT DISTINCTNESS

A. Borodin

University of Toronto, Toronto, Canada[1]

F. Fich

University of Washington, Seattle, Washington[1]

F. Meyer auf der Heide

Johann Wolfgang Goethe Universität Frankfurt a. M., Fed. Rep. of Germany[1]

E. Upfal

IBM Research Laboratory, San Jose, California

A. Wigderson

Mathematical Science Research Institute, Berkeley, California[1]

Abstract

In "A Time Space Tradeoff for Sorting on non-Oblivious Machines", Borodin et al. $[B-81]$ proved that to sort n elements requires $TS = \Omega(n^2)$ where T=time and S=space on a comparison based branching problem. Although element distinctness and sorting are equivalent problems on a computation tree, the stated tradeoff result does not immediately follow for element distinctness or indeed for any decision problem. In this paper, we are able to show that $TS = \Omega(n^{\frac{3}{2}})$ for deciding element distinctness (or the sign of a permutation).

1 This work was done while the authors were visiting the IBM Research Laboratory in San Jose.

I. Introduction

Time-space tradeoffs are one of the more classical issues in complexity studies. Cobham's $[C-66]$ seminal paper establishes such tradeoffs for the restricted Boolean model of one-tape Turing machines. A number of time- space tradeoffs were established for both the Boolean and arithmetic circuit models (see Tompa $[T-80]$). Within these models, merging was essentially as difficult as sorting. For the problem of sorting $\{x_1, x_2, ..., x_n\}$ from an arbitrary linearly ordered set, the appropriate model is the comparison based branching program. Such programs are labelled directed acyclic graphs derived from comparison computation trees by identifying common subtrees. Following Cobham, space (or capacity) is measured as the $\log_2$(*# of nodes)* in the program and time (as for computation trees) is the length of the longest path. Borodin, Fischer, Kirkpatrick, Lynch and Tompa $[B-81]$ established the "near optimal" bound of $TS = \Omega(n^2)$ for sorting but were not able to establish a similar result for any decision problem, conjecturing that such a result should hold for the problem of determining element distinctness (i.e. $f(x_1, x_2, ..., x_n) = true$ iff $x_i \neq x_j$ for all $i \neq j$).

We are not able to establish the result as conjectured, but we are able to show $TS = \Omega(n^{\frac{3}{2}})$. Since there is no need to output during the computation, we need to find an appropriate notion of progress and show how this progress is constricted by a bound on the space. It turns out that once the appropriate progress notion is made, the basic outline of proof parallels the development in the sorting result.

II. The Model and Proof of the Main Result

Let $\{x_1, x_2, ..., x_n\}$ be elements chosen from an arbitrary linear order $[D, \leq]$. A comparison branching program is a labelled directed acyclic graph. Each non-sink node has outdegree three and is labelled by a comparison $x_i : x_j$, with one outdegree for each of the three possible outcomes $<, =, >$. The sinks are labelled accept and reject. An input $<x_1,x_2,...,x_n>\varepsilon D^n$ follows a path in a program P in the obvious way determined by the comparisons, and we define acceptance of a set $L\subset D^n$ as usual.

We consider the set $L=\{<x_1,x_2,...,x_n>|x_i\neq x_j\}$. We say that $<x_1,x_2,...,x_n>\varepsilon L$ is ordered by the permutation π if $x_{\pi(1)}<x_{\pi(2)}<...<x_{\pi(n)}$. It is clear that π determines the comparison path τ that $<x_1,x_2,...,x_n>$ follows in any comparison tree or branching program. Clearly, τ must terminate in an accepting node. Moreover, it is easy to see that τ must contain a comparison for every "adjacent" pair $x_{\pi(i)}:x_{\pi(i+1)}$, $1\leq i\leq n-1$. Otherwise, we can set $x_{\pi(i+1)}=x_{\pi(i)}$ and still follow the same path τ (and erroneously accept). The number of adjacent pairs tested on a path will measure the progress for any π. Once we establish the following main lemma, we can follow the same proof structure as in Borodin et al $[B-81]$.

Main Lemma: Let T be a comparison computation tree of height (=time) t. For every c there exists an α so that if $t\leq\alpha\sqrt{n}$ then for all S the fraction p of input permutations π for which T follows a path containing more than S comparisons of adjacent pairs is bounded by $p\leq\frac{1}{c^S}$.

Proof of Main Lemma: Let τ be a computation path of length $t\leq\alpha\sqrt{n}$. There are at most $r\leq 2t$ elements x_i that are involved in some comparison in τ. τ determines a partial order on r elements. We will compute the fraction of permutations π following τ for which we have made at least S comparisons $x_{\pi(i)}:x_{\pi(i+1)}$. Let σ be any total order of the r elements consistent with τ. We bound the fraction for each σ as follows:

There are $\binom{n}{r}$ ways to assign ranks to the accessed elements. We now bound the number of rank assignments under the constraint that at least S adjacent pairs have been tested. There are $\binom{t}{s}$ ways to choose the S pairs and then $\binom{n}{(r-s)}$ ways to assign ranks to the r elements. (If $x_j<x_k$ is one of the S adjacent pairs, fixing the rank of x_j fixes the rank of x_k).

$$\text{Hence, } p \le \frac{\binom{t}{s}\binom{n}{(r-s)}}{\binom{n}{r}} = \binom{t}{s}\frac{r(r-1)...(r-s+1)}{(n-r+s)...(n-r+1)} \le t^s\frac{r^s}{(n-r)^s} \le 4^s\left(\frac{t^2}{n}\right)^s \quad \text{for } \alpha \le \frac{1}{2}$$

$$\le (\frac{1}{c})^s \quad \text{for } \alpha \le \frac{1}{2\sqrt{c}}. \ \square$$

With the main lemma now established, we proceed exactly as in Borodin et al [$B-81$].

Theorem: Let P be a time T, space S comparison branching program for deciding element distinctness on n elements. Then $TS = \Omega(n^{\frac{3}{2}})$.

Proof: Consider P in stages, where each stage represents $t = \alpha\sqrt{n}$ steps where we choose α sufficiently small so that c=4 in the main lemma. Without loss of generality, $S \ge logn$, since each of the possible comparisons appears at least once in the program, which therefore has at least $\binom{n}{2}$ nodes.

Let q_i be the fraction of input permutations (of distinct elements) for which P has compared at least iS adjacent pairs by the end of the ith stage. Using the main lemma, we will show that $q_i \le i(\frac{1}{2})^S$. Hence $q_i < 1$ for $i \le \frac{n}{S}$. This in turn implies that there must be at least $\frac{n}{s}$ stages so that $T \ge \frac{n}{s}\alpha\sqrt{n}$. Otherwise, there will be a permutation for which some adjacent pair has not been tested, forcing a contradiction as previously explained. Thus $TS \ge \alpha n^{\frac{3}{2}}$.

To establish the claimed bound for q_i, we can consider each of the 2^s nodes at the end of stage i to be the root of a *subtree* of height t. That is, expand the branching program for stage $i+1$ into at most 2^s computation trees. For each such tree at most a fraction $(\frac{1}{4})^s$ of all $n!$ permutations can have more than S adjacent pairs tested. (Note that this is independent of the permutations that actually arrived at the root of this tree). Hence, $q_{i+1} \le q_i + 2^s(\frac{1}{4})^s \le (i+1)(\frac{1}{2})^s$ by induction on i with q_0=0.

$\square$

It is easy to see that the same proof establishes the same bound for determining the sign of a permutation. In this case, if not all adjacent pairs have been tested, we can change the ordering of some pair and thereby change the sign.

III. The Obvious Open Questions

Since we do not know how to improve the known upper bound of $TS = O(n^2 logn)$ for element distinctness (this upper bound holding even for sorting), the most obvious open question is whether or not $TS = \Omega(n^2)$. To see why the existing proof techniques do not extend, we note that we are only exploiting the space bound at the start of each stage. If we allow a stage to be $O(n)$ steps (as in the sorting lower bound) then we can decide distinctness in $O(\log^2 n)$ stages using only constant width at the beginning of each stage. (Simply partition the elements into $O(logn)$ blocks of size $O(\frac{n}{logn})$, and then each stage can test a pair of blocks for distinctness by sorting). We still conjecture that $TS = \Omega(n^2)$ holds for deciding distinctness but any proof will have to frequently exploit the space bound.

Perhaps the most important extension of our results is to the Boolean branching program model. In Borodin and Cook [$B-82$] the sorting lower bound is extended to the setting of sorting n integers in the range $[1, n^2]$, the input represented by a string of $2nlogn$ bits. This lower bound is made possible since we have an explicit notion of progress, namely how many ranks have been established. Our comparison lower bound exploits the fact that we could also find a "monotone" concept of progress, that of "adjacent pairs tested". For the Boolean or "R-way model" (see Borodin and Cook [$BC-82$]) this concept does not apply. The difficulty of this issue is realized when one notes that in the comparison model, "silent sorting" (i.e. being able to infer the sort from the comparison paths) is equivalent to deciding element distinctness (see Reingold [$R-72$]) whereas in the Boolean or R-way model, silent sorting is trivial (simply look at each input once). Thus far, we still have not established a non trivial time-space lower bound for any specific decision problem in the Boolean setting.

References

[$BC-82$] Borodin A. and Cook S., A Time-Space Tradeoff for Sorting on a General Sequential Model of Computation, SICOMP 11(2), May 1982, pp. 287-297.

[$B-81$] Borodin A., Fischer M., Kirkpatrick D., Lynch N., Tompa M., A Time- Space Tradeoff on Non-Oblivious Machines, J.C.S.S. 22(3),June 1981, pp.351-364.

[$C-66$] Cobham A., The Recognition Problem for the Set of Perfect Squares, Research Paper RC-1704, IBM Watson Research Center, Yorktown Hights, N.Y., April 1966.

[$R-72$] Reingold E., On the Optimality of some Set Algorithms, J. ACM 19, 1972, pp.649-659.

[$T-80$] Tompa M., Time-Space Tradeoffs for Computing Functions Using Connectivity Properties of their Circuits, J.C.S.S. 20(2), 1980, pp.118-132.

Parallel Machines and their Communication Theoretical Limits

K. Rüdiger Reischuk
Institut für Theoretische Informatik
Technische Hochschule Darmstadt
6100-Darmstadt
West-Germany

1. Introduction

In the past few years the interest in parallel algorithms and parallel machine architecture has grown enormously. After many problems concerning sequential computations have been settled and since new technologies make the development of large parallel systems feasible parallel computation is a new challenge for theoretical computer scientists. Let us consider typical complexity measures like parallel time, hardware size and information exchange. For many computational problems it is unknown whether and how a good speedup can be achieved on a given parallel machine with respect to an efficient sequential solution. There are two main reasons for this ambiguity: some serialism inherent to the problem and/or communication bottlenecks. The latter are caused by a large information flow between the processing elements which is necessary, but cannot be supported efficiently by the parallel architecture.

Our main concern will be the communication problem, but it cannot totally be isolated since both limitations may interfere. For example it might be possible to transform a sequential computation in a way that allows a fast parallel simulation, but at the expense of generating (among others) additional information flow. Lower bounds due to limited communication facilities have been established by combinatorial or algebraic methods. Some of these are already well known from the sequential case, for example crossing sequence arguments, some are extensions of known methods to the parallel envirement, for example to count connected components, and some like Ramsey arguments seem to be new.

In the literature one can find a variety of parallel computation models, uniform or nonuniform centralized controlled or distributed. In the centralized case one can further distinguish between single and multiple instruction machines. Distributed systems may operate synchronously or asynchronously. We will study the communication aspect in the strongest setting, that means nonuniform machines where processing elements perform individual operations synchronously. This excludes effects due to other reasons. Yao pioneered the case of 2 processors cooperatively computing a boolean function by exchangig bits where initially the inputs are distributed evenly [Y 79]. This paper was followed by a sequence of results which now enable us to know the communication complexity of the boolean 2 processor world quite well [H 86]. These results have implications, for systems of more than 2 processors which form a line or other simple configurations [T 84] and VLSI circuits [MS 82, JK 84].

The computational models we will consider here are large parallel machines where each processor has strong computing power. Let n denote the number of inputs and p the number of processors. In general p will be a function of n, sometimes even unbounded. For simplicity we only consider functions which depend on all inputs.

The communication between processors may be established by different means. In the most stringent case this is done by static communication links that connect a processor with some others. Communication takes place only over these links. Thus we get a graph or *network*. For algorithmic design machines with a common or shared memory consisting of m cells, $1 \leq m \leq \infty$, are more pleasant. Each processor has random access to any of these cells. This model is therefore called *parallel random access machine*.

As an intermediate step one may consider *multiple channel broadcasting networks* where each processor may send information by broadcasting on private or shared (multiple access) channels. To receive messages in each step a processor has to select one channel to listen to. If exactly one message is sent over that channel the communication between the two parties succeeds. Compare with [GL 83, LYG 85].

Finally in the *parallel computation tree* model one does not care how communication is realized. A processor can use all results computed by its colleagues at previous steps. Parallel random access machines are further classified according to how simultaneous access of different processors to the same memory cell is managed. The spectrum includes models for which this is totally forbidden and those without any restrictions. Due to physical constraints it seems unrealistic that any large parallel RAM can actually be built. Instead such a machine has to be simulated in the network or broadcasting model.

But even theoretically powerful networks like complete binary trees or cube-connected cycles [PV 81] have physical design problems as Schorr observes [83]. While their graph-theoretic diameter is only $O(\log p)$ and therefore connections between any pairs of processor can be established fast, a realization in $d = 2$ or 3 dimensions has to put each processor at distance $\delta = \Omega(p^{1/d})$ from almost all others, the geometric radius. Thus a simple communication requires time $\Omega(\delta)$ in most cases and the auther concludes that even arbitrary large parallel computers only allow a small polynomial speedup compared to the old-fashioned Turing machine.

Fortunately as long as technology is not to close to the absolute limit ($p = \infty$, computation speed = speed of light) the constants involved in the time bounds of this simulation matter quite a lot. Thus it still makes sense to strive after logarithmic parallel time or for the more flexible models after even faster computations. In this respect it is important to understand the power of the different communication mechanisms and their limitations. To get to the point in most cases it is sufficient to consider simple, sequentially well known computational problems in the parallel environment. In the following we try to review some of the recent research on this subject.

2. Fixed connection models

If a problem consits of independent pieces of small size one can easily find an efficient implementation on a parallel machine. Information exchange between processors handling different parts is not necessary. Therefore the interesting cases are functions that require a large flow of information. Below several properties of functions will be defined that imply a certain amount of communication necessary to compute such a function.

The absolute minimal communication delay of a network depends on the distances between input and output ports. If the n inputs are distributed evenly among $p \leq n$ processors and each processor has only a small number of direct neighbours most distances will be at least of the order $\log p$. This gives the trivial bound $\Omega(\log n)$ on communication complexity of $p = n$ processor networks for almost all n input funtions, in particular for all functions with 1 output which depends on all inputs. For several problems parallel algorithms are known that on specific networks achieve a total time bound of this order, see for example [S 80,GK 84]. For $p \leq n$ the lower bound becomes $\Omega(\frac{n}{p} + \log p)$ assuming that the sequential complexity is at least linear. Thus for $p \leq n/\log n$ the communication bottleneck might disappear. This is not the case for functions that require a larger amount of data movements like routing or sorting in networks for which the lower bound can be improved to $\Omega(\frac{n}{p}\log p)$.

The routing problem requires n items initially distributed among the processors to be sent simultaneously to specified adresses. If these adresses are not known beforehand but depend on the relative order of the items we are confronted with the sorting problem. Both problems are fundamental and have received a lot of attention. For a detailed overview the reader may consult [BH 85]. Routing, (resp. sorting) provides a way for a network to simulate the information flow in a shared memory where simultaneous access to a single cell is not (res. is) possible [LPV 81, MV 84, U 84, U 84a, UW 84, V 84]. Galil and Paul show how efficient universal networks can be obtained that way [GP 83].

3. Shared memory models

We already mentioned that different communication facilities have been proposed for parallel machines where processors have access to a common memory. Let us assume that each step of a parallel RAM consists of three parts: first each processor may read one cell of the common memory, then do its internal computation and finally try to write into one cell. The PRAC [LPV 81] may not perform any simultaneous access, the PRAM [FW 78] may perform simultaneous reads, while the WRAM model [*SV* 81, G 82] also allows simultaneous writes. One can also find the names EREW-, CREW-, resp. CRCW-PRAM for exclusive, resp. concurrent read, resp. write. The fourth possibility ERCW has not been considered because to realize simultaneous writes seems more difficult than simultaneous reads. But Snir gives an example where only the absence of concurrent reads slows down a computation, and this cannot be compensated by the concurrent write option [S 85].

To resolve write conflicts of a WRAM some convention is needed. Let CRAM (C for common) denote the model in which simultaneous writes to a cell are only allowed if the processors involved try to write a common value. In the ARAM model (A for arbitrary) the conflict is solved nondeterministically, an arbitrary processor succeeds in changing the memory content to its individual value. Such a machine computes a function f if for all inputs x it stops with $f(x)$ regardless which processors win these competitions. Alternatively one may totally order the processors and agree that always the processor of highest rank succeeds. In this case we will use the notation ORAM (O for ordered, some authors call the model priority PRAM).

These are the versions of a WRAM that have been studied. But one may also consider other ways to resolve write conflicts, for example a cell is changed to the maximum value that processors try to write into it (MRAM). Obviously an algorithm for a CRAM can also be implemented on an ARAM and an ARAM algorithm also works on an ORAM. Further it is easy to see that an MRAM can simulate an ORAM without loss of efficiency. The weakest of these concurrent write models, the CRAM, needs only a constant number of steps to simulate one step of any other machine if the number of processors is increased to p^2 and the size of the memory to $m+p$ (compare [K 81]). It even suffices if there exist only p cells into which a single value, let us say 1, can simultaneously be written by several processors. Thus if we do not care about the size of the machine all conflict resolution mechanisms are equivalent. Later we will see that this does not hold for fixed size.

A random access shared memory gives the possibility of arbitrary information flow from one processor to another. Furthermore even if no form of simultaneous access is allowed there is still some sort of communication with unbounded degree hidden. The fact that no processor writes into cell c in step t may have large "entropy". Certainly at most $\log(p+1)$ since the events "processor P_i tries to write into c at t" are mutual exclusive. On the other hand even in the stronger ORAM model where simultaneous writes are possible and resolved by ranking the fact that some processor actually wrote only gives a similar amount of information.

Thus we cannot expect the logarthmic lower bound due to bounded communication degree to hold in general. In fact some nontrivial functions can be computed much faster.

4. The power of concurrent read

If one item has to be duplicated n times this can be done on a $p = n$ processor parallel RAM by 1 simultaneous read operation. But it requires $\log n$ time without this option regardless of the number of processors. A more interesting prototype of problem is searching in a linear ordered list considered in [S 85]. Given n numbers $x_1 < x_2 < \ldots < x_n$ and some y find the interval $[x_i, x_{i+1}]$ into which y falls.

Searching does not allow a good speed-up. One can show that p-ary splitting essentially is the optimal strategy for a p-processor machine. To implement this method efficiently all processors have to be informed about the new search interval without loss of time before each recursive step. In a concurrent read model this is no problem, thus the time complexity of linear search is $\Theta(\log n/\log p)$ on a p processor PRAM or WRAM and at least a speed-up of order $\log p$ is possible. Snir shows that on the contrary a PRAC requires $\max\{\frac{1}{2}(\log n - \log p), \sqrt{\log n}\}$ steps. For small p the communication bottleneck prevents almost any improvement with respect to the 1 processor case and even arbitrary many processors achieve little speedup.

This result is proved by estimating the maximal possible information flow and therefore holds regardless of the computational power of processors. Furthermore a PRAC of size $p = n$ can solve the problem in $0(\sqrt{\log n})$ time by compressing long sequences of inputs into a single symbol. The PRAC time complexity for the searching problem in a purely information theoretic sense is therefore determined as $\Theta(\sqrt{\log n})$. If memory cells cannot store (resp. in addition processors cannot compute) such encodings the time complexity increases to $\Theta(\log n/\log\log n)$ (resp. $\Theta(\log n)$).

These lower time bounds hold for arbitrary finite number of processors and infinite common memory. Originally the results were stated for comparison based machine models in which processors were only allowed to compare inputs. Order equivalent inputs had to yield identical communication patterns. In general it is much easier to obtain lower bounds for such a structured computation model. Fortunately the number of different communication patterns can be made finite even in the unstructured parallel RAM model.

As soon as this finitness condition is fulfilled and the input domain can be arbitrary large one can apply an elegant and powerful combinatorial technique, Ramsey theory, to structure the seemingly chaos. On a smaller input domain one is guaranted to find a nicely structured computation. Recently this method has successfully been applied to various problems in parallel computation theory. But to be fair we will not suppress its drawback. The bounds on the size of the original domain, these are called Ramsey numbers, are extremly large, much larger than one would ever like to compute with. Thus this method cannot prove that for problems of moderate size chaotic programming gives no advantage.

5. The power of concurrent write

The weakest concurrent write machine, the CRAM, can compute any function of finite domain in just two steps. First for every possible input configuration the (not)-identity with the given input is checked by a simultaneous write operation and then a fast table look-up is performed for the single configuration found not to disagree. This shows that unbounded information flow is possible in constant time. But the method in general requires an exponential number of processors which limits its practical significance.

The boolean or of n bits is a prototype of function to show that even without an exponential blowup concurrent writes can be very powerful. The property we need is that switching any bit of the or of n zeros to one changes the function value. Let us call such a configuration *critical*. Thus when computing the or at point 0 it seems necessary that from any input information can flow to the output in case that bit is switched. If processors cannot simultaneously write into a cell the situation looks like the bounded degree case. Suprisingly $\log_2 n$ is not a lower bound [CD 82, R 82] instead an upper bound $\log_\alpha n$ can be obtained with $\alpha = 2.61..$ for the or function and $\alpha = 3$ for another function identical to the or in the critical configuration [(CDR 85)]. To achieve these bounds it is necessary for a PRAM to exploit the hidden information flow described in section 3.

If the communication pattern is fixed (machines with this property are called *oblivious*), then one can show that for the critical configuration the $\log_2 n$ lower bound actually holds even if concurrent writes are allowed. In contrast to the WRAM the advantage of nonoblivious computations for a PRAM is not too large. Infinitely many processors still require $\log_\alpha n$ steps with $\alpha = 4.79..$ to compute a function with a critical configuration like the or. But note that this result depends heavily on the fact that outside the critical region simultaneous writes are not allowed, too.

Since the input domain of the or is rather small, the proof cannot use Ramsey methods, instead we have to analyse the information flow directly. Let the size of a critical configuration be the number of inputs of which switching changes the function. Almost all boolean functions have a large critical configuration. Hence in the boolean case also for the PRAC and PRAM model $\Omega(\log n)$ is a communication theoretic lower bound (almost everywhere). Simon shows that every 1 output boolean function that depends an all inputs must have a critical configuration of size $\Omega(\log n)$ [S 82]. Thus in no case a parallel RAM without concurrent writes can compute a boolean function faster than $\Omega(\log\log n)$. This bound is best possible.

These last claims seem to contradict the result from above that an n processor PRAM can search a list of size n in constant time. The difference is that unlike the list searching problem in general no information about the relative order of inputs is available a priori. This information is extensively used to avoid write conflicts in the fast search algorithm. If the domain of the searching problem is extended to a full cartesian product, for example by generating a special symbol in case the input list is not ordered, the time complexity becomes logarithmic.

6. The impact of the individual computing power

The searching problem showed that the communication bottleneck of a PRAC can be compensated to a certain extent by giving each processor more computational power. In this section we will study this tradeoff for the most powerful parallel RAM, the WRAM, and exhibit relations to other computational models.

Let us consider machines where the instruction set of processors is somewhat closer to reality. Besides the access operations to private and common memory, direct or indirect, only boolean operations on pairs of bits and comparisons and arithmetic operations on $0(\log n)$ size numbers are allowed. Stockmeyer and Vishkin show an interesting connection to circuits of unbounded indegree [SV 84]. Modulo small polynomial differences in hardware size the parallel time complexity of both models is of the same order.

Almost all boolean functions have exponential circuit complexity regardless of whether the indegree is bounded or not. Thus for this restricted class of machines the question of very fast polynomial size parallel computation becomes only interesting for specific functions of low sequential complexity. In this respect the parity function, the sum of n bits mod 2, has attracted much attention. By the work of Yao and Hasted its essentially optimal depth-k circuits are known, their size is $\exp(\Theta(n^{\frac{1}{k-1}}))$ [Y 85, H 85]. Hence the same lower bound holds for the corresponding machine model. In particular it implies that a polynomial size machine requires time $\Omega(\log / \log\log n)$. An algorithm matching this bound can easily be found and also be extended to the ordinary sum function on natural numbers provided inputs and outputs are given in binary notation.

This observation suggests an alternative model in which natural numbers may be arbitrary large, but have to be treated as atomic elements. Processors may perform comparisons of numbers or arithmetic operations. If we further abstract from the communication mechanism by a shared memory we arrive at the *parallel computation tree* (PCT) model [Y 82, MR 84], a generalisation of both the well knowm algebraic computation trees [B 83] to the parallel envirement and of Vailant's parallel comparison trees [V 75] to arithmetic computations.

A PCT with p processors gets as inputs real numbers and in one step performs p arithmetic operations or comparsions on previonsly computed functions and then splits according to the outcome of these comparisons. Thus one may expect a branching factor up to 2^p which means very powerful communication facilities. But it can be shown that the actual outdegree is only a polynomial in p depending on what kind of arithmetic operations are available.

Now consider languages like the knapsack problem which divide the n-dimensional space into many connected components. The height (= parallel time) of a PCT solving such a problem is lowerbounded by its outdegree and the number of leaves necessary to cover all components. This way nontrivial lower bounds on the parallel time complexity have been proved [Y 82, MR 84].

These bounds can be transferred to the corresponding WRAM model dealing with natural numbers. The advantage of this method is that explicit bounds on the maximal size of inputs can be given which are much smaller than in the combinatorial approach using Ramsey arguments. Furthermore these algebraic arguments can be combined with the information flow approach for the PRAM to yield a $\log n$ lower bound for a WRAM computing the sum of n numbers [R 85].

The same resul has been obtained by purely informationtheoretical methods [I 84, R 85a]. In this case processors may perform arbitrary operations, and still the input size can be kept moderately small. To prove these logarithmic lower bounds the following functional property of the sum is used and is the only needed: whenever a single x_i of an input vector $x = x_1, \ldots, x_n$ is changed, where x and i may be arbitrary, the function takes another value. We call this property *supercritical*, it seems to require an extensive information exchange that cannot be conducted other than in a binary tree fashion. A simple proof for this result using Ramsey's theorem can be found in [MW 85], but as already mentioned one has to consider very large numbers.

Finally Beame applies the random restriction method of Yao and Hastad directly to WRAMs rather than using the detour via the circuit model [B 85]. This way he does not have to limit the computational power of processors. The result is an $\Omega(\sqrt{\log n})$ lower time bound for the boolean sum mod 2 computed by a polynomial size machine.

7. Comparison problems

Concerning exclusive reads we already considered the searching problem. For the concurrent write model with inputs given in binary notation the results in [CSV 84, Y 85] yield the following classification of comparison or order type problems. On the one hand there are problems like finding the maximum of n numbers or merging two sorted lists of size $\frac{n}{2}$ that have constant depth circuits of polynomial size in the input length. Others like sorting n numbers or the boolean threshold functions to which parity can be reduced require exponential size. The same result holds for the corresponding bit-orientated WRAM model. A polynomial size machine cannot sort faster than in time $\Omega(\log n/\log\log n)$.

Since the boolean or is equivalent to the maximum, resp. can be solved by sorting the bit vector a parallel machine without simultaneons writes needs at least logarithmic time. Remember that this holds regardless of the machine size and the operation sets of processor. Merging however can be performed much faster by a PRAM. Borodin and Hopcroft describe the implementation of an $0(\log\log n)$ algorithm on an n-processor machine where inputs may be arbitrary large numbers [BH 85].

For the following results the number of processors is a critical parameter because for large p ($p = \binom{n}{2}$ generally suffices) comparison problems can be solved in constant time on certain parallel models. We will restrict to the case where the number of processors equals the number of inputs. Furthermore the write conflict resolution makes a difference. The computational power of processors may be arbitrary.

To find the maximum of n numbers an $0(\log\log n)$ algorithm for a CRAM is described in [SV 81]. Recently Fich et al. prove a corresponding lower bound for the stronger ORAM model [FMRW 85]. Valiant already established the last result for a parallel comparison tree which with respect to communication facilities is at least as powerful [V 75]. But its computational power is restricted since processors can only compare inputs. The proof for the ORAM again relies on a Ramsey argument, but the technique is more involved than former ones. Using Valiant's adversary strategy, Ramsey methods are applied iteratively to find nicely structured computations on subsets of the input domain that in addition give as little information about the ordering of the inputs as possible. Note that an MRAM finds the maximum in 1 step.

For the merging problem Borodin and Hopcroft show that their $\log\log n$ algorithm is asymtotically optimal on a parallel comparison tree. As for the maximum it should be possible to extend this result to a parallel machine with unlimited computing power.

Let us close this section with two more results on the sorting problem. We gave several examples that on parallel machines with restricted communication or computing power this problem requires logarithmic or almost logarithmic time. Meyer auf der Heide and Wigderson consider the unrestricted ORAM model, but do not allow more than n processors [MW 85]. They show that nicely structured computations of an ORAM can be simulated by a generalisation of parallel comparison trees, called *parallel merge trees*.

Instead of comparing pairs of inputs processors can merge sorted lists of certain length in a single step. It is shown that parallel merge trees have depth $\Omega(\sqrt{\log n})$. Thus an ORAM capable to sort very large numbers requires the same amount of time. This time bound also follows from Beame's result for the parity function, but even for sorting an n-bit vector with a polynomial size machine.

Since the best known upper bound is $0(\log n/\log\log n)$ it remains an open problem to close this gap for the unrestricted class of machines. In case of parallel comparison trees Häggkvist and Hell have shown that the upper bound is sharp if $p = 0(n \log^k n)$ for some k [HH 81].

8. Write conflict resolution and communication bandwidth

For a shared memory machine the size m of the common memory is called the *communication bandwidth*. The lower bounds above hold for polynomial bandwidth, in some cases it may even be unbounded or infinite. The technique to simulate the different WRAM versions efficiently required to square the number of processors and to increase the communication bandwidth by p. Thus except for very small memories the bandwidth can be kept on the same order.

In [VW 83] ORAMs are considered with arbitrary many processors, but bandwidth $m = 0(\frac{n}{\log^2 n})$. The authors show that such small bandwidth generates a communication bottleneck for functions they call *sensitive*. The condition is that for every input vector there exists a large critical configuration. By an information flow argument an $\Omega(\sqrt{\frac{n}{m}})$ lower bound can be obtained which is optimal.

For sublinear bandwidth Fich et al. prove several separation results between the concurrent write models CRAM, ARAM and ORAM [FRW 85]. The main result is that for $m = 0(p^{1-\epsilon})$ such a machine requires $\Theta(\log p)$ steps to simulate one step of a machine with less restrictive write conflict resolution than itself.

Finally one may compare the concurrent write mechanisms without restricting the bandwidth, but fixing the number of processors. A result in this direction was abtained in [FMRW 85] for the problem to decide whether n given numbers are mutually distinct. For $p = n$ this problem can be solved by an ARAM in constant time, which is not possible on a CRAM.

9. Conclusion

We have tried to structure a variety of papers on communication in parallel systems. How much information exchange is necessary for fast computations and how can this be realized on different models of parallel machines? This overview cannot be complete, nor did we try to present any technical details. The interested reader is encouraged to look into the cited literature.

Although we dealt with fast parallel computations the preparation of these notes had to be done in a very short time using an ordinary sequential algorithm. We ask to excuse any deficiencies caused by this fact.

References:

[B 83] **M. Ben Or,** *Lower bounds for algebraic computation trees,* Proc. of the 15th ACM An. Symp. on Theory of Computing, 1983, 80-86.

[B 85] **P. Beame,** *Lower bounds for very powerfull parallel machines,* Technical report, 1985.

[BH 85] **A. Borodin, J. Hopcroft,** *Routing, merging and sorting on parallel models of computation,* J. Comp. and Syst. Sc. 30, 1985, 130-145.

[CD 82] **S. Cook, C. Dwork,** *Bounds on the time for parallel RAMs to compute simple functions,* Proc. of the 14th ACM An. Symp. on Theory of Computing, 1982, 231-233.

[CDR 85] **S. Cook, C. Dwork, R. Reischuk** *Upper and lower time bounds for parallel random access machines without simultaneous writes,* SIAM J. Comput. 14, 1985.

[CSV 84] **A. Chandra, L. Stockmeyer, U. Vishin,** *Constant depth reducibility,* SIAM J. Comput. 13, 1984, 423-439.

[FMRW 85] **F. Fich, F. Meyer auf der Heide, P. Ragde, A. Wigderson,** *One, two, three ... infinity lower bounds for parallel computation,* Proc. of the 17th ACM An. Symp. on Theory of Computing, 1985, 48-58.

[FRW 85] **F. Fich, P. Ragde, A. Wigderson,** *Relations between concurrent-write models of parallel computation,* Technical report, 1985.

[FW 78] **S. Fortune, J. Wyllie,** *Parallelism in random access machines,* Proc. of the 10th ACM An. Symp. on Theory of Computing, 1978, 114-118.

[G 82] **L. Goldschlager,** *A universal interconnection pattern for parallel computers,* J. ACM 29, 1982, 1073-1086.

[GL 84] **A. Gottlieb, C. Kruskal,** *Complexity results for permuting data and other computations on parallel processors,* J. ACM 31, 1984, 193-209.

[GP 83] **Z. Galil, W. Paul,** *An efficient general-purpose parallel computer,* J. ACM 30, 1983, 360-387.

[H 85] **J. Hastad,** *Improved lower bounds for small depth circuits,* Technical report, 1985.

[H 86] **B. Halstenberg,** *Kommunikationskomplexität,* Diplom Arbeit, Universität Bielefeld, 1986

[HH 81] **R. Häggkvist, P. Hell,** *Parallel sorting with constant time for comparisons,* SIAM J. Comput. 10, 1981, 465-472.

[JK 84] **J. Jaja, P. Kumar,** *Information transfer in distributed computing with application to VLSI,* J. ACM 31, 1984, 150-162.

[K 81] **L. Kucera,** *Parallel computation and conflicts in memory access,* Inf. Proc. Let. 14, 1982, 93-96.

[LPV 81] **G. Lev, N. Pippenger, L. Valiant,** *A fast parallel algorithm for routing in permutation networks,* IEEE Trans. on Computers 30, 1981, 93-100.

[LYG 85] **G. Landau, M. Yung, Z. Galil,** *Distributed algorithms in synchronous broadcasting networks,* Proc. of the 12. ICALP, 1985, 363-372.

[MR 84] **F. Meyer auf der Heide, R. Reischuk,** *On the limits to speed up parallel machines by large hardware and unbounded communication,* Proc. of the 25th IEEE An. Symp. on Foundations of Computer Science, 1984, 56-64.

[MS 82] **K. Mehlhorn, E. Schmidt,** *Las Vegas is better than determinism for VLSI circuits,* Proc. of the 14th ACM An. Symp. on Theory of Computing, 1982, 330-337.

[MV 84] **K. Mehlhorn, U. Vishkin,** *Randomized and deterministic simulation of PRAMS by parallel machines with restricted granularity of parallel memories,* Acta Informatica 21, 1984, 339-374.

[MW 85] **F. Meyer auf der Heide, A. Wigderson,** *The complexity of parallel sorting,* Proc. of the 26th IEEE An. Symp. on Foundations of Computer Science, 1985, 532-540.

[P 84] **J. Parberry,** *A complexity theory of parallel computation,* Dissertation, University of Warwick, 1984.

[PV 81] **F. Preparata, J. Vuillemin,** *The cube-connected cycles: a versatile network for parallel computation,* Com. of the ACM 24, 1981, 300-309.

[R 82] **R. Reischuk** *A lower time-bound for parallel random access machines without simutaneous writes*, IBM Research Report RJ3431, 1982.

[R 85] **R. Reischuk,** *Simultaneous writes of parallel random access machines do not help to compute simple arithmetic functions*, Technical report, Universität Bielefeld, 1985, to appear in J. ACM.

[R 85a] **R. Reischuk,** *An information theoretic lower bound for WRAMS*, Technical report, Universität Bielefeld, 1985.

[S 80] **J. Schwartz,** *Ultracomputers*, ACM Tr. on Progr. Lang. and Systems, 2, 1980, 484-521.

[S 82] **H.U. Simon,** *A tight $\Omega(\log\log n)$ - bound on the time for parallel RAM's to compute nondegenerated boolean functions*, Information and Control 55, 1982, 102-107.

[S 83] **A. Schorr,***Physical parallel devices are not much faster than sequential ones*, Inf. Proc. let. 17, 1983, 103-106.

[S 85] **M. Snir,** *On parallel searching*, SIAM J. on Computing 14, 1985, 688-708.

[SV 81] **Y. Shiloach, U. Vishkin,** *Finding the maximum, merging and sorting in a parallel computation model*, J. of Algorithms 2, 1981, 88-102.

[SV 84] **L. Stockmeyer, U. Vishkin,** *Simulation of parallel random acces machines by circuits*, SIAM J. Comput. 13, 1984, 409-422.

[T 84] **P. Tiwari,** *Lower bounds on communication complexity in distributed computer networks*, Proc. of the 16th ACM An. Symp.on Theory of Computing, 1984, 109-117.

[U 84] **E. Upfal,** *Efficient schemes for parallel communication*, J. ACM 31, 1984, 507-517.

[U 84a] **E. Upfal,** *A probabilistic relation between desirable and feasible models of parallel computation*, Proc. of the 16th ACM An. Symp. on Theory of Computing, 1984, 258-265.

[UW 84] **E. Upfal, A. Wigderson,** *How to share memory in a distributed system*, Proc. of the 25th IEEE An. Symp. on Theory of Computing, 1984, 171-180.

[V 75] **L. Valiant,** *Parallelism in comparsion problems*, SIAM J. on Computing 4, 1975, 348-355.

[V 84] **U. Vishkin,** *A parallel-design distributed-implementation (PDDI) general-purpose computer*, Theoretical Computer Science 32, 1984, 157-172.

[VW 83] **U. Vishkin, A. Wigderson,** *Trade-offs between depth and width in parallel computation*, Proc. of the 24th IEEE An. Symp. on Foundations of Computer Science, 1983, 146-153 and SIAM J. on Computing 14, 1985, 303-314.

[Y 79] **A. Yao,** *Some complexity questions related to distributive computing*, Proc. of the 11th ACM An. Symp. on Theory of Computing, 1979, 209-213.

[Y 82] **A. Yao,** *On parallel computation for the knapsack Problem*, J. ACM 29, 1982, 898-903.

[Y 85] **A. Yao,** *Separating the polynomial-time hierarchy by oracles*, Proc. of the 26th An. IEEE Symp. on Foundations of Computer Science, 1985, 1-10.